Also in the Variorum Collected Studies Series:

C. STEPHEN JAEGER
Scholars and Courtiers: Intellectuals and Society in the Medieval West

GORDON LEFF
Heresy, Philosophy and Religion in the Medieval West

PATRIZIA LENDINARA
Anglo-Saxon Glosses and Glossaries

RODNEY M. THOMSON
England and the Twelfth-Century Renaissance

RICHARD W. PFAFF
Liturgical Calendars, Saints and Services in Medieval England

PATRICK MCGURK
Gospel Books and Early Latin Manuscripts

GILES CONSTABLE
Culture and Spirituality in Medieval Europe

WALLACE MARTIN LINDSAY
Studies in Early Medieval Latin Glossaries

PATRICK SIMS-WILLIAMS
Britain and Early Christian Europe
Studies in Early Medieval History and Culture

SUSAN REYNOLDS
Ideas and Solidarities of the Medieval Laity
England and Western Europe

ROSAMOND MCKITTERICK
Books, Scribes and Learning in the Frankish Kingdoms, 6th–9th centuries

CHARLES W. JONES AND WESLEY STEVENS
Bede, the Schools and the Computus

DAVID N. DUMVILLE
Britons and Anglo-Saxons in the Early Middle Ages

VARIORUM COLLECTED STUDIES SERIES

Studies in the Transmission
of Wyclif's Writings

Drawing of Wyclif found before a copy of his *De mandatis*, in Prague Castle Archives, Metropolitan Chapter Library, C.38, f.17rb.

Anne Hudson

Studies in the Transmission of Wyclif's Writings

Taylor & Francis Group

LONDON AND NEW YORK

First published 2008 by Ashgate Publishing

2 Park Square, Milton Park, Abingdon, Oxfordshire OX14 4RN
711 Third Avenue, New York, NY 10017

Routledge is an imprint of the Taylor & Francis Group, an informa business

First issued in paperback 2018

This edition © 2008 by Anne Hudson

Anne Hudson has asserted her moral right under the Copyright, Designs and Patents Act, 1988, to be identified as the author of this work.

All rights reserved. No part of this book may be reprinted or reproduced or utilised in any form or by any electronic, mechanical, or other means, now known or hereafter invented, including photocopying and recording, or in any information storage or retrieval system, without permission in writing from the publishers.

Notice:
Product or corporate names may be trademarks or registered trademarks, and are used only for identification and explanation without intent to infringe.

British Library Cataloguing in Publication Data
Hudson, Anne, 1938–
  Studies in the transmission of Wyclif's writings. –
  (Variorum collected studies series)
  1. Wycliffe, John, d. 1384 2. Reformation – Early movements
  I. Title
  270.5'092

  ISBN 978-0-7546-5964-8 (hbk)
  ISBN 978-1-138-37526-0 (pbk)

Library of Congress Cataloging-in-Publication Data
Hudson, Anne, 1938–
  Studies in the transmission of Wyclif's writings / by Anne Hudson, Margaret Hall.
     p. cm. – (Variorum collected studies series 907)
  Includes bibliographical references and index.
  ISBN 978–0–7546–5964–8 (alk. paper)
  1. Wycliffe, John, d. 1384. 2. Reformation – Early movements.
  I. Hudson, Anne, 1938– II. Title.
  BX4905.H83 2008
  270.5092–dc22

2007046406

VARIORUM COLLECTED STUDIES SERIES CS907

CONTENTS

Acknowledgements		ix–x
List of Abbreviations		xi–xiv
I	Introduction: Wyclif's works and their dissemination (*first publication*)	1–16
II	From Oxford to Prague: the writings of John Wyclif and his English followers in Bohemia *Slavonic and East European Review* 75. London, 1997	642–657
III	The Hussite catalogue of Wyclif's works (*first publication*)	1–35
IV	Cross-referencing in Wyclif's Latin works *The Medieval Church: Universities, Heresy, and the Religious Life: Essays in Honour of Gordon Leff*, Studies in Church History, Subsidia 11, eds P. Biller and B. Dobson. Woodbridge: Boydell and Brewer, 1999	193–215
V	The development of Wyclif's *Summa theologie* *John Wyclif: Logica, politica, teologia*, eds M. Fumagalli Beonio Brocchieri and S. Simonetta. Florence: SISMEL – Edizioni del Galluzzo, 2003	57–70
VI	Wyclif's Latin sermons: questions of form, date and audience *Archives d'histoire doctrinale et littéraire du moyen age* 68. Paris, 2001 Additional Appendix from *Aspects of the 'Publication' of Wyclif's Latin Sermons, Late-Medieval Religious Texts and their Transmission: Essays in Honour of A.I. Doyle*, ed. A.J. Minnis. Woodbridge: D.S. Brewer, 1994	223–248 124–126
VII	*Accessus ad auctorem*: the case of John Wyclif *Viator* 30. Los Angeles, CA, 1999	323–344

VIII	Trial and error: Wyclif's works in Cambridge, Trinity College MS B.16.2 *New Science out of Old Books: Studies in Manuscripts and Early Printed Books in Honour of A.I. Doyle*, eds R. Beadle and A.J. Piper. Aldershot: Scolar Press, 1995	53–80
IX	Wyclif and the north: the evidence from Durham *Life and Thought in the Northern Church c.1100–c.1700: Essays in Honour of Claire Cross, Studies in Church History, Subsidia 12*, ed. D. Wood. Woodbridge: Boydell and Brewer, 1999	87–103
X	*Peculiaris regis clericus*: Wyclif and the issue of authority *The Growth of Authority in the Medieval West*, eds M. Gosman, A. Vanderjagt and J.R. Veenstra. Groningen: Egbert Forsten Publishing, 1999	63–81
XI	*Poor preachers, poor men*: views of poverty in Wyclif and his followers *Häresie und vorzeitige Reformation im Spätmittelalter*, ed. F. Šmahel. Munich: Oldenbourg, 1998	41–53
XII	The king and erring clergy: a Wycliffite contribution *The Church and Sovereignty c.590–1918: Essays in Honour of Michael Wilks, Studies in Church History, Subsidia 9*, ed. D. Wood. Woodbridge: D.S. Brewer, 1991	269–278
XIII	Notes of an early fifteenth-century research assistant, and the emergence of the 267 articles against Wyclif *English Historical Review 118*. Oxford, 2003	685–697
XIV	Which Wyche? The framing of the Lollard heretic and/or saint *Texts and the Repression of Medieval Heresy*, eds C. Bruschi and P. Biller. York: York Medieval Press, 2003	221–237
XV	Wyclif texts in fifteenth-century London (*first publication*)	1–18
XVI	The survival of Wyclif's works in England and Bohemia (*first publication*)	1–43
Appendix I: additional notes		1–4
Appendix II: supplement to manuscript listings		1–16

CONTENTS   vii

Index of Wyclif's works discussed   1–4

Index of manuscripts   5–9

General index   10–14

> This volume contains xiv + 376 pages

PUBLISHER'S NOTE

The articles in this volume, as in all others in the Variorum Collected Studies Series, have not been given a new, continuous pagination. In order to avoid confusion, and to facilitate their use where these same studies have been referred to elsewhere, the original pagination has been maintained wherever possible.

Each article has been given a Roman number in order of appearance, as listed in the Contents. This number is repeated on each page and is quoted in the index entries.

Asterisks in the margins are to alert the reader to additional information supplied at the end of the volume in Appendix I: additional notes.

ACKNOWLEDGEMENTS

Although the papers printed here bear a publication date of 1991 or later, the research that they reflect was begun around 1970. My investigations began from the English writings that have been associated with Wyclif and his followers, the Lollards, and I have continued to edit a series of texts from that background. In 1972, thanks to help from the British Council, I spent a month in Prague and a shorter time in Vienna studying the Bohemian copies of Wyclif's Latin works, and looking for Latin sources of Lollard texts. The papers here represent the fruits of that and many subsequent visits to those two cities, and to libraries elsewhere in the British Isles, Europe and the United States. Because the manuscripts that they investigate are so far-flung, re-checking details from them, and bringing together manuscripts and secondary sources, has not been invariably possible: I deplore any errors, inconsistencies or omissions, but ask for understanding of this problem (which, with improving technology, may diminish in the future). In nearly forty years of research I have accumulated innumerable debts for help and encouragement, not all of which can be itemized here. But my vast debt to the almost invariable helpfulness of the many library assistants I have encountered will be clear from the index of manuscripts; I would like to single out for particular gratitude those in the Bodleian Library in Oxford, in the manuscript rooms of the Österreichische Nationalbibliothek, the Prague University (now National) Library and the Prague Metropolitan Chapter Library (remembering particularly the help given in the last two before 1989). My visits to Prague in the early days would have been impossible without the help of Ilona Hamplová, and to her and her husband Parviz I owe an immense debt for continuing friendship. To mention individual scholars who have been generous in their help is to risk the omission of others for no good cause beyond brevity: my debt to some scholars is evident from the *festschriften* to which several papers here were originally contributed. Not so evident is my gratitude to other friends, especially to František Šmahel, Vilém Herold, Ivan Hlaváček and Jiří Kejř in Prague, Peter Biller, Maureen Jurkowski, Alison McHardy in England, James Carley, Ann Hutchison and George Rigg in Toronto, Helen Barr, Jeremy Catto, Kantik Ghosh, Vincent Gillespie and Ralph Hanna in Oxford. Pamela Gradon remains the scholar and friend to whom I am most indebted: until her death in 2002 she shared many of those memorable visits to Central European libraries (working on the *Postilla*, of which research sadly little reached publishable form), discussed Wycliffite topics repeatedly, and was consistently a stimulus to further investigation. I am also very grateful to Dr Marek Suchy, of the Metropolitan Chapter Library in Prague, for facilitating the production of the plate used as a frontispiece, and for obtaining permission for its appearance here. My thanks also go to Ashgate for their acceptance of the volume for inclusion in the Variorum series, and to the editorial staff for all their help.

The author and publisher gratefully acknowledge the following institutions and publishers for their kind permission to reproduce the papers included in this volume: *Slavonic and East European Review*, London (for paper II); Ecclesiastical Historical Society, London (IV, IX, XII); SISMEL - Edizioni del Galluzzo, Florence (V); Librairie Philosophique J. Vrin, Paris and Boydell & Brewer Ltd, Woodbridge (VI); *Viator*, Los Angeles, CA (VII); Ashgate Publishing Ltd, Aldershot (VIII); Egbert Forsten Publishing, Groningen (X); Oldenbourg Wissenschaftsverlag GmbH, Munich (XI); Oxford University Press, Oxford (XIII); Boydell & Brewer Ltd, Woodbridge (XIV).

ABBREVIATIONS

Included here are only those abbreviations used in the new material, and those that are not expanded at any point in the individual reproduced papers. Since publishers' conventions do not in all respects agree, for some items the following list includes alternatives (but not noting differences in italicization); the first of these is that used in the new material here.

AHDLMA	*Archives d'histoire doctrinale et littéraire du moyen âge*
Arnold	ed. T. Arnold, *Select English Works of John Wyclif* (3 vols., Oxford, 1869–71).
Bale, *Catalogus*	John Bale, *Scriptorum illustrium maioris Brytannie ... Catalogus* (2 vols., Basel, 1557–9).
Bale, *Index*	*Index Britanniae scriptorum: John Bale's Index of British and Other Writers*, eds R.L. Poole and M. Bateson, revised C. Brett and J.P. Carley (Cambridge, 1990).
BIHR	*Bulletin of the Institute of Historical Research*
BL	London, British Library
BLR	*Bodleian Library Record*
BN	Paris, Bibliothèque nationale
CBMLC	*Corpus of British Medieval Library Catalogues* (London, 1990–).
CCR	*Calendar of Close Rolls*
CPR	*Calendar of Patent Rolls*
EETS	Early English Text Society (volumes without prefix are in the Original Series, those prefixed ES are in the Extra Series, those prefixed SS in the Supplementary Series).
EHR	*English Historical Review*
Emden, *Cambridge/ BRUC*	A.B. Emden, *A Biographical Register of the University of Cambridge to 1500* (Cambridge, 1963).

Emden, *Oxford*/ BRUO	A.B. Emden, *A Biographical Register of the University of Oxford to A.D.1500* (3 vols., Oxford, 1957–9).
EWS	*English Wycliffite Sermons*, eds P. Gradon and A. Hudson (5 vols., Oxford, 1983–96).
Friedberg	ed. E. Friedberg, *Corpus iuris canonici* (2 vols., Leipzig, 1879–81).
FZ / *Fasc. Ziz.*	*Fasciculus zizaniorum*, ed. W.W. Shirley (Rolls Series, 1858).
G & C	Cambridge, Gonville and Caius College Library
HBS	*Henry Bradshaw Society Publications*
HUO	*The History of the University of Oxford ii Late Medieval Oxford*, eds J.I. Catto and T.A.R. Evans (Oxford, 1992).
JEH	*Journal of Ecclesiastical History*
LB	A. Hudson, *Lollards and their Books* (London, 1985).
Matthew	ed. F.D. Matthew, *The English Works of Wyclif hitherto unprinted* (EETS 74, 2nd edn., 1904).
MGH	*Monumenta Germaniae Historia*
MLGB	N.R. Ker, revised by A.G. Watson, *Medieval Libraries of Great Britain* (2nd edn., London, 1987).
MMBL	N.R. Ker, completed by A.J. Piper, I.C. Cunningham and A.G. Watson, *Medieval Manuscripts in British Libraries* (5 vols., Oxford, 1969–2002).
MS	*Medieval Studies*
Netter, *Doctrinale*	Thomas Netter of Walden, *Doctrinale antiquitatum fidei catholicae ecclesiae*, ed. R. Blanciotti (3 vols., Venice, 1757–9, reprinted Farnborough, 1967) – quoted by book and chapter number, followed in brackets by volume and column number
NRA	National Register of Archives, *formerly* Public Record Office (PRO)
ns	new series
ODCC	eds F.L. Cross and E.A. Livingstone, *The Oxford Dictionary of the Christian Church* (3rd edn., Oxford, 1997).

ODNB	*Oxford Dictionary of National Biography* (printed version Oxford 2004, online version 2004 and updated).
OHS	Oxford Historical Society
ÖNB / Vienna / ONB	Vienna, Österreichische Nationalbibliothek
PBA	*Proceedings of the British Academy*
PL	Patrologia latina
PMK / Prague MK	Prague, Metropolitan Chapter Library
PNM / Prague NM	Prague, National Museum Library
PR	A. Hudson, *The Premature Reformation: Wycliffite Texts and Lollard History* (Oxford, 1988).
PUK / Prague UK	Prague, University (now National) Library
RS	Rolls Series
SCH	*Studies in Church History*
SCH, S / Subs	*Studies in Church History, Subsidia*
Sharpe	R. Sharpe, *A Handlist of the Latin Writers of Great Britain and Ireland before 1540* (Turnhout, 1997).
SS	*Surtees Society Publications*
STC	eds A.W. Pollard and G.R. Redgrave, Revd. K.F. Panzer et al., *A Short-Title Catalogue of Books printed in England, Scotland and Ireland ... 1475–1640* (3 vols., London, 1976–91).
Summary Catalogue	eds F. Craster et al., *A Summary Catalogue of Western Manuscripts in the Bodleian Library* (7 vols., Oxford, 1922–53).
T / Th / Thomson	W.R. Thomson, *The Latin Writings of John Wyclyf* (Toronto, 1983) – numbers prefixed with these refer to the <u>items</u> in Thomson's catalogue.
TCC	Cambridge, Trinity College Library
TCD	Dublin, Trinity College Library
TCWB	eds H. Barr and A. Hutchison, *Text and Controversy from Wyclif to Bale: Essays in Honour of Anne Hudson* (Turnhout, 2005).
WB	eds J. Forshall and F. Madden, *The Holy Bible ... made from the Latin Vulgate by John Wycliffe and his Followers* (4 vols., Oxford, 1850, reprinted New York, 1982).
Wilkins	ed. D. Wilkins, *Concilia Magnae Britanniae et Hiberniae* (4 vols., London, 1737).
WS	Wyclif Society Publications – abbreviations used for individual works are mostly self-explanatory,

	but the following collections should be noted: *Op.min.= Opera minora*, ed. J. Loserth (WS, 1913), *Pol.Wks. = Polemical Works*, ed. R. Buddensieg (2 vols., WS, 1883).
ZSRG	*Zeitschrift der Savigny-Stiftung für Rechtsgeschichte*

I

Introduction: Wyclif's Works and their Dissemination

John Wyclif was an unusually prolific author, and his writings had a profound effect on those who came in contact with the ideas expressed within them: there can be no other medieval scholar who could plausibly be accused of causing civil rebellion in England, heresy in England and central Europe, and revolution in Bohemia, and all almost entirely through the written word. The papers collected here look at various aspects of this remarkable output: its content, its assembly and structure, its dissemination and the various attempts to suppress it, together with a closer investigation into the thought of some of the texts. Before turning to the particular focus in each paper, it may be useful to look briefly at Wyclif's written output as a whole, concentrating on the genesis of some individual texts.

Thomson in his valuable catalogue *The Latin Writings of John Wyclyf* lists 435 works by Wyclif, a number inflated by his decision to list each of the sermons, and each of the prologues and books of the *Postilla super totam Bibliam*, under a separate heading; a more realistic number would be around 150, but for ease of reference Thomson's work numbers are here used throughout.[1] The uniformity imposed by any catalogue listing inevitably disguises the heterogeneity of the material covered. Here I am less concerned with the variety of topics discussed in those 150 writings, and more with what, for want of a better term, must be described as 'publication', the way in which a text was (or was not) released by the author to a public, whether individual, institutional or general.[2] Some of Wyclif's works were probably never intended for such release: the two surviving determinations against the Carmelite John Kenningham (T378 and 380), incompletely preserved in only a single manuscript, record an early

---

[1] Two can be removed: T391 and T51, for which see Appendix II under these numbers; both are extracts from other works. T40, 41, 42, 43 and less certainly 44 could be unrecognized extracts or paraphrases from longer texts dealing with the eucharist.

[2] Wyclif's logical and purely philosophical works (T1–21) are less fully discussed here than they should be: in part this is the result of my own interests and expertise, but some of them are unprinted, and others are available only in unsatisfactory early editions (only T11 and T17 have been adequately edited in modern form).

academic encounter, whilst the debates with William Woodford only survive, if at all, overlaid with later polemic either in sections of Wyclif's own texts or in the Franciscan's writings against Wyclif.[3] In origin these debates were part of the normal academic interchange, and need not necessarily have been directed to a wider audience than the Oxford schools. Other works, however, were designed for a particular public purpose: the two texts concerning the activities of the papal collector Arnald Garnier in 1377 (T397 and 398) appear to have been written as a contribution to the attempts by the civil authorities to stem the outflow of English money to Rome (or rather to Avignon).[4] In this case whether Wyclif sought their wider transmission is unclear.[5] The brief which Wyclif provided to justify the invasion of the Westminster sanctuary in 1378 was similarly originally written to satisfy a particular political purpose, and was apparently used at the Parliament in Gloucester that year; but in this case Wyclif recycled the material, and his answers to the subsequent objections, to form the core of his own *De ecclesia* (T32), later described as part 7 of his *Summa theologie*.[6] Here it would seem the resulting text was certainly designed for publication, almost (granted the limits of manuscript dissemination) in the modern sense of that word.

The relation of the Parliament brief to the finished *De ecclesia* seems clear, at least in terms of the direction of revision. But this is not always so apparent. An important case is *De eucharistia minor confessio* (T39), a brief expression of Wyclif's final view of the nature of the central sacrament: here the date in a single copy, 10 May 1381, as against nine which are undated, has been taken as authoritative.[7] More importantly, the whole of the text as it is extant in all English copies is paralleled in *De apostasia*;[8] but which came first, *Confessio* or

---

[3] For Woodford see *ODNB* and bibliography there; the status of the disputes with Uthred (T381) is considered below no. IX 96–101.

[4] For Wyclif's objections to the demands for payments see Thomson p. 250 and *ODNB*.

[5] Both are found in Bohemian copies, only the second in an English manuscript (and that later and from a source hostile to Wyclif, namely *FZ*, Oxford Bodley e Mus.86).

[6] For the problematic structure of this work see below nos. IV–V. Two English manuscripts (TCD 242 and Florence BLaur.Plut.XIX.33) preserve just chapter 7 from *De ecclesia*, the section which seems most likely to reflect Wyclif's first contribution; but, since their texts are essentially identical to copies of the complete work, it seems that they must be regarded as secondary extracts.

[7] The dated manuscript is Oxford, MS Bodley 703, whose major contents are anti-Wyclif texts by William Woodford; for the other copies see T39 and here Appendix II.

[8] In the longer work they are pp. 213/2–16, 219/32–221/13, 222/40–229/37, 230/21–231/9; it will be noted that the same sequence is followed in both shorter and longer works. This relationship was recognized by the scribe of one of the Bohemian copies in his note 'Exponitur ista pro confessio doctoris de sacramento eukaristie libro de apostasia capitulo 16 circa g' (PUK

De apostasia? The four Bohemian copies of this *Confessio* have an extension which itself is likewise paralleled elsewhere, in the epistle sermon for the feast of Corpus Christi.[9] It may seem not unreasonable to argue that the Bohemian extension does not go back to Wyclif, but is the result of a secondary comparison of two texts on obviously related subjects. But is the opening of the *Confessio* a series of extracts from *De apostasia*? The usual answer to that question has been negative – the originary status of the *Confessio* has not been regarded as open to dispute. That answer may be right; but since the date normally given to *De apostasia* is 1379–80, or well before 10 May 1381, it should be recognized as in some respects difficult. The *Confessio minor* could be a short definitive statement extracted from the longer work by a hostile critic anxious to refute Wyclif.[10] Whether Wyclif himself ever authorized the *Confessio minor* seems to me highly questionable.

The prolonged attempt by his opponents, many but not all of them ecclesiastical, to silence Wyclif resulted in other statements that gained variable currency. Thomson distinguishes two texts associated with the abortive attempt to bring him to trial at the meeting of the Canterbury convocation in March 1378. The first of these, the *Protestacio* (T399), survives only in various manuscripts of the historical writings associated with St Albans;[11] the second, entitled *[Libellus] ad parliamentum regis* (T400) is found independently in both English and Bohemian manuscripts.[12] Both consist of a series of eighteen points with supporting evidence: whilst the points remain unchanged, the evidence varies between the two versions; the list of views was produced by an opponent, on this occasion pope Gregory XI in his bull issued in May, but

---

XI.E.3 f.54v; the final 'g' is the usual indexing device in academic books – for which see further below no. VII 330–31).

[9] *Sermones* iii.278/7–286/30; the copies are two in PUK XI.E.3, and one in ÖNB 1387 and 4343; there is an extract from the Bohemian extension in Brnc Mk 109, f.179v headed 'doctor ewangelicus in Confessione fidei Sepe confessus sum subdit inter cetera'. The Hussite catalogue explicit, mentioned by Thomson T39 n.11, presumably derives from a misreading of the Bohemian penultimate word *ipsis* as *episcopis*.

[10] Apart from the manuscript now BL Royal 7 B.iii, three copies have association with religious orders (Bodley 703 with the Franciscans, Bodley e Mus.86 with the Carmelites, Cambridge Jesus College 59 with the Durham Benedictines), and two (Eton College 47 and BL Harley 635) are collections including anti-Wyclif materials in the hand of John Malberthorp, fellow of Lincoln College and later of Eton (see *MMBL* ii.686–8).

[11] See *St Albans Chronicle* i.198–210 and see here Appendix II; Thomson's main heading is unfortunate since *Protestacio* is not used in the manuscripts of 399 (though it is in two of 400), which describe the text rather as *Declaraciones*.

[12] The English tradition is, however, poor, consisting of Oxford Bodleian Arch.Selden B.26 and e Mus.86 (*FZ*); BL Additional 5902 is declaredly a post-medieval copy of the first of these.

the evidence was contributed by Wyclif himself.¹³ The differences between the two are puzzling: the general drift of each answer is the same in both texts, but, whilst there is some overlap of authorities, mostly biblical but occasionally patristic or canonistic, this is not complete; there is no clear differentiation between audiences, nor any clear mark of corruption through transmission.¹⁴ Whether both versions should be regarded strictly as Wyclif's is unclear: the freestanding text has the better claim, but that in Walsingham's *Chronicle* is not self-evidently a later sophistication. Certainly independent, but equally not well evidenced in England, is yet another defence (T401) that Wyclif produced to Gregory's nineteen conclusions. This one, judging by its address to 'tam seculares quam clerici' (FZ p. 488/25) and by its tone, was certainly intended to gain a wide circulation. Yet despite its preservation in ten Bohemian copies, only a single one is found in England even if that seems to derive from an Oxford and perhaps well-informed source.¹⁵ Not evidenced at all in English copies is the longer tract concerning 33 articles (T402): here there are two French copies, and eight Bohemian texts plus an extract.¹⁶ The text was not used by Netter, and whether its disappearance should be regarded as fortuitous is unclear.

Some of the uncertainties so far discussed could be the result of the activities of men other than the author, whether opponent, chronicler, polemicist or simply the scribal editor. But it is clear that, in addition to the changes of mind that are reflected on topics such as the eucharist, Wyclif often worked under extreme pressure of time, at least until his withdrawal to Lutterworth in the autumn of 1381. This resulted both in the obvious incompleteness of some works, and in the reusing of material with variable amounts of revision – of the latter *De ecclesia* is a very clear example. The most evident of the incomplete texts are two, the *De dominio divino* (T23–25) and the *Opus evangelicum* (T374–377). To take the simpler case first: the fourth book of the latter ends in all four

---

¹³ The bull did not reach England until the autumn. In both texts the seventh condemned conclusion is ignored with consequent renumbering of the remainder.

¹⁴ The freestanding version, T400, is called variously *libellus* (in Bodleian e Mus.86), *protestacio* (in Oxford Bodleian Arch Seld.B.26 (and BL Additional 5902), Paris BN lat.3184 start and PUK XI.E.3) and *conclusiones* (at the end of the same Paris copy and ÖNB 3929); ÖNB 1387 has no title at either end.

¹⁵ Bodleian Arch Seld.B.26, ff.85va–87vb; the manuscript is composite, this item preceded by T400 (and at the start Gregory XI's bull against Wyclif in the version sent to Oxford university) and followed by T383 forming part 3 of the whole.

¹⁶ The two French copies are Paris BN lat.3184, Vatican Borgh.lat.29; in addition to the Bohemian copies listed by Thomson should be noted PMK D.105, ff.201–219v and the extracts in Padua Antoniana 226, f.260r–v with conclusions 1–5 only (the main content of the manuscript is Holcot on the *Sentences*).

surviving copies, two English and two Bohemian, with the scribal colophon 'Auctoris vita finitur et hoc opus ita'.[17] The incompleteness is immediately apparent from the fact that the subject of this book, announced at the start as a commentary on John 13–17 (ii.287/5), has not reached the end of the first of those chapters, and that the fourth book has only fourteen chapters as compared with over sixty for each of the others.[18] But it seems to me that the incompleteness may be much more considerable than this that there is not just a failure to reach the end of the declared text because of the interruption of death, but that what remains is of the whole only a first draft. As has been noted by scholars before, even as a commentary this work is very strange: alongside the expected quotation of the biblical source to be expounded, there are also very long *verbatim* quotations, often extending to over a printed page, from a limited range of patristic commentaries, Jerome and pseudo-Chrysostom on Matthew, Augustine on John.[19] Whilst it is entirely credible that the heavy use of these texts reflects the restricted availability of books to Wyclif in Lutterworth (these, it may be supposed, he owned himself), the technique is drastically different from any found earlier.[20] It seems possible that what we have is, in effect, a first draft of a work that was intended to be reworked into a more digested whole – in this the authority of the fathers would be fully demonstrated, but the quotations would have been curtailed to fit Wyclif's own argument. Whatever its status, however, the *Opus evangelicum* was evidently released in its incomplete form after Wyclif's death, and gained some circulation: numerous conclusions from it in the 1411 Oxford condemnation make clear its availability there, and, although the number of surviving manuscripts is not enormous, it was, to judge by the likely date of the two, evidently transmitted to Bohemia fairly early.[21]

---

[17] TCC B.16.2, f.460vb, TCD 241, p. 332a, PUK IV.A.18, f.202va, ÖNB 1647, f.298va; there is an extract from book I, caps.52–8, in PMK C.38, ff.175ra–82rb.

[18] There is some minor discrepancy between the manuscripts, English as against Bohemian, in the chapter divisions and hence numbering in books 2 and 3, but this does not make more than a single number's overall difference.

[19] For Jerome see PL 26.15–218, for pseudo-Chrysostom PG 56.611–946; the Augustine used is mostly from the sermons, PL 38–9, but also the commentary on John, PL 35.1379–1976.

[20] The inclusion in the third book, virtually unaltered (e.g. ii.132/2–134/9 = *Op.Min.*359/33–362/12, 180/8–13, 34–40 = 363/22–364/1, 181/6–25 = 364/1–20), of long sections from Wyclif's own independent and highly polemical commentaries on Matthew 24 (T373), can be paralleled in the use of the *De sex iugis, De incarcerandis fidelibus* or *De religione privata* in the sermons discussed below. Thomson's table p. 215 regarding text 372 is not helpful: all the parallels between the brief commentary and *Opus evangelicum* cited are sequential quotations from Matthew 23, and since both texts are expositions of this chapter the identity is only to be expected.

[21] For the first point see here no. XIII; the two Bohemian copies PUK IV.A.18 and ÖNB 1647 both date from c.1400.

More puzzling is the incompleteness of the *De dominio divino*. All surviving copies, one English and four Bohemian, preserve it in the same form: a first book where the text stops in mid sentence near the start (to judge by the length of those preceding) of chapter 19, a second book which halts equally abruptly a fair way through chapter 5, and a third that ends with a complete sentence but not at the end of the argument in chapter 6. All scribes note the incompleteness of each book, and some leave space evidently in the hope of obtaining a more satisfactory exemplar.[22] The English copy was owned in Oxford in 1403, and one of the Bohemian copies, ÖNB 1294, was made in England at Braybrooke in Northamptonshire in 1406 or 1407 (see below no. XIV 234–6); it must thus be assumed that, if any more of the text ever existed, that material had been lost sight of at a very early stage. It was not quarried in the 1411 Oxford enquiry but does appear, with a variant only in the final explicit of the third book, in the Bohemian catalogue;[23] the references in the three copies of the index to the text, and in the biblical index in which it was included, do not extend beyond the material now known.[24] The explanation of this curious state of affairs may lie in one simple fact: the *De dominio divino* was not included within the *Summa theologie*, even though it was evidently understood as closely related to it, or more precisely as a prologue to it, by both the Bohemian catalogue and the lists that probably preceded this.[25] As will be argued below, the twelve books of the *Summa theologie* underwent varying degrees of revision, by Wyclif himself in his last years and possibly by his disciples after his death. It is tempting to see the surviving state of *De dominio divino* as an indication of what a major Wyclif tract looked like before that revision. In this case the abandonment of the text, if that is what happened, cannot have been because Wyclif lost interest in the subject – far from it. The issue of true dominion underlies a large part of his later writing, and the work would seem to be the logical first step of a sequence which is then carried into the first three parts of the *Summa theologie*. Why then was it omitted from the *Summa*? and, if my

---

[22] The copies are Gonville and Caius 337/565, ff.68r–127v, ÖNB 1294, ff.212ra–251vb, 1339, ff.1ra–89vb, 3929, ff.114rb–170rb, 3935, ff.13ra–48ra; the first was not known to R.L.Poole, the editor of the Wyclif Society edition.

[23] See below no. III items 101–3; the last book is shown there as ending 'habentur hic', as against the ending in all manuscripts 'donare dicitur'; it seems hard to base much on this discrepancy.

[24] For these see below no. VII; the index in ÖNB 3935 ff.1ra–11va is headed 'Registrum primi libri de dominio divino', but all three books are covered.

[25] See below no. III. For the wording see entry 100 'Summa eiusdem in theologia continet duodecim libros in se. Primus est liber mandatorum (ie *De mandatis*), presupponens tres libros de dominio divino'.

suggestion about its state is correct, why was it not finished, albeit at a late date? A possible answer is that by the time Wyclif reached Lutterworth, where the revision of the books of the *Summa* was undertaken, he had lost sight of the text, and had no draft, however fragmentary, to complete.[26] It is credible that the fragments that survive represent Wyclif's consolidation of lectures he had given, soon after the event, but that the work was broken off or abandoned for more pressing concerns; if the text was not available to him in the final years in Lutterworth, it is understandable that his disciples thought it best, when the fragmentary materials surfaced, to leave them in their incomplete state. Perhaps it is not insignificant that the Czechs, Faulfiš and Kněhnic, copied *De dominio divino* at Braybrooke, not Oxford.[27]

De dominio divino was not, for whatever reason, revised; *De ecclesia*, on the other hand, underwent substantial reshaping. The processes of revision found in the twelve books of Wyclif's *Summa theologie* and in his five sets of sermons are examined in the papers that follow and do not need repeating here. But it is worth adding to the evidence three instances that are not covered below. The first is what is now known as book 3 of the *De logica* (T3). Superficially this book completes the sequence of books 1–2, works which have usually been ascribed to an early stage in Wyclif's career.[28] Two English manuscripts (now in continental collections), fragments of a third, and one Bohemian copy contain both 2 and 3, thus confirming the coherence at least of these two books.[29] All this points to a unified transmission of the whole, or at least of books 2–3. The incorporation, unattributed, of an extract from book 2 in the so-called *Logica Oxoniensis*, an assemblage of teaching materials put together in the last third of the fourteenth century, would seem to indicate that nothing exceptional or

---

[26] The rarity of cross-references to *De dominio divino* may support this, especially in contrast to their frequency in *De civili dominio*: in *De mandatis* 34/20 is a reference to *De dom.div.* chapter 1 (5/6), and at 38/4 to chapter 3 (22/2); there is one unspecific reference at 16/10; in *De civ.dom.* iii.183/16 there is a single unspecific reference.

[27] Though G & C 337/565 was in the hands of three Oxford masters in 1403 (see *LB* p. 79).

[28] Book 1, a very elementary text-book, is normally dated to c.1360, book 2 to the following three years, and Thomson dates book 3 as '1363?'. Manuscript preservation of book 1 as a whole is not good, but one of the two continental copies (ÖNB 4523) also contains book 2.

[29] Respectively Assisi Biblioteca Communale 662, ff.1ra–109va and Escorial e.II.6, ff.1ra–76vb; the fragments are now Oxford Bodleian MS Lat.misc.b.27 (for which see my paper in *BLR* 19 (2006) 244–50), PUK V.E.14, ff.1r–176v. PMK N.19, ff.129ra–166ra and PUK V.H.33, ff.1r–28r contain only book 2; PUK IX.E.3, ff.1–176r only book 3. Despite Jeremy Catto's doubts (*HUO* ii.190 n.47) about the traditional numbering of *De logica* in three books (as in T1–3), the headings visible in the newly discovered fragments support it.

objectionable was found in that section at least.[30] Yet in the 1411 list of 267 errors extracted from Wyclif's works appear twenty quotations from *De logica* book 3, quoted under the title of *De arte sophistica*. Location of those quotations in the dense and poorly edited text is not easy, but sufficient of the citations can be traced to be sure that *De logica* 3 as we know it is indeed in question, and that the quotations are as close to its text as those from more readily accessible texts.[31] Looking at the subject matter of these 'errors', their relevance to Wyclif's views on the eucharist is all too plain: if these are a fair sample of what Wyclif was teaching around 1363, then it is incomprehensible that the authorities took so long to indict him for teaching error on this sensitive subject before their attack of 1381. That the text as we have it, and as it was extracted by the 1411 investigators, could represent a version dating from much later in Wyclif's life is suggested by a reference towards the end of book 3 to the present time as 'mille trecenti et 83 anni' (iii.183/39). Thomson described this date as 'deeply suspect', and offered as possible explanations either scribal error, or authorial revision of just this sentence – the latter he evidently thought highly improbable in the light of Wyclif's later preoccupations. But the surviving four copies of this section all give the same date.[32] And, as the 1411 scrutiny perceived, the argument of large parts of this book are far from being irrelevant to Wyclif's final positions. It seems much more likely that *De logica* book 3 as it survives should be regarded as a version revised by Wyclif at the end of his life, and that the earlier, less contentious, version was suppressed with complete success.

Much less clear is the textual history of *De benedicta incarnacione* (or *De verbi incarnacione* T22). Here there are four copies of English origin, four of Bohemian; one of the English copies is heavily abbreviated, so that its evidence is unhelpful.[33] The Wyclif Society edition by Edward Harris unfortunately

---

[30] See L. de Rijk, '*Logica Oxoniensis:* an attempt to reconstruct a fifteenth century Oxford manual of logic', *Medioevo* 3 (1977), 121–64 especially pp. 144–5; see Oxford, New College MS 289, ff.37r–38r where *De logica* ii.75/3–83/14 is quoted without attribution.

[31] Thus in Wilkins' text conclusion 159 is traceable to *De logica* ii.85/14, 167 to iii.69/24, 169 to iii.137/13, 170 to iii.137/33, 171 to iii.141/40, 172 to iii.142/6 and 173 to iii.151/8; it will be noted that the quotations here are sequential through the text as now known.

[32] See Assisi f. 101vb where the date is written 'mille trecenti octoginta 3^{es} anni', Escorial f.71rb '1383', PUK V.E.14 f.162v and IX.E.3 f.158r in both of which is found 'mille trecenti et 83 anni'. For discussion of the date to a similar conclusion see M. Wilks, reprinted in his *Wyclif: Political Ideas and Practice* (Oxford, 2000), pp. 55–8.

[33] The English copies are Cambridge Gonville and Caius 337/565, ff.128r–178r, Oxford Oriel 15, ff.225ra–243ra, Pavia Biblioteca Universitaria 311, text disrupted by misbinding ff.91va–b, 93ra–97vb, 62ra–71vb, 108ra–130rb, and abbreviated London BL Royal 7 B.iii, ff.66r–74v; the Bohemian copies PMK D.35, ff.1r–77v, ÖNB 1387, ff.75ra–104vb, 4307, ff.115r–157v, 4504, ff.37r–110v; Harris did not use the Cambridge, Pavia and Prague copies.

provides a conflated text, using two of the English copies (including the abridged one) and three of the Bohemian; a full understanding of the situation will not be possible until the work is reedited using all manuscripts. But it is clear even from Harris's edition that there are some major oddities in the transmission: at least four passages, two of them of considerable length, are missing from some copies. For the most part it is the English copies that lack them, the Bohemian which provide them; but this is not always the case – and, as with the *De veritate sacre scripture* example discussed in no. IV 202–5 below, the English scribes sometimes show awareness of the anomaly.[34] But, in comparison with the case of *De logica 3*, the responsibility for the variant forms is much less clear: do the discrepancies go back to Wyclif, to his assistants who continued the revision of his works, or to scribal error? The witnessing of the two forms of text do, however, emphasise that more than one copy of the text travelled to Bohemia.

Much more complicated is the state of the text in Wyclif's most widely disseminated work, the *Dialogus* or *Speculum ecclesie militantis* (T408). Of this there are twenty-four surviving copies, two of them English, the remainder continental and mostly Bohemian.[35] The Wyclif Society edition is here even more unsatisfactory than in the last instance: A.W.Pollard produced a conflated text from the evidence of only nine of the copies, and it is very difficult at times to discover the basis for his readings. The work itself is a brief summary of many of Wyclif's views, presented as a dialogue between *Veritas* and *Mendacium*; in Pollard's edition it falls into 36 chapters plus an epilogue. But many of the copies either do not number the chapters at all or cease to do so as the text progresses; some do not specify the speakers, or even mark the shift from one to the other. The major divergences, however, occur from chapter 28 onwards; in what follows I have specified chapter numbers from Pollard's edition, but many of the copies involved do not mark these or have variant numbers. One

---

[34] The Royal manuscript is so abbreviated that its affiliations in the discussion cannot be traced; its evidence is not included here. The passages are pp. 68/19–25 present in ÖNB 1387, 4307 and Prague but missing from the three English copies and ÖNB 4504; 75/18 missing from all English copies but present in all Bohemian; 134/31–136/25 present in all Bohemian copies, missing from Pavia without notice, and from Oriel and Cambridge with a marginal note of the defect and supplied at the end of the text (f.177v) in the latter; 168/24–170/15 present in all Bohemian copies, again missing from Oriel and Pavia without notice, and from Cambridge again with a marginal note and supplied at the end (f.178r). It is worth noting that the indexing letters found only in ÖNB 4307 (see below no. VII) require the presence of the third and, less clearly, of the fourth passage in the text.

[35] See Thomson's listing; Oxford Bodleian MS James 3, a seventeenth-century transcript of extracts from the text, does not include any of the material relevant here, and has been omitted (but see below no. XVI).

of the two English copies and fourteen of the continental copies conclude the text with Pollard's chapters 28–30 and 33–36, omitting his chapters 31–32 and the Epilogue.[36] Three further continental copies are very close to this arrangement, but differ in that they contain chapter 32 after chapter 36 and finally the Epilogue; all three recognize that these last two chapters may not be in their correct position with a rubric stating that the following material had been extracted *per falsos fratres*.[37] Only one Bohemian copy, ÖNB 3932, contains all of Pollard's text (a manuscript unknown to Pollard), but in the order chapters 28–31, 33–36, 32, Epilogue. The remaining English manuscript, now Manchester Rylands Eng.86 is Pollard's authority for his arrangement of the chapters, but it is an uncertain witness:[38] its text proceeds, with numbered chapters, up to and including 28, a marginal note there (f.114v) reads 'Hic deficiunt 4^{or} capitula, scilicet 29. 30. 31. 32' before providing chapters 33–36 ending on f.116v; the missing four chapters appear ff.118r–121r (though lacking most of 30, Pollard 63/20–69/18, because of the loss of two leaves after f.118v); but there is no sign of the Epilogue. So this one English copy provides the chapter ordering, albeit its scribe left out four of them at first writing, but Bohemian copies attest chapter 32 and they alone have the Epilogue; chapter 31 appears only in the Rylands copy plus one of the Bohemian manuscripts. How can this extraordinary situation be explained? It should first be said that the absence of chapters 31–32 from most copies cannot be a simple case of homeoteleuton in their archetype: neither the conclusion of chapters 30 and 32 nor the opening of chapters 31 and 33 offer opportunity for this. Subject matter is another possible cause: chapters 31–32 deal with endowment in particularly outspoken terms, and with some references to specifically English history – but this did not deter the scribe of ÖNB 3932.[39] Similar interests are voiced in the poorly attested Epilogue.[40] The explanation given in three of the Bohemian copies for their eccentric positioning of chapter 32 and the Epilogue is unlikely to have

---

[36] These are Florence Laurentian Plut.XIX.33 (the English copy), Brno UK Mk 62, Florence Bibl.naz.cen. Conv. sopp.E.3.379, Olomouc KK C.O.118, Olomouc SV I.V.34, PMK B.17/1 and C.38, PUK VIII.F.13 and X.C.23, ÖNB 1622, 3930, 4302, 4515, 4536 and Vatican Borgh.lat.29. The copies in Munich BSB clm 15771, ff.35r–50r, and ÖNB 4701, ff.41r–57r, end incomplete before this part of the text; the material in ÖNB 1337, ff.166ra–168va, though largely derived from the *Dialogus*, does not overlap with this section.

[37] These are ÖNB 1338, f.76rb, 1387, f.160va and 4505, f.24r.

[38] There is a description of the manuscript in Ker *MMBL* iii.409–11, but his account of the contents of ff.118r–121r needs modification: f.118r–v does indeed contain Pollard's cap.29 and 30 to 63/20, but ff.119r–120r contain cap.31, f.120r–121r cap.32 – Ker was misled by the eccentricities of the chapter numbering in the various copies and the edition.

[39] See, for instances, *Dialogus* pp. 70/1, 72/14, 29 for English references in chapter 31.

[40] See pp. 87/25, 90/1 with its discussion of the correct interpretation of Magna Carta.

any authority: neither section expresses any particular hostility to the fraternal orders – chapters 19 or 25–26 would seem more obvious targets for extraction by the friars.

Further oddities occur within the text present in all copies: at least two substantial passages are missing from many of the manuscripts.[41] The *Dialogus* was translated into Czech and survives in a single manuscript: unfortunately, however, the manuscript is defective because of the loss of leaves, so that, whilst the two omissions just mentioned are also not present here, no evidence is offered about the final chapters.[42] Later English use of the work likewise casts uncertain light on the textual situation: fifteen passages were extracted from the text by the 1411 committee, but none of them derives from the end of the text relevant here.[43] Netter made considerable use of *Dialogus* in his *Doctrinale*, especially in the first books and the last, quoting and, as usual, providing chapter numbers. There seem, however, to be a larger number of discrepancies between those given in the printed edition of Netter and those provided in Pollard's text than can be attributed to errors in transmission, whether in manuscript or in the early prints; but it is hard to see any sequence in the mistakes that would allow for an explanation.[44] What is clear, however, is that Netter did have access to a version of the *Dialogus* which contained chapter 31, and also at least part of the material missing from chapter 30 in one of the two English manuscripts.[45] It is not easy to draw any conclusions from this state of affairs. Some of the problems may well be scribal: the Manchester manuscript does not inspire confidence, either in its overall layout or in the peculiarities of its witness to this particular text.[46] But it is hard to avoid the conjecture that the *Dialogus* was another of the texts that underwent authorial revision over time,

---

[41] 59/26–60/3 (chapter 28) against perpetual endowments is missing from all copies other than Manchester, Vatican Borgh.lat.29 and ÖNB 3932, 61/28–62/5 (chapter 29) from all copies other than Manchester alone.

[42] Prague National Museum III.B.11, ff.181r–210v; it was published by M. Svoboda under the title *Překlad Viklefova Dialogu* (Prague, 1909); f.205v ends at the equivalent of the Latin p. 53/19 (chapter 26), ff.208r–209v contain parts of chapters 28 and 29, pp. 58/17–63/6, f.210r–v parts of chapters 35 and 36, pp. 82/14–84/15 – chapter numbers are not given in the Czech version.

[43] Conclusions 141–155 in Wilkins' edition (iii.345–6); these mostly follow the text ordering, and 155 derives from chapter 27.

[44] Thus, for instance, Netter II.23 (i.362) chapter given as 16 should be 11 (*Dialogus* 21/22), II.75 (i.545) chapter given as 14 should be 24 (p. 50/19), II.66 (i.591) chapter given as 6 should be 4 (p. 9/2).

[45] He quotes chapter 31 (p. 71/34) at II.75 (i.649) as chapter 32, and material he describes as from chapter 30 (p. 67/18) at IV.36 (i.943).

[46] For other comments on this manuscript see below no. XVI.

and that the extant manuscripts derive their oddities from archetypes made at different stages of the text's development.[47] And again multiple exemplars, reflecting different stages of the textual history, seem to have gone to Bohemia. This is a text for which a new edition is urgently needed, though whether all the questions that can currently be raised could be satisfactorily answered remains to be seen.

The *Dialogus* evidently gained wide circulation, and its fierce argumentation in favour of Wyclif's most radical views makes that easy to explain. At the other end of the spectrum are texts for whose existence we only have indirect evidence. The Hussite catalogue specifies that Wyclif wrote a *Postilla in totam Bibliam*, though admits that 'it is not available today'.[48] Only the commentary on the New Testament (and that lacking one for the Apocalypse T371) survives from Bohemia; from England material for roughly the second half of the Old Testament, starting from Job, is also available though lacking now Proverbs to Ecclesiasticus (T320–324, 328–344). Whether Wyclif ever compiled a commentary on the opening books must remain uncertain;[49] it is possible that he did and that, given the uncontroversial nature of almost the whole of the known material, it remains to be discovered, probably in an unattributed state. More certain evidence of existence are the two references to a commentary on Aristotle's *Meteora*, one in the listing of Syon abbey and the other in the catalogue of a Carolinum college in Prague (see below no. XVI) – the chance that there is any connection between these two is too remote to weaken the case. Syon also provides a reference to a copy of a letter by Wyclif to John of Gaunt, duke of Lancaster, a letter whose content and date it would be fascinating to recover (see below no. XVI); Peter Partridge's miscellany, now Oxford Bodleian MS Digby 98, also, according to its prefixed medieval list of contents, originally contained many letters by Wyclif at a point where now only two stubs remain.[50] Thomson's listing only includes a small handful of letters, though the boundary between these mostly public missives and more extensive tracts is a difficult one to define; interestingly, however, several of them (including the most personal, T395, 396 and 404 save for the *FZ* copy) survive only in Bohemian copies.

---

[47] It should be noted that progressive deterioration in the continental tradition will not account for the situation since it does not cover the rearrangement that sets chapter 32 after 36.

[48] See no. III item 99.

[49] For reasons to think he did comment on the Wisdom books (T325–7) see below no. XV.

[50] See R. Hanna, 'Dr Peter Partridge and MS Digby 98', in *TCWB* pp. 41–65 esp. 51–2: the possibility that the surviving material that comes shortly after these two stubs on ff.185r–v also derives from a lost work by Wyclif seems to me a strong one.

Many uncertainties remain about the transmission of Wyclif's works to Bohemia: we may know the names of two or three of the *colporteurs*, but they cannot singlehanded have carried copies of all the writings which reached Prague. Who were the others? Where, when and under whose guidance did they obtain their exemplars? The possibility that some texts migrated not direct from Oxford to Prague but through more complicated academic channels is confirmed by the colophon to the very imperfect copy of *De civili dominio* (T28–30) in which the student scribe notes that Wyclif's views on dominion were debated at Paris on 16 January 1381.[51] There seems no reason to question this claim, especially when it is remembered that Jerome of Prague later fell foul of the authorities in Paris, as well as in Heidelberg and Vienna, for disseminating Wycliffite views.[52] At about the same date, Nicholas Biceps in Prague seems to have been aware of the dangers for eucharistic orthodoxy inherent in Wyclif's philosophical views: there is no evidence that Biceps ever visited England, but he was in touch with academic debate in western Europe.[53] The three copies of the reply to Strode's ten questions (T385), all Bohemian, end with a colophon recording that the text was found in the papers of Robert Stonham when he died at the Council of Pisa in 1409;[54] these point to another mode of dissemination. Transmission across the whole continent, in academic or ecclesiastical circles, is by no means peculiar to the writings of Wyclif. What is more unusual is the dramatic effect those writings had on the wider world outside such circles. Even if current Czech scholarship tends to play down the seminal importance of Wyclif in the thinking of Hus and his followers, and hence on the events that followed in the years after Hus's death at Constance, in such an account many questions remain to be answered. Quite apart from his direct tributes to Wyclif, Hus himself quoted a large number of Wyclif's works

---

[51] See Paris BN lat.15869, f.103r.

[52] For Jerome of Prague there are a number of sources: for F. Šmahel's contributions see the list in his *Die Prager Universität im Mittelalter* (Leiden, 2007), p. viii n.10; also Z. Kaluza, 'Le chancelier Gerson et Jérôme de Prague', *AHDLMA* 51 (1984), 81–126; V. Herold, 'Magister Hieronymus von Prag und die Universität Köln', *Miscellanea Mediaevalia* 20 (1989), 255–73; M.H. Shank, '*Unless you believe you shall not understand': Logic, University and Society in late medieval Vienna* (Princeton, 1988), pp. 176–9. I. Kořán, 'Knihovna Mistra Jeronýma Pražského', *Český časopis historický* 94 (1996), 590–600 printed a list of books owned by Jerome, at least three of which contained material by Wyclif.

[53] See further W. Zega, *Filozofia Boga w 'Quaestiones Sententiarum' Mikołaja Bicepsa* (Warsaw and Bydgoszcz, 2002) – an English summary appears pp. 225–7.

[54] The manuscripts are PUK III.G.16, f.87v; V.G.19, f.258v and ÖNB 3929, f.276ra; for Stonham see Emden *Oxford* ii.1789–90. The existence of the colophon in all copies makes it clear that the note was copied along with the text itself; Buddensieg's note (*Pol.Wks* i.xxxi) misled Emden into assuming that the third manuscript actually belonged to Stonham.

in his own texts on many subjects;⁵⁵ the dominating position of the English Wycliffite Peter Payne in Hussite affairs continued through to the middle of the fifteenth century.⁵⁶ Even firmer testimony to Wyclif's continuing centrality is the number of copies of his works from Bohemia that survive to the present, despite the ravages of political and ecclesiastical conflict that have affected central Europe over six centuries.

The papers here deal entirely with Latin works, and almost entirely with texts that can with fair certainty be attributed to Wyclif himself; my own conviction is that, even though the probability that Wyclif himself at various points taught in English must be strong, that teaching is preserved only in Latin.⁵⁷ The writings composed and disseminated by his followers, whether in Latin or more frequently in English, are numerous and important enough to deserve separate treatment; some in Latin share the Bohemian transmission found for Wyclif's own Latin works, but the vernacular writings are entirely an insular matter. A few points of general comparison may perhaps be made here. As the final chapters here mention, it is much more difficult to trace ownership of vernacular writings than of Wyclif's Latin texts in the period between the master's death in 1384 and the 1530s: this is partly a reflection of the concentration by the orthodox persecutors of Lollardy on lay suspects, with the consequent destruction of evidence both by the officials of the church and by the anticipation of the suspects themselves (who, even if they retained the books, avoided adding, or removed, any mark of ownership), but partly the result of the fact that the institutional libraries of the period were almost exclusively under the control of the church and their books consequently, whatever their content, almost exclusively in Latin. In simple terms, manuscripts of vernacular texts containing texts of Lollard origin are, even excluding copies of the Wycliffite Bible, more numerous than those surviving in England of Wyclif's own Latin texts, but their whereabouts until the modern period is

---

⁵⁵ See, for instance, listings in the indices to the texts by Hus, *De ecclesia*, ed. S.H. Thomson (Cambridge, 1956), p. 241, *Polemica*, ed. J. Eršil (Prague, 1966), p. 503, *Postilla Adumbrata*, ed. A. Molnar (Prague, 1975), p. 655, *Questiones*, ed. J. Kejř (Turnhout, 2004), p. 200.

⁵⁶ For Payne's career see Šmahel in *ODNB*. Another later testimony to the frequency and range of quotations is the *Confessio Taboritarum* (ed. A. Molnar and R. Cegna, Rome, 1983), see index p. 425.

⁵⁷ If Walsingham's allegation that Wyclif had preached about 1377 'running from church to church around London' (*Chronicon Angliae*, ed. E.M. Thompson, RS 1874, p. 117) is credited, then the *Sermones quadraginta* may in part at least have originated in English. It seems to me that Wyclif's practical involvement in the Bible translation project is improbable, if only on grounds of his time.

Introduction: Wyclif's Works and their Dissemination

hardly ever traceable.[58] But, if ownership by a religious institution was more regularly declared and offered a better chance of preservation in the medieval period, the dispersal and destruction of the contents of those libraries in the sixteenth century altered the picture decisively, as the final chapter here argues. And, although the religious changes of that later period might in England be thought to work towards a renewed interest in Wyclif's anticipation of many of the reformers' convictions, the advocacy of Bale and Foxe arguably came too late to salvage many copies from those earlier libraries. Latin books perhaps suffered more than texts in the vernacular: on the one hand they were regarded as outmoded in the increasing demand for theology in a language that all could understand, whilst on the other their medieval Latin was derided as a poor distortion of the rediscovered model of Ciceronian style.

The story of the transmission of Wyclif's writings is one for which there is a surprising amount of evidence. In some ways it is an idiosyncratic case: the content of those writings aroused extremes both of support and of anathema, and both contributed to a multiplication of copies and their transport over long distances. But the Latin language had equally facilitated a similar dissemination of many other, often less polemical, texts by many other writers. Equally, the energy for revision of texts discussed here is not peculiar to Wyclif: indeed, in late fourteenth-century England revision could almost be said to have reached epidemic proportions (Langland, Gower, Chaucer, the chronicles associated with St Albans all provide familiar examples); the indexing efforts described below (no. VII) can be paralleled frequently, even if little modern research has been done into this phenomenon.[59] In many respects then, the story here is not atypical, however much its details may surprise those unfamiliar with the period. What is, however, perhaps remarkable is the fact that so much detail is traceable for an author whose views were condemned within his own lifetime, and whose works and followers were persecuted so energetically both in England and on the continent. The fathers at the Council of Constance in 1415–17 who condemned a list of Wyclif's views, ordered the exhumation and burning of his body with the scattering of the ashes in unconsecrated ground, sent Jan Hus and later Jerome of Prague to the stake as impenitent advocates of teachings

---

[58] By my reckoning there are 45 surviving manuscripts of Wyclif's Latin works that are of English origin; noting only copies of the Wycliffite sermons, of the *Glossed Gospels*, the revised versions of Rolle's Psalter commentary and of the *37 Conclusions*, all of which require normally a complete and sizeable volume, the count of vernacular English manuscripts is 54 – beyond which there is a large number of manuscripts which in whole or in part consist of shorter Wycliffite works.

[59] For a particularly ambitious undertaking, the *Tabula septem custodiarum* see R.H. and M.A. Rouse, *Registrum Anglie* (*CBMLC* 2, 1991), pp. xcviii–cxxvi; see here also nos. VII and IX 90.

they attributed to Wyclif, would surely have been startled if they had realised that so many copies of so much material would survive their efforts and those of their successors. Books in this case may be said to have overcome bonfires.

From Oxford to Prague: The Writings of John Wyclif and his English Followers in Bohemia

AENEAS SYLVIUS PICCOLOMINI, later Pope Pius II, in his *Historia Bohemica*, tells how the books of the heresiarch John Wyclif had been brought to Prague by a man of noble Bohemian blood, by name Putridus Piscis, who had been studying in Oxford.[1] Aeneas does not assert that this was the first appearance of Wyclif's books in Central Europe, but he plainly saw the story as significant — symbolic if not originatory. Since any consideration of the transmission of Wyclif's writings is bound to tell the colourful story of the Bohemians Mikuláš Faulfiš and his friend Jiříz Kněhnic, despite the breach of chronology I shall start with it. In 1406–07 these two spent some time in Oxford, where they obtained through the good offices of Peter Payne a testimonial, with the seal of the University attached, attesting that Wyclif was of upright life, pre-eminent in the knowledge and exposition of scripture, outstanding in his writing and teaching, and had never been condemned for heresy.[2] They also paid their respects at the grave of Wyclif in Lutterworth, where in typical tourist fashion they chipped a fragment from the tombstone to take back with them as a memento of their visit.[3] Less predictably, they also spent some time at two small villages, each about sixty miles from Oxford though in opposite directions; in both their purpose was to copy texts written by Wyclif. At Kemerton, west of Oxford, they copied the *De ecclesia*; at Braybrooke, north-east of Oxford, they copied the *De dominio divino*. They also

---

[1] See *Historia Bohemica*, Helmstedt, 1699, pp. 49–50. Any paper on the present subject must owe a large debt to the magisterial work by František Šmahel, and notably to his paper 'Doctor Evangelicus super omnes evangelistas: Wyclif's Fortune in Hussite Bohemia', *Bulletin of the Institute of Historical Research*, 43, 1970 pp. 11–34, and I wish also to record my own gratitude for his generosity over many years.

[2] The testimonial does not survive in the Oxford archives or in English medieval records, though in the sixteenth century it must have been available in England, since it was copied into the manuscript now British Library MS Cotton Faustina C.vii fol. 125^{r-v}; from there it was printed by D. Wilkins, *Concilia Magnae Britanniae et Hiberniae*, 4 vols, London, 1737, III, p. 302. A Bohemian copy is to be found in Prague University Library MS XI.E.3, fol. 1.

[3] See F. Palacký (ed.), *Documenta Mag. Iohannis Hus vitam, doctrinam, causam in Constantiensi concilio actam... illustrantia*, Prague, 1869 (hereafter *Documenta*), p. 313.

somewhere made a copy of the *De veritate sacre scripture*, and checked their version in the early weeks of 1407 in Oxford. Kemerton and Braybrooke must have been then, as they are now, tiny hamlets off any main route, though close to good roads. But the reason for the availability of Wyclif's texts in either is not hard to seek: Braybrooke was the main residence of Sir Thomas Latimer, the Lollard knight whose credentials as a Wycliffite are least open to challenge; Kemerton was in 1406 the living of Robert Lychlade, expelled from Merton College, Oxford in 1395 for his adherence to heretical views, though reinstated by Henry IV in 1399, a living to which he had been instituted by Sir William Beauchamp, another suspected Lollard knight.[4]

The enterprise of Faulfiš and Kněhnic evidently gained wide publicity in Bohemia: Hus recounted a story concerning Faulfiš's experience in England.[5] The Oxford testimony concerning Wyclif was repeatedly mentioned in the judicial process against Jerome of Prague that took place in Vienna in 1410, declaredly because Jerome himself had often publicly mentioned it.[6] This and the stories about the chip off the tomb and the copying of the books were remembered in 1415 proceedings against Hus in Constance.[7] From the wording of Aeneas Sylvius it would seem that the two Bohemians took back to Prague several books. But miraculously one single volume survives, now Vienna Österreichische Nationalbibliothek (hereafter ÖNB) 1294; and it is from the annotations to the three texts there that the itinerary I describe can be discovered.[8]

The story of these two Bohemians has many interesting aspects, and raises many central questions, both in the history of English Wycliffism and in the history of the fortunes of Wyclif and Wycliffism in Central Europe. It is only the second of these that is directly relevant here. The first point is the relative lateness of their journey: why did two Bohemians come in search of Wyclif texts as late as 1406? By that time Wyclif's ideas were well known in Prague, and by my reckoning some sixteen manuscripts of Wyclif's works written before that date by Bohemian scribes are known to survive.[9] Certainly most of these surviving manuscripts are of Wyclif's logical or philosophical works, but this is not true of all, and, even if it were true, those philosophical

---

[4] For Latimer, Beauchamp, Hoke and Lychlade, see Anne Hudson, *The Premature Reformation: Wycliffite Texts and Lollard History*, Oxford, 1988 (hereafter *The Premature Reformation*), pp. 90–91, 100–01, 153–54, 164; for Latimer, see also K. B. McFarlane, *Lancastrian Kings and Lollard Knights*, Oxford, 1972, pp. 139ff.

[5] Hus, *Opera omnia*, II, *Česká nedělní Postila*, ed. J. Daňhelka, Prague, 1992, p. 148.

[6] L. Klicman (ed.), *Processus iudiciarius contra Jeronimum de Praga habitus Viennae a. 1410–1412*, Prague, 1898 (hereafter *Processus iudiciarius*), pp. 15, 18, 22, 24, 31, 34.

[7] Palacký (ed.), *Documenta*, p. 313; compare *Historia Bohemica*, p. 49, 'pleraque volumina'.

[8] See the edition of *De dominio divino* by R. L. Poole, London, 1890, pp. ix–xii.

[9] For details of the extant manuscripts of Wyclif's works see W. R. Thomson, *The Latin Writings of John Wyclyf*, Toronto, 1983; I have accepted the dates there given.

texts are far from purveying throughout the innocent orthodoxy that some modern critics have assumed. The possibility that Faulfiš and Kněhnic came to England in search not of new texts but of *authoritative* copies of what was already known in Prague is one that is implied by the care with which they validated in the margins the sources of their material — the *De veritate sacre scripture* was *correctus graviter* (fol. 119ᵛ) in Oxford. It is a possibility to which I shall return later.

If these two named seekers were not the first to bring Wyclif's works to Bohemia, when had those first texts arrived? The question is difficult to answer. Without the circumstantial details of names, dates and places, such as are offered by this story, evidence is much harder to piece together. The earliest hint comes in the comments of Mikuláš Biceps on the view of John Wyclif that Christ was in the consecrated host *solum figuraliter et non realiter* (Prague Metropolitan Chapter Library [hereafter PMK] MS C. 19, fol. 158); the basis of this lies in the opinion that *est* in biblical language often indicates metaphorical and not literal predication — *est* in *hoc est corpus meum* should be compared with *ego sum vitis vera* or *ego sum pastor*. The date of Biceps's shrewd comment is apparently 1377–79 — a very early date since it is usually held that Wyclif himself did not directly preach remanence until 1379 or 1380, and that it was that preaching that directly led to the first formal condemnation of him published in England.[10] Biceps's comments need not imply that he had himself *read* any of Wyclif's texts: he could have heard tell of Wyclif's position in the schools through ordinary academic channels. Any astute philosopher, and in that category we must surely include Wyclif himself, could perceive plainly where his earlier speculation about universals must end. One place where Wyclif's views, albeit on a topic other than the eucharist, were under discussion at the latest by 1381, was Paris: at the end of a partial copy, apparently a student abbreviation, of the *De civili dominio*, appears a note that on 16 January that year a debate was held in the university there on Wyclif's doctrine of dominion.[11] Certainly those views on dominion were known in Rome by 1377, in part probably purveyed by the

---

[10] See E. Stein, 'Mistr Mikuláš Biceps', *Věstník Královské české společnosti nauk*, 4, 1928 (1929), pp. 39–56 (p. 43n.), and D. Trapp, 'Clm 27034: Unchristened Nominalism and Realism at Prague in 1381', *Recherches de théologie ancienne et médiévale*, 24, 1957, pp. 320–60 (pp. 349, 355–56); the early date was questioned by S. H. Thomson in a review in *Speculum*, 38, 1963, p. 117, but has been confirmed by F. Šmahel, 'Universalia realia sunt heresis seminaria', *Československý časopis historický*, 16, 1968, pp. 797–818.

[11] Now Paris, Bibliothèque Nationale fonds. lat. 15869, fols 70–125ʳ, the note fol. 103ʳ; Thomson's account of this manuscript is not accurate, since it contains abbreviated sections from all three books of the work.

English Benedictine Adam Easton, and resulted in Gregory XI's attempt to procure the condemnation of the Oxford master.[12]

Central to the whole question are two factors: the amazing mobility of scholars throughout the late medieval period, and, fundamental to that mobility, the existence of a *lingua franca* used by academics whether English, French, Roman or Bohemian. Just as the Irishman Richard FitzRalph could purvey the outcome of his discussion with the Armenian schismatics to the whole of Western Europe in Latin, so could boundaries entirely disappear in the travels of the ideas of Wyclif. For those travels were, so far as I have been able to see, entirely those of *Latin* Wyclif and Wycliffite works — of texts in English there is no trace at all, of texts that might conceivably have left England in English guise only a minute handful of arguable cases. In Prague the longstanding reputation of Oxford's university must have helped the rapid dissemination of Wyclif's works: from 1367 the statutes of Prague University allowed for the dictation to copying scribes of texts originating only from Prague itself, Paris or Oxford — as will be seen, this method was certainly used for the multiplication of copies of some Wycliffite texts.[13]

In the case of Biceps it is possible that the ideas travelled independently, and in advance of, the texts in which Wyclif fully argued them. Also, since Biceps is not known to have visited England, his knowledge, however extensive it may have been, was probably acquired from a source intermediate between Oxford and Prague. Attempts to explain the transfer of Wyclif's texts to Bohemia have concentrated on direct contacts with England. Mention is always made of the marriage of Richard II and Anne of Bohemia in January 1382, an alliance which obviously must have brought some of her countrymen to England and which may have fostered traffic in both directions; the fact that Anne's ownership of vernacular scripture is mentioned by Wyclif himself in one of his late works encourages the notion that this alliance was indeed significant.[14] Probably independently of this, the Czech Adalbertus

---

[12] See W. A. Pantin, 'The *Defensorium* of Adam Easton', *English Historical Review*, 41, 1936, pp. 675–80; the sole surviving manuscript is now Vatican lat. 4116; for Gregory XI's bull concerning Wyclif, see E. M. Thompson (ed.), *Chronicon Angliae*, London, 1874, pp. 175–83.

[13] See *Monumenta Historica Universitatis Carolo-Ferdinandeae Pragensis*, 2 vols, Prague, 1830–32, I, pp. 13–14, 40–42.

[14] J. Loserth, 'Über die Beziehungen zwischen englischen und böhmischen Wiclifiten', *Mitteilungen des Instituts für österreichische Geschichtsforschung*, 12, 1891, pp. 254–69; R. L. Poole, 'On the Intercourse between English and Bohemian Wycliffites in the Early Years of the Fifteenth Century', *English Historical Review*, 7, 1892, pp. 306–11; R. F. Young, 'Bohemian Scholars and Students at the English Universities from 1347 to 1750', *English Historical Review*, 38, 1923, pp. 72–84; and R. R. Betts, 'English and Czech Influences on the Hussite Movement' in Betts, *Essays in Czech History*, London, 1969, pp. 132–59. For Wyclif's mention of Anne see his *De triplici vinculo amoris* in *Polemical Works*, ed. R. Buddensieg, 2 vols, London, 1883, I, p. 168.

Ranconis (Vojtěch Raňkův z Ježova), after spending time himself in Oxford around 1360, at his death in 1388 left money for the establishment of scholarships to assist Czech scholars to study theology or the arts at Oxford or Paris.[15] Adalbertus is not known to have commented on Wyclif's views, though he was a supporter of the Czech 'pre-reform' movement and also the proud possessor of the autograph copy of FitzRalph's *De pauperie salvatoris*, a text which underlies Wyclif's teaching on dominion — and which, like the copy of a Sentences commentary of the mid-fourteenth-century Oxford Carmelite Osbert of Pickingham (now PMK C.105), he may well have obtained in Oxford.[16] We do not know the names of the beneficiaries of Adalbertus's bequest. One possible recipient was Jerome of Prague, who certainly studied in Oxford from about 1399 to 1401, and who may have returned a few years later. Jerome declared later in his life that he took back with him to Prague from England copies of Wyclif's *Dialogus* and *Trialogus* and two texts dealing with the eucharist — whether these were the long *De eucharistia* and *De apostasia* or two of the shorter tracts in which Wyclif set out his views of this topic is unfortunately unclear.[17]

With Jerome we come back from the realms of speculation and inference to the hard facts of specified manuscript transmission, even if those books, unlike Vienna 1294, do not survive. But again Jerome's visit in 1399–1401 is too late to explain the whole story. And Jerome's admission came at his trial at the Council of Constance in 1416, some sixteen years after the event — there is no need to doubt its veracity in outline, but is the specific detail of the individual texts involved reliable? The *Dialogus* and *Trialogus* had by then become the *summae*, respectively popular and academic, of Wyclif's thought. Equally, can we accept the detail of Hus's reply to the taunts of the Englishman John Stokes in 1411, when he claimed that he had had Wyclif's books for twenty years and more?[18] And Hus's claim is also infuriatingly vague — which Wyclif texts were available in 1391 or earlier? We should probably not take the dates in either story too precisely, any more than we should build too much on the words of Hus at his trial in 1415, reported by

---

[15] J. Kadlec, *Leben und Schriften des Prager Magisters Adalbert Rankonis de Ericinio*, Beiträge zur Geschichte der Philosophie und Theologie des Mittelalters, 4, Münster, 1971, pp. 11–12, 37, 59.

[16] Now Vienna Österreichische Nationalbibliothek 1430; see K. Walsh, 'The Manuscripts of Archbishop FitzRalph of Armagh in the Österreichische Nationalbibliothek, Vienna', *Römische Historische Mitteilungen*, 18, 1976, pp. 67–75 (p. 67).

[17] H. von der Hardt (ed.), *Magnum oecumenicum Constantiense Concilium*, 6 vols, Frankfurt, 1699 (hereafter *Magnum oecumenicum*, IV, p. 649. For Jerome, see F. Šmahel, 'Leben und Werk des Magisters Hieronymus von Prag', *Historica*, 13, 1966, pp. 81–111, especially p. 89; see also V. Herold, 'Wyclif und Hieronymus von Prag' in R. Työrinoja *et al.* (eds), *Knowledge and the Sciences in Medieval Philosophy*, 3 vols, Helsinki, 1990, III, pp. 212–23.

[18] *Contra Iohannem Stokes*, in J. Erši (ed.), *Magistri Iohannis Hus Opera omnia: 22 Polemica*, Prague, 1966, p. 60/21.

Peter of Mladoňovice, that twelve years earlier, that is in 1403, Wyclif's theological works had not yet reached Bohemia — a claim that is directly at odds with Jerome's.[19] And Jerome of Prague in 1410 was said to have heard about Wyclif's logic during a stay in Paris — the indirect link appears as important as the direct, precise dates are hard to validate.[20]

If traces of named Bohemian visitors to England are few, it is even more difficult to discover evidence at the early period for English travellers to Prague who might have taken Wyclif's texts with them. By late 1414 or the beginning of 1415, Peter Payne, the helper in Oxford in 1406 of Faulfiš and Kněhnic, had followed them back to Prague, and entered Hussite history.[21] It would have been strange if Payne had *not* taken Wyclif and Wycliffite works with him, and Harrison Thomson argues that it is to Payne that the indexes of Wyclif's works (to which I will return later) are due, and that Payne's hand is to be seen in annotations in a number of Wyclif manuscripts now in Vienna.[22] But, even if Payne's contribution to Hussite knowledge and understanding of Wyclif was considerable, it is impossible on chronological grounds to maintain Payne as the 'founding father' of Wyclif texts in Bohemia.

The evidence for that early period up to c. 1410 is for the most part fragmentary and unspecific. Wyclif's name and the outline of some of his ideas were certainly known in Prague within a few years of his death in 1384, if not before. Around that time the Prague archbishop Jan of Jenštejn in his defence of Church property spoke of Wyclif as *heresiarcha nephandissimus*.[23] Before 1400, on the other hand, Stanislaus of Znojmo wrote a tract on universals so imbued with Wyclif's philosophy that it was printed in 1905 amongst the works of the English master.[24] But specificities of texts are usually hard to pin down before the end of the 1390s. Clearly dated to 1397 is one manuscript, now Prague University Library (hereafter PUK) III.G.10; this contains four of Wyclif's major philosophical works, the *De universalibus, De tempore, De ydeis* and *De materia et forma*. Though the standard listing of Wyclif's works assigns dates between 1368 and 1372 for all of them, it seems likely that some

---

[19] Palacký (ed.), *Documenta*, p. 280.
[20] Klicman (ed.), *Processus iudiciarius*, p. 22; compare von der Hardt, *Magnum oecumenicum*, p. 646.
[21] See 'Peter Payne in England' in Betts, *Essays in Czech History*, pp. 236–46; A. B. Emden, *An Oxford Hall in Medieval Times*, 2nd edn, Oxford, 1968, pp. 125–54; for further details and references, see Hudson, *The Premature Reformation*, pp. 99–103.
[22] S. H. Thomson, 'A Note on Peter Payne and Wyclyf', *Medievalia et Humanistica*, 16, 1964, pp. 60–63.
[23] The text was written in 1382, but survives in a copy of June 1385: see J. Sedlák, *Studie a texty*, 2 vols, Brno, 1913–15, II, p. 105.
[24] M. H. Dziewicki (ed.), *Miscellanea philosophica*, 2 vols, London, 1905, II, pp. 1–151; for details of manuscripts, see F. Šmahel, *Verzeichnis der Quellen zum Prager Universalienstreit 1348–1500, Mediaevalia Philosophica Polonorum*, 25, 1980, pp. 21–22.

of them as we have them had undergone revision by Wyclif later in the 1370s.[25] All these works reappear in the manuscript now in Stockholm, Lat.A.164, accepted as an autograph copy by Jan Hus himself and dated to 1398; the copy of *De universalibus* was made from two exemplars, one of them the extant manuscript of 1397.[26] The earliest surviving dated manuscript of one of the directly theological and polemical works, the *De symonia*, is from 1401, now Vienna ÖNB 3937; two years later, from 1403, is a copy of the *De eucharistia* (PUK VIII.G.32) accompanying the philosophical *De trinitate*.[27] These are all dated by their scribes. But on palaeographical evidence more can be added: for instance the two Bohemian copies of the *Opus Evangelicum*, finished by its author as all scribes noted 'et vita sua', come from *c.* 1400 (now ÖNB 1647 and PUK IV.A.18). After the date of the visit to England of Faulfiš and Knĕhnic comes a flood of Bohemian copies, though it may seem that this must in large measure be a case of *post hoc et non propter hoc*.

Direct evidence, whether of testimony by sympathizers and by opponents, or from the colophons of manuscripts, thus provides distressingly little unambiguous information. Can anything be learned by a study of the texts themselves? In the first place, it is important to recognize how much our knowledge of Wyclif's works owes to Bohemian scribes. The most recent listing of those works, by Williel Thomson, completing the work of his father S. Harrison Thomson in 1983, gives a total of 435 works; that figure, which, for convenience in listing manuscripts, treats the sermons as 244 separate items instead of four collections plus four outriders, can more realistically be reduced to about two hundred. Of these, about half survive *only* in Bohemian copies. This half includes a number of Wyclif's most important texts: the complete *De civili dominio*, *De ecclesia*, *De officio regis*, *De potestate pape*, *De eucharistia*, the *Supplementum Trialogi* and a large number of the shorter polemical tracts. It should be stressed that this survival does not indicate that the texts in question are Hussite revisions or compilations of Wyclif's works: enough English evidence survives to show that the reason for their sole survival in Bohemia lies in the more efficient destruction in England of works offensive to the orthodox hierarchy of the Church. There may always have been more copies of some of the late tracts in Hussite Bohemia than there ever were in England; but the works themselves are genuinely those of the English master.

Some 130 manuscripts containing Wyclif's works in Bohemian hands survive. And it is clear that even that large number does not fully

---

[25] See Thomson, *Catalog*, nos. 11–2, 18, 20; for revision in the first see the edition by I. Mueller, *De universalibus*, Oxford, 1985, pp. xix–xxxviii.
[26] Ibid., pp. xli–xlii, lxxxvi.
[27] See colophon in the first fol. 137ᵛ, and in the second fol. 82ᵛ.

represent the original total: so much can be proved without recourse to speculation concerning the losses by natural causes and by deliberate destruction, whether medieval or modern. The evidence for this claim lies in a remarkable catalogue of Wyclif's works which was made by 1415, and which is found in three medieval copies and one later version, all now in Vienna.[28] There is absolutely no reason to think that this catalogue originated outside Bohemia, and Prague seems its most credible source. The catalogue gives a list of the titles, incipits and explicits, and for most cases the number of chapters when this is more than one; it is alphabetically ordered by incipit. Its *raison d'être* seems to be the recognition or identification of Wyclif's genuine writing; there is no indication that it is a finding list, since no library or place is mentioned. The motive for the compilation seems to be friendly — there is no cause to suspect that this is an identification kit for the extirpation of the books in question — the three medieval copies are all in manuscripts containing Wyclif's works, and the author comments rather sadly at one point that 'today we do not have all of the *Doctor Evangelicus*'s commentary on scripture'.[29] The listing is both accurate and comprehensive. Accurate in that only two works are included that firmly should not have been: in both cases the texts in question are by disciples of Wyclif and not by the master himself, a fact that the incipit of one of the two should have revealed. The four further works that cannot now be identified amongst Wyclif's writings may indeed be genuine: their topics, as revealed by their titles, are all within his range and words in the incipits and explicits of two are characteristic parts of his vocabulary.

Of the two hundred or so works I have suggested we should calculate as a fair tally of Wyclif's output, these Hussite catalogues contain all but about thirty. Amongst those omitted are a dozen or so which may never have achieved circulation in England, let alone in Bohemia; most are brief, some summary statements of views that Wyclif elaborated at more length elsewhere, some occasional pieces originating in response to a particular situation. A few are early academic productions, such as the commentary on Aristotle's *Physics* or the interchange on biblical interpretation with Kenningham.[30] One or two may be summaries produced not by Wyclif himself but by a disciple. The only notable area in which the catalogues are surprisingly reticent is that of the

---

[28] ÖNB 3933, 3935, 4514, and the later copy 7980; prints of the first three are to be found in *Polemical Works* (see note 14 above), 1, pp. lix–lxxiv; see Anne Hudson, 'The Hussite Catalogues of Wyclif's Writings' in J. Pánek, M. Polívka and N. Rejchrtová (eds), *Husitství, Reformace, Renesance: Sborník k 60. narozeninám Františka Šmahela*, 4 vols, Prague, 1994, 1, pp. 401–17.

[29] ÖNB 3933 fol. 196vb (Buddensieg 1, p. lxvi): 'postilla super totam bibliam que hocce non habetur'.

[30] Thomson, *Catolog*, nos. 6, 378–80.

philosophical works: given the early interest in Prague in this aspect of Wyclif's output, it is unexpected that four of the sections of the first book and four of the second of the *De ente* are missing — though only a single Bohemian copy of each survives. This absence, and the paucity of copies, may suggest that Wyclif's philosophical reputation in Bohemia rested upon four tracts, *De universalibus, De tempore, De trinitate*, and *De ydeis*.

The catalogues show that six works by Wyclif now not extant in Bohemian copies must have been at the time they were compiled, since they are entered with correct incipits and explicits.[31] Conversely, there are nine texts accepted as by Wyclif which today *are* to be found in Bohemian copies but which are not included in the catalogues; all save one are relatively insignificant and brief, the exception being the reply to ten questions of Wyclif's Oxford colleague Strode (T385).[32] The scholarship of the catalogues bears witness to a more varied tradition of Wyclif's writings in Bohemia than is now extant. For instance, all five surviving Bohemian copies of the *De statu innocencie* (T27) are incomplete, ending at best in chapter six; but the catalogue states that the work has ten chapters and gives an explicit corresponding to the end of that chapter ten in the complete text; that complete version is now only found in two copies of English origin.[33] The surviving ten Bohemian copies of *De tempore* lack the final chapter thirteen; but the explicit of that text in the catalogue suggests that this last chapter must have been known on the continent.[34] The expertise shown by the catalogues is remarkable, the discrimination exemplary. Who made them, and where? That information, alas, is withheld. But, given the thoroughly academic form of the enterprise, Prague seems the most likely place where the scholars could have been found to devise and compile the listing, and where the books could have been available to produce the information.

The information of the catalogues is relatively simple to analyse, and can add details to the picture of the fortunes of Wyclif in Bohemia. Much more laborious to investigate are the copies themselves: how reliable are their texts, in so far as that can be assessed? Are all surviving copies derived from a single exemplar brought to Bohemia from England? Some of the problems in answering either question are

---

[31] Ibid., nos. 381–83, 405, 420, 423.

[32] The other eight are ibid., nos. 41–43, 392, 406–07, 433–34; the reason for the absence of T385 may be the fact that the colophon to all three surviving copies includes the name of Robert Stonam, who had actually owned the text, but who may in haste have been taken for the author.

[33] Cambridge, Gonville and Caius College 337/565 and Trinity College, Dublin 241.

[34] ÖNB 3933, 4514 and 7980 give the explicit as *per consequens modo instat orationis suffragium* (3935 omits the first two words), which seems to be a conflation of the end of cap. 12 *ab eo oracionis suffragia* and of cap. 13 *per consequens modo instat*.

obvious from what has already been said. If no English copy survives, how can the accuracy of the Bohemian text be assessed? For a few texts, and for some passages, it may be possible to check the Bohemian readings against the quotations of Wyclif to be found in the polemics composed by his English opponents in the fifty years after the heresiarch's death. Most useful in this regard is the material recorded by the Carmelite Thomas Netter of Walden, who in his vast *Doctrinale* quotes many long extracts from some texts. The texts which Netter most frequently used are, however, not those for which information would be most welcome, in this enquiry at least — in other words, not those for which we are now dependent exclusively on Bohemian copies.[35]

A more fruitful route of investigation seems to be to look with more care at the textual transmission of those works where both English and Bohemian copies survive. Currently this is difficult: the publishing endeavours of the Wyclif Society began in 1883 and ended in 1921, and the editions produced are not adequate for this purpose. This is largely because more manuscripts have come to light since that time, but partly because what interested the editors was in principal measure Wyclif's ideas and not the transmission of the texts, and hence they are not sufficiently meticulous in the recording of variants for detailed analysis of the quality of an individual manuscript to be made. Two more recent editions, both of philosophical works, the *De trinitate* and *De universalibus*, use all known copies, but again are not exhaustive in their record of variants.[36] If their editors' assurances are to be believed, in both cases the Bohemian manuscripts form a group, credibly descended from a single exemplar. This is not a surprising conclusion in the instance of the *De trinitate*, where only a single English copy survives; it is more disappointing with the *De universalibus*, for which five English copies survive but which Ivan Mueller, the editor of the tract, sees as standing as a group over against the fifteen Bohemian and two Polish copies, all of which in his stemma derive from the same hyparchetype (the copy now in Venice written by a German scribe, possibly working in Ferrara, seems closely allied to the English group).

Loserth, in his 1886 edition of the *De ecclesia*, knew all three surviving complete manuscripts. Whilst the copy, now Vienna ÖNB 3929, seems to be a close copy, mistakes and all, of Faulfiš's version made in England (ÖNB 1294), the third, now PUK X.D.11, descends from an archetype anterior to this and superior in some respects to it — confirming that

---

[35] The most accessible edition is that by B. Blanciotti, 3 vols, Venice, 1757–59 [reprint, Farnborough, 1967]; Netter apparently did not, for instance, have ready access to either *De dominio divino* or *De civili dominio*, and of the sermons used only those on the Sunday epistles.
[36] For the second see note 25 above; the first was edited by A. du P. Breck (Boulder, CO, 1962).

more than one exemplar of this text must have come to Bohemia.[37] In my own work on the texts of Wyclif's major writings, a more multifarious textual tradition has certainly emerged in the *De veritate sacre scripture* than was known to Rudolph Buddensieg in his edition for the Wyclif Society of 1905–07. The interesting detail for the present purpose concerns a passage covering the end of chapter seven and beginning of chapter eight, a passage which is found in five of the surviving manuscripts but is missing from the remaining seven that cover this section. Two of the manuscripts that include the section are English, two Bohemian; the fifth is Faulfiš's Vienna ÖNB 1294. Conversely, three of the manuscripts that omit the passage are English, four Bohemian.[38] There are further complications: in all three of the English copies that include the passage there is an indication that the scribes realized that their exemplar(s) were untrustworthy at that point, and Vienna 1294 likewise has a marginal note at the start, acknowledging that the passage does not appear in all copies. But equally, one Bohemian scribe of a copy without the passage (Prague UK III.B.5) noted marginally 'hic est magnus defectus'. Two deductions from this seem legitimate: first, that the surviving Bohemian copies derive from two English traditions, one of which contained the passage and the other of which did not; secondly that, in addition to a surprisingly widespread consciousness of the problem at this point in the text, there is a remarkable concern with correctness, shown most clearly in Vienna 1294, but not only there.

Part of that concern is connected with the fact that the omission covered a chapter break, and that this in turn affected the numbering of subsequent chapters. This mattered to users of the *De veritate* for two reasons: characteristic of all Wyclif's longer works, particularly of his middle period, is frequency of cross references within the work itself and to other of his own writings — these references are usually by chapter number; similarly, chapter numbers are used in the summaries and indexes to Wyclif's works, both of which had their beginnings in England but which developed into a major concern in Hussite Bohemia.[39] The Vienna manuscript produced by Faulfiš and Kněhnic contains a summary of the *De veritate*, though in a different and slightly later hand; it at first conflates the two chapters into a single one at the

---

[37] See Loserth's edition (London, 1886), pp. xvii–xxii.
[38] Other manuscripts in the first group are Oxford, Bodley 924; Cambridge, Peterhouse 223; PMK A.84; and PUK VIII.C.3; those in the second are Cambridge, Queens' College 15; Dublin, Trinity College 243; London, British Library Royal 7.E.x; PMK B.53 and C.38; PUK III.B.5; and Olomouc, Kap.K.C.o.115; this problem is discussed in my paper 'Cross-referencing in Wyclif's Latin Works' (forthcoming).
[39] A brief summary of the English origins is in Hudson, *The Premature Reformation*, pp. 104–06; the most important Bohemian indexes are to be found in PUK X.E.11, PMK C.118 and ÖNB 1725.

point of this passage, but then corrects to make the single summary cover two chapters, and amends subsequent chapter numbers. The usefulness of cross references, or of indexes and summaries, depends entirely on accuracy of numbers.

The Faulfiš story is partly memorable because of its colourful detail; but its importance lies more in the accident that here we have names, dates and places, on the one hand, and, on the other, the actual copy these men made, guaranteed by their own annotations to the text. The crucial nature of the concatenation can be seen if the case is compared with that of Jerome of Prague: none of the five Bohemian copies of the *Trialogus* and none of the nineteen Bohemian copies of the *Dialogus* can reasonably be conjectured to have been made by Jerome, nor brought back by him from England. Hence we raise questions even about the veracity of his testimony.

The title of my article implies that I should say something about the works of Wyclif's English followers that reached Bohemia. Two major Latin texts are most widely found. The first of these is an alphabetical set of *distinctiones*, the *Floretum* or, in its abbreviated form, the *Rosarium*, giving a vast assemblage of material from the Bible, the Fathers, canon law, a few medieval authorities and from Wyclif on a wide range of theological, ethical and ecclesiological subjects.[40] Over twenty-five Bohemian copies of some version of these texts are known to me, and I do not doubt that more remain to be discovered. In each case, of the *Floretum* and of the *Rosarium* there is a little evidence (though one could find some evidence for it in the former) that all copies descended from a single hyparchetype — in other words, that only one copy of each was brought from England. When this occurred is unclear: the earliest dated copy of the Floretum in Bohemia was written in 1413 (PUK V.B.2); the first copies of the *Rosarium* are two dated by their scribes as 1417 (PUK IV.G.19 and PMK D.16), and are said to have been taken down at the *pronunciatio* of Magister Mathias at Prague University. This Magister Mathias also dictated the second major English Wycliffite text, the Apocalypse commentary known from its first words as the *Opus arduum*; the copy testifying to this appears immediately after the *Rosarium* in Brno University Mk 28, where his surname is said to be *Engliš*.[41] Magister Mathias Engliš is found in Hussite records with the alternative *Mathias de Hnatnice*; the man was certainly Bohemian, was a friend of Faulfiš, and subsequently participated in a number of Hussite missions between 1424 and 1440. How did he come by his byname

---

[40] For my own papers on these two see Hudson, *Lollards and their Books*, London, 1985, pp. 13-42, originally published in 1972 and 1974; they were also studied by J. Kejř, '"Rosarius" — domnělé dílo slovenského husity', *Studie o rukopisech*, 14, 1975, pp. 83-110, and Kejř, 'Ještě jednou o "Rosariu"', *Studie o rukopisech*, 15, 1976, pp. 103-06.
[41] Hudson, *Lollards and their Books*, pp. 43-65, especially p. 45.

Engliš? Should we add his name to the small tally of known Bohemian visitors to England who, to judge by his later activities, could well have acted as a *colporteur* of Wycliffite texts?[42] Not associated with any Hussite name is the text surviving now in three Hussite copies in Vienna, written by a *discipulus* of the *Doctor evangelicus*, and showing by reference to the oath and declarations of the king at his coronation that the king has the right and duty of correcting errant clergy; since the coronation materials are distinctively English, the text must originate far from its present home.[43]

The *Floretum* and *Rosarium*, albeit more modestly, survive in copies in England; like the short text on the coronation oath, the *Opus arduum* does not — all thirteen manuscripts are in continental libraries, none of them in an English hand, most in Bohemian libraries and hands. Internal testimony proves that the commentary was written in England between Christmas 1389 and Easter 1390 by an anonymous academic imprisoned by the bishops for his Wycliffite views. How the text got out of that episcopal prison, let alone how it arrived in Bohemia, is entirely unknown.[44] Easier to explain is the way in which William Thorpe's *Testimony* travelled, an account, certainly fictionalized, of his long conversations in August 1407 with his captor, Archbishop Arundel. The *Testimony*, as it survives in two Bohemian copies, is in Latin, whereas the original was almost certainly in English; whether the translation was done before or after the text's migration is not clear, though both extant Latin copies descend from a single exemplar with two interpolations of certain Hussite origin.[45] Peter Payne might well have brought this text, as he might equally have brought the Latin version of a 1406 sermon by his predecessor as Principal of St Edmund Hall, Oxford, William Taylor, a single copy of which is found without attribution in Prague (PUK III.G.11).[46] Did Payne also bring a copy of the letter of Richard Wyche to his English friends, dating from a few years earlier, around 1402–03 when he was under investigation by the Bishop of Durham, that survives uniquely in the same manuscript? In 1410, Wyche wrote to Hus himself: though he laments the fact that he knows Hus only by repute, he shows himself aware of Hus's troubles in Prague and of the fact that one of his *coadjutores in evangelio* was named *Jacobellus*. The allusions in Hus's reply to the long time taken for

---

[42] See F. M. Bartoš, 'A Delegate of the Hussite Church to Constantinople in 1451–1452', *Byzantinoslavica*, 24, 1963, pp. 287–92, and ibid., 25, 1964, pp. 69–74.
[43] See my paper 'The King and Erring Clergy: A Wycliffite Contribution', *Studies in Church History Subsidia*, 9, 1991, pp. 269–78.
[44] See note 41 above.
[45] See my edition in *Two Wycliffite Texts*, Early English Text Society, 301, 1993, pp. xxvi–xlv.
[46] The English text was edited in ibid.; for the Latin see 'William Taylor's 1406 Sermon: A Postscript', *Medium Aevum*, 64, 1995, pp. 100–06.

Wyche's letter to reach him are unfortunately not clear enough for certain interpretation.[47] The year 1410 was also the date of a letter from the Lollard Sir John Oldcastle to the Bohemian nobleman Voksa of Valdštejn (Wallenstein), and of the sending of four letters from the Scottish preacher Quentin Folkhyrd to Bohemia.[48] This last is the more mysterious, since the letters, whilst couched in unimpeachably Wycliffite terms, lack any specificity to Bohemian affairs, and their author's connections with Central Europe are hard to trace — yet they survive in at least two copies, and were translated into Czech.

The interests of the English texts to an audience remote geographically from the setting in which they were originally written seem diverse: the two long texts are readily explicable — the *Floretum/Rosarium* as an invaluable reference tool of a familiar academic kind, the *Opus arduum* as a commentary on a book central, especially, to later Hussite concerns, with a sympathetically similar polemical outlook. The shorter texts are less readily comprehensible and most certainly express unambiguously an anticlericalism and antipapalism common to Hussitism and to Wycliffitism, along with various other shared or closely similar opinions. Association with named Wycliffites was in some instances probably crucial. And, because of the paucity of *named* travellers, we probably underestimate the extent of the interchange between Prague and England and also the knowledge of, and interest in, English Wycliffite affairs in the Hussite world of the early fifteenth century. This is certainly suggested by two further texts. The first is a lament of the English *pauperculi sacerdotes* under persecution by Archbishop Arundel, probably from about 1411, found in a Bohemian manuscript otherwise filled with Wyclif's writings.[49] The second is

* perhaps the most unexpected of the emigrants: this is the poem *Heu quanta desolacio Anglie prestatur*, which uses the satirical refrain line beginning *wyth an O and an I* found in several poems of English origin — this is the one place where English words are found in Hussite manuscripts. I now know of five copies of this particular poem, two in

---

[47] Wyche's earlier letter to his disciples, found in PUK III.G.11 fols 89ᵛ–99ᵛ, was printed by J. Loserth, 'The Trial of Richard Wyche', *English Historical Review*, 5, 1890, pp. 530–44; the letter to Hus is in K. Höfler (ed.), *Geschichtschreiber der husitischen Bewegung in Böhmen* (Fontes Rerum Austriacarum ... Scriptores, vi), Vienna, 1865, pp. 210–12, from PUK XI.E.3 fols 112ᵛ–13.

[48] Oldcastle's letter is edited by Loserth, 'Über die Beziehungen zwischen englischen und böhmischen Wicklifiten' (see note 14 above), pp. 266–69, from PUK XIII.F.21 fol. 146; Oldcastle also wrote, probably between 1411 and 1413, to Wenceslas of Bohemia (printed by Loserth, ibid., pp. 268–69, from Herrnhut I.61). Folkhyrd's letters were printed from Bautzen VIIIº–7 fols 106ᵛ–09ᵛ, and in the Czech version by Sedlák, *Studie a texty* (see note 23 above) ii, pp. 182*–96*, and from the Latin text in PUK X.E.24 fols 391ᵛ–93ᵛ by J. H. Baxter (ed.), *Copiale Prioratus Sancti Andree*, London, 1930, pp. 230–36.

[49] Printed from British Library Cotton Faustina C.vii by F. M. Salter, *Snappe's Formulary and Other Records*, Oxford Historical Society, 80, 1924, pp. 130–32; ÖNB 3932 fols 89ᵛᵇ–90ʳᵇ.

England, one now in Rome, but in a manuscript probably of French origin, and two of certain Bohemian origin.[50] What is odd about this case is that the poem deals, in highly allusive fashion, with the events in Oxford and London in 1381-82 concerning the condemnation of Wyclif and the reactions of his immediate followers and opponents. Some individuals, such as Nicholas Hereford and Peter Stokes, are named; others are mentioned under veiled descriptive terms; the poem was plainly an academic production only meant to be comprehensible by those 'in the know' — and certain parts remain in their reference entirely obscure to us. It seems to have little to offer to an audience twenty, let alone forty, years later than the events it mocks, nothing at all to Hussites many hundred miles away. Yet the English personal and place names, as well as the text itself, are preserved with quite remarkable fidelity.

Any conclusion to all this may seem at first sight hazardous and uncertain: so much is obscure; so little hard evidence has come to light; so many major questions remain unanswerable. But I think the outlook is not all bleak: with more investigation I believe more can be discovered — not much, I conjecture, in the way of named Bohemians in England, nor, without great luck, the copies they actually took back. More in the way of deductions from a closer scrutiny of known copies: Harrison Thomson's observation in a number of Vienna manuscripts of annotations in a hand with perceptibly English letter forms may not be, as he thought, identifiable with that of Payne, but it does testify to English influence in Bohemia; and that recognition has recently been capped by Malcolm Parkes's spotting of similar English-type letter forms and flourishing in a Wolfenbüttel Bohemian Wyclif manuscript — explicable according to Parkes as imitation of an English exemplar.[51] Equally, a new and more complete and acute survey of the copies of individual texts may, as I suggested with the *De veritate*, throw some light on the multiplicity of copies taken to Bohemia. Scrutiny of colophons, followed by the tracking of the names found with their histories, in addition to pointing to possible contacts, may also indicate

---

[50] The poem was printed by T. Wright, *Political Poems and Songs ... from the Accession of Edward III to that of Richard III*, 2 vols, London, 1859-61, I, pp. 253-53, from British Library Cotton Cleopatra B.ii, fols 60-63; the other manuscripts are Bodleian Digby 98, fols 198^r-^{v}, Vatican Pal. lat. 994, fols 158-160, Vienna ÖNB 3929 fols 223^v-225 and PMK D.12, fols 217^v-22. The identification of the Stokes mentioned in the poem with the later adversary of Hus made in Eršil's edition of Hus's *Contra Iohannem Stokes* (see note 18 above), p. 10, is erroneous.

[51] See Thomson, 'A Note on Peter Payne and Wyclyf' (see note 22 above); the Wolfenbüttel manuscript is Helmstedt 565, containing Sermones I and III (the latter in a better text than was known to its editor Loserth); I am grateful to Professor Parkes for his comments on the manuscript.

the concern to disseminate materials of English origin in Bohemia. We may be able to *name* few of the *colporteurs*, but, if all the books transported between England and Prague were put together, they would far outweigh the ability of Faulfiš's and Kněhnic's horses to carry them.

III

The Hussite Catalogue of Wyclif's Works

Wyclif's influence and reputation in Hussite Bohemia have long been subjects of debate and disagreement. The condemnations of both Wyclif and Hus produced in 1415 at the Council of Constance asserted and assumed a close connection between the two, a connection which the utterances of Hus himself at his investigation did little to dispel even though his denial of certain charges, especially relating to the eucharist, implied his independence of Wyclif in some major ideas.[1] The high esteem in which Wyclif was held by Hus's followers has been traced by František Šmahel, who drew attention to the most striking claim made in Bohemia: that Wyclif was '*doctor evangelicus super omnes evangelistas*', and could be accounted the fifth evangelist.[2] Such evaluative statements, however significant for the originator and the receivers of them, are plainly polemical and cost little effort to make, even if the consequence of using them might be significant. Much more effort must have been needed to produce the listing of Wyclif's works, which is the subject of the present chapter. That the catalogue was produced in Bohemia, and not in England, seems fairly clear: all copies of it derive from Bohemia, and there is no trace of it or of any comparable efforts at the English end. The adversaries of Wyclif in England in the fifteenth century would have found such a listing valuable in their attempts to eradicate the master's works and influence;[3] the later admirer and cataloguer of those works, John Bale, would surely have used it to advantage had it been available to him.[4]

The catalogue survives in three medieval copies, all now in the Österreichische Nationalbibliothek (henceforward ÖNB) numbered 3933, 3935 and 4514; there is also a further post-medieval copy in the same library's collection in MS

---

[1] For an account in English of the trial, including the translation of some documents, see M. Spinka, *John Hus at the Council of Constance* (New York and London, 1965), see especially pp. 213, 265–7; a more recent study of the legal processes of the trial is J. Kejř, *Die Causa Johannes Hus und das Prozessrecht der Kirche* (Regensburg, 2005).

[2] See F. Šmahel, '*Doctor Evangelicus super omnes evangelistas*: Wyclif's Fortune in Hussite Bohemia', *Bulletin of the Institute of Historical Research* 43 (1970), 16–24, reprinted with a few bibliographical updatings in his *Die Prager Universität im Mittelalter* (Leiden, 2007), pp. 467–89.

[3] See no. XIII.

[4] See no. XVI.

7980. Rudolf Buddensieg printed the first three, and parts of the fourth, in the introduction to his edition of Wyclif's *Polemical Works*; this edition was without notes or commentary, and is hard to use.[5] Johann Loserth, in his 1925 revision of W.W. Shirley's *A Catalogue of the Original Works of John Wyclif* utilized the materials Buddensieg printed,[6] as did W.R. Thomson in his *The Latin Writings of John Wyclyf*.[7] The material in these four manuscripts clearly represents a single cataloguing endeavour. Mistakes in each medieval copy which are not replicated in any of the others suggest that none of them is the cataloguer's original manuscript, but that each derives from independent scribal miscopying of that original;[8] the post-medieval list in 7980 is stated at the start to derive *ex duobus libris manuscriptis*, one of which, as will be explained, could well have been 4514.[9] The edition here uses a fresh transcription of ÖNB 3933 as its basis, and includes only those variants from the other copies that might throw light either on the work described, or on the transmission of that text in Hussite Bohemia.

The three medieval manuscripts in which the material is found are all collections of Wyclif's Latin texts; in each of them at least one of those texts is ascribed, either by name or by the usual Latin by-name *Doctor evangelicus*.[10] In MS 3933 (A) the catalogue occurs at the end of the volume, ff.195va–196vb, in a quire whose only other content, preceding this in the same hand, is an index to Wyclif's *De blasfemia*; the same scribe seems to have provided also the index to *De officio regis* which occurs on ff.58ra–62va following the text itself (ff.1ra–57rb) and in the same quire.[11] Although the hand of the items between these two indexes is that of a different scribe, it seems clear that the entire manuscript has been together throughout.[12] There is no date in the manuscript, but paleographically Thomson suggests c. 1415. On the pastedown inside the front cover the book is stated to belong to Paul of Slawkowicz who graduated

---

[5] See *Polemical Works* i.lix–lxxxiv; as will be described later, Buddensieg omitted the second half of the catalogue as found in MS 7980. He printed each copy separately.

[6] Loserth's revision, as its title implies, does not include the English works attributed to Wyclif that were included by Shirley: *Shirley's Catalogue of the Extant Latin Works of John Wyclif* (London, [1925]). Shirley's catalogue was published in Oxford, 1865.

[7] Thomson uses the catalogue throughout his listing as *VC*, but makes no overall comment on its reliability or status (see his p. xx).

[8] See items 2, 46, 47, 49 below for examples.

[9] See below pp. 4–5.

[10] The other contents can be seen most readily from Thomson's index (pp. 316–17).

[11] For the indexes see below no. VII.

[12] The hand of *De officio regis* could be identical with that of the indexes, but the greater informality of the latter makes certainty difficult. The medieval list of contents on the front pastedown includes the index to *De blasfemia* but not the present catalogue.

as Bachelor of Arts from Prague University in 1395.[13] In this copy gaps are left in the catalogue apparently to accommodate further items (see further below p. 4 concerning the layout) that might come to notice. The manuscript was number 8 in the Carolinum manuscripts sent to Kaspar von Niedbruck, and has been in the Vienna library ever since.[14] In ÖNB 3935 (B) the catalogue appears on ff.223va–224v, at the end of a quire completing Wyclif's *De blasfemia* (here without index). It is dated by the scribe 1453,[15] but this should be understood to date the catalogue only, since it seems probable that this was added into blank leaves at a date after the writing of the preceding and following texts; an index to *De dominio divino* appears at the start of the manuscript in a separate quire preceding the text itself.[16] The scribe seems to have felt pressed for space since he extended his writing into the margins all round the text; but again a few gaps are left for the addition of more items. Ownership of the volume is not declared, but derivation from the Carolinum collection has again been asserted.[17] The copy of the catalogue in ÖNB 4514 (C), ff.102v–104v, again appears after *De blasfemia* plus its index, here in the same hand as that text; the copy of *De blasfemia* is dated (f.86r) 1432.[18] Again the material concludes a quire, but it is not clear that it was added later: no gaps are left for further additions, though the listing ends neatly at the foot of f.104v.[19] Again no personal ownership is

---

[13] See J. Třiška, *Životopisný slovník předhusitské Pražské Univerzity 1348–1409* (Prague, 1981), p. 439 who says that he gave PUK V.D.12 and IX.D.7 to the (Bohemian) nation; he also owned ÖNB 4937, a miscellany of Wyclif items.

[14] See K. Schwarzenberg, *Katalog der kroatischen, polnischen und tschechischen Handschriften der Österreichischen Nationalbibliothek* (Vienna, 1972), p. 32. See further below no. XVI.

[15] This is the date accepted in F. Unterkircher, *Die datierten Handschriften der Österreichischen Nationalbibliothek von 1451 bis 1500* (Vienna, 1974), p. 106 and plate 38; Buddensieg had given the date as 1473, Thomson as 1423.

[16] There seem to be several hands in the manuscript, corresponding to booklet divisions that separate both texts and quires. The hand of ff.223va–224v is not found elsewhere in the manuscript; for the main part of the list two columns are used but for items 94–115 the full width of f.224v.

[17] K. Schwarzenberg, 'Bücher der Österreichischen Nationalbibliothek aus dem Prager Karolinum', *Biblos* 19 (1970), 97–103 and 20 (1971), 103 at no. 46; this draws on, and in certain aspects modifies, the information in F.M. Bartoš, 'Vzácný dokument z dějin knihovny Karlovy University', *Jihočeský sborník historický* 17 (1948), 31–4.

[18] Accepted F.Unterkircher, *Die datierten Handschriften ... von 1401 bis 1450* (Vienna, 1971), p. 100.

[19] The hand of *De blasfemia*, its index and the catalogue seems to be the same as that of ff.1r–26v that contain a commentary on *Cantica canticorum* probably not by Wyclif (see Thomson GSpur 3); the hand of *De officio regis*, ff 105r–182r filling quires 9–15, is probably different.

declared, but once more this seems to have been included in the package of Carolinum manuscripts sent to von Niedbruck.[20]

Buddensieg's report of the post-medieval copy, ÖNB 7980 (D), is seriously defective: he oddly seems to have noted only the opening section of its copy on ff.5r–6v and to have failed to see that the list continues after other material on ff.11r–12v and contains all that he had thought to be missing.[21] The material that interrupts the catalogue includes a list of books mainly by Hus in the Bohemian College in Prague, a second briefer list of Wyclif's works (which Buddensieg transcribed),[22] and a quire of smaller format (numbered ff.1ª–23ª) containing various other lists, again mainly of works by Hus, in more than one hand;[23] after the catalogue, ff.13r–24v contain an independent text incomplete at the end in yet another different hand. The catalogue here is headed by the scribe (f.5r) Ex *duobus libris manuscriptis: Incipiunt nomina librorum M.Joan Wycleff iuxta ordinem alphabeti*.

The organization of the Wyclif catalogue in all four manuscripts is the same: the information provided aimed to include for each work the title, the number of chapters, the opening and the closing words of the text. Sometimes one or two of these items are not forthcoming, but, especially in the layout of A (3933) and B (3935), its absence is regularly marked by a gap left by the scribe. The list is alphabetized by the opening letter of the incipit, even though in all copies the title is placed above this. In A and B two colours of ink are used: red for the title and the number of chapters, and for the abbreviation *fi* (ie *finis*) between the incipit and explicit, black for the words of the latter two. In the concluding section of the catalogue, where the items of the *Summa theologie* are listed, the same format is used, though here the ordering is according to the sequence of the books rather than by the incipit first letter.

From the detailed readings of the four copies it is possible to see that they fall into two groups. First, and most clearly, C (4514) shares a number of errors with D (7980): as well as more minor omissions and mistakes, both copies lack all cross references, lack item 42 and make a sequence of omissions between items 76 and 79 (see notes below for details). As originally written D replicates all the mistakes of C, adding a few, mostly by misinterpretation of letters, figures

---

[20] The number 33 is found on the front board; see Schwarzenberg (note 17) p. 102 at no. 33.

[21] The last two words given by Buddensieg *18 Conclusiones* are catchwords at the foot of f.6v, taken up by the first item on f.11r.

[22] Printed by Buddensieg, *Polemical Works* i.lxxxiii-lxxxiv

[23] For the material on f.23a^{verso} see below no. XVI 33. The manuscript as it stands is a collection of originally independent papers subsequently fitted together, in diverse hands but all post-medieval.

or abbreviations of its own; there is every reason to think that D's main source was C. But D was corrected at one point (see note to item 75) marginally after its first writing – this was presumably from the second copy to which allusion is made in its heading. A (3933) and B (3935) are likewise closely related, though neither is a copy of the other. Their proximity is clear from their sharing of the correct readings where CD are mistaken. But each manuscript has independent mistakes: B lacks the titles for *Quattuor imprecaciones* (71, also omitted CD), *De trinitate* (83, also missing from CD) and *Epistola missa ad simplices sacerdotes* (90, also omitted CD), omits any attempt at the surname of the recipient of the set of *Responsiones* (78, also omitted CD), and gets one step behind with the titles to two items because of an earlier omission (see notes to 92–3). As is clear from the information given, B is in many of these errors aligned with CD; the three are also in agreement in their placing of the general note about Wyclif's other works at the end rather than after item 93. But A is not perfect: its reading for the explicit of item 47 seems to be a conflation, but one where CD provides a better version (see note), its cross reference from item 84 to item 79 seems inferior to the fuller version provided by B, and its anticipation of the *De mandatis* in the general note on the *Summa theologie* at item 100 seems awkward. Many of the apparent mistakes shared by all four manuscripts could derive from the compiler's original text: most obviously, the absence of titles or of number of chapters could derive from absence of that information in any readily recoverable form from the actual books that the compiler consulted; absence of an explicit might likewise derive from the compiler's suspicion that the text in front of him was incomplete (it is notable that no text lacks an incipit). Other mistakes, notably over the number of chapters or individual words in the incipits and explicits could be attributable either to the compiler, whether incompetently or because of his use of a defective copy of the text, or to a subsequent hyparchetype. But a few apparent confusions or errors may credibly derive from mistakes in that hyparchetype rather than in the original: cases are discussed below regarding items 2, 29 and 51. In general, however, it is striking how little variation there is in the four copies, considering that the nature of the text required precise accuracy in the copying of words and numbers that in isolation have little meaning.

Apart from the minutiae of the catalogue, which will be analysed following the text itself, a number of general questions arise. First, what was the purpose of the catalogue? Explicitly no evidence is provided to answer this question: two of the three medieval lists (A and B) have no heading, while one (C), followed by the post-medieval copy (D), simply describes what follows as a list of the books of John Wyclif in alphabetical order. Implicitly, given the information that the compiler chose to provide and the order in which he chose to display it, it seems reasonable to infer that the purpose was to establish a list of the accepted works of the *Doctor evangelicus*, against which the authenticity of further copies of the texts themselves, whether anonymous or with attributions that for some reason might be doubted, could be verified. The author's biography was evidently of no interest in this undertaking, nor was the chronology of the works' composition; the content of each work was equally not relevant here (chapter analyses and indexes provided to many of the major works fulfilled this need);[24] nor was the catalogue a finding list for copies of the works – even though, as will be argued below, its very existence implies the accessibility somewhere in Bohemia of the texts listed.

Secondly, what was the model for such a catalogue of the works of a single writer? In searching for this, it seems important to look for a combination of the features of this catalogue: the focus on a single writer, the inclusion of title, book and chapter numbers, incipit and explicit, and the exclusion of any biography of the author or summary of the work in question: the catalogue is at one and the same time austere in its limitations and scholarly in the information it offers. From this standpoint, though an ultimate influence may have been Augustine's *Retractiones*, often seen as the antecedent to all later medieval bibliographical tools, this does not provide explicits but conversely offers, as the title would lead one to expect, discursive material on the subject matter of the text in question, even if only on a few aspects of that.[25] Equally another influential medieval reference work, Jerome's *De viris illustribus*, covers, as its title implies, a wide range of people; again its entries are not in the schematic form found here.[26] The influence of these two patristic models in the later medieval period seems overwhelming, but they cannot be the immediate pattern for the instance here. The closest credible model I have so far found appears to be the list of authors and their works which is appended to many copies of the *Manipulus florum*, the handbook compiled in the thirteenth century in Paris by Thomas of Ireland.[27] This list, although it covers a large number of authors from pseudo-Dionysius and Augustine onwards, is an austere list of authors, their works with indication of number of books (but not chapters), and their incipits

---

[24] See below no. VII.

[25] See PL 32.583–656. R.H. Rouse and M.A. Rouse have discussed the influence of this work and the development of bibliographical tools in a number of places: note particularly the papers reprinted in *Authentic Witnesses: Approaches to Medieval Texts and Manuscripts* (Notre Dame, 1991), especially pp. 469–94.

[26] See PL 23.601–720.

[27] See R.H. Rouse and M.A. Rouse, *Preachers, Florilegia and Sermons: Studies on the 'Manipulus florum' of Thomas of Ireland* (Toronto, 1979).

and explicits.[28] The handbook was very popular in the later medieval period, and nine probable Bohemian copies are listed by the editors, Richard and Mary Rouse.[29] The *Manipulus florum* index likewise influenced Henry of Kirkestede, a Benedictine of Bury St Edmunds in England working in the middle and third quarter of the thirteenth century, in his *Catalogus de libris autenticis et apocrifis*.[30] But here most authors are provided with an initial biography, varying in length from a few brief words to several lines. If the Wyclif catalogue had originated in England, it would be tempting to wonder whether Kirkestede's work could have influenced the compiler; but, since there is no evidence that the latter's efforts were known outside England, the model of Thomas of Ireland seems more likely.

Turning to the coverage of the catalogue, over a hundred works of Wyclif are provided with a title and incipit, with number of books and chapters where their length is so divided; many, but not all of these, are also furnished with an explicit. Thomson's 1983 catalogue offers a much higher number, but only because he, unlike his medieval forerunner, numbered each sermon and each book of the *Postilla in totam Bibliam* separately.[31] The medieval catalogue has a few straight duplicates: *De statu innocencie* (T27) is listed in the opening section as well as amongst the books of the *Summa theologie* (see items 93 and 105), similarly the Sunday epistle sermons (T176–234) appear in the opening section and in the comment that follows (see items 42 and 96); the complete *Opus evangelicum* (T374–7) is detailed (items 52–5), but two of the four books have already appeared independently in their alphabetical position (items 24 and 31); two minor works are listed more than once (T390 at items 2 and 4, T394 doubtfully at items 29, 67 and 91). Of the works recognized by Thomson as authentic works of Wyclif, some thirty do not appear in the medieval catalogue.[32] The larger number of the texts that are missing comprise philosophical works: thus

---

[28] See the print of this list, pp. 251–301, based on Paris BN lat.15986 and 15985, both according to the Rouses in the author's hand.

[29] See their descriptions, pp. 311–405, manuscripts now in Budapest (1), Prague (8), plus one possible instance now at Wake Forest University, USA.

[30] See the edition again by R.H. Rouse and M.A. Rouse (*CBMLC* 11, London 2004), and note the analysis in the introduction pp. lxxxiv-cxxv on the compilation of the *Catalogus*.

[31] Thomson recognized 435 works; using the same methodology as the medieval compiler, this comes down to about 115.

[32] Thomson fails to identify five works that seem to me clearly identified in the medieval catalogue (items 2, 23, 27, 33 and 98); it is not clear to me why he mentions ÖNB 7980 alone as recording T7. Since the publication of Thomson's list two works have been added to the tally, neither of them mentioned in the medieval catalogue: these are (i) an elementary logical text *Summa summularum*, found partially in Harvard University Library Houghton Lat.338, Oxford Bodleian Lat.misc.e.79, ff.44v–45v and Seville, Biblioteca capitular y Columbina Cod.5–1–12,

only four parts of the *Summa philosophie* which in Thomson's account totals thirteen books appear in the catalogue, even though at least one Bohemian copy of all thirteen survives.[33] Likewise absent are three other early works: two of these (T4 and T6) only survive in a single manuscript, whilst the third (T5), though known in eight extant copies of which four are Bohemian, often travelled anonymously or attributed to another author.[34] Equally early and missing from the catalogue are three texts only known now in a single English manuscript, Cambridge Corpus Christi College 103: these are *De actibus anime* (T4) and Wyclif's side of the dispute with the Carmelite John Kenningham.[35] In the last case the preservation of parts of an informal debate in the Oxford schools was probably fortuitous; there is no sign that news of it ever reached Bohemia. Similarly transient in nature (if not in their interest for the development of Wyclif's hermeneutics) are some texts from Wyclif's later career which do not appear in the catalogue: the *Protestacio Johannis Wyclif* (T399) is recorded by the chronicler Thomas Walsingham under 1378, but appears nowhere else and its immediate origination from its declared author may be dubious; both the *De fide sacramenti* (T40) and the slightly longer *Peticio ad regem et parliamentum* (T403) seem dateable to the months between Wyclif's reception of the condemnation of Courtenay in August 1381 and the Blackfriars Council of May-June 1382, but neither is known outside England.[36] Some texts, however, that do survive in Bohemian copies did not find their way into the catalogue: three short texts on the eucharist (T41-3) fall into this category, the latter two of which are indeed only known from Bohemia; brevity may have led to the omission of other texts apparently well known in Bohemian manuscripts (and often not known in England).[37]

---

ff.43ra–45vb (see below Appendix ii, item 1a); and (ii) a lost commentary on Aristotle's *Meteora*, recorded in the library of the Bohemian nation in Prague and in Syon Abbey library in England.

[33] See T7–10, 13–16, 19; for T13 the Bohemian ÖNB 4307 is the only surviving manuscript.

[34] See *Johannis Wyclif: Summa insolubilium*, ed. P.V. Spade and G.A. Wilson (Binghamton, 1986).

[35] T378–80; as Thomson explains, the record of this dispute is fragmentary, and it is likely that more exchanges occurred than are now traceable.

[36] T40 occurs only in Cambridge Trinity College B.14.50, an informal collection of mainly English Wycliffite material (see *LB* pp. 25–7); T403 is recorded by Thomson only in the English manuscript now Florence Biblioteca Laurenziana Plut.XIX.33, ff.23v–26v, but has recently been discovered by James Carley in London BL Cotton Vitellius E.xii, ff.79r–81r. The text which Thomson describes under T391 is in fact a coupling of two extracts from the *Sermones quadraginta* and should not be regarded as a separate text.

[37] This covers T406, T407, T433 and T434, and to a less evident extent T392. The colophon at the end of T385 indicating that the text was found amongst the papers of Robert Stonham at his

Survival to the present in Bohemian manuscripts is, however, not a safe guide to inclusion or exclusion from the catalogue. In addition to the texts just mentioned which are absent from the catalogue though extant in Bohemian copies, there are conversely seven works included by the cataloguer though now not known to survive in manuscripts of Bohemian origin. Three of these, T381–3 (= here items 36, 78 and 48 respectively), are responses to individual Benedictine opponents, in the first case Uthred of Boldon, in the second and third William Binham; the first two survive in only a single manuscript of non-Bohemian origin.[38] The other four, T405, 420, 423 and 428 (= here items 12, 69, 80 and 74 respectively) are all late polemical texts, none of them well attested even in English copies.[39] In addition, some of the entries reveal the presence in Bohemia of versions of texts different from any now attested there: most strikingly, all five surviving Bohemian copies of *De statu innocencie* (T27=93 and 105) are incomplete, ending at their most extended in chapter 6, but the catalogue states that the text has ten chapters as the English copies witness and gives an explicit which corresponds to that version. Differences in chapter numbers between the catalogue and the attested text may in some cases result from the mechanical miscopying of numbers in the former; this must be suspected where incipit and explicit both agree with the text as usually found;[40] in the case of *De veritate sacre scripture* (T31= item 109), the discrepancy from the printed text arises from a division in the textual tradition of the work that is attested both in English and Bohemian copies;[41] the number of chapters given in the *Dialogus* (T408 = item 5) does not agree with that found in any surviving copy of that very diversely divided work.[42]

So far, all the evidence points towards a compilation of considerable care and discrimination. It is in the light of that evidence that one must consider the six items entered which are not known to present-day scholars amongst the output of Wyclif. These are items 9, 15, 30, 35, 49 and 51, and the details can

---

death at Pisa in 1409 may explain the absence of this text from the catalogue (see above no. I 13).

[38] The single manuscript, which also contains the third, is now Paris BN lat.3184, a manuscript that also contains two other Wyclif works (T400 and 402) belonged to Laurence Bureau, a doctor of Paris who died in 1504; Thomson describes the manuscript as of French origin, and notes the date 1396 on f.125v (at the end of an item way beyond the Wyclif texts which end f.54v).

[39] The first, third and fourth survive in Manchester Rylands MS Eng.86, the first and third also in Florence Laurentian MS Plut.XIX.33; the second is found only in Vatican MS Borghiana lat.29.

[40] As, for instance in items 112, 114 and 19; see the notes below on these items.

[41] See note to the item, and here below no. IV 202–6.

[42] See here no. I.

be seen below. Four of these (9, 15, 35 and 51) were, to judge by the chapter numbers given, texts of some length. The titles, and/or the incipits of most are credible productions of Wyclif (titles 15, 30, 49, incipits 9, 15, 35). In some cases (despite their declared length) it is possible that they will be recognized as extracts from other Wyclif texts. But even without such verification, the survival of works that are accepted as genuine in only a single manuscript should make us pause before dismissing these as erroneously included. One work certainly should not have been entered: the incipit of item 37 *Discipulus quidam venerabilis doctoris* should have made clear to the compiler that this is not a work by the *Doctor evangelicus* himself.[43] Item 45 is a second, albeit less clear, case: the text *De necessitate futurorum* is known from two Bohemian copies, but, though much of the material reflects Wyclif's ideas and even phraseology, Loserth's view that the text as it stands was put together by one of Wyclif's disciples has found general acceptance.[44] Here there was no obvious reason for the compiler to doubt an attribution if he had found it in a manuscript.

The accuracy of the catalogue is in most of its details remarkable. Where then, and how, was it compiled? If, as I have argued, the work is of Bohemian origin, then Prague seems the obvious answer to the first question. The compiler evidently had access to a collection of the works of Wyclif, even if all were not available to him at one time, that is remarkable in its range and completeness. Equally, the method of the compiler is definitively scholarly: he is not distracted by comments outside the strict limits of the bibliographical information he considered essential – in the very rare instances where additional detail is provided, as when he comments that the whole of the *Postilla in totam Bibliam* is not available in Bohemia (item 99), or the chronology of the *Sermones quadraginta* and *Sermones viginti* (items 41 and 72), these are related to that bibliographical aim. Only Prague seems likely to have been able to provide the materials and the scholarship to achieve that objective, and this may be confirmed by the claim in the post-medieval copy of the catalogue (D f.8r) that the briefer listing derives *Ex registris vniuersitatis et collegii Caroli 4°*, referring to the founder of Prague University.[45] Much more obscure are the processes of compilation, though some analogous efforts can be traced. The listing of the books of

---

[43] See below no. XII for the text in question.

[44] The copies are PUK V.F.9, ff.68v–75v and ÖNB 4937, ff.28r–34v, unascribed in both. See the entry in Thomson p. 308, and J. Loserth, 'Die ältesten Streitschriften Wiclifs', *Sitzungsberichte der kaiserlichen Akademie der Wissenschaften in Wien, Phil.-Hist.Klasse* 160/2 (1908), 1–74 at pp. 68–70 – Loserth there quotes from it a sentence referring to the view of *venerabilis Doctoris Evangelici* in the third person.

[45] The wording is, however, ambiguous since it may merely describe where the seventeenth-century copyist found the material not its origin.

Wyclif's *Summa theologie* is found independently of the complete catalogue in some Bohemian manuscripts that contain only one or two of the *Summa*'s component parts, though without the incipits and explicits provided here: thus a listing of books similar to that found here as items 100–115 and including, as this does, the uncertain relation of *De dominio divino* to the *Summa*, is found in Prague UK X.G.1, PMK C.38 and Vienna ÖNB 1339.[46] Such an elementary list may underlie that part of the catalogue, since it is noteworthy that, with the exception of the double entry for the *De statu innocencie*, the parts of the *Summa* are dealt with outside the main alphabetical listing. Rather different in kind, but attentive to the bibliographical detail apparent in the catalogue are the lists of contents prefixed to a number of Bohemian manuscripts that specify titles and incipits of the works that follow: instances are ÖNB 1337 f.ii^v and 4527 front pastedown and in PUK III.G.11 front flyleaf, all of which are in the hand of the main scribe of the texts that follow, and all of which are assemblages of many brief texts.[47] The inclusion of the incipits seems the most distinctive resemblance, but it should be noted that whilst in the first manuscript the number of chapters is specified (even though many of the texts have only one), in the second it is not, though the folio number of the start of the text is, perhaps more usefully, provided – in the third neither piece of information is given.[48] Again such listing may have been utilized by the compiler of the catalogue, but the absence of explicits from these simpler cases make it clear that the compiler could not have taken all his information from such a source.

Is it possible to suggest which manuscripts could have been available to the compiler? At first glance this seems a foolish question. But the survival of eight manuscripts which appear to have been the major part of a 'collected works of Wyclif' make it tempting to wonder whether these could have provided the compiler with his evidence. After all, such a collection of works from one writer must represent a comparable scholarly endeavour to the catalogue itself, even if the manual labour involved in the one vastly outweighs that in the second. This set of manuscripts, seven now in Vienna, one in Wolfenbüttel, is described below (no. XVI). But though some relation between these two

---

[46] In the first preceding a copy of T26 *De mandatis*, in the third before copies of T23–5 *De dominio divino* itself, T26 *De mandatis* and T27 *De statu innocencie*; in the first and third the material is in the hand of the main scribe; in the second it occurs after the index to *De mandatis* and before the text itself.

[47] See Thomson's index of manuscripts for the full Wyclif contents, though the last also contains material not by Wyclif.

[48] The order of the information in the two is also different: in the first the sequence is title, number of chapters, incipit; in the second folio number, incipit and then title; the length of the incipits in these and the catalogue is not regularly the same.

III

enterprises, of copying and of cataloguing, whichever way the influence may have gone, seems attractive, the evidence is against it. The inclusion of items in the catalogue that are not found in the extant eight volumes is not conclusive: it is highly likely that further volumes have been lost or were never completed. Much more telling is the inclusion of texts in the eight extant volumes not listed in the catalogue.[49] Though the veneration for the *Doctor evangelicus* that lies behind both enterprises is similar, a more direct relationship between the two seems unlikely. In addition, the tools available to the cataloguer were probably more diverse than a coherent neat assemblage of texts. Though the absence of some titles may not be indicative, the fact that several texts lack explicits may suggest that the compiler used lists for some of his items that were not accompanied by the texts themselves; the absence of chapter numbers might point in a similar direction.[50]

To speculate further about the circumstances of the compiling of this catalogue seems unfruitful; in particular, even if Prague is accepted as the place of production, no name can be put to the scholar(s) involved. Though there is at first sight a similarity between this effort and the indexing of individual works by Wyclif (for which see below no. VII), in its most remarkable aspect, namely its completeness and accuracy of detail over a range of texts, the catalogue is quite different: for the indexes only a single work is needed at a time, for the catalogue access to many texts is the imperative prerequisite. The index of Wyclif's discussion of biblical passages (for which see below no. VII 338–40) is a closer parallel to the catalogue, but even this in comparison makes use of a relatively small range of texts. The achievement of the catalogue is hard to over-estimate: its comprehensiveness but fastidiousness in excluding material not by the master, and its accuracy of detail, put it far beyond the subsequent listing of Wyclif's works by John Bale, or indeed by any of Bale's successors and rivals, down at least to Johann Loserth in his 1925 list. To find a comparable medieval listing of the works of a single author seems impossible. As such it is powerful testimony to Bohemian scholarship and also to Bohemian regard for the *Doctor evangelicus super omnes evangelistas*.

---

[49] These are T406, 407, 433 and 434; all are admittedly short, but other comparably brief texts find their place in the catalogue.

[50] Absence of title is not necessarily indicative of this since many copies of Wyclif's works lack such headings in the manuscripts.

The edition

The text is given here from ÖNB 3933 (A), since this appears to be the earliest copy. The layout of the text there in the main part of the list (nos. 1–93) usually gives the title in red (here shown boldface), followed by the number of chapters (sometimes prefixed by *ca*, in red, followed on the next line by the incipit and explicit in black, separated by the abbreviation *fi* (= *finis*, here represented by a double diagonal slash; this layout is also followed in the final section (nos. 94–115). There is some minor variation from this ordering, either by omission (of title, explicit or number of chapters) or by rearrangement (chapter numbers may follow the explicit rather than the title). These variations have been replicated here. Abbreviations have been expanded whenever possible, but in a few cases where a word is simply left unfinished the shortened form is retained. The gaps which the scribe left at the end of each incipit letter, apparently for the insertion of further items, are not reproduced here. The initial numbers are supplied for convenience of cross reference to the notes; the numbers prefixed by T in the final column give the catalogue numbers of the works in Thomson. Full variants from the other three copies (ÖNB 3935=B, 4514=C, 7980=D) are not given, since they mainly alter spellings or offer readings inferior to those of A; where variant readings may possibly contribute to identifying the works in question, or their transmission in Bohemia, they are quoted in the notes. As has been argued, B is very closely related to A, D to C. Neither C nor D leaves any gaps for new entries; those in B are fewer and less regular. A table concording Thomson's numbers with the Hussite catalogue numbers here is on pp. 34–5.

III

1 **De ordine christiano.** ca.5   T414
   Ad declarandam veritatem. // et libere acceptanda.

2   ca.3   T390
   Amice preclare ex scriptis. // fidei lucem veram

3 **Littera parua.**   T387
   Amice karissime.

4 **De octo questionibus propositis discipulo**   T390
   Amice preclare ex scriptis vestris. // insensibiliter introducunt

5 **Dialogus, et intitulatur speculum ecclesie militantis**   T408
   Cum ydemptitas sit mater. // facilius cognoscantur. 39

6 **Trialogus. Supplementum eius quere in v.**   T47
   Cum locucio ad personam. // secundum quemlibet beatorum. 100

7 **De officio pastorali libri duo.**   T53
   Cum duplex debet esse officium. // Domini regis regum

8 **De noua preuaricancia mandatorum.** ca.8   T415
   Cum secundum veritatis testimonium. // a bonis homines spoliantes

9 **De duodecim legibus.** ca.8   TGIntro
   Cum philosophi pseudoapostoli so. // in clericis iam peruersis

10 **De oracione dominica**   T424
   Cum heresi diebus istis. // laude dignum. c.8

De salutacione angelica quere in q.

11 **De perfectione statuum.** ca.6   T426
   Cum viantes et specialiter fratres. // populo predicantes

12 **De seruitute ciuili et dominio seculari.** ca.6   T405
   Cum secundum philosophos sit relativorum. // multiplici atque graui

III

The Hussite Catalogue of Wyclif's Works   15

13 **Contra bella clericorum et vocatur cruciata.** 10   T411
    Cum secundum fidem catholicam, Ro.8. // sacerdotibus deputandum

14 **De speculo secularium dominorum.** ca.5   T409
    Cum veritas fidei eo plus. // concorditer inuehendum

15 **De quodam periculoso mendacio nouiter practisato.** 5   TGIntro
    Cum paruus error et insensibilis. // aliis modicum deleantur

16 **De materia et forma.** ca.   T20
    Cum materia et forma sint vniversalia. // animam essenciam preter Deum

17 **De concordacione fratrum.** ca.4   T432
    Cum Christus sit primus et nouissimus. // mencacio sit fundatum

18 **De septem donis Spiritus Sancti.** ca.8   T50
    Cum Spiritus Sanctus sit tercia persona trinitatis. // multipliciter prophetat

19 **Expositio textus Matt.23.** ca.12   T372
    Cum sapiencia Dei patris. // in istis perfidis sine fine

20 **De vaticinatione.** ca.2   T45
    Cum secundum sanctos spectat ad of // ecclesie est sedata

21 **De condempnacione 19 conclusionum**   T401
    Cum secundum apostolum Heb.xi. // et pie in euangelica paupertate

22   T300
    Cum autem Spiritui Sancto appropriatur. // in Anglia germinare

23 **Epistola**   T202
    Cum prelati contencionum. // suos acucius puniendi

24 **Liber tertius de sermone Domini in monte super Matt. quere in 1.74**
    T376
    Completo tractatu primo ewangelium. // appetent se non esse

III

25 **Sermones de tempore per circulum anni super ewangelia**   T54–
    Cum deus vndiquaque plenus abhor.

26 **Triginta tres conclusiones.**   T402
    Cristus Deus noster caput vniuersalis ecclesie. // compendiosius dabit pacem

27 **De confessione siue de Eukaristia et penitencia.** 6   T44
    Duo sunt sacramenta precipua. // constancius confiteri

28 **De oracione et ecclesie purgacione.** 5   T46
    Dicturus de oratione. // quomodo sunt ab ecclesia expellenda

29   T394
    Dictum est de gradibus ecclesie. //

30 **De comodis conuenientibus ex reductione cleri ad ordinem Christi**
    Dictum est in solutione cuiusdam argumenti. //

31 **Quartus liber de sermone Domini in monte super Matt.** 14   T377
    Dictum est superius quod tercius tractatus. // sed disserere pocius disputator

32   T418
    Duo sunt genera hereticorum. // obseruanciam faciendo

33 **Recommendacio assumencium gradus**   T299
    Dominus vobiscum, Ruth 2. // cum corpore resumendum

34 **De quadam questione pro thesauris retinendis in regno quere in h. forma juramenti**   T398
    Dubium est vtrum regnum Anglie. // regni inpediat in futurum

35 **De responsione cuiusdam doctoris. Quere in j.q.s. partes dominices**
    Doctor quidam veritatis catholice. // aut cesset finaliter altibore 8

36 **Responsiones ad argumenta cuiusdam monachi quere in q.S. et j.**
    T381
    Doctor meus reuerendus et magister. // et subtilia argumenta

III

37 **Raciones 6 vtrum licet seculari clerum delinquentem castigare**
                                                                                                                  TGDub.16
    Discipulus quidam venerabilis doctoris e. // laicos mortaliter peccantes

38 **De diabolo et membris eius**   T430
    Fertur quendam fratrem inflatum. // de ecclesia Jesu Christi

39 **De demonio meridiano. In c. et v. habes fere talem.**   T300
    Frons meritricis facta est populo. // in Anglia germinare

40 **Epistola missa pape. In h. et v. plures epistole.**   T404
    Gaudeo plane. // patens condicio antichristi

41 **40 sermones compositi dum stetit in scolis quere 20 sermones in R. Rogate etc.**   T257–96
    Hora est iam nos de sompno. //

42 **Epistolarum sermones de tempore per circulum anni.**   T176–234
    Hora est iam nos de sompno. //

43 **Epistola missa Lincoliensi episcopo. In G. et v. plures quere**   T396
    Humilis seruus Christus et deuotus. // et testimonio confirmetur

44 **Forma iuramenti Arnoldi de Granario collectoris Domini pape. Quere in D. questionem.**   T397
    Hec est forma iuramenti. // fuit gracius repetita

45 **De necessitate futurorum**   TGSpur.1
    Impugnante quodam ingenioso. // in veritate poterit defensare

46 **De vniuersalibus. ca.15**   T11
    In purgando errores circa vniuersalia. // aperit agressuros

47 **De tempore**   T12
    In tractando de tempore. // pro quibus modo instat orationis suffragium

48 **De responsione quere in d. Q et v**   T383
    Inter alia doctor meus reuerendus. // rationali et honesta

III

49 **De dissensione facta in Romana ecclesia**   TGIntro
    Iam incidit tractare de ista

50 **Exhortacio cuiusdam doctoris**   T389
    Labora sicud bonus miles. // concedat dominus veritatis

51 **De octo beatitudinibus.** 21
    Licet totum ewangelium. // quasi vna sit anima

52 **De sermone Domini in monte super Mt. et diuiditur in 4 libros**   T374
    Licet totum ewangelium. // *prime partis* sufficiunt pro presenti. 62

53 **Secunda pars sic incipit**   T375
    Sequitur in textu ewangelii. // ex Dei gracia surgere. Explicit tractatus de sermone Domini in monte diuisus in 2 libros ad similitudinem scripti Augustini.

54 **Tercius liber sic incipit** 74   T376
    Completo tractatu primo ewangelii. // non appetent se non esse

55 **Quartus liber sic incipit** 14   T377
    Dictum est superius quod tercius tractatus est. // potius dusputator. Hec Augustinus

56 **De fundacione sectarum.** 16   T431
    Motus sum per quosdam veritatis a. // ecclesia sit ablata

57 **De eo qui contra Spiritum Sanctum peccat**   T52
    Non peccat in Spiritum Sanctum ad sensum est. // cuius huiusmodi sunt prelati

58 **Deteccio perfidie sectarum antichristi**   T421
    Paulus docet Eph.4. // est questio ventilata

59 **De mendacio fratrum**   T419
    Pseudofratres putant quod non licet. // Gregorii omelia 6 in fine

60 **De incarnatione Verbi** T22
   Prologus Prelibato tractatu etc.
   Quia autem spiritualizer viantibus. // eiusdem Domini nostri Jesu Christi

61 **Decem et octo conclusiones** T400
   Protestor publice ut sepe alias. // stare pro ewangelica paupertate

62 **Responsiones ad argumenta cuiusdam emuli veritatis. 18** T388
   Quidam socius quem suppono esse e. // regulariter talem legem

63 **Responsio ad argucias monachales contra 44 conclusiones** T384
   Quidam doctor vtinamque veritatis. // mendacii nequicia dominetur

64 **Responsiones ad argumenta Radulfi z Strode** T386
   Quia secundum philosophum sanctum est prehonorare. // tocius ecclesie causatiui

65 **De amore quere plures responsiones in d. j. et s.** T393
   Quidam fidelis in Domino querit. // miserie dirumpamus

66 **De salutacione angelica que sequitur statim oracionem dominicam**
   T425
   Quamuis autem salutacio angelica. // rose proprietatibus senciendum

67 **De gradibus cleri** T394
   Quidam secularis probus zel. // multipliciter illum mundum

68 **De dissensione paparum. Et est alius paruus qui eciam sic incipit**
   T410
   Quia ista monstruosa dis. // est in clericis iam peruersis

69 **De versuciis antichristi** T420
   Quamuis diabolus ex naturali

70 **Exposicio textus Matt.24** T373
   Quia ewangelicum istud. // sit melius intellecta

71 **De 4 imprecacionibus** T417
   Quia clerus regni Anglie. // rationabilis ex fide scripture

III

72 **Sermones 20 compositi in fine vite sue. Et debent stare post 40 sermones: quere in h**   T237–56
    Rogate que ad pacem //

73 **Differencia inter peccatum mortale et veniale**   T51
    Restat nunc discutere. / sine discrimine nesciunt

74 **Contra religiones priuatas et intitulatur purgatorium secte Christi**
        T428
    Sepe assumptum est vt fides. // irremissibile multis regnis

75 **De quatuor sectis nouellis et eorum erroribus 12**   T429
    Secundum tres virtutes theologicas. // ad ecclesie prodessendum

76 **De Christo et suo aduersario antichristo**   T412
    Secundum catholicos ecclesia est. // a Christi vestigiis deuiare

77 **De nouis ordinibus**   T422
    Secundum apostolum Eph.6. // in parte cognoscere ex scriptura

78 **Responsiones ad alium doctorem**   T382
    Secundum doctor meus Willelmus Rynnan. // libro 2° partis 2 ca.7

79 **De corpore Christi quere in T alium maiorem tractatum**   T39
    Sepe confessus sum et adhuc. // quantum in episcopis est

80 **De contrarietate duorum dominorum suarum parcium ac eciam rerum**   T423
    Sicut est vnus verus et summus. // triumphante ecclesia exstante 8

81 **De citacionibus friuolis et aliis versuciis antichristi**   T413
    Si papa uel eius vicarius. // sibi seruiat libertate

82 **De fide catholica.** ca.8   T49
    Suppositis dictis de fide ca. // Christi et diaboli stabilire

83 **De trinitate**   T17
    Superest inuestigare de distinccione. // per communem essenciam communicacionem essencie

84 De eukaristia. Quere paruum tractatum in s. T38
Tractando de eukaristia. // in Christo Iesu finaliter obseruare

85 De ydeis T18
Tractando de ydeis. // habet ideam propriam in Deo

86 De compositione hominis. ca.8 T21
Tria mouent me ad tractandum. // alibi satis sepe

87 De triplici vinculo amoris T427
Tria sunt vincula amoris. // regulam legis Dei

88 De sex iugis T141–2, 145–7
Vt simplices sacerdotes zelo a. // huiusmodi nouitates

89 Epistola missa episcopo Cantuariensi T395
Venerabilis in Christo pater et domine.// legislator

90 Epistola missa ad simplices sacerdotes T416
Videtur meritorium bonos colligere. // taliter operando

91 De gradibus cleri et ecclesie militantis T394
Videtur autem sanctis doctoribus. // multipliciter istum mundum

92 Supplementum trialogi id est de dotacione ecclesie et debet stare inmediate post trialogum ca.10 T48
Vtrum clerus debuit dotacionem. // adiutorio postulando

93 De statu innocencie T27
Vt supradicta magis. // de dominio clericorum. ca.10

Nota multi sunt alii libri Magistri Johannis Wiclif, videlicet [94] proprium sanctorum, [95] commune sanctorum, et [96] epistolarum dominicalium. Eciam est [97] summa sua in theologia que in Boemia habetur, [98] summa in logica tres tractatus, [99] Postilla super totam bibliam que hocce non habetur, et quam plures aliis libri.

Summa eiusdem in theologia continet 12 libros in se: Primus est liber mandatorum, presupponens [100] tres libros De dominio diuino, quorum prologus sic incipit Cum quilibet christianus T23

III

101 Primus liber sic incipit et habet 19 ca^a.
    In tractando de dominio

102 Secundus sic incipit et habet 5 ca^a.   T24
    Iam vlterius restat

103 Tercius sic incipit et habet 6 ca^a.   T25
    Redeundo iam 3° ad materiam. // habentur hic

104 Liber primus de mandatis sic incipit et habet ca.30   T26
    Premissa sentencia de dominio in communi. // dicitur aliena

105 Secundus de statu innocentie ca.10   T27
    Vt supradicta magis ap. // de dominio clericorum

106 Tercius de dominio ciuili, et continet in se tres libros.
    Primus sic incipit. 44 cap.   T28
    Tractando de ciuili dominio. // conferat liber vite

107 Secundus sic incipit, et est quartus in ordine, habens 18 cap^a.   T29
    Licet capitulo 37 rogarem obnixius. // aduersarios crucis Christi

108 Tercius incipit, et est quintus in ordine, continens 27 ca^a.   T30
    Vt supradicta de lege Christi. // procuratorie sic orare

109 Sextus de veritate sacre scripture. 31 ca^a.   T31
    Restat parumper discutere. // diffusius pertractare

110 Septimus de ecclesia. 23 ca^a.   T32
    Quia nonnulli eciam illi. // de isto alibi

111 Octauus de officio regis. 12 ca^a.   T33
    Consequenter ad ordinem clericalem. // partem suam

112 Nonus de potestate pape. 13 ca^a.   T34
    Iam vltimo restat. // membrum diaboli ad infernum

113 Decimus de symonia. 8 ca^a.   T35
    Post generalem sermonem. // totam ecclesiam semper regnat

114 **XI^{us} de apostasia**. 18 ca^a. T36
   Restat vlterius ponere aliud principium. // hoc venerabili sacramento

115 **XII^{us} de blasfemia**. 18 ca^a. T37
   Restat succintte de blas. // ministerium limitare

Notes

It is clear that the scribe of D had difficulty with the form of certain numerals, notably 5 and 7, reading the first usually as 7; variation in D which concerns 5/7 confusion only is not noted in the commentary below. Where no comment is made on an entry, it can be assumed that the information given agrees with the text as that is given in Thomson's *Catalog* for the relevant number.

1. T414; AB give five chapters as the printed text, whilst C gives three (for which none of the extant copies gives support), and D omits any number.

2. No title is given for this entry which is in fact a conflation of two items. T390 *De octo questionibus pulcris* supplies the incipit, but T435 *De solucione Sathane* the explicit; ACD state that the text has 3 chapters, B that it has 2 (T390 is not divided into chapters, nor, despite Buddensieg's edition, *Pol.Wks*.ii.391–400, is T435). The origin of the confusion is unclear: since the incipit of T435 is 'Quantum ad obiectum fratrum', its expected entry position is much later in the catalogue, but it is perhaps possible that a copy (no longer surviving) omitted the first word. T390 appears again as no. 4, but T435 is not entered elsewhere.

3. T387 is a very brief (10-line) letter, and given the few details here the identification must be regarded as tentative; the text survives only in six Bohemian copies. C adds after the incipit of AB 'epistola parua est', having omitted the title; D's alteration of 'karissime' to 'christiane epistola prima est' may be a misreading of an entry identical, or similar, to C's; neither variant corresponds to further words in T387.

4. T390 makes a second appearance with correct title, incipit, explicit and lack of chapter division in AB; in the explicit CD substitute for 'insensibiliter' the reading 'misericorditer' (not attested in the copies collated by Loserth).

5. T408 is the most widely attested of Wyclif's Latin works, with 25 surviving manuscripts; the title here combines two forms, of which *Dialogus* is the usual continental form, *Speculum ecclesie militantis* that found in two surviving English copies and in Vatican Borghese lat.29 described by Thomson as French. The second title comes from the end of chapter 36 in the edited text (p. 85/28). See above no. I for the variation in copies of this text. The number of chapters given here, 39, is more than in any surviving copy (where 37 is the maximum); but many copies do not number the chapters at all. The explicit given is that of a final chapter found only in four copies (see above no. I 9–11).

6. T47; the cross reference is to no. 92; C and D omit this instance as all other similar directives. The division of the *Trialogus* into four books is not mentioned here, though it is regular in the copies, and the number of chapters is one short of the total of the four books in its edited form.

7. T53: here the number of books but not of chapters is given; the incipit is of the first book, the explicit that of the second.

8. T415.

9. As Thomson p. 305 observes, this is not now recognizable as a work by Wyclif, though its title and especially its incipit make it a credible production. The second word is not entirely certain: A, B and C, apart from the ending, have the same abbreviation as is found in the incipit of 12, but D has here unabbreviated *pharisei*. The same explicit is given for no. 68 whose other details, but not these words, relate to T410; equally that text has only a single chapter. However, at the end of T410 in ÖNB 3929 the scribe noted 'Non est hic finis quia deberent esse octo capitula': this could derive from the catalogue here, but it should be noted that there may be independent evidence of a longer form of the text in the collection at Syon (O.36, see V. Gillespie, *Syon Abbey* (*CBMLC* 9, 2001), pp. 318–19).

10. T424; the cross reference, omitted from CD and included only marginally in B, is to item 66.

11. T426.

12. T405; no Bohemian copy now survives.

13. T411; the alternative titles are both found in ÖNB 1337 and 3933, but *Cruciata* is commoner (ÖNB 3929, 3930, 4527, 4536, PMK D.50, PUK V.F.9).

14. T409.

15. Thomson p. 305 regards this again as a credible work by Wyclif though no longer surviving. The final word of the incipit is probably *insensibilis* in AB (with the same central abbreviation as in the explicit to no. 4), *misserabilis* in CD, but in all copies heavily abbreviated.

16. T20: although the text survives in many Bohemian copies, all of the catalogue manuscripts leave a gap for the number of chapters (actually 9).

17. T432.

18. T50. The incipit and explicit are correct, but, though Buddensieg's edition has 9 chapters, it is clear that most copies do not number chapters even if they divide the material. ÖNB 3933, the base for this edition, contains a copy of the work, ff.76vb–80vb, and numbers the final chapter as 9 (f.79vb).

19. T372. In the printed edition the number of chapters is 14, not 12 as here stated; however, again some copies do not number the chapters, and Rylands 86 and ÖNB 4527 number the last 12 (see Loserth's edition p. 350).

20. T45.

21. T401.

22. T300 in part: no title appears in any copy of the catalogue perhaps because the incipit given is that of chapter 3 of the text; the full text with title appears as no. 39, with a cross reference back to this entry in AB.

23. See T202. Thomson does not recognize this as a freestanding work, but only as a part of the sermon on the epistle for the second Sunday after Easter. As I have argued (see no. VI 231), this was not its original form. A freestanding text with the incipit and explicit here survives in five Bohemian copies (PMK D.123, PUK III.G.11, ÖNB 1337, 1387 and Olomouc C.O.118) with the titles *De prelatis contencionum* or *De incarcerandis fidelibus*; in none of them is it described as *Epistola*.

24. T376: the details are correct, with the number 74 relating to the chapters of book 3 alone. The cross reference (missing from CD) is to nos. 52–5 where all four books are detailed.

25. T54– : the incipit is that of the prologue to this set of sermons, a prologue absent from the one surviving English copy of the set. Unfortunately, the absence of an explicit and of a number of sermons makes it impossible to know how the cataloguer's set ended: for the problems of the concluding items of all three sets of Wyclif's sermons see here no. VI.

26. T402. The alternative title (found in PUK V.F.17), but not given here, is *De paupertate Christi*, but the usual title where given is that here (as in ÖNB 4343, PMK B.17/1, PUK III.G.11 and Paris BN lat.3184).

27. T44: the text is common in Bohemia but does not survive in England, though Netter knew it, see *Doctrinale* V.138 (ii.799).

28. T46: the details are correct, but only a single copy (ÖNB 1337) survives.

29. Probably T394. None of the copies recognizes a title, and in AB a line gap is left for this. But the apparent incipit picks up the title given in several copies, *De gradibus cleri*. However, this title with the proper incipit of the text is given at 67. It is thus possible that this incomplete entry relates to a completely different, and lost, work.

30. The identity of this text is unclear (and is apparently unmentioned by Thomson); its title and incipit are credible as works of Wyclif; it could be part of another longer text.

31. T377: the details are mostly correct, though as Wyclif's opening paragraph makes clear (*Opus evangelicum* ii.287/5), the basis here is John 13–17 not Matthew. The number 14 relates to the chapters of Wyclif's book. In the explicit (not present in CD), the second word in the text is *differre*.

32. T418: the brief text survives only in a single copy (ÖNB 1337) with the title *De duobus generibus hereticorum* and the final word of the explicit there is *paciendo*.

33. T299: the incipit and explicit identify the text, itself surviving only in Bohemian copies. The title is interesting: it is entirely compatible with the content (which is a sermon on graduation day), but is not found in any of the

surviving five manuscripts (three give no title, ÖNB 1337 and 3929 offer the vague description *Sermo pulcer*).

34. T398, with cross reference in AB to 44.

35. The identity of this text is unclear, and both title and incipit are unhelpful; AB indicate that the text had 8 chapters, but this information is missing from CD. The final word of the explicit in A and C is *altibore*: since these two copies are not usually in agreement textually, this reading is probably correct (B's *a labore* and D's *alii bonorum* being attempts to interpret a word with which they were not familiar). The word *altibore* is not attested in Lewis and Short or in the *Dictionary of Medieval Latin from British Sources* (London, 1975–), but is presumably a form of the latter's *altiboare* 'to proclaim aloud' recorded there only once from the tenth century. Once Wyclif's works are available in scannable form, this work (if it survives) should be readily traceable. The cross references, omitted from CD, could be to 48, any of 62–4, and 78 respectively. Thomson does not appear to comment on this entry.

36. T381: there is only a single, and non-Bohemian, copy of this text against Uthred of Boldon, but the details agree. The similarity between the cross references in AB here and for 35 leads to the speculation that 35 could be another, lost, part of Wyclif's argument with Uthred (for which see below no. IX 96–101).

37. The identity of this text is not in doubt, but, as the incipit makes clear, it should not have been included in the catalogue since it is by a follower of Wyclif. The text only survives in three Bohemian copies (ÖNB 3928, 3932 and PUK X.E.9), although its English origin is clear from its use of the clauses in an English king's coronation oath: see edition here no. XII.

38. T430.

39. T300: the first cross reference is to 22, where chapter 3 alone is listed without title, but the second is obscure since none of 88–93 is identical with this (both cross references are omitted from CD).

40. T404; the cross references (omitted from CD) are to 43 and 89–90 (or possibly to 89 alone, as having, like 40 and 43, a personal addressee).

41. T257–96: the number of sermons and the incipit identifies this as the *Sermones quadraginta*, usually dated (on grounds of content apart from this description) as written between 1375 and 1377 (see no. VI appendix here and references there given). The cross reference, omitted CD, is to 72 (see comments there).

42. T176–?234: as with 25, the absence of an explicit and of any number for the sermons makes the entry less useful than could be wished; for the problems see here no. VI. This item is omitted from CD entirely, presumably

because the incipit is identical with that of 41, leading either to inadvertent eyeskip or to deliberate suppression as an erroneous duplication.

43. T396; cross references (omitted CD) are to 40 and 89(–90), as at 40 above.

44. T397: the cross reference (omitted CD and added marginally in B) is to 34, which itself refers in AB to this item.

45. The text is described in Thomson GSpur.1, but its authenticity is denied. Two copies of a text with this incipit and explicit survive (PUK V.F.9, ff.68v-75v and ÖNB 4937, ff.28r–34v), but without attribution in either.

46. T11: the incipit is that of chapter 1 and not of the analysis that often precedes the text (see below no. VII 324–6). The second word of the incipit is correct in A, but B (altered by correction) and CD supply instead *impugnando*.

47. T12: again the incipit is that of chapter 1 and not of the analysis. The explicit of chapter 12, with which all Bohemian and German copies end, is *in spiritum sanctum subtrahendo ab eo oracionis suffragia*; English copies add a thirteenth chapter whose ending is *et per consequens modo instat*. The form given in A (shortened in B by the omission of *pro quibus modo*, words sophisticated in C to *per conuersus modo* and in D to *per consequens modo*) appears to be a blend of these two forms. It is tempting to think that the absence of specification of chapter numbers from all four copies reflects an awareness of diversity in this text's transmission.

48. T383, identifiable from the incipit and explicit. The text in question does not survive in a Bohemian copy, but is the response of Wyclif (probably his second) to objections brought against his views on the relation of the clergy to civil dominion and civil law by William Binham and others. This section is edited by J. Loserth, *Opera minora* pp. 422/22–430/5, where it is run on without a gap to the end of T382, as in the sole surviving copy of that text (Paris BN lat.3184, ff.49r–52v); three other English copies of T383 attest this text alone. The cross references in AB are obscure: Wyclif's first response to Binham is here 78 (which should give a reference to *S*), but this is ignored apparently in favour of other responses: *d* is probably to item 35 where a similar set of references is found, *Q* to one of 62–4, but the identity of the text meant by *v* is unclear.

49. Thomson (p. 305) accepts this as a genuine, though lost, work by Wyclif: the title is certainly credible, but the incipit is uninformative and there is no explicit. Variant readings in the title are likewise unhelpful: AC's *dissensione* is replaced in B by *dissensionibus* and in D by *dispensatione*; AB's *ecclesia* by CD *curia*. The subject matter was evidently the papal schism.

50. T389.

51. The entry is a puzzle though the only significant variant in the four copies is that CD give the number of chapters as 12 not 21. The title suggests T390 *De octo questionibus pulchris*, but this is correctly entered as no. 4; the incipit given is identical to that for 52, and could be an incorrect anticipation of that; the explicit is not helpful for identification.

52–5. T374–7, the four books of the *Opus evangelicum*, listed here because of the incipit of the first. The number of chapters for books 3–4 is given marginally in A only, none of the copies having the same information for book 2; the earlier separate listing of books 3 and 4 at nos. 24 and 31 provide this information in all copies. Book 2, which, if entered separately, should appear between 74 and 83 has 60 chapters. All surviving copies of the work end with the colophon *Autoris vita finitur et hoc opus illa*, and it is clear that the cataloguer here knew no more of the text. The note under 53 (omitted CD) about Wyclif's model for the book division is found at the end of book 2 in three surviving copies (TCC B.16.2 f.404rb, ÖNB 1647 f.176vb, PUK IV.A.18 f.123rb, not in the fourth, TCD 242 f.99rb).

56. T431; CD give the number of chapters as 6, but the higher 16 is correct.

57. T52; the first word of the incipit should be *nemo*, but all copies here have *non*.

58. T421.

59. T419: the second word of the incipit in the edited text is *publicant* (with variant *replicant*), rather than the index's *putant* (AB, omitted CD); the first two words of the explicit gave CD trouble and were replaced by *gregis occulta*.

60. T22: the incipits of both the analysis and the text proper are given in AB but the second is omitted from CD; the analysis stands at the start in all surviving copies, Bohemian and English.

61. T400: the text, which does indeed cover 18 conclusions, is variously headed in the surviving ten copies, English and Bohemian; see above no. I 3–4.

62. T388: the surviving copies have 17 chapters, not 18 as here (Loserth's text, *Opera minora* p. 312/13 adds the words *Et hec dicta sufficiant pro presenti* to the explicit given here).

63. T384.

64. T386: B substitutes *Rudolfi* for the first name, whilst BD interpret *z* as *et*.

65. T393. The cross references (omitted CD) are to 35, 48 (in both of which entries there are comparable references) and perhaps 78.

66. T425. In two of the three surviving copies of the text (ÖNB 1337 and 3929) this does indeed follow straight on from T424 on the Lord's prayer; but

in the third (ÖNB 4505, ff.207r–209r) only 425 is found (and conversely in TCC B.15.28, ff.128r–130r only T424). See here the directive after 10.

67. T394.

68. T410: the title and incipit are those of this text, but the explicit is not (it should be *per simulata mendacia tamquam fidem*). The same explicit is found for item 9, itself an obscure entry. The cross reference here (omitted CD) is also unexplained: if it is to item 9, the incipit of that is different.

69. T420: only a single non-Bohemian copy survives.

70. T373.

71. T417: A has the title only in the top margin, in faint darker ink and probably in a different hand; no title appears in BCD.

72. T237–56, the *Sermones viginti*, whose existence as a set is not recognized in TCC B.16.2, and is difficult to discern from Loserth's edition or Thomson's listing; see here no. VI. That the cataloguer is correct about the dating of these sermons is certain from the copious references to contemporary events of the period 1381–3 found in them (see here no. VI 239–43). The close linking of this set with the *Sermones quadraginta* by the cataloguer – *debent stare post 40 sermones* – is not entirely explicable: quite apart from their divergent dates, only in two manuscripts (TCC B.16.2 and ÖNB 3928) do the two sets stand together, and in both cases the later sermons are placed before the earlier set. The cross reference in AB is to 41.

73. T51. Neither the cataloguer, nor Thomson, nor most remarkably Loserth (who printed this short work at the end of his edition of *De mandatis*) noticed that this is an extract from *De civili dominio* iii.cap.24 (which Loserth had edited some twenty years previously). See Appendix II no. 51.

74. T428: only a single English copy of this text survives, with the title here.

75. T429. C omitted the explicit of this text, jumping to that of 77; as originally written D followed this error. But marginally in D, in the same hand but perhaps at a different time, the information contained under item 76 was added and marked for insertion in the text.

76. T412. Entry omitted from C, and added in D (see above).

77. T422. CD only contain the explicit, wrongly attached to item 75 (see above).

78. T382: the surname is only preserved, incorrectly, in A: it should be *Binham*. It is surprising that there is no cross reference to 48: see this for more details. The text here only survives in a single, non-Bohemian copy. Again CD share a substantial error: both jump from the incipit of this text to the explicit of item 79 without correction in either copy.

79. T39: the title and incipit are identifiable with this work, and the cross reference in AB to no. 84 is clear. Two forms of this text survive: a brief

version in English copies, with an explicit *veritas vincet eos*, and a longer version in all continental copies with the explicit *quantum in ipsis est*; it is the latter (with corruption of the penultimate word) that the catalogue reflects. The shorter version corresponds to sequential passages in *De apostasie*, whilst the extension in the longer version parallels sequential passages in T209, a sermon on the epistle for Corpus Christi day. See above no. I 2–3.

80. T423: the number of chapters given in AB is correct; only two copies, both of English origin, survive.

81. T413.

82. T49.

83. T17: the title is given only in A, and there the incipit and explicit appear in a somewhat darker ink from the rest of the listing.

84. T38: the incipit given is that of the text proper, not of the analysis which in all surviving copies appears at the start; the text has nine long chapters, but the catalogue does not note the number. The cross reference in AB is to no. 79. B, but not A, notes the present item as *magnus tractatus*.

85. T18: the text is unprinted, but the manuscripts divide it into five chapters.

86. T21: the number of chapters in all surviving copies is 7, not 8 as given here.

87. T427.

88. Thomson does not recognize this as a free-standing text but, as with no. 23, only as parts of five epistle sermons T141–2, 145–7. See below no. VI 232 for evidence that suggests that the text began in the form catalogued here, and that it was subsequently broken up for insertion in the five sermons; eight Bohemian copies preserve the material as a single text, with the title (where provided) as given here.

89. T395.

90. T416; the title is given only in A.

91. T394. The item is entirely omitted from CD, whilst the title in B is that of 90 (where it was omitted but with a gap left by B). This is the third appearance of the text: see before at 29 and 67. Here the incipit is that of chapter 3 (Loserth, *Opera minora* p. 142/16), a point at which many scribes seem to have perceived a gap between questions. Despite the equivalence of the explicits of 67 and this, and the similarity of title of all three, no cross references are found at any of them.

92. T48. B erroneously gives the title of 91 before the incipit and explicit of 92, as a result of the misattribution of the title of 90 to 91. ACD all recognize the text as an appendix to the *Trialogus*, here no. 6, though in only one of the four surviving copies of this does it stand after that text (ÖNB 4505, whereas in ÖNB 1387 the *Supplementum* stands earlier in the manuscript with other

unrelated texts before the *Trialogus*, and in ÖNB 1338 and 3929 the latter text does not appear). The text is usually described as *De dotacione ecclesie* in medieval sources (cf Netter, *Doctrinale* II.1 (i.247) where both titles are recognized).

93. T27. Again B's errors over the titles of 91 and 92 are continued, and the title for 92 appears prefixed to the information here. CD have no title for this entry, and that in A appears to have been slightly erased. The information is repeated at no. 105, and it is unclear why this single, and briefest, part of the *Summa theologie* should alone be entered in this part of the catalogue. It is worth noting also that the explicit given here and at 105 is that of the two surviving English copies of the text: the five Bohemian manuscripts all end before this, and at differing points, and all in fewer chapters than 10 (four at p. 509/6 in chapter 6, one at p. 482/9 in chapter 2); it is thus clear that a full version of the text did reach Bohemia.

From this point, as has been noted above p. 4, the form of the catalogue changes: for convenience of discussion identifying numbers have been inserted. Entries for nos. 94–9 are in abbreviated form, before the final entries, 100–115, resume in a style similar to the opening material. The section covering 94–9 is placed first in A, and this is followed in the present edition; in BCD the same information is given at the very end after item 115.

94. T115–142: the sermons for specified saints' days.

95. T143–?173: the sermons for the *Commune sanctorum*; for the uncertainty about the closing of this set see here no. VI.

96. T176–?234: also entered more fully at 42; again the closing is unclear (see here no. VI).

97. This anticipates the fuller listing at 104–15.

98. Without more detail it is not absolutely clear what is meant here. Thomson lists as T1–3 the tracts *De logica, Logice continuacio* and *De logica tractatus tercius*; he suggests that the second and third of these may not be connected to the first, and that the *tercius* in the title of the third may derive from a division of the second into two parts (but see above no. I 7–8). The first is a very elementary tract, with no title in either surviving copy (ÖNB 4523 and Erfurt SB Ampl.Q°253). The only copy of T2 which also has T1, ÖNB 4523, has no heading at the start of the T2.

99. T301–371. The whole bible is not covered in the surviving copies, either English or Bohemian, at least so far as has been recognized to date: missing are the Old Testament books before Job and (save for a possible lost copy at Syon, see here no. XV 12–13) of Proverbs, Wisdom and Ecclesiasticus. From Bohemian sources only the New Testament commentary survives. The quotations in Cochlaeus's *Historia Hussitarum* (Mainz, 1549), pp. 498-9, to which V. Mudroch, 'John Wyclyf's *Postilla* in Fifteenth-Century Bohemia', *Canadian*

Journal of Theology 10 (1964), 118–23 draws attention, derive from a text by Rokycana but again draw only on the New Testament.

100. A has a fuller form of this note than any of the other copies, all of which omit the words *primus ... mandatorum*; since that text is listed below at 104, it is possible that A's reading is here incorrect. It is worth noting that none of the descriptions of the books of the *Summa theologie* mentions the analyses for the work in question (unlike the entry for T22 at no. 60 above).

101–103. T23–25: the uncertain relation of the *De dominio divino* to the ensuing twelve books of the *Summa* is similarly noted in those listings of the latter that have been discussed above p. 11. The details of the books, including the note of the incipit to the Prologue in 100 (and accepting AB's 19 for the number of chapters in book 1 as against CD's 29), are correct apart from the final explicit which in the extant copies reads *secundum legem humanam donare dicitur*. Thomson (p. 42 n. 3) suggests that this indicates the Bohemians knew a slightly longer text; but, if so, it cannot have been much more extended since the number of chapters here agrees with the texts (Thomson's note, p. 44 n. 23 of seven chapters in book 2 derives from Buddensieg's misreading of AB here). See above no. I 6–7.

104. T26: the penultimate word of the explicit is recorded by Loserth p. 474/18 as a variant to his printed *discitur*.

105. T27: details as at 93 above.

106–108. T28-30: the analysis that follows each book in the single surviving complete copy (ÖNB 1341 of books 1–2, 1340 of book 3) is ignored here.

109. T31: the state of the text and the number of chapters (31 or 32) is discussed below no. IV 202–6; the cataloguer evidently knew the shorter form.

110. T32.

111. T33.

112. T34: the number of chapters in all copies here is given as 13. The two complete copies of the text (PMK C.73 and PUK III.F.11) both number the last chapter 12 (the former divides the final chapter after p. 386/26, the latter after p. 382/10, both without chapter number). The index to the text recognizes 13 chapters, as implicitly do references in the biblical index, but unfortunately the analysis only extends to the end of chapter 11 (for all of these tools see below no. VII).

113. T35.

114. T 36. All but one of the extant copies of the text have 17 chapters, not 18 as here. The one exception is Wolfenbüttel 306, where chapter 3 is divided at p. 49/17 and consequently has 18 chapters. The surviving indexes to the work, and the biblical index, only recognize 17 chapters.

115. T37.

III

Index to the Hussite catalogue: the first column gives the numbers in Thomson's catalogue, the second the item numbers here.

1–3	98	53	7
4-10	missing	54–114	25
11	46	115–75	94–5
12	47	141–2, 145–7	88
13–16	missing	176–234	42, 96
17	83	202	23
18	85	237–56	72
19	missing	257–96	41
20	16	299	33
21	86	300	22, 39
22	60	301–71	99
23	101	372	19
24	102	373	70
25	103	374–7	24, 31, 52–5
26	104	378–80	missing
27	93, 105	381	36
28	106	382	78
29	107	383	48
30	108	384	63
31	109	385	missing
32	110	386	64
33	111	387	3
34	112	388	62
35	113	389	50
36	114	390	2, 4
37	115	391–2	missing
38	84	393	65
39	79	394	?29, 67, 91
40–43	missing	395	89
44	27	396	43
45	20	397	44
46	28	398	34
47	6	399	missing
48	92	400	61
49	82	401	21
50	18	402	26
51	73	403	missing
52	57	404	40

405	12	426	11
406–7	missing	427	87
408	5	428	74
409	14	429	75
410	68	430	38
411	13	431	56
412	76	432	17
413	81	43–4	missing
414	1	435	2
415	8		
416	90	GDub16	37
417	71	GSpur1	45
418	32		
419	59	unknown	9
420	69	unknown	15
421	58	unknown	30
422	77	unknown	35
423	80	unknown	49
424	10	unknown	51
425	66		

IV

CROSS-REFERENCING IN WYCLIF'S LATIN WORKS

ONE of the most immediately striking features of all of Wyclif's major writings, whether philosophical, theological, or polemical, is the frequency with which cross-references are found both between different chapters or parts of the same work and between works other than the current one.[1] The frequency of cross-referencing is variable. In the philosophical works and the intermediate tracts traditionally placed before the twelve-part *Summa theologie*, links are not enormously numerous. The first text to show a plethora of them is *De civili dominio*: here on average one instance occurs roughly every other page, more frequently in parts I and III, in other words some 600 in all. This habit continues with slight abatement in *De veritate sacre scripture*, and into *De ecclesia*. Thereafter the remaining parts of the *Summa* show a diminishing number, still further reduced in the *De eucharistia*. Cross-referencing is relatively common in the three long sets of sermons composed after Wyclif's retirement to Lutterworth, and in the *Sermones quadraginta* written *dum stetit in scholis*.[2] The device is obviously in origin an academic one, and it is worth observing that some of the major works which were written

---

[1] In this study Wyclif's works are quoted from the editions of the Wyclif Society (WS: 1883–1921), with the addition of *De officio pastorali*, ed. G. V. Lechler (Leipzig, 1863); *Trialogus*, ed. G. V. Lechler (Oxford, 1869); *Summa de ente libri primi tractatus primus et secundus*, ed. S. H. Thomson (Oxford, 1930); *De trinitate*, ed. A. du P. Breck (Boulder, 1962); *De universalibus*, ed. I. J. Mueller, with A. Kenny and P. V. Spade, 2 vols (Oxford, 1985). Texts in the WS editions are cited by title, followed if necessary by volume name (*Op. min.* = *Opera minora*, *Pol. Wks* = two volumes of *Polemical Works*). As far as possible, references are given by (volume), page and line number, the last being supplied if necessary, without counting any headings. W. R. Thomson's *The Latin Writings of John Wyclyf: An Annotated Catalog* (Toronto, 1983), though its details need some correction, provides an invaluable catalogue of the manuscripts of the texts; Thomson's numbering of the texts is used here, prefixed with T. In references to manuscripts I use 'Vienna' to refer to those in the Österreichische Nationalbibliothek there, 'Prague MK' to refer to the Metropolitan Chapter Library there, and 'Prague UK' to refer to the National, formerly the University, Library there; BL is used for London British Library, TCC for Trinity College Cambridge.

[2] I have considered the implications of those in the *Sermones quadraginta* and *Sermones viginti* in 'Aspects of the "publication" of Wyclif's Latin sermons', in *Middle English Religious Texts and their Transmission: Essays in Honour of A. I. Doyle*, ed. A. J. Minnis (Cambridge, 1993), pp. 121–9.

after Wyclif left Oxford have few if any: in the *Trialogus* the virtually complete absence of internal linkings could be explained as the result of a perception that the orderly organization of the whole obviated the necessity for such an aid, but this explanation does not seem relevant to the final *Opus evangelicum*.[3] Cross-referencing has previously been observed by students of Wyclif, and has traditionally been used in the attempt to order his vast output chronologically, and to put dates to individual works.[4] But this is to jump to conclusions – to assume that the references are authorial and that the works in which they occur were composed as a whole at one time. The discussion here will suggest that there are questions to be answered in regard to the former assumption, and substantial objections to the latter. More modestly, I hope here to use the cross-references to throw light on the ways in which Wyclif's works were written, put together, and 'published'.

Two preliminaries must first be made clear. First, the existing editions of Wyclif quickly proved to offer inadequate documentation for this enquiry. Most simply, more manuscripts of many of the texts edited in the Wyclif Society have come to light; these may offer conflicting or more complete evidence. More worryingly, it also became clear that neither the text, nor the variants cited from those manuscripts known to the editors, were always an accurate record of their witness.[5] In some cases this is probably the result of the editors' reliance on amanuenses, whose work they were either unable or unwilling to check; in others it seems likely that the alteration was deliberately though silently made, to fit in with the editor's understanding of the passage to which reference was intended. These deficiencies in the printed texts have meant that I have felt obliged to check all cross-references across all manuscripts currently known, whether or not they had been quarried by the editors; this has been a slow business, since some thousand or so references scattered through many texts across numerous manuscripts in several countries are

---

[3] There seems to be only a single internal link in the *Trialogus*: this is the unspecific one in bk ii.14 (123/16) back to *sententia primi libri*.

[4] The most notable examples have been S. Harrison Thomson, 'The order of writing of Wyclif's philosophical works', *Českou Minulostí práce* (Festschrift in honour of V. Novotny), ed. O. Odložilík, J. Prokeš, and R. Urbánek (Prague, 1929), pp. 146–65; I. J. Mueller, 'A "lost" *Summa* of John Wyclif', *SCH.S*, 5 (1987), pp. 179–83. Thomson (*Latin Writings*) draws together the evidence from this source with other scraps of internal and external testimony.

[5] Thus, for instance, the three complete manuscripts of *De ecclesia*, all allegedly used by Loserth, all unambiguously give references to chapter 22 despite the text's 20 at 257/1, and all have 25 as against the text's 27 at 467/29 (no variants given at either place).

involved, and it has not been possible to check all cases for a second time.[6]

The second preliminary concerns terminology. The term 'cross-referencing' can cover a wide variety of linking devices. At its most general, phrases such as *ut patet alibi*, *ut dictum est in multis locis* can be used; but these are of little interest, since they have no indicative force concerning individual works. They have been ignored in the present study. Much more interesting are those links which offer specific references. The simplest form is a plain specification of work: 'ut patet ex dictis in Trialogo', found in the brief *De fide catholica* (*Op. min.* 116/21), since the title is that of one of Wyclif's final works, offers no problems. But the titles of some of his works are far from being so distinctive as this: 'ut patet in materia de ydeis/de universalibus' may be a reference to two of Wyclif's works *De ydeis* and *De universalibus*, but the nouns are common ones and may not incorporate a title at all. Here some discretion is needed, unless further specification of chapter clarifies the position. The opening 'ex dictis de statu innocencie' in *De quattuor sectis novellis* (*Pol. Wks* i.270/14) leads to the assumption of a reference to Wyclif's brief work of that name, until it is noted that the following words are 'et de statu post finale iudicium', for which no equivalent work is known to survive; the conclusion must be that neither is a cross-reference. It should also be observed at the start that two of the phrases most frequently employed incorporate ambiguity: *ut patet* and *ut dictum est* would normally be translated 'as appears' and 'as is said', but do they imply anything about order or about chronology? Even if both naturally suggest that the material is already available, it is less clear whether any implications of sequence and/or of time should be drawn. The second could equally well be translated 'as has been said', thus more clearly implying chronology but again leaving sequence uncertain. Even the simple verb *est* can apparently be ambiguous in this context: *De potestate pape* specifies at one point 'de istis autem in tractatu *De sacramentis* est sermo lacior' (278/5), and yet a good deal later in the text is found 'sicut dicam, si Deus voluerit, in materia *De sacramentis*' (382/10) – the first must apparently indicate an existing text, though the second looks forward to writing it in the future. The importance of these ambiguities will become clear later.

[6] One defect in my first investigations that it has been impossible completely to remedy was my failure to record whether a manuscript had the usual Arabic or less commonly Roman numerals (or spelt out the word); this turned out very occasionally to be of interest. The various editors' usage does not follow that of their base manuscripts.

IV

Turning to the cross-references themselves, usually in Wyclif's works these take the form of the chapter (or sermon) number, together with some indication of work; no lettered subdivisions of chapters or sermons are used, though very rarely words such as *in fine* may give further help in location.[7] When the reference is to another part of the same work, *huius* is usually substituted for any fuller title. The indication of work may take the form of title, or of the number of the part in a longer sequence, or of both. Examples of the first, without the obscurity mentioned above, would be 'ut recitavi in tractatu *De incarnacione*' (T32 *De ecclesia* 126/28 referring to T22 *De benedicta incarnacione*). Examples of the second are 'vide hoc libro 2° tractatu primo capitulo 4to' (T9 *Purgans errores circa veritates in communi* 7/7 referring to T14 *De intelleccione dei*, book II tract 1 of the *De ente*), 'ut ostenditur 25 capitulo libri 5' (T31 *De veritate* ii.216/9 referring to T30 *De civili dominio* iii.71, the fifth book of the *Summa theologie*). The third fashion, as the most cumbersome, is the least common: an example is 'ut tactum est tractatu *De tempore* capitulo 3 et ita libro 6' (T19 *De potencia productiva dei ad extra*, TCC fol.143rb, to T12 *De tempore*, book 6 of the first part of *Summa de ente*). Where reference is to a freestanding work, without numeration in a larger collection, the title has to be the identifying mark. But habit seems to vary somewhat in references to the *Summa de ente* and the *Summa theologie*: to the former either title or book and part might be used, though increasingly the title seems to have been preferred. In the *De civili dominio*, the *De veritate* and the *De ecclesia* references within the *Summa theologie* are almost always by book-number and chapter;[8] but in the fewer indications of the subsequent parts there is an increasing tendency to use titles, and this becomes the invariable method in references to the *De symonia*, *De apostasia*, and *De blasphemia*.

The sections that follow show some of the kinds of evidence produced by these cross-references. Because all sections of the philosophical *Summa de ente* have still not been edited, and a printed source to which recourse can be made is consequently not available, I shall

---

[7] Lettered subdivisions of chapters or sermons are provided in many but not all of Wyclif's works, but not in all copies; the evidence suggests that this device, necessary for the provision of indexes, was added very soon after Wyclif's own lifetime. For a provisional statement about the device and the indexes see my *PR*, pp. 104–8; a fuller analysis will be published soon.

[8] This numbering implies the twelve-part order, as known from Thomson and the WS editions; for questions about the date when that order was established see below, pp. 207 ff.

largely avoid this area.⁹ The sermons will also not be included here: the two short sets, the *Sermones quadraginta* and the *Sermones viginti* have been discussed elsewhere, whilst in the remaining three long groups cross-references form one element in a larger argument about their composition, and will be examined at more length in another paper. * The main theological and ecclesiological works, most of them assembled into the twelve sections of the *Summa theologie*, will form the core of the present study.

I

The simplest evidence produced by listing the cross-references in Wyclif's works is a number of titles, apparently of texts by the author himself, that are unfamiliar to the reader of the modern editions. A number of these are identifiable with sections now incorporated into other texts, and seem to point to varying processes of revision. The first example has been recognized since 1977, when a work *De religione* by Wyclif was noted by Eric Doyle from references in William Woodford.[10] Doyle deduced from Woodford's quotations and references that *De religione* consisted of *De civili dominio* iii chapters 1–3, followed by *De apostasia* chapters 1–2. Whether, as Doyle suggests, the *De religione* was originally a section of *De civili dominio* iii (with the two chapters of *De apostasia* replaced after the three of this), or whether it was an independent work subsequently split up by Wyclif between the two now known tracts, does not emerge from Woodford's testimony. But a *De religione* is mentioned within Wyclif's own texts, in *De civili dominio* ii.236/30 and in *De blasphemia* 50/25. These confirm that its opening was incorporated into the opening chapters of *De dominio civili* iii.[11] However, *De blasphemia* also refers to material that was once in the *De religione* under its new home: 'dictum est autem 2° capitulo *De apostasia*' (203/9) is correct for the latter text as we know it, even though it seems originally to have been *De religione* chapter 5.[12] In

---

[9] Mueller, 'A "lost" *Summa*', and the introduction to his edition of *De universalibus*, pp. xxxiii-xxxviii, covers some of the problems, and suggests the original existence of a third *summa*, of which only parts survive.

[10] E. Doyle, 'William Woodford, O. F. M., and John Wyclif's *De religione*', Speculum 52 (1977), pp. 329–36.

[11] The first is to *De civ. dom.* iii.19/36–20/2, the second more vaguely to *De civ. dom.* iii cap. 1; the first involves a reference forward (for which see below pp. 210 ff).

[12] Similarly 'ut patet libro 5° capitulo 3' (*De blasphemia* 203/19) incorporates the book

comparison with the other examples to be considered, it seems fairly certain that it existed as a separate tract and that it was split up by Wyclif himself.

Another text whose existence the cross-references support is *De adnichilacione*: this is referred to in *De benedicta incarnacione* 76/18, 78/30, *De statu innocencie* p. 476/6, and *De eucharistia* 52/11. Dziewicki in his volume for the Wyclif Society entitled *De ente* (1909) included as the final item three chapters, 12–14, of the final tract of the second book of the *Summa de ente*, the *De potencia productiva dei ad extra*, which, he noted, are headed in Trinity College Cambridge B.16.2 (the only manuscript he knew) *De adnichilacione*; in fact that heading covers chapters 12–16.[13] Thomson (p. 35) dismissed the idea that *De adnichilacione* was ever a separate tract, though he seems to think the designation is Wyclif's, not just scribal: he argues that the heading was 'a kind of shorthand tag' for 'a distinctive and recognizable portion of a long and somewhat unwieldy treatise'. There is certainly no sign of any break in the text of *De potencia productiva* in the other manuscript, Prague UK IX. E.6 – but then there are few headings of any description in that copy, even where an undisputed break occurs in Trinity.[14] It seems likely that the indications that an originally separate *De adnichilacione* once existed should be added to the other evidence suggesting that what we now have as the separate thirteen tractates of the *Summa de ente* is a late redaction of earlier material which almost certainly was of different shape and subdivision.[15]

Other allusions are to works hitherto not recognized. First a *De heresi* is mentioned in *De ecclesia* (69/2, 87/25, 298/18). Since all specify it as 'book 6', this must be identified with the final chapter of the *De veritate sacre scripture*. This begins (iii.274/18) 'postremo incidentaliter ad tractatum *De veritate scripture* restat tractare de heresi' (and cf. end iii.309/25), which may suggest that an originally independent tract is

---

number of *De civili dominio* iii within the *Summa theologie*; 'ut expositum est 2° capitulo *De apostasia*' (220/11) must involve a scribal error in the chapter number (albeit found in all extant copies), since the material in question seems to be chapter 3, p. 31.

[13] The title appears as a running title on fols 151r-156r above chapters 12–16, and chapter 12 begins with an illuminated capital of a kind normally found in the manuscript only for a new item.

[14] The Prague copy, fols 16r and 51r, does not mark off in any way the start of *De sciencia dei* and *De potencia productiva* respectively.

[15] See Mueller, 'A "lost" *Summa*', and intro. to *De universalibus*. It should be noted that a reference in *De trinitate* 166/19 establishes *De ente predicamentali* as the fifth tract of *De ente* book 1, even if this was not its original status.

being incorporated.[16] A *De mendacio* is again mentioned in *De ecclesia* (43/23, 159/30). This may likewise be a part of the *De veritate*, this time chapters 16–20 (ii.1–129); here there is no sign of 'marking off' in the wording; but the subject is certainly right, and the first reference in the *De ecclesia* precedes the title with 'ut patet libro 6' – *De veritate* is the sixth book of the *Summa theologie*. More intriguing is the *De cessacione legalium* found in *De symonia* (51/2 and 76/25), and in *Sermones* ii.259/37. The obvious objection to this as a work by Wyclif is that it alludes to Grosseteste's treatise of this name.[17] That this may not be the right answer is indicated both by the fact that *Lincolniensis* has not been mentioned hitherto in *De symonia* (though he is at 88/20 and 103/8, neither is a reference to the *De cessacione legalium*), and also by the inappropriateness of the subject matter to which this reference is allegedly relevant. In addition to the cross-references, John Bale lists a work of the same title under Wyclif's name, and gives an incipit for it 'Redeundo autem ad propositum de'; this is *not* the incipit of Grosseteste's work, which itself is included by Bale under the latter's name with the right incipit.[18] Bale's evidence provides the essential clue: the incipit he gives is that of the penultimate chapter in the edition of *De veritate sacre scripture*, whose subject is indeed the continued validity of law if the officers imposing it cease to exist. This seems to be a third section of the *De veritate* that may have had independent existence before being incorporated.

A *De privilegiis* is mentioned in *De officio regis* (1/2), and *De ecclesia* (276/14, 304/12, 343/12). These references seem likely to allude to chapters 8–11 (157/25–250/16) of *De ecclesia* itself, as it now stands. Privilege is indeed the subject of those chapters (though chapter 12 continues it). The first reference in *De ecclesia* (cap. 13) is in full '11 capitulo *De privilegiis*',[19] and plainly refers to the citation of Matthew 10 and Luke 10 in chapter 11 (248/2–6); the second 'sicut dixi in

---

[16] A reference in *De civili dominio* ii.113/12 'considerans dicta de heresi vii capitulo' seems to be to chapter 7, ii.58/8 ff. of the same book, and not to the *De heresi* specified in *De ecclesia*.

[17] Wyclif knew this work, as is evident from *De veritate sacre scripture* iii.104/10–14, 106/12–107/4 and elsewhere.

[18] *Scriptorum Illustrium maioris Brytannie* . . . *Catalogus* (Basel, 1557–9) i.452, Grosseteste i.306.

[19] *11* appears in Vienna 1294 and Vienna 3929, *20* in Prague UK X. D.11; for a possible cause of the discrepancy in the last see below p. 201. The punctuation given, recognizing a title, is my own, Loserth's being inconsistent; manuscript rubrication can here, as elsewhere, not be regarded as significant because of its frequent omission even with undoubted titles.

materia *De privilegiis*' and the last 'ut patet superius tractatu *De privilegiis*' is less specific, but implies that the tract is part of the current work. Here there is less reason to look to an independent tract, and it may be that the title only refers to a subdivision of a longer work.

Less clear are the remaining references. *De maximo et minimo* appears in *De veritate* (ii.121/7)[20] and in *De ecclesia* (572/5); the most likely candidate for this is chapter 7 of *De logica tractatus tercius*.[21] Other cases, where a philosophical work seems to be in question are: *De continuacione* (*De benedicta incarnacione* 53/18) which could be either chapter 9 of the same work or chapter 20 of *De ente predicamentali* (T13); *De accione* (*De ente* 195/26) which might be an allusion to *De ente predicamentali*, especially chapter 10. The identity of *De anima*, mentioned in *De benedicta incarnacione* (203/19, 230/18) and *De ecclesia* (422/2), is unclear: the obvious answer of *De actibus anime* (T4) seems from the subject matter in question improbable, and the answer may lie in a lost commentary on Aristotle's text of the same name which Mueller, on other grounds, has suggested once existed.[22] Other cases where the nature of the text is less clear are *De perplexitate* (*De dominio divino* 126/21); *De Christo* (*De veritate* iii.118/11).[23]

II

These titles could in some instances (though not in that of *De religione*) point not to modification of earlier plans but simply to subdivision of the work in question. But smaller details of the cross-references make it clear that revision must in some cases be in question. A simple case concerns *De ecclesia*. The organizational problems of *De ecclesia* are obvious to anyone who reads the text attentively: though part of it apparently relates to Wyclif's advice given to the Parliament at Gloucester in 1378 concerning the Shakyl and Haulay sanctuary

---

[20] With the addition 'et in materia de composicione continui'.

[21] See the opening words of this chapter, p. 129/2.

[22] Mueller, 'A "lost" *Summa*', p. 182; Wyclif's commentary on Aristotle's *Physics* survives in one copy now in Venice (T6 Biblioteca San Marco, Marciana lat. VI.173, fols 1ra–58vb), and his commentary on the *Meteora* once existed in the Prague Carolinum library (list 2, no. F7 in the facsimile in J. Bečka, J. Benda, *Katalogy Knihoven Kolejí Karlovy University* (Prague, 1948).

[23] The context of the first is entirely unhelpful; for the second the editor, R. Buddensieg, suggests tentatively *De benedicta incarnacione* 36/15 ff.

case, it is not clear which section if any was actually presented there and equally the number of opponents to which other sections of the material on this topic were directed is obscure.[24] One oddity in this text is the frequency with which the cross-referenced chapters are incorrectly given in all the available witnesses. The number of surviving manuscripts of this text is not enormous: three complete manuscripts (Vienna 1294 (A), Vienna 3929 (A1), Prague UK X. D.11 (B)), one containing only chapters 1–3, and two containing chapter 7.[25] The situation may be set out as follows: cross-references involving chapter 1–2 are unchanging and correct; a reference to a chapter 10 should be to existing chapter 2 (84/20), two to 12 should be to 3 (177/19, 181/6), one to 14 should be to 5 (388/4), one to chapter 16 should be to 7 (223/12), one to 18 should be to 8 (223/7), one to 20 should be to 11 (276/14), four to 22 should be to 13 (340/26, 343/18, 372/23, 516/27).[26] It is hard to make complete sense of this: it seems certainly to imply that material has been removed between existing chapters 2 and 3, but the number of chapters taken out seems to vary between eight, nine, and ten; assumption of further excisions of chapters later on still cannot produce a single coherent explanation. Unfortunately, there are no useful references to *De ecclesia* in other Wyclif works. Netter, whose quotations from Wyclif's works are usually furnished with identifiable bibliographic details, and are often long enough for checking, seems not to have used this text.[27] But the possibility of intermediate stages, perhaps more than one, in the compilation of the

---

[24] See Thomson, pp. 58–60, and references there given; the historical background to this text, and to other allusions by Wyclif to the case, are being studied by Peter Griffin (Trinity College, Cambridge). The full textual problems cannot be set out here.

[25] The sigils are Loserth's, and reflect his belief that the second was a copy of the first. The incomplete versions are respectively Wolfenbüttel Herzog August Bibliothek, Guelf. 1126 fols 46–84v, Trinity College Dublin 242, pp. 398–403 and Florence Biblioteca Laurenziana, Plut. XIX.33 fols 30–32v. Vienna ÖNB 3934, fols 148r-151r contains notes from various Wyclif works including this.

[26] These details are those of Loserth's base text without his emendations, Vienna ÖNB 1294; variants to them are as follows: 388/5 all copies, despite Loserth's record, have 14; 223/12 A1 has 6; 276/14 A and A1 have 11 as is correct by the printed text but B has 20; 340/26 A's reading 13 is a marginal correction to 22, A1 has 22, B has 13; 343/18 A's reading is again a correction of 22 to 13, A1 and B have 22; 372/23 A's reading is again 22 corrected to 13, with 13 in the margin, A1 has 13; 516/27 again A corrects 22 to 13, with 22 and 13 both in the margin, A1 along the line crosses through 22 and writes 13, B has 13.

[27] His *De ecclesia et membris eius* is T48, now called the *Supplementum Trialogi*, or *De dotacione ecclesie*; see *Doctrinale Antiquitatum Fidei Catholicae Ecclesiae*, ed. B. Blanciotti, 3 vols (Venice, 1757–9).

text as we know it would seem to be the most probable background to the muddle that remains.

A much more complicated case is the *De veritate sacre scripture*. Here the problem rests not in a discrepancy of references between numbers and actual text, but relates to one divergence between the manuscripts in regard to their inclusion or omission of the section i.151/19–167/8, covering the end of chapter 7 and beginning of chapter 8. Of the twelve manuscripts that contain this part of *De veritate*, six omit this material: Queen's Cambridge 15 (C), BL Royal 7 E.x (R), Prague UK III. B.5 (Q), with a marginal note *hic est magnus defectus*, Prague MK B.53 (K), Prague MK C.38 (S), Olomouc Kapitolni Knihovna C. O.115 (O). The section is present in six: Vienna 1294 (A), but with a marginal note 'vide bene quia aliqui non habent hoc ab isto loco usque ad signum tale' – the sign appears again at i.167/8; Trinity College Dublin 243 (D), but the section was omitted at its proper place by the original hand and was added by another on the opening flyleaves in an odd order;[28] Bodley 924 (B), but with a marginal note (p. 47), 'item cum logica abhinc usque ad hoc + ut 5° folio post non creo' and a corresponding mark at the end of the passage; Peterhouse 223 (P), but marked at either end by marginal pointing hands, and by a new line leaving a blank in the text; Prague UK VIII. C.3 (Z) and Prague MK A.84 (X) in neither of which is there any comment.

At first sight the cause of the problem seems to have been eye-skip: p. 151/18 ends a sentence 'ex intento et institucione et ordinacione legiferi dantis legem sic falsam, ut decipiat', and the omitted section ends 'in casu scripturam sacram et scripturam ut decipiat'. The omission, if such it is, must have arisen very early in the tradition. Scribes of the earlier manuscripts of insular origin seem to have been particularly aware of a difficulty: Vienna 1294, though written by Bohemian scribes, was corrected in Oxford in 1406,[29] and the Bodley, Dublin, and Peterhouse copies all indicate a problem. Only Prague UL III. B.5 of the true continental copies shows awareness of corruption.

This apparent scribal omission has ramifications in the cross-referencing within the *De veritate*. As has been said, it crosses a chapter

---

[28] On fols 2v–3 appear i.159/1–167/8 with the marginal note *capitulum 8*, then on fols 3-3v pp. 151/19–158/20 with no indication of misplacement; the order perhaps reflects an exemplar two of whose leaves had been reversed from their proper order (the two chunks of material each run to 208 lines in print).

[29] See colophon fol 119vb 'in vigilia Purificacionis Sancte Marie Oxonie per Nicolaum Faulfiss et Georgium de Knyehnicz'.

division, and its inclusion or omission should affect the subsequent numbering of the remaining chapters. No chapter numbers of any kind are found in Prague MK C.38 (itself an incomplete copy ending i.368/18). Numbering that is correct for the inclusion of the passage is found in Vienna 1294, Peterhouse Cambridge 223 and Prague UK VIII. C.3; numbering that is correct for the omission in BL Royal 7 E.x, Queens' Cambridge 15, Prague MK B.53, Prague UK III. B.5, Olomouc and Trinity College Dublin 243 – notwithstanding the subsequent addition of the missing material at the start of the last copy. Prague MK A.84 has only sporadic numbering but, despite the fact that it includes the passage, those numbers that occur after chapter 7 could only be correct for a text without it.[30] It is not clear whether the inconsistencies in Bodley 924's numbering are independent of this particular problem, or whether they too reflect it.[31]

There is, however, a further complication. As with most of Wyclif's major works, an analysis of the text survives in certain copies.[32] For the *De veritate* an analysis up to chapter 21 (according to the numbering of the edited text) survives in four copies: Vienna 1294, Trinity College Dublin 243, Prague UK III. B.5 and Prague MK B.53. The second of these is certainly of English origin; the first, despite the copying of the main text in England, could have been written in Bohemia since the analysis (along with an index by opening) is in a different hand from the main text and in a separable quire.[33] The content of the analysis in all four copies is identical. Significant for the present purpose is that the analysis *of chapter 7* moves straight from material identifiable with the text at i.148/1 to other material at i.167/14, ignoring all matter in the dubious section. For the two Prague manuscripts this is reasonable, and produces no oddities about the numbering of subsequent chapters since neither copy contains the dubious section – their analysis corresponds with their text. In the Dublin copy the analysis likewise corresponds to the text *as originally written*, with its chapter numbering but without the added material at the start. But the scribe involved in

---

[30] The text ends incomplete in chapter 18 (i.287/8).

[31] Chapters 1–11 are correctly marked, allowing for the inclusion of the passage; chapter 12 is again numbered 11, and the remaining chapters are one too low for the text – though sporadically visible plummet notes record the correct form.

[32] Whether these analyses were authorial or scribal is not entirely clear, but, as is evident in the present case, the origin of many if not all can be proved to be English, since they are found in both insular and Bohemian copies in identical form.

[33] Analysis fols 125va–127rb, index fols 120ra–125rb; the whole forming quire 13 of eight leaves, as opposed to the ten-leaf quires elsewhere.

IV

the analysis in the Vienna manuscript noticed the problem: he continued through the analysis of chapter 7 as that appears in the other copies, but then went back and added *et 8* in the central margin for insertion after 7, continuing then to analyses for what he described as chapters 9–21; these correspond to the edited text 9–21, but to the other analysis copies chapters 8–20. This may suggest only that the analysis was made from a manuscript that lacked the section. The same may be the explanation also for the fact that the index of biblical passages discussed in Wyclif's writing, an index preserved in two Bohemian manuscripts, likewise is only accurate for a copy without the section.[34]

The question of the original state of the text evidently interrelates with the cross-references: this passage should enable decisions to be made also about the authority of the cross-references. If the passage at the end of chapter 7 and beginning of chapter 8 (according to the edited text) were original – as the explanation of eyeskip would imply – then any original cross-references to chapters after 7 should reflect its presence. Conversely, if the cross-references are scribal, then correctly those copies which omit the passage should have numbers one lower than those which contain it in all cross-references involving chapters 8 onwards. But in fact the situation is more complicated and in its complexity provides no help towards the resolution of either the originality of this short passage or the responsibility for the linkings. Two cross-references seem to require inclusion of the passage in *all* manuscripts available: iii.23/2 'ex capitulo vicesimo' refers back to ii.137 chapter 20, but *20* is found without significant variation (ABCDKOQ in which KOQ should have *19*, Z has *secundo* by evident misreading of *20* as *2°*); iii.104/4 'dictum est vicesimo primo huius' refers back to ii.164 chapter 21, but *21* is found in all available manuscripts (ABCDKOQZ in which KOQ should have *20*). So far this would seem to confirm that the omission of pp. 151/19–167/8 was a scribal error, and that the cross-references continued as if no loss had occurred. But more mysteriously in four places lower figures appear, and in those manuscripts that *include* the passage as well as in those that do not: ii.139/30 'sicut in parte tactum est supra capitulo 16', where the reference is to ii.30 chapter 17 (found in ABCDKOPQZ, where

---

[34] Prague UK IV. G.27 fols 1ra–35vb and Vienna 4522 fols 24–108v; the first is dated 1461, the second is itself undated though another item in the manuscript was copied in 1423.

ABDOPZ should have *17*); ii.140/18 'ut recitatur supra 16 capitulo', where the reference is to ii.44 chapter 17 (found in the same group of manuscripts); ii.154/23 'ut narratur 17' where the reference is to ii.83 chapter 18 (found in the same group of manuscripts); iii.245/18 'ut expositum est 16 huius sexti' to chapter 17 (again in the same group, though P's text stops before this point).[35] These four cases might seem to suggest that the cross-references were inserted after the original composition and to a copy that lacked the original end of chapter 7 and beginning of chapter 8. The only way to explain their presence in manuscripts that *do* have that section would be to assume that the insertion was done on the hyparchetype of the defective copies *prior* to the realization of the eyeskip.

But was it eyeskip? Both *De ecclesia* and *De potestate pape* contain references back to *De veritate*; some of these throw no light on the situation (either because they are too general, are incomplete, or because they refer to material before chapter 7), but all the relevant examples provide a chapter number that is only correct on the assumption that the passage omitted was *not* part of the text as known.[36] Much of the evidence seems to point to a different explanation of the 'missing' passage: that it is not an omission by a careless scribe in a hyparchetype, let alone by a series of careless scribes who coincidentally omitted the same piece, but that it was in fact added to the text at a date subsequent to the completion of the whole and the first 'publication'. Consideration of the content of the passage may confirm this: the opening chapters of the *De veritate* are very largely uncontroversial, concerned with the status and value of scripture, and the need for all Christians to understand it. This subject runs through to the middle of chapter 7 and is continued immediately after the 'missing' section. But the end of chapter 7 and beginning of chapter 8, as edited by Buddensieg, deals with more dangerous topics and in more tendentious terms: the alleged infallibility of the pope, the worldly jurisdiction of the clergy, the identification of heresy, with loaded language such as 'glose sinistre, ut quidam doctor tradicionis

---

[35] A fifth possible case is at iii.256/9 where 'ut exponitur supra capitulo 18' refers to ii.100 chapter 19; but only B has a number here, whilst ACDKOQZ leave a gap, but B should read *19*.

[36] Thus *De ecclesia* 239/13 refers to chapter 25 (edited text iii.55/11 chapter 26), 257/15 to chapter 24 (iii.12/5 chapter 25), 297/33 to chapter 20 (ii.155 ff. chapter 21); *De potestate pape* 1/7 refers to chapter 14 (i.375 chapter 15); all available manuscripts of each text offer the same number.

humane et mixtim theologus' (153/22), 'corpus ecclesie malignancium' (154/15). Difficult though impressionistic judgements of this kind may be to establish, there seem to be signs of embattled defence in this section which is characteristic enough of much of Wyclif's later writing but not, up to this point and indeed for several chapters beyond, of the *De veritate*.

The implications of this local, but extremely knotty, problem seem to be various. If, as has been suggested, the passage from the end of chapter 7 to beginning of chapter 8 was an authorial addition rather than its absence being the result of a scribal eyeskip, then it must point to revision of the *De veritate*. If this is correct, the revision extended to the modification of some but not all of the existing cross-references within the text. The existence of some copies without the passage would imply that circulation of the text began prior to revision; but the proportion of copies showing awareness of the problematic status of the passage (whether that was of a defect or of addition) suggests a remarkable interest in the authority of the text, and an apparent ability to collate at least parts of an exemplar against another source – 'controlled dissemination' seems not out of the question.

But if a possible explanation is available for *De veritate*, no such solution emerges in the case of another part of the *Summa theologie*. The *De officio regis* (T33) was placed as the eighth book of the *Summa theologie* by the compilers of the Hussite catalogue of Wyclif's works, and has been accepted as such by modern editors and cataloguers.[37] It follows on from *De mandatis*, *De statu innocencie*, the three books of *De civili dominio*, *De veritate sacre scripture*, and *De ecclesia*. Internal evidence of subject matter suggests a date after the Westminster sanctuary case of 1378 discussed in *De ecclesia* (see 157/29 and less explicitly 169/20), and after Urban VI's Bull of November 1378 (see 120/17); but disillusionment with Urban VI has, to judge by his description as 'papa noster' (123/6), not yet set in.[38] The text as a whole is much better organized than the three works that precede it in the *Summa*,

---

[37] The Hussite catalogues are printed (with some mistakes and the omission of the second half of the last copy) by Buddensieg in *Pol. Wks* i.lix–lxxxiv; the earliest manuscript is dated *c.* 1415. Some consideration of their evidence appears in my article, 'The Hussite Catalogues of Wyclif's Works' in *Husitství, Reformace, Renesance* i (in honour of František Šmahel), ed. J. Pánek, M. Polívka, N. Rejchrtová (Prague, 1994), pp. 401–17.

[38] Arguments against articles of the *abbas de Cartesii* have not yet proved enlightening (98/6 ff., 128/35 ff., 130/18 ff.); John de Usk was Abbot of Chertsey from the 1370s to 1400, but no text by him seems to survive.

with fewer digressions or outbursts. The editors, Alfred Pollard and Charles Sayle, say (p. xxii) 'With chapter VIII there can be no doubt that the *De officio regis* originally came to an end'; but the remaining four chapters deal with four objections mentioned at the start of chapter 9 (217/13, and picked up at the start of the next two chapters 231/2 and 245/26) which are relevant to what precedes and legitimately extend the discussion. The amount of cross-referencing in this text is small in comparison with the three works before it in the *Summa*, but *De mandatis*, *De civili dominio* books i and iii, and *De ecclesia* are mentioned; the reference to 'libro 6 *De pastorali officio*' (163/17) could well be to *De veritate sacre scripture*, the sixth book of the *Summa*, and not to the *De officio pastorali* (T53), though the subject matter would allow either.

But there are in the *De officio regis* half a dozen puzzling references to statements in chapters 33, 34, 36, 38 and two in 39 of another work; one of these last is specified as 'libri proximi'. The 'liber proximus', the *De ecclesia*, has only 23 chapters (and even the assumption of an originally longer work, above p. 201, would not give 39). The only work likely to be relevant that has the requisite number of chapters is *De civili dominio* i. One of the six seems certain to be to this work (231/1 '39 capitulo' to *De civ. dom.* i. 274/9 ff.), and a second seems likely (195/28 '38' to *De civ. dom.* i. 267/7 ff.); but in each case the chapter number in the printed *De civili dominio* is one lower than that in the *De officio regis* reference. Three further references in the latter seem to be to *De civili dominio* ii, but here the numbering is hopelessly discrepant (125/13 'superius 34 capitulo' to *De civ. dom.* ii. 58 ff., chapter 7; 212/1 '39 capitulo' to ii.39/7 ff., chapter 5; 249/29 '33 capitulo' again to ii.39/7 ff., chapter 5). The first instance, 'ex dictis 36 capitulo' (119/3) is difficult to locate. The three known manuscripts of *De officio regis* do not differ in regard to any of these.[39] Unless these references are simply crazy, the implications are bewildering in their ramifications. In terms of their ideas and subject matter, *De officio regis* would make a very reasonable follow-on to *De civili dominio* i. Much of books ii-iii of that latter work is taken up by Wyclif's responses to objections, some of them following on from the 1377 Bull of Gregory XI, to book i; they could thus hardly have been planned from an early

---

[39] The printed edition is based on Vienna 4514 with correction from Vienna 3933; Prague UK X. D.11, which may be earlier than these, was known to, but not used by, the editors.

stage.⁴⁰ *De veritate* and *De ecclesia*, as has been seen, have clear signs of heavy revision, involving the amalgamation of tracts that may well have had independent origins. So *De civili dominio* book i as the 'liber proximus' to *De officio regis* is not impossible. The absence of specification of work from all but one of the six references could suggest that the two works were very closely connected in the author's mind.

There is, however, conflicting evidence. The last suggestion does not begin to deal with the problem of the apparent allusions in *De officio regis* to book ii of *De civili dominio*, allusions which might suggest that some material that we know in that latter book was at the time of the writing of the former in book i. Equally references in *De veritate sacre scripture* specify it as book 6 of the *Summa* (iii.245/18, 301/11, 305/25) and *De civili dominio* iii as book 5 (ii.216/9, 250/13, 21 etc.), a numeration only correct on the now accepted ordering (in which *De officio regis* is part 8). Yet *De civili dominio* iii.447/14 observes 'ut 6 libro propono diffusius exponere' in regard to subject matter involved in any of *De ecclesia*, *De officio regis*, or *De potestate pape*, but not to the subject matter of *De veritate sacre scripture* which is now the sixth book. Certainly the text of *De civili dominio* rests on evidence of extreme fragility, even for Wyclif's case where burning by his opponents has drastically reduced the number of manuscripts: only a single copy of the whole survives (Vienna 1341 for books i-ii, 1340 for book iii), together with an extensive but poor student's copy of about two thirds.⁴¹ But the 1411 Oxford condemnation, which listed forty-four erroneous passages from it, thought the *De civili dominio* had three books, and the cross-references elsewhere in Wyclif's own writings will only work on that assumption.⁴²

III

Turning from the detail of individual texts to consider whether any general conclusions can be drawn, the first obviously important

---

⁴⁰ Cf. Catto, 'Wyclif', pp. 206-7.

⁴¹ Paris Bibliothèque nationale lat.15869 contains (*pace* Thomson, *Latin Writings*, pp. 49, 51) book i, book ii caps.1-12 (lacking ii. 110/21-129/1), book iii. 512/21-538/18, 626/19-647/31 somewhat disordered.

⁴² Thus *De potestate pape* 9/14 'ut tangitur 21 capitulo 5 libri' to *De civ. dom.* iii. 425, or to *De veritate* in *De officio regis* itself as 'libro 6' (52/29). For the 1411 condemnation see Wilkins, *Concilia*, 3, pp. 339-49; the items from *De civili dominio* are nos. 176-219.

question about all these cross-references is whether they originate from Wyclif's own efforts or whether they were scribal additions. The possibility that they were scribal additions is suggested by the presence of a few marginal cross-references found in the early and (perhaps unjustifiably) prominent manuscript, Trinity College Cambridge B.16.2.[43] It would be readily comprehensible if all the cross-references had started off in such fashion and had been subsequently incorporated into the text. But, though this is a credible hypothesis, there is little or no hard evidence to support it. The references visible in the margins of this manuscript are not replicated at all in other copies of the texts against which they are found, whether marginally or in the text. I have made no systematic search for new cross-references introduced into the margins of Bohemian copies. Some of these manuscripts are very heavily annotated, and such an investigation would take a long time.[44] But were there widespread intrusions of new cross-references from the margins *into the texts themselves*, this would certainly have come to my notice in checking those links printed in the editions; I have not been aware of any cases. Conversely, the presence of cross-references embedded within all texts is entirely stable at the same places through all copies of the texts in question; an almost exhaustive survey of surviving manuscripts has revealed a remarkable uniformity of presence of cross-references at the same places in all extant copies. There are, of course, cases where scribes evidently misread or miscopied numbers – numbers are particularly susceptible to such error; but such cases are few, and in any case do not obscure the intention to provide a cross-reference.[45] This uniformity must, at its lowest, indicate that this means of facilitating access to the texts was provided in the hyparchetype of all copies of the work in question – if

---

[43] Those I have noted are in the sermons, and are recorded by Loserth in his footnotes to i.309/27, 347/12, 354/6, 362/18, ii 13/11, 107/31, iii.27/29, 110/31, 220/3.

[44] S. H. Thomson, 'A Note on Peter Payne and Wyclyf', *Medievalia et Humanistica*, 16 (1964), pp. 60-3, sought to associate marginalia in seven Vienna manuscripts that he thought to be in a distinctively English hand with Peter Payne, the fugitive Lollard who reached Prague in 1415. Thomson's hypotheses are open to question on a number of fronts.

[45] An instance of visual confusion is *De mandatis* 40/5 where a forward reference to 'tractatu 3 capitulo 10' (i.e. *De civili dominio* i cap. 10) leads to fourteen manuscripts' reading of the chapter as *14*; this probably goes back to an exemplar like Gonville and Caius Cambridge 337/565 which indeed here has Arabic *10* where the second numeral could readily be read as *4*. The forms of certain numerals, notably 5 and 7, in Bohemian script, equally misled several of the Wyclif Society's editors, and produced errors in the printed texts.

the author did not provide them, then a redactor/redactors must have worked with remarkable consistency over a very considerable body of Wyclif's works. With remarkable consistency but not complete uniformity: if a redactor were inserting these references with an eye to 'publication', then one might expect that the same form, of title or of part number, would be used throughout. The sort of fluctuation found is more characteristic of activity over a period of time, an individual scholar's natural tendency to favour one form at one time and another subsequently or to vary by oversight or by stylistic preference even within a single work.

Another piece of evidence that at first sight might point towards scribal origin is the fact that quite a number of these references are in some degree incomplete: most commonly chapter numbers are not entered, as 'patet tractatu *De tempore* capitulo –' (*De dominio divino* 112/7), 'patet ex dictis *De divino dominio* tractatu 1 capitulo –' (*De civili dominio* i.127/4); occasionally the reference is even more defective 'ut exposui capitulo – libri –' (*De officio regis* 7/15, probably referring back to one of the first five books of the *Summa theologie*). But on reflection these deficiencies seem more easily explicable on the hypothesis of authorial origin for the references. Why should a scribe, let alone a redactor charged with providing this means of access to the texts, insert a reference which he could not complete? Perhaps the scribe or redactor hoped to be able to complete the reference subsequently, and failed to do so. But the multiplication of unverifiables does not make this an attractive line of argument.

As may have been noticed from some examples, including one just quoted, references may be explicitly forward as well as backward – explicitly, since they use a future tense in the verb attached or indicate position forwards by an adverb. Thus 'ut posterius dicitur *De sciencia dei*' (*De intelleccione dei* 99/24, the first tract of book 2 of the *De ente*, referring to *De sciencia dei*, itself the second tract of the same book); 'ut patet infra tercio huius capitulo 43' (*De mandatis* 316/32, the first book of the *Summa theologie*, referring to *De civili dominio* i.358, itself the third book); 'ut planius intelligatur tractatus *De symonia*' (*De veritate* iii.310/2, referring forward to a later book of the *Summa*). Some of the references that may be supposed to direct forwards are not marked as such: thus 'vide libro tercio *De humano dominio*' (*De dominio divino* 204/27 referring to *De civili dominio* part i). From the statement at the end of *De statu innocencie* it would appear that Wyclif intended the *De dominio divino* to precede any treatment of human dominion.[46]

The issue of forward allusions seems to form the nub of any debate about the origins of the cross-references. If the origin were editorial (which term I use here to cover both the activities of a scribe and those, presumably more organized, of a redactor), then forward allusions would be as simple to provide as backward ones. If the editor had only the single text on which he was working, then references either way could only be within that text. If he had a range of texts, then the extent of references could be greater and should encompass all available works irrespective of their date or order. Only if the editor had guidance about the date or ordered sequence, could he correctly indicate outside the single work futurity or completion, *posterius* from *superius*, by verb tense, or by adverb. Unambiguous *verbal* indications of future by means of verb tense or adverbs are comparatively rare; as was said at the outset, 'ut patet' or 'ut dictum est' are open to either retrospective or forward interpretation. The number of certain references forward, whether within a single work or between different works, is actually very small – though it does exist – and is far outweighed by the vast number unambiguously, or at least most naturally understood, as alluding backwards. This in itself points against the idea of editorial activity: on simple grounds of probability more forward references would be likely on that hypothesis. There can be no doubt that the presumed aim of the operation, to facilitate access to all Wyclif's texts, would be much better achieved had there been more forward references; such references could also have allowed for the indication that Wyclif had modified a view expressed in his early works in writings from later in his career, and so have reduced the appearance of inconsistency in regard to certain opinions.

Here the question of the origins of these cross-references interlocks with that of date: can a reference within one work to another work provide a chronology of the one text to the other? If, for instance, *De veritate sacre scripture* refers, without clear indication by verbal tense or by adverb, to *De civili dominio* iii (as at ii.216/9 of the former to iii.71 of the latter, cited above p. 208), does this necessarily imply that *De veritate* is the later composition? In view of the evidence adduced above

---

[46] *De statu innocencie* 524/19–25; it should be noted that all five continental manuscripts of the text end before this point, chapter 10 only existing in the English manuscripts Trinity College Dublin 243 and Gonville and Caius Cambridge 337/565.

concerning the modification of texts, including here both works, I think this must be regarded as dubious – at least in that simple formulation.

Looking in detail at the clear cases, it is striking that the largest number of apparently forward references occur in parts of the *Summa de ente*, the philosophical collection in two books of respectively seven and six parts, whose organization and content has been shown to have been authorially modified in major ways.[47] To summarize the cases that seem proven: I.i *De ente in communi* refers to II.i *De intelleccione dei*; I.ii *De ente primo in communi* refers to II.i *De intelleccione dei*, II.iv *De trinitate* and II.v *De ydeis*; I.iii *Purgans errores circa veritates in communi* refers to I.v *De universalibus*, II.i *De intelleccione dei*, II.iii *De volucione dei*; I.iv *Purgans errores circa universalia in communi* refers to II.v *De ydeis*; I.v *De universalibus* refers to II.iv *De trinitate* (and also to T22 *De benedicta incarnacione*, outside the *Summa*); I.vi *De tempore* refers to a 'tractatu de substancia', probably to be identified with I.vii *De ente predicamentali*;[48] I.vii *De ente predicamentali* refers to II.i *De intelleccione dei*, II.iii *De volucione dei* (with which it has a substantial overlap of two chapters), and II.v *De ydeis*; II.i *De intelleccione dei* refers to II.ii *De sciencia dei*, II.v *De ydeis* (and again to *De benedicta incarnacione*); II.ii *De sciencia dei* alludes to II.iii *De volucione dei*, II.iv *De trinitate* and II.v *De ydeis*; II.iv *De trinitate* in its reference to 'ut patebit in materia *De eucharistia*' (111/3) probably intends a pointer to the section *De anichilacione* which, as previously mentioned, forms a section of II.vi *De potencia productiva dei ad extra*.[49] Such a display is exactly what might be expected if an author worked through previously written material as he assembled it into a single coherent whole.

The contrast with the works of Wyclif's theological and ecclesiological maturity is striking, despite the fact that some texts of that maturity, notably *De civili dominio*, show the densest concentration of cross-referencing. *De dominio divino* contains three allusions, all of

---

[47] See references above, nn. 4 and 9; for the effects of this reorganization on the availability of exemplars to at least one scribe see my paper 'Trial and error: Wyclif's works in Cambridge, Trinity College MS B.16.2', in *New Science out of Old Books: Studies . . . in Honour of A. I. Doyle*, ed. R. Beadle and A. J. Piper (Aldershot, 1995), pp. 53–80.

[48] Accepting the view of S. H. Thomson, 'Order of writing', p. 161 (c), and his suggestion of chapter 5 of that text.

[49] See above p. 198. For reasons of space full references to the other cases cannot be given; most are deducible from S. H. Thomson and Mueller's articles above n.4 and from W. R. Thomson's observations on his texts T7-19 (though some cases in each that seem to me dubious have been ignored here).

them vague, to a book 'de humano dominio' – should this be italicized, as an alternative title to what became known as *De civili dominio*?[50] *De mandatis*, the first section of what came to be described as the *Summa theologie*, has two more specific allusions to *De civili dominio* i, and two acknowledgements of outline intentions to discuss the power of the pope and simony.[51] Amongst the vast array of the device in *De civili dominio* in book i just six refer to book ii, one to book iii, whilst in book ii two only refer to book iii.[52] Quite apart from the tiny fraction of these forward pointers, two factors are worth observing: that all seven of those in book i derive from four chapters (40–3) and hence might reflect authorial revision of that section. Secondly and more significantly, much of *De civili dominio* ii and iii represent Wyclif's defence of his views in book i against their heretication by Gregory XI's Bull and the ensuing outcry of opposition from William Woodford and other critics – exactly the situation in which forward reference, if entered by a redactor working at a date later than composition, would be most helpful. The remaining examples of forward pointing in the *Summa theologie* are very few and unhelpful; many have already been mentioned in another context.[53] To summarize: the final paragraph in T31 *De veritate sacre scripture* anticipates a 'tractatus De symonia' (T35), though T32 *De ecclesia* (342/28) speaks of it as written; T34 *De potestate pape* mentions twice, once in the future, a tract *De sacramentis*, T35 *De symonia* more specifically calls it *De eucharistia*, whilst T37 *De blasphemia* speaks of it as written.[54] The contrast with the *Summa de ente* is striking.

It should be noted that all the early manuscripts contain the references, whether these point backwards or forwards. One of the earliest surviving manuscripts, the extract from *De potestate pape* in Trinity College Dublin 115 probably of 1380, unluckily does not involve a cross-reference.[55] Oriel College 15 of *De benedicta*

---

[50] See 204/26, 224/12 and 255/20; the first has a future verb, the second and third know that this is a 'third book' and the third that the matter is to be found in chapter 7.

[51] Respectively 40/5 'tractatu 3 capitulo 10', 316/32 'infra tercio huius capitulo 43'; 360/1 'de ista materia cum tangit potestatem pape dicetur inferius', 380/17 'quomodo autem omnes simoniaci sunt heretici est alibi longus sermo' (all manuscripts are unanimous in their witness to the books).

[52] See i.315/17, 330/28, 337/4 (repeated 14, 27) 341/14 (linked to 345/7), 393/5; i.394/5 (repeated at 20), 394/13; ii.209/26, 212/20.

[53] See above pp. 208 ff for details.

[54] Respectively 278/6 and 382/10 (for which see above p. 195); 110/27; 22/31.

[55] The extracts from *Sermones quadraginta* in Exeter College Oxford 6 (for which see J.van Banning, *JThS*, ns, 36 (1985), pp. 338–49) omit the only reference 'ut alias ostendi'.

incarnacione, written by Nicholas Fawkes of Glastonbury Abbey in 1389, has the full panoply of references, as found in the later copies. The two early copies of parts of *De civili dominio*, Durham Dean and Chapter Reg. N of 1391 with chapters 24, 26–7 of book iii, and Paris BN lat.15869, a student copy of not much later than 1381, with two-thirds of the whole, likewise record them (even if curtailed in the latter case by the scribe's abbreviation of parts of the work). There seems to be no stage in the known textual history of any of the writings without these references. After prolonged work with this bulk of evidence, my own conclusion is that the majority derive from authorial insertion: the absence of any significant body of forward references, especially in the *Summa theologie*, seems the strongest evidence for this. But equally traces of authorial revision and recasting are abundant in the philosophical works and in the texts of the *Summa theologie*;[56] the stage at which cross-references were provided cannot be assured, even if they were provided authorially. On their own, it seems, cross-references may be a hazardous means of establishing chronology.

This negative conclusion does not, in my view, end their interest. The evidence of titles and of certain details of cross-referencing seem to make a strong case for the view that the *De veritate sacre scripture* and the *De ecclesia* underwent considerable revision before they reached the state in which modern scholars know them from the Wyclif Society editions. Indeed, those editions give a misleading impression of a settled text in regard to many of Wyclif's works. Scrutiny by Ivan Mueller of the references in the philosophical works pointed to major reorganizations in that area, apparently undertaken at least in part much later than the original writing of the texts. Michael Wilks some years earlier than Mueller drew attention to evidence that Wyclif revised his presumably early *De logica tractatus tercius* (T3) in the 1380s, incorporating into it ideas concerning the eucharist that he certainly had not arrived at in the 1360s.[57] This revision explains why this work, under the title of *De arte sophistica*, was examined by the Oxford investigators before the 1411 condemnation.[58] Wyclif's *Sermones*

---

[56] See Mueller, 'A "lost" *Summa*' and intro. to *De universalibus* for material on the former.

[57] M. Wilks, 'The early Oxford Wyclif: papalist or nominalist?', *SCH* 5 (1969), pp. 93–4; it should be noted that the date 1383 (iii.183/39) appears in all four surviving manuscripts (written out as 'mille trecenti octoginta 3' in Assisi Biblioteca Communale 662), and so is unlikely to be a scribal error (as Dziewicki i.vii, knowing only one manuscript, suggested).

[58] See Wilkins, *Concilia*, 3, p. 346, and for some of the notes of the investigators Hudson, *PR*, pp. 83–5.

Cross-referencing in Wyclif's Latin Works

quadraginta certainly underwent reorganization before the 'publication' of the collection, though in this case it is less clear whether either collecting or reorganizing was done by Wyclif himself.[59] Anyone who tries to compare a manuscript of the *Dialogus* (T408) with the printed edition is likely to find that the numbering and order of the later chapters are seriously discrepant.[60] Loose ends, whether of the kind considered here or as evidenced in other ways, abound.[61] None of this, unwilling though Thomson, Wyclif's latest cataloguer, was to recognize revision,[62] should surprise us. Wyclif was a busy man, both as an academic and as a political controversialist, often with many tracts under way simultaneously, answering objections and questions with ferocious energy as soon as they arose. He had every reason himself later to endeavour to tidy up his output, to incorporate the answers to immediate problems into a larger whole, to adjust for afterthoughts, for new arguments and new situations. But, to complicate the situation, his early disciples likewise had every reason to organize their master's output; the provision of indexes to many of the major works, necessitating the prior provision of subdividing letters to each chapter or sermon, seems certainly attributable to their devotion.[63] One conclusion does, however, seem certain: the cautionary one that dating any of Wyclif's texts is even more hazardous than has hitherto been apprehended, and that in particular cross-references should not alone be trusted.

---

[59] See 'Aspects of the "publication" of Wyclif's Latin sermons'.

[60] Pollard's edition provides a conflated text with few variants, and used only nine of the twenty-five manuscripts now known.

[61] The Hussite catalogues provide further indications, as I have shown in 'Aspects of the "publication" of Wyclif's Latin sermons'; the evidence provided by the passages duplicated from one work to another will be considered elsewhere. Allusions to Wyclif by near contemporary writers, whether friends such as Hus or foes such as Woodford, are rarely detailed enough for use in this matter; Netter's evidence is an exception to this general rule.

[62] In addition to the examples already given, T391 is another clear instance: this snippet, surviving in only one manuscript, is not a 'letter' (as suggested in Thomson's article 'John Rylands Library MS Eng.86: an unnoticed piece by John Wyclyf', *MS* 43 (1981), pp. 531–6 and repeated in the *Catalog* p. 241) but two extracts from *Sermones quadraginta* (*Sermones* iv.200/27–201/5 plus 233/10–26) strung together with a few words at the beginning and middle.

[63] See *PR*, pp. 104–6 for a preliminary statement.

V

THE DEVELOPMENT OF WYCLIF'S *SUMMA THEOLOGIE*

In its printed form in the Wyclif Society's edition Wyclif's *Summa theologie* presents a reassuringly clear structure: seventeen volumes covering twelve books – or ten if the *De civili dominio* is counted as a single book rather than as three[1]. The *Summa* there issued consists of *De mandatis divine, De statu innocencie, De civili dominio* (in three books), *De veritate sacre scripture, De ecclesia, De officio regis, De potestate pape, De symonia, De apostasia, De blasphemia*[2]. Twelve books were recognized by the Hussite cataloguers who early in the fifteenth century put together their list of Wyclif's works, with title, number of chapters, incipits and explicits; they also entitle those twelve *Summa in theologia*[3]. Williel Thomson, in the completion of his father, Samuel Harrison Thomson's modern catalogue, likewise accepts twelve books; he goes further in dating these twelve in sequence between 1375 and 1381[4]. Modern critics, including those who have not taken heed of some rather hesitant reservations in Thomson's notes, have assumed from these points that the development of Wyclif's theolo-

---

1. Apart from the *Postilla in totam Bibliam*, a work still unprinted, most of Wyclif's writings were published by the Wyclif Society between 1883 and 1921; they were edited by various scholars, without standardization of method, and to differing levels of competence. References are to the volumes in this edition unless otherwise indicated, though many of the points have been checked against the manuscripts whether or not these were used by the editors. In references to manuscript collections the following abbreviations will be used: ONB for Vienna Österreichische Nationalbibliothek, PMK for Prague Metropolitan Chapter, PUK for Prague National, formerly University, Library. In all citations, whether from manuscript or edition, modern punctuation and capitalization has been provided; in editions page numbers are followed by a slash and the line number, the latter discounting all headings.

2. In the Wyclif Society's edition each book appeared in a separate volume with three exceptions: the brief *De statu innocencie* appears at the end of *De mandatis, De civili dominio* book 3 appears split between two volumes, and *De veritate sacre scripture* in three.

3. The earliest copy, ONB 3933, is dated c.1415. For the catalogue see the print by Buddensieg in *Polemical Works* I. LIX-LXXXIV, and my discussion *The Hussite Catalogues of Wyclif's Works*, in *Husitství, Reformace, Renesance*, vol. 1, ed. J. Pánek, M. Polívka, N. Rejchrtová, Prague 1994, pp. 401-17.

4. W. R. Thomson, *The Latin Writings of John Wyclyf*, Toronto 1983; Thomson numbers Wyclif's works, and these numbers will be used here preceded by T – the *Summa* is T26-37.

gy and ecclesiology can be traced simply by following the changes through these long works[5]. The purpose of the present paper is to suggest that this path is too easy, and that the stages by which this twelve book assemblage came into being were far more complex, were spread certainly up to Wyclif's death in 1384 and perhaps beyond, and that the processes of revision which some parts have undergone are only traceable in part – but in sufficient part to alert the critic to the need for caution.

When the concept of a *Summa in theologia* was reached is not clear. The *terminus ante quem* is certainly the lists of its books which are found in Hussite copies of Wyclif's works, two of which are probably antecedent to the Hussite catalogue and formed its model; the earliest of these lists of which I am aware are of c.1410[6]. These lists, which vary to some degree between copies, give a confusing multiple description, some of which is also reflected in the Hussite catalogue. One description recognizes only three parts *De dominio divino, De dominio status innocencie, De dominio hominis post lapsum* – the first is evidently the work of that title later placed outside the *Summa*, the second is recognizable as the second book of the *Summa*, whilst the third may be *De mandatis* or *De civili dominio*[7]. Another description, declaredly deduced from the end of *De statu innocencie*, lists *De mandatis, De dominio angelorum* and *De dominio clericorum*; the last of these is presumably *De civili dominio*[8]. The third listing gives the order of twelve books as we know them, and calls the group *Summa theologie*[9]. Whether any such *Summa* was perceived in England seems far less clear: despite the poor preservation of the majority of the twelve books in

---

5. See, for instance, before Thomson's listing, G. Leff, *Heresy in the Later Middle Ages*, Manchester 1967, vol. 2, pp. 495-8 and subsequent discussion; more recently, M. Lambert, *Medieval Heresy: Popular Movements from the Gregorian Reform to the Reformation*, Oxford revd.edn. 1992, pp. 227-42.

6. PMK C.38, f.16va and ONB 1339, front pastedown; the material in PUK X.G.1, flyleaf 1, is perhaps slightly later but its information overlaps closely with these two.

7. ONB 1339, front pastedown: «In hoc volumen continentur infrascripti libri: liber primus, secundus et tertius *De dominio diuino*, omnes incompleti; *Liber mandatorum* siue *Decalogus*, completus et perfectus; Item liber *De statu innocencie* eciam incompletus». The brevity of the last, in comparison with many of Wyclif's works, may have given the impression that it was incomplete; but the observation may anticipate the ensuing description.

8. This is the third listing in ONB 1339: «Secundum aliam quotacionem iste est ordo: primus liber est *De dominio diuino*, secundus *De dominio status innocencie*, tercius *De dominio hominis post lapsum*; hoc patent in *Tractatu status innocencie* in fine vbi addendum dicit ad primum tractum *De mandatis*, ad secundum librum *De dominio angelorum*, ad tercium *De dominio clericorum*»; see *De statu innocencie* p. 524/15-25. This is the first description given in PMK C.38, f.16va, and PUK X.G.1, flyleaf 1.

9. ONB 1339 «Iste est ordo librorum summe sue in theologia...»; PMK C.38 «Summa theologie continet duodecim libros...».

Wyclif's home country, it might be expected that Wyclif's opponents, and most importantly the methodical and exhaustive Thomas Netter, would have mentioned it – so far as I can see they do not[10]. Nor do any of the manuscript copies of any book of the *Summa* written in England indicate in heading or colophon any consciousness of that book's part in a larger whole – each book is presented as freestanding[11]. Even in Bohemia presentation of a text as part of a numbered sequence is very rare[12]. The omission of the *De dominio divino* from the twelve-book numbering evidently gave rise to surprise amongst the Bohemians; the exclusion of *De eucharistia* (T38), although apparently not observed by medieval readers, may likewise seem odd. Is the concept of a *Summa* a cataloguer's invention?

Notwithstanding this scepticism, the reader of Wyclif's works, however inattentive to such details, may well wonder what the problem is: Wyclif scatters numerous cross references to his own other productions through out these twelve books, and throughout texts such as the *De dominio divino* and *De eucharistia* which might appear to be outliers of the *Summa*[13]. Even granted that he does not claim a *Summa*, so many of these involve the numbers of books that such a structure implicitly emerges, at least in part. These cross-references appear regularly in all manuscripts of the texts in question, both those used for the Wyclif Society editions and those discovered since; inevitably the transmission of numbers involves some scribal error, but the choice between variants in these cases is usually clear. The difficulty comes when one comes to try to put them all together: variation in mode of reference is discernible, inconsistencies emerge of a kind that cannot be explained by simple incompetence in copying, references appear to apparently unknown works. To give examples of each of these. First variation in mode: whilst the first six of the twelve books are regu-

---

10. Netter's *Doctrinale antiquitatum fidei catholicae ecclesiae* is most readily available in the edition by B. Blanciotti, Venice 1757-9, reprinted Farnborough 1967. Netter's quotations are regularly cited by work and chapter, or sermon, number.

11. For the manuscripts see Thomson's listings. Typical are the headings and colophons of Trinity College Dublin 243 (formerly C.1.24), containing *De veritate sacre scripture*, *De symonia* and *De blasphemia*, with simple book titles and no indication of any connection between them.

12. It is regularly found in those parts (1-5, 10-12) of the *Summa* present in the set ONB 1339-43; that this was intended as a complete «works of Wyclif» (though now lacking some volumes) is evident from the distinctive layout common to all volumes, the use (rare in Bohemian copies) of parchment rather than paper, the inclusiveness of content but absence of duplication (save for two very brief texts). A further volume of the set is now Wolfenbüttel Herzog August Bibliothek Cod.Guelf 565, a stray that owes its present location to Flaccius Illyricus.

13. I have studied these cross-references in more detail in *Cross-referencing in Wyclif's Latin Works*, «Studies in Church History, Subsidia», 11, 1999, pp. 193-215.

larly referred to by number, the second six never follow this form but are always described by title (though *De ecclesia* is never mentioned by either method)[14]. The density of cross-references is most striking in *De civili dominio* which has around 600 of them, almost all to parts of that work or to *De mandatis*; equally it is remarkable that in only a very small number of instances do internal references in *De civili dominio* use the three book numbers of that work rather than the part numbers within the entire *Summa*[15]. There seems no easy explanation for the change of method between the first six and the last six books if the whole is regarded as a twelve-part sequence.

Other inconsistencies are less striking but more important. The *De officio regis* in the Hussite catalogue forms book eight of the *Summa*, preceded by *De ecclesia*, a work which in the printed edition has 23 chapters; in *De officio regis* are six references to statements in chapters 33-39, in one specified as being *libri proximi* – *proximus* in Wyclif regularly has the meaning of «the immediately previous»; all of these are constant in all three manuscripts[16]. The only work which has the requisite number of chapters is *De civili dominio* i, but this, as the *Summa* stands, is five books prior to *De officio regis*. Two of the six references seem fairly certainly to be to this work[17]. Three, however, are more readily explicable as allusions to *De civili dominio* book 2 – though the chapter numbers are not correct[18]. An intention to follow a study of civil dominion generally with an immediate examination of the office of kingship makes admirable sense – and we recall that books 2 and 3 of *De civili dominio* are largely concerned to answer the objections of others, including Gregory XI in his 1378 bull, to the theses of book 1[19]. Books 2 and 3 were in some sense from the start afterthoughts. But the idea of *De officio regis* as a follow-on to *De civili dominio* may have lasted longer to a period when those afterthoughts had been penned: in the third part is a reference to «VI libro propono diffu-

---

14. For example of the numerical method, in *De civili dominio* I.19/9 «quod dictum est tractatu 1 capitulo 5» refers to *De mandatis* chapter 5 (p. 34/15ff); or the title method, in *De blasphemia* p. 220/11 «dictum est autem 3 capitulo *De apostasia*» (p. 19ff, actually chapter 2).

15. For the exceptional cases see *De civili dominio* II. 132/11, 145/12, 167/37, III. 271/5, 313/32.

16. See *De officio regis* pp. 119/3, 125/13, 195/28, 212/1, 231/1, 249/29; the most explicit is the penultimate «contra 3 dicta 39 capitulo libri proximi». The Wyclif Society editors knew of, but did not fully use, PUK X.D.11, ff.130rb-210va.

17. See p. 231/1 to *De civili dominio* I. 274/9ff, and p. 195/28 to the same text 267/7ff.

18. See p. 125/15 «superius 34 capitulo» to *De civili dominio* II. 58ff chapter 7; p. 212/1 «39 capitulo», to II. 39/7ff chapter 5; p. 249/29 «33 capitulo» to the same as the last.

19. See Wyclif's protestation II. 114/27; book 2 begins with reference to the opposition of an Oxford

sius exponere» (III. 447/14) the subject of expropriation, a reference that is reflected in *De officio regis* (pp. 36ff), but not in *De veritate sacre scripture* which is now the sixth book.

If this case points towards twofold modification of any plan in the light of immediate circumstances by the addition of bulky but unforeseen arguments, other evidence suggests that the books as we have them result from the amalgamation of materials that originally were independent. Eric Doyle back in 1977 suggested that William Woodford's quotations of a *De religione* by Wyclif were explicable from chapters 1-3 of *De civili dominio* chapters 1-3 and chapter 1-2 of *De apostasia*, and that Wyclif had subsequently split *De religione* and suppressed it as an independent work;[20] Doyle did not notice that there are two references within Wyclif's own texts that confirm this[21]. Cross references of a similar kind within Wyclif's writings suggest that this was not a unique case: *De ecclesia* seems to incorporate a once-independent tract *De privilegiis* as chapters 8-11, whilst *De veritate sacre scripture* apparently absorbed *De mendacio* as chapters 16-20, *De cessacione legalium* as chapter 31, *De heresi* as chapter 32[22]. Though no cross references reveal the loan, *De apostasia* incorporates in four sections the whole of the *De eucharistia minor confessio*, dated in one manuscript 10 May 1381[23].

The case of *De ecclesia* is one where the status of the surviving text has before been questioned, albeit often perfunctorily[24]. Though part of it relates to Wyclif's advice given to Parliament in Gloucester in the aftermath of the Shakyl and Haulay sanctuary case of 1378, it is not clear which sec-

---

Benedictine (II.1/9), and allusions to this continue; *iste doctor* in book 5 cap. 17 (III. 329/23) seems to have no antecedent, but caps. 18-19 are an answer to William Woodford's *De dominio civili clericorum* part I. Cf. J. I. Catto, 'Wyclif and Wycliffism at Oxford 1356-1430', in *The History of the University of Oxford II: Late Medieval Oxford*, ed. J.I. Catto and T.A.R. Evans, Oxford 1992, pp. 202-5.

20. E. Doyle, *William Woodford, O.F.M., and John Wyclif's «De religione»*, «Speculum», 52, 1977, pp. 329-36.

21. See *De civili dominio* II. 236/30 and *De blasphemia* 50/25.

22. See my discussion in the article cited n. 13, pp. 197-200.

23. The latter is printed in *Fasciculi zizaniorum*, ed. W.W. Shirley, Rolls Series 1858, pp. 115-32; the date derives from Oxford MS Bodley 703 f.57ra. The sections in *De apostasia* are pp. 213/2-16, 219/32-221/13, 222/40-229/37, 230/21-231/5; the identity was noticed by the scribe of PUL XI.E.3, f.54v heading to his first copy. All Bohemian copies of the text include the longer conclusion, itself paralleled in *Sermones* III. 278/7-286/30, printed by I. H. Stein, *An unpublished fragment of Wyclif's «Confessio»*, «Speculum», 8, 1933, pp. 503-10; the direction of the «borrowing» cannot be regarded as certain.

24. Thomson sub T32; cf. H. B. Workman, *John Wyclif: a Study of the English Medieval Church*, Oxford 1926, vol. 1, pp. 321-4.

tion if any was actually presented there, and equally the number of opponents to which arguments are directed is obscure; the whole reads as a dossier on the case, badly sorted out afterwards[25]. Thus there are many indications of debate: extant chapter 14 opens «antequam respondeam ad magistrales obiectus», chapter 15 comments «quidam doctor qui sui gracia misit mihi tres conclusiones huic materie pertinentes», chapter 16 starts «post hec dubia respondendum est ad magistrales argucias quas doctores obiciunt contra dicta»; more provocatively chapter 15 also notes «episcopus Roffensis dixit mihi in publico parlamento stomachante spiritu quod conclusiones mee sunt dampnate». Internal cross-references again should increase scepticism about the coherence of the whole: they point to a massive reduction in the number of chapters, but are not compatible with a single reorganization[26]. It has usually been thought that the core of *De ecclesia* is chapter 7, a conjecture that is supported by the fact that two manuscripts preserve this alone[27]. Here, if nowhere else, revision must be conceded – but revision that must have been complex and may never have been completed.

Looking at the subject matter of the several books even in general terms would suggest a lack of coherent scheme. Critics have often argued that the impetus at the start was towards an analysis of authority, an analysis which sprang from Wyclif's reading of FitzRalph's views of dominion and from his radical development of those views; this analysis was fostered by R.L.Poole's inclusion of FitzRalph's *De pauperie Salvatoris* books 1-4 as an appendix to the Wyclif Society edition of *De dominio divino*[28]. But such a perception involves, of course, an anticipation of the *Summa* in the *De dominio divino* which stands outside it – and it is worth remembering that, if this was the starting point, Wyclif seems to have had difficulty in getting the sequence under way, since all three books of *De dominio divi-*

---

25. For a recent summary account of the affair see N. Saul, *Richard II*, New Haven and London 1997, pp. 36-8. Respectively *De ecclesia* pp. 299/10, 332/20, 359/5 and 354/22.
26. See my discussion (note 13) pp. 200-202; it should be noted that Loserth, the editor of the work for the Wyclif Society, emended many of the references in his text. The tract in its surviving form has 23 chapters, but some references seem to imply that a further ten chapters must once have existed: for instance, p. 223/7 reads in the manuscripts «iuxta conclusionem secundam capituli XVIII», referring to material (p. 173/11) currently in chapter 8.
27. MSS Trinity College Dublin 242 (once C.1.23) and Florence Biblioteca Laurenziana Plut. XIX. 33. See, for instance, Catto pp. 210-11.
28. See pp. 273-476. For Wyclif's debt to FitzRalph see, for instance, M. Wilks, *Predestination, Property and Power: Wyclif's Theory of Dominion and Grace*, «Studies in Church History», 2, 1965, pp. 220-36; Leff pp. 546-9, Lambert pp. 236-7, and compare A. Gwynn, *The English Friars in the Time of Wyclif*, Oxford 1940, pp. 71-3, and K. Walsh, *A Fourteenth-Century Scholar and Primate: Richard FitzRalph in Oxford, Avignon and Armagh*, Oxford 1981, pp. 377ff.

no are evidently unfinished, the last two seriously so[29]. But, granted such an uncertain start, the first three books of the *Summa* follow a coherent sequence, even if *De statu innocencie*, as Wyclif comments, is something of a digression which should come if anywhere before *De mandatis*[30]. If my deduction concerning the references in *De officio regis* is correct, then that text was first designed to come after what we know as *De civili dominio* I. This is a neat sequence of four parts, from divine absolute authority, to the ordained authority of the divine in relation to mankind before and after the fall, to human authority and its limitations in general terms, and finally to the authority of the king, the paradigmatic medieval ruler. Into this is the comprehensible intrusion of parts II and III of *De civili dominio*, an adventitious set of answers to objections – a parenthesis, albeit a gigantic one, into the sequence. The remaining six books are less obviously attached in subject matter. Certainly, the opening six chapters of *De ecclesia* as it stands deal broadly with the topic, before the contemporary concerns of the sanctuary case take over[31]; given the muddle about chapter numbers it seems reasonable to think that it was originally longer, or at least was intended to be. *De potestate pape* obviously moves to the actual government of the church, starting at its organizational head. And under the polemical titles, and even more polemical content, of the last three sections, *De symonia, De apostasia, De blasphemia*, is to be found a consideration of other orders in the church, particularly the «private religions» of the monks and friars, but also subordinate episcopal officials such as deans and archdeacons.

But the formal linking of these last three books is not to *De potestate pape* but to the major interruption which I have omitted: *De veritate sacre scripture*. In the final paragraph of that work Wyclif announces his intention next to turn to simony; *De symonia* opens «After the general discussion of heresy it remains to consider its parts. Three of them exist, symony, apostasy and blasphemy»[32]. I mentioned that the final chapter of

---

29. The incompleteness of the text is observed, either by overt comment or by the leaving of blank space, by the scribes of manuscripts ÖNB 1294, 1339, 3929, 3935 and Cambridge, Gonville and Caius College 337/565.
30. For Wyclif's comment see *De statu innocencie* p. 475/3 and cf. p. 524/19.
31. Though there is a reference to Urban VI in chapter 2 (p. 37/29), and to the cardinals' accusations against him in chapter 4 (p. 87/20), there appears to be no allusion to the sanctuary affair in the first six chapters.
32. *De veritate* III. 309/25 «Istud itaque dixerim pro nunc in comuni de heresi, ut sciatur ex fructu veritatis scripture notare et cavere hereticos, et ut planius intelligatur tractatus *De symonia*, quam, si

De veritate indeed is a section *De heresi*. So were the final books intended to follow immediately on the consideration of scripture? or are these sentences a hangover of an earlier stage when *De heresi*, and perhaps its associated *De cessacione legalium* (now the penultimate chapter of *De veritate*), were freestanding tracts? or were all of them parts of a different whole? As with *De ecclesia*, *De veritate* starts with a fairly uncontroversial six and a half chapters, at which point there is a section of much more aggressive argument to the middle of chapter 8, before a return to less polemical material as far as at least the end of chapter 11 – that section of aggressive argument is missing from six of the twelve surviving manuscripts available for this part, though one of those lacking it and four of those having it show some awareness of a textual problem at this point[33]. Revision is the simplest way to explain this local situation, but that local dislocation may well point to a more serious reorganization. A discussion of the standing of scripture is, of course, germane to the picture of christian authority which was Wyclif's concern in *De dominio divino* and its successors. But it is much less evident either that it *must* come after *De civili dominio* – logically it should surely come before *De mandatis* at the latest – or that Wyclif shows any consciousness of this as its determined position within its rambling length. And yet the cross references to it specify it as part 6 of a whole, its position in the sequence as we know it[34].

It is at this point that the question of the responsibility for these cross references becomes unavoidable: were they inserted by Wyclif as he wrote? or were they added by him, or by another, in revision or as a facilitating means of guidance for users of this vast assemblage of materials? Three general points need to be borne in mind: first, the vast majority (though not absolutely all) of them are references backward if the usual sequence of texts is accepted; second, the device is not restricted to the *Summa theologie* but is found in the *Summa philosophie* and, to a more limited extent, in other academic works by Wyclif even those written after his departure to Lutterworth; thirdly, all the manuscripts of the various works of all types agree in the positioning of these innumerable references and, with

Deus voluerit, propono diffusius pertractare»; *De symonia* p. 1/2 «Post generalem sermonem de heresi restat de eius partibus pertractandum. Tres autem sunt maneries heresis plus famose: scilicet symonia, apostasia et blasfemia.»

33. See my article n. 13, pp. 202-206.
34. See cross references within the text itself III. 301/11, 305/25, and in *De ecclesia* pp. 43/23, 45/15, 47/23, 68/21, 69/2, 87/27, 181/27, 199/4, 215/9, 239/13, 297/33, 298/18 (but compare 257/15 «ut dictum est 24 cap. libri proximi» to *De veritate* III. 12/5 (chapter 25 of the edited text).

the reservation already made about occasional scribal miscopying of numbers, about their content[35]. If the device is not part of Wyclif's original writing, it must have been introduced *before* the release of the archetype copy of *any* of the works. Yet I have already indicated reasons why it is hard to see them, at least in every detail, as part of Wyclif's original writing: if the *Summa* has undergone as much reshaping as I have suggested, then cross references must have needed adjustment. Sometimes adjustment is visible: earlier I mentioned the survival of references to *De religione*, a work absorbed in two parts into two distinct works – here original allusions were not adjusted – but in *De blasphemia* one old allusion remains but one reference to the absorbed material is to its new home, *De apostasia* chapter 2 instead of *De religione* chapter 5[36]. Elsewhere adjustment has not occurred, as in the misleading references in *De ecclesia* and *De officio regis* that I described earlier.

Does all this matter? I would suggest that it does, and seriously. Precise historical references within the parts of the *Summa*, and contemporary allusions to it, are few. Within the texts 24 March 1378 is said to be *hodie* in chapter 11 of *De veritate*[37]; discussion of the Westminster sanctuary case in chapter 7 of *De ecclesia* dates that as after 11 August 1378 and the ensuing discussions as November of that year or slightly later; in *De blasphemia* it seems possible to trace the precise point within chapter 13 when news of the June 1381 Peasants' Revolt reached Wyclif[38]. But my analysis so far should have made clear that, whilst these may date certain chapters, they need not date an entire text.

The same is true of external allusions that might allow dating. Gregory XI's 1377 bull lists 19 arguments, most of which are verbally traceable to book I of *De civili dominio*[39]. Margaret Harvey's recent examination of Adam Easton's *Defensorium ecclesiastice potestatis* has confirmed Pantin's

---

35. These points are illustrated in my paper (n. 13) pp. 208-14; for the inclusion of cross references in works which, as we have them, date from after Wyclif's retirement see, for instance, *Sermones* 1 pp. 136/6, 154/27, 3 pp. 26/29, 114/23, 4 pp. 47/29, 67/4 (the last two within the late *Sermones viginti*).
36. See *De blasphemia* pp. 203/9 «2 cap. *De apostasia*» but 50/25 «dictum est in tractatu *De religione* 2 cap.»
37. *De veritate* I. 258/6.
38. See the change in subject matter that occurs at the start of chapter 13, where Wyclif interrupts his sequential discussion of the ninth branch of blasphemy, that manifested by the monastic orders, to comment forcefully on the Revolt. These observations are discussed in my paper «*Poor preachers, poor men*»: *Views of Poverty in Wyclif and his Followers*, in *Häresie und vorzeitige Reformation im Spätmittelalter*, ed. F. Šmahel, Munich 1998, pp. 41-53.
39. The footnotes to the Wyclif Society edition identify these.

suggestion that Easton was the reader of Wyclif's text – he had asked for a copy to be sent to him in Avignon – and that he excerpted these arguments for the pope[40]. Allowing for the passage of Easton's letter written in November 1376, the sending of the book and its perusal, this would seem to give us a date of early 1376 at the latest for the completion of Wyclif's work. But Harvey showed also that Easton shows knowledge of views which are *not* in book i of *De civili dominio* but in book II or III – and indeed some of Gregory XI's list are closer to the formulations in those later books. Harvey proposes that these views were available to Easton as *dicta*, statements noted down from Wyclif's lectures or sermons[41]. This highly persuasive suggestion implies that *De civili dominio* II and III, far from being wholly reactive to Gregory's bull and its English protagonists as sometimes assumed, incorporate views antedating 1377, views probably propounded first as Oxford lectures and dealing with opposing views as they appeared; the extremism of arguments in those books cannot be regarded simply as the polemic of a man confronted by his own condemnation and determined to resist – they reflect a much more deep-seated radicalism.

Similar problems arise when critics try to date Wyclif's arrival at the formulation for the eucharist which produced the final condemnation in the Blackfriars Council of 1382. His public prevarications are familiar ground, and it is usually stated that it was not until 1379 or 1380 that his full explanation was reached[42]. But this explanation, which sees a progressive move from academic orthodoxy to unacceptable remanence faces

* problems. First Nicolas Biceps in Prague as early as 1378 seems to have seen that Wyclif's philosophical views about accidents and substances had implications for the eucharist that go beyond contemporary orthodoxy[43].

---

40. *Adam Easton and the Condemnation of John Wyclif, 1377*, «English Historical Review», 113, 1998, pp. 321-34; see W. A. Pantin, *The «Defensorium» of Adam Easton*, «English Historical Review», 51, 1936, pp. 675-80, and also his edition *Chapters of the English Black Monks*, «Camden Society», 3rd series 54, 1937, pp. 76-7 for the letter of Easton.

41. In fact Easton had asked in his letter (see last note) for «copiam dictorum cuiusdam magistri Iohannis Wyclyf ... et copiam cuiusdem libelli quam edidit de potestate regali per diversa capitula idem doctor». This suggests he was aware of the existence of both book and less formal notes.

42. See, for instance, Workman II. 408-9, Leff pp. 549-57, Lambert pp. 233-4, J. H. Dahmus, *The Prosecution of John Wyclyf*, New Haven 1952, pp. 81-2; compare M. Keen, *Wyclif, the Bible, and Transustantiation* in *Wyclif in his Times*, ed. A. Kenny, Oxford 1986, pp. 1-16 at pp. 9-16, and Catto pp. 194ff.

43. E. Stein, *Mistr Mikuláš Biceps*, «Vestník Královské české společnosti nauk», 4, 1929, pp. 39-56 at p. 43n; D. Trapp, *Unchristened Nominalism and Realism at Prague in 1381*, «Recherches de théologie

THE DEVELOPMENT OF WYCLIF'S *SUMMA THEOLOGIE*   67

Second, if improbably Wyclif failed to understand what Biceps had perceived until 1380, then how are references plainly indicative of remanence in the texts of *De dominio divino*, the supposedly earlier *De potencia productiva dei ad extra* and even more strikingly the *De logica tertia* purportedly from Wyclif's period as an artist to be explained?[44] Interpolation? Revision?

If Wyclif's own writings offer difficulties concerning dating, these two instances from Easton and Biceps suggest that the solution is not likely to derive from the testimony of his enemies or of his followers. The dilemma is that this testimony needs to be both early and precise. Anything written after 1384 may reflect the final form in which Wyclif left a text, and may well be made with the hindsight of the condemnations of his views which were publicized at least from the Blackfriars Council in 1382 onwards. Equally the case of Easton's probable access to *dicta* for *De civili dominio* book 2 reminds the modern critic of the extent to which academics learned of their contemporaries' views through informal channels, channels that might be both written and oral[45]. Easton's evidence is particularly important since for *De civili dominio* book 1 it gives precise chapter locations; in this it is, so far as I can see, unique amongst material written early and probably *before* Wyclif's death[46]. The date of Easton's citation thus becomes a matter of some importance: does the *Defensorium* in its extant form date from around the time of Gregory XI's condemnation, or is it later? Harvey suggests a date between April and September 1378, the first indicated by the dedication of the whole to Urban VI and the second by the absence of reference to the papal schism. The first of these

---

ancienne et médiévale» 24, 1957, pp. 320-60 at pp. 349, 355-6; the early date has been confirmed by F. Šmahel, «*Universalia realia sunt heresis seminaria*», «Československý časopis historický», 16, 1968, pp. 797-818.

44. See, for instance, *De dominio divino* 232/10ff; chapters 12-16 of *De potencia*, of which only the first two are printed in *Johannis Wyclif De ente*, Wyclif Society 1909, pp. 287-315; *De logica tertia* p. 137/1ff. But the last text has certainly been revised: p. 183/39 gives the date as 1383, and the inclusion of tenets from it (under the title of *De arte sophistica*) in the 1411 Oxford condemnation (see D. Wilkins ed., *Concilia Magnae Britanniae et Hiberniae*, Oxford 1737, vol. 3, p. 346) point to its reflection of Wyclif's advanced views.

45. The familiar case of the exchange of notes between Wyclif and William Woodford, both of them in Oxford, recounted by the latter in his *Quaestiones de sacramento altaris contra Wyclefum* question 63, and printed in translation by A. G. Little, *The Grey Friars in Oxford*, «Oxford Historical Society», 20, 1891, p. 81.

46. See Harvey's references pp. 323-4. Netter certainly gives such exact references, but the *Doctrinale* was not begun until the second decade of the fifteenth century. Other opponents cite usually by work alone, and are later than 1384.

dates seems firm, at least for the completion of the whole; the second, since it is negative and reasons could be envisaged for the omission, may be slightly less persuasive[47]. If the chapter references to book I of *De civili dominio* were in place in Easton's *Defensorium* by 1378, then we must probably assume that the copy of Wyclif's sent out to him at Avignon at the end of 1376 had that book in substantially the form we know, as far as its chapter divisions are concerned[48]. But it is worth insisting that this was only one book of the *Summa*, not the whole. And it is doubly infuriating that the *De civili dominio* is perhaps the most fragile of all Wyclif's works in its manuscript history: only a single copy of the complete text survives, books 1-2 in ONB 1341 and book 3 in ONB 1340. The French copy of most of book 1 and parts of books 2-3 is, despite its early date, and despite the intriguing mention of the recantation of its views forced on a Paris student in 1381 recorded at the end of book 1, hard to see as an independent witness to an authorial state of the work[49].

I have not space here to pursue all the ramifications of the case. But I should like to make two points, a warning and a suggestion. To start with the warning, one which is implicit in all I have been saying: that extreme caution should be exercised in dating any of the works as we have them, and consequently of dating, or seeing a chronological sequence in, the development of Wyclif's ideas. What we have, I would suggest, is largely a collection of substantially revised texts, manifesting perceptibly complex and incomplete adjustment. All dates must be treated with extreme caution: only one copy of Wyclif's *Confessio minor*, usually assumed to have been issued on 10 May 1381, is actually dated (the other nine are not), and that is the copy in a collection of the works of Wyclif's Oxford opponent William Woodford – it may be reliable, but then again it may not[50].

---

47. Harvey p. 322. I am very grateful to Dr Harvey for discussing the evidence with me; she is not to be blamed for my hesitation in accepting her apparently firm case. She confirms that the second copy of the *Defensorium*, that in Seville, Biblioteca Capitular y Colombina MS 57-1-7, contains exactly the same text as that she used, Vat. Lat. 4116.

48. Easton refers to a «second tractate» that includes chapter 18, and to chapter 26 as from the «tractate *De iure*»; but these could reflect Easton's mental sectioning of the book rather than any formal divisions in his copy of Wyclif's work.

49. Paris Bibliothèque nationale, fonds lat. 15869, ff.70-125; book 1 is somewhat abbreviated, after which appear book 2 caps. 1-12 (but missing II. 110/21-129/1), and book 3 chapters 24 (to IV. 538/18 only) and 27 (disordered). For the note see f.103. Almost all the cross references within the material included are in place. The other copies listed by Thomson under T28-30 are very brief extracts (or the Bohemian index).

50. See above, n. 23 for the text. The dated copy is MS Bodley 703; the other undated nine manu-

More radically I should like to suggest that this incomplete revision was part of an enterprise undertaken by Wyclif, probably with the help of friends, at Lutterworth between late 1381 and his death in December 1384 to establish a body of materials that would identify the *Doctor evangelicus* as an *auctoritas* on a par with, say, Wyclif's hero Robert Grosseteste, even perhaps with Augustine, whom Netter saw as Wyclif's model[51]. For this enterprise it was necessary to bring together the multiplicity of works, long and short, academic and political, finished (and, if Easton's evidence is indeed dated to 1378, perhaps *De civili dominio* book 1 formed the model) or incomplete, into a coherent set of sequences. Some texts, for instance two dealing with the issue of papal demands for taxation (T397 *De iuramento Arnaldi* and 398 *Responsio ad quesita regis et concilii*) and two immediate replies to Gregory XI's bull (T400 *Libellus ad parliamentum regis* and 401 *De condemnacione xix conclusionum*), all four probably from 1377-8, had escaped beyond reach – they had been intended for a specific audience, and it was later impossible or at least imprudent to try to recall them[52]. The revision was in differing degrees minimal or drastic: *De blasphemia* seems little modified, *De ecclesia* and probably *De veritate sacre scripture* much more radically reshaped. Revision was also sometimes perfunctory or incomplete, and may have been done on texts that had already been reworked; my examples hitherto will amplify this claim. At this late stage only did the concept of a *Summa theologie* come into existence, and the cross references were, even if not added *de novo*, at least much expanded and systematized. Differences in the format, between numbered books and titles, may suggest that more than one person was involved in the enterprise. Some ten years ago Ivan Mueller demonstrated the traces of a similar process of revision and tidying up in the evolution of the earlier *Summa philosophie*, and suggested that relics of yet another *Summa*, heavily biassed towards commentary on Aristotle, may be discernible in inexplicable cross references within that and within *De*

---

scripts are Cambridge Jesus College 59, Eton College 47, London BL Royal 7 B. III, Oxford Bodleian e Mus. 86, all of them English in origin plus Bohemian ONB 1387 and 4343, and PUK XI.E.3 with two copies (Brno UK Mk 109 f.179v has an extract from the Bohemian continuation).

51. For Wyclif's respect for Grosseteste see R. W. Southern, *Robert Grosseteste: The Growth of an English Mind in Medieval Europe*, Oxford, 2nd ed. 1992, pp. 298-307. Netter's comment is *Doctrinale* book V cap. 16 (ed. cit. II. 108).

52. Thomson dates the two texts about papal demands for taxation to 1377/8. A date after the death of Edward III seems assured for T397, since there is reference to «our king» *licet in etate iuvenili florenti* (see edition by G. Lechler, *Johann von Wiclif und die Vorgeschichte der Reformation*, Leipzig 1873, vol. 2, pp. 579/2).

actibus anime[53]; that case can now be strengthened by evidence of a lost commentary by Wyclif on Aristotle's *Meteora* known from medieval library catalogues of Syon Abbey and of Prague University[54]. Wyclif during his final years at Lutterworth worked at the summary that would provide an overview of all these texts, the *Trialogus*[55].

Beryl Smalley in 1953 suggested that «Had Wyclif kept quiet, his *Postilla* would doubtless have become a classic. It would be on the shelves of Duke Humfrey [in the Bodleian Library Oxford] in some early printed edition»[56]. But this is surely a case of hindsight: had Wyclif kept quiet, the conventional views on scripture purveyed by almost all of the *Postilla* would have had little to attract a printer a century later. I would like to propose a different scenario: that, had Wyclif not been forcibly *kept quiet* at Lutterworth for the last three years of his life, we should have been left with a plethora of short pieces, fragments, lecture notes, even more inconsistent and self-contradictory than is discernible from the *Summa theologie* that the Wyclif Society printed – typical detritus from the study of an academic who dabbled in politics. At Lutterworth that detritus was converted into the *magnum opus* that established for the Hussites, and for later scholars, the *auctoritas* of the *Doctor evangelicus*.

---

53. I. Mueller ed., *De universalibus*, Oxford 1985, vol. 1, pp. XXXIII-XXXVIII, and his article *A «lost» Summa of John Wyclif*, «Studies in Church History Subsidia», 5, 1987, pp. 179-83. Cf. Catto pp. 188-9.
54. For the first see Thomson's note 1 p. 13; for the second «Wigleff super Metheorum» in list 2 as F.7, reproduced in facsimile *Katalogy Knihoven Koleji Karlovy University*, ed. J. Bečka and J. Benda, Prague 1948, p. 32; see now *Syon Abbey*, ed V. Gillespie, Corpus of British Medieval Library catalogues, 9, London 2001, p. 450.
55. Edited G. V. Lechler, Oxford 1869.
56. B. Smalley, *John Wyclif's «Postilla super totam Bibliam»*, «Bodleian Library Record», 4, 1953, pp. 186-205 at p. 205.

VI

WYCLIF'S LATIN SERMONS:
QUESTIONS OF FORM, DATE AND AUDIENCE

Résumé
Le théologien radical anglais du Moyen-Age tardif Jean Wyclif a laissé de nombreux sermons. Bien qu'édités par Loserth pour la Wyclif Society, ils n'ont pas fait l'objet d'autant d'études que ses autres écrits philosophiques ou théologiques. Cet article veut analyser les manuscrits qui conservent les sermons et comment ils les classent, la date de ceux-ci et le public auquel ils étaient destinés.

Abstract
Wyclif, the late medieval English radical theologian, left a large number of Latin sermons, but these, although printed by Loserth amongst the editions of the Wyclif Society, have been less frequently studied than his other writings. The purpose of the present paper is to examine the manuscript preservation and arrangement of the sermons, their date of origin and the audience for whom they were intended.

Zusammensetzung
Johann Wyclif, der radikalische englische Theologe des Spätmittelalters, hat viele Predigten geschrieben, die aber in Vergleich mit seinen anderen philosophischen oder theologischen Texten ganz selten studiert wurden. Der Vorsatz hier ist die handschriftliche Erhaltung und die Ordnung der Predigten zu untersuchen, ebenfalls ihren originalen Zeitpunkt und die Zuhörerschaft wofür sie zusammengesetzt waren.

John Wyclif was famous, some contemporaries would have said notorious, as a preacher: the Benedictine chronicler Thomas Walsingham reports that in the late 1370s Wyclif had charmed the ears of the Londoners, nobles as well as ordinary people, through his frequent sermons, so enticing them to his heterodox and seditious opinions[1]. All that remains of those sermons is forty of them, apparently put together as a collection several years after their preaching, and known as the *Sermones quadraginta*[2]; the early fifteenth-century Hussite catalogue of Wyclif's writings describes them as preached by Wyclif « dum stetit in scolis »[3]. Much more extensively preserved are the sermons that Wyclif apparently wrote in his parish of Lutterworth between his departure from Oxford in the autumn of 1381 and his death on 31 December 1384. Of these there are over 180 arranged in three cycles, on, respectively, the dominical gospels, the Sanctorale (Proprium followed by Commune) gospels, and on the dominical epistles; in each set there is a handful which does not fit the set description given, and a second handful of uncertain location[4]. There is also a further collection of just twenty sermons, the *Sermones viginti*, on various texts from the Psalms as well as from the gospels and epistles; the Hussite cataloguer described these as composed « in fine vite sue »[5].

The purpose of the present paper is primarily to look at the three cycles of sermons, and at the puzzles they offer in regard both to their currently known form and to their intended audience; the *Sermones viginti* will also be briefly examined, but the much better known *Sermones quadraginti* from Wyclif's earlier career will not[6]. Loserth's edition of all these sermons was made from Trinity College Cambridge MS B. 16.2 (henceforward C), the only surviving English copy of any

---

(1) See THOMAS WALSINGHAM, *Chronicon Angliae*, E. M. THOMPSON (ed.), Rolls Series, 1874, p. 116; *Historia Anglicana*, H. T. RILEY (ed.), Rolls Series, 1863-4, I. 324-5, 363.

(2) The collection was printed by J. LOSERTH, *Iohannis Wyclif Sermones* IV, Wyclif Society, 1890, p. 197-492 as nos. 23-62. For details of manuscripts of these, and of other works by Wyclif, see W. R. THOMSON, *The Latin Writings of John Wyclyf*, Toronto, 1983, nos. 257-96 (numbers from this listing will henceforth be preceded by T); all references have been checked from the manuscripts themselves, and this explains a few differences (a and b indicate first and second columns, r and v recto and verso – where no indication is given, the recto and a single column are implied). The dating of these sermons has been studied by W. MALLARD, « Dating the *Sermones Quadraginta* of John Wyclif », *Medievalia et Humanistica*, 17 (1966), p. 86-105, and independently in G. A. BENRATH, *Wyclifs Bibelkommentar*, Berlin, 1966, p. 378-86; their rearrangement is studied in A. HUDSON, « Aspects of the "Publication" of Wyclif's Latin Sermons », in *Late-Medieval Religious Texts and their Transmission: Essays in Honour of A.I. Doyle*, A. J. MINNIS (ed.), Cambridge, 1994, p. 121-9.

(3) The catalogue is printed from four manuscripts in R. BUDDENSIEG, *John Wiclif's Polemical Works in Latin*, Wyclif Society, 1883, I. LIX-LXXXIV; for its origins see A. HUDSON, « The Hussite Catalogues of Wyclif's Works », in *Husitství – Reformace – Renesance* I, J. PÁNEK, M. POLÍVKA, N. REJCHRTOVÁ (eds.), Prague, 1994, 401-17.

(4) Printed by J. LOSERTH as *Iohannis Wyclif Sermones* I-III, Wyclif Society, 1887-9; the sermons are Thomson 55-236.

(5) Printed *Sermones* IV. 24-197 as nos. 3-22 (Loserth's description « Sermones mixti » should, for reasons explained in Hudson [1994], 126-7, be ignored); Thomson nos. 237-256.

(6) A new manuscript of this early set has recently been identified by Siegfried WENZEL in Pembroke College Cambridge MS 199, f. 142ra-221vb: see his paper « A New Version of Wyclif's *Sermones quadraginta* », *Journal of Theological Studies* 49 (1998), p. 155-61.

save the *Sermones quadraginta*, and the only known copy in which all the sermons of the three cycles are to be found. That manuscript, codicologically well presented though it is, is for almost all of the large number of Wyclif's works which it offers textually poor [7]. For set 1 on the Sunday gospels Loserth also knew the copies in Vienna, Österreichische Nationalbibliothek (henceforth ONB) 3934 and 4529, and for set 2, the Sanctorale sermons, the same library's 3928 and 3931; these he collated. He knew no other manuscript of set 3, the Sunday epistle sermons. Since Loserth's edition two important manuscripts of the sermons have been identified in the Helmstedt collection in the Wolfenbüttel Herzog August Bibliothek, Guelph collection (henceforth Wo): 565 which contains both Sunday gospel and Sunday epistle sermons, and 306 which contains the Sunday epistle sermons only [8]. Loserth was aware of a few copies of single sermons or of small selections, including most importantly a copy of five of the epistle sermons in Herrnhut, Archiv der Brüder-Unität ABII.R.1.16.a [9], and of nine from the *Sermones viginti* in Prague University Library (henceforth PUK) III.G.11 [10], ff. 112r-141r. A few more copies of single sermons, mostly from the epistle set or from the *Sermones viginti*, have also come to light [11].

Equally, neither Loserth nor Thomson was aware that thirty-four of the main epistle cycle plus four more (in order Thomson nos. 200-234, 297, 235-6, and then 185) are used as prothemes to Jan Hus's Latin Sunday gospel sermons from the collection known as the *Leccionarium* in PUK III.B. 19 [12]. This use in the section of Hus's work that covers the season from Easter Sunday to the end of Trinity, is, of course, secondary, and it appears to be unique amongst the main manuscripts of

(7) For the manuscript see A. HUDSON, «Trial and Error: Wyclif's works in Cambridge, Trinity College MS B. 16.2», in *New Science out of Old Books: Studies in Manuscripts and Early Printed Books in Honour of A. I. Doyle*, R. BEADLE and A. J. PIPER (eds.), London 1995, p. 53-80; at p. 65-8 are collected comments on the quality of Trinity's text. The manuscript is not fully or correctly foliated; the numbering given here is explained in my paper.

(8) These were first identified by H. KÜHN-STEINHAUSEN, «Wyclif-Handschriften in Deutschland», *Zentralblatt für Bibliothekswesen* 47 (1930), p. 626-7. Thomson gives the full details of their evidence for the sermons.

(9) See details in Thomson nos. 200-3, 208. Thomson also gives details of the single sermons, though the discussion that follows here will explain some of the apparent oddities. The Herrnhut manuscript has the appearance of a notebook written by various Hussite hands; several leaves are loose and no quiring is possible. The sermons appear f. 35-8 (T200 complete), 41-42v (T201 begins 199/25 because of loss of the previous folio), 48-51v (T202 complete), 55-56v (T203, ends deliberately incomplete 215/17), 145-147 (T208, ends incomplete in mid quotation 271/23 at foot of leaf, no continuation on verso). The material attached to the first four of these is very similar to, but not in every respect identical with, that from Hus described below.

(10) For other contents of this manuscript see further below.

(11) See italicized entries under T200, 202, 241, to which should be added for T252 ONB 3927, f. 120va-121vb.

(12) The identity of the Wyclif material was recognized by J. TRUHLAR, *Catalogus codicum manu scriptorum Latinorum, qui in c.r. bibliotheca publica atque universitatis Pragensis asservantur*, Prague 1905-6, I. 166, but appears to have passed unnoticed by Wyclif scholars since then. The presence of T297, 235-6 will be explained below (p. 247). The oddity is T185 which is appended on f. 249-250v where it ends incomplete at III. 72/21 at the foot of f. 250v (and is not accompanied by any other material).

the *Leccionarium*[13]. Despite its isolation in this regard, the editor of the Hus material tells me that PUK III.B. 19 is one of the two most authoritative copies[14]. In small part the Herrnhut selection that Loserth knew (see above) may derive from a copy close to this, but its extent is tiny in comparison. For the text of Wyclif's sermons this Prague manuscript, extensive though its coverage is, cannot be regarded as significant: a half of the sermons are complete, but the rest are curtailed[15]. Interesting though this use of Wyclif's sermons may be as evidence for the influence of the *Doctor evangelicus* in Bohemia, influence also demonstrated by the other selections, none of these would allow substantial improvement of the text. The two Wolfenbüttel copies, on the contrary, allow for innumerable corrections to be made to the text of the epistle and gospel sermons.

Leaving aside the issue of further manuscripts, Loserth's edition, invaluable though it is to have a printed text, is not by modern standards adequate: Loserth emended the text of Trinity, both conjecturally and by comparison with other copies available to him, with only irregular notice of the fact in his variants. The critic who relies on the printed edition alone is likely to be occasionally misled, and more frequently puzzled by what is found both in the main text and even more by statements and omissions in the variants. Loserth was, however, badly hampered by his unavoidable reliance on Trinity for the third set; other manuscripts, and notably the two in Wolfenbüttel, regularly allow for the correction and completion of the text[16].

The medieval list of contents in Trinity, following the headings provided by the scribe, divided the sermons into four groups; these groups are reflected in the main in the four volumes of the printed edition[17]. As edited by Loserth, the first part is headed by a section entitled editorially *Praefatio;* this note does not appear (as Loserth in his variants faithfully reports) in the Trinity College manuscript, though it does occur in the two Vienna copies and in that in Wo 565, and furnishes

---

(13) Hus's sermons in this set for the seasons from 1 Advent to the end of Lent have been edited by A. VIDMANOVÁ-SCHMIDTOVÁ, *Leccionarium bipartitum pars hiemalis*, Prague, 1988; since III. B.19 does not include this section, the manuscript is not mentioned there. F. M. BARTOŠ and P. SPŮNAR, *Soupis pramenů k literární činnosti M. Jana Husa a M. Jeronýma Pražského*, Prague, 1965, no. 92 list the manuscripts of both sections of the work (including this) but without details of the full coverage and contents which (as the edition mentioned here makes clear) vary considerably from copy to copy. Short quotations from Wyclif found throughout these sermons are not relevant to the present discussion.

(14) I am very grateful to Prof. Anežka Vidmanová for this information, for confirming that no other manuscript has these extensive prothemes, and for a copy of her paper « K textové tradici letní části Husova Leccionaria bipartita », *Listy filologické* 109 (1986), p. 147-55.

(15) Thomson nos. 200-3, 205, 209-10, 214-15, 219-21, 223-4, 226, 228-9, 232 are complete; the remainder usually lack the second part (see below for this division).

(16) Trinity lacks many chapter numbers and even book titles in biblical references, and has a number of lacunae and mistakes recognized by Loserth (see, for instance, III. 89/21, 106/15, 107/18, 111/12, 116/13-20, 121/2, 133/31-2, 206/7, 25-6, 486/36); at III. 435/26 the continental reading is confirmed as original by NETTER's citation of the same passage *Doctrinale antiquitatum fidei catholicae ecclesiae*, B. BLANCIOTTI (ed.), Venice, 1757-9, I. 388. For sermon 27 of set 3 see below p. 232.

(17) See plate 6 in HUDSON (1995); for divergence see below p. 239 ff.

the incipit for the set in the Hussite catalogues[18]. The authenticity of the note is a matter of considerable importance, since it purports to explain both the arrangement of the sermons that follow and also the occasion of their composition. The sermons, we are there told, have been put together by « quilibet fidelis » (3) « in illo ocio quo a scolasticis ociamur »(9), and are « sermones rudes ad populum »(11). The « quilibet fidelis » seems certainly identifiable with Wyclif: the incipit of this preface is given in the Hussite catalogue under the heading « Sermones de tempore per circulum anni super ewangelia », the set is attributed at the end of both the Vienna copies, and extracts from them are faithfully quoted under Wyclif's Latin byname, *Doctor evangelicus*, in the early Lollard *Floretum*[19]. From the remainder of the description it has reasonably been concluded that the sermons were assembled in Lutterworth for the congregation there, and that the *ocium* of which mention is made is the absence of teaching duties in the Oxford schools. To the suitability of the sermons that follow to a small town congregation it is worth returning later. Following this autobiographical information comes an account of the coverage: this is to be Sunday by Sunday through the year. More particularly this aim is spelt out. The year can be divided into six parts: the first is the four Sundays of Advent, the second the five Sundays between the first after the octave of Epiphany to Septuagesima, the third with nine from then to the Sunday before Easter (i.e. Palm Sunday), the fourth with six from Easter to Ascension, the fifth with three from Ascension to Trinity Sunday inclusive, the sixth from the first Sunday after Trinity to the end of that season contains at most 25 Sundays. This, we are told (2*/4-6), makes a total of 52 sermons, the number of weeks in the year. But, since at the Christmas season many occasions, including Sundays, are concerned with the festivities of saints, the number of sermons has been augmented to cover these. The sermons that follow this description accord with it: the 52 are found as promised using the gospel lections of the Sarum ritual[20]. A group of five is added after the sermon for 4 Advent; these use the Sarum gospels for the Sunday within the octave of Christmas, for the feasts of the Circumcision, the Epiphany, the Sunday within the octave of the Epiphany and the octave of the Epiphany (nos. 5-9 respectively), three of which need not fall on a Sunday[21]. The basic fivefold division of the liturgical year is marked in Wo 565 by marginal headings through the text[22]. It is plain that the provision is not designed to fit the actual requirements of any individual calendar year: if the Epiphany season has five Sundays after its octave, implying a late Easter, then the Trinity season must be substantially shorter than 25 Sundays. The maximum requirement to cover the eventualities of

---

(18) See *Polemical Works* I.LXI.

(19) For the quotations see C. VON NOLCKEN, « Notes on Lollard citation of John Wyclif's writings », *Journal of Theological Studies* 39 (1988), p. 411-37.

(20) I have used J. WICKHAM LEGG, *The Sarum Missal*, Oxford, 1916

(21) Cf. the note from ONB 3934 and 4529 printed by Loserth in the variants to I. 28/24; the note is also found in Wo 565 f. 8vb.

(22) See f. 20ra-rb, 29vb, 47rb, 58vb, 65rb.

VI

228

any liturgical year is provided. Despite the stress placed on the precise occasion of each sermon in the prefatory note, only the Wolfenbüttel 565 copy regularly includes headings indicating these; Trinity notes the occasion of only four[23].

The ensuing two sets have no parallel prefatory note. The first sentence of the Sanctorale sermons refers back to the first set, before continuing to the Sarum gospel for the *Missa in gallicantu* on Christmas day[24]; the opening sentence of the first Sunday epistle sermon, that for 1 Advent, claims that the epistles are of equal authority with the gospels (III. 1/4) – possibly to be understood as implying that these sermons are to follow those on the latter. In all surviving manuscripts of the Sanctorale sermons, the Proprium (Thomson nos. 115-42) precede the Commune sermons (Thomson nos. 143-73), and in all the Proprium departs from the norm of sermon manuscripts in starting provision with Christmas rather than with the feast of St. Andrew (here at the end). Sarum is the basis of the Sanctorale, though the Proprium has a reduced coverage in view of Wyclif's disapproval of non-biblical saints; the celebration of many of the biblical saints is muted (Bartholomew [no. 21] and Michael [no. 26] are not mentioned by name in the sermons for their feasts), whilst only two non-biblical saints are included, Sylvester (no. 6) and Martin (no. 17), and for the first the only mention is a decidedly derogatory remark about the pope's sin in accepting endowment (II. 37/33). Wyclif does not use every lection provided in Sarum for the Commune, but it is hard to see any significance in his selection[25]. Given his own statements, and the often even more extreme views of his followers, it is not easy to see when many of this sequence of sermons could be used : Grosseteste might be a candidate for celebration under the heading of a common of a confessor and bishop (nos. 50-51), but to provide a name for a Wycliffite confessor and abbot (no. 55) or virgin and martyr (no. 58) taxes ingenuity.

The provision of epistle sermons in set 3 matches that of gospel sermons in set 1 except in two regards. Set 3 has three sermons for Christmas day : 5 for the mass *in gallicantu*, 6 for that *in mane*, and 7 *ad magnam missam* (as indicated unusually in Trinity, as well as more fully in Wolfenbüttel 565)[26]. Christmas is marked by only a single gospel sermon, placed as the first of set 2, the Proprium Sanctorum, and using the lection for the mass *in gallicantu*. Set 3 also provides an epistle sermon for Corpus Christi day at its appropriate place after Trinity Sunday

---

(23) Whether Wo 565 obtained these headings from an English exemplar is unclear : the Sunday lections used in England and Bohemia (judging by Hus's usage for the latter) were identical save for the period after the Epiphany where the Sarum rite was one Sunday in advance of the Bohemian order (T64-67, 186-9 are lections in Bohemia for the Sunday within the octave to the third Sunday after the octave respectively). Interestingly Wo 565, and Wo 306 for the second group, give the Bohemian occasions here.

(24) *Sermones* II. 1/4 «Continuando sermones sanctorum cum sermonibus dominicis incipiendum a festo Sancti Sanctorum... » [« in joining up the sermons of the saints to the Sunday sermons, it is right to begin from the feast of the Saint of saints »].

(25) For a comparison with that in the *English Wycliffite Sermons*, see the edition by P. GRADON and A. HUDSON, Oxford, 1983-96, I. 10-11.

(26) The occasions given by Loserth (III.contents list), and taken thence by Thomson (T181-2) for 6 and 7 are incorrect. The time of 7 is noted by Wyclif's parallel III. 55/4.

(T209); the gospel sermon for that day is not found in set 1 elsewhere. Trinity lacks all indication of occasion through the Sanctorale sermons, and has only ten indications in the Epistle set; the headings in Loserth's content lists depend upon the sequence in the Sarum ritual. Wolfenbüttel 565 usually provides correct placing in the Epistle set, but this is less well preserved in Wolfenbüttel 306; the two Vienna manuscripts of the Sanctorale set offer a fair number of occasions, usually correctly[27].

So far the arrangement is not remarkable. Despite the illogicality in the placing of sermons for the Christmas season, divided haphazardly between all three sets, such an irregularity can be frequently paralleled both in sermon collections and in missals. None of the surviving copies of Wyclif's sermons departs from the disposition of Trinity[28]. But at the end of each of the three sets more divergence is found; details of the final items in each are given in the appendix.

The Trinity manuscript, as Loserth notes in his variants, concludes set 1 with a sermon for 25 Trinity followed by the colophon «Explicit pars prima». The scribe ended the sermons on the Proprium (T142) with «Explicit secunda pars. Incipit tercia», provided a major capital for the initial letter of the next sermon (T143), and started numbering afresh with the Commune sermon; he continued as far as sermon 18 (T160) before abandoning this for some reason, going back and crossing «Explicit... tercia» through, together with the numbers 2-18, and substituting numbers continuous with the Proprium. The erroneous description of the part was, however, evidently not corrected until after the heading for the epistle set was written: that was first described as part four and only subsequently modified to three[29].

The main plan for the three sets is clear, and is borne out by all the surviving manuscripts that contain any significant part of them. It has been noted that the majority of these major manuscripts (C, Wo 565, ONB 3934 of set 1; C, ONB 3928 of set 2; C and Wo 565 of set 3) number the sermons in each set with considerable fidelity[30]. The significance of these numbers in fact extends beyond the facilitation of the scribal task in copying a long work. The sermon numbers are used within the sermons themselves in an extensive series of cross references of the kind «ut patet sermone...» with, if necessary, the addition of either «huius», that is «huius partis», or «prime/secunde partis». The purpose is to point the user of the sermons towards other discussions of the same topic or text elsewhere in the

---

(27) ONB 3931 heads two consecutive sermons in the Commune, Thomson nos. 146-7, as for the feasts of St. Mark and St. Laurence; the first of these duplicates the provision of Thomson no. 126, whilst the second appropriation would doubtless have been unacceptable to Wyclif since it honours a non-biblical saint.

(28) Though the illogical disposition of Christmas-tide sermons is matched (but not identical) in the vernacular Wycliffite sermons, some scribes attempted to change the ordering; see *English Wycliffite Sermons* I. 19-27.

(29) See plate 9 in HUDSON (1995), above n. 7.

(30) ONB 4529 of set 1, ONB 3931 of set 2 and PUK III.B. 19 (unsurprisingly given the sermons' attachment to those of Hus) do not use numbers. Wo 306 has numbers from 1-30 in set 3, usually at the top of the column in which the sermon begins.

collection; the effect, particularly in the direction outside the current set, is to draw the whole assemblage of 181 sermons into a single unit. The device is one that is found even more frequently than here in many of Wyclif's earlier writings, notably in the major works of his public career such as the *De civili dominio* and *De veritate sacre scripture;* this has been examined elsewhere[31]. As in these earlier uses of the device, all the references are backward in the sequence. The implication of this seems certainly to be that they were inserted at the composition of the sermons by the author – any subsequent redactor, wishing to make more accessible the preaching of the *Doctor evangelicus* would surely have included forward references.

These cross references are found in all manuscripts at the same points in the texts, and with remarkable though not complete unanimity concerning the sermon number. They offer a valuable check on the reliability of each copy. Loserth's reliance on Trinity can be seen once again to be too great, and his handling of its evidence equally cavalier. One apparent cross reference at III. 157/31 (sermon 20) is almost certainly a mistake: C reads « ij s' 33^{0}» (*not* « xxxiv » as emended by Loserth), whilst both Wolfenbüttel copies have instead a reference to Isaiah 33. The allusion to Isa. 33 : 1 fits the context exactly, and the Trinity scribe doubtless misread « ys. 33 » in his exemplar. Here Loserth, having only Trinity, cannot be blamed[32]. These cross references help with the establishment of the concluding sermons of each set, as will be seen from the examination of the problems in this area in the appendix.

All the evidence suggests that the complete cycle, consisting of three sets, respectively probably of sixty sermons in the first, sixty-one in the second and sixty-two in the third, was planned and executed by Wyclif as a whole. That it was intended as it stands to be read as a whole is clear from numerous links, even beyond the cross references already discussed. At the start of many sermons are indications that the ensuing discussion takes up where the preceding sermon in the same set stopped : but, if the three sets had been used as their headings and lections would indicate, there would have been at least one and (with the likely intervention of at least one saint's day) perhaps more sermons preached between the discussions – but such indications are always within the single set[33]. As will be seen later, all the signs are that set 3 as it stands was written sequentially, with contemporary events at the forefront of Wyclif's mind, whereas such events are of less immediate concern in set 1. The antecedents of the vast enterprise are, however, less clear. How far was this immense collection a new work? or did it

---

(31) See A. HUDSON, « Cross referencing in Wyclifs Latin Works », *Studies in Church History Subsidia* 11 (1999), p. 193-215.

(32) Elsewhere his practice is more confusing : at I. 260/11 (sermon 39) his text reads « supra Sermone XXXIIII$^{°}$ »; the variants record Trinity as having « XXXVI » (actually Arabic numerals are used), but add « recte XXXVII ». The conjecture is correct (the reference is to I. 248/3ff in sermon 37), and is confirmed by Wo 565 and ONB 3934; Loserth's text reading appears to derive from ONB 4529, though this is nowhere stated.

(33) See, for instance, I. 57/32, 185/28, 200/1, 393/17, 398/30; II. 7/20, 244/3, 392/32, 400/17; III. 88/9, 97/8, 105/27.

make over materials, whether in sermon or other form, that Wyclif already had to hand ? A number of pieces of evidence need to be considered.

First, within the Sanctorale and epistle sets there are, as Thomson recorded, substantial passages which occur in Bohemian manuscripts in a different form. The first of these is a text which in its independent guise is known as *De sex iugis*, the yokes being the various links, between Christ and the faithful, husband and wife, parents and children, masters and servants, rulers and subjects, neighbours, that draw *currum Christi*[34]. Eight copies of this tract survive, all of Bohemian origin, and it is entered under this title in the Hussite catalogue of Wyclif's works[35]. In the sermons the yokes are rather inconsequentially introduced, and are arbitrarily divided between Sanctorale sermons that are not all consecutive : the first in sermon 27 (Thomson 141), the second and third in 28 (T142), the fourth in 31 (T145), the fifth in 32 (T146) and the sixth in 33 (T147). This sequence incidentally confirms the prior positioning of the Proprium before the Commune (141-2 are in the former, the remainder in the latter). Thomson's failure to list *De sex iugis* as a separate tract implies that he thinks the Bohemian copies of it are derivative from the sermons[36] But the direction of borrowing is almost certainly the reverse, with the implication that the 'lifting' was authorial and not merely scribal. This seems a reasonable deduction because the independent tract makes much more coherent sense than the divided sections within sermons whose themes otherwise barely relate to the yokes. That the incorporation was authorial seems probable from the fact that without these sections the sermons would be significantly shorter than the usual length found in the cycle. This is most striking where the second and third yokes are together expounded in sermon 28 : in the printed edition the entire sermon extends to six and a half pages, an average length in the cycle, but without the yokes it would be only two pages, substantially shorter than any other sermon[37]. It must surely be reasonable to think that, for whatever reason, an existing tract has been split up to provide much material for five sermons[38].

---

(34) The independent tract was printed by G. LECHLER in his *Johann von Wiclif und die Vorgeschichte der Reformation*, Leipzig, 1873, II. 591-605, in the English translation by P. LORIMER, *John Wiclif and his English Precursors* 2 t. version, London, 1878, II. 358-70.

(35) For the latter see *Polemical Works* I.LXXVIII. The manuscripts (folios are given in Thomson p. 122) are ONB 1337, 3928 (a second copy in addition to the material's incorporation in the set 2 sermons), 3932, 4343, 4522, Prague Metropolitan Chapter (henceforward PMK) C. 116, D. 123 and N. 48 (this last appears to have been lost since the 1970s, and cannot be checked).

(36) He gives information at the start of the set (p. 122) and then only in the footnote to his 141 (p. 131 n. 1); the work is not included in the alphabetical lists of titles of Wyclif's works (p. 334-5), though it does appear in those of incipits and explicits (p. 318-33).

(37) In the following list the first number refers to the opening of the sermon, the third to its close and the second to the start of the yoke(s) : II. 195/24-202/20-203/38; 204/1-205/39-210/25; 227/1-232/6-234/6; 234/8-237/21-240/30; 240/31-244/3-247/13.

(38) Adaptation was only slight but attentive : at the end of the first the tract's « De observatione istorum mandatorum decalogi patet alibi » (359/27) has been altered in its final two words to « superius parte prima » (II. 203/38), an allusion to sermons 13-22 of set 1 discussed below p. 233.

The situation in the epistle set is less clear-cut. Here Thomson's opening list notes the independent existence of two sections found in the sermons, but each doubles material in only a single sermon; again Thomson plainly thinks that the independent sections are extracts from the sermons. The first, whose independent title reveals its polemical subject, *De prelatis contencionum* or *De incarcerandis fidelibus*, duplicates part of epistle sermon 27 (T202, *Sermones* III. 209/11-212/40); the second, entitled by modern editors *De religione privata II*, duplicates part of epistle sermon 29 (T204, *Sermones* III. 230/21-239/31)[39]. Once more all the copies, five of the first and five of the second, are Bohemian; only the first appears as a separate work in the Hussite catalogue where it is described as *Epistola*[40]. The first of these duplicates is well fitting to its sermon context; again the sermon would be rather short (only three and a quarter pages) without it. Loserth's text as printed from Trinity lacks a substantial part of the polemical section, as this is represented both in all other copies of the sermon and in all copies of the independent tract[41]. It seems probable, however, that this is simply a scribal error on the part of the Trinity scribe (the material could well represent a column or a side of his exemplar), rather than a reflection of the stages of authorial composition[42]. The second passage with a parallel seems more of an unrelated appendix in the sermon, and its addition makes the sermon unusually long (turning a normal six-page length into over fifteen). But all three complete manuscripts of the epistle set include the material[43]. In both cases it seems reasonable to assert Wyclif's responsibility for the present state of the sermons, though to accept that he was incorporating already existent material. The direction of one other parallel seems simpler to determine: the whole of the epistle sermon for

---

(39) The first was printed in J. LOSERTH, *Johannis Wyclif Opera minora*, Wyclif Society, 1913, p. 92-7, the second in *Polemical Works* II. 524-36.

(40) The copies of the first are in ONB 1337, 1387, Olomouc Kapitolní Knihovna C.O. 118, PMK D. 123, PUK III.G. 11 (all folio references given Thomson p. 143); it appears in the catalogue *Polemical Works* I.LXI. The title *De prelatis contencionum* is found in the medieval list of contents in ONB 1337, *De incarcerando fideles* (sic), in that in PUK III.G. 11, and in the colophon of the Olomouc copy, *De incarceracione* in PMK D. 123. The copies of the second text are ONB 3930, 4527, PUK X.E. 9, Wolfenbüttel 669 and Naples Biblioteca Nazionale VII D. 9, ff. 156v-162r (not known to Thomson). The title is found in the list of contents at the start of PUK X.E. 9 and ONB 3930, though the heading to the latter and the colophon to Wo 669 describes it as 'posicio'; the text in the Naples copy is headed « Posicio evangelici doctoris Husonis », which led W. BRANDMÜLLER, « *Fata libelli*: Eine Hussitica-Handschrift aus Neapel », *Annuarium Historiae Concilii*, 11 (1979), 142-70 at p. 164 to ascribe the work to Hus (a mistake corrected by B. KOPIČKOVÁ and A. VIDMANOVÁ, *Listy na Husovu obranu z let 1410-1412*, Prague, 1999, 163-4).

(41) C lacks after « fratres suos » III. 212/13 the material found in *Opera minora* p. 95/26-97/9.

(42) It is found in Wo 306, 565, PUK III.B. 19 and Herrnhut copies of the sermon, and in all copies of the independent tract. Thomson (T202 and n. 3) describes the extra material in the independent tract, as « an obviously later diatribe », but without providing any evidence; he seems unaware that the other copies of the sermon version include it. The note « de non incarcerando fideles » in the Herrnhut manuscript f. 50 above this section may indicate only the content, rather than knowledge of it as an independent tract (no indication is given of the start or finish of that).

(43) Though the copy of this sermon in PUK III.B. 19 ends just at the point where this section should start, this should not be seen as textually significant since the *dubia* of the second half of many sermons (see below p. 238-9) is often omitted from this manuscript.

Corpus Christi day apart from the opening paragraph (III. 278/7-286/30) is found in four Bohemian copies of the *De eucharistia minor confessio*, appended without note of any separation to that text as it is found in five medieval English copies [44]. The first part of the *Confessio*, dated in a single copy 10 May 1381, is itself parallel to four sections of the *De apostasia* [45]. Whatever the direction of borrowing between the *Confessio minor* and the *De apostasia*, it seems fairly clear that the Bohemian version of the former derived its appendix from the sermon.

No such duplicated passages are known within the Sunday gospel set of sermons. But one potentially separable unit is remarked by the author: in sermon 13 Wyclif announces « Circa istum sermonem et novem sequentes (ut mandatus sum a quodam devoto layco) propono compendiose dicere sentenciam mandatorum » (I. 89/22). This intention is faithfully accomplished [46]. No copy of this material independent of its sermon context is known, nor does it correspond to anything in the Hussite catalogue. Certainly to form an independent tract the material would require some modification of the first sentences on each commandment which, at least in some cases, link the discussion to the preceding subject matter of the sermon in question. Perhaps the existence of Wyclif's *De mandatis*, to judge by the number of surviving copies one of his most widely disseminated writings, was felt to fulfil the need for his teaching in this area [47].

The instigation of this examination of the commandments recalls the wording of the prefatory note to set 1, that the sermons are *rudes ad populum* – even if the *devotus* was educated, he was declaredly *laycus*. Throughout this set and in the Sanctorale there is a consciousness of a possible, if not sole, congregation whose theological competence might be limited and whose attention might have to be retained by explanation: « dilatanda est materia sermonis secundum quod expedit populo audienti » is a typical observation [48]. Many of these observations seem directed towards a sympathetic preacher who would use the sets as a resource for his own sermons : as for instance, « alias autem laudes ex istis potest predicator elicere et ad devocionem populi quantumcunque libuerit declarare » (I. 38/15).

---

(44) Printed by I. H. STEIN, « An unpublished fragment of Wyclif's *Confessio* », *Speculum* 8 (1933), p. 503-10; Stein did not recognize the equivalence, nor did Thomson under 209. In his entry for the *Confessio minor* T39, Thomson lists the manuscripts of both longer and shorter versions without differentiating the two (his explicit is of the shorter version), or mentioning Stein's article; all continental copies are of the longer version. Since Stein's paper (and also unlisted by Thomson) an extract from the longer version has come to light in Brno University Library Mk 109, f. 183r-v (corresponding to the *Sermones* version III. 284/13-285/6) headed « doctor ewangelicus de Corpore christi Sepe confessus sum ».

(45) *De apostasia* 213/2-16, 219/32-221/13, 222/40-229/37, 230/21-231/9; the only copy with a date is that in MS Bodley 703, where the text appears in an anthology of William Woodford's anti-Wycliffite writings. The first copy of the long *Confessio* in PUK XI.E. 3 notes above the text, f. 54v, « Et ponitur ista confessio (*altered from* professio) doctoris de sacramento eukaristie libro de appostasia capitulo 16 circa g » (the last indicating the subdivision of chapter 16).

(46) At I. 89/24-92/38, 98/3-99/26 105/11-107/20, 111/33-114/3, 118/11-121/4, 126/35-128/2, 130/32-133/20, 138/25-140/13, 144/8-146/3, 153/1-154/3.

(47) For manuscripts see T26.

(48) *Sermones* I. 130/30, compare I. 35/29, 38/15, 128/3, 133/11, 165/1, 192/12, 197/3, 223/1; II. 79/12, 158/36, 159/6, 202/21, 219/30, 226/30, 247/5, 282/36, 285/11, 419/23, 459/19.

The first set seems peculiarly aware of the teaching needs of the parish priest, a consciousness that Sunday gospel sermons are the traditional locus for the preaching of pastoralia[49]: in addition to the exposition of the commandments, the Pater noster is discussed in sermon 29, the five bodily senses in sermons 30-31, the seven works of spiritual mercy in 37, the seven works of corporal mercy in sermon 39 and the creed in sermon 44. Though Wyclif's usual polemical targets are well castigated, only one reference appears in set 1 to an apparently precisely contemporary debate: in sermon 9 the arguments of « quidam doctor de ordine fratrum Minorum » who had boasted of the need for salvation of membership in a religious order such as his own are savaged[50]. Academic instincts are here reined in, though sometimes only superficially: « sed difficultates istius materie relinquo scolasticis credens quod ista sentencia vulgo sufficiat » (I. 296/16)[51]. But if the preacher's attention is still partly on a congregation beyond his old academic world, the scholarly interests of a lifetime are evidently impossible to put wholly aside: issues of necessity, predestination, the identification of Christ with his members, the Trinity in the sublunary world, on whether intellect or desire is the higher force seem unlikely topics to keep the sympathy of a Lutterworth congregation[52]. Some hints of a clerical audience creep in: « et utinam nos sacerdotes istam racionem... notaremus et... satisfaceremus Deo in nostris subditis et in donis Dei nobis propriis laboraremus continue, sicut sumus indubie debitores »[53].

The Sanctorale sermons reflect a similar division of concerns: what use, the third sermon asks, are logic, natural philosophy and mathematics? all are « vana curiositas theologorum »[54]. Expounding Matt. 10: 7-8, the preacher sententiously observes « debet predicator predicare populo quomodo assistente tanto adiutorio pro beatitudine instancius laboraret, et quomodo cautelis dyaboli retardantibus resisteret. Et ista magistri materia est sufficiens pro quibuscunque sermonibus populo predicandis » (II. 283/4)[55]. But, as the comment elsewhere « sed verba exhortacionis dimissa ista materia sunt congruencie auditorii applicanda » (II. 226/30) perhaps ruefully acknowledges, some parts are more suitable than others to an unsophisticated audience. How much of the discussion of lightning (248/20ff), of the properties of salt (376/15ff and again 394/23ff) or of light (380/17ff, 384/20ff and 400/15ff) would have been comprehensible to a congregation in Lutterworth seems questionable. Even if the disquisitions on the desirable disendowment of the clergy, or on the evils of avaricious pilgrims and sham cripples (341/10ff), might well have found sympathy from such hearers,

---

(49) See H. L. SPENCER, *English Preaching in the Late Middle Ages*, Oxford, 1993, chapter 5 and especially p. 207-16.
(50) *Sermones* I. 62/8ff.
(51) Compare I. 8/33, 61/1, 142/3, 310/8, 333/1, 371/23, 400/33.
(52) Respectively I. 281/29, 344/1, 261/10, 9/10, 351/1.
(53) See I. 381/10, and compare 291/8.
(54) *Sermones* II. 18/12; for the antischolastic tone compare II. 172/26, 277/9.
(55) Compare II. 226/30.

other complaints about the contemporary ecclesiastical world would seem likely to have appeared remote and irrelevant.

Precisely dateable references are few in either of these two sets. In both the theology and ecclesiology of Wyclif's final years are firmly in place: denial of current explanations of the eucharist is frequent, together with the identification of the friars as leaders of the opposition to Wyclif's own sacramental views; castigation of the failings of the contemporary church, coupled with a demand for disendowment as the only hope for reform, is strident; the primacy of scripture and the need for clerical preaching to the laity is constantly reiterated[56]. But immediately dateable contemporary events do not seem to be of consuming interest: there is perhaps a distant allusion to the Peasants' Revolt (I. 126/2), but without the anguish that this event excited in *De blasphemia;* the papal schism is mentioned surprisingly rarely and then with little of the abhorrence shown in other late tracts[57].

It is, however, from the third set that the world of Lutterworth seems particularly to have faded from the preacher's attention, and the affairs of Oxford and London repeatedly and insistently excite emotional comment. Allusions to an unlearned audience are rare and distant[58]; one comment, in which the wisdom of a preacher is said to be perceptible from the way in which he suits his utterance to his hearers «Quid enim valet predicare rudi populo subtilitates Trinitatis increate?» seems to invalidate a Lutterworth congregation as the intended listeners to any of these sermons[59]. Despite one reference to *hodie* (114/25), the written word seems dominant: material is describes as *supra* (66/31), *in isto capitulo* (IV. 499/29); the tract *De papa* is mentioned by name, allusions made to less specific discussions[60].

More striking are the increasing references to contemporary affairs, and especially to Wyclif's own experiences. A recent case of fraternal immorality not far from Oxford is deplored (III. 219/33). The arguments of «quidam pseudo-frater idiota nimis ignarus» against the disendowment of bishops are answered at length (III. 37/3-40/4), as the original impetus of the sermon is lost. Wyclif's own public and academic past is frequently recalled: «*solebam* docere populum

(56) See, for instance, of the first I. 110/16, 164/22, 400/14, II. 192/25, 241/38, 454/22; of the second I. 132/9, 155/37, 244/18, II. 38/5, 71/15; of the third I. 125/13, 289/5, II. 418/3, 451/31.

(57) For Wyclif's concern with the Revolt see my discussion in «*Poor preachers, poor men:* Views of Poverty in Wyclif and his Followers», in *Häresie und vorzeitige Reformation im Spätmittelalter*, F. ŠMAHEL (ed.) Munich, 1998, p. 41-53; for the schism see II. 70/19 and note the absence of reference to it at II. 434/3 where the issue seems relevant. The vaguely-worded allusion to an alliance between the king, persuaded by the council of bishops and clergy, and the pope to despoil «pauperes regni» (I. 383/22) may refer to negotiations that preceded the Despenser crusade.

(58) For example III. 55/4 «istam autem epistolam et eius evangelium *in principio erat verbum* non expedit laicis particulariter reserare sed dicere illis in compendio quod utrumque istorum evangeliorum diffuse declarat ut fidem», even though «circa istam epistolam dubitant et variant multi scolastici... musitant multi infatuati moderni... sed fideles derident istum errorem et istas argucias sophistarum». Rare acknowledgements of the laity are III. 69/27, 105/21, 120/18, 145/9, 383/1, 428/35.

(59) *Sermones* III. 341/13; but see the anti-scholastic jibes at III. 83/7, 138/18.

(60) Respectively 43/30, 180/7, 181/31, 182/40, 196/21, 262/36, 429/19.

contra questores et indulgencie venditores » (28/1, my emphasis, and cf 47/16), « in castris scolasticis sepe dixi » (199/19, concerning Christ's purging of the church), his declaration of the primacy of scripture has been inadequate « tractando istam materiam absconderem veritatem, nunc equivocando, nunc ipsam sub communi involucro abscondendo, et nunc veritatem pusillanimiter reticendo, vel propter superbiam vel propter adiutorium ordinis quem non adeo impugnabam, vel propter timorem servilem » (263/3). There seem to be two oblique references to an episode more explicitly described in the *Trialogus*, when Wyclif agreed not to use the terms « substantia panis materialis aut vini » outside the schools[61]. The precise date of this promise, and to whom it was made, are both unfortunately unknown, but 1381 seems a likely year; it is tempting to think that the promise was one element in the negotiations (between whom?) that allowed Wyclif to retreat to apparently untrammelled ministry in Lutterworth, and which resulted in the Blackfriars condemnation of his views but not of his person. One sermon has a fairly open reference to the means by which pope Gregory XI came by the evidence on which to base his 1377 condemnation of Wyclif's views : « quidam... canis niger » (188/34), that is a Benedictine, later specified as « dictus Tolstanus » or « sui catuli dicuntur reportasse usque ad curiam Romanam sed nimis ydiotice... qui artem mendacii tamquam virtuosam Oxonii introduxit » (189/5)[62]. The Benedictine in question appears to have been Adam Easton (of which *Tolstanus* is a relatively easy scribal misreading), who indeed requested from Avignon a copy of Wyclif's *De civili dominio*, extracts from which he refutes in his *Protectorium*[63]. Another « canis niger », this time unnamed, appears later (246/28 and 252/10ff); these two sections are quoted in the Carmelite *Fasciculi zizaniorum*, declaredly from sermon 31-2 (though actually found in sermons 30-1) in the third set of sermons, identifying the Benedictine as William, monk of Ramsey, and as *Wellys* – if the surname is reliable, the christian name should be John, and the monk in question a participant in the Blackfriars Council[64]. Wyclif explains « Voco autem istum dampnum et sibi similes canes magni (Wo 306 and 565 : canem nigrum), quia sic vocauit Carmelita publice predicando me vulpem et ipsos canes vulpem illam usque ad exitum insequentes » (III. 246/34). The Carmelite was probably Peter Stokes, sent by archbishop

---

(61) *Trialogus* 375/18; cf *Sermones* III. 283/38 and more distantly 316/5.

(62) Loserth prints *tolstanus;* the name in the two Wolfenbüttel manuscripts is probably to be read as *colstanus*, with a misreading far from uncommon of an English hand's *t* as *c*. Thomson's acceptance of Whitney's suggestion of Waldeby (T199) should be ignored. The two Wolfenbüttel copies also make unlikely Loserth's suggestion (III. 59 note 2) that the 1377 condemnation is mentioned earlier in sermon 8 (III. 59/1) : those copies specify « Gregorius secundus », making the reference one to a much earlier pope's pronouncements on absolution.

(63) See M. HARVEY, « Adam Easton and the Condemnation of John Wyclif, 1377 », *English Historical Review* 113 (1998), p. 321-34, and her *The English in Rome, 1362-1420*, Cambridge, 1999, p. 199ff.

(64) *Fasciculi zizaniorum*, W.W. SHIRLEY (ed.) Rolls Series, London, 1858, p. 239-41 quoting III. 246/28-247/3 and 251/31-3, 252/10-15, 253/1-5, 25-31, 254/22-6, 255/26-8, 256/3-5, 32-7; for Wells see A.B. EMDEN, *A Biographical Register of the University of Oxford to A.D. 1500*, Oxford, 1957-9, III. 2008.

Courtenay to report on the activity of Wyclif and his followers in late 1381-2[65]. In the sermon for Corpus Christi day reference is made to the preacher's own arguments concerning the eucharist, arguments which his opponents could not answer (280/26); the debate involved «quidam secularis» (280/26), «catuli» (280/28), «catulus quidam» (281/32), and «canes» (281/40), all, no doubt, identifiable to a contemporary Oxford audience but hardly to one in Lutterworth.

From this point on in the epistle sermons, after sermon 34, reference is recurrently made to the events of the Earthquake Council, the Council that in the course of May 1382 produced the condemnation of ten heresies and fourteen errors, allegedly drawn from Wyclif's writings, though without naming their author. The first reference in sermon 35 is somewhat guarded: Wyclif has evidently heard of the earthquake (292/14) which he anticipates to be a portent of trouble to come (292/21-294/23). Sermon 41 is much better informed: twenty-four articles were condemned by three bishops and twenty-four doctors of theology (347/3), and the twenty-first is quoted (347/7-9); again the arguments of a «catulus» against it are summarized[66]. Two sermons later the council is expressly named: «error nimis periculosus a synodo Terremotus in Anglia» (370/2), and the seventeenth conclusion quoted and discussed; the church is troubled by this Earthquake Council (373/38). Sermons 43 to 46, 50, 51 and 54 all discuss in detail one or more of the items condemned, covering eight of the conclusions, some of them repeatedly[67]. In turn the last of these was quoted in the Carmelite dossier of anti-Wycliffite materials, the *Fasciculi zizaniorum*[68].

It is tempting to see a chronological sequence behind these changes, not only within the third set but within the entire collection. If the preface to the first set is indeed reliable, then the cycle cannot have been begun (at least in the form in which we now have it) before late October 1381, the latest date at which Wyclif is known to have been in Oxford[69]. Sunday gospel sermons, followed by those on the Sanctorale, employed Wyclif at Lutterworth through the winter and early spring. Reports of the months' troubles in Oxford became more frequent as Wyclif began the epistle set, recalling academic disputes of the previous years both within the university and in the wider field of papal condemnation. By the

---

(65) Stokes's activities, more public in 1382 after Wyclif's departure from Oxford, are described in my paper «Wycliffism in Oxford 1381-1411», in *Wyclif in his Times*, A. KENNY (ed) Oxford, 1986, p. 67-84 at p. 68-73. The date when Stokes first came to Oxford is unclear, but his mission to assist in the extirpation of Wyclif's ideas is plain (see *Fasciculi zizaniorum* p. 275-7). Another possible Carmelite is John Kenyngham, who early engaged in debate with Wyclif over his interpretation of scriptural language (*ibid.* p. 4-103); he reappeared as a signatory to the Blackfriars condemnation of Wyclif's views (p. 286) and preached the sermon after the ensuing procession (*Knighton's Chronicle 1337-1396*, G.H. MARTIN (ed.) Oxford, 1995, p. 260).

(66) For the conclusions see *Fasciculi zizaniorum* p. 277-82.

(67) See 369/37 (17), 380/1 (19), 390/15 (21), 391/29 (17), 392/5 (1) 398/32 (14), 436/1 (2), 440/37 (2), 467/38 (7), 468/30 (general) 469/4 (1), 471/28 (18).

(68) See p. 283-5 where sermon 54, III. 468/30-469/2 is quoted together with extracts from the *Trialogus* (374/24-375/6, 376/14-22, 377/6-21, 339/5-16).

(69) From the pledge note including Wyclif's name of a copy of Gratian's *Decretum* (now BL Royal 10 E.ii) deposited in an Oxford loan chest on 23 October 1381.

time he was writing the last twenty epistle sermons he had been notified of the full Earthquake Council list, and of some of the maneouverings that led up to its compilation [70]. The change in tone and in specificity within what had been planned as a single work can be paralleled in *De blasphemia*: this, purportedly arranged to describe twelve «tortores» of the contemporary church, is first subverted by Wyclif's anger at the moves against him in Oxford in the early months of 1381, and then further and more seriously hijacked by his reactions to the Peasants' Revolt of early June 1381 [71].

One further point about these three sets of sermons should be examined: the question of whether they incorporated, beyond the precise parallels that have already been examined, substantial revisions from earlier works by Wyclif. Perhaps the most important extant evidence for this, concerning the relation between these sermons and the *Postilla in totam Bibliam*, must be left for separate discussion by Pamela Gradon. But the view that earlier versions of Wyclif's Latin sermons existed was put forward some years ago by Michael Wilks in explanation of the English Wycliffite sermon cycle: the writer of these last, he claimed, «was working off the manuscripts of Wyclif's Latin sermons before these were revised and augmented» [72]. Wilks provided no evidence to support his claim, but the very detailed subsequent examination by Pamela Gradon of the relations between English and Latin sermons produced details that could reflect such a process of revision in the latter [73]. Certainly there are a significant number of places where the English sermons appear to mirror phrases or arguments from the Latin, but with minor discrepancies; one explanation of these last, though not always the only possibility, is the availability to the English writer of a variant version of the Latin. It is notable that the English sermons do not use the sections paralleled in the *De sex iugis, De incarcerandis fidelibus, De religione privata* or *Confessio minor;* more significantly, given the generally less technical nature of the material, there is no trace of Wyclif's discussion of the ten commandments in the sequence of Sunday gospel sermons (I.nos. 13-22). But, if these are to be regarded as additions made in revision of an earlier version, it is hard from the evidence of the English to generalise beyond these. Many of the Latin sermons conclude with a section, sometimes more than half of the whole sermon, in which a question is debated; these, academic in style as well as normal subject matter, are often marked in the manuscripts with a marginal *dubium* or *questio* [74]. But, whilst it would be credible that these are later additions to earlier and simpler versions, they are not invariably unrepresented in the English sermons; this is the more

---

(70) See, for instance, the comments 373/37ff, 435/40ff, 468/30ff.

(71) Described in HUDSON (1998, above n. 57), p. 44-7.

(72) M. WILKS, «Misleading manuscripts: Wyclif and the non-Wycliffite Bible», *Studies in Church History* 11 (1975), p. 147-61 at p. 159.

(73) See *English Wycliffite Sermons* III.XCIX-CXLVIII.

(74) See, for instance, I. 3/27, 12/37, 18/30, 26/13, 31/1 etc., text and Loserth's record of the marginal material.

interesting because of the relative lack of academic sophistication in the latter[75]. Looking even at the Latin sermons, it is not clear that this division of material is fundamental. Though usually the opening section is primarily exegetical, whereas the *dubium* leaves the lection and is often polemical, this is not invariably the case[76]. It should finally be noted that the two Hussite copies of the epistle sermons, which often omit the end, do not systematically eliminate references to events contemporary with the original writing, and certainly cannot be used in support of an earlier, less controversial version of the sermons[77].

If the hypothesis above concerning the dating of sets 1-3 as they now exist is credible, then it may make it somewhat easier to account for the *Sermones viginti*, about which little here has so far been said. The set is known from three manuscripts. In Trinity College Cambridge B. 16.2 it is not recognized by the scribe as a separate entity but the sermons are nos. 3-22 of the fourth part of the sermons (preceded by T235-6 on the epistle and gospel for the dead, and followed by the *Sermones quadraginta*, again not recognized as a group, and ending with T297-8). In the other two full copies, ONB 3928 and 3931[78], the group is acknowledged as such by a numbering system, though each only contains nineteen sermons (the ninth of the Trinity collection is missing) and no rubric is given at beginning or end. In both of these the copy was made with the last five (16-20) of Trinity's sermons first, followed by the opening eight plus ten to fourteen; in each the scribe then indicated by numbering that this order was incorrect, restoring the Trinity order[79]. Prague University Library III.G.11

---

(75) See, for instance, the notes to English sermons 33/48-76 (giving parallels from I. 75/16-77/4), 43/55-82 (I. 142/6-20, 143/7ff), 51/31-9 (I. 199/9-14); English and Latin in these instances are dealing with the same lection, and this seems a more persuasive case than those where a different lection is in question since the parallel Latin material might have been found from Wyclif but outside the sermons.

(76) Thus in set 1, the first sermon has polemical material before the *dubium* (2/31-3/26), whilst the *dubium* deals with matters concerning the creation; but the second on the text *Erunt signa in sole et luna et stellis* (Luke 21 : 25), despite the *dubium* announced (12/37), hardly distinguishes the two sections in subject or in distance from the lection.

(77) Thus, as has been mentioned, both PUK III.B. 19 and Herrnhut include complete sermon 27 which incorporates *De incarcerandis fidelibus*; PUK retains references to the Earthquake Council in sermons 35, 44-6 and 51 and to the earlier debate involving Wells in sermon 30.

(78) ONB 3931 has, as Loserth noted, a curious error in T254 : in the midst of a quotation from Scripture (IV. 169/27), the scribe switches to a section from the sermon on the dedication of a church, T112, transcribing a lengthy portion (I. 383/19-385/10) before reverting to the end of the biblical quotation. Although the return starts a new column, there is no sign by the scribe, or by the marginal annotator, of any awareness of disruption. The mistake seems certainly to have arisen from misplacement of a folio in an exemplar, not necessarily the immediate exemplar of ONB 3931; the same manuscript's version of T112 has the passage here in the correct place, f. 147va-148ra.

(79) ONB 3928 numbered the set straight through to 19, whilst ONB 3931 added at the end to make up the 20 the independent graduation day sermon (T299, but his descriptive title should be ignored) which followed in the manuscript (f. 201vb-203ra) as in 3928; see my discussion (1994), p. 126-8. ONB 3928's copy of T245, appearing earlier in the manuscript (see appendix), has a marginal '20' beside it, though the head of the column gives the number of the sermon starting there as '60'. Two isolated copies of sermon 16 are found in ONB 3927 f. 120va-121vb and 3932 f. 207va-209rb.

VI

240

contains sermons 1-3, 5-8, 10-11 and 19-20 (as these appear in Trinity), but not continuously, not completely in this order and with no indication of derivation from a set[80]. To add to the complication, both Vienna manuscripts contain the sermon placed as no. 9 in Trinity, a sermon on John 6 : 37 for the dead, but place it elsewhere along with another for the same occasion[81].

Accepting the ordering of Trinity for this group, an ordering which, with a possible query about the ninth, is mirrored in the numbering of both Vienna copies and confirmed by the incipit given to the set in the Hussite catalogue[82], comparison with the liturgical structure of the three longer sets and of the *Sermones quadraginta* as those survive in manuscript leads one to look for a similar structure here. Such a liturgical order is traceable in the last nine sermons, from St. Andrew's day to All Saints' day[83], but it is not to be found in the first eleven; accepting the copying order in the Vienna manuscripts will not rectify this, but indeed in the splitting of the sanctorale material makes its absence more acute. There is further difficulty about the dating of this collection. Sermons 6-10 inclusive lack any immediately contemporary reference; the last of these, indeed, deals with oral confession in less vehemently negative terms than might be expected from Wyclif at the end of his life[84]. Sermon 1 could well be a defence of conclusion 19 of the Blackfriars Council, the issue being that of general as opposed to special prayer; sermon 4 could likewise be partly directed against the errors concerning the friars there condemned[85].

But in the remaining thirteen sermons the dominant issue is that of the Despenser crusade, the campaign led by the bishop of Norwich in support of Urban VI to Flanders[86]. This enterprise, on which Wyclif also wrote two independent tracts, was undertaken from 16 May 1383 until the bishop's return in

(80) The sermons are in manuscript order f. 112-116 T237, f. 116-119v T238, f. 119v-122v T239, f. 122v-126v T241, f. 126v-130 T242, f. 130-133v T243, f. 133v-137 T244, f. 137-141 T247, f. 260v-264v T255, f. 264v-268v T256, f. 268v-271v T246. Insofar as they are recorded in the opening list of contents, they are identified by biblical text. The manuscript is a collection of mainly Wyclif and Hus texts, together with two of English Wycliffite origin (see my paper « William Taylor's 1406 sermon : a postscript », *Medium Aevum* 64 (1995), p. 100-106).

(81) Both after T236, ONB 3928 f. 126va-128rb, ONB 3931 f. 140vb-142va; T236 in both follows set 2; see appendix for acceptance of this as the correct position for 236.

(82) See *Polemical Works* I.LXIV incipit « Rogate que ad pacem ».

(83) T248-56. Sermon 16, described by Thomson (T252) as « Epistle for the Mass de non virginibus », whilst technically correct, uses the lection traditionally found for the feast of Mary Magdalen, 22 July (see Legg p. 293); this seems intended here (though she is not mentioned), and fits the sequence, after Sts. Peter and Paul (no. 15, 29 June) and before the Assumption (no. 17, 15 August).

(84) See *Sermones* IV. 101/13ff which condemns Innocent III's imposition of mandatory annual confession, but admits that in certain circumstances oral confession may be useful. The opening reference to the need of careful teaching of both eucharist and penance (95/32) nonetheless suggests a late date.

(85) In sermon 1 see IV. 27/8-33/38; in sermon 4 IV. 50/6-53/10, 56/3-8 deal with the friars, conclusions 23-24 at Blackfriars, whilst the intervening section reverts to the issue of prayer, 56/8-57/33 is a more outspoken statement on oral confession (conclusion 5).

(86) PUK III.G. 11 sermon 5, both in the initial list of contents and in the heading itself, is described as ' Sermo optimus contra cruciatam '.

disgrace to face impeachment in parliament on 26 October[87]. Despenser had been granted bulls by Urban, allowing him to offer indulgences to those who would fight in his cause, in March 1381, but the preaching of the crusade gathered momentum eighteen months later from the autumn of 1382 when in parliament the Commons supported the raising of troops under the bishop[88]. It seems likely that Wyclif's allusions in his sermons derive from this latter period, since this cause seems to have taken over from the Blackfriars Council as the focus for his polemic. Equally it seems probable that news of the disastrous outcome of the Crusade had not reached Lutterworth when the sermons were written: no mention is made of the impeachment of Despenser, an event which would surely have delighted Wyclif, nor of the full tally of English losses. What excites Wyclif's attention in the crusade is the confirmation of all his strongest convictions concerning the evils of the contemporary papacy and prelacy, more interested in worldly wealth and temporal power than in spiritual matters, involved in the most appalling form of war where one christian seeks to kill another, and issuing indulgences *a pena et culpa* to those who will support their cause. Those indulgences, and the close association of the friars with their preaching, excite particular wrath: sermons 2, 3 and 11-13 are notably concerned with them, and 14-19 all mention them. The reference to «hodie» in sermon 12 (IV. 117/33), on the epistle for St. Andrew's day, suggests that it was intended for use on 30 November 1382. If this is right, and the others can be similarly attributed to the occasions for which their lections are appropriate, then twelve can be dated between that feast and 29 September 1383[89]. The last sermon is based on the epistle for All Saints day, 1 November; if it was intended for that day then 1383 is probable but not proven: there is reference to excuses made for war by pope and bishops, and a rejection of «totum papale officium» as «venenosum», but the indulgences still loom larger than the actuality of the crusade[90]. Despenser was impeached in parliament on 26 October, so that it is credible that news would have

---

(87) See M. ASTON, «The Impeachment of Bishop Despenser», *Bulletin of the Institute of Historical Research* 38 (1965), p. 127-48, and further references in *English Wycliffite Sermons* IV. 146-51; also M. WILKS, «Roman candle or damned squib? The English Crusade of 1383», in *Wyclif: political Ideas and Practice*, Oxford, 2000, p. 253-72. Wyclif's independent tracts are *De dissensione paparum* (T410), described in the colophon to the text in ONB 1337, 4527 and PUK X.E. 9 as «epistola missa ad episcopum Nortwicensem propter cruciatam», and *Cruciata* (T411), *Polemical Works* II. 567-76 and 579-632.

(88) See ASTON, p. 132-6; *Rotuli Parliamentorum* (London, 1783), III. 140 dated 6 October 1382.

(89) After sermon 12 (T248) would come in sequence 13 (T249) Purification epistle 2 February 1383; 10 (T246) Ash Wednesday epistle 4 February 1383; 11 (T247) Friday after Ash Wednesday (see Legg p. 54 and not as Thomson states) 6 February 1383; 2 (T238), assuming this is based on part of the Psalm used on 4 Lent (Legg p. 79), 1 March 1383; 3 (T239) for the same occasion (this sermon appears to be a continuation of 2 though its tone is less vehement); 14 (T250) for the feast of John the Baptist, 24 June 1383; 15 (T251) for that of Sts. Peter and Paul 29 June 1383; 16 (T252, not as Thomson allocates its occasion) for that of Mary Magdalen 22 July 1383; 17 (T253) for the Assumption 15 August 1383; 18 (T254) for the nativity of the Virgin 8 September 1383; 19 (T255) for Michaelmas 29 September 1383.

(90) See 195/27-196/31, 195/4, 197/18ff.

not reached Lutterworth by 1 November[91]; what is less easily explained is the rarity of any direct allusion to the sequence of battles and defeats that had preceded this. But, if the choice of lection has any diagnostic force in regard to date, then composition of the majority of sermons in this group between the end of November 1382 and the beginning of the following November seems most probable; there is nothing in the content to forbid such a conclusion.

The *Sermones viginti*, like the *Sermones quadraginta* from the beginning of Wyclif's active preaching life, are almost certainly an anthology rather than a set written to a predetermined design; unlike the earlier collection, the *Sermones viginti* have not been reorganized into a single coherent liturgical sequence. I have argued elsewhere that the extant arrangement of the larger group was probably imposed by an editor working from Wyclif's materials after his death[92]. The smaller group likewise seems to originate in a similar way, assembling the master's sermons, providing four references back to the first set that Wyclif had put together[93], and one to the *Trialogus*[94], but not the cross references within the group that are found in the *Sermones quadraginta*.

Whether all of the *Sermones viginti* should be described as written «in fine vite sue» is obscure. Of the sermons within the group that lack immediately contemporary reference, it is tempting to see two, those on the lections for Easter Monday (6) and for Rogation Monday (7) as self-exhortatory, the first on the avoidance of despair and the second, taking up from that, on predestination and the need for faith in scripture. We are told of the need for a «disposicio... quod homo in iugi Dei ministerio perseveret, nunc orando nunc scribendo vel studendo et omnino communicando cum sanctis sciolis, ne homo ex solitario studio in materia et forma inutili profundatus capciose temptacioni dyaboli sit aptatus»[95]. But to see this as directed towards the writer himself may be an anachronistic modern interpretation. Five of the sermons not fixed in date by internal allusion, nos. 4-8 (T240-244) and 20 (T256) can from their lections be assigned to liturgical occasions; these could be fitted around the dateable sequence in the larger group[96]. But this would still leave two sermons unplaced, the first and ninth (T237, 245)[97].

Insofar as any single audience can be deduced from the *Sermones viginti*, it again seems to be one nearer to the central powers of church and state than could have been found in Lutterworth. The polemic against the Despenser crusade seems designed to draw to the attention of those who could stop it the full horror of its blasphemy: «crux autem ista [sc.that of the crusade] cum non sit crux domini

---

(91) See *Rotuli Parliamentorum* III. 153.
(92) See my 1994 paper (above n. 2).
(93) See IV. 47/29 (to I. 107/22 and I. 210/24), 67/4 (to the exegesis in sermon 1 of set 1), 93/16 (incomplete reference without sermon number, probably to I. 272/21)
(94) See IV. 46/9.
(95) *Sermones* IV. 71/22.
(96) T240 for the same occasion as T246, T241-244 between T239 and T250, T256 after T255.
(97) T245's status is uncertain, as the appendix explains.

Jesu Christi, videtur quod sit crux sui adversarii Antichristi »[98]. The friars appear as its chief advocates but have mixed motives, and may covertly be supporting Clement rather than Urban, and aim « ad regnum Anglie seducendum »[99]; in any case there are friars on both sides, both relying on the claim « Papa noster sic precipit et concedit, ergo verum » (sermon 12, IV. 121/29). But « totum papale officium est venenosum » (sermon 20, IV. 195/4), and « Ego autem non consencio quod regnum Anglie vel aliquis christianus laboret ad proximos hostiliter invadendum » (sermon 16, IV. 156/24).

Wyclif's own three sets comprise in all 183 sermons, whilst the two editorial groupings add a further 60. Only two others survive. One is a graduation day sermon (T299), not surviving in any manuscript of English origin, but extant in five Bohemian copies and duly registered in the Hussite catalogue of Wyclif's works as a separate entity under the title *Recommendacio assumencium gradus;* though none of the extant manuscript so entitle it, the subject matter confirms the correctness of the catalogue's description[100]. It must be an early work, given the benevolence of the speaker's mood and his enthusiasm for the academic process. This marks it out from the *Sermones viginti*, to which one of the Vienna copies of that group attaches it[101]. The other is a brief fragment, extant only at the very end of the Trinity copy of the sermons, and based on the gospel for Tuesday in Whitsun week; it is primarily concerned with simony in the clerical world, and particularly amongst the private orders[102]. Despite its apparently limited circulation, it provided the immediate source of an extra vernacular sermon attached in three manuscripts to the cycle of English Wycliffite sermons[103]. A legacy of 245 sermons bears witness to the importance which Wyclif repeatedly asserted to attach to preaching; it was one which also bore fruit in the even larger number, 294 in all, arranged by his English followers into five sets. His Latin by-name, the *Doctor evangelicus*, is an accurate description.

Appendix

The purpose of this appendix is to consider the intended position of a handful of sermons whose location in the manuscripts is variable. The problems are complicated, and the schematic arrangement below aims to make the situation as clear as possible.

---

(98) Sermon 14, IV. 135/30.
(99) Sermon 5, IV. 61/12 and 11, IV. 111/15.
(100) *Polemical Works* I.LXI; the text is printed by Loserth in *Sermones* IV. 511-15. In ONB 1337 and 3929 the item is described as « Sermo pulcer ».
(101) Note IV. 515/11-23; see discussion above p. 239 and n. 79.
(102) T298; Trinity f. 363ra-rb; Loserth IV. 502-505; it is not in the Hussite catalogue.
(103) See the account and text in *English Wycliffite Sermons* III. 319-23.

VI

1. Loserth's edition can be grouped into the following categories; his arrangement is mirrored in Thomson's numbering:

I. Preface (T54)
    1-57 Sunday gospel sermons (T55-111)
    58 Dedication of a church gospel (T112)
    59 Sunday after dedication gospel (T113)
    60 Octave of dedication gospel (T114)

II. 1-28 Proprium sanctorum (T115-142)
    29-59 Commune sanctorum (T143-73)
    60 Ascension day gospel (T174)
    61 Corpus Christi day gospel (T175)

III. 1-59 Sunday epistle sermons (T176-234)

IV [104]. 1 Epistle for dead (T235)
    2 Gospel for dead (T236)
    3-22 [*Sermones viginti*] (T237-56)
    23-62 [*Sermones quadraginta*] (T257-96)
    63 Dedication of a church epistle (T297)
    64 [Gospel for Tuesday in Whitsun week] (T298)
    [65] [Graduation day sermon] (T299)

2. The main manuscripts witnessing the sermons are the following, with their ordering shown using Thomson numbers. Manuscripts having single sermons, or an apparently eclectic collection such as PUK III.G.11, are not included here since they cannot help towards determination of original order or grouping. Contents of the included manuscripts other than the sermons are not indicated here.

    a) Trinity College Cambridge B.16.2

Sermons divided into four groups: there is no division within the four (apart from the cancelled attempt to differentiate at the start commune from proprium sermons), but here numbers are separated to highlight those sermons not clearly associated with a set:

  i) T55-111, described as part 1, numbered 1-57
  ii) T115-173, described as part 2, numbered 1-59 [105]
     T174-5 numbered 60-61
     T112-114 numbered 62-64
  iii) T176-234, described as part 3, numbered 1-59

---

(104) For reasons given in my 1994 paper, I have suppressed Loserth's titles for the different sections of this volume, supplying instead more traditional or, where no such exists, more useful descriptions.

(105) For the original division of this part into two, see above p. 229.

VI

WYCLIF'S LATIN SERMONS : QUESTIONS OF FORM, DATE AND AUDIENCE   245

    iv) T235-6 ⎫
        T237-56 ⎬ described as part 4 [106], numbered 1-60 [107]
        T257-96
        T297-8 ⎭

b, c) Vienna ONB 3934 and ONB 4529
    T54
    T55-111   (1-25 numbered in 3934 only)
    T112-114

d) Wolfenbüttel 565
    T54
    T55-111   most numbered 1-57
    T176-234   most numbered [1]-59
    T297   numbered 60
    T235-6   numbered 61-2 [108]

e, f) Vienna ONB 3928 and ONB 3931
    T115-173   most numbered 1-59 ⎫
    T236   numbered 59 (sic) ⎬ in 3928 only ; no numbers in
    T245 [109]   numbered 60 ⎭ 3931
    T175
    T112-114
    T252-256 ⎫
    T237-244 ⎬ reordered to run T237-244, 246-56
    T246-251 ⎭
    T299
    T257-294 numbered from 5-38, found in 3928 only as a separable section of the manuscript

g) Wolfenbüttel 306
    T176-234 some numbers at the start only (completed in modern pencil)
    T297
    T235-6 [110]

h) Prague UK III.B. 19 (see above p. 225-6)
    T200-234
    T297
    T235-236
    T185

---

(106) The list of contents on f. 2v describes this « Quarta pars de epistolis in sanctorum festivitatibus cum aliis diuersis sermonibus continet sermones 64 » (see HUDSON, 1995, plate 6).

(107) T293 is omitted from the numbering, the number 58 is used twice, and T297-8 are unnumbered.

(108) The text of T236 seems to have given the scribe much trouble, since, uncharacteristically, a number of gaps are found ; presumably his exemplar for this sermon was obscure.

(109) Both manuscripts have at the end of this sermon « Expliciunt ewangelia de sanctis ».

(110) The whole sequence is concluded f. 209va « Et sic est finis epistolarum ».

i) Vienna ONB 3932
   T257-295 [111]

j) Pembroke College Cambridge 199
   T257-65, 267-96 [112]

k) Lambeth 23
   T257-84 (remainder lost, but index implies its original presence)

3. From this it emerges that five groups are established:
   57 Sunday gospel sermons (T55-111) – stable in 4 MSS
   59 Sanctorale sermons, Proprium preceding Commune (T115-173) – stable in 3 MSS
   59 Sunday epistle sermons (T176-234) – stable in 3+ MSS
   20 *Sermones viginti* (T237-56) – attested in 3 MSS, order more unstable, uncertainty about T245
   40 *Sermones quadraginta* (T257-96) – attested in 5 MSS

4. Of variable position and attestation:
   T112-114 gospels associated with church dedication
   T174 Ascension day gospel
   T175 Corpus Christi day gospel
   T235-236 epistle and gospel for dead
   T245 gospel for dead
   T297 epistle for dedication of church
   T298 gospel for Tuesday in Whitsun week
   T299 graduation day sermon

i) T112-14: Loserth places these at the end of set 1 (followed by Thomson in his listing); no explanation of this is given. This is correct, despite the absence of them from Wo 565 and their placing by C at the end of the Sanctorale. The main evidence for this is the statement at the beginning of T60 (I. 393/17) « Omnia ista tria evangelica alludunt dedicacioni ecclesie et cum quodlibet eorum contingit legi in die dominica, ideo decrevi per eorum quodlibet transcurrendum »[113]. In addition a cross reference confirms that this was the original position of T60: in the epistle set is a reference to « sermo 60 prime partis » (III. 26/29), alluding to this sermon (I. 401/21)[114].

---

(111) The omission of the final sermon of the set is not accidental, since the same hand on the following leaf of an intact quire continues to *De sex iugis*.

(112) See Wenzel's article (above n. 6) for the oddities of this manuscript.

(113) Whilst this satisfactorily fixes their position, the assertion that all three would fall on a Sunday is puzzling; if correct, it would imply that the second and third must fall on the same day, and this would uniquely provide two gospel sermons for the same calendar date. It seems likely that what Wyclif means is that all three occasions *could* fall on a Sunday.

(114) This is the reading of Wo 565 and Wo 306; Trinity's reading, reported without comment by Loserth, is in the text « sermone LXXX » with, in the margin « sermone LXXX prime partis ». Since Wo565, which contains set 1, has only 57 sermons in it and, like Wo 306, does not anywhere have the relevant sermon, the reference must derive from the exemplar of these two copies.

ii) T174-5 : T174 is unique to C[115]; T175 follows it in C and occurs in ONB 3928 and 3931, and in all three it is found after (though with differing immediate antecedents) the Sanctorale sermons. This position seems unhappy : both occasions are variable in calendar date (and hence unlike the Proprium part of that sequence) but fixed in liturgical placing (unlike either part of the Sanctorale). Despite this a cross reference within the Ascension day sermon « ut exponitur sermone 57 » (II. 446/38) alludes to material in sermon 57 of the Sanctorale set (II. 416/18ff), without the set number that would be necessary for another set. The Corpus Christi day sermon, though not independently fixed, would seem a natural follower to the sermon for Ascension day.

Hence it seems that a position for these two at the end of the Sanctorale set must be accepted.

iii) T235-6 and T297. In Wo 565, Wo 306 and PUK III.B. 19 these three occur in the order T297, T235-6; in C T235-6 occur together, but some distance from T297. Loserth (IV.xv) described T297 as intended for the Dedication of a church; in this he was followed by Thomson, who could have supported such a placing from the headings found in Wo 565 and 306 to this item. Despite this heading, the subject matter of this sermon has much of relevance to the office of the dead, the office for which T235-6 are appropriate[116]. Since two of the sermons, T235 and 297, are based on epistles, placing at the end of set 3 would be logical; but, on the other hand, locating sermons for the office of the dead at the end of the Commune sanctorum set (as is done by ONB 3928 and 3931) also makes sense. It would seem, however, that this latter position is not correct. Cambridge's copy of the epistle set ends with a statement that seems contradictory : « De isto inferius » (III. 520/ 36, T234), contradictory in that it requires something to follow. Material in T235 contains material that would explain this allusion (IV. 9/8ff and especially 10/29ff). Within T235 is a reference back to sermon 59, without part number : this is correct for the epistle set (IV. 6/29 back to III. 518/3ff, sermon 59). Netter in his *Doctrinale*, written in the 1420s to confute Wyclif and his followers, described T297 as sermon 60 of the epistle set[117]. It thus seems likely that all three should be attached to the end of the epistle set, in the order T297, T235, T236.

iv) For the position of T245 see above p. 240 where it is suggested that it belongs where C places it, as the ninth of the *Sermones viginti*.

---

(115) Though another copy may have been in the possession of Jerome of Prague. In the list published by I. KOŘÁN, « Knihovna Mistra Jeronýma Pražského », *Český časopis historický* 94 (1996), p. 590-600 appears as item 14 (p. 593) « Sermones de tempore incipiunt ante Ascensionem ». As Kořán notes, this is the incipit of the sermon T174. The eccentric opening suggests the collection was not a coherent cycle but an eclectic selection.

(116) See LEGG, p. 203, 431-2.

(117) *Doctrinale*, II. 274, referring to *Sermones* IV. 500/6; for reasons that are not clear, Netter's frequent references sometimes describe the epistle sermons as set 2, sometimes as set 3.

v) T298 and T299 : the first of these is unique to C and its status is uncertain (see above p. 243); T299 is a sermon entirely independent of the sets described here (see above p. 243).

5. The most probable original arrangement of the five extant sets of sermons, in order of their composition was thus :

Sermones quadraginta, T257-96
Set 1 : 60 sermons, T55-111 plus T112-14
Set 2 : 61 sermons, T115-173 plus T174-5
Set 3 : 62 sermons, T176-234 plus T297, T235-6
Sermones viginti, T237-56.

Additional Appendix

The *Sermones Quadraginta* have long been recognized to date from a much earlier period of Wyclif's career than the longer sets that make up Loserth's and Trinity's first three groups.[16] The fifteenth-century Hussite catalogues' note *dum stetit in scolis* is shown by internal references in most of these sermons to be essentially correct. Quite apart from the more tempered tone of allusions to the religious orders and the papacy than is normal in the productions of Wyclif's last years, and the absence of any reference to heterodox notions of the eucharist, a few precise indications of date make it possible to suggest dates between January 1375 and September 1379 for many of the sermons. Where these sermons were preached is less clear: *dum stetit in scolis* may be correct as a dating indication, but several of the sermons may have been preached in London rather than in Oxford - they would then be examples of the sermons which Walsingham alleged Wyclif had delivered in these years, 'running from church to church around London'.[17] Almost simultaneously in 1966 two scholars, William Mallard and Gustav Benrath, produced a closer analysis of the *Sermones Quadraginta*, assigning precise dates and an order to several of the sermons.[18] On eleven of the forty they agree; Mallard with varying degrees of hesitation placed twenty more, and assigned six further doubtful dates.[19] More important for the present purpose is the fact that the ordering of the sermons that can be established from internal references cannot, even on the more conservative listing agreed by both Benrath and Mallard, be reconciled with the manuscript order. Using the sermon numbers as these appear in the surviving manuscripts, but arranging them in the order agreed by these two scholars, with those only dated by Mallard in italics, the following sequence is established:

---

[16] See, for instance, Loserth Sermones iv.v, or H. B. Workman, *John Wyclif* (Oxford, 1926), ii.206-7.

[17] Thomas Walsingham, *Chronicon Anglie*, ed. E. M. Thompson, Rolls Series (London, 1874), p. 117, dated 1377.

[18] W. Mallard, 'Dating the *Sermones Quadraginta* of John Wyclif', *Medievalia et Humanistica*, 17 (1966): 86-105; G. A. Benrath, *Wyclifs Bibelkommentar* (Berlin, 1956), pp. 378-85. I have substituted the manuscripts' sermon numbers for those derived from Loserth's muddled edition in vol. iv; Loserth's numbers are used by Mallard and Benrath, but can be translated from Thomson's listing.

[19] Some of the second category seem reasonable, but I am not sure that his assumption that Wyclif would never have preached more than a single sermon on one Sunday is unchallengeable - indeed, does Walsingham's derogatory comment imply that Wyclif broke that convention in his evangelical zeal?

6; *9, 12-13, 16-17*; 37, 33-5, 40, 38, 1; *4*; *7, 8, 10-11*; *14-15, 19, 22-23*; 39, 2-3; *18, 20, 24-25*; 29[20]

As is clear, not merely are sermons 1 and 2-3 late in the chronological sequence, but there is no pattern of rearrangement; only in one case are more than two sermons found together *both* in chronology and in manuscript sequence.

The rationale behind the manuscripts' *re*organization of these 40 sermons is easy enough to see: from sermon 1 to sermon 36 they have been arranged into the sequence of a single liturgical year, though the sermons vary in their use of gospel or epistle lection, and sometimes a Sunday is doubly provided whilst others are entirely omitted.[21] Sermon no. 37 (T293) backtracks from 22 Trinity to 19 Trinity, whilst no. 38 (T294) is for 25 Trinity; the full quota of forty is made up by a sermon on the lection for a virgin and martyr from the Sarum Commune Sanctorum and by one for the dedication of a church. But this secondary organization was not the only 'editorial' change. Cross references were also provided. Four of these are in the same format as those already described in the other sets: *ut patet sermone* – with a number inserted finally. These numbers are found in all copies, but can only be correct on the liturgical arrangement that the manuscripts follow – they cannot be correct chronologically.[22] It should be noted that, unlike those in sets 1-3, these are all four *forward* references in regard to manuscript position. More of the cross references are of the form *ut dixi sermone proximo* or *proxima dominica* (*proximus* in Wyclif regularly means previous, not following) and these are more puzzling. Some are, of course, indecisive: *proxima dominica* at the start of sermon 17 (iv.321/14), alluding to sermon 16 (iv.320/3ff.) is correct by Mallard's extended chronology, since these two are dated by him 11 and 6 April 1376 respectively, and by manuscript order where they are for Good Friday and Palm Sunday. Others are correct only by the rearranged liturgical order of the manuscripts: thus the reference to *in sermone proximo* in manuscript order 20 (iv.349/10), alluding to the matter of 19 (iv.340/13) does not work for the chronological order at least on Mallard's arrangement, since 20 is there separated from 19 by six other sermons.[23] Such references must have been added after the reorganization. Yet others, however, cannot work on the manuscript order: most of these are in the opening sentence of sermons, where the preacher makes plain his intention of continuing a previous discourse to the same congregation – this evidence is, indeed, the major plank in the case by which

---

[20] Sermon 1 (T257) is dated by Benrath to 30 November 1376, Advent Sunday and St Andrew's day (see iv.197/23 and 198/36), and that is accepted here; Mallard thinks the bulk of the sermon from that date, the remainder from three years later. The semi-colons mark breaks in the dating of the sermons, for which see summaries in Benrath p. 386, Mallard p. 105.

[21] Thus, for instance, there are two sermons, nos. 8-9 (T264-5), on the gospel for Sexagesima Sunday, two, nos. 15-16 (T271-2), on the epistle for Palm Sunday, three, nos. 17-19 (T273-5) on the gospel for Good Friday; but the fourth to the ninth Sundays after Trinity lack provision of any kind. No. 26 (T282) for the Assumption is places between sermons for the third and tenth Sundays after Trinity, a common but not invariable position for the feast.

[22] *Sermones* iv.202/6 referring to sermon 38 (iv.468/2) in no. 1, iv.213/4 to sermon 39 (iv.476/20) in no. 3, iv.432/14 to sermon 37 (iv.464/1) in no. 33; the form of reference at iv.309/5, no. 14, is different in form *sermone de dominice 19* (to no. 37, again iv.464/1), but must have been inserted after a liturgical arrangement had been settled.

[23] Mallard dates 20 as 18 April 1378, 19 as 27 March 1377 (pp. 94-97, summary p. 105).

Mallard and Benrath have been able to build up their chronology. Thus what is now sermon 38 refers twice (iv.469/38, 474/14) to material preached *dominica proxima*, but that material is now in sermon 40 (iv.485/20, 489/6) – both Mallard and Benrath agree that these two were preached sequentially, on 23 and 16 November 1376 respectively.[24]

What are we to conclude from all this about the 'publication' of the *Sermones Quadraginta*? I would suggest that we must deduce editorial activity, putting together a round number of Wyclif's early sermons – it is highly improbable this is more than a small proportion of the total output of his preaching *dum stetit in scholis*, and parts of some other early sermons may well have been worked into the three coherent sets by Wyclif himself. A liturgical arrangement was the best way to make this material accessible to others at a later date. Some cross references were added at this stage. But no systematic attempt was made to remove the indications of the previous order. All of the surviving indications of the older order are verbal rather than numeric – that is they are of the form *sermone proximo, superius*, or of date, and hence might be more difficult than a sermon number for a reviser to spot and modify for subsequent copying. It would, I think, seem likely that this rather slovenly editorial activity was done by someone other than Wyclif himself. On the other hand, since the references almost without exception appear in all surviving manuscripts, whether English or Bohemian, it must have been undertaken before the hyparchetype was written.[25]

---

[24] Another instance is in sermon 16 (iv.315/34) where material in sermon 13 (iv.300/19) is stated to have been preached *proxima dominica*; Mallard dates 16 as 6 April 1376, 13 as 30 March 1376 (see summary p. 105).

[25] Lambeth omits the reference in 3 (iv.213/4), whilst in 2 (iv.206/32) and 3 (iv.217/16) the two Vienna manuscripts have less precise references. But Prague University Library V.H.27, which contains three sermons from this group (nos. 17–19, T273–5), reproduces the three references found within them.

VII

ACCESSUS AD AUCTOREM: THE CASE OF JOHN WYCLIF

In the fifty years after the death of their author on 31 December 1384 the writings of John Wyclif, the *Doctor Evangelicus*, obtained an unusually wide circulation. Though investigated in England from 1377 onwards, finally outlawed (unless inspected and, improbably, approved) from the issue of Archbishop Arundel's *Constitutions* in 1409, and destroyed either individually or in fires such as that in 1410 at Carfax in Oxford or in 1411 in London, the assiduous copying continued.[1] Much of this was by Bohemians, following the interest shown at the University of Prague from the late 1370s onwards; opposition was encountered in that part of central Europe, and a fire in Prague to destroy manuscripts of Wyclif antedated that in Oxford by some nine months, but at least until the 1430s those works were still being much transcribed.[2]

Wyclif wrote a very large number of texts, some of them brief and others long. Both produced, from the viewpoint of anyone interested in the opinions of the *Doctor Evangelicus*, problems of access. With the short texts there could be difficulties of identification: how could the genuine works be differentiated from those on similar subjects composed by later followers? or indeed, in cases such as Wyclif's anti-fraternal polemics, from texts on comparable subjects but in no way connected in origin with Wyclif? The answer found to this problem was an identification list, a list of titles, incipits, and chapter (or sermon) numbers. Such a list was in existence in Bohemia by 1415, and survives in three medieval and one post-medieval copies. It is an admirably comprehensive document; only two texts are included that certainly should

---

[1] Wyclif's works are quoted here from the editions of the Wyclif Society (1883–1921), with the addition of *De officio pastorali*, ed. G. V. Lechler (Leipzig 1863); *Trialogus*, ed. G. V. Lechler (Oxford 1869); S. H. Thomson, *Summa de ente libri primi tractatus primus et secundus* (Oxford 1930); *De trinitate* ed. A. du P. Breck (Boulder 1962); *De universalibus*, ed. I. J. Mueller, with A. Kenny and P. V. Spade, 2 vols. (Oxford 1985); many of the shorter works are collected in the Wyclif Society's volumes entitled *Opera minora* (*Op.min.*) and *Polemical Works* (*Pol.Wks.*). W. R. Thomson's *The Latin Writings of John Wyclyf* (Toronto 1983), though its many details need occasional correction, provides an invaluable catalog of the manuscripts of the texts; Thomson's numbering of the texts is used here, prefixed with T. In references to manuscripts the following abbreviations are used: ÖNB for Vienna Österreichische Nationalbibliothek, PMK for the Prague Metropolitan Chapter Library, PUK for the Prague National (formerly University) Library, BL for London British Library, G&C for Gonville and Caius College Cambridge, TCC for Trinity College Cambridge; TCD for Trinity College Dublin; columns are indicated by a and b, where no other indication is given the recto of a folio is implied. For the growing opposition to Wyclif in England see A. Hudson, "Wycliffism in Oxford 1381–1411," in *Wyclif in his Times*, ed. A. Kenny (Oxford 1986) 67–84; idem, *The Premature Reformation: Wycliffite Texts and Lollard History* (Oxford 1988) 60–119; and J. I. Catto, "Wyclif and Wycliffism at Oxford 1356–1430," in *The History of the University of Oxford* 2: *Late Medieval Oxford*, ed. J. I. Catto and T. A. R. Evans (Oxford 1992) 175–261.

[2] For the bonfire in Prague see H. Kaminsky, *A History of the Hussite Revolution* (Berkeley 1967) 72–77; more generally, the paper by F. Šmahel, "'Doctor Evangelicus super omnes evangelistas': Wyclif's Fortune in Hussite Bohemia," *BIHR* 43 (1970) 11–34 remains the most useful survey in English.

not have been, and few of Wyclif's works that are known to have been available in Bohemia are omitted. That list has been examined elsewhere.³

The long works offered a different difficulty: how to find material on any particular topic within one work of several hundred columns, let alone across several such writings? The polemicist had an obvious need for some means of access; the preacher, who wanted to check the *Doctor Evangelicus*'s comprehension of a passage before committing himself, equally urgently required help. Three answers to these problems were found in the fifty years before the Council of Basel, and it is the purpose of the present paper to examine each. All three stand as testimony to the serious and scholarly concern of Wyclif's followers, whether in England or in Bohemia; all three have some interest in the development of the *accessus ad auctorem* in the later medieval period.⁴

Before proceeding to the analysis, a few cautions must be given about the evidence presented. Almost all of the works to be discussed have been edited, with few exceptions in the Wyclif Society between 1883 and 1921. Invaluable though those editions are, they are inadequate for the present purpose: more manuscripts have come to light since they were produced; the interest of their editors was in Wyclif's ideas and not, except rarely, in the minutiae of the manuscripts involved; and the recording of certain information vital for the present purpose was fitful at best. Work, volume, page, and line numbers will be used where possible in the references here, but it has been necessary to derive most of the information direct from the manuscripts.⁵ Secondly, the dating of Hussite manuscripts is a study that has hardly begun. I have endeavored to verify all scribal specification of date, but have accepted Thomson's dating where only paleographical evidence is available.⁶

I

The first mode of access to his longer writings is the provision of chapter by chapter summaries that are found attached to a number of Wyclif's works. Thomson, often following the divergent usage of the editors, describes them variously as prologue (T38), proem (T12), or analysis (as in his note to the Gonville and Caius manuscript of this text, p.25 n.1); but all are of the same form and the same name should be used for all. Analysis seems better than either of the other terms, since the aim is plainly a sequential guide to the content of each part of the relevant work; as will be seen, the

---

³A. Hudson, "The Hussite Catalogues of Wyclif's Writings," in *Husitství, Reformace, Renesance: Sborník k 60. narozeninám Františka Šmahela*, ed. J. Pánek, M. Polívka, N. Rejchrtová (Prague 1994) 1.401–417; they were printed, slightly inaccurately, in *Pol.Wks.* 1.lix–lxxxiv.

⁴Preeminent in the studies of this topic are the numerous publications of Richard and Mary Rouse: see, in particular, *Preachers, Florilegia and Sermons: Studies on the "Manipulus Florum" of Thomas of Ireland* (Toronto 1979), esp. 7–42; the papers reprinted as chapters 4–7 in *Authentic Witnesses: Approaches to Medieval Texts and Manuscripts* (Notre Dame 1991); and their introduction to *Registrum Anglie de libris doctorum et auctorum veterum*, Corpus of Medieval Library Catalogues 2 (London 1991).

⁵Those manuscripts are scattered over many libraries in various countries; practical considerations have precluded the possibility that all the information here given could be rechecked after the notes had been taken; the same practical problems have made it impossible in every case to complete inadequate notes taken on a previous visit. I have endeavored to recheck those points on which my argument here depends; but I am aware that some other details may prove inaccurate, and even more that my examples may be expanded from other copies that I have not (at least since beginning to collect this information) considered.

⁶For manuscripts in Vienna, F. Unterkircher, *Katalog der datierten Handschriften in lateinischer Schrift in Österreich* 1–4 (Vienna 1969–1976) is useful; there is no equivalent volume for Prague manuscripts.

position is not always at the start, as "prologue" or "proem" would suggest. Other possibilities would be "epitome" or "summary," but neither adequately reflects the apparent desire to capture in order the main arguments of each section. An earlier English parallel to these analyses are the *intentiones* of the Dominican Robert Kilwardby for a number of patristic works: again, chapter by chapter summaries are provided.[7]

Analyses are found of the following works: T (= Thomson) 11 *De universalibus*, T12 *De tempore*, T22 *De benedicta incarnacione*, T26 *De mendatis*, T29–30 *De civili dominio* 1–3, T31 *De veritate sacre scripture*, T32 *De ecclesia*, T33 *De officio regis*, T34 *De potestate pape*, T35 *De symonia*, and T38 *De eucharistia*.[8] The first two of these works are primarily of philosophical interest; the remainder are theological or, increasingly as the sequence progresses, ecclesiological in concern. Although the list covers some of Wyclif's most important works, it does not include all the longest texts: among the early philosophical writings the *De ydeis* might have been expected to acquire a summary, while of the later productions the *Trialogus* might seem an obvious candidate for such analysis (though its fairly clear overall structure may have made one seem redundant). Three parts of the *Summa theologie* do not appear with analyses: *De statu innocencie*, whose brevity may have discouraged the effort, and the last two books, *De apostasia* and *De blasphemia*.

Attestation for these analyses is variable. All eight copies of T22 *De benedicta incarnacione* contain one, as do all eight copies of T35 *De symonia*, the three copies of T33 *De officio regis*, and the seven of T38 *De eucharistia*.[9] On the other hand, of the three surviving complete copies of *De ecclesia* ÖNB 1294 and 3929 do not contain an analysis; it is found only in PUK X.D.11, but then separate from the text and added later after other items in the manuscript.[10] Only two of the twenty-three copies of *De universalibus*, and one of the thirteen of *De tempore*, lack the analysis, though in each case one of those without it derives from England.[11] The extent of the analyses is somewhat variable, depending only in part on the complexity and cohesion of the chapter summarized. Thus the analysis of the forty-four chapters of *De civili dominio* 1 covers twenty-one columns of relatively small format in the one surviving copy, the individual chapter summaries varying from just four to twenty-five lines in the modern printed edition. In general the prime concern is the main argument, but some authorities discussed may be mentioned.[12] The extent of the analysis, however, seems to vary more considerably between works than the argument of each complete text

---

[7]The first to draw attention to these, and to Kilwardby's indexes, was D. A Callus, "The 'Tabulae super originalia patrum' of Robert Kilwardby OP," in *Studia Mediaevalia in honorem ... R. J. Martin* (Bruges 1948) 243–270, supplemented by his "New Manuscripts of Kilwardby's *Tabulae super originalia patrum*," *Dominican Studies* 2 (1949) 38–45. According to R. H. Rouse, reported by M. B. Parkes, "The Provision of Books," in Catto and Evans (n. 1 above) 245 and n. 183, almost all surviving copies of the tools described by Callus are of English origin.

[8]For an explanation of the Thomson numbers see n. 1 above. Most but not all of the analyses are printed along with the texts; those which are not are those for T26, T31, T32, T33 and, inevitably since the text has not been printed, T12.

[9]Details of the manuscripts are listed in the appendix below.

[10]Text fols. 1ra–130rb, analysis fols. 212ra–214vb.

[11]Respectively the Escorial manuscript (of English origin) and ÖNB 4307 (Bohemian), and TCC B.16.2 (English). The last may originally have been provided with a copy: it could have been accommodated on the now excised section of fol. 57 at the end of the text.

[12]In the printed edition (n. 1 above) 1.443–460. For instances of authorities, Grosseteste and Hostiensis in that for chapter 40, 1 Cor. 9 and Matt. 18 in that for chapter 41.

could justify: though the summary of *De universalibus* lengthens as the chapters proceed, all are longer than the very perfunctory analysis provided for *De tempore*; the chapter analysis of *De eucharistia* is more extensive and mentions major authorities cited, while those of *De officio regis* and, even more, *De symonia* are cursory and refer to almost no authorities.

It seems reasonable to think that these analyses originated in England rather than Bohemia: where the text survives complete in English copies, the analysis is found along with it in at least one copy, as with T11 *De universalibus*, T12 *De tempore*, T22 *De benedicta incarnacione*, T26 *De mandatis*, T31 *De veritate sacre scripture*, T35 *De symonia*. In the remaining cases there is no complete text in a manuscript of English origin; since an analysis is never found without a copy of the text in the same codex, origin in England in these cases cannot be proved. The question then arises of whether Wyclif himself initiated these analyses. Harrison Thomson, in the article in which he first identified the contents of Gonville and Caius 337/565, implied that the prefatory paragraph and analysis of *De mandatis* were written by Wyclif himself.[13] W.R. Thomson (p. 51 n. 1) extends this ascription to the summaries of the three books of *De civili dominio*. The significant differences between the prefatory paragraph on the one hand, and the remainder and other analyses on the other, are the announcement in it of material to come, alluding rather obscurely to two previous discussions in three books, and to an intention to write a further on topics that can credibly be identified with the subjects of *De mandatis*, *De statu innocencie*, and *De civili dominio* book 1,[14] and the use of a first-person verb against the usual third-, which apparently was the basis of Thomson's assumption.[15] This paragraph has the strongest claim to be Wyclif's; no other analysis contains a first-person pronoun or verb. Furthermore, while the recent edition of *De universalibus* contains a print of the Latin text of its analysis, no corresponding English translation is found in the companion volume; on inquiry of Anthony Kenny for the reason for its omission, it appeared that Kenny considered the analysis to have failed to understand the content of the text to such a degree that it could not be by Wyclif.[16] Origin among the master's followers seems most probable for all but the single paragraph, but the device was certainly of English origin, and the surviving evidence would suggest that in all probability all known analyses migrated to Bohemia from England.

There is one oddity about four of the surviving analyses: they are incomplete in all copies. For the *De mandatis* an analysis of only the first twenty-two of the thirty chapters is found, for the *De veritate* of only twenty-one (or twenty) of its thirty-two

---

[13]S. H. Thomson, "A Gonville and Caius Wyclif Manuscript," *Speculum* 8 (1933) 197–204, here 202–203; Thomson claimed the entire analysis to be unique, but it is found also (though not printed in the edition) in ÖNB 1339 and PMK C.38–only the prefatory paragraph (pp. 201–202/20) is unique.

[14]Printed ibid. 201–202; the other two copies begin at "Capitulum primum" (202/21). One of the two three-book works is certainly *De dominio divino*; equally the final sentence appears to allude to material now known in *De civili dominio* 2 (2.233–258).

[15]In the first line *decrevi*—unless this is a mistake for *decrevit*.

[16]Dr Vilém Herold, who earlier discussed and printed the same analysis in *Filosofický Časopis* 18 no. 6 (1970) 999–1009, tells me that he shares Kenny's doubts about its origin. I am grateful to both scholars for their help.

VII

ACCESSUS AD AUCTOREM   327

(or thirty-one) chapters,[17] for *De ecclesia* of only twelve of its twenty-three chapters, for *De potestate pape* for only eleven of its twelve chapters; in the first and last cases the summary breaks off in mid sentence. The last might be dismissed as an accident of preservation: only two copies of the entire text survive, and in both manuscripts the analysis is separated from the text itself—it would be possible to assume that both copies derive from a defective exemplar. Equally the defect in that for *De ecclesia* might be accidental: only a single copy of the analysis survives, again separated from the text, so the error could be either again a defective exemplar or a mistake by the scribe of the surviving copy.[18] The other two are more difficult to dismiss. Three copies of the *De mandatis* analysis are known, one in an English, two in Hussite copies; all end at the same place, the end of chapter 22—no copy of the text itself ends, whether by design or by accident of preservation, at this point.[19] Four copies of the *De veritate* analysis exist, one in an English manuscript, one written by Hussite scribes in England, and two Bohemian; again, no surviving copy of the text ends at the point where the analysis stops. Textual history may explain all these four cases, but the coincidence would seem a strange and unlikely one. Insofar as this oddity is indicative of the origin of this mode of access, it points against Wyclif's authorship.

One further peculiarity should be mentioned, this time involving *De tempore*. This text survives in two forms: with twelve chapters in ten manuscripts, and with the addition of a final thirteenth chapter in three more. All evidence indicates that the version of the text that reached Bohemia was that in twelve chapters; the long-awaited edition may elucidate the status of the final chapter found in the three English copies.[20] The analysis, found in all copies save for TCC, always extends to thirteen chapters, though the summary for the last is even briefer than the remainder: "Capitulum 13 resumendo methaphysicam(?) de quidditate temporis declaratur." In Hus's own copy that sentence is crossed through, though the date at which the emendation was made is unclear. In the other nine Hussite copies, and in Pavia of English origin, the twelve-chapter text is thus accompanied by a thirteen-chapter analysis.[21] In the remaining three English copies the thirteen-chapter summary is found: in G&C, now lacking the text that should have followed,[22] in TCD 242, where two copies are found,

---

[17]The variable number of chapters derives from the absence, in six of the available twelve copies, of the end of chapter 7 and beginning of chapter 8 (1.151/19–167/8); see my discussion in "Cross-referencing in Wyclif's Latin Works," *Studies in Church History, Subsidia* 11 (1999) 193–215

[18]For *De potestate pape*, PMK C.73 text fols. 161va–259va, analysis fols. 263ra–264va (the latter is a separable quire, the remainder blank), and PUK III.F.11 text fols. 134vb–223ra, analysis fols. 226va–228rb—these two manuscripts share the same contents in identical order; for the *De ecclesia*, PUK X.D.11 text fols. 1ra–130rb, analysis fols. 212ra–214vb.

[19]Two copies of the text begin at chapter 15, CUL Ii.3.29 fols. 1–49vb and TCC B.15.28 fols. 1–255, and one, Paris BN lat.15869 fols. 109–112v ends in mid-sentence in chap. 7 (p. 56/5).

[20]A. du P. Breck promised an edition in his paper "John Wyclyf on Time," in *Cosmology, History and Theology*, ed. W. Yourgrau and A. Breck (New York 1977) 211–218, and discussed its progress in 1985, but no further news has been heard. The Hussite catalogs (Hudson, n. 3 above) give the explicit of the text as that of the twelve-chapter version, though, perhaps significantly since it departs from their usual practice, they do not specify the number of chapters it contains.

[21]See appendix for the remaining manuscripts. Contrary to W. R. Thomson's statement (n. 1 above) 25, Pavia Biblioteca Universitaria 311 has only twelve chapters. The summary in the Venice copy (as some others) does not number the chapters, and runs this sentence on to the preceding matter.

[22]The analysis ends at the foot of fol. 48v, with the catchwords "incipit in tractando de tempore," the end of quire 4; all that remains of quire 5, fols.49–51, is blank (judging from the offset of some letters from

and in Lincoln 159 with the matching text.[23] Presumably the explanation both for the state of the text itself, and for the eccentric state of the analysis, must lie in textual corruption. It must likewise be assumed that all surviving copies of the analysis go back to a hyparchetype that lacked all but the first words of its final paragraph; only Hus, or a later user of his copy, paid sufficient attention to its matter to amend the summary to match the text copied.[24]

II

The second method of facilitating access is considerably more complicated: the provision of indexes to a text. Any index must consist of a series of verbal entries that pick up words or ideas found in the text, together with references that will locate the entries within that text. The provision of such an index, taken for granted in modern scholarly works, was a difficult business in the time of scribal copying: the easier part was the realization that alphabetization of the items would facilitate finding material from an index, and this, at least as far as alphabetization by first letter, is common to all the methods to be described here. But unless the text were verse, laid out in lines, and the ruling of each sheet in each copy were rigorously controlled, no two copies of a text would correspond in their layout to the extent necessary to make an index as we know it workable. In ÖNB 3930 a brief index is found both for the long *Trialogus* and for the much shorter *Dialogus* (without its epilogue), but these refer only by folio number to the texts that follow, and hence are not transferable to any other copy.[25] The entries in the index appear to pick up marginal side-notes through the text in red—the same red ink that numbered the folios. One Hussite copy of *De mandatis* repeats the same method.[26] Hus provided a similar index to his copies of four works, *De tempore*, *De ydeis*, *De materia et forma*, and *De universalibus*, though using for the most part simpler single-word entries; again, these pick up side-notes in the text.[27] The scrappy index to *De trinitate*, found at the end of ÖNB 4316, seems to attempt this kind of tool: few references are filled in, but those that are seem to fit the folio references of this text.[28]

Equally unsatisfactory was the device of indexing by opening (two facing pages): each opening was numbered at the top of both leaves, and the columns (in all cases

---

fol. 48v, it is not a modern fill-in); fol. 52, which begins T21 *De composicione hominis*, appears to be in the same hand as quire 4.

[23]TCD 242 fols. 171vb–189vb text, fols. 171va–vb and 189va–190ra analysis (the first copy does not number the chapters, while the second does); Lincoln 159 fols. 319ra–333va text, fol. 333va–vb analysis.

[24]In Stockholm MS Lat.A.164 the analysis fol. 1r–v precedes the text itself.

[25]Again details of manuscripts are given in the appendix. In this case the numbers in the index refer to the medieval, not the current, folio numbering of the texts; the copying of both is dated 1414. For the discrepancy between the copies of the *Dialogus* (which certainly goes well beyond this issue), see T408.

[26]Brno Mk 38, text fols. 29va–164ra, index fols. 164ra–166va, using the medieval foliation of the text from 1 through 134; the keys to the index entries are entered usually in the margins of the text.

[27]Stockholm MS Lat.A.164, fols.134v–135v; the hand is the same as that of the text. The manuscript also contains a *Replicacio de universalibus* by an unknown Prague master (see the description by J.Danhelka, "Das Zeugnis des Stockholmer Autographs von Hus," *Die Welt der Slaven* 27 [1982] 225–233), fols. 77–86; but the numbers found in the index apparently do not include these folios and there are no side-notes on them—the index pertains solely to Wyclif.

[28]The text is fols. 1–79v, the index, which is not in the same hand, fols. 130v–132v. The first two chapters of *De trinitate* in ÖNB 3935 have been marginally divided into numbered subsections (25 in the first, 14 in the second), but no surviving index makes use of them.

with Wyclif texts, such indexes are found in two-column manuscripts) lettered at the top *a–d* (these letters might be omitted after the start of the text). Again, transference from one copy to another required alteration of all the references. But the method nevertheless is found in copies of several texts: *De veritate sacre scripture, De ecclesia, De symonia, De eucharistia,* and *Opus evangelicum.* All are relatively brief, and are certainly more perfunctory than those provided by the method described later.[29] One of the manuscripts involved, ÖNB 1294 with the first two indexes listed, was made in England by Mikuláš Faulfiš and Jiří Kněhnic, but the indexes are in a hand not found elsewhere in the manuscript and the opening numbers and column letters are added in that same hand; whether the device was copied in England, or made after the manuscript had been taken back to Bohemia, thus, is not clear.[30] Bohemian initiation of this type of indexing seems certain in the case of the third and fourth examples in ÖNB 3927, where, in addition to the indexes already mentioned, after fourteen further items, all by Wyclif but otherwise apparently random, a composite index keyed by opening is found in the same hand as the texts.[31]

The difficulties involved in indexing by folio or opening are graphically illustrated in two further cases. PMK A.71/1 contains a text of *De mandatis,* followed by an index in a separate hand and in a new quire. The text references in the index extend from 1 to 120; such a numbering does not relate to the folios or openings of this manuscript, but to numbers entered somewhat fitfully at the head of the folios between the two columns. The verbal part of the entries corresponds to that found in the index in Brno Mk 38 described above. But in the Brno manuscript, when the scribe copied the first item in the index he first provided the number *101*; this he then cancelled and wrote *113*. At the same point in PMK A.71/1 the number given is *101*. This lower number is correct for the added numeration in the Prague copy, just as *113* is correct for the folio in Brno. The correction makes it plain that the lower number, and the Prague added numeration, derive from an index by either folio or opening to a copy extending to 120—the scribe of Brno, after an initial mistake, updated the folio numbering, while the copyist of Prague inserted the old numeration throughout his text. The Prague method was evidently less satisfactory, since precision within the folio is lacking in the indication of change.[32] A very similar situation can be seen in

---

[29] For instance, in ÖNB 3927 the index to *De symonia* contains only two entries under *H* and three under *I,* while that for *De eucharistia* has only five under *B* and three under *R.*

[30] For these two see Hudson *Premature Reformation* (n. 1 above) 90–9 , 100–101; and A. Hudson, "From Oxford to Prague: The Writings of John Wyclif and His English Followers in Bohemia," *Slavonic and East European Review* 75 (1997) 642–657. The texts are respectively fols.1ra–119vb with index fols. 120ra–125rb, and fols.128ra–207vb with index fols.208ra–210va; the index to *De ver.* is followed by the analysis (fols. 125va–127rb) in a separate quire (13^8 against normal quires of ten), that to *De ecclesia* uses blank leaves in quires 21–22. The openings for the first are numbered 1–120, for the second in a separate sequence 1–81.

[31] The items are fols. 1ra–49vb, the index fols. 50ra–51va followed by fol. 52 blank; the section is a separable booklet of four twelve-leaf quires followed by one of four—the same separation is found for *De symonia* followed by index (fols. 53ra–74rb and 74va–vb, fols. 75–76 blank, quires 6–7 of twelves), and *De eucharistia* (with T252 a sermon unnoticed by Thomson after it) plus index (fols. 77ra–120rb, 120va–122ra, index fols. 122ra–123vb, fol. 124 blank, quires 8–12). The texts are in order T432, 414, 44, 421, 394, 300, 395, 404, 384, 417, 393, 431, 426, 49; all are polemical, but their subject matter is diverse and other texts of comparable material do not appear.

[32] At the end of the PMK A.71/1 text is a note which may be an obscure indication of the date 1403 (see the editor's text note to p. 474/18), but since the index is not in the same hand this may not be relevant to its

ÖNB 3932, in which indexes to the *Dialogus* (without epilogue) and *Trialogus* are found.[33] The verbal part of the entries is identical to indexes to the same texts found in ÖNB 3930, in which referencing is by folio. But in ÖNB 3932 the *Dialogus* entries are numbered from 237 to 256, the *Trialogus* entries from 121 to 230; this numeration relates not to the folios or openings of the manuscript but to red numeration entered marginally. Again, a corrected numbering in ÖNB 3930 reveals the relation between the two: the scribe first numbered the opening of the text of the *Dialogus* in red as 237, before correcting it to 1. Since ÖNB 3930 is dated 1412–1414 while ÖNB 3932 was copied in 1418, the former cannot have been derived from the latter but must have taken the numbering from an exemplar common to both.[34] It seems clear that the two indexes in both manuscripts derive from a volume having the *Trialogus* on folios/openings 121–230 followed by the *Dialogus* on folios/openings 237–256, with indexes for each text.

The methods used so far are difficult to transfer, and depend for their accuracy not only on copying but also on conversion. A simpler method was to index simply by book and chapter. Two Hussite copies of parts of the *Postilla super totam bibliam* have brief alphabetical indexes using biblical book and chapter number for references; the two are entirely independent of each other. That in ÖNB 1342, on the opening flyleaves (pastedown and fol. i r–v), gives the impression of one done by a user of the present copy, with long gaps left between letters for further entries. The second, that in PUK III.F.20, is more ambitious (fols. 199v–202v), and usually gives an approximate verbal indication of position within a chapter (*post principium, in medio, ante finem* etc.). Both, but particularly the second, could be regarded as indexes to the biblical text rather than the commentary, even if certain passages are interpreted in conventional ways (e.g., *eukaristie sacramentum, purgatorium* etc.). More adaptable, but still providing only a rough guide to content, is the index by chapter only, found in nine copies of *De officio pastorali*; a list in a tenth which lacks any numbers corresponds to the verbal items of the others.[35] Given the brevity of the chapters in this work, the method was sensible: its enormous virtue over those previously mentioned is that it could be transferred without modification from copy to copy.

In the majority of Wyclif's texts, however, a chapter runs for several folios, in terms of the modern printed edition even up to about fifty pages; some refinement of use of those chapter numbers was necessary if an index was to be of any assistance in access. The usual solution depended upon the arbitrary division of each chapter (or sermon, in the case of preaching material) into a variable number of sections marked by letters entered in the margins of the text. The device is an extension of that found in medieval Bibles, where each chapter is divided into from four to seven sections, a–

---

making. The Brno text is dated 1414; that its index was made from the exemplar of Prague's not from Prague itself is shown by the correct assignation of material to folio (a task impossible, as explained, from Prague).

[33]In ÖNB 3932 a third set of index entries for *De eucharistia* appears fols. 209va–210vb after the text, fols.157ra–207va, but, since no references have been inserted, the method intended is unclear.

[34]In ÖNB 3930 see the dates fols. 20vb, 124vb, 196rb, in 3932 fol. 90rb; Unterkircher 4.187–188 (n. 6 above) lists the former but not the latter.

[35]See appendix for these copies. Comparable indexing of the *Dialogus*, a text of similar length, would have been impossible given the fluctuating chapter divisions and the suppression of all such divisions in many manuscripts.

d or *a–g*.³⁶ Similarly in these non-biblical works the index used both chapter number and section letter.³⁷ It was an essential requirement of the method that the marginal section letters should be copied along with the text, and that the transcriber should locate them precisely where he found them in his exemplar—since a new section regularly begins where there is a sentence division, this should not have proved too difficult. The number of subdivisions of a chapter obviously depended on the length of the average chapter in the work in question: for instance, in *De civili dominio* 1, chapters 1–10 are each divided simply into two, A and B, while chapter 42 was divided into sixteen parts, A–Q.³⁸ Chapters 43–44 differ again: in 43 after the sequence A–V the numbers 12–21 appear, while in 44 after A–C, X–Y are found the numbers 2–11, followed by D–Y. An annotator queried whether the text should be rearranged to accommodate the sequence implied by the numbers. This seems improbable, but a second annotator observed that, though the text is correct, an index he had seen implied the rearrangement. Such an index (for which see below) is that in PUK X.E.11, where for instance on fol. 277va various entries under *ecclesia* place material noted as sections 2–11 in chapter 43.

This method is found in three extant English manuscripts of Wyclif's works: Lambeth 23 of the *Sermones quadraginta*,³⁹ TCD 242 of the *Opus evangelicum*, and CUL Ll.5.13 of the *De mandatis*.⁴⁰ It is much more common in Bohemian manuscripts: actual indexes are found there together with the texts of *De dominio divino*, of *De mandatis*, of *De officio regis*, of *De symonia*, of *De blasphemia*, and of *Trialogus*. In addition to these are the manuscripts in which, though no index is found, marginal subdividing letters appear alongside the text so that they could be used with one.⁴¹ From this evidence of marginal subdivision it must be concluded that, apart from other copies of the works just mentioned, the following works were provided with indexes: *De tempore*, *De benedicta incarnacione*, *De civili dominio*, *De apostasia*, *De eucharistia*, *Sermones* set 1, and *Sermones* set 3. It is also worth noting that subdivi-

---

³⁶In many copies of the Wycliffite Bible the letters are used as precision keys in the calendar of lections accompanying the text. The device originated from the Dominicans of Saint-Jacques in Paris in the early thirteenth century: see Rouse and Rouse (n. 4 above) *Preachers* 34, *Registrum* ci–ciii; and O.Weijers, *Dictionnaires et répertoires au moyen âge* (Turnhout 1991) 25.

³⁷Indexes of this type are common in English manuscripts of that favorite of Wyclif and his followers, the *Opus imperfectum in Matthaeum* attributed to Chrysostom; see the introductory volume to a new edition by J. van Banning (Turnhout 1988) ccxlvi–cclvi.

³⁸The letters are not printed in this first volume of the edition, but were included by Loserth, the editor of parts 2–4. The sequence and notes are recorded (not altogether accurately) by Lane Poole, the editor of part 1, *De civ.dom.* 1.xii–xvi; but not knowing the index, he did not understand the verb *registravit* used by the second annotator.

³⁹The text is now incomplete, ending in sermon 28, *Sermones* 4.397/3, fols. 258ra–280vb; the index covers the full text fols. 256rb–257ra. The index numbers extend to "41," but it appears that, rather than the set having in that copy contained an extra sermon, a division must have been introduced somewhere in 32–33 (all references are traceable in the set as normally found, but while those up to 31 correspond to the printed text, those later are all one too high). My comments on this index in *Premature Reformation* (n. 1 above) 104–106 are incorrect and should be ignored.

⁴⁰TCD 242 text fols. 2ra–162va, index fols. 204va–208vb; the latter is wrongly stated to be a "table for the codex" by M. L. Colker, *Trinity College Library Dublin: Descriptive Catalogue of the Mediaeval and Renaissance Latin Manuscripts* (Aldershot 1991) 1.434–435. A prefatory note (fol. 204va) explains the purpose of the index as being to make the preceding material more accessible CUL Ll.5.13 text fols. 2ra–108va, index using a single column fols. 112r–129v.

⁴¹For the manuscripts involved see appendix.

sion of at least the sermons in set 3 was used by the English compiler of the *Floretum*, a text datable before 1396.[42]

Despite this long list there are some unexpected exceptions: no copy of T34 *De potestate pape* has marginal letters, though in fairness it must be noted that only two complete copies survive. More surprisingly, none of the twelve extant complete or substantial copies of T31 *De veritate sacre scripture* has the marginal dividing letters—a considerable oddity given the extreme length of the chapters in that work. But in the second case an extract from the text survives that utilizes such a division: in PMK D.123 seven passages are located within the whole by means of letters of the kind explained here.[43] Where multiple copies survive with the lettered subdivision, spot checking suggests that, with one exception to be discussed below, their placement is constant.

The index to the *Sermones quadraginta* in Lambeth 23 is intriguing: the manuscript is a composite one, containing Nequam on the Canticles, sermons of Januensis (i.e., Jacobus de Voragine), distinctions attributed to Cestrensis (i.e., Ranulph Higden), with Wyclif's work, duly attributed in the medieval contents list on the pastedown and in the index toward the end.[44] The whole, however, if not planned from the start, was brought together by a series of indexes, all of which work in the same way. Marginal letters appear throughout dividing the chapters, sermons, or distinctions, and the four indexes (with inversion of the order of the last two items) appear on fols. 252ra–257va.[45] Lambeth 23 belonged to the Durham Benedictine house, and from the miniature of Saint Cuthbert has been thought to have been written there.[46] The Durham house seems to have been much concerned at the end of the fourteenth century with the acquisition, and in some cases the making, of indexes to a wide variety of texts.[47] The three extant English Wyclif indexes overlap only in one case with these Bohemian tools: there is no Continental index to *Sermones quadraginta*, and the Bohemian index of the *Opus evangelicum* by opening in PUK IV.A.18 seems to be entirely independent of that in TCD 242 by book, chapter, and subsection. Only for the *De mandatis* are both English and Continental examples by the same method found. The items for the two indexes seem to be independent (or at least the Bohe-

---

[42] For the compilation see my papers reprinted in A. Hudson, *Lollards and Their Books* (London 1985) 13–42, and see C. von Nolcken, "Notes on Lollard Citation of John Wyclif's Writings," JTS n.s. 39 (1988) 411–437. The second citation in the *Floretum* under *sequi Christum* (von Nolcken 436) is to "sermone 21a" where the final letter correctly indicates the start of the sermon as the location.

[43] Thus in the margins fol. 168 E, fol. 169 F, fol. 169v F, fol. 170 G, fol. 170v H, fol. 178v D, fol. 179 E; the extracts extend from fol. 160 through fol. 181v in two sequences.

[44] As M. R. James, *A Descriptive Catalogue of the Manuscripts in the Library of Lambeth Palace* (Cambridge 1932) 37–39, comments, the quiring of the manuscript is impossible to verify because of the tight binding, and incomplete quire signatures and catchwords. The Wyclif sermons are in the final two quires, which appear to be twelves, with the final leaf of the second lost; two more quires would have been needed to complete the set. To judge from the dirt and marking on it, the present final leaf, numbered (but incorrectly) fol. 280, was evidently without the remainder for some time before the present binding was done.

[45] A second index to the distinctions was added by a later hand fol. 257va–b; this provides a subject key to the first headword index, and would have had to be used with it.

[46] See N. R. Ker, *Medieval Libraries of Great Britain: A List of Surviving Books: Supplement to the Second Edition*, ed. A. G. Watson (London 1987) 31; for the miniature see James (n. 44 above) 38. I have discussed the manuscript further in "Wyclif and the North: The Evidence from Durham," *Studies in Church History*, Subsidia 12 (1999) 87–103.

[47] No full study of this yet exists, but see, for example, Durham Cathedral Library MSS A.III.35, A.IV.8, B.I.13–16, B.II.29, B.III.27–29, B.III.31, B.IV.30, B.IV.32, B.IV.42–43.

mian index has modified any insular antecedent). Equally the division of chapters, though similar, is not identical: thus, for instance, in chapter 27 the English manuscript has subdivisions a–t but the Bohemian copy a–x, with consequently divergent placing.[48] The discrepancies are not great, but apparently indicate independence of origin.

The account of the indexes appearing with copies of a work does not, however, exhaust the evidence. Four manuscripts, all Bohemian, are found with groups of indexes *without* the texts covered. The most extensive is PUK X.E.11 which contains fifteen indexes, and nothing else; nine of these appear again in PMK C.118, three in ÖNB 1725, and two in PUK IV.G.27. PUK X.E.11 appears to warrant most attention, since two of the indexes there are provided with an explicit colophon attributing them to Peter Payne, together with another which associates more with Payne, and many are dated.[49] The fifteen indexes, all written in the same hand, are these:

1. fols. 1ra–30va to T31 *De veritate sacre scripture*, attributed to *Petrum Anglicum dictum Peyne*, finished "in die dionisij," i.e., 9 October 1432.
2. fols. 30vb–45rb to T32 *De ecclesia*, unattributed, dated feria 2 after the feast of Saint Nicholas, i.e., 6 December 1432.
3. fols. 45va–55ra to T33 *De officio regis*, unattributed and undated.
4. fols. 55rb–72va to T34 *De potestate pape*, unattributed but dated vigil of Epiphany 1433, i.e., 5 January.
5. fols. 72va–76ra to T35 *De symonia*, unattributed but dated 1433.
6. fols. 76rb–92rb to T36 *De apostasia*, dated five days before Purification 1433, i.e., 28 January.[50]
7. fols. 92va–113vb to T37 *De blasphemia* without title, dated Sabbath before Sexagesima 1433, i.e., 14 February.
8. fols. 113va–146ra to T47 *Trialogus*, dated feria 2 post Judica 1433, i.e., 30 March.
9. fols. 146rb–167va to T38 *De eucharistia*, dated feria 3 post Domine ne longe 1433, i.e., 7 April.
10. fols. 167va–172vb to T20 *De materia et forma*, attributed to Payne, and dated 4 feria post Reminiscere 1433, i.e., 11 March.

The scribe then continues "Hoc totum scriptum predictum in 15 sexternis compilatum est per reuerendum Magistratum Petrum Anglicum dictum Peyn."

11. fols. 173ra–175rb to T12 *De tempore*, declaredly not to be attributed to Payne and dated 5 before Pudentiana 1433, i.e., 14 May.
12. fols. 175va–177ra to T18 *De ydeis*, undated and again specifically said not to have been compiled by Payne.
10a. fols. 177rb–181va to T20 *De materia et forma*, repeating that of fols. 167v–172v, unattributed but dated vigil of Easter 1433, i.e., 11 April.

---

[48]*De mandatis* p. 406; CUL places *t* against line 13, PMK C.38 places *X* against line 9. This is not an isolated discrepancy: other examples are x 360 line 3 PMK *p*, line 26 CUL *q*, p. 361 line 5 PMK *Q*, line 18 CUL *r*, line 29 PMK *R*; p. 380 line 19 CUL *o*, PMK *R*, p. 381 line 18 CUL *p*, line 21 PMK *S*.

[49]The dates in the manuscript are given by the liturgical calendar (e.g., the first is "in die dionisij") but are here also translated into modern month and day form.

[50]But the scribe also says "et fuit 2ª feria"—28 January was a Wednesday, not a Monday, in 1433.

The scribe then notes that he does not know the responsibility for the last three indexes (*tria vltima registra*); seven largely blank leaves then follow (after fol. 182 six not numbered).
> 13. fols. 183ra–205vb to T23–25 *De dominio divino*, dated 3 before Ascension 1433, i.e., 18 May.[51]
> 14. fols. 206ra–230vb to T26 *De mandatis*, dated 6 before Trinity 1433, i.e., 1 June, "when the ambassadors from the Council of Basel were in Prague, two bishops and doctors."
> 15. fols. 231ra–359ra to T28–30 *De civili dominio* 1–3, dated from Sunday before Pudentiana to before the feast of Saint Matthew, i.e., between 17 May and 21 September.

The quiring of the manuscript confirms that the last three items form two separate booklets, the first with items 13–14, the second with item 15. Within the opening section no division into booklets is possible.[52] The scribe's assertion of Payne's responsibility for the indexes in fifteen sexternions (fol. 172vb) comes indeed within the fifteenth quire.

Before the credibility of the attribution is considered, it may be useful to list the other copies, where the indexes are all anonymous and undated:
> (i) PMK C.118, in order, to T38 *De eucharistia* (fols. 1–16), T37 *De blasphemia* (fols. 16v–32v), T33 *De officio regis* (fols. 33–40v), T35 *De symonia* (fols. 41–44), T32 *De ecclesia* (fols. 44v–56), T31 *De veritate sacre scripture* (fols. 56v–82), T34 *De potestate pape* (fols. 82v–96v), T36 *De apostasia* (fols. 97–110), T23–25 *De dominio divino* (fols. 111–130v)[53]
> (ii) ÖNB 1725 to T23–25 *De dominio divino* (fols. 1–31v), T26 *De mandatis* (fols. 33–67v), T28–30 *De civili dominio* (fols. 81–236)[54]
> (iii) PUK IV.G.27 to T28–30 *De civili dominio* (fols. 36ra–124vb), T26 *De mandatis* (fols. 125ra–146va)[55]

It will be observed that the order of the final three items in PUK X.E.11, said by the scribe to be of uncertain origin, is precisely that of the three in the Vienna collection, ÖNB 1725.

It is important to notice that, so far as random spot-checking is reliable, the indexes found in these four manuscripts appear to be identical with those found in Bohemian manuscripts of the respective texts. The only possible exception to this generalization

---

[51] But the scribe adds "Mense Junij et fuit eodem die ut" (nothing further)–the latest possible date of Ascension is 3 June, and that only occurred in the fifteenth century in 1451.

[52] The first section is 1–13^{12} (fols. 1–156), 14^{10} (fols. 157–166), 15^{12} (fols. 167–178), 16^{10} (fols. 179–182 plus six unnumbered blank leaves), with signatures 1–16 mostly still visible; the second section is 17–20^{12} (fols. 183–230); the third, 21–29^{12} (fols. 231–338), 30^{16} (fols. 339–354), 31^{12} (fols. 355–361 plus blank unnumbered leaves), the first ten of which (quires 21–30) the scribe numbers quires 1–10.

[53] Quiring 1–8^{12} (fols. 1–96), 9^{14} (fols. 97–110), 10–11^{12} (fols. 111–134); the whole written in the same clear Bohemian hand. At the end of the first index is a copy, not recorded by Thomson, of T417.

[54] Quiring 1^{12} (fols. 1–12), 2–3^{10} (fols. 13–32), 4–6^{12} (fols. 33–68), 7^{12} (fols. 69–80 all blank), 8–20^{12} (fols. 81–236). All are in the same hand, on parchment, and, despite the different format imposed by index rather than text, this is apparently a companion volume to the set of Wyclif's works now incompletely preserved in ÖNB 1337–1343, 1647, and Wolfenbüttel 565.

[55] Quiring 1–3^{12} (fols. 1–35, 25 being repeated), 4^{14} (fols. 36–50), 5–9^{12} (fols. 51–110), 10^{14} (fols. 111–124), 11–12^{12} (fols. 125–146 plus the final two leaves of quire 12 cut out); the scribe's quire number 7 on existing quire 10 shows that quires 4 onwards could have stood without the first three—fols. 1–35 are in a hand different from the rest, and contain the biblical index to be described below.

appears to be the index to T35 *De symonia* found with the text in PUK X.E.9, which is slightly shorter than that found in the index collections, PUK X.E.11 or PMK C.118 (though the index found with the text in ÖNB 4536 seems to be identical with the latter two).

The dating attached to the indexes in PUK X.E.11 is the first question to consider. The first nine items form a credible sequence, with copying from the autumn of 1432 through to 7 April 1433. But the remaining four items of the opening section, items which cannot in this copy be reordered, are dated 11 March, 14 May, no precise date, and 11 April respectively. Leaving aside these four, work on items 13–14 in the second booklet follows on from the first. The rather unclear colophon to the last item, the vast index to *De civili dominio*, appears to indicate copying between 17 May and 21 September 1433—again, a credible enterprise. The problematic section is that with items 10–12 and the duplicate 10a. For all but these, the colophons plainly indicate a sequence of *copying* indexes, not of their creation (if only because of their scope, on which see further below). The only explanation for the problematic section seems to be the copying of dates from an exemplar; it is unfortunate that none of the indexes in this section is found anywhere else. That dates might be blindly copied is suggested by an oddity at the end of the index to *De civili dominio*: after the final book, chapter, and letter reference the scribes of both PUK IV.G.27 and PUK X.E.11 wrote "1426," for which the only explanation seems to be that it is the date of the writing of their common exemplar.

Equally important is the reliability of the scribe's ascription of two of these indexes to Peter Payne, and of his more general rubric (fol. 172vb). Harrison Thomson, taking up a suggestion of Bartoš, argued that all the indexes found in the three Prague manuscripts (presumably excepting those said *not* to be by Payne—though this is not clear) were to be ascribed to Payne, and he himself added to these the indexes in ÖNB 1725.[56] Bartoš's evidence for his suggestion was an assertion of Jan Przibram that Payne had made "tabulas abbreviatas" of Wyclif's works.[57] But *tabulas abbreviatas* might describe equally well what are here called "analyses." The case is less clear-cut than Harrison Thomson seems to have realized. In the first place, the information proferred by the scribe of PUK X.E.11 is by no means unambiguous. Most puzzling is the note on fol. 181va that he does not know the responsibility for the last three indexes: since he ascribed that for *De materia et forma* to Payne on fol. 172vb, his disclaimer on 181va can hardly refer back to the three immediately preceding indexes, which would include the duplicate copy (fols. 177rb–181va)—if the scribe did not notice the identity, he is scarcely a reliable witness; if the note instead refers forward, however, he is apparently ignoring the blank leaves and linking the second and third booklets to the first. Whatever the explanation, the extension of Payne's responsibility to the three

---

[56]S. H. Thomson, "A Note on Peter Payne and Wyclyf," *Medievalia et humanistica* 16 (1964) 60–63 at 61–62; his view is followed by his son W. R. Thomson (n. 1 above) in his notes to the relevant manuscripts under T20 (not observing that the second anonymous index is identical to the first), T23–26, T28–38, T47. This view is also followed by W. R. Cook, "Peter Payne, Theologian and Diplomat of the Hussite Revolution," Ph.D. thesis (Cornell 1971) 163–171 with some corrections of Thomson's details and 384–386 (though some manuscript information needs emendation).

[57]F. M. Bartoš, *Literární Činnost M. Jana Rokycany, M. Jana Příbrama, M. Petra Payna*, Sbírka Pramenu k Poznání Literárního Života Československého Skupina 3, číslo 9 (Prague 1928) 101–102; the quotation is to be found in J. Cochlaeus, *Historiae Hussitarum* (Mainz 1549) 231, where it is dated 1429.

final indexes in PUK X.E.11 seems unwarranted: it selects attribution as reliable while dismissing its withholding as mendacious.

More seriously, it must be accepted that PUK X.E.11 is not clearly the earliest of the four manuscripts whose indexes overlap with it. Though PUK IV.G.27 is certainly later, being dated 1446 in a colophon (despite the copied "1426" noted above), PMK C.118 is paleographically dated as ca.1410 and ÖNB 1725 as first half of the fifteenth century.[58] All nine of the indexes in PMK C.118, the chief contender for the earliest place, appear in PUK X.E.11 as well; one of the shared nine (to *De dominio divino*) is not associated with Payne's name in PUK X.E.11, although another (to *De veritate sacre scripture*) is expressly attributed to him there.

But the question of dating extends beyond these four collections of indexes. The same indexes occur along with the texts to which they relate, and two of these are dated: the index to T47 *Trialogus* in ÖNB 4505 is itself dated 1429, while in ÖNB 4514 the text and index of *De blasphemia* are in the same hand with the copying of the text dated 1432. These dates are not incompatible with attribution to Payne, though they confirm the dating in PUK X.E.11 as scribal. Underlying any of the indexes, and a crucial first step toward their making, is the lettered subdivision of the chapters. Such subdivision occurs, in relevant texts, in a number of manuscripts earlier than PUK X.E.11.[59] The difficulty with this evidence is that it is usually hard to be sure that the marginal lettering was done by the original scribe at the time of the text's copying, and not added later. Thus, in PUK V.A.3 the copying of *De mandatis* is dated 1404 and in PUK VIII.G.32 the copying of *De eucharistia* is dated 1403; but in neither case is it absolutely certain that the marginal letters were entered at those dates. If that could be regarded as likely, then such indexes must antedate Payne's arrival in Bohemia.[60] The particular attribution of two indexes to Payne also raises interesting questions. That for *De materia et forma* appears nowhere else but in PUK X.E.11, and none of the twelve extant manuscripts of the text itself has the chapter subdivisions.[61] The index to *De veritate sacre scripture*, attributed to Payne in PUK X.E.11, appears without ascription in the (probably) earlier PMK C.118; but again the surviving twelve copies of the text lack marginal chapter subdivisions which alone make the tool usable (particularly given the extreme length of the chapters in this work)—the sole evidence for knowledge of these divisions is in one set of extracts from the work (PMK D.123). If Payne can certainly be credited with these two, then it

---

[58]These are the dates assigned by W. R. Thomson, who (n. 56 above) accepted the attribution of all to Payne.

[59]Namely, leaving aside those only dated as first half of the fifteenth century (where a firm date is given, this derives from a statement in the manuscript, others are paleographical assignments from Thomson), T11 in PUK VIII.F.1 of 1410, T23–25 in ÖNB 1339 of ca. 1410, T26 in PUK V.A.3 dated 1404 and PMK C.38 of ca. 1410, T28–30 in ÖNB 1340–1341 of ca. 1410, T35–37 in ÖNB 1343 ca. 1410, T37 in ÖNB 3933 of ca. 1415, ÖNB 3935 dated 1423, T38 in ÖNB 1387 of ca. 1410 and PUK VIII.G.32 dated 1403, T47 in ÖNB 4505 dated 1429 (not 1439 as Thomson states).

[60]The first certainly dated event known for Payne is 6 October 1406 when he procured for the Bohemians Faulfiš and Knĕhnic a letter from Congregation at Oxford University, with the university's seal attached, attesting to Wyclif's orthodoxy (Hudson *Premature Reformation* [n. 1 above] 100–101 and references there). But since Congregation consisted of the regent masters, it must be assumed that Payne had entered the university at the latest by the late 1390s. The hand of CUL Ll.5.13 is late fourteenth century.

[61]Thomson T20 omits the copy in Pavia, Biblioteca Universitaria 311, fols. 35vb–37vb, 98ra–107vb, fol. 48ra (the quires, and leaves within certain quires, are disordered and misbound); the copy is of English provenance.

would seem that his efforts can have borne singularly little fruit, and it may suggest that he was working to a pattern that already existed. It is tempting to think that the more general attribution (PUK X.E.11 fol. 172v), rather than indicating precise authorship for all that precedes, was an acknowledgment on the part of the scribe of the English origin of indexes based on chapter subdivisions—though an earlier traveler, rather than Payne, seems the likely conveyor of the device.

The scope of the indexes in this pattern is variable, and not entirely in proportion to the length of the text in question. Again this variation is most easily explicable on the basis of diverse responsibility. The text of *De apostasia* is roughly two and a half times as long as *De symonia*, but its index (if we use PUK X.E.11 as a yardstick) is over four times as long.[62] The most extensive index by far is that for *De civili dominio*, with over five hundred columns; that to *De veritate sacre scripture*, a text which is apparently close to *De civili dominio* in length, runs to only 120 columns.[63] There is also divergence in the type of entry. All extend beyond the single word (such as Hus used in his copy of Wyclif's philosophical works for the index by folio; see above). But the brief index to *De ydeis*, said not to be by Payne, is fairly perfunctory: entries such as "Equivocacio triplex," "In deo res quomodo sunt," or "secula seculorum" are typical. In the index to *De civili dominio*, entries such as "Castigari a subditis debent prelati scilicet quilibet seruatis" or "Castigacionem dominorum secularium non evacuat sacerdotalis dignitas" (fol. 241vb) are more characteristic in length. The number of entries per column, and hence the absolute length of an index, obviously varies in accordance with the length of the verbal material that precedes the text reference(s). In the case of *De civili dominio* about twenty verbal entries per column seems average, giving a daunting total of some ten thousand entries.

There is some evidence that the laborious process of indexing was preceded by marginal annotation of the text. If we look, for instance, at the single complete copy of *De civili dominio* 1 in ÖNB 1341, it is striking that many of the notes in the top and bottom margins that draw attention to the matter discussed are identical in wording to entries in the index to the text.[64] Rational, however, though such a sequence might be, given the inevitable closeness of text and entry, proof in this regard seems impossible to achieve.[65] The degree of alphabetization of these indexes needs brief comment, comment that must be regarded as provisional. One example, that to *De mandatis* taken from PMK C.38, was used by Loserth for the index to the Wyclif Society's edition.[66] In all of the indexes simple ordering by initial letter is provided, and the whole is often marked out, whether by line gaps, rubrication, or both, into separate letters.

---

[62]*De apostasia* in the printed edition is 254 pages, the index 65 columns; *De symonia* is 113 pages, its index 15 columns.

[63]This is a judgment based on the printed editions: *De civ.dom.* text runs to 1364 pages; the edition of *De ver.sac.scrip.* is more extravagant in the print size and in the annotation, and thus its 989 pages may exaggerate its length.

[64]For instance fol. 127ra bottom margin "Appellacio triplex a particulari ecclesia errante" (cf. text 1.391/7) appears in PUK X.E.11 fol. 235ra; fol. 131vb "vtrum peccatum sit catholicum" (text 1.405/20), PUK X.E.11 fol. 319ra "peccatum videtur esse catholicum."

[65]S. H. Thomson (n. 56 above) 61–63 argued that annotations in a number of Hussite copies are in an English hand which he suggests is Payne's, and that these were indeed preliminary stages in the compilation of the indexes. Considerably more work would be needed, however, to turn this hypothesis into certainty.

[66]*De mandatis* (1922) 537–567.

Beyond that there is more variation. It is usual for the items under the same general lemma to be in the order of the text, with the inevitable rider that related discussions are not brought together.[67] But there is an attempt to go further by juxtaposing entries which use grammatically related forms (for instance, listing those with the opening *regem* or *regis* with *rex*). This last observation, and the indexer's choice (not always readily perceptible as logical) of headword point up the difficulties of alphabetization at any but the most elementary level.

III

There remains a third device used to render Wyclif's works more accessible, a device that in some ways is the most remarkable. This is an index of biblical passages discussed by the *Doctor evangelicus* in his various works. It is found in two copies, ÖNB 4522 fols. 24–108v (the rest of the manuscript has fols. 1–21 an index to a commentary on the *Sentences*, plus after the biblical index T53, T409, T42 and *De sex iugis* fols. 109–144v, and other non-Wyclif material fols. 145–188), and PUK IV.G.27 fols. 1ra–35vb (followed by other indexes—see above). The index seems to be the same in the two copies. Neither copy has any ascription of authorial responsibility, though Harrison Thomson extended Payne's work to this (which he apparently knew only in the Prague copy).[68] The first item in ÖNB 4522 is dated 29 August 1423, and is said to have been copied in Basel (fol. 21); but that item is in a different hand from the biblical index and may not have had any connection in origin with it.[69] The copy in PUK IV.G.27 is dated at the end 1461.[70]

The number of works covered by this biblical index is large:[71] T12 *De tempore*, T22 *De benedicta incarnacione*, T23–25 *De dominio divino*, T26 *De mandatis*, T28–30 *De civili dominio*, T31 *De veritate*, T32 *De ecclesia*, T33 *De officio regis*, T34 *De potestate pape*, T35 *De symonia*, T36 *De apostasia*, T37 *De blasphemia*, T44 *De confessione* (Thomson's *De eucharistia et penitencia*), T47 *Trialogus*, T48 *Supplementum Trialogi*, T49 *De fide catholica*, T53 *De officio pastorali*, T384 *Responsiones ad argucias*, T393 *De amore*, T394 *De gradibus cleri*, T395 *Epistola missa ad archiepiscopum*, T402 *De 33 questionibus*, T404 *Epistola missa ad papam*, T408 *Dialogus*, T409 *Speculum secularium dominorum*, T414 *De ordine christiano*, T415 *De nova prevaricis mandatorum*, T422 *De novis ordinibus*, T426 *De perfectione statuum*, T427 *De vinculo amoris*, T431 *De fundacione sectarum*, T432 *De concordia fratrum* plus

---

[67]For the difficulties of compiling alphabetical indexes before the use of slips see L. W. Daly, *Contributions to a History of Alphabetization in Antiquity and the Middle Ages*, Collection Latomus 90 (1967) 86–90.

[68]S. H. Thomson (n. 56 above) 63; this is odd since he listed ÖNB 4522 erroneously (61) as a manuscript having annotation in the hand he thought to be Payne's.

[69]The first item fols. 1–21r is in quires 1–2, after which there are two blank folios; the biblical index forms the second booklet whose quires are numbered 1–7 by the scribe (existing quires 3–8^{12} [24–95], 9^{12} plus 1 [96–108]). A sixteenth-century note inside the front cover records that the manuscript came from Lymburg (modern Nymburk).

[70]The copy is thus fifteen years later than the other indexes that follow (see above). The name of the scribe is concealed by an anagram "Nomen scriptoris si tu cognoscere vellis Jo libi Prima sit (these last two marked for reversal) han sequens nes que suprema," i.e., Johannes ?

[71]Much larger than Thomson p. 47 n. 9 indicates. An earlier notice of the index in ÖNB 4522, with a more accurate indication of its coverage, is J. Loserth, "Die ältesten Streitschriften Wiclifs," *Sitzungsberichte der Kaiserlichen Akademie der Wissenschaften in Wien*, phil.-hist. Klasse 160.2 (1908) 68.

De sex iugis and *De incarcerandis fidelibus*.[72] Three isolated references draw attention to a major gap in coverage: the most obvious source of biblical discussion, the sermons, along with other exegetical work such as the *Opus evangelicum*, diatribes based on Matthew 23 and 24 (T372 and 373) and, perhaps less surprisingly, the *Postilla in totam Bibliam*, are not included.[73] The sermons are quarried just three times; their absence elsewhere, and that of the other texts, if not because of their inaccessibility, could have been because it was relatively easy to discover major discussions of biblical passages within these works, though the Sarum use of the sermons could have caused problems for a Bohemian, and the possibility does not cover incidental quotation outside the lections. Less easily explained is the absence of T38 *De eucharistia*. Conversely the appearance of the single work *De tempore* from Wyclif's philosophical output may seem surprising; even more surprising is the relative frequency of references to it. Commonest, however, are citations from the *Summa theologie* (where the only absentee is the brief *De statu innocencie*), especially *De mandatis*, *De veritate sacre scripture*, and *De potestate pape*, and from the *Trialogus*. Predictably it seems impossible to discover the manuscripts used for the index.[74]

The form of the biblical index is most readily seen in the Prague manuscript. Each leaf is ruled in two columns, with a second ruling close to the left-hand edge of each. The biblical book is entered within the main column in usual medieval order from Genesis to Apocalypse, and the chapter number in the narrow column; both of these are in red. There follows a brief biblical phrase (e.g., Luke 22[:26] "Vos autem non sic"), followed by a reference, or a string of references, to Wyclif's works. The copy in ÖNB 4522 is unfinished: the rubricator has not supplied either book names or chapter numbers; the material so far as it goes, however, seems to be identical with the Prague manuscript. The scale of the enterprise is again extraordinary. While it is impossible to come to an exact estimate of the number of references, some idea may be gained from an example: a single side of the Prague copy (fol. 24r) covers Luke 11–16, with 50 entries and some 114 references to Wyclif's works. Even allowing that the New Testament coverage is denser than that for the Old, a rough guess suggests about five thousand references to Wyclif.

The form of those references is that found in the previously described set of indexes to individual works. Most texts are located by title, heavily and not altogether consistently abbreviated (e.g., "4 3^g" indicates book four of the *Trialogus*), chapter, and subdividing letter. For works with more than one part, *De dominio divino*, *De civili dominio*, *Trialogus*, and *De officio pastorali*, indication of part is given. A glance at the two lists that use this method, work indexes (see above) and biblical index, makes it plain that the coverage of the latter is much greater than surviving evi-

---

[72]For these two see respectively T141 n. 1 and T202 n. 1; the first was printed as a separate work (in which form it appears in eight Bohemian manuscripts, and is recognized by the Hussite catalog), by G. Lechler, *Johann von Wiclif und die Vorgeschichte der Reformation* (Leipzig 1873) 2.591–605. the second (in five Bohemian copies, and described as *Epistola* by the Hussite catalog) by Loserth in *Op. min.* 92–97. W. R. Thomson (n. 1 above) does not recognize either as an independent work.

[73]T101 is described correctly as "de sermonibus dominicalibus 47" under Matt. 5, T137 as "sermone de sanctis 23" and T125 as "sermone de sanctis 11" under Matt. 1 (PUK IV.G.27 fols. 19rb and 18va respectively).

[74]Though there is a substantial overlap of sixteen of the shorter texts and ÖNB 1337, a further twenty-eight of that volume's shorter items are not involved in the index.

dence for the former. It also reveals that a large proportion of minor works must have had the marginal subdividing letters, even though no copy with them now survives.[75] Checking back from the Wyclif text to the index reveals something of the method, and reinforces respect for the industry and conscientiousness of the workers. I took three sections at random: *De officio regis* chapter 4, *De blasphemia* chapter 12, *De fundacione sectarum* chapters 9–11.[76] This showed, as might be expected from the verbal keys, that references without quotation are only very rarely listed. But of texts quoted only two were missed; thirty-five were correctly entered, and only one mistaken chapter reference occurred.[77] The sequence of references to subdivisions in the chapters of *De fundatione sectarum* was entirely credible. A considerable effort had been made to order the biblical references within the chapter: while such ordering might seem simple in a chapter as familiar as Matthew 5, it must have needed much more effort in, for instance, Romans 13.

What was the model for this index to biblical exegesis? This type of tool seems to be the most difficult to parallel, of the tools reviewed here. A tempting model would be the *Tabula septem custodiarum*, described by the only scholars to make a systematic study of it as "a collection of references to incidental passages, in the works of the Fathers and a few later authors, which expound specific passages of Scripture; the references are presented in the order of the text of the Bible"—adjusting for the single author here only involved, this is precisely a description of the tool for Wyclif.[78] The *Tabula* survives in around a dozen copies, all of them English, and appears to date from the first decade of the fourteenth century; its compilation derives from the Oxford Franciscan house. The connections between Oxford Greyfriars and Wyclif and his early followers is a subject that deserves closer scrutiny than can here be given, but the possibility that the *Tabula* formed the inspiration for the Wyclif index is a tempting one. Unfortunately, no surviving copy of the Franciscan tool has (so far as I have been able to trace) annotation that would connect it with the Wycliffites; on the other hand, as the Rouses pointed out to me, Wycliffite interest could explain the burst of copying of the *Tabula* at the end of the fourteenth and beginning of the fifteenth centuries by scribes and for patrons outside the order, after nearly a century when it was apparently confined to the Oxford Franciscans.[79] The chief problem in this hypothesis remains, of course, the absence of any evidence for an English circulation of the Wyclif biblical index, and indeed any certainty about its insular origin. But, given the English analogies cited for the analyses and work indexes, analogies which suggest a strong interest in access tools, the possibility that this device likewise went to Bohemia along with Wyclif's texts should not be forgotten.

---

[75]For instance PUK IV.G.27 fol. 21ra in a string of references for Matt.18[.15] "si autem peccaverit in te frater tuus" appear locations in *De fundacione sectarum* 9A, 12B (*Pol.Wks.* 1.47/14, 59/7), and *De perfeccione statuum* 6G (*Pol.Wks.* 2.478/13).

[76]In the first two the subdividing letters are entered in the margins of the printed editions. I took three chapters of the last to obtain a section of roughly comparable length.

[77]Those omitted were *De officio regis* 80/7 (Rom. 13.6) and *De blasphemia* 182/4 (Prov. 17.22); the mistake was *De blasphemia* 184/21 where the chapter is listed as "20" against correct "12" (the letter, "L," is correct, the biblical text 1 Reg.2.12).

[78]Rouse and Rouse, *Registrum* (n. 4 above) xcviii–cxxvi, quotation at ci. I am much indebted to Richard and Mary Rouse for discussions of this parallel.

[79]See details about the manuscripts, ibid. cli–clxix.

IV

This welter of detail reveals one clear point: the devotion of Wyclif's disciples, whether in England or in Bohemia, to the task of making his works accessible. Analysis and index were not, it seems, alternatives: both survive, or may reasonably be deduced to have existed (where subdividing letters but no index exist) for T11 *De tempore*, T22 *De benedicta incarnacione*, for nine of the twelve parts of the *Summa theologie* (T26, 28–35), and for T38 *De eucharistia*. At first the plethora of different types of work index, by chapter by folio or opening, by sectioning the existing chapter or sermon division, seems confusing. On further scrutiny, some traces of reasoning emerge: that chapter division is sufficient for texts such as *De officio pastorali* or *Dialogus*, though both attracted further subdivision in the biblical index. There appears to be some overlap of effort between at least some of the indexes by folio, opening, or section throughout a text. Equally it seems clear that in the long run the method of lettered subdivisions for chapters or sermons was, to judge by its greater frequency, that found most convenient. But the very diversity of method attests to the perceived urgency of the task. That few English manuscripts show signs of this activity is less surprising than that traces of analysis and of index by subdivision of chapters or sermons can be found in copies from Wyclif's home country; only the biblical index seems unique to Bohemia. In some part this may be a reflection of the systematic destruction of Wyclif's texts in England: of the major theological and ecclesiological works that have been involved in the present paper, no complete copy of *De civili dominio*, *De officio regis*, *De potestate pape*, *De eucharistia*, or *Trialogus* survived both that process and the less targeted depredations of time. But in part, of course, it reflects the growing importance of Wyclif's precise words and thoughts for Hussite disciples: it is notable that analyses, the rougher guide, are relatively well exemplified in English copies, while the more precise indexes are not. Those indexes, whether by work or by biblical citation, must have been collaborative enterprises—to attempt to ascribe all to one man, whether Payne or any other, is singularly to fail to grasp the enormity of the undertaking. For such collaboration English Wycliffites could again provide a model: the *Floretum/Rosarium* handbook, the Wycliffite Bible translation and revisions, the *Glossed Gospels* in their various versions, all derive from similar effort, and from comparable scholarship.[80] Just as the Hussites gave currency to, but did not originate, Wyclif's title as *Doctor Evangelicus*, so in the devices examined here they showed themselves to outdo the English disciples of their hero.

---

[80]See, for a summary account of all these, Hudson *Premature Reformation* (n. 1 above) 106–110, 231–258.

APPENDIX

Here are listed the manuscripts involved in the various categories described above. Where total numbers are given for the attestation of a text, fragments and extracts are generally omitted.

1. Analyses (brackets indicate those that are printed in the editions listed in note 1 above)

T11 *De universalibus* (1.1–14) TCC B.16.2, fol. 23ra–vb; Gonville and Caius 337/565, fols. 47–48v; Lincoln Cathedral 159, fols. 290ra–291rb; Pavia Biblioteca Universitaria 311, fols. 1ra–2rb; Krakow Biblioteka Jagiellonska 848, fols. 3ra–4ra; 1855, fols. 86–87v; PMK L.36, fols. 139ra–40rb; M.54, fols. 1r–4v; PUK III.G.10,fols. 70–72v; IV.H.9, fols. 1ra–3ra; V.H.16, fols. 1–4; VIII.F.1, fols. 1ra–2va; VIII.G.6, fols. 1–3; VIII.G.23, fols. 1–5; XXIII.F.58, fols. 3–5; Stockholm Kungliga Biblioteket Lat.A.164, fols. 87–88v; Vatican lat.4313, fols. 1ra–2rb; Venice Biblioteca Marciana Lat.VI.172, fols. 27va–29va; ÖNB 4523, fols. 58–60v; 5204, fols. 1–4; Wroclaw Biblioteka Uniwersytecka IV.F.7, fols. 304ra–305va [*not* Escorial e.II.6, ÖNB 4307]

T12 *De tempore* Gonville and Caius 337/565, fol. 48v; TCD 242, fol. 171va–b and again fols. 189vb–190ra; Lincoln Cathedral 159, fol. 333va–b; Pavia Biblioteca Universitaria 311, fol. 48ra–va; Krakow Biblioteka Jagiellonska 848, fol. 72va–vb; PMK M.54, fol. 170r–v; N.19, fol. 88rb–va; PUK III.G.10, fol. 31r–v; IV.H.9, fol. 95ra–b; VIII.F.1, fol. 87ra–va; XXIII.F.58, fol. 75r–v; Stockholm Kungliga Biblioteket Lat.A.164, fol. 1r–v; Venice Biblioteca Marciana Lat.VI.172, fol. 1ra–va; ÖNB 4316, fol. 85r–v [*not* TCC B.16.2]

T22 *De benedicta incarnacione* (1–2) Gonville and Caius 337/565, fol. 128; London BL Royal 7 B.iii, fol. 66 (abbreviated like its text); Oxford Oriel 15, fol. 225ra; Pavia Biblioteca Universitaria 311, fol. 91va–b; PMK D.35, fol. 1r–v; ÖNB 1387, fol. 75ra; 4307, fol. 115; 4504, fol. 37 [*all*]

Introductory note to T26, T27, and T28 Gonville and Caius 337/565, fol. 181

T26 *De mandatis* (to chapter 22 only) Gonville and Caius 337/565, fols. 181–2; PMK C.38, fols. 173va–174va; ÖNB 1339, fols. 234rb–236rb [*not* five English MSS nor ten Continental MSS]

T28 *De civili dominio* i (i.443–60) ÖNB 1341, fols. 144vb–152vb

T29 *De civili dominio* ii (ii.275–83) ÖNB 1341, fols. 252ra–254vb

T30 *De civili dominio* iii (iv.648–62) ÖNB 1340, fols. 261ra–266ra

T31 *De veritate sacre scripture* (omitting last eleven chapters) TCD 243, fols. 4ra–5vb; PMK B.53, fols. 274–8; PUK III.B.5, fols. 1ra–3ra; ÖNB 1294, fols. 125va–127rb [*not* four English MSS nor four Continental MSS]

T32 *De ecclesia* (to chapter 12 only) PUK X.D.11, fols. 212ra–214vb [*not* ÖNB 1294, 3929; Wolfenbüttel Guelf 1126]

T33 *De officio regis* PUK X.D.11, fols. 210va–212ra; ÖNB 3933, fols. 1ra–2ra; 4514, fols. 182–184 [all]

T34 *De potestate pape* (pp. 398–406) (to chapter 11 only) PMK C.73, fols. 263ra–264va; PUK III.F.11, fols. 226va–228rb

T35 *De symonia* (pp. 115–118) TCD 243, fol. 157rb–vb; PUK X.E.9, fols. 69–70v; ÖNB 1343, fols. 35va–36vb; 1622, fols. 83–84; 3927, fol. 53ra–va; 3937, fol. 115ra–va; 4504, fols. 1–2; 4515, fols. 27–28; 4536, fols. 133–134v [all]

T38 *De eucharistia* (pp. 1–10) PUK IV.D.22, fols. 130bisra–132ra; VIII.G.32, fols. 1–3v; XI.E.3, fol. 15r–v; Vatican lat.4313, fols. 31rb–32ra; ÖNB 1387, fols. 1ra–2ra; 3927, fols. 77ra–78ra; 3932, fols. 157ra–158rb

ACCESSUS AD AUCTOREM 343

2. Indexes
   a) by folio or opening
   T17 *De trinitate* ÖNB 4316, fols. 130v–132v
   T26 *De mandatis* Brno Universitni Knihovna Mk 38, fols. 164ra–166va
   T31 *De veritate sacre scripture* ÖNB 1294, fols. 120ra–125rb
   T32 *De ecclesia* (printed pp. 589–596) ÖNB 1294, fols. 208ra–210va
   T35 *De symonia* ÖNB 3927, fol. 74va–b
   T38 *De eucharistia* ÖNB 3927, fols. 122ra–123rb; 3932, fols. 209va–210vb (numbers missing)
   T47 *Trialogus* ÖNB 3930, fols. i ra–ii rb (flyleaves)
   T374–377 *Opus evangelicum* PUK IV.A.18, fols. 203ra–207vb
   T408 *Dialogus* ÖNB 3930, fol. ii va–vb (flyleaf)
   Also composite index to various texts, (a) to T11, 12, 18 20 by folio in Stockholm Kungliga Biblioteket Lat.A.164, fols. 134v–135v; (b) to T44, 49, 300, 334, 393, 394, 395, 404, 414, 417, 421, 426, 431, 432 by opening in ÖNB 3927, fols. 50ra–51va

   b) Index by transferred folio or opening numbers
   T26 *De mandatis* PMK A.71/1, fols. 277ra–279va
   T47 *Trialogus* ÖNB 3932, fols. 91ra–92ra
   T408 *Dialogus* ÖNB 3932, fol. 90va–vb

   c) Index by (book and) chapter only
   T53 *De officio pastorali* Brno Universitni Knihovna Mk38, fol. 29ra–va; PMK F.20, fols. 154v–155v; PUK III.G.11, fol. 27bisr–v; V.F.9, fols. 147v–148v; X.E.9, fols. 67–68v; X.H.17, fols. 31–32; XII.F.21, fols. 61v–63; ÖNB 4527, fol. 226ra–vb; 4536, fols. 96v–98; PUK X.C.23, fol. 194ra–rb (numbers missing)
   T345–70 *Postilla* on New Testament (a) ÖNB 1342, pastedown–fol. i v (flyleaf); (b) PUK III.F.20, fols. 199v–202v (entries differ)

   d [i]) Index by (book and) chapter and subdividing letter (no folios are given for those volumes that are solely indexes—contents set out above)
   T11 *De tempore* PUK X.E.11
   T18 *De ydeis* PUK X.E.11
   T20 *De materia et forma* PUK X.E.11
   T23–5 *De dominio divino* PMK C.118, PUK X.E.11, ÖNB 1725; ÖNB 3935, fols. 1ra–11va
   T26 *De mandatis* (a) CUL Ll.5.13, fols. 112–129v; (b) (printed from PMK C.38 pp.537–567) PUK IV.G.27, X E.11, ÖNB 1725; PMK C.38, fols. 1ra–16vb; PUK X.G.1, fols. 1ra–19rb
   T28–30 *De civili dominio* 1–3 PUK IV.G.27, X.E.11, ÖNB 1725
   T31 *De veritate sacre scripture* PMK C.118, PUK X.E.11
   T32 *De ecclesia* PMK C.118, PUK X.E.11
   T33 *De officio regis* PMK C.118, PUK X.E.11; ÖNB 3933, fols. 58ra–62va
   T34 *De potestate pape* PMK C.118, PUK X.E.11
   T35 *De symonia* PMK C.118, PUK X.E.11; PUK X.E.9, fols. 126–131; ÖNB 4536, fols. 187va–191va
   T36 *De apostasia* PMK C.118, PUK X.E.11
   T37 *De blasphemia* PMK C.118, PUK X.E.11; ÖNB 3933, fols. 185ra–195rb; 4514, fols. 86r–102v

T38 *De eucharistia* PMK C.118, PUK X.E.11
T47 *Trialogus* PUK X.E.11; ÖNB 4505, fols. 209v-227v
T257-96 *Sermones quadraginta* Lambeth 23, fols. 256rb-257ra
T374-7 *Opus evangelicum* TCD 242, fols. 204va-208vb

d [ii]) Manuscripts having the indexing letters necessary for use with indexes under d [i]— where these are printed in the editions, an asterisk follows the title
T11 *De universalibus* PUK VIII.F.1
T22 *De benedicta incarnacione* ÖNB 1387 (cap.1 only), 4307
T23-5 *De dominio divino* ÖNB 1339, 3935
T26 *De mandatis* CUL Ll.5.13; PMK C.38, PUK V.A.3, X.G.1, ÖNB 1339
T28-30 *De civili dominio* 1-2* ÖNB 1340; *De civ. dom.* 3* ÖNB 1341
T31 *De veritate sacre scripture* PMK D.123 (extract only)
T32 *De ecclesia** ÖNB 1294
T33 *De officio regis** ÖNB 3933
T35 *De symonia* PUK X.E.9, ÖNB 1343, 4536
T36 *De apostasia** ÖNB 1343, 3935
T37 *De blasphemia** PMK C.73; ÖNB 1343, 3933, 3935, 4514
T38 *De eucharistia* PUK VIII.G.32, ÖNB 1387
T47 *Trialogus* ÖNB 4505
T53 *De officio pastorali* ÖNB 1337
T54-111 Sunday gospel sermons Wolfenbüttel Guelph 565
T176-236 Sunday epistle sermons Wolfenbüttel Guelph 565
T257-296 *Sermones quadraginta* Lambeth 23

The four manuscripts containing indexes apart from the texts, all by (book), chapter and subdividing letter:
PMK C.118 to T23-25, 31, 32, 33, 34, 35, 36, 37, 38
PUK IV.G.27 to T26, 28-30
PUK X.E.11 to T12, 18, 20, 23-25, 26, 28-30, 31, 32, 33, 34, 35, 36, 37, 38, 47
ÖNB 1725 to T23-25, 26, 28-30

e) Index to biblical passages discussed by Wyclif are found in: PUK IV.G.27, ÖNB 4522

VIII

Trial and Error: Wyclif's works in Cambridge, Trinity College MS B.16.2

The most extensive manuscript of Wyclif's Latin writings now surviving in England is Trinity College Cambridge MS B.16.2: it contains twelve of Wyclif's relatively early logical and philosophical tracts, four sets of sermons that comprise virtually all of the reformer's extant preaching materials, and the four books of the *Opus Evangelicum*, finished, as this and the only other manuscript of English workmanship state, 'Autoris vita finitur et hoc opus ita'. The manuscript can hardly be described as neglected, since the majority of its contents have been printed, but the printed descriptions of it are all in some degree unsatisfactory. In addition no consideration appears to have been given to the make-up of the manuscript, or the reasons that lie behind its arrangement and contents, and no comprehensive survey has been ventured of its overall textual value. It is the purpose of this paper to offer a beginning to this study – a beginning only, since the manuscript is extremely complex and investigation of it raises perhaps more questions than it solves.[1]

I

Physically the manuscript is an impressive one: approximately 410 mm by 300 mm overall, 300 mm by 195 mm written space, each parchment folio divided into two columns with about 70 lines to each. There are now 439 folios plus two small portions, but, as will be seen, more than a further 20 have been cut away.[2] There is a foliation in ink, and a pagination in pencil; neither is complete nor correct. Following a request that the manuscript might be refoliated, and that, to elucidate its complex make-up, quires a and b and all missing leaves should be included in the numbering, some renumbering was undertaken, but not on the majority of leaves, and older numerations have not been struck through. This latest foliation, inadequately though it has been entered in the manuscript, has been followed here.[3] Each quire is now numbered on the right-hand lower corner of the first recto folio; this numbering agrees with the description here. The sections and quiring are as follows:

i paper flyleaf; a⁴ leaves 3–4 cut away; (1: fols 5–22) 1¹², 2⁶ leaves 1 and 4–6 cut away; ‖ (2: fols 23–58) 3¹², 4¹² leaf 1 cut away, 5¹² leaves 3, all but top left inner quarter of 11, and all 12 cut away; ‖ (3: fols 59–158) 6¹² leaf 2 cut away, 7–8¹², 9¹⁴ leaves 4–6 cut away, 10–11¹², 12⁶ leaf 6 cut away, 13¹², 14⁸ leaf 8 cut away; ‖ (4: fols 159–376) 15–30¹², 31¹⁴ leaf 14 cut away, 32¹² leaves 7–12 cut away save top inside quarter of leaf 7; ‖ (5: fols 377–464) 33–39¹²; b⁴ leaves 1–2 cut away; i paper flyleaf.

The double slashes in the quiring mark divisions between the sections of the manuscript; as will be seen, no work traverses a quire boundary at any of these divisions. Apart from the first (after quire 2), which was ignored, these sections correspond to the four divisions noted by the medieval scribe who listed the contents of the manuscript on fol. 2v (see Plate 6).[4] The nature of the contents certainly reflects a divided structure for the manuscript. There are few quire signatures, and none of them seems helpful.[5] Catchwords are regularly found, and those of interest are noted in the account of the contents below. Some, but not all, of the leaves lost from the manuscript were almost certainly blank; in one or two cases where a text would have ended in the first column of a leaf now lost it is tempting to wonder whether an incriminating colophon has been removed. The most eccentric part of the manuscript is that consisting of the first three sections indicated by the quiring; this will be considered further below in section III. The incipit for the second folio of text in the entire volume is *infima et minime*.

The manuscript, despite the fivefold division indicated by the quiring above in conjunction with the contents, was evidently planned throughout on the same scheme. Furthermore, even if the five sections were designed as booklets, and the decision to bind these booklets together was a secondary one, annotation makes it plain that from a very early stage in its history the manuscript has been in its present form (see below, section III, for further details). The layout of all sections of the manuscript, itself not a simple matter, is consistent throughout. James was not explicit about the number of hands, though he noted that a new scribe began work at the start of the fourth section.[6] Two scribes is certainly too conservative an estimate: it is hard to be sure how many there are. Dr Doyle suggests that there are eight: (1) fols 5r^a–19v^a, 23r^a–37r^b (fols 20–22 cut away); (2) fols 37v^a–46v^b; (3) fols 47r^a–57r^a, and fols 377r^a–460v^b; (4) fols 59r^a–157r^a; (5) fols 159r^a–173v^a 20 lines from foot, and fols 255r^a–288r^b line 14; (6) fols 173v^a 19 lines from foot–fol.

194v^b, and fols 288r^b line 14–290v^b; (7) fols 195r^a–254r^b, and fols 291r^a–363r^b; (8) fols 365r^a–371r^a. He dates all the hands except the last as s. xiv/xv, the last as s. xv in. All hands are of a kind found in university manuscripts of the end of the fourteenth and beginning of the fifteenth centuries, blending features of anglicana formata and modified textura.[7] The parchment throughout has the yellowish tinge, especially on the hair side, described by Malcolm Parkes as typical of Oxford manuscripts; the ink used by most of the scribes is distinctly brownish in colour.[8] The provenance of the manuscript will be discussed further in section V.

The decoration of the volume is also apparently the work of more than one person. One style of illuminated capitals appears on fols 5, 9v, 13v, 16v, 46, 59, 84, 108, 131, 151, 201v, 224v, 307v, 377, 403, 427, 455 (see Plates 7–10); these are all in blue, red and gold, and the last seven are extended around the whole leaf. A second, of slightly different style but of comparable size, appears on fols 23, 23v, 159, 255 (in quires 3, 15 and 23), using orange, blue and gold (see Plate 11). Within the text, at chapter or sermon openings, the capitals are mostly blue with red flourishing, but a few are in the reverse with the red a purplish tint; though the general style is maintained throughout, the details of execution vary.

The binding is of leather over boards and dates from the seventeenth century, though the spine has been renewed at a later date with matching leather. On the front and back covers are arms incorporating those of Thomas Neville, master of Trinity College from 1593 to 1615, and dean of Canterbury from 1597. Neville gave this manuscript, and many others, to the College; a number of Neville's gifts came from the medieval library of Christ Church Canterbury.[9] The library of Canterbury College Oxford, a dependency of Christ Church Canterbury, possessed a volume of Wyclif's sermons in 1443, but the second folio given reveals that it was not the present Trinity manuscript.[10]

II

Contents[11]

fol. 2v (quire a) list of contents (Plate 6); fols 3–4 cut away.

Part 1

Quires 1–2 [A.I.D. hand (1); running-heads in the form book number centrally on verso and facing recto, tract number in outer verso margin, title in outer recto margin].

1. fols 5r^a–9v^a *De ente in communi* (Th.7; c.1.1); colophon: *Explicit tractatus primus primi libri de ente in communi quo ad eius noscibilitatem veritatem et ampliacionem.* Text edited from this copy by S. H. Thomson (Oxford, 1930), pp. 1–61. Only other known manuscript Vienna, Österreichische Nationalbibliothek (ÖNB), 4307, fols 158r–167v.
2. fols 9v^a–13r^b *De ente primo in communi* (Th.8; c.1.2); heading at start runs on from preceding item: *Incipit tractatus ⌐secundus⌐ eiusdem libri de ente primo* (the number is added in a different, but medieval, hand); colophon: *Explicit tractatus secundus libri primi de ente primo.* Text edited from this copy by S. H. Thomson (Oxford, 1930), pp. 62–112. Only other known manuscript again Vienna, ÖNB, 4307, fols 167v–177r.
3. fols 13r^b–16r^b *Purgans errores circa veritates in communi* (Th.9; c.1.3 *de veritatibus in communi*); heading at end of fol. 13r^b: *Incipit tractatus tercius eiusdem libri purgans errores ⌐circa⌐ veritates in communi*, text begins fol. 13v^a; colophon: *Explicit tractatus tercius purgans errores circa veritates in communi.* The scribe on fol. 14r^b notes that material at the end of chapter 2 is missing, and leaves the last thirteen lines of the column blank. Text edited from this copy by M. H. Dziewicki, *Johannis Wyclif De Ente: Librorum Duorum Excerpta* (WS 1909), pp. 1–28. Only other known manuscript, not used by Dziewicki, is Vienna, ÖNB, 4307, fols 177v–184r.
4. fols 16r^b–19v^a *Purgans errores circa universalia in communi* (Th.10; c.1.4 *de vniuersalibus incompletus*); heading on fol. 16r^b: *Incipit tractatus quartus purgans errores circa universalia in communi*, text begins fol. 16v^a; no colophon at end. Fol. 17 (the first of quire 2) was cut away, containing most of chapter 2 and the beginning of chapter 3 (the stub is too narrow to see where chapter 3 began).[12] Text ed. Dziewicki, as item (3), pp. 29–48; found also, unknown to Dziewicki, in Vienna, ÖNB, 4307, fols 185r–190r. Fol. 19v is blank apart from 16 lines at the head of col. a, fols 20–22 (leaves 4–6 of quire 2) cut away, possibly blank but see below pp. 63–4.

Part 2

Quires 3-5 [A.I.D. hands (2) and, quire 5, first stint of (3), cf. part 5;

running heads in form of title centrally on verso and facing recto, with usually chapter numbers in the outer margins].

5. fols 23r^a–45r^b *De universalibus* (Th.11; c.1.5 *de vniuersalibus completus*) preceded by an analysis of the text; no title at beginning or end, but running head *de vniuersalibus*. Lacks chapter 10 lines 218–589 because of loss of leaf after fol. 34 (leaf 1 of quire 4, stub present fol. 35). Edited as *Tractatus de universalibus* by I. J. Mueller (Oxford, 1985), using this manuscript along with Lincoln, Cathedral Chapter Library, MS 159 (formerly C.1.15) as base text. There are twenty-one further manuscripts. Mueller (pp. xxxii–xxxiii) suggests that the addition of the *De universalibus* was an afterthought, and that the *De tempore* originally was intended to follow item (4); see further section III.
fol. 45v blank.

6. fols 46r^a–57r^a *De tempore* (Th.12; c.1.6 *de tempore incompletus*); no title at beginning or end, but running head *de tempore*. The end of cap. 4 and beginning of cap. 5 is lost because leaf 3 of quire 5 (fol. 49) has been cut out. The text ends twelve lines down column a of fol. 57r, and the lower half of that column and the outer column of the leaf, together with the whole of the next leaf (leaf 12 of quire 5) were cut out. This latter may have been blank, since nothing of the *De tempore* is lost. Unpublished. Found in fifteen other manuscripts.

Part 3

Quires 6–14 [A.I.D. hand (4); running titles as in part 1].

7. fols 59r^a–67r^a. *De intelleccione dei* (Th.14; c.2.1); no title at beginning or end, but running-head *liber ij^{us} ... tractatus primus* and the title of the tract given in the upper margins. A leaf (fol. 60) that contained the end of chapter 1 and beginning of chapter 2 is cut away after fol. 59 (Dziewicki p. 57 line 29).[13] Edited from this manuscript by Dziewicki, as items (3–4) above, pp. 49–112. Also found in Prague, National Library, IX.E.6 (1762), fols 1r–15v; this copy was not known to Dziewicki (the lost material is Prague fols 2v mid–4v top).[14]

8. fols 67r^a–83v^b. *De sciencia dei* (Th.15; c.2.2). There is no heading immediately before the text, but running heads and chapter numbers

show a change of item; at the end, extending into lower margin: *Explicit de sciencia dei.* (see fol. 139r–v below). Unpublished. Also found in same Prague MS as item (7), fols 16r–51r.

9. fols 84r^a–108r^a *De volucione dei* (Th.16; c.2.3); no initial heading, but final colophon *Explicit tractatus compilatus a M.J.W. de volucione dei etc* (see Plate 7); running heads confirm the title. Leaves 4–6 (fols 98–100) of quire 9, containing the end of cap.11, the whole of cap.12, and the start of cap.13, have been cut away (see edition p. 229 line 35 and note p. 230). Edited from this manuscript by Dziewicki, as items (3–4) above, pp. 113–286. Also found in same Prague MS as item (7), fols 56r–96r, unknown to Dziewicki.

10. fols 108r^a–131r^a [*De trinitate*] (Th.17; c.2.4 with title as heading); heading at start *Incipit tractatus eiusdem de personarum distinccione*; no colophon at end.[15] Edited using this manuscript along with others by A. duP. Breck (Boulder, Colorado, 1962). Six other manuscripts contain the text.

11. fols 131r^a–137v^a *De ydeis* (Th.18; c.2.5). No heading at start, text ends *Explicit tractatus compilatus de ydeis secundum M. Johannem W. &c.* Unpublished. Text survives in fifteen other copies.

Fol. 138 (leaf 6 of quire 12) is cut away. The folio was probably blank since fol. 137v^b has the catchwords to fol. 139r^a (text actually cancelled – see below); this must at least imply that the folio was removed (or known to be blank) at a very early date.

Fols 139r^a–139v^b, ending three-quarters down col. b, contains the end of chapter 12 of *De sciencia dei*, marked marginally *va...cat*. The same material occurs before at fols 83r^a–83v^b, where it forms the end of the tract that ends there at the foot of the second column on the verso. Fol. 83 is the first leaf of quire 8, fol. 139 is now the first leaf of quire 13. For the implications of this change of plan see below, section III.

12. fols 139v^b–157r^a *De potencia productiva dei ad extra* (Th.19; c.2.6); no heading at start, colophon at end *Explicit tractatus Magistri J.W. de potencia dei*. As Thomson notes (p. 35), the running heads on fols 151–6 inclusive, above chapters 12–16, read *de adnichilacione*, but, though such a title is appropriate to the subject matter of chapters 12–14, it is not in his view to the last two; Thomson rejects the idea that these chapters ever formed a separate *tractatulus*, but it is perhaps worth keeping an open mind on the question since Trinity's heading may not be accurate in its delimitation.[16] Chapter 12 also has an illuminated capital at its start (fol. 151), as if it were a new

tract (see Plate 8). The writer of the initial list of contents (fol. 2v) recognized the division of the text, and his analysis reflects the running-heads: he listed 2.6 as 'Sextus de potencia productiua dei ad extra continet 16 capitula vbi in 5 capitulis vltimis tractatur de adnichilacione'. Chapters 12–14 only edited from this manuscript by Dziewicki, as above item (7), pp. 287–315. Apart from this copy only a single fragment of the text survives, in the same Prague MS as item (7), fols 51r–55v ending ten lines from the end of chapter 2 in Trinity, fol 142r^b.

Fol. 158 cut away, and the catchwords to item 13 appear on fol. 157v.

Part 4

Quires 15–32 [A.I.D. hands (5)–(8), the change-overs not corresponding to a break between items, for distribution see above pp. 54–5; running heads usually in the form of part number centrally on verso and recto, with sermon number within those parts in the outer margins of each column].

13. fols 159r^a–201r^b Fifty-seven *Sermones super evangelia dominicalia* (Th.55–111; c.3.1 specifying 57 sermons). Edited by Loserth *Sermones* i (WS 1887), using this manuscript as base text.[17] No heading at start. Text ends fol. 201r^b nine lines down the column: *Explicit pars prima. Incipit pars secunda.* Set also found in three continental manuscripts, Vienna, ÖNB, 3934, 4529, and Wolfenbüttel, Herzog August Bibliothek, Cod. Helmstedt 565. It should be noted that Trinity lacks the preface to the set found in all three continental copies. Loserth's edition also may imply that occasions are given for each sermon in Trinity: they are not, save for Th.71, 73, 75.

14. fols 201v^a–251v^a Sixty-one *Sermones super evangelia de sanctis* (Th.115–175; c.3.2 specifying 64 sermons, and hence including the three in item 15 below); no heading at start, no colophon at end, running-head *ij pars*. The set was originally divided in half by the scribe after no. 28 (Th.142; fol. 224v^a), with the deleted rubric *Explicit secunda pars. Incipit tercia.* This corresponds with the end of the Proper of the Saints, and precedes the Common; the sermons of this latter group were first numbered from 1–18, before the numbers were altered to 29–61 in accordance with the removal of the division. Edited by Loserth *Sermones* ii (WS 1888). This set is found

in two continental manuscripts, Vienna, ÖNB, 3928 and 3931.
15. fols 251v^a–254r^b Three sermons, for the dedication of a church, the Sunday following, and the octave (Th.112–114; c.3.2 see item (14) above); the occasions are not stated in the manuscript, where no headings appear. In two continental copies of the dominical gospel sermons, Vienna, ÖNB, 3934 and 4529, they are attached to that set, while in two more, Vienna, ÖNB, 3928 and 3931, they follow the sanctorale set as here. Trinity, however, is the only copy with no rubric between Th.175 and 112, and the running heads continue the numeration, 62–4. There is then an erased explicit *Explicit ... super euangelia* .... Loserth included these three sermons at the end of *Sermones* i (WS 1887), 378–404.
fol. 254v is blank, but the catchwords to the next item have been entered at the foot.
16. fols 255r^a–307v^a and 365r^a–371r^a Fifty-nine *Sermones super epistolas* (Th.176–234; c.3.3 specifying 59 sermons); no heading at start. The set was written straight through up to Th.229 on fol. 307v^a, where the scribe wrote *Explicit prima pars epistolarum et quarta in ordine/ Incipit pars secunda ⌜epistolarum⌝ et quinta in ordine*; in this *quarta* has been cancelled and ⌜*iij*⌝ substituted, and *quinta* likewise cancelled and ⌜*iiij*⌝ substituted, all the changes are in a different hand (see Plate 9). A marginal note (printed Loserth iii. 473) then points out that sermons incorrectly omitted at this point are to be found later; a symbol ties this to fol. 365r^a where Th.230–4 follow, forming the sole contents of quire 32, which was a normal quire of parchment; the text ends 22 lines down fol. 371r^a and the rest of fol. 371 and fols 372–376 are cut away – presumably the rest of the leaves (to the end of quire 32) were blank. Edited by Loserth *Sermones* iii (WS 1889); the whole of this set is found in two continental manuscripts, but some individual sermons and one run of sermons are found in others, again mostly on the continent.
17. fols 307v^a–363r^b Sixty-four miscellaneous sermons (Th.235–98; c.3.4 specifying 64 sermons described as *de epistolis in sanctorum festiuitatibus cum aliis diuersis sermonibus*). For the altered heading on fol. 307v^a, see item (16) above. The text on fol. 363r^b ends three lines from the bottom of the leaf without a final rubric, and fol. 363v is blank and fol. 364 cut away (end quire 31); there are no catchwords to the next quire. Since Loserth used this manuscript to print *Sermones* iv (WS 1890), the edition follows the sequence of sermons found here, and Thomson's numeration (Th.235–98) in turn

follows Loserth. But the sermons do not belong to a single set, unlike the three sets here, items (13), (14), (16). Thomson nos 237–56 form a set known in the medieval period as *Sermones Viginti*, nos 257–296 as the *Sermones Quadraginta*; the remaining sermons (Th.235–6, 297–8) seem not to fit into either group but to have been isolated survivals.[18] The *Sermones Quadraginta* survive as a whole in the same order in three other manuscripts, the *Sermones Viginti* in two others but in a different order.

For fols 365–376 see above item (16).

Part 5

Quires 33–39 [A.I.D. hand (3) second stint, cf. part 2; running-heads in the form of book number centrally, with title at outer margins, on verso and recto].

18. fols 377r^a–460v^b *Opus evangelicum* in four books (Th.374–7; c.4.1–4). The text ends two-thirds of the way down fol. 460v^b with the note 'Autoris vita finitur et hoc opus ita'. No heading or colophon. Edited by Loserth (2 vols WS 1895–6), using this manuscript as base text. There are three other complete manuscripts, and one fragment. fols 461–2 cut away, 463–4 blank.

III

The details above attempt to describe the manuscript as it now stands. It is clear, however, that the present state of the volume reflects a number of modifications that were undertaken during its making. These modifications affect especially the first three sections of the manuscript. The simplest of these changes to explain concerns the third section, quires 6–14. Here quires 8–12 inclusive were added after quire 13 had at least been begun: material on fol. 139, leaf 1r-v of quire 13, and marked for omission by marginal *va ..cat*, are repeated on leaf 1r-v of quire 8. Evidently in origin item 8 *De sciencia dei* was to have been immediately followed by item 12 *De potencia productiva dei*. Subsequently the exemplar(s) for items 9–11 came to hand, together with some indication that these tracts belonged between the two as originally written. Consequently the final part of *De sciencia dei* was rewritten on the first leaf of quire 8, and the three new items were copied (filling the rest of quire 8 plus new quires 9-12); the end of *De sciencia dei* as first written was cancelled (on the first leaf of what became quire 13). The changes had been made before the provision of the running heads and list of contents at the start of the manuscript.[19] These running heads (for which more fully see below) are not interrupted between present quires 6–14, describing the tracts as numbers 1–6 of book II. In the only other surviving manuscript of either tract, Prague, National Library, IX.E.6 (1762), *De sciencia dei* immediately precedes *De potencia productiva* (fols 16–51 and 51–55v respectively, the latter tract defective).[20] The exemplar for the tracts, which in Trinity now intervene between the two, may thus have come to the scribe's hand later, but in a form that suggested to him that this material belonged between the two.[21] There is certainly evidence in cross-references between the tracts to suggest that the order eventually achieved was correct.[22] The catchwords at the end of quire 12 are those to the *cancelled* material at the start of quire 13; this was presumably entered to ensure the right sequence despite the cancellation.

Much more obscure is the original state of the first and second sections of the manuscript, quires 1–2 and 3–5 respectively. The material in section 1 seems superficially straightforward, though quire 2 is badly mutilated. The texts have a coherent set of running heads, numbering them as tracts 1–4 of book I; these running heads correspond to the sections set out in the opening list of contents. But these running heads are not continued through quires 3–5: here only the title of the work is given. It seems fairly clear that quires 3–5 were added to the manuscript as an afterthought, apparently after the provision elsewhere of the running-heads, though equally apparently before the compilation of the list of contents since the two works are included in this latter in their present position.[23] The scribe at the start of *De universalibus* seems to be that of the opening items, but the third scribe who wrote quire 5, completing *De tempore*, appears elsewhere in part (5) of the manuscript. It has been suggested that the copies of *De universalibus* and *De tempore* were added as two separate stages.[24] Quires 3–5 cannot now be separated into distinct booklets, since the second item begins on leaf 12 of quire 4; but the present format may be misleading. The last leaf of quire 4 seems of a more substantial kind of parchment from that of the remainder of the quire (or of the following quire), the hand on that leaf is that of the preceding item and different from that of the immediately following material, and the join up of quires 4 and 5 is not very neatly made.[25]

It might possibly seem that fol. 46 was an extra leaf to 'bridge in' the copy of *De tempore*. But this does not explain the stub, fol. 35, which appears to be conjoint to this leaf at the start of quire 4; material from the *De universalibus*, equivalent to a folio's length, has been lost at this point (edition chapter 10 lines 218-589). Two words that are all that survive on this stub, on the verso about seven lines from the bottom of the writing space in what would have been the inner margin, read (when the abbreviations have been expanded) *est relacio*. Credibly this relates to *De universalibus* cap. 10 line 581, possibly as a marginal comment since it does not correspond exactly to the wording of the text; this would be precisely in the right place in the lost material. The change of hand at the end of quire 4, one folio into the copy of the *De tempore*, suggests that *De universalibus* came to hand and was written after the copy of *De tempore* had been made: *De tempore* could originally have begun on one of the missing leaves of quire 2 – this could have been removed when *De universalibus* became available, and the material recopied at the end of quire 4.[26] In any case it seems that the change in the quality of parchment for fol. 46 is probably fortuitous, and that the leaf was always part of quire 4.

But the reason for the intrusion of items 5–6 on the inserted group of quires 3–5 is tied up with the whole issue of Wyclif's conception of what has come to be known as the *Summa de ente*. This is not the appropriate place to investigate the question fully, nor am I competent to do so. But a little needs to be said. As book I stands in the modern catalogue, it consists of seven tracts; for all but two of these the manuscript evidence is poor - the exceptions are the *De universalibus* and the *De tempore*. The first four tracts are found only in the present manuscript, items (1)–(4), and in Vienna, ÖNB, 4307; in the latter manuscript they are found in the same order and with the same tract numbering attached to them. There they are immediately followed by *De ente predicamentali*, a tract which is there numbered in one running head (fol. 193v) as tract 5, and of which this is now the only surviving copy.[27] Vienna, ÖNB, 4307 does not contain *De tempore*; more interestingly, it contains *De universalibus*, but as a separate and unnumbered tract earlier in the manuscript.[28] It seems that Beer may well have been right in suggesting that in the Trinity manuscript tract 4 of book I was at first intended to be followed, as in Vienna, by the *De ente predicamentali*.[29] This would have taken roughly 26 leaves in the format of Trinity, that is, it could have been completed in the missing leaves 4–6 of quire 2, fols 20–22, plus most of a further two quires of twelve leaves.[30] In addition to the running heads in Vienna, *De ente predicamentali* is described in *De trinitate* as the fifth tract.[31] Such an arrangement in the English manuscript was, however, upset when *De universalibus* and the *De tempore* became available, and by the evidence – which apparently seemed to the compilers of Trinity overwhelming – that these two tracts should stand after tract 4. Consequently the compilers removed the start of *De ente predicamentali* by excising leaves 4–6 of quire 2 (fols 20–22), and removing the next two quires. In their place were inserted the copies of the two new works, on three quires. For some reason the compilers did not reintroduce *De ente predicamentali* after the new material.³² That the *De universalibus* and *De tempore* were written somewhat later than the other tracts of book I of the *Summa* can be argued on other grounds.³³ That these two tracts were finally intended by Wyclif to stand before the *De ente predicamentali* appears from a cross reference in the *De tempore* to it: *probatum est tractatu septimo de quantitate*.³⁴ The interest of this puzzle derives not only from the development of the Trinity manuscript, but because that development seems possibly to reflect changes in Wyclif's own conception of his philosophical *Summa* and to throw light on the modification of that work.

A brief description has been given above of the running heads and the list of contents in the Trinity manuscript. Both were evidently designed to bring together an unwieldy bulk of material and to facilitate the use of its texts. As has been said, in the philosophical works, with the exception of the *De universalibus* and *De tempore*, the running heads normally consist of tract number at the top left corner of the verso leaf, book number in the form *liber*...(number) centrally on verso and facing recto, and title at the top right-hand recto corner; below these at the outer edge of each column is the chapter number (see Plate 7). In the *De universalibus* and *De tempore* the title is given in full centrally on each verso and recto, below which on some folios, but not all, are found the chapter numbers at the outer edge of the columns (see Plate 10). The list of contents for this section of the manuscript divides the material into two books, giving tract number, title and an indication of the number of chapters for each (see Plate 6). In the fourth part of the manuscript, fols 159–371, containing the sermons, the running heads normally consist of the part number centrally, below which the sermon-number is entered at the outer edge of each column (see Plate 9).³⁵ Normally these numbers are repeated in the margin beside the start of each sermon. In the final part of the manuscript the running heads consist of book-number centrally on both verso and recto, and book title at the extreme outer edge of verso and recto. The running heads in parts 1–3 and 5 of the manuscript are in the same hand as that of the initial list of contents, but those in section 4 seem to be in another hand. An early annotator has also been through the first folios of part 4 of the manuscript, adding at the outer upper corners of the folios a very brief précis of the material to be found below, but this rapidly becomes very fitful. That annotator may also have been the scribe who supplied the list of contents (fol. 2v, see Plate 6).

IV

The Trinity manuscript may be the most extensive witness to Wyclif's writings now in England, but what of its textual value? No final judgement can yet be made: three complete texts (items 6, 8, 11) and a large part of a fourth (item 12) have not yet appeared in critical editions, and of the remaining texts only four (items 1, 2, 5 and 10) have been critically edited from all known surviving copies in recent years. Trinity was used for the Wyclif Society editions of the remainder, but the nineteenth-century editors were ignorant of crucially important copies against which Trinity could be judged.[36] The verdict must therefore remain open, but a little can be said. In the first place the account of the manuscript above makes it less than surprising that the textual value of Trinity's copies varies from work to work: the piecemeal construction of parts 2–3 in itself suggests a multiplicity of exemplars. Equally, the chronological range of composition, from the early philosophical works to the final *Opus Evangelicum*, must suggest that, even had Trinity's immediate exemplar (improbably) been a single large manuscript, the textual history of the works that made it up cannot have been identical for all works.

Of the modern editors, subsequent to the Wyclif Society publications, who have worked with Trinity, S. Harrison Thomson in his edition of tracts 1–2 of the first part advances the rosiest view of its textual value. Comparing it with only a single other copy, Vienna, ÖNB, 4307, he observed 'I find this scribe [of Trinity] to have been as scrupulously careful as could reasonably be expected, and to have given us an exceedingly good text.'[37] Breck in his edition of the *De trinitate*, for which more manuscripts (albeit all of Bohemian origin) survive, was considerably more cautious: 'of uneven quality ... Often the scribe has failed completely to understand the material with which he is working'.[38] Most recently Mueller, with even more copies available, including three others of English origin, suggested that Trinity, together with the copy in Lincoln Cathedral, Chapter Library, MS 159, stand closest to Wyclif's original, but that, despite this, they should be regarded as 'at best representatives of the third generation of descent'.[39] As has been seen, *De universalibus* was added to the philosophical section of the manuscript at a stage after most of it had been completed; that the copy is not qualitatively the same as that of the *De trinitate* should not surprise.

Turning to those items in that philosophical section for which inadequate editions were produced by Dziewicki (items 3, 4, 7, 9 and part of 12), or for which no edition has yet been published (items 6, 8, 11 and the rest of 12), a few tentative comments may be made.[40] Firstly it is worth considering the relationship between Prague, National Library, IX.E.6 and Trinity: common material are items (7–9), and part of item (12) in Trinity. In Prague these tracts are in the order 7, 8, 12, 9. As explained above, it seems clear that the scribe of Trinity originally intended item (12) to follow item (8), and that the whole of quires 8–12 with their contents (items 9–11) was added after the writing of at least the start of item (12); in fact, since item 12 runs to the end of quire 14, there is no reason why that item should not have been completed before the writing of items (9–11). What immediately led the organizer of Trinity to insert items (9–11) is unclear. But cross references within Wyclif's own writings suggest that he was right to do so.[41] Despite the evidence concerning the original ordering of the tracts in Trinity, the relationship between its text and that of Prague does not seem to be particularly close.[42] In all four tracts Prague does not provide chapter-numbers, often omits any division between chapters, and even does not mark a new tract at the start of the *De sciencia dei* and the *De potencia productiva*. Also there are errors or gaps in each manuscript that are not reproduced in the other.[43] The two texts of *De volucione dei* seem to be more discrepant than the other three: Prague entirely omits chapters 9–10 (ed. pp. 202 line 16–221 line 22),[44] and also lacks the end of chapter 13 (ed. pp. 231 line 28–233 line 13), absences that cannot be explained by loss of leaves in the surviving manuscript.[45] On the other hand, some references are complete in Prague where they are incomplete in Trinity.[46] But equally a reference to Augustine's *De diversis quaestionibus 83* (garbled in Dziewicki's edition, p.128 line 20) is correctly to the 28th question in Trinity, but incorrect in Prague (fol. 59r to q. 20). In general it would seem that Trinity and Prague are not particularly close to each other in their texts.

The question also arises of the relation between the duplicate copies of the last section of the *De sciencia dei* in Trinity (fols 83 and 139), the second of which (as it now stands in the manuscript) was written first. In two cases the first copying was better than the second: a reference to Job

12 (Trinity fol. 139v^a and Prague fol. 50r) is correct against one to Job 13 (Trinity fol. 83v^a), actually Job 12:17; and one to 1 Cor. 12 (Trinity fol. 139v^b, Prague fol. 51r) is preferable to one to 1 Cor. 11 (Trinity fol. 83v^b). One oddity is worth noting: Trinity fol. 139v^b wrote *ponit distinctionem*, Prague fol. 51r *ponit* (gap) *hanc distinctionem*, but Trinity at its second writing fol. 83v^b has *ponit in terminis hanc distinctionem*. From this it would seem clear that the copy of this section made later but now standing first in the manuscript was not made from the earlier. In general, despite the two biblical references, the later copy seems better than the earlier, and certainly there are substantial differences between them.

The scholar who worked most extensively with Trinity was Loserth in his editions of the *Sermones* and of the *Opus Evangelicum*. His comments concerning the text of the former are largely unfavourable: 'the text is faulty, full of more or less serious blunders' ... 'sometimes we find such gross mistakes that we are led to doubt whether the scribe understood the meaning of the text'.[47] Loserth knew all the complete copies of the sanctorale sermons (vol. ii), and his judgement can be confirmed. Not only are there frequent defects, often omissions, in Trinity, but this copy lacks the headings specifying the feast days for each sermon; since the choice of lections depended upon the English Sarum rite, it seems probable that the headings found in the two Vienna manuscripts were inherited from an English exemplar better than Trinity.[48] A similar argument can be used in regard to the headings of the Sunday gospel and epistle sermons, found complete in Wolfenbüttel, Helmstedt, 565 (a copy unknown to Loserth) but almost entirely absent from Trinity.[49] This Bohemian manuscript would have allowed Loserth to improve considerably his edition of the epistle sermons, where he only had Trinity for all but four sermons.[50] Loserth, though apparently with some misgivings, followed at most points the order of the sermons in Trinity; in this he was unwise, though how unwise was concealed until more manuscripts came to light. The ending of the first three sets differs between extant copies, and this is not the right place to examine the issue of correctness. Trinity was a particularly unfortunate guide for the sermons which Loserth printed as volume iv, covering fols 307v^a–363r^b. These 64 sermons are presented in Trinity as a single sequence, without division or heading beyond a number.[51] From other copies, and from references in the fifteenth-century Hussite catalogues, it is clear that among this assemblage two separate groups can be distinguished, the early *Sermones Quadraginta* and the late *Sermones Viginti*.[52] In neither set are Trinity's readings very satisfactory.[53] It seems possible that the corrections to the numbers in the sanctorale group (see above p. 59) imply that a second exemplar was available at least when the changes were made.

Loserth knew the Dublin manuscript (TCD 242, *olim* C.1.23) in addition to Trinity for the *Opus Evangelicum*; he thought both had been copied from the same exemplar, that each had independent mistakes, but that the Dublin copy was generally more careful (i. v–vi).[54] Trinity, he also observed, omitted the whole of part III chapter 57, a chapter shown to be original by the sequence of biblical exegesis (the contents list on fol. 2v gives 72 chapters in part III, a number which corresponds with Trinity's omission in the text). Two further manuscripts of the text are now known, Vienna, ÖNB, 1647 and Prague, National Library, IV.A.18; it seems clear that both are closer to the Dublin copy than to Trinity, but are not descended from it.[55]

From all this detail a conclusion emerges that antecedently might seem surprising: Trinity's textual value, despite its early palaeographical date, is not high. Only in the *De ente in communi* and *De ente primo in communi* does it appear to be the best surviving copy, and then only against a single Bohemian manuscript dated 1433. Over a wide range of texts, texts whose antecedent history cannot have been identical, the Trinity scribes transmitted inferior versions. How far back in the textual history this inferiority goes will only be possible to assess when (if ever) all of the works have been critically edited to modern standards. But it is striking that, despite the fact that many scribes were involved in producing Trinity, the most characteristic fault, noted by Loserth repeatedly and by Breck, is careless omission, often by eyeskip, of phrases, sentences or even in *Opus Evangelicum* part iii a whole chapter.[56] Handsome in appearance Trinity may be, but this is hardly matched by accuracy of text.

V

Can anything be said about the origins of the manuscript? Neither scribe nor medieval owner added his name or affiliation to the volume.[57] Ian Doyle's keen eye picked out the form of the capital I used at the start of items or chapters in the opening sections of the manuscript as unusual, and perhaps characteristic of Oxford productions (see Plates 10 and 11).[58] Given the likely dating of Trinity's production around 1400, an Oxford origin would have seemed out of the question to scholars twenty years ago; but now, with the increasing acknowledgement of continuing interest in, and even loyalty towards, Wyclif's views in Oxford up to the end of the first decade of the fifteenth century, the possibility must be taken seriously.[59] Professional scribes with the competence to copy technical philosophical and theological works would probably have been readily available there, even if their efforts were not here above reproach;[60] it is striking that four of the eight scribes (3, 5, 6 and 7, of which only 3 could possibly have copied the two sections, now separated, consecutively) worked each two stints separated by material of some length, suggesting their availability over a period of time. Whether the necessary exemplars would have been available in Oxford is a question hard to answer. The *Opus Evangelicum* was composed at Lutterworth, but it, like the *Trialogus*, its *Supplementum* and some short works of the same origin, was available to the committee at Oxford who produced a list of condemned extracts from fourteen of Wyclif's texts in 1411.[61] As has been mentioned (p. 55), Canterbury College in 1443 possessed a copy of some at least of the sermons; but the scanty extant library lists, coupled with fifteenth-century suppression of Wyclif's works, make it hard to know whether they would have been available around 1400 when Trinity was in the making.[62]

Another intriguing question is the possibility that the Trinity volume was to be one of a complete corpus of Wyclif's works.[63] It is striking that Trinity does *not* contain any of the twelve books of the master's *Summa theologie*, nor the *De dominio divino* or *De eucharistia* that respectively form a prologue and an appendix to that whole; judging by the modern editions, these fourteen would, along with the *Dialogus*, *Trialogus* and its *Supplementum* require another two volumes the size of Trinity. This would still leave some early works leading in to the *Summa Theologie*, the shorter, mostly polemical writings, and the whole of the *Postilla in totam Bibliam* – perhaps another two volumes. This may be to envisage too grandiose a scheme; but the presence in Trinity of major sequences from Wyclif's early and late career, but almost nothing from the middle, suggests that the volume might not have been intended to stand on its own. Absence of those middle period works cannot be the result of avoidance of heretical material – the censured ideas are present in the *Sermones* and *Opus Evangelicum*, even if less fully argued. No trace of any such further volumes survives.

The nearest analogy in size and layout to Trinity are the fragments of a manuscript found as binding leaves in another Trinity College Cambridge manuscript, O.4.43; but, even from the tiny proportion of the whole that survives, it is clear that this was not exclusively a Wyclif collection.[64] Lincoln Cathedral, Chapter Library, MS 159 part 3 is of similar format, containing copies of *De universalibus* and *De tempore*; whether this section was originally part of a larger Wyclif whole, let alone whether that whole contained any of the more obviously controversial works, is irrecoverable.[65] Neither of the Wyclif manuscripts now in Dublin, albeit that they include some of these controversial works, is of a format of anything like the splendour of Trinity.[66] Even more of a working copy is Cambridge, Gonville and Caius College, MS 337/565.[67] This last certainly derives from Oxford: it was owned by Henry Bryt, fellow of Queen's in 1403–4, John Mychel, probably connected with Exeter College in 1403, and John Gosele.[68] Its contents are entirely Wyclif: *De universalibus*, *De tempore* (now a fragment: only the initial analysis survives), *De composicione hominis*, *De dominio divino*, *De benedicta incarnacione*, *De mandatis*, *De statu innocentie* – an interesting but unattributed collection of works from the early middle period of Wyclif's life, with a large amount of marginal notation.[69] If Trinity B.16.2 is indeed of Oxford origin, no more striking contrast could be found than this between the scholars' working copy now at Caius and the presentation style of Trinity. But, as so often in Wyclif studies, the available proof here of provenance falls short of the modern investigator's desire.

Notes

1. Ian Doyle's contribution to this chapter will be apparent in the suggestions directly attributed to him, but its extent as usual far exceeds these; my gratitude is great, but he should not be blamed for my misunderstandings or misinterpretations of his comments. I should also like to thank Dr Malcolm Parkes for discussion of the problems in the manuscript, and the editors for suggesting numerous improvements to the first version of this paper.
2. The most complete description is by M. R. James, *The Western Manuscripts in the Library of Trinity College Cambridge* i (Cambridge, 1900), 513–15. Other descriptions appear in the editions of individual works, for which see above, pp. 56–61.
3. The folio numerations given in the editions of the various works in the manuscript, and in other material relating to it, all differ in varying degrees from this and from each other according as the editors followed or partially corrected one of the numbering systems entered more fully in the manuscript; discrepancies have not been noted here. The editions of Wyclif's works are, unless otherwise indicated, those published by the Wyclif Society (WS) (1883–1921).
4. James i. 514 prints this list.
5. Quires 3 and 7 are both marked *f*; quire 8 is marked *h*, quire 13 *n* (allowing for quires 9–12 as *j-m*); all these are in plummet. Quires 23–4 are signed *g* and *h* respectively in ink (signatures which puzzlingly do not allow for all the previous quires in section 4); quire 32 (a supplementary

quire) is signed *a* in plummet.
6. James i. 515.
7. See M. B. Parkes, *English Cursive Book Hands 1250–1500* (Oxford, 1969), plates 5(i) and (ii), 7(ii) and 17(i).
8. See M. B. Parkes, 'The Provision of Books' in *The History of the University of Oxford, ii: Late Medieval Oxford*, ed. J. I. Catto and R. Evans (Oxford, 1992), pp. 407–83 at p. 417; the present manuscript is not mentioned in this chapter.
9. James pp. viii, xxii; James in *The Ancient Libraries of Canterbury and Dover* (Cambridge, 1903) gives details about the Christ Church holdings, and the surviving books are listed in N. R. Ker, *Medieval Libraries of Great Britain* (London, 2nd edn 1964), pp. 29–40. The Manuscript Cataloguer at Trinity College, Jonathan Smith, very generously gave me the information that Neville's arms are combined with those of Bulmer and of Alban of Middleham.
10. See the inventory of William Thornden, taken when he entered office as Warden in 1459, item 23 with the second folio *methaphisicis* (W. A. Pantin, *Canterbury College Oxford* i (Oxford Historical Society, new series vi, 1947), p. 12 item 23). This is identifiable with *Sermones* i.4/6. Even if the section of the Trinity manuscript containing the *Sermones* ever stood alone, its second folio incipit would have been *voluntatem* (on eras.) *dei* (*Sermones* i. 12/12 see variant for this reading). Since the name of R[obert] Lynton is appended to the entry in the inventory, the book probably came to Canterbury College by his gift; Lynton was Warden from 1443–8.
11. References are given following 'Th.' to the numbers in W. R. Thomson, *The Latin Writings of John Wyclyf* (Toronto, 1983), and following 'c.' to the initial contents list in the manuscript, by the scribe's section and number the title in that list agrees with that in the text unless otherwise noted). To save space the incipits and explicits of each text are not repeated here unless they differ from those printed in Thomson; indication is, however, given of any title or attribution.
12. Notice of the Vienna MS, and a text of its chapters 2–3 as far as the end of the loss in Trinity, was provided by S. H. Thomson, 'A "Lost" Chapter of Wyclif's *Summa de Ente*', *Speculum*, iv (1929), 339–46.
13. Though Dziewicki observed this (see his note p. 57), he ran the text straight on as if nothing were lost, and inserted at p. 58 l ne 9 a heading for chapter 2 which is without justification in the manuscript. In fact chapter 2 can be proved to have begun on the recto of the lost leaf since on the remaining stub part of the red flourishing that surrounded the opening letter can still be seen.
14. As noted by I. H. Stein, 'Another "Lost" Chapter of Wyclif's *Summa de Ente*', *Speculum*, viii (1933), 254–5, though the edition there promised of the material missing in Trinity from items (7) and (9) seems never to have appeared.
15. Despite the title given, which is repeated in the abbreviated running titles, the text is described as *tractatu[s] de trinitate* in cross references in, for instance, *De universalibus* p. 40 line 319 or p. 86 line 32.
16. There are cross references to *tractatus de Anichilacione* in *De eucaristia* p. 52 line 11, in *De benedicta incarnacione* pp. 76 line 18, 78 line 30, and in *De statu innocencie* p. 476 line 6; none of these specifies a chapter and hence are useless for the limits of the tract.
17. In this manuscript the sermons printed by Loserth at the end of this set (Th.112–14) come later: see below item (15).
18. I have considered the composition of the *Sermones miscellanei* in 'Aspects of the "Publication" of Wyclif's Latin Sermons', in *Late-Medieval Religious Texts and their Transmission*, ed. A. J. Minnis (Woodbridge, 1994), pp. 121–9, and hope to elucidate other obscurities in the transmission of all four sets of sermons in Trinity elsewhere.
19. The running head on fol. 139r is *De potencia productiva dei ad extra*, the title of the work that actually begins on fol. 139v^b, that on fol. 139v *Tractatus sextus*.
20. The text breaks off two-thirds of the way down a verso leaf, almost at the end of chapter 2, = Trinity fol. 141r^b nine lines from the end of that chapter.

21. See below section IV for the question of the relationship between the Prague and Trinity copies.
22. See numerous cross-references to *De volucione dei* as tract 3 (e.g. *De ente predicamentali* pp. 156 line 13, 178 line 34), to *De ydeis* as tract 5 (in *De sciencia dei* Trinity fol. 77v^b); there seems to be no tract number given in references to the *De trinitate* nor to *De potencia productiva dei ad extra*.
23. There is an alteration to this list of contents concerning tract 4 of book I, though it seems doubtful whether it is significant: the scribe first wrote *Quartus de vniuersalibus et continet*, then struck through the last two words and continued *incompletus et continet 5 capitula*. Tract 5 is described as *de vniuersalibus completus*.
24. This is implied somewhat obscurely by Mueller in his edition of *De universalibus*, pp. xxxii–xxxiii.
25. Fol. 46v ends *cum quantitas non sit mag*, the original catchword has been erased and *magnitudo* written rather messily by a hand different from the main hand on either fol. 46v or fol. 47, and fol. 47 begins *magnitudo set ipsa est passio*.
26. The possibility that fol. 46 was itself originally the lost leaf 6 of quire 2, and that the stub with its two words was therefore originally leaf 1 of that quire seems unlikely. Unfortunately, the material missing from item (4), *Purgans errores circa universalia in communi*, because of that loss, printed from the Vienna manuscript by Harrison Thomson (1929, above n. 12), does offer a possible opportunity for these two words at p. 345 line 25 – equally, this is at about the right place of the text in relation to the position of the marginal words, though, as with the alternative explanation above, it is not an exact correspondence. But the identity of hand between fol. 46 and that of the now immediately preceding *De universalibus*, together with the fact that quire 2 lacks not one but three leaves at its end, makes this a less probable suggestion.
27. Ed. R. Beer (WS London, 1891), see his partial description of the Vienna manuscript pp. v–ix.
28. See Mueller (1985), p. lxiii. The comments regarding the Vienna manuscript in J. A. Robson, *Wyclif and the Oxford Schools* (Cambridge, 1966), p. 126 seem to be based on a misreading of Beer: that the manuscript belongs together, and cannot be split between a part containing the *De universalibus* and the remainder, is shown by the alternating stints of the two scribes (Mueller p. lxii).
29. Beer pp. viii–ix.
30. Judging by S. Harrison Thomson's editions of items (1-2), one whole folio of Vienna corresponds roughly to one side of Trinity; *De ente predicamentali* is fols 190v–242v in Vienna. There are a large number of spaces left in the text (fols 199v–200r, 203r–v, 207v–208r, 217v, 232v), suggesting that the scribe felt his exemplar to be obscure or untrustworthy.
31. See Breck p. 166, alluding to *De ente predicamentali* pp. 15ff.
32. The 'bridging in' of the two intact quires could have been difficult: if the start of *De ente predicamentali* had been on original fol. 20, then three leaves would have needed to be supplied, whereas quire 5 only had one leaf probably blank (fol. 58). Certainly, by the time the list of contents was made, any trace of the text had been suppressed.
33. See Robson pp. 129–30, Mueller pp. xxii–xxxviii, the latter of which should be taken to modify S. H. Thomson, 'The Order of Writings of Wyclif's Philosophical Works', in *Českou minulostí práce, věnované profesoru Karlovy university Václavu Novotnému*, ed. O. Odložilík, J. Prokeš and R. Urbánek (Prague, 1929), pp. 146–65 and the dates in Thomson (1983), nos 11 and 12. See also J. I. Catto in *The History of the University of Oxford, ii: Late Medieval Oxford* (Oxford, 1992), pp. 188–92.
34. See Thomson p. 27, referring to Vienna, ÖNB, 4316 fol. 108v; the reference is also found in this form in at least nine other manuscripts of *De tempore* (I have checked all but the Krakow, Stockholm, and Venice MSS).
35. In the vast majority of cases no occasion is entered for any sermon (despite the appearance of this information in the contents lists provided by Loserth's edition); the only exceptions to this are in the cases of Thomson nos 71–3, 75, 176–82, 195, 199–200 (14 out of 244 sermons).

36. Notably Vienna, ÖNB, 4307 in the case of items (3–4), Prague, National Library, IX.E.6 in the case of (7), (9) and (12), and the two Wolfenbüttel manuscripts of the sermons.
37. Ed. cit. p. xiii; cf. Thomson's view of the Vienna copy (p. xv) 'a vastly inferior text'.
38. Ed. cit. p. xix.
39. Ed. cit. p. lxxxv.
40. S. H. Thomson corrected a few readings of Dziewicki's edition of item (4) from Vienna, ÖNB, 4307 in 'A "Lost" Chapter of Wyclif's *Summa de ente*', *Speculum*. iv (1929), 339–46 at p. 346; more cases could certainly be found.
41. See above n. 22.
42. Prague's text of the *De potencia productiva dei ad extra*, item (12) in Trinity, ends before the extract edited by Dziewicki from Trinity begins.
43. Thus in *De intelleccione dei* 81 line 6 T[rinity]'s reading (garbled by the edition) omits by eyeskip a reference to Aristotle's *De anima*, whilst P[rague] has the number needed at 110 line 11; in the *De sciencia dei* T is incorrect (fol. 75r^a) in its reference to *ad Ro.5* against P's correct *ad Ro.xj* (fol. 33v), actually Rom. 11:33, but P leaves a gap (fol. 41r) after *non prioritate* not found in T (fol. 78v^b) *non prioritate conuenit*; in *De potencia productiva* T's reference fol. 142r^b to Augustine's *De civitate dei* book 10 chapter 31 is correct against P's fol. 55v to book 15 chapter 13, but at T fol. 139v^b eyeskip has produced a nonsensical passage where a reference to Duns Scotus, *doctor subtilis*, commentary on *Sentences* I d.43 has been omitted (P fol. 51r).
44. This absence could be related to the fact that the material appears as caps 17–18 of *De ente predicamentali* (pp. 157 line 6–178 line 34), a text only found in Vienna, ÖNB, 4307.
45. The absent material should have started in the middle of fol. 76r and two lines from the bottom of fol. 83v respectively.
46. E.g. T p. 185 line 24 reference simply to Augustine *De doctrina christiana* book 2, where P, fol. 72r, supplies chapter 32; T p. 189 line 36 reference just to *Matthew*, where P fol. 73r correctly adds chapter 26.
47. *Sermones* i. xxxvi; cf iii. iv.
48. See Loserth's variants to ii. 5 line 3–4, 7 line 17, 8 line 19–20 etc. The other copies are Vienna, ÖNB, 3928 and 3931.
49. They are found fitfully but not at identical places in Vienna, ÖNB, 4529 and 3934 of the Sunday gospel sermons; in the Sunday epistle sermons Wolfenbüttel, Helmstedt 306, again unknown to Loserth, has them more partially. Trinity differs from the three continental copies in lacking the preface to set 1.
50. Nos 5–7 and 10 were available to him in TCD 242, and his variants for those sermons show how often this corrected Trinity. Wolfenbüttel 306, and the limited evidence of Prague, National Library, III.B.19 for Th.200–234, 235–6, 184–5 (see my review of Thomson, *Journal of Ecclesiastical History*, xxxv (1984), 629), confirm the inferiority of Trinity for this set.
51. 1–58 are sequentially numbered, but then follows one (Th.293) without a number, then one numbered again 58, 59–60, and finally two unnumbered sermons.
52. Vienna 3928 contains both sets, but as separate items, fols 193r^a–253r^b and 139r^a–185r^a respectively, the second in differing order. See above n. 18 and W. Mallard, 'Dating the *Sermones Quadraginta* of John Wyclif', *Medievalia et Humanistica*, xvii (1966), 86–105. The Hussite catalogues are printed in *Polemical Works*, ed. R. Buddensieg (WS London, 1883) i. lix–lxxxiv.
53. Again continental copies preserve some occasion headings which are likely to go back to the original; see also Loserth's variants to these sermons.
54. This judgement seems fair: see variants to i. 69 line 6 and 103 line 27 for Trinity in the right against Dublin, but 85 line 36–7, 88 line 23–4, 95 line 36–7 for Trinity's frequent eye-skip omissions.
55. For instance, all three lack Trinity's errors at i. 53 line 22, 220 line 9, 221 line 37, ii. 147 line 36, 291 lines 19–21, but the Hussite copies have the passage lost in Dublin at ii. 312 lines 10–14; both these copies have the chapter missing from Trinity. The Prague copy lacks all chapter

numbers, and both (as noted by Loserth i. vi for the two English copies) appear to have discrepancies over chapter division and order.
56. Chapters 55–63 inclusive all begin with the words 'Sequitur in textu Matthei', though the ends of each chapter should have made the error avoidable.
57. The only medieval scribble is on the penultimate leaf, b^3, 'Esto pedana mee calige pars, sine numella, Inde pedanabo caligas vel fune ligabo'.
58. The capital is triangular, resembling a capital in vernacular manuscripts; the space left by the scribes at these points anticipated the triangular shape. Doyle noted its use also in Bodleian MS Bodley 716, the copy of Wyclif's *Postilla* (Th.345-71) that belonged to Bury St. Edmunds; see A. G. Watson, *Catalogue of Dated and Datable Manuscripts c.435–1600 in Oxford Libraries* (Oxford, 1984), i. 20–1 and ii. plate 248. It also occurs in Oxford, Oriel College, MS 15, containing amongst other works Wyclif's *De benedicta incarnacione* and Oxford, New College, MS 134, both Oxford productions.
59. The earlier view is typified by the comments of K. B. McFarlane, *John Wycliffe and the Beginnings of English Nonconformity* (London, 1952), pp. 115–16, 126, 156–7, 183–4; for more recent modifications see my *The Premature Reformation* (Oxford, 1988), pp. 60–119, and J. I. Catto, 'Wyclif and Wycliffism at Oxford 1356–1430', in *The History of the University of Oxford, ii: Late Medieval Oxford*, (Oxford, 1992), pp. 175–261.
60. See M. B. Parkes 'The Provision of Books', ibid., pp. 407–83.
61. See D. Wilkins, *Concilia Magnae Britanniae et Hiberniae A.D. 446–1717* (London, 1737), iii. 339–49; some of the working materials are in Oxford, Magdalen College, MS 99, fols. 176r–8v, 257r–61v.
62. See *Premature Reformation* pp. 84–5 for known Oxford copies.
63. For the possibility of a comparable scheme manifested by a group of continental manuscripts (to which should be added Vienna, ÖNB, 1341) see my review of Thomson (above n. 50) p. 630.
64. Described by F. A. C. Mantello, 'The Endleaves of Trinity College Cambridge MS O.4.43 and John Wyclif's *Responsiones ad argumenta cuiusdam emuli veritatis*', *Speculum*, liv (1979), 100–103; the Wyclif text is preceded by the end of a letter of Grosseteste. The leaf size of the surviving fragments is *c.* 295 mm by 220 mm but the top of each leaf has been cut off.
65. See R. M. Thomson, *Catalogue of the Manuscripts of Lincoln Cathedral Chapter Library* (Cambridge, 1989), pp. 127–9; leaf size is *c.* 395 mm. by 280 mm.; the two items are in separate sets of quires but a medieval hand has been through numbering the quires of the whole volume thus showing that the present book must have been assembled early; *pace* Thomson, the two Wyclif items seem not certainly in the same hand.
66. TCD 242 and 243, see M. L. Colker, *Trinity College Library Dublin: Descriptive Catalogue of the Mediaeval and Renaissance Latin Manuscripts* (Aldershot, 1991), i. 433–7.
67. See M. R. James, *A Descriptive Catalogue of the Manuscripts in the Library of Gonville and Caius College* (Cambridge, 1907–8), i. 380–1, and more fully S. H. Thomson, 'A Gonville and Caius Wyclif Manuscript', *Speculum*, viii (1933), 197–204.
68. For the first two see A. B. Emden, *A Biographical Register of the University of Oxford to A.D. 1500* (Oxford, 1957–9), i. 294, ii. 1332; Thomson (art. cit. above) seems not to have been aware of the ownership.
69. The first two items form a single group of quires, with the analysis of *De tempore* breaking off at the end of quire 4, and each of the following items is in a separable group of quires; all groups of quires are in different, though similar, hands, apart from the possible reappearance of the hand of the analysis at the start of *De composicione hominis*; the parchment throughout is of the brownish Oxford type.

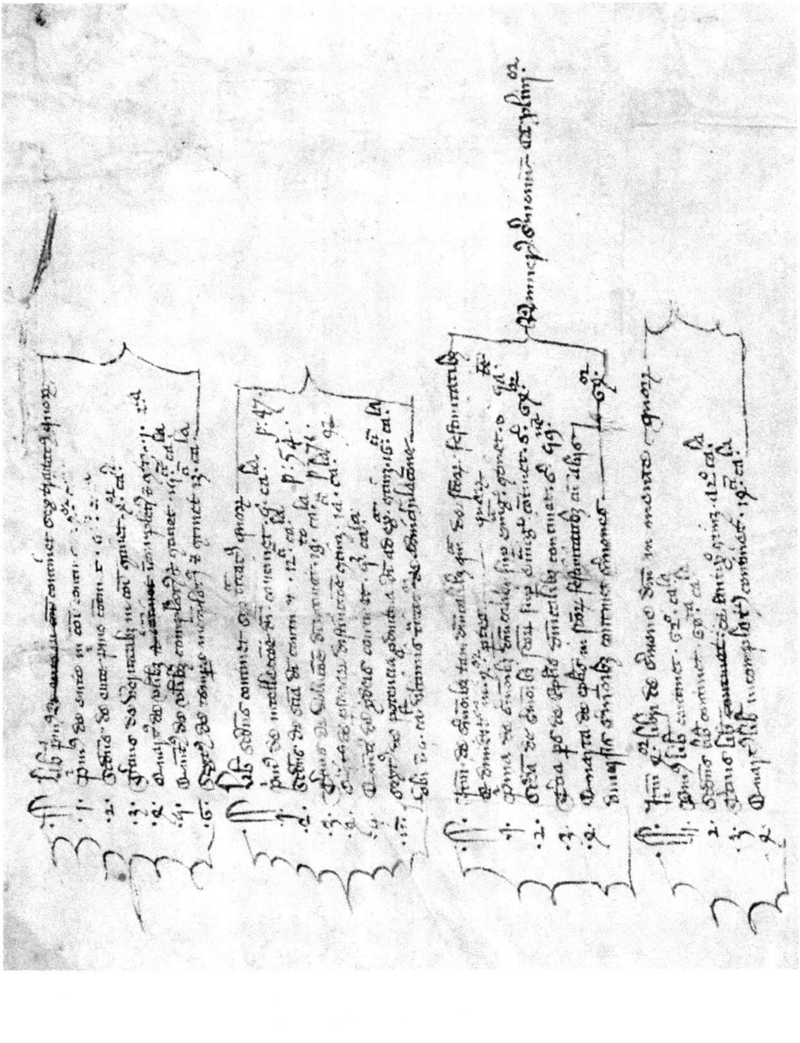

VIII

Wyclif's works, Trinity College MS B.16.2   75

PLATE 6   Cambridge, Trinity College MS B.16.2, fol. 2v, top half (reduced).

PLATE 7 Cambridge, Trinity College MS B.16.2, fol. 108r, top third (reduced).

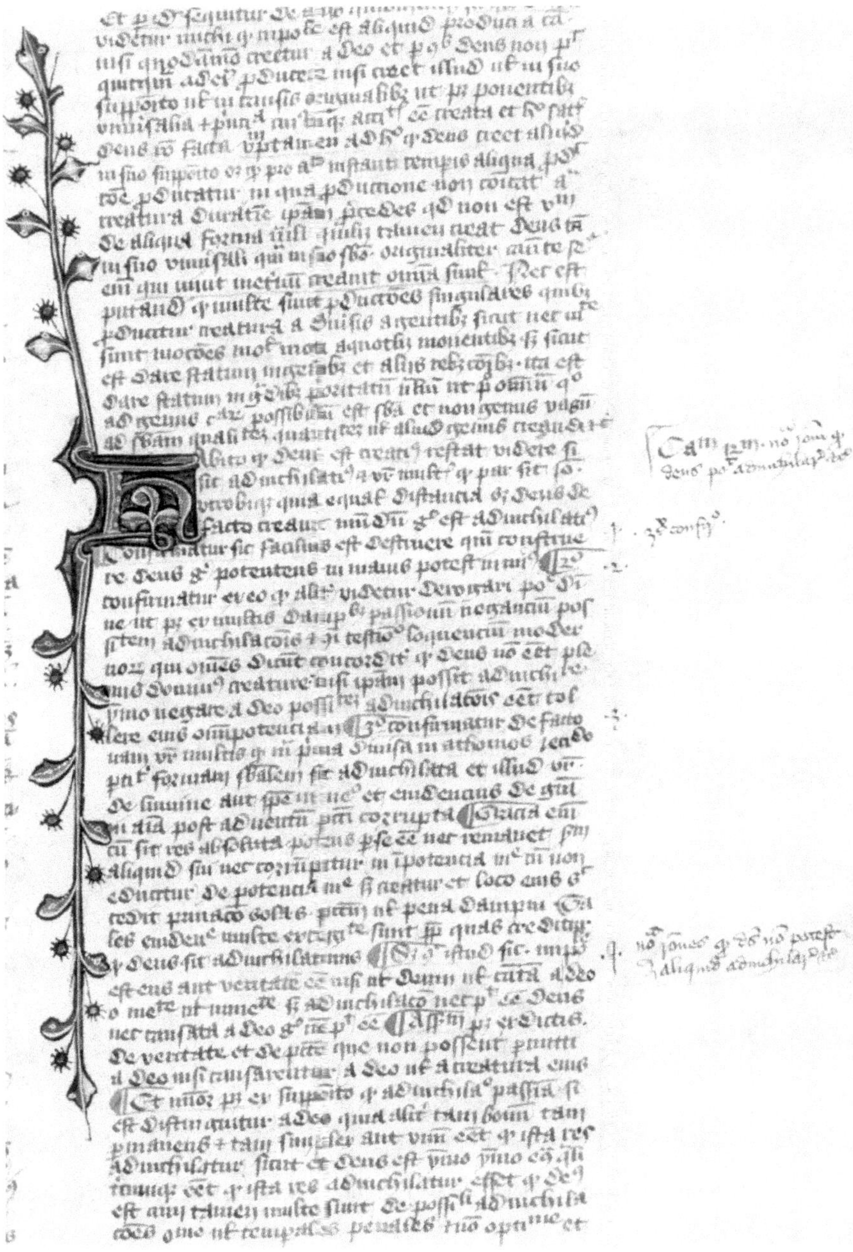

PLATE 8   Cambridge, Trinity College MS B.16.2, fol. 151r, lower half of col. b (reduced).

VIII

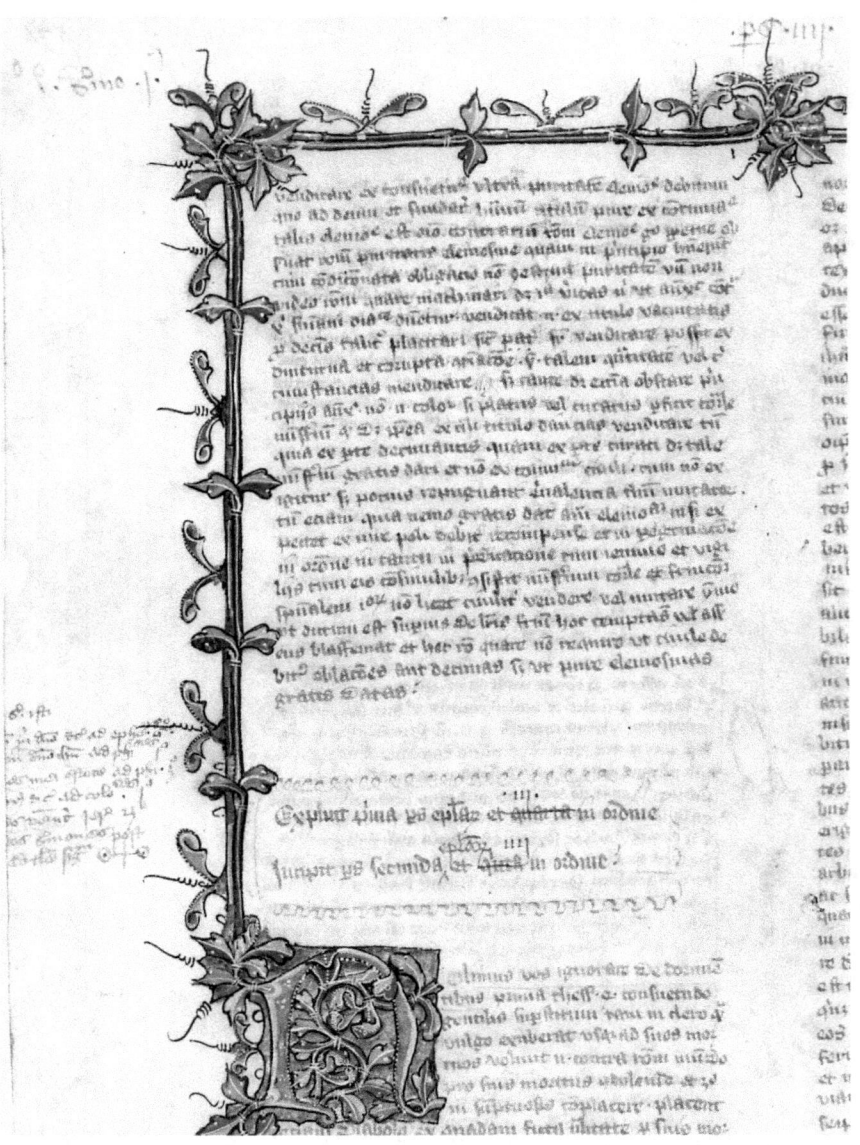

PLATE 9   Cambridge, Trinity College MS B.16.2, fol. 307v, upper half of col. a (reduced).

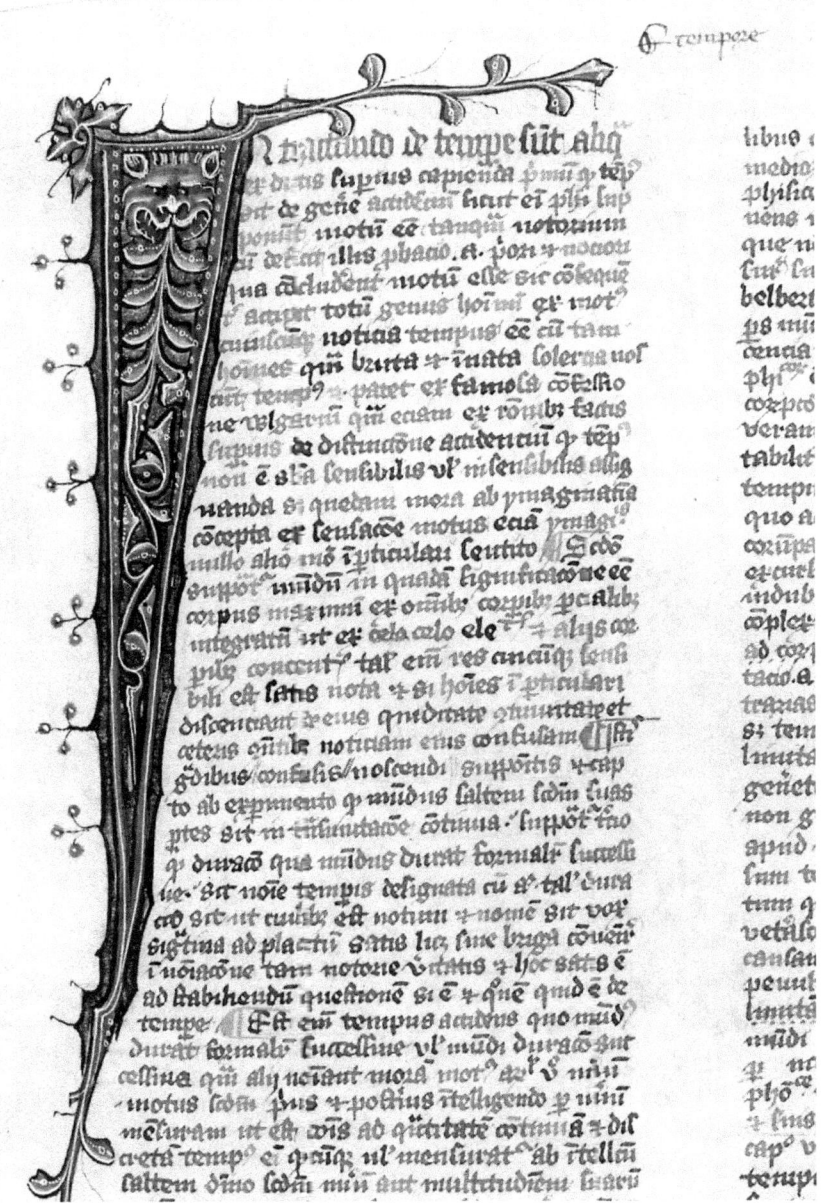

PLATE 10 Cambridge, Trinity College, MS B.16.2, fol. 46r, upper portion of col. a (reduced).

PLATE 11 Cambridge, Trinity College, MS B.16.2, fol. 23v, lower portion of col. b (reduced).

IX

WYCLIF AND THE NORTH: THE EVIDENCE FROM DURHAM

THE present-day hamlet of Wycliffe stands on a small spit of level ground on the south bank of the river Tees, some seven miles east of Barnard Castle, at a point where the north bank rises in a high cliff; the churchyard stretches almost to the river bank. The claim that John Wyclif takes his name from the village cannot, unless further documentation is discovered, be finally proved; but it seems a reasonable one. Robert Wyclif, a clerk in the diocese of York, acted on behalf of John in 1371 in regard to tithes from an alien priory granted to the latter by the king, and again in 1376 to pay part of the annates claimed by the papal collector Arnald Garnier for the prebend of Caistor, a prebend from which Wyclif was displaced by the appointment of the papal provisor Philip Thornbury.[1] Robert was presumably a relation, perhaps John's nephew, and was a well-documented figure in the York and Durham dioceses up to his death in 1423, when his will included gifts to the church and poor of Wycliffe; his most notable position was that of chancellor and receiver-general for bishop Walter Skirlaw of Durham between 1390 and 1405.[2] Another Wyclif, with the Christian name of William, was rector of Wycliffe from 1363 to at least 1365, when he was granted a licence to study at Oxford for two years; this was at least William's second visit to the University, since he is recorded as a fellow at Balliol in 1361.[3] Confusingly, two John Wyclifs were ordained simultaneously to the orders of subdeacon, deacon, and priest at three ceremonies between March and September 1351, one the son of William 'de Wykliff' and the other the son of 'Simon de

---

[1] See PRO E159/147 and for the second W. E. Lunt and E. B. Graves, *Accounts rendered by Papal Collectors in England, 1317–1378* = Memoirs of the American Philosophical Society, 70, (Philadelphia, 1968), p. 504.

[2] For Robert see H. B. Workman, *John Wyclif*, 2 vols (Oxford, 1926), 1, pp. 45–8; the will is partly printed in J. Raine, ed., *Wills and Inventories ... of the Northern Counties*, 1, SS, 2 (1835), pp. 66–8, and partly in L. Baker, ed., *Testamenta Eboracensia*, 1, SS, 4 (1836), pp. 403–5.

[3] See Emden, *Oxford*, 3, p. 2106; York Reg. Thoresby, 11, fol. 291v.

Wycliff'.[4] At the last occasion both were presented on the title of Egglestone Abbey, a title also recorded for the first when he was ordained deacon (at which point the second was presented on the title of Kirklees). The precise significance that should be attached to these titles is unclear, but Robert Swanson has suggested that 'certain houses were being designated to provide titles in particular localities'.[5] If this is correct, then Egglestone, a Premonstratensian abbey, may confirm the connection of John Wyclif with this area: the abbey is some five miles west of Wycliffe, on the south side of the Tees, nearer to Barnard Castle.

Wyclif travelled south to Oxford about the time of his ordination or slightly before; he is first recorded as steward at Merton College in 1356, by which time he was a probationary fellow. But his election as Master of Balliol by December 1360 makes it possible that his first affiliation as a student had been to that college, a northern foundation which maintained close connections with the York diocese.[6] After this, however, it is difficult to trace any direct connections between Wyclif and the area from which he came, even though Robert's assistance may suggest that he did not entirely lose touch with it. John's most northerly living was that of Fillingham, a benefice in Balliol's gift, to which he was promoted by the college in 1361; Fillingham, in the diocese of Lincoln, is some nine miles north of the cathedral city.[7] In 1362 preferment as canon of York was requested for him by Oxford University; this was not granted, and a canonry at Westbury on Trym, near Bristol, was given instead.[8] Thereafter Wyclif's life was concentrated in Oxford and London, until his retirement to his final cure at Lutterworth, following the 1381 furore over his eucharistic teaching.

If Wyclif lost touch with the north, however, some in his home

---

[4] York Reg. Zouche, 10A, fols 50v-51r, 52r, 53r; one was ordained as acolyte on 18 Dec. 1350 (ibid., fol. 49v).

[5] R. N. Swanson, 'Titles to orders in Medieval English episcopal registers', in H. Mayr-Harting and R. I. Moore, eds, *Studies in Medieval History presented to R. H. C. Davis* (London, 1985), pp. 233-45 at p. 242; compare J. A. Hoeppner Moran, 'Clerical recruitment in the Diocese of York, 1340-1530: data and commentary', *JEH*, 34 (1983), pp. 19-54 at pp. 30-1.

[6] Merton Record 3690, and 4.16, p. 12; Balliol Archives E.1.38b; for Balliol's early northern associations see J. Catto, 'The first century of Balliol men, 1260-1360' in J. Prest, ed., *Balliol Studies* (London, 1982), pp. 3-16, and J. Jones, *Balliol College: a History, 1263-1939* (Oxford, 1988), pp. 1-20.

[7] Lincoln Reg. Gynewell 9, fol. 172r.

[8] *Calendar of Entries in the Papal Registers Relating to Great Britain and Ireland: Petitions to the Pope, A.D.1342-1419*, ed. W. H. Bliss (London, 1896), 1, pp. 390, 392.

Wyclif and the North

territory retained, or discovered, an interest in him. The Tees at Wycliffe formed the medieval boundary between the dioceses of York and Durham, and it is at Durham that concern about Wyclif can be traced for some time in the last part of the fourteenth and into the following century. The cathedral priory had, of course, a house in Oxford for its students, Durham College, and it will emerge below that in at least one case this can be shown to have been the route through which information about Wyclif and his ideas was transmitted; it was probably the regular pathway.[9] The simplest evidence of this interest consists in the copies of Wyclif's texts that derive from Durham. Even though the proportion of Durham books to have been preserved is unusually high, the fact that three codices with Wyclif texts survive from Durham is remarkable: many of his writings do not survive in any manuscript of English origin, and no other religious house can be associated with more than one surviving manuscript.[10] Perhaps the simplest of these manuscripts is that, now Jesus College Cambridge 59, in which, on folios 140v-144v, is a copy of Wyclif's *De eucharistia minor confessio*; on folio 10 is the note 'de communi libraria monachorum dunelm'. The text here is in the shorter form in which it appears in all English copies, is not dated, but concludes with the colophon by the scribe of this text 'Confessio Wicklyf'.[11] The volume as a whole consists of a copy of William of Paris's *De fide et legibus*, together with a series of short texts and extracts; in the medieval list of contents on folio 1v the colophon is expanded 'Confessio Joh' Wyclyff

---

[9] See R. B. Dobson, *Durham Priory: 1400–1450* (Cambridge, 1973), pp. 343–59, and more briefly idem, 'The Black Monks of Durham and Canterbury Colleges: comparisons and contrasts', in H. Wansbrough and A. Marett-Crosby, eds, *Benedictines in Oxford* (London, 1997), pp. 61–78; for the library see A. E. Coates, 'The Library of Durham College, Oxford', *Library History*, 8, no. 5 (1990), pp. 125–31.

[10] For the survival of Wyclif's texts see W. R. Thomson, *The Latin Writings of John Wyclyf* (Toronto, 1983), though some corrections and additions are needed; medieval ownership of some English copies can be traced in N. R. Ker, ed., *Medieval Libraries of Great Britain: a List of Surviving Books*, 2nd edn (London, 1964), and A. G. Watson, ed., *Supplement* (London, 1987).

[11] Thomson, *Latin Writings*, no. 39 lists the other copies; only that in MS Bodley 703, where it appears alongside anti-Wyclif texts by William Woodford, is dated to 10 May 1381, and it is from there that the dating in *Fasciculi Zizaniorum* (ed. W. W. Shirley, RS, [1858], pp. 115–32, at p. 115 n. 2) is taken. The shorter version of the *Confessio* consists of statements found in exactly the same form in Wyclif's *De apostasia*, ed. M. H. Dziewicki, WS (1889); whether the shorter text should be regarded as extracts from the longer, or as an earlier statement subsequently incorporated in it, is not clear. The longer version, which survives only in Hussite copies, was printed by I. H. Stein, 'An unpublished fragment of Wyclif's *Confessio*', *Speculum*, 8 (1933), pp. 503–10.

IX

de sacramento altaris'.¹² Though the date of copying is not specified within the manuscript, the book was present in the library at Durham by 1395: it is identifiable from the *secunda folio* wording in the list of the *Libraria claustralis* taken in that year.¹³

The *Confessio* is a short text. More substantial evidence for interest in Wyclif is the copy, now incomplete because of the loss of the final quires, of his *Sermones quadraginta*, now Lambeth Palace Library MS 23.¹⁴ This is a large and, even in its defective state, imposing volume with five items, listed in two medieval hands on the front pastedown: Alexander Nequam's commentary on the Song of Songs (folios 1ra–143vb), the Lenten sermons of *Ianuensis* (folios 144ra–198vb), a set of *distinctiones* attributed to *Cistrensis* (folios 199ra–250ra), the opening entries of Bromyard's *Opus trivium* (folios 250ra–251vb), and 'sermones Magistri Johanni Wiclyf ad simplices sacerdotes satis catholici'.¹⁵ These final sermons begin on folio 258ra and end at the foot of folio 280vb in number 28 of the forty;¹⁶ the quiring because of a very tight modern binding is not absolutely clear, but a new quire of twelve leaves probably begins with folio 258, and a second, also of twelve, survives minus its final leaf; rubbing and creasing on folio 280v suggest that the book was unbound for some time. But, although this might suggest that the Wyclif material is a separable booklet, immediately before it, from folios 252ra to 257vb, are medieval indexes to the four complete items of the volume; that to Wyclif's sermons is on folios 256rb–257ra, headed 'Incipit tabula sermonum Wycliff', and it is followed by the index to the third item.¹⁷ The

---

¹² See the list of contents in M. R. James, *A Descriptive Catalogue of the Manuscripts in the Library of Jesus College Cambridge* (London, 1895), pp. 93–4; the list, including this item, is partly repeated in the margins of fol. 2r in another medieval hand. There are two scribes, the Wyclif text being in that which also wrote fols 2r–9v and 140r–151r.

¹³ *Catalogi veteres librorum ecclesiae cath. Dunelm.*, ed. J. Raine, SS (1838), p. 72, 'intelligitur' – this is now fol. 3 of MS Jesus College 59.

¹⁴ See M. R. James, *A Descriptive Catalogue of the Manuscripts in the Library of Lambeth Palace* (Cambridge, 1932), I, 37–9; the sermons were edited by J. Loserth, *Iohannis Wyclif Sermones*, 4, WS (1890), pp. 197–492.

¹⁵ For the first text see F. Stegmüller, *Repertorium biblicum medii aevi*, 2 (Madrid, 1950), no. 1168; the second is listed without mention of this manuscript by J. B. Schneyer, *Repertorium der Lateinischen Sermones des Mittelalters*, 3 (Münster, 1971), pp. 238–46; *Cistrensis* is Ranulph Higden, and the text is mentioned by J. Taylor, *The 'Universal Chronicle' of Ranulf Higden* (Oxford, 1966), p. 184; for Bromyard's work see L. E. Boyle, 'The date of the *Summa praedicantium* of John Bromyard', *Speculum*, 48 (1973), pp. 533–7, reprinted in *Pastoral Care, Clerical Education and Canon Law, 1200–1400* (London, 1981).

¹⁶ See Loserth, *Sermones*, p. 397/3, 'et adulter lex'.

¹⁷ Even if the order of the indexes may indicate the original ordering of the texts (a

Wyclif and the North

Wyclif index uses sermon numbers and subdividing letters a–m; these subdividing letters are entered in the margins of the sermons themselves, and the sermon numbers appear in the outer margins beside the start of each. All the evidence therefore suggests that the four items belonged together from an early stage.

Evidence for Durham ownership is as unequivocal as in the case of Jesus College 59: it consists primarily in the medieval pressmark '$1^a.5^{li}$.M' found on the front pastedown, a typical Durham form and accepted by Neil Ker.[18] M. R. James identified the bishop within the capital on folio 1 as St Cuthbert holding the head of King Oswald.[19] The indexing of all four items certainly corresponds with the Durham concern for such methods of access. The date of the manuscript seems on paleographical evidence to be c.1400. It is interesting that, as in Jesus 59, Wyclif's text is attributed – here in the list of contents and at the start of the index, though not at the start of the text itself. 'Satis catholici' in the list of contents may indicate an awareness that certain other works by the same author might not be so described.

More interesting than either of these is the copy of three chapters from the *De civili dominio* to be found anonymously as folios 109r–124v in a paper volume now Registrum Papireum (N) in the Durham Dean and Chapter Library.[20] The beginning of the text seems to come on the fourth leaf of an eight-leaf quire, without a heading but with a space left for a capital that has not been provided; the first chapter ends on folio 117v and is immediately followed on the next line by the second, that in turn ends folio 121 and is similarly followed by the third; this ends in the middle of folio 124v, after which there is a gap of about

---

hypothesis that the present binding and lack of many catchwords and signatures makes impossible to verify or disprove), the medieval list of contents indicates that the present order was early established. The entries from Bromyard, fols 250ra–251vb, are in the same hand as the *Cistrensis* text, but end eleven lines before the bottom of fol. 251vb – the incompleteness again may suggest that *Cistrensis* originally stood after the Wyclif sermons.

[18] Ker, *Medieval Libraries*, p. 73. Alan Piper identifies the hand of the pressmark with that of Dr Thomas Swalwell: 'Dr Thomas Swalwell, Monk of Durham, Archivist and Bibliophile (d.1539)', in J. P. Carley and C. G. C. Tite, eds, *Books and Collectors 1200–1700: Essays presented to Andrew Watson* (London, 1997) pp. 71–100, at p. 81, and attributes additional information in the list of contents here and in MS Jesus College Cambridge 59 to him (p. 92 n. 61).

[19] Neither is named, but the identification seems probable. In the decoration at the foot of fol. 1r is a blank shield.

[20] Thomson, *Latin Writings*, nos 28–30, lists this incompletely. I owe many of the details that follow about this manuscript to the great generosity of Dr Alan Piper and Dr Ian Doyle of Durham. On fols 11r–13r appear copies of some of the material connected with Pope Gregory XI's condemnation of Wyclif in 1377.

IX

five lines, and then just under ten lines of a different text is added, apparently in the same hand.[21] The text from folio 116r onwards is increasingly defective because of damage to the outer edges, damage repaired by modern blank paper; by the end only about half of each line remains. The other contents of the manuscript are largely formulary materials. Its date appears, from the fact that these are largely in one hand (the hand also of the Wyclif text) and on paper with the same watermark, to be 1391 or shortly after; the latest document is dateable to 1391 (that on folios 104v-105r). Since the documents all relate to Durham Cathedral Priory, it seems reasonable to conclude that the volume was compiled there in 1391 or shortly afterwards.

The Wyclif chapters are those known to modern readers as chapters 24 and 26-7 of book iii of *De civili dominio*.[22] Neither author nor the title of the work from which the chapters were drawn are named. The subject matter of the chapters concerns, in the first instance, the difference between mortal and venial sin, a subject announced in the first sentence of chapter 24. The opening of chapter 24 exists as an apparently independent work in three Bohemian copies, though each ends at a different point; none of these copies has a title, but the text was recognized as freestanding by the catalogue of Wyclif's works made by his early Bohemian disciples, where it is called *Differencia inter peccatum mortale et veniale*.[23] But none of these contains chapters 26-7, whose subject matter extends beyond this limited issue. Chapter 27, which deals with various questions about the value of prayers for the dead, exists alone as the last item in an English Wyclif manuscript, now Florence Laurenziana Plut. XIX. 33, folios 174r-182v; the main item here is the *Trialogus*, and this is accompanied by nine short works and two extracts (the other being chapter 7 of *De ecclesia*).[24]

---

[21] It is difficult to identify this snippet since about half of each line is now lost; the final word 'prescitorum' makes it tempting to look in Wyclif, but I have so far not succeeded in finding it.

[22] The whole work was edited by R. L. Poole and J. Loserth, 4 vols, *WS* (1885-1904); the chapters are iv.512/21-562/7 and 603/9-647/31.

[23] See Thomson, *Latin Writings*, no. 51; the text was printed by J. Loserth and F. D. Matthew at the end of their edition of the *De mandatis*, *WS* (1922), pp. 527-33, apparently without recalling that the same material had been included in *De civili dominio*, iv. Of the three manuscripts Prague UK V. E.17 is the longest, whilst Prague MK A.71/1 (not A.70, as in Thomson) ends p. 532/8, and Prague MK C.38 ends p. 531/4. In the Bohemian catalogue, R. Buddensieg, *John Wiclif's Polemical Works*, *WS* (1883), i.lxiv, lxxi and lxxviii, the explicit given is that of the longest form.

[24] See in manuscript order, Thomson, *Latin Writings*, nos 431, 412, 423, 383, 403, 413, 32

Wyclif and the North

If the Bohemian manuscripts are to be understood as preserving a version of the material of chapter 24 prior to its incorporation into the *De civili dominio*, was the Durham material likewise a more extensive discussion that was independent? Or is it to be understood as an extract from the longer work? Fortunately this question can be answered with some certainty. It is characteristic of Wyclif's writings, particularly of those written before his withdrawal from Oxford, to contain within them cross-references to discussion of comparable subjects elsewhere in his output; if these cross-references were not provided by Wyclif himself (as seems most likely), they were certainly inserted before the dissemination of the texts in which they appear.[25] One of the texts in which these references occur most prolifically is *De civili dominio*. Unusually there are none in that part of chapter 24 of book iii that overlaps with the Bohemian tract, a fact that may support the original existence of this as an independent entity. But in the remaining part of that chapter and in chapters 26–7 there is the usual scatter of them: most of them are to be found in the Durham copy, despite the fact that inevitably some have been lost in the damage done to the outer margins.[26] The references are in the form of chapter number in relation to *De civili dominio* iii itself, or of chapter and book number in relation to the earlier four books of the *Summa theologie* (and often to the present book itself when the context leaves ambiguity); those in the section here in question cover *De civili dominio* ii as well as iii. Obviously a reference such as 'ut patet 17 et 18 capitulis 4 libri' (iv.532/27) is meaningless save in regard to a complete copy of the book in question. Since Durham contains such references without significant modification, it must be concluded that the section in Registrum N derives from a complete text of *De civili dominio* ii-iii. Whether that complete text was itself in Durham depends upon whether the extract was derived directly or indirectly from it; to answer this question there seems no evidence beyond the suspicion that more of the cross-references might have been dropped as useless if there were more than a single stage of transmission.

---

ch. 7, 415, 408, 47, 405 and 30 ch. 27. The manuscript's content was first properly identified by I. H. Stein, 'The Wyclif manuscript in Florence', *Speculum*, 5 (1930), pp. 95–7.

[25] I have discussed these references, and their implications, in my paper 'Cross referencing in Wyclif's Latin Works', *SCH.S*, 11 (forthcoming).

[26] In ch. 24 the references are found at iv.526/14, 531/22, 532/27, 534/22, 538/28; in the later section references still available and present are those at iv.602/9, 610/38, 612/2, 630/24, 635/9 (where Durham has ch. 13 not 23 as the printed text), 639/13, 645/1, 645/9.

IX

At least one further Wyclif volume, a volume now lost, can be associated with Durham. Robert Rypon, monk of Durham, almoner there in 1390-1, prior of the dependency at Finchale from 1397 until some time before 1405, and subprior back at Durham in 1408, gave three books to Durham College Oxford; one of these was described as 'Summa Wyclyffe'. The gift is listed in a catalogue dating from c.1390-1400, under the heading of 'Libri logice'.[27] Though two *summae* can be discerned amongst Wyclif's works, the philosophical *Summa de ente* and the later *Summa theologie*,[28] it seems improbable that Rypon's title is so precise: these should have been listed in the catalogue under 'Libri philosophie' and 'Libri theologice' respectively. It is more probable that all or part of Wyclif's *De logica* were in Rypon's gift.[29] Rypon was a noted preacher, whose sermons (preserved in BL MS Harley 4894) contain a number of attacks on the Lollards.[30]

Less remarkable than these is the list of 'Conclusiones extracte de trialogo M. Jo. Wyclyff per T. Archiepiscopum Cant. & eius consilium prouinciale dampnate' found in the Priory Registrum Magnum (III), folio 119v. 'T' here is Thomas Arundel, and the list is that presented to the Canterbury Convocation in February 1397.[31] Much later, in 1433, Thomas Gascoigne mentions that he copied a letter of Archbishop Arundel concerning Wyclif to the University of Oxford in 1411 from a book containing also the forty-five Conclusions condemned at Basle and Oxford; the book was in Oxford 'in Collegio Dunelmae'. To judge by this and later allusions to the book, it was apparently a collection of conciliar and provincial material; Gascoigne says that it was given to

---

[27] For Rypon see Emden, *Oxford*, 3, p. 1618; for the gift W. Pantin in H. E. Salter, W. A. Pantin, and H. G. Richardson, eds, *Formularies which bear on the History of Oxford c.1204-1420*, OHS, ns 4 (1942), pp. 243 and n. 77, 245. The direct information concerning books at Durham College is not revealing: beyond this three lists survive, one of 1315 (too early for Wyclif), the second of c.1400, and the third of 1409 list books sent to Oxford and, unsurprisingly, do not contain works by him: see H. E. D. Blakiston, 'Some Durham College Rolls', *Collectanea*, 3, OHS, 32 (1896), pp. 1-76, at pp. 35-41.

[28] See Thomson, *Latin Writings*, nos 7-19, 26-37; Pantin suggested the first of these as the more probable.

[29] Ibid., nos 1-3; all three books were of early date though the third part was at least partly revised late in Wyclif's career – reflected in the eucharistic material which led to the censure of some items from this work, under the title *De arte sophistica*, in 1411: see D. Wilkins, *Concilia magnae Britanniae et Hiberniae*, 4 vols (London, 1737), 3, p. 346.

[30] For instance, BL MS Harley 4894, fols 32v, 40r, 77v; the sermons were quoted extensively by G. R. Owst, *Preaching in Medieval England* (Cambridge, 1926) and *Literature and Pulpit in Medieval England*, 2nd edn (Oxford, 1966).

[31] See Wilkins, *Concilia*, 3, pp. 229-30.

Wyclif and the North

Durham College by Robert Burton, a member of the English delegation at the Council of Basle.[32] A second Durham copy of Wyclif's forty-five Conclusions condemned at Constance is to be found in York Minster XVI.I.1, written by the monk Robert Emyldon junior, amongst a collection of largely patristic materials. Emyldon was in Oxford, where he probably assembled this material, between 1435 and 1444.[33] Swalwell, the later antiquary of Durham, noted Wyclif's burial place and the later burning of his bones in two of his annotations.[34]

Beyond the preservation of Wyclif's writing and conclusions at Durham and in its dependent college in Oxford during the decades around 1390–1410, there is earlier evidence for interest in the controversialist from the northern Benedictine house. Within a collection of formulary letters appear five which relate to the intended journeys of two monks to Oxford to answer the attacks of John Wyclif on the Benedictine order. The first four concern a 'Dominus W.', for whom the first and third offer a letter of recommendation to another prelate, whilst the second and fourth respond.[35] The responses reveal somewhat more than the other two: in the second letter we learn that 'W' was about to journey 'ad studium Oxon.', to engage with 'magister Iohannes', a troubler of 'our order' in scholastic debate, whilst in the fourth the opponent's name is given as 'magister I. de W.', who 'multiplices utrobique ventilavit opiniones, que cedere poterunt in grave preiudicium et detrimentum ecclesiastice stabilitatis.' But from the second it appears that the abbot of St Alban's had sent advice that the time was not ripe for such a debate and that it should be postponed.[36] The scribe's own index to the letters amplifies the initials of the offender to 'J. Wyclyff'.[37]

---

[32] *Loci e libro veritatum*, ed. J. E. Thorold Rogers (Oxford, 1881), pp. 116, 157, 164–5; see Emden, *Oxford*, 1, pp. 319–20.

[33] N. R. Ker and A. J. Piper, eds, *Medieval Manuscripts in British Libraries iv Paisley–York* (Oxford, 1992), pp. 706–9, item 14, and Emden, *Oxford*, 1, p. 642. I am much indebted to Alan Piper for drawing this to my attention. That this collection is unlikely to be the one Gascoigne saw appears from the divergence between its other contents and those mentioned by Gascoigne (see n. 32). The Constance condemnation is in J. D. Mansi, *Sacrorum Conciliorum Nove et Amplissima Collectio*, 27 (Venice, 1784), cols 632–4.

[34] See Piper, 'Dr Thomas Swalwell', pp. 97–8, n. 131.

[35] For these four see Salter, Pantin, and Richardson, *Formularies*, pp. 231–3, and introductory note by Pantin, pp. 222–3.

[36] The letters appear in sequence in Durham Cathedral MS C.iv.25, fol. 39r, letters A-D.

[37] See ibid., fol. 88r; Pantin appears to have overlooked this index.

IX

The fifth letter is rather fuller, and appears to relate to a very similar but distinct attempt to engage with Wyclif: a chapter of the Black Monks, either at provincial or general level, in view of the current hostility in certain quarters to their order, had ordered 'John de A.' to reply to John Wyclif (named in full in the heading) in scholastic acts; but members of the King's Council had forbidden John to air any opinions in the schools which might lead to schism or disruption, and consequently the order is countermanded.[38] Pantin, who first drew attention to this letter, suggested that 'John de A.' should be identified with John de Acley (or Aycliffe), a monk at Durham who can be traced from 1373 until 1420/1,[39] and who was certainly in Oxford at various dates in the 1370s where, for some part of that decade, he was prior of the Durham cell there. Although neither this letter nor the earlier group mentions Durham, the title of the collection as a whole states that it derives 'de officio cancellarie monachorum Dunelmie', when Robert of Langchestre was chancellor and then 'feretrarius'; this fixes the compilation in the 1390s, and makes it a reasonable deduction that 'dominus W' in addition to 'John de A.' were Durham monks. The most probable date for both the intended answers to Wyclif would seem to have been c.1377-8, at the time of the arrival in England of Gregory XI's bulls against Wyclif, bulls which related to nineteen conclusions drawn from the *De civili dominio*.[40] The *Fasciculi Ziza-niorum* records, following the text of Wyclif's *Responsio*, that about this time the King and his Council (given the date the second must have been the more important) had imposed silence on Wyclif.[41] It would seem that all the authorities, secular as well as ecclesiastical, were anxious to preserve the peace rather than to decide on the controversial issues at stake.

Those two efforts to oppose Wyclif were aborted, apparently before anything was set down in writing. But 'dominus W' and 'John de A.' were not the most celebrated Durham monks to be involved in the battle: Uthred of Boldon, monk of Durham, at various times warden

---

[38] W. A. Pantin, 'A Benedictine opponent of John Wyclif', *EHR*, 43 (1928), pp. 73-7; this letter is in the same manuscript fols 59v-60r, letter E, and the index (fol. 84v, again missed by Pantin) specifies the subject as 'J. de Wiclyff'.

[39] Alan Piper has corrected Emden's dates: the death is recorded in the year May 1420-May 1421 (Dean and Chapter Library Durham, Bursar's Accounts 1420-1).

[40] See Walsingham, *Chronicon Anglie*, ed. E. M. Thompson, RS (1874), pp. 180-1, 174-5, *Historia Anglicana*, ed. H. T. Riley, 2 vols, RS (1863-4), I, pp. 352-3, 346-7.

[41] *Fasciculi Zizaniorum*, p. 271; for the text see Thomson, *Latin Writings*, no. 398.

of Durham College in Oxford, prior of Finchale, and subprior of Durham, exchanged fire with Wyclif perhaps more than once. The details of this contest are, unluckily, hard to chart, despite the relatively ample records of Uthred's career.[42] Only a single determination from Wyclif, challenging Uthred's views on three issues, has been preserved; from Uthred's side no text that directly and exclusively opposes Wyclif survives, though several seem to refer to views that he had favoured.[43] The *Determinacio ad argumenta magistri Outredi* is found in only a single manuscript, now in Paris, along with three other ascribed Wyclif texts.[44] In confirmation of the limited circulation indicated by the one surviving manuscript is the fact that the text was not known to the makers of the Bohemian catalogue.[45] The three views which Wyclif opposes are set out as conclusions at the start: they state respectively that (i) in every condition, whether before the fall or after, the priestly condition is better than that of a layman; (ii) that in no situation may the secular power on its own authority judge the priesthood; (iii) that anyone instructing or urging kings, princes, or secular rulers that they should on their own authority deprive the Church of tithes or dues, even if the Church should err, is arguing the king's destruction and the destruction of the souls of the lay rulers.[46] Since Wyclif states that Uthred had disseminated these views 'more

---

[42] Brief biographies of Uthred are to be found in Emden, *Oxford*, I, pp. 212–13; W. A. Pantin, 'Two treatises of Uthred of Boldon on the monastic life', in R. W. Hunt, W. A. Pantin, and R. W. Southern, eds, *Studies in Medieval History presented to F. M. Powicke* (Oxford, 1948), pp. 363–85; M. D. Knowles, 'The Censured Opinions of Uthred of Boldon', *PBA*, 37 (1951), pp. 305–42; J. I. Catto in J. I. Catto and T. A. R. Evans, eds, *The History of the University of Oxford ii Late Medieval Oxford* (Oxford, 1992), pp. 184–6; D. H. Farmer, 'New Light on Uthred of Boldon', in Wansbrough and Marett-Crosby, eds, *Benedictines in Oxford*; a full modern biography is much needed.

[43] For Wyclif's text see *Opera minora*, ed. J. Loserth, WS (1913), pp. 405–14; for Uthred's responses see the manuscript details given in Pantin, 'Two treatises', pp. 364–5, and the edition of two of the relevant texts (for which see below) by C. H. Thompson, 'Uthred of Boldon: a study in fourteenth century political theory' (Manchester Ph.D. thesis, 1936) to which the following comments are much indebted.

[44] BN, MS lat.3184, fols 46v–48r; for the other texts see Thomson, *Latin Writings*, nos. 402, 382–3, 400; the unprinted Paris catalogue suggests that an inscription dated 1396 on fol. 125v in Breton may indicate its origin; it subsequently belonged to Laurence Burelli, doctor of Paris (see fol. 1v) who died in 1504.

[45] See above, n. 23.

[46] *Opera minora*, p. 405/9–20. Thompson, 'Uthred of Boldon' 1, p. 55, n. 1, notes that Wyclif p. 406/1–3 (*recte* p. 405/9–12) is closely similar to Uthred's fol. 25, 'pro quilibet hominis progressu versus suum terminum naturalem, sive in via innocencie sive lapsus excellencius, semper fuisset et foret sacerdocium quam hominis dominium pro eodem.'

suo ad informacionem scole Oxoniensis seminavit' (p. 405/6), implying that he is answering a spoken rather than a written text, it is not surprising that the precise wording given by Wyclif has not yet been traced in any of Uthred's surviving writings. The preservation of those writings is in any case rather poor, and only a small part of them is available in print.[47] But Uthred's views as retailed by Wyclif are entirely consonant with those to be found in his *De regalia et sacerdocio, De naturali et necessaria connexione ac ordine sacerdotalis officii et regalis, De dotacione ecclesie sponse Christi* and *Contra garrulos dotacionem ecclesie inpugnantes*, all of which are to be found only in a single Durham manuscript.[48] The first and second opinions are very close to Uthred's wording in the second of these tracts; the third is more extreme than Uthred's wording, but is consonant with his views in this and the ensuing two tracts.[49] Wyclif's reporting of Uthred's opinions continues later in his answer.[50]

The date of the exchange between Wyclif and Uthred is not altogether simple to establish. Uthred seems to have been in Oxford for much of the time between 1347 and about 1367, in which year he was appointed prior of the Durham dependency of Finchale.[51] Thompson, editor of the last two of the tracts mentioned, suggested that the first three of the four at least were written before 1367, and that the second might have been the subject of Uthred's inception *determinatio* for his M.Th., which would place this in 1357.[52] Even if the

---

[47] The position is little different now from that described by Pantin in 1948: Pantin, 'Two treatises', printed extracts from two texts, noted the edition of two more relevant here in Thompson's thesis 'Uthred of Boldon', and observed the inadequacy of the edition of the only lengthy text printed, that of *Contra querelas fratrum*, by M. E. Marcett, *Uthred de Boldon, Friar William Jordan and 'Piers Plowman'* (New York, 1938), pp. 25-37.

[48] Durham Cathedral Library, MS A. IV.33, respectively fols 1r-23r, 24r-64v, 69r-99v, 99v-110r; the last two (not the last three, *pace* Pantin, 'Two treatises', p. 364, n. 6) were edited by Thompson, 'Uthred of Boldon', vol. 2.

[49] Ibid., fol. 46v: 'restat ut semper et pro semper temporis regale officium fuerit, sit et erit sacerdocio subalternum et ipsum sacerdocium ... regali officio dignius sit in gradu', and fol. 54r, 'videtur quod hec violencia gladialis spoliandi, cruciandi etc. non ad sacerdocium se extendat sicut ad populum laicalem', quoted Thompson, 'Uthred of Boldon', 1, p. 60, n. 1 and p. 64 n. 1; see also 1, p. 28 where he suggests that Wyclif might have been answering another lost tract on the issue of disendowment, but this seems to me, whilst possible, not a necessary deduction.

[50] See *Opera minora*, pp. 406/1, 13, 407/19, 409/13, 411/15, 412/29.

[51] Pantin, 'Two treatises', p. 363, Emden *Oxford*, 1, p. 212.

[52] Thompson, 'Uthred of Boldon', 1, pp. 10-16, 31-5. He argues (p. 31) that the interchange between Uthred and Wyclif arose from the question of papal tribute that was discussed by Parliament in 1366; but on neither side does this seem to me to be the main

Wyclif and the North

mention of the papal Schism in the second text is the result of a later revision, such dates seem somewhat improbable.[53] The issue of disendowment, on which Uthred's second tract reflects, and his third and fourth concentrate, becomes visible as a major concern in 1371 with the argument of the two Austin friars, John Bankin and another, who may have been Thomas Ashborne, at the Parliament that year in favour of confiscation of ecclesiastical wealth in support of the war effort against France. Since the advocates of the secular powers then, and in the comparable instance two years later involving the Franciscan John Mardisley and the Austin Ashbourne, were friars, it would be entirely in accordance with Uthred's hostility to the fraternal orders over other matters if he had been provoked by these cases to take up the cudgels on these new issues.[54]

If Wyclif's determination against Uthred can shed any light on the date of Uthred's discussion of the question of disendowment, then a date for the latter in the mid 1370s seems much more likely than one in the 1360s. Wyclif's assertion of the powers of the secular ruler over the Church, powers which include those of the removal of ecclesiastical temporalities not only in case of national need, but also of the moral turpitude of the clerical order, was most stridently proclaimed in what became the first book of his *De civili dominio*; this was the text from which Pope Gregory XI, acting almost certainly on the prompting of the Benedictine Adam Easton, who had obtained a copy of the work from England, took the conclusions condemned in his 1377 bull.[55] Allowing the time necessary for the rumour

---

concern – and reticence would certainly have not stopped Wyclif from trenchant comments on that topic. For other objections to such an early date, see J. Loserth, 'Die ältesten Streitschriften Wiclifs', *Sitzungsberichte der Kaiserlichen Akademie der Wissenschaften in Wien*, Phil.-Hist. Klasse 160.2 (Vienna, 1908), pp. 9-11, 25-6.

[53] Thompson, 'Uthred of Boldon', 1, p. 90 quotes the passage from the Durham MS A.IV.33, fol. 49v 'fuit in ecclesia Iesu Christi monstrum christianis omnibus dolorosum, scilicet duo capita reputata, cum tamen solus Christus caput sit super omnem ecclesiam que corpus ipsius est', but does not mention the implication for date.

[54] For the sequence see M. Aston, '"Caim's Castles": Poverty, Politics, and Disendowment', in R. B. Dobson, ed., *The Church, Politics and Patronage in the Fifteenth Century* (Gloucester, 1984), pp. 45-81, at p. 51; for the second J. I. Catto, 'An alleged Great Council of 1374', *EHR*, 82 (1967), pp. 764-71. For Uthred's two surviving antifraternal tracts see Pantin, 'Two treatises', p. 364; Pantin dates them to c.1366-8; a recent review of Uthred's position is G. L. Dipple, 'Uthred and the friars: Apostolic Poverty and clerical dominion between FitzRalph and Wyclif', *Traditio*, 49 (1994), pp. 235-58.

[55] See W. A. Pantin, 'The *Defensorium* of Adam Easton', *EHR*, 51 (1936), pp. 675-80; also Thomson, *Latin Writings*, nos 23-30 and references given there; Catto, *History of the*

concerning its content to reach Easton, for the passages of the demand from Avignon to Norwich and of the book back, for Easton to digest its content and persuade the Pope of its dangers, a composition date for *De civili dominio* i of between 1374 and 1376 seems most likely.[56] Wyclif in his determination against Uthred refers to his previous discussion of the issues involved; though it is hard to point to precise passages that Wyclif had in mind, it seems reasonable to think that he was referring to the debate, carried on in academic discussion as well as in writing, that culminated in *De civili dominio* i.[57] That Uthred should have visited Oxford in the 1370s is not improbable: in May 1374 he was certainly in London, defending papal claims against the secular ruler.[58] Even later in 1380 or 1381 he travelled again to London in connection with negotiations concerning the Durham house in Oxford.[59] A date for the exchange between 1378 and 1380 would seem most probable, and would avoid the need to postulate later revision to accommodate Uthred's allusion to the Schism.

The tone of Wyclif's tract against Uthred has been described by a recent critic as 'more courteous and deferential' that that of his riposte to Uthred's fellow-Benedictine William Binham.[60] Such a view may be too simplistic. There seems to me to be a degree of exaggeration in Wyclif's tone that points towards sarcasm and condescension: this reaches its climax towards the middle of the determination when, having set out a further argument advanced by Uthred, Wyclif exclaims,

---

University, pp. 202–4. See, now, for conformation of this suggestion, and for the care with which Easton had read and excerpted Wyclif's work, M. Harvey, 'Adam Easton and the condemnation of John Wyclif, 1377', *EHR*, 113 (1998), pp. 321–34.

[56] Our knowledge of this book depends on two witnesses: Vienna, Österreichische Nationalbibliothek, MS 1341, and BN MS lat. 15869, a Paris student's somewhat abbreviated copy, made soon after 1381; these two agree in all matters relevant to the present issue.

[57] See *Opera minora*, pp. 405/8, 22, 410/34, 414/35 as observed by Loserth and mentioned by Thomson, *Latin Writings*, p. 230; Catto, *History of the University*, p. 203 suggests that Uthred may have been the first to raise the issues of endowment and papal taxation in the schools, though he does not set a firm date for this.

[58] See Pantin, 'Two treatises', pp. 363–4, with reference to *Eulogium historiarum*, 3 , ed. F. S. Haydon, RS (1863), p. 337; also Catto, 'An alleged Great Council'.

[59] *Durham Account Rolls*, 3, ed. J. T. Fowler, SS, 103 (1901), p. 591.

[60] Thomson, *Latin Writings*, p. 231; the text against Binham is *Opera minora*, pp. 415–30.

Wyclif and the North

O quam gratum esset communicare cum homine, qui vellet sic subtiliter et seriose procedere, dimissis ambagibus et difficilibus argumentis mendicare manifesta mendacia. Tunc enim dilucidaretur utrobique materia et non seminarentur inutiliter verba utriusque scandalose.[61]

Similarly, at the end of the text Wyclif seems to lose patience with the argument, simply referring Uthred to his previous discussions: 'Et tantum pronunc dixerim doctori meo reverendo ad conclusiones et subtilia argumenta.'[62] Whether Uthred could have been the 'dominus et socius de ordine sancti Benedicti inter omnes valentes Oxon.' to whom Wyclif refers at the start of *De civili dominio* ii is uncertain.[63] At various points in this book and in book iii Wyclif answers, sometimes declaredly and at length, sometimes more allusively, the objections that had been raised against him.[64] Here the objections were to Wyclif's proposition that clerics could be so guilty that it was legitimate and meritorious for secular lords to remove their temporalities, an issue close to that of the third conclusion raised at the start of the independent tract against Uthred. The objections seem to have been made publicly in St Mary's Church, and we may recall Wyclif's comment on the publicity with which Uthred had proclaimed his views 'ad informacionem scole Oxoniensis'.[65] Again the wording of the apparent quotations by Wyclif from his opponent's arguments have not so far been traced. Uthred is a likely candidate, but was doubtless not the only Benedictine in Oxford who had been affronted by this view.

Durham interest in Wyclif can then be traced back at least to the mid 1370s; it seems to have persisted into the early fifteenth century, well after Wyclif's death and the heretication of his own views and those of his followers. Whether or not it was first aroused by Uthred of Boldon's academic encounters with the secular master cannot be demonstrated, but these encounters and the issues debated in them may reasonably be seen to have fostered the concern. The surviving

---

[61] *Opera minora*, p. 409/23.
[62] Ibid., p. 414/36.
[63] *De civili dominio*, ii.1/9.
[64] For instance, book iii, chs 18–19 are an answer to William Woodford, O.F.M.'s *Determinatio de civili dominio*, itself an answer to Wyclif's first book of the same title.
[65] See *De civili dominio*. ii.5/19 coram tam sciolo et venerabili auditorio in ecclesia beate virginis Oxonie' (with which compare *Opera minora*, p. 405/6); the discussion extends through the first four chapters.

IX

Durham copies of Wyclif's writings suggest, however, an interest that went beyond that particular conflict. The extract from *De civili dominio* iii may suggest, as I have argued, that a complete copy of that work was once in Durham; but the extract itself is not on the face of it particularly contentious, dealing primarily with the distinction between venial and mortal sin (though it includes Wyclif's deduction that anyone in mortal sin lacks dominion). The *Sermones quadraginta* likewise, as the medieval maker of the list of contents in the manuscript observed, are 'satis catholici', even if they may be an edited version of more controversial sermons preached in the 1370s.[66] Only the *De eucharistia confessio* is overtly heretical in a way that even a casual reader could not miss.

These three, together with the subsequent listings of Wyclif's errors and with the allusions to other books owned by Durham, make it tempting to suggest that, after a period of interest and investigation in Durham, discretion became the better part of valour, and the holdings of Wyclif's texts were reduced. By the first years of the fifteenth century Durham's bishop, Walter Skirlawe, was engaged in proceedings against a group of Wyclif's followers in the diocese.[67] The fullest evidence for this comes unusually from the Lollard side: the Latin letter from Richard Wyche, apparently smuggled out of the Bishop's prison to his friends, provides an account of efforts by the Bishop and his officials to obtain from him an unambiguous statement of his views.[68] The Bishop was assisted by at least one layman and by a large number of clerics of various orders. Most of the latter are mentioned at best by their office, but Wyche provides a few names; one of these is 'monachus qui vocatur Rome', almost certainly the Durham Benedictine Thomas Rome, who had been at Durham College from 1391 to 1396 and who returned there as warden from 1409 to 1418.[69] A much more prominent part in the investigation was played by one whom

---

[66] W. Mallard, 'Dating the *Sermones Quadraginta* of John Wyclif', *Medievalia et Humanistica*, 17 (1966), pp. 86–105, and A. Hudson, 'Aspects of the "Publication" of Wyclif's Latin Sermons', in A. J. Minnis, ed., *Late-Medieval Religious Texts and their Transmission: Essays in Honour of A. I. Doyle* (Woodbridge, 1994), pp. 121–9.

[67] See M. G. Snape, 'Some evidence of Lollard activity in the diocese of Durham in the early fifteenth century', *Archaeologia Aeliana* ser. 4, 39 (1961), pp. 355–61.

[68] The letter survives only in one Bohemian manuscript, now Prague University Library, III. G.11, fols 89v–99v, where it has no heading, but is entered in the medieval list of contents on the front medieval flyleaf. It was printed by F. D. Matthew, 'The trial of Richard Wyche', *EHR*, 5 (1890), pp. 530–44.

[69] Emden, *Oxford*, 3, pp. 1587–8; see Matthew, 'Richard Wyche', p. 539.

Wyclif and the North

Wyche only describes as *Cancellarius*: at the date of the affair this was none other than Robert Wyclif. Perhaps it is not coincidental that Wyche's letter should be one of the rare Lollard texts that names the founder of the sect: 'bonus Wicleff'.[70]

---

[70] Matthew, 'Richard Wyche', p. 536.

X

Peculiaris regis clericus:
Wyclif and the Issue of Authority

The Lollard Peter Payne arrived in Prague by the spring of 1415, having fled from England the previous year. The immediate cause of his departure at that particular point is not clear: involvement in the Oldcastle rebellion of January 1414 is an obvious motive, though Payne may have left before this and his name has not so far been found amongst the suspects, apprehended or sought.[1] But, even if the academic Payne had himself been lucky or prudent enough to avoid direct participation, he would not have needed much foresight to perceive that his standing as a Lollard would leave him in an exposed position in the rebellion's aftermath.[2] Payne would have been well aware of the extension of royal and ecclesiastical powers in the previous thirty years, and must have suspected that advantage would be taken of the rebellion to increase those powers yet further. From the

---

[1] For Payne's career, and the date of his arrival in Bohemia, see in English R. R. Betts, 'Peter Payne in England', in his *Essays in Czech History* (London, 1969), pp. 236-246; A. B. Emden, *An Oxford Hall in Medieval Times* (Oxford, 1968²), pp. 125-161; and some further details in my *The Premature Reformation: Wycliffite History and Lollard Texts* (Oxford, 1988), pp. 99-103; expanding these (currently in Czech, but to be published in *The New Dictionary of National Biography*) see F. Šmahel, 'Curriculum vitae Magistri Petri Payne', in: *In memoriam Josefa Macka (1922-1991)*, eds. M. Polívka and F. Šmahel (Prague, 1996), pp. 141-160.

[2] There is no full-length modern study of the revolt or its leader; for partial recent comments see E. Powell, 'The Restoration of Law and Order', in: *Henry V: The Practice of Kingship*, ed. G. L. Harriss (Oxford, 1985), pp. 53-74 and the same author's *Kingship, Law and Society: Criminal Justice in the Reign of Henry V* (Oxford, 1989), pp. 141-167; C. Allmand, *Henry V* (London, 1992), pp. 280-305. Margaret Aston in 'Lollardy and Sedition, 1381-1431', first published in *Past and Present* 17 (1960), 1-44, argued that the Oldcastle revolt was the logical outcome of Wyclif's views; this, as the following paper may indicate, seems to me unpersuasive.

arrival of pope Gregory XI's bulls condemning some of the early political views of John Wyclif in the autumn of 1377, new legislation was progressively introduced to control, and then to eradicate, Wyclif's teaching wherever it might be found.³ The chief stages of this process are familiar enough: in 1401 the bill *De heretico comburendo* had enacted for England the penalty for heretics long familiar on the continent.⁴ Before this had come a number of edicts for the searching out of books containing Wycliffite views, and for the apprehension of those owning, reading or listening to them; equally in 1392 investigation was required into the conventicles in which Lollard opinions were being taught and discussed.⁵ In 1407 archbishop Arundel set out his Constitutions, which attempted to control more effectively the sources of Lollard teaching: in the universities issues of doctrine recently disputed were not to be discussed, wardens of halls were to question their students monthly on their theological opinions; no cleric was to preach outside his own benefice unless licensed by the diocesan (a provision which had to be hastily modified to allow continuance of fraternal preaching); translation of the Bible was henceforth forbidden, and ownership of existing vernacular scriptures required episcopal approval both of the translation and of the owner.⁶ In

---

³ For the bulls see Walsingham's *Chronicon Angliae*, ed. E. M. Thompson (Rolls Series, 1874), pp. 173-183; the early stages of the legislation are outlined by H. G. Richardson, 'Heresy and the Lay power under Richard II', *English Historical Review* 51 (1936), 1-28.

⁴ *Statutes of the Realm* ii (London, 1816), 125-8; for the background and implications of this legislation see A. K. McHardy, '*De Heretico Comburendo*, 1401', in: *Lollardy and the Gentry in the Later Middle Ages*, eds. M. Aston and C. Richmond (Stroud, 1997), pp. 112-126.

⁵ For the legislation against books and conventicles, see *Premature Reformation*, pp. 174-180. See also N. Saul, *Richard II* (New Haven/London, 1997), pp. 299-303.

⁶ The Constitutions are printed in D. Wilkins, *Concilia Magnae Britanniae et Hiberniae*, 4 vols. (London, 1737), iii.314-19; see also C. R. Cheney, 'William Lyndwood's *Provinciale*', in his *Medieval Texts and Studies* (Oxford, 1973), pp. 158-184.

1406 major parliamentary legislation authorised extensive enquiry and arrest of suspects.[7]

As this summary indicates, both secular and ecclesiastical powers were involved in the suppression of Wycliffism: royal letters, parliamentary action, episcopal and provincial edicts all played a part; much pressure was put both by the archbishops of Canterbury and by the kings on the authorities of the University of Oxford, from which Wycliffism had sprung, to extirpate the heresy.[8] The ill-advised action of Sir John Oldcastle after his conviction for heresy in 1413 in raising civil revolt inevitably increased the anxiety of the secular authorities to stamp out all sympathisers wherever they might be found, an anxiety the more frenzied through the ensuing three years of Oldcastle's own continued evasion of arrest.[9] The county by county investigations are couched primarily in terms of searches for rebels, their supporters and their concealers, but the occasional mention of beliefs makes it clear that this was primarily because civil disobedience is easier to trace than intellectual opinion. The extent of the surviving records makes plain the thoroughness of the enquiries, and the anxiety of the central powers.

That Payne was right to leave for Bohemia is also clear from the further energies that Henry V's archbishop Henry Chichele put into stamping out heresy. His register records the trials of a number of major Lollards whom Payne must have known, if not personally at least by repute: Thomas Drayton, patronised by the Cheyne family,

---

[7] *Rotuli Parliamentorum* iii (London, 1767), 583-584, and see Allmand, pp. 287-288.

[8] For this see *Premature Reformation*, pp. 82-103 and J. I. Catto, 'Wyclif and Wycliffism at Oxford 1356-1430', in: *The History of the University of Oxford*, vol 2: *Late Medieval Oxford*, eds. J. I Catto and T. A. R. Evans (Oxford, 1992), pp. 175-261; the basic documents for some of the enquiries are in *Snappe's Formulary and other Records*, ed. H. E. Salter (Oxford Historical Society 80, 1924), pp. 90-193.

[9] See above n. 2; an unpublished thesis by C. Kightly, 'The Early Lollards: A Survey of Popular Lollard Activity in England, 1382-1428', Ph.D. thesis (York, 1975) contains the most exhaustive survey of the enquiries available, though M. Jurkowski, 'New Light on John Purvey', *English Historical Review* 110 (1995), 1180-1190 has shown that more can be found.

three of whom had participated in the Oldcastle revolt; William Taylor, predecessor of Payne as Principal of St. Edmund Hall in Oxford, Lollard preacher and friend of Drayton; Robert Hoke, the long-serving rector of Braybrooke from 1401-1425, the former home of the late Sir Thomas Latimer, the most certain of the Lollard knights of Richard II's reign; Richard Wyche, apprehended for heretical views back in 1401 by the bishop of Durham, correspondent of John Hus in 1410, and perhaps related to William Thorpe.[10] Whether Payne carried with him from England to Prague any books is not formally recorded; but his porterage would be an easy explanation for the presence in Bohemian copies of Latin versions of material written by Taylor, Thorpe and Wyche.[11] Chichele was also tireless in the pursuit of other Lollards, great and small, whether in his own diocese or outside; it is clear that he urged on, even if he did not instigate, enquiries in the Norwich diocese by bishops Wakeryng and Alnwick, and that he took over from bishops Repingdon and Fleming the prosecution of Lollards from various parts of their extensive Lincoln diocese.[12] Over a period of years he refined the mechanisms for the investigation of suspects, the processes required of the ecclesiastical officers, the rules of abjuration, the penalties for relapse, and even in 1427 worked to-

---

[10] *The Register of Henry Chichele, Archbishop of Canterbury 1414-1443*, ed. E. F. Jacob, 4 vols. (Oxford, 1938-1947), see i.cxxix-cxliv for a general discussion, for Drayton iii.107-9, Taylor iii.67-9, 108, 158-73, iv.203, Hoke iii.105-12, and Wyche iii.56-7. All are discussed in *Premature Reformation*; all but Hoke are involved in the material edited in *Two Wycliffite Texts* (EETS 301, 1993), pp. xvii-xxv, xlv-lix.

[11] For these see *Two Wycliffite Texts*, and 'William Taylor's 1406 Sermon: a Postscript', *Medium Aevum* 64 (1995), 100-106; for more light on the Oxford background to some of the activity see M. Jurkowski, 'Heresy and Factionalism at Merton College in the early Fifteenth Century', *Journal of Ecclesiastical History* 48 (1997), 658-681.

[12] See M. Aston, 'William White's Lollard Followers', reprinted in her *Lollards and Reformers* (London, 1984), pp. 71-99 and references there given; the cases of Drayton and Hoke derived from the Lincoln diocese.

wards the production of a list of questions against which a suspect's heterodoxy or orthodoxy might be determined.[13]

By 1430 then, fifty years after Wyclif's views on the eucharist had outgrown academic debate to become public knowledge, England's rulers had acquired vastly more extensive powers. For the first thirty years of that period it seems clear that the lead was taken by the ecclesiastical hierarchy, even if they necessarily had to involve secular officials and secular law to effect their aim of extirpating what they saw as heresy. Two energetic and determined archbishops of Canterbury, William Courtenay and Thomas Arundel, had used every weapon in their hands, helped first by the preoccupations of Richard II with other troubles, and then by the weak position, particularly weak financial position, of Henry IV.[14] Henry Chichele, Arundel's successor in 1414, was no less uncertain in his objectives, but the Oldcastle revolt had given him the enthusiastic support of his king, Henry V.[15] By 1430 all the legislation and procedures used to ensure orthodoxy in England up to the Reformation were in place. And up to the 1530s it continued to be used: though no certain figure can be given even for those burned by the secular powers for heresy after being handed over by the ecclesiastical courts, let alone for those investigated by episcopal officials on suspicion of heterodoxy, records from the first thirty years of the sixteenth century from Canterbury,

---

[13] See *Chichele Register* (n. 10), i.cxxix-cxlv; also my paper 'The Examination of Lollards', reprinted in *Lollards and their Books* (London, 1985), pp. 125-140.

[14] See J. Dahmus, *William Courtenay, Archbishop of Canterbury 1381-1396* (University Park and London, 1966); M. Aston, *Thomas Arundel: A Study of Church Life in the Reign of Richard II* (Oxford, 1967), and R. G. Davies, 'Thomas Arundel as Archbishop of Canterbury, 1396-1414', *Journal of Ecclesiastical History* 24 (1973), 9-21; Arundel's major rôle during the reign of Henry IV in persuading the king to legislate against the heretics is described in P. McNiven, *Heresy and Politics in the Reign of Henry IV* (Woodbridge, 1987). For a reconsideration of Lancastrian reaction to Oldcastle and Lollardy see P. Strohm, *England's Empty Throne* (New Haven/London, 1998).

[15] E. F. Jacob, *Henry Chichele* (London, 1967) is a general biography, but the introductory sections to Jacob's edition of Chichele's archiepiscopal register more fully surveys his activities.

Lincoln, Lichfield, Winchester, Salisbury and London dioceses bear witness to extensive and continued enquiries and convictions for heresy, all of them in some cases ending in the death penalty.[16]

Did the heresy in question deserve such persecution? Was the assumption of such wide-ranging powers over men's opinions, practices, and reading justified by the ideas that were being propagated or the actions that ensued from them? Why did Wyclif arouse such deep hostility – for, as I have urged in more detail elsewhere, there can be little doubt that his ideas were the root cause of this persecution right up to the 1530s. The central issue presented by the ecclesiastical opposition, to judge from its primary mention in most polemic and in condemnations whether of Wyclif or of his followers, was the eucharist: Wyclif, after many years of prevarication, had finally declared the current explanations of the changes to the elements at the words of consecration were philosophically and physically unacceptable, and that Christ was present in the host only *figuraliter*, *sacramentaliter*, *virtualiter*.[17] Some of his followers had gone further to argue that, not only did the substance of bread and wine remain after the consecration, but that the mass was purely commemorative, a memorial.[18] But, although this was the issue on which, to judge by the records, many enquiries centred and some hinged, it may be legitimate to doubt whether the eucharist was the source of the original hostility to Wyclif. In later investigations the eucharist, like the issues of images and pilgrimages that follow it in frequency of mention, provided simple questions to which unambiguous answers should be obtainable even from uneducated people by unsophisticated officials – does material

---

[16] The cases are reviewed in J. A. F. Thomson, *The Later Lollards 1414-1520* (London, 1965); for amplification of some of the sixteenth-century material see *Premature Reformation* pp. 446-507, and S. Brigden, *London and the Reformation* (Oxford, 1989). The Canterbury material has recently become more accessible in N. Tanner's edition *Kent Heresy Proceedings 1511-1512* (Kent Records 26, 1997).

[17] For the stages by which Wyclif came to his conclusions see J. A. Robson, *Wyclif and the Oxford Schools* (Cambridge, 1966), pp. 131-133, 184-189, and Catto (above n. 8), pp. 213-214 and his paper 'Wyclif and the Cult of the Eucharist', *Studies in Church History Subsidia* 4 (1985), 269-286.

[18] See *Premature Reformation*, pp. 284-285.

bread remain after the words of consecration? should images of saints be honoured? is pilgrimage a worthy religious exercise?[19] Even in the first instance with opposition to Wyclif himself it seems clear that the eucharist was the turning point, not the source of the trouble: Wyclif's inability to accept transubstantiation had been an unavoidable implication of his philosophical standpoint from the early 1370s onwards (and had been apprehended as such as far away as Prague by 1378), but, after many years of prudent evasion, he had played into his enemies' hands by preaching unambiguously on the subject in English, and encouraging his disciples to follow suit.[20] Even so, and even granted that by 1380 eucharistic doctrine at least for lay consumption had been defined too closely to make such preaching welcome, it is hard to see that the eucharist could have posed such a profound threat to the stability of church, let alone state, that such repressive measures were the inevitable outcome. The eucharist might have been the last straw, but the camel's back was already breaking – or, less flippantly, the eucharist was the convenient immediate cause to achieve a long desired end.

It will be noticed that up to this point I have avoided using the term 'authority', the theme word of this collection. This has been a deliberate omission, because it is a word of particular significance in the context of Wyclif's thought, and one that I should like to suggest stands ultimately at the centre of the furore that Wyclif caused in England. 'Authority' is, I take it, the best modern equivalent to Wyclif's term *dominium*, best because, unlike the modern use of 'dominion' it focusses not on material goods but only on moral, legal or psychological power. Wyclif's teaching on *dominium* is, as is well

---

[19] See the lists of questions in the paper mentioned n. 13, in the first questions 1-4, 26-31, and in the second 1-4, 18-21. Looking at the 1428-1431 enquiries of bishop Alnwick of Norwich, ed. N. P. Tanner, *Heresy Trials in the Diocese of Norwich, 1428-31* (Camden Society 4th series 20, 1977), all three issues recur repeatedly.

[20] See references in n. 8 above, also M. Aston, 'Wycliffe and the Vernacular', reprinted in her *Faith and Fire: Popular and Unpopular Religion, 1350-1600* (London, 1993), pp. 27-72; for the understanding in Prague see my paper 'From Oxford to Prague: The Writings of John Wyclif and his English Followers in Bohemia', *Slavonic and East European Review* 75 (1997), 642-657, at p. 644.

known, a development of the views of Richard FitzRalph as set out in his *De pauperie Salvatoris*: true dominion, authority, inheres by right only in God, and can only be transmitted to a human when that human is in a state of grace; hence no man in a state of mortal sin can rightfully exercise authority.[21] The obvious anarchic force of such a doctrine was, of course, apprehended by Wyclif and circumvented by his immediate qualification that only God could know whether any human at any particular time was in a state of grace. Wyclif first set out his thoughts on this in *De dominio divino*, a work that was apparently never finished. He argued it much more extensively in *De civili dominio* book i, a work which must have been finished by early 1376 since Adam Easton, a Benedictine of Norwich resident in the Avignon curia, that year requested a copy of it from England because of the rumours he had heard of its scandalous content. Easton's perusal of that copy seems to have been the immediate cause of the set of bulls issued by Gregory XI in June 1377 in which Wyclif's views on dominion were condemned, characterized as a revival of the abhorred doctrines of Marsilius of Padua and John of Jandun, and the English authorities were adjured to bring Wyclif to correction.[22] The bulls reached England in the late autumn, but, despite some activity to effect their aim, Wyclif escaped trial; the recent death of Edward III, followed by news of that of Gregory XI, and the ensuing Schism, coupled with some protection from John of Gaunt and perhaps others in the royal circle, postponed serious attack.[23] But Wyclif certainly

---

[21] See M. Wilks, 'Predestination, Property and Power: Wyclif's Theory of Dominion and Grace', *Studies in Church History* 2 (1965), 220-236 and the references given in *Premature Reformation*, pp. 359-362; the first four books of FitzRalph's *De pauperie Salvatoris* was printed as an appendix to Wyclif's *De dominio divino* by R. L. Poole (Wyclif Society, 1890), pp. 259-476.

[22] For the bulls see above n. 3; the activities of Easton, from which the dating of *De civili dominio* can be deduced, are described by W. A. Pantin, 'The *Defensorium* of Adam Easton', *English Historical Review* 51 (1936), 675-680, and Catto (above n. 8) pp. 183-184, 202-204. See further M. Harvey, 'Adam Easton and the Condemnation of John Wyclif, 1377', *English Historical Review* 113 (1998), 321-334.

[23] J. H. Dahmus, *The Prosecution of John Wyclyf* (New Haven, 1952), pp. 35-73.

did not abandon his views, and, as I shall indicate, drew out their implications in a number of more outspoken texts.

Before looking at these texts, I should quickly mention the traditional disregard in which Wyclif's views on dominion have been held. It has been argued, with especial persuasiveness by Gordon Leff, that these views are of purely theoretical force, without practical implication. If God alone can know the state of grace of king or bishop, then no consequence can follow in this world – king and bishop can continue untrammelled in the exercise of his power.[24] But, leaving aside the further arguments that Wyclif based on his theory, this is surely too simpleminded a conclusion. The theory makes plain, in the first place, that true authority inheres not in the office but in the officer: respect or obedience rightly depends not on 'the king' or 'the throne' but on the state of the soul of Edward III and Richard II, not on 'the pope' or 'the bishop' but on Urban VI or Thomas Arundel. Furthermore, though God may be the ultimate arbiter of an individual's state of grace, it may not be too difficult for the human subject to make a shrewd guess about the status of, say, pope Boniface VIII or, to take an example nearer in time and place, Henry Despenser, nominally bishop of Norwich but actually more at home with the sword than the crozier, leader in 1383 of the disastrous expedition to Flanders to support Urban VI against Clement VII in which many civilian Urbanists as well as many English soldiers perished.[25] Even if judgment could not be given on earth, sufficient doubt could be cast to undermine the theoretical basis of many claims to dominion, secular or ecclesiastical.

Investigation of Wyclif's own exploration of his theory of *dominium* bears out the immediacy of its implications. Here I should like to concentrate on one work, the *De officio regis*.[26] As we know

---

[24] G. Leff, *Heresy in the Later Middle Ages*, 2 vols. (Manchester, 1967), ii.546-549.

[25] M. Aston, 'The Impeachment of Bishop Despenser', *Bulletin of the Institute of Historical Research* 38 (1965), 127-148; for Lollard views on the crusade see my discussion in *English Wycliffite Sermons* (in collaboration with Pamela Gradon), 5 vols. (Oxford, 1983-1996), iv.146-151.

[26] Eds. A. W. Pollard and C. Sayle (Wyclif Society, 1887); references to all texts are given by page and line numbers, the two separated by a slash.

Wyclif's *De officio regis*, it forms the eighth book of his *Summa theologie*, a collection of twelve tracts concerning the sources of law and of society, and of their abuses. The coherence and sequence of that *Summa* seems to go back to Wyclif himself, though its precise articulation was (to judge from cross references between its twelve books) the result of a complex, and probably now not in every aspect recoverable, process of revision late in its author's life.[27] *De officio regis* now stands after the *De ecclesia*, itself one of the most heavily edited books; it may originally have been intended to stand rather after *De civili dominio* i, of whose ideas it is to a considerable degree an extension.[28] Unlike some parts, there seems little sign of revision in *De officio regis*, and its date seems fairly clear: the 1378 Shakyl and Haulay case is mentioned, but is apparently no longer a matter of intense concern (157/29); the papal Schism with its two rivals is more frequently deplored (120/17, 121/13, 123/6, 219/25, 226/7), but of these rivals Urban VI is still *papa noster* (121/24) – Wyclif's doubts about the acceptability of the Roman pope certainly chrystalized into condemnation fairly rapidly.[29] 1379, with completion towards the end of that year, seems a reasonable dating. The coherence of the text is also unusually clear: digression is unwontedly rare, and when con-

---

[27] For the sequence of texts and the manuscripts in which they occur see W. R. Thomson, *The Latin Writings of John Wyclyf* (Toronto, 1983), nos. 26-37. Evidence about the arrangement of the twelve parts derives in the main from internal cross references almost certainly provided by Wyclif: see my forthcoming paper 'Cross-referencing in Wyclif's Latin Works', in: *The Medieval Church: Universities, Heresy and the Religious Life. Essays in Honour of Gordon Leff*, eds. P. Biller and R. B. Dobson (*Studies in Church History Subsidia* forthcoming).

[28] A reference at 231/2 to *39 capitulo libri proximi* (*proximus* in Wyclif regularly means 'previous' not 'following') seems clearly an allusion to *De civili dominio* (eds. R. L. Poole and J. Loserth, Wyclif Society 1885-1904) i.274/9ff, though that book now stands four books earlier in the *Summa*; other comparable references are discussed in my paper. Books ii and iii of *De civili dominio* consist of replies to objectors to book i, and hence cannot have been part of any original plan; but the interposition of *De veritate sacre scripture* and *De ecclesia* is less easy to explain.

[29] The Shakyl and Haulay case is reviewed by Dahmus, pp. 74-82. For Wyclif's condemnation of Urban VI see the development of references in *De potestate pape* discussed by H. B. Workman, *John Wyclif*, 2 vols. (Oxford, 1926), ii.74-5.

temporary argument is mentioned it is relevant to the established subject of the section and does not lead to polemic beyond that subject – the most extensive such case is the discussion in chapters 5-6 of the four arguments of the Abbot of Chertsey, John of Usk. The 1887 editors of *De officio regis*, Alfred Pollard and Charles Sayle, stated in their preface (p. xxii) that the text originally ended with chapter 8, and that the four ensuing chapters were an addition. The only evidence cited for this is the opening words of chapter 9 that four questions are to be considered *Ulterius pro complemento finali* (217/13). But the phrase is probably without implication for the overall structure;[30] certainly the remaining chapters deal with topics strictly relevant to what has preceded, issues concerning oaths, excommunication and war.

The clarity of the text's structure is matched by the style which, compared with the tortuousness of some of Wyclif's writing, is for the most part straightforward. Even though the audience must be supposed to be a clerical one, given the language and the constant appeal to canon law, the model of the 'mirror for princes' seems plain: this is a tract to guide the advisors to the young Richard II in his education for kingship. Those advisors are crucial: *totum regnum debet diligenter ad salutem et virtutem regis attendere sed specialiter eius domestici. ... notaret rex de clericis eius domesticis quod sint ydonei et diligentes ad suum officium exequendum* (52/22).

The starting point of Wyclif's argument is traditional enough: the king is the vicar of God (4/26), or of Christ in his divinity, *in temporalibus* (13/2);[31] the priest is the vicar of Christ's humanity (137/18), *in spiritualibus* (13/2). Where Wyclif diverges from current thought is in his definition of the extent of 'temporal' as opposed to 'spiritual' affairs: the clergy have no rightful claim to inalienable rights over property, any more than they can have any exemption from the law of

---

[30] Similar phrases recur at the start of chapters throughout Wyclif's work, and it would be unwise to base theories of structural modifications on them; see, for instance, the opening of each of chapters 3-7 of *De symonia*, ed. S. Herzberg-Fränkel and M. H. Dziewicki (Wyclif Society, 1898).

[31] The antiquity of the distinction is recognized by Wyclif in *Sermones* iii.211/14, ed. J. Loserth (Wyclif Society, 1887-1890), where it is attributed to Augustine.

the secular ruler – to talk of the temporalities of a bishop or of the pope is properly a contradiction in terms. Because priestly honour is dependent on removal from the world, a priest aspiring to worldly honour gravely reduces ecclesiastical dignity (42/4).

Wyclif's views on dominion in the *De officio regis* form a crucial appendix to the outline adumbrated in *De dominio divino* and more clearly enunciated in *De civili dominio* i. Right at the start Wyclif makes a distinction between *potestas* and *dominium* (17/25): *potestas* is the temporal ability to rule, *dominium* the divine authority for doing so. But because of the different areas of rule of king and priest, *potestas* is more relevant to the first. *Regia potestas, que est ordo in ecclesia, stat cum mortale, eciam in prescito* (10/33). *Prescitus* is in Wyclif another technical term, meaning one foreknown by God to damnation, in opposition to the *predestinatus*, one similarly foreknown to salvation. Such a doomed man can notwithstanding wield *potestas*: *tyrranni, eciam presciti (...) habent potestatem informem ad regendum et dominandum, sed illa potestas non est dominium* (17/25). There is then for the king no immediate danger from Wyclif's view of *dominium*: the king's power extends over all the realm, and hence over all persons and temporalities in it (66/4). The obedience due to the temporal ruler is unrestricted, whether or not that ruler is in a state of grace.[32] The subject may attempt to persuade the ruler towards action more in accord with law, and particularly scriptural law; but in the last resort obedience is required – the vice of a bad king may be deplored but as ruler he must be loved (17/2). Only very briefly does Wyclif allude to the problem of the incorrigible tyrant: comparing the loyalty owed by the christian to Christ with that owed by the subject to the king, Wyclif acknowledges one difference despite the similarity: *favet autem homo nature hominis non solum resistendo sed eciam*

---

[32] Even in regard to the clergy, Wyclif's teaching can only by distortion be regarded as Donatist; see, for instance, *De ecclesia*, ed. J. Loserth (Wyclif Society, 1886), 448/14: *prescitus eciam in mortali peccato actuali ministrat fidelibus, licet sibi dampnabiliter, tamen subiectis utiliter sacramenta*; cf. *Sermones* i.273/37, 275/36, iii.47/13.

occidendo (201/15) – an idea he notably fails to develop.³³ But the king owes the obligation of good rule to his subjects; most ominously, indeed one might say with perceptive prescience for events in 1381, Wyclif comments that nothing more destroys a kingdom *quo ad vitam politicam, quam immoderate aufferre ab inferioribus bona fortune* (96/25).³⁴ On the issue of war Wyclif's message was of more dubious appeal to the secular powers: though he conceded the theoretical possibility that there might be just causes for a war, he observed that justice could hardly be sustained once war has been joined – the evils inseparable from the prosecution of warfare evidently incline him towards pacifism, though his statements remain somewhat equivocal.³⁵

Much more contentious ground is reached, however, in Wyclif's consideration of the clerical estate: whilst the king has no authority over the sacraments, he has authority over the ministers of the sacraments in exactly the same form as over the laity (197/2). Consequently clerical claims to exemption from civil law and civil taxation cannot be accepted; the priesthood's allegiance to the pope is in dangerous conflict with the obedience owed to the king.³⁶ Historically before the donation of Constantine the pope was the emperor's liege-

---

³³ In *Sermones* ii.238/27-240/13 Wyclif discusses two kinds of dominion, *iuste et iniuste*, but it is noteworthy that he insists that servants should obey even bad lords, and that the discussion of rebellion allows its legitimacy only in the case of resistance to evil clerics.

³⁴ Compare his later comments in *De blasphemia*, ed. M. H. Dziewicki (Wyclif Society, 1893) from chapter 13 onwards. I have discussed these in: 'Poor preachers, poor men: Views of Poverty in Wyclif and his Followers', in: *Häresie und vorzeitige Reformation im Spätmittelalter*, ed. F. Šmahel (Munich, 1998), pp. 41-53.

³⁵ See the whole of chapter 12, especially pp. 261/4ff, 262/8ff, 271/13ff, 272/21ff, 276/17ff; the subject is also discussed in *De civili dominio* ii. caps. 17-18, and *Sermones* iv.209/31ff and 312/3ff.

³⁶ Wyclif was, of course, writing in a long tradition of discussion of these issues. See particularly M. Wilks, '*Reformatio Regni*: Wyclif and Hus as Leaders of Religious Protest Movements', *Studies in Church History* 9 (1972), 109-130, and in a more general context his book *The Problem of Sovereignty in the Later Middle Ages* (Cambridge, 1964).

man (202/4); this is for Wyclif the proper model for the relation of clerical and secular ruler. The archbishop on his admission swears allegiance to the king on behalf of the clergy (69/24), and the implications of this should be observed; no foreign cleric, whatever and from whomever his mission, should be admitted without a similar oath (108/2, 164/1, 203/23); the claims of friars and other religious that they owe direct obedience to the pope and consequently are exempt from English obligations are invalid (206/1); the pursuit of claims abroad is improper (154/2). Bishops hold authority from the king (119/25), and should pay heed not to canon law or to Roman civil law but to *iuri civili regni nostri* (193/19). On the other hand, despite the allegiance owed by the clergy to the king, the office of a cleric is not compatible with involvement in temporal administration: the duty of the priest is the preaching of God's word, and that is a full-time occupation (154/23). At a later stage in Wyclif's career this hostility to clerks in secular offices became much more pronounced: commenting, not without regret, on the slaying of archbishop Sudbury by the 1381 rebels, Wyclif *observes Quid, rogo, pertinet ad archiepiscopum occupare cancellariam regis, que est secularissimum regni officium?*[37] The king's duty extends to positive action: he, and his deputies, should enforce the residence of parish clergy (163/7).

Most materially, of course, this leads to a consideration of the temporal wealth of the church and its political implications. Given his conception of the duty of priests, and of the limitation of 'spiritual matters', and his insistence on the life of poverty set by Christ and his apostles as the model for subsequent clergy, the logic of Wyclif's condemnation of the wealth of the church is unassailable. He acknowledges that the laity cannot escape from the responsibility of having provided this: the progenitors of the kings of England irreligiously and foolishly endowed the church (213/10), and the lords through endowment corrupted the church (215/1). The intention of such gifts may have been reasonable – they were to *be bona pauperum, patrimonium Christi*, but they have entirely diverted the clergy

---

[37] *De blasphemia*, p. 194/16; see my paper '*Hermofodrita or Ambidexter*: Wycliffite Views on Clerks in Secular Office', in: *Lollardy and Gentry* (above n. 4), pp. 41-51.

from their function. Disendowment is the only solution: *Res igitur sacras, super quibus rex habet capitale dominium, debent usui quem limitarunt leges ecclesie mancipare* (183/14). And Wyclif is not reluctant to draw out the implications of this theory in strictly practical terms: it is lawful for the king to tax the clergy, and obligatory for the clergy to pay without exemption (9/24, 66/24); claims to the inalienability of clerical wealth are ludicrous since their logic would imply that no priest can purchase anything (208/18, cf, 63/25); the king may lawfully pull down a church and build a tower in time of attack, or melt chalices to pay his soldiers – *lapides vivi sunt meliores saxis terrestribus* (185/9). Even the more immediate payments of tithes and offerings to parish priests should be dependent upon the fulfilment by the individual curate of his spiritual office: the laity may legitimately withhold tithes from one who is non-resident, or who even though present does not preach and minister effectively to his flock – the layman being the judge (59/26, 87/13).

Such a programme might be viewed with equanimity by the secular rulers, but it could hardly be tolerated by the ecclesiastical hierarchy and its allies. Wyclif's programme was developed by his followers both before and after his death in 1384. Lollard schemes for disendowment have been much discussed, and need no further exemplification here.[38] But other limitations on the powers of the priesthood were likewise advocated; the multitude of evidence cannot here be fully reviewed, and I shall limit my comments to a brief look at four texts. The *Tractatus de regibus* may date from the 1380s, and has been described by its editor as being 'an epitome of the master's theories on the relations between church and state'.[39] Despite its brevity, and, compared with Wyclif's own sophistication, its crudity of argument, the basic claims are still in place: reiterating the familiar claim

---

[38] See most fully M. Aston, '"Caim's Castles": Poverty, Politics and Disendowment', reprinted in her *Faith and Fire* (above n. 20), pp. 95-131 and references there.

[39] Edited by J.-P. Genet, *Four English Political Tracts of the Later Middle Ages* (Camden Fourth Series 18, 1977), pp. 5-19; the single manuscript is Oxford, Bodleian Library MS Douce 273, ff.37v-53. Genet, p. 3, dates the text, perhaps more firmly than the evidence assures, from the allusion (p. 18/1) to the persecution of [Lollard] preachers.

(here attributed to Augustine) that the king is the vicar of God and the priest the vicar of Christ, the author goes on to concentrate on the king's *regale* (8/19ff). The maintenance of this is the king's supreme duty, and requires his retention of his subjects, the wealth of his kingdom and honour. It follows from this that those encroaching on the king's domination of any of these is a traitor. Priests assailing any of these fall under the same condemnation: the king may even be a traitor to his own office when he allows a priest to take over anything that should rightfully be the king's (8/24ff). Any cleric, including any friar, who claims exemption from the king's law is arguing *that kyngus bene not fulle lordes of her kyngedome* (10/14); private religious have been introduced by the popes, and these diminish the *regale* of lords *and thus, by processe of tyme, my3t tho londe be conquerid al into tho popis honde as other rewmys bene* (11/8) – *Summe men sayne that if tho pope were lorde of al thinge in this londe that is in tho dede honde of prestys, he were more lorde than oure kynge* (11/18). The author is in no doubt about why this situation is not remedied: it is a simple reflection of the excessive power of the clergy over the king and over the legal processes of his realm – the king has been duped into allowing the clergy to imprison men who teach the truth about *them And sithen leve of enprisonynge comes to hem by graunt of kynges, tho kynges that 3yven hem leve, approven synne that comes therof* (18/20). The *Tractatus* seems to have gained little circulation itself, but its arguments are found at greater prolixity in many other Lollard tracts.

The *Tractatus* deals with complex concepts in a relatively straightforward way. Two other Lollard texts attempt to confront the political issues within a more astute framework. The first of these is a Latin work by a *discipulus Doctoris Evangelici* which survives in three Hussite copies; this argues the case not only for the right, but also for the duty, of a secular ruler to punish erring clergy, proving the case by means of the wording of the king's coronation oath.[40] Despite

---

[40] Edited in 'The King and Erring Clergy: a Wycliffite Contribution', *Studies in Church History Subsidia* 9 (1991), 269-278; the manuscripts are Prague University

Peculiaris regis clericus

the preservation of the text, origination in England is assured by the distinctively English form of the oath; its date is less certain since the wording is compatible with the oath sworn by both Richard II and Henry IV. Comparable in technique is a longer vernacular text that draws on the oath sworn by a bishop to the pope on taking up his office: the oath is divided into twenty-three subsections, each of which is shown to impinge on the proper allegiance of a cleric to his secular sovereign.[41] Date here is more certain: allusion is made to the two popes, Urban VI and Clement VII, indicating origination between 1378 and 1389. Again this text is much concerned with the conflict between royal and papal *regaly*: to the author the two powers are only compatible if the pope reverts to Peter's understanding of his position, and withdraws entirely from temporal wealth and its associated powers. The mere fact of swearing the oath to the pope renders the bishop a traitor to the king (ff. 2, 7v, 11); the division between the secular powers and the ecclesiastical encourages division amongst the people, and this leads to rebellion (f. 5v); the intention of the distribution of wealth to the clergy was *to make hem trewe dispensatours of here godis to pore nedy men, takyng of the same godis a resonable lyuyng* (f. 8), but this has been diverted to the enrichment of the church.

More significant than the individual charges in these two texts, since these charges can be replicated over and over again in Lollard texts, is the structure of these two texts. Both imply access to sources which, whilst not obscure, would hardly occur to writers not versed in political discussion, whether secular or ecclesiastical. The vernacular text draws heavily on canon law, with the conventional form of references to it supplied in the margins. In this it shares in a common Wycliffite technique; another text with similar concerns and equal erudition is the *Thirty-Seven Conclusions of the Lollards*, where use is also

---

Library X.E.9, ff.206-207v, Vienna, Österreichische Nationalbibliothek 3928, ff.189-90 and 3932 ff.155v-156.

[41] Found in London, British Library MS Additional 24202, ff.1-13v.

made, along with the usual panoply of patristic references, of canon law commentators.[42]

It is, I would suggest, in the light of texts of this kind, by Wyclif and by his followers, that the extension of civil and ecclesiastical powers between 1380 and 1430 should be seen. Wyclif the master and his disciples, whether writing in Latin or in the more accessible vernacular, were arguing about immediate political issues, in practical terms and with inside information. Nicholas Hereford's Ascension day sermon in 1382, in which he exhorted his congregation to press the king towards disendowment of the church, if necessary by rebellion – this, remember, less than a year after the Peasants' Revolt – is only remarkable for its crudity:[43] most Wycliffites preferred a more sophisticated approach, through political, indeed parliamentary, argument. To the king as secular monarch Wyclif and Lollardy offered no direct challenge; indeed, their blueprint for the commonwealth strengthened the authority of the king, both materially through the confiscation and taxing of accumulated church wealth, and administratively through the substitution of a single political allegiance for the division between royal and papal lordship. But to Courtenay, Arundel, Chichele and the multitude of their clerical subordinates, Wycliffism represented a challenge in some ways more profound than any devised by Henry VIII. There can be no surprise, therefore, that the ecclesiastical hierarchy used all its powers, directly and indirectly, to thwart that challenge. And Wyclif would have seen the irony that a sequence of kings, Richard II, Henry IV and Henry V, allowed themselves to be manipulated by their clerics to put down those who had most to offer them. Wyclif described himself, probably about 1378, as *peculiaris regis clericus*; some forty years later Lollards described

---

[42] Printed under the title *Remonstrance against Romish Corruptions in the Church*, ed. J. Forshall (London, 1851); see, for instance, p. 15.

[43] The sermon was edited by S. Forde, 'Nicholas Hereford's Ascension Day Sermon, 1382', *Medieval Studies* 51 (1989), 205-241.

Henry V as the modern equivalent of the gospel high priest, the *princeps presbiterorum, princeps sacerdotum*.[44]

---

[44] *Opera minora*, ed. J. Loserth (Wyclif Society, 1913), 422/24; for the later taunt see Walsingham *Historia Anglorum*, ed. H. T. Riley, 2 vols. (Rolls Series 1863-1864), ii.306; and Thomas Netter of Walden, *Doctrinale Antiquitatum Fidei Catholicae Ecclesiae*, ed. B. Blanciotti, 3 vols. (Venice, 1757-1759), i.486. Though Allmand (above n. 2, pp. 304-305) has argued that not only 'Henry was the clergy's protector, but their master, too', the biblical resonance of the phrase makes clear the hostility of its origin.

XI

Poor preachers, poor men:
Views of Poverty in Wyclif and his Followers

Thomas Walsingham, in the course of his blood-curdling story of the Peasants' Revolt of 1381, gave an account of the sermon of John Ball before two thousand Kentish men assembled on Blackheath before their entry into London[1]. Ball's text, according to Walsingham, was not a biblical one but two lines of English verse:

    Whan Adam dalf and Eve span,
    Wo was thanne a gentilman?

Whether Walsingham was aware that the lines were not new, and had been used some years previously by no less a worthy than bishop Brinton, is unclear[2]. More interesting is his summary of the contents of Ball's ensuing sermon: all men had been created equal by God, who, had he wished there to be lords and servants, would have created these two orders in Eden; consequently all men should live as equals. To bring about this situation, men should strive first to kill the great lords of the kingdom, then the judges, justices and juries of the kingdom; then they should sieze the land of those they knew to be harmful to the community; there would then be peace and security in the future, equal liberty, nobility, dignity and power[3]. Ball's words so pleased the company, Walsingham adds, that they ac-

---

[1] *Thomas Walsingham*, Historia Anglicana, ed. *Henry T. Riley* (Rolls Series, London 1863–4) ii.32–3, largely reproduced in Walsingham Chronicon Angliae, ed. *Edward M. Thompson* (Rolls Series, London 1874) 321–2; in addition to Walsingham, the most important, near-contemporary accounts of the Revolt are those of the Anonimalle Chronicle, 1333–1381, ed. *Vivien H. Galbraith* (Manchester 1927), and of *Henry Knighton*, Chronicon ed. *Joseph R. Lumby* (Rolls Series, London 1889–95) ii.130–144. A convenient collection of these and other, mostly chronicle, accounts translated into modern English is The Peasants' Revolt of 1381, ed. *R. Barrie Dobson* (London ²1983).
[2] *Mary A. Devlin* (ed.), The sermons of Thomas Brinton, Bishop of Rochester (1373–1389) i, in: Camden Society third series 85 (1954) 154; Devlin dates this sermon to 12 March 1374. For other medieval English citations, which suggest that this is a traditional verse, see *Bartlett J. Whiting* and *Helen W. Whiting*, Proverbs, Sentences and Proverbial Phrases from English Writings mainly before 1500 (Cambridge Mass., London 1968) A38.
[3] The Anonimalle Chronicle 137–8 contains a comparable account of Ball's advice to the rebels, though not presented as a sermon, as a result of which Ball 'fuist tenu entre les comunes come une prophete'.

claimed Ball their future archbishop and chancellor of the kingdom; Ball alone was worthy of the first – saying that the present archbishop was a traitor to the commons and the kingdom, and that he should be beheaded wherever he might be found.

As Walsingham's audience would have appreciated, Ball's final exhortation had been followed to the letter in the events that ensued: Simon Sudbury, archbishop of Canterbury and chancellor of England, was beheaded by the rebels outside the Tower of London[4]. Equally, though it is not clear from other sources that the move actually had the approbation of the Revolt's leaders, the palace of the Savoy, the London house of John of Gaunt, duke of Lancaster, was sacked by the mob; that this may have been not wanton destruction nor greed for rich plunder, but in pursuit of Ball's ideal of human equality, is suggested by the report that the gold and rich jewels were thrown into the Thames and that the rebels themselves punished those of their fellows who kept any for themselves[5]. Walsingham, after this damning narration, reproduces Ball's letter to the commons of Essex, a letter of much less blatant instigation to rebellion, and then smugly concludes the history of Ball by narrating how Ball was hung, drawn and beheaded at St.Albans in July 1381 in the presence of the king, the body then being quartered and the four parts sent to four cities of the realm[6].

The interest of this story for my present purpose lies in the fact that it appears as part of the narrative of Ball's trial, and occurs immediately after another claim by Walsingham: Ball 'docuit et perversa dogmata perfidi Johannis Wiclyf, et opiniones quas tenuit, et insanias falsas'. This claim in more ambivalent terms is made by Knighton when, in his account of Wyclif, he describes Ball as his precursor, the John the Baptist as it were; the later collection of materials, the *Fasciculi Zizaniorum*, describes Ball as Wyclif's *sequax*[7]. The views which, Walsingham alleged,

---

[4] For recent commentary on the Revolt see The English Rising of 1381, ed. *Rodney Hilton* and *Trevor H. Aston* (Cambridge 1984), Essex and the Great Revolt of 1381, ed. *W. H. Liddell, R. G. Wood* (Essex Record Office 1982), and *Nicholas Brooks*, The Organization and Achievement of the Peasants of Kent and Essex in 1381, in: Studies in Medieval History presented to R. H. C. Davis, ed. *Henry Mayr-Harting, Robert I. Moore* (London and Ronceverte 1985) 247–70.

[5] For the sack of the Savoy see primarily *Walsingham* Hist.Angl. i.457 repeated in Chron.Angl. 288–9; *Knighton*, 134–5; Anon.Chron. 141–2.

[6] Hist.Angl. ii.33–34, Chron.Angl. 322; a fuller account of letters sent out by the rebels under various names including that of Ball is to be found in *Knighton*, 138–40, They have been discussed a number of times; see most recently *Richard F. Green*, John Ball's Letters: Literary History and Historical Literature in: Chaucer's England: Literature in Historical Context, ed. *Barbara A. Hanawalt* (Medieval Studies at Minnesota 4, Minneapolis 1992) pp.176–200; *Steven Justice*, Writing and Rebellion: England in 1381 (Berkeley, London 1994); and my paper: Piers Plowman and the Peasants' Revolt: a Problem Revisited, in: Yearbook of Langland Studies 8 (1994) 85–106.

[7] *Knighton*, ii.151 'Hic [i.e. Wyclif] habuit praecursorem Johannem Ball, veluti Christus Johannem Baptistam, qui vias suas in talibus opinionibus praeparavit, et plurimos quoque doctrina sua, ut dicitur, perturbavit'; Fasciculi Zizaniorum, ed. *Walter W. Shirley* (Rolls Series, London 1858) 273.

Views of Poverty 43

Ball had been disseminating for twenty years and more, certainly anticipated his Blackheath sermon: he had castigated both secular lords and ecclesiastical figures, but he had also long taught that no-one should give tithes unless he were richer than the parson to whom those tithes should be paid, and had urged that tithes and offerings should be withheld if it appeared that the payer led a better life than his curate[8].

The connection of Wyclif with the Peasants' Revolt of 1381 is, of course, an issue that has been long and hotly debated, and is one without any easy resolution[9]. The coincidence of the Revolt with the ecclesiastical challenge to Wyclif's teaching on the eucharist in Oxford in the spring of the same year means that no chronicler of religious affiliations – and that covers almost all the consecutive histories of the Revolt – can avoid the charge of confusing the two affairs. Wyclif's *Confessio*, his response to the condemnation of his eucharistic views by the Oxford committee headed by William Berton, is dated 10 May 1381[10]; the Revolt reached the outskirts of London on 13 June – the feast, as Margaret Aston has recently reminded us, of Corpus Christi day[11]. Wyclif's deplorable departure from theological orthodoxy in regard to the church's central sacrament retrospectively validated the 1377 condemnation of pope Gregory XI, a condemnation which had never been fully endorsed in England; that condemnation had selected a number of Wyclif's earlier opinions on dominion, the temporalities of the church and the ability of the secular powers to correct erring clerics[12]. To a dispassionate observer it might seem that those opinions, whilst hostile to the temporal aspirations of the clergy, were hardly incitement to the kind of civil rebellion that erupted in the Peasants' Revolt. But chroniclers of Walsingham's stripe could argue, with persuasive if not always logical force, that sedition against the secular powers was the in-

---

[8] Hist.Angl. ii.32, Chron.Angl. 320–1. Walsingham's twenty years was no exaggeration: Ball had certainly been in trouble with the authorities since 1355 at the latest; see *Alison McHardy, The Church in London 1375–1392* (London 1977) xviii, 86, and *Margaret Aston*, Corpus Christi and Corpus Regni: Heresy and the Peasants' Revolt, in: Past and Present 143 (1994) 3–47 at 21–3.
[9] See *Herbert B. Workman*, John Wyclif: a Study of the English Medieval Church (Oxford 1926) ii.237–40; *K. Bruce McFarlane*, John Wycliffe and the Beginnings of English Nonconformity (London 1952) 99–100; *Joseph H. Dahmus*, The Prosecution of John Wyclyf (New Haven 1952) 82–85; *Margaret Aston*, Lollardy and Sedition, 1381–1431, reprinted in her Lollards and Reformers (London 1984 – the paper first appeared in 1960) 3–7; *Dobson*, (above n.1), 373; my comments in: The Premature Reformation (Oxford 1988) 66–9.
[10] Fasc.Ziz. 115–32; the deliberations of the Oxford committee are 109–13. The date is given on the copy of the text in Oxford MS Bodley 703, f.57ra. A longer version appears in four Hussite copies, and the continuation is printed by *I. H. Stein*, An unpublished fragment of Wyclif's Confessio, in: Speculum 8 (1933) 504–510. The whole of the text reappears in Wyclif's De apostasia, ed. *Michael H. Dziewicki* (Wyclif Society 1889) 213/2–16, 219/32–221/13, 222/40–229/37, 230/21–231/9 and the continuation, after a few lines, Wyclif Sermones iii, ed. *Johann Loserth* (Wyclif Society 1889) 278/7–286/30.
[11] *Aston*, Corpus Christi.
[12] The condemnation appears in *Walsingham*, Hist.Angl. i.345–356, the views pp.353–6.

evitable extension of Wyclif's doctrine of dominion and of his attack on the material wealth and power of the church[13].

It is not my purpose here to argue this case yet again. Whatever their polemical motivation, and however much that motivation slanted their judgment and consequently the accuracy of their reporting, many ecclesiastical contemporaries undoubtedly saw a connection between Wyclif's teaching and the Revolt. Wyclif's own comments on that Revolt in his *De blasphemia* have been taken by some critics as indicative of his hostility to the aims of the Revolt, and consequently of the improbability of his involvement with its course or its leaders[14]. But such critics, it seems, have concentrated on one or two remarks to the exclusion of their wider context. Wyclif did indeed deplore the beheading of the archbishop by *rurales* (190/20); it would have been better if the secular authorities had removed the cause of contention, the excessive temporalities of the church, in time to stop such an attrocity. The punishment exacted by the populace was indeed cruel and in their anger the rebels 'non plene fecerunt ad regulam' (190/17); but provocation had been offered by ecclesiastical incarceration of *bona pauperum* which should have been transferred to the relief of the community (190/25). As he had outlined earlier, 'particio indebita bonorum fortune est precipua causa perturbacionis ecclesie' (33/1), or 'inprovida distribucio bonorum fortune ex ceco titulo elemosine facit nimis magnam perturbacionem ecclesie' (89/22) – the only change was the extension of that explanation from the church to the whole realm.

These statements, ambiguous at best, are, however, only the starting point in *De blasphemia* for Wyclif's much more extensive reflection upon the state of the country and upon the circumstances that could have produced the Revolt, an event which had evidently shocked even if it had not entirely surprised him. Like many of Wyclif's major works, the *De blasphemia*, the last book of his *Summa theologie*, fails to adhere closely to the plan and structure outlined at the start: a definition of blasphemy in the church, and an analysis of its twelve branches. Equally, like many of his writings, the text as it has been preserved, in seven complete manuscripts and two extracts, might appear to represent a partially revised or altered version of what Wyclif had originally written – the ninth branch of blasphemy, though its identity in the monastic orders is clear, is never fully described[15]. But the apparent defect occurs precisely at the point at which references

---

[13] And not only chroniclers: the Cistercian William of Rymington in his XLV Conclusiones written before autumn 1383 accused Wyclif of stirring up disturbances in London and elsewhere, and most notably on Corpus Christi day (i.e. 1381); see Oxford MS Bodley 158, f.202 where it forms part of the prologue – notably Wyclif in his reply (printed Opera Minora, ed. *Johann Loserth* (Wyclif Society 1913) 201–57 failed to deal with this charge.

[14] Text ed. *Michael H. Dziewicki* (Wyclif Society 1893); for these critical deductions see the discussions listed above (n.9), *McFarlane*, 99–100, is most sceptical; but note *Workman*, ii.241–3; *Dahmus*, 85; *Aston*, 4.

[15] The twelve branches are described as tortores, and the analysis begins in chapter 4 (54/15ff.) with the pope; the ensuing chapters deal with the cardinals, the bishops and the archdeacons (caps. 5–7), with penance and implicitly confessors (caps. 8–11), with rural deans and cursorily rectors and inferior priests (cap. 12), as the second to eighth tortores. Chapter 13

to the Peasants' Revolt intrude. Rather than later modification then, it seems more probable that the interruption reflects the precise chronology of Wyclif's writing. The opening twelve chapters allude many times to the debates of early 1381 in Oxford, and comment with new venom on the activities of the friars both in long established vices and in apparently new hostilities (such as their reluctance to share their books)[16]. But, though Wyclif's earlier ideas that Walsingham alleged resurfaced in the popular rising of 1381 are certainly repeated in these early chapters, the first overt mention of the Revolt is in chapter 13[17]. The remainder of the tract, though it adheres superficially to the analysis of the ninth to twelfth branches of blasphemy, is, it seems to me, dominated by that Revolt[18].

The interest of those reflections for my present purpose lies in the way in which they combine many of Wyclif's long-held views about the correct relation of church and state with the precisely contemporary situation. The ideals, expressed in largely timeless terms in *De civili dominio* i, from which Gregory XI on the information of Adam Easton drew the condemned views in 1377, are now translated into concrete proposals for immediate and urgent political action[19]. The criticism of the actual ecclesiastical set-up had always been anchored all too blatantly in contemporary affairs, but the warnings that had accompanied that criticism could be shown in the second half of *De blasphemia* to have been fulfilled in the Revolt. The exhortations of *De officio regis*, that mirror for the young prince Richard II, a work of uncharacteristic terseness and coherence that may originally have been intended to follow directly on *De civili dominio* i, now require immediate political implementation[20]. The seven petitions to the king that are incorporated into *De*

opens with the identification of the ninth as the possessioners (188/2), but within two pages Wyclif turns to the Revolt. Though the tenth to twelfth are identified in caps. 14–18, the discussion is constantly diverted into issues connected with the contemporary disturbances. The complete copies of the tract, all but one of them Hussite (including two not used by Dziewicki), do not appear to differ significantly in the text offered.

[16] See for the first 62/8, 89/27; for the second for instance 75/20, 86/12 and the charge concerning books 21/5.

[17] For instance 52/28ff., 77/35ff., 81/15ff., 93/27ff., 109/19ff., 156/23ff.

[18] *Dziewicki* in his introduction (vii-viii, xxxiii-xxxiv) implies that the Revolt is only seriously considered in chapter 13, though he mentions the later allusion to it in chapter 17 (267/10). Dziewicki (vii-viii) points to two allusions in the text that might refer to the Despenser crusade of 1383 (156/27, 191/29), but, as he says, they are uncharacteristically unspecific and probably refer to skirmishes incited by the papal rivals before that.

[19] For the condemned views see above n.12; all but three of the nineteen are verbally identifiable, mostly in sequence, in: *Reginald L. Poole* and *Johann Loserth* (eds.), De civili dominio, 4 vols. (Wyclif Society 1885–1904) i.251–84, whilst the fourth, eighth and last are summaries of material to be found in the book. For Easton's involvement in supplying the information see *William A. Pantin*, The Defensorium of Adam Easton, in: English Historical Review 51 (1928) 675–80; I am grateful to Dr Margaret Harvey, who is currently preparing a fuller study ✻ of Easton's Defensorium, for confirmation of Pantin's suggestion.

[20] The possibility that the De officio regis, *Alfred W. Pollard, Charles Sayle* (eds.) (Wyclif Society 1887), may have been intended to stand earlier in the Summa theologie arises from some cross-references in the text to chapters 'libri proximi' which seem only explicable as allusions

blasphemia chapter 17 (270/12–271/26) repeat old demands, demands that had been condemned by Gregory XI, but their significance is now altered[21]. The fourth is expressed tersely in Wyclif's accustomed terms: 'quod regni comunitas non oneretur talagiis insuetis, antequam totum patrimonium, quo clerus dotatur, deficiat. Patet, quia omnia ista sunt bona pauperum caritative exponenda ad eorum egenciam, vivente clero in perfeccione primarie paupertatis' (271/7). But this is the theorem that culminates from the preceding demonstration that the Revolt could have been stopped if the king, as he should, had taxed the clergy: 'si igitur clerus possessionatus, thesaurarius bonorum pauperum, reddidisset regi ipsorum pedagium, quomodo staret ista dissensio, inferens tantum malum?' (190/33). The sixth 'Quod rex nullum episcopum vel curatum mancipet suo ministerio seculari. Patet: quia aliter tam rex quam clerus foret proditor Jesu Cristi' (271/17) takes its force from the earlier assertion in regard to archbishop Sudbury (194/16) 'Quid, rogo, pertinet ad archiepiscopum occupare cancellariam regis, que est secularissimum regni officium?'

Wyclif acknowledged that the punishment exacted by the *populus* on the clergy in the Revolt was excessive *quantitate*, *qualitate* and *modo* (196/20–197/34) – in quantity, in that property not life should have been removed; in quality, because it was wrong to have killed the archbishop without allowing him to defend himself against his accusers; in manner, because malefactors, even the clergy, are entitled to punishment commensurate to their crime, because punishment should not be attempted against the secular rulers, and because judgment should not be given without due consultation. But the remedies Wyclif outlined to the dire situation of the country can hardly be regarded as comforting to either religious or secular leaders: the temporal possessions of the clergy 'potest quietare comunitates et dominos, ac de remedio perpetuo talis periculi providere' (201/20), and, even more provocatively, 'est enim error intollerabilis quod rex vel alius dominus regni super eius populum tiraniset' (197/39).

Dominating the whole of the last six chapters of *De blasphemia* is a profound anger, against the clergy, against the king, against the lords, for their collusion in allowing the country to come to a pass such that rebellion of this kind could occur. Despite the concern with the rejection of his own views of the eucharist, and his evident pain at the participation of the friars in that rejection, Wyclif constantly recurs to the issues of the Revolt: it is argued against him that many saints have defended clerical temporalities, and that by the same logic as he urges their deprivation could the deprivation of unjust secular owners be justified; but 'tam necessaria est illa sentencia, quod inpossibile est pacificare regna vel clerum complete

to De civili dominio i. A fuller analysis of these references, and of my suggestion that De officio regis may have been directed towards the young king, will be presented elsewhere.
[21] For instance, the demand for confiscation of clerical wealth in the fourth (271/7) repeats the sixth and seventeenth condemned points (Hist.Angl. i.354–355) found in De civili dominio i.267/12 and 265/29 respectively; the final rejection of clerical powers of excommunication (271/20) picks up errors nine and ten (Hist.Angl. i.354) from De civili dominio i.274/15, 276/7.

solvere sua debita, nisi illa sentencia fuerit per principes practisata' (283/30ff.). Whatever the doubts about the theory that Wyclif had urged since *De civili dominio* i, the question was now, and had been for some time, a practical one – and to that there was only one answer.

How far is this wisdom after the event? can the concern for the commons, the apprehension of poverty as well as injustice as the underlying causes of unrest, be traced in Wyclif's earlier writings? does this search for a practical remedy outlast the immediate aftermath of the Revolt? did his followers continue the message of *De blasphemia*? In the rest of this paper I should like to begin to address these questions. Much has been written about Wyclif's theory of dominion, and about his views on fraternal begging, in both cases much about his debt to FitzRalph; though these matters are germane to any full consideration of the questions, I do not want here to go over this ground again[22]. Equally, though it is so central to my subject that I shall briefly return to it at the end, I shall not discuss all the thinking of Wyclif and his followers on the subject of disendowment[23]. What seems to deserve fuller scrutiny is Wyclif's views on the third estate: we know his views on *poor preachers* but what did he think about *poor men*?

In common with many earlier commentators, Wyclif did not condemn riches out of hand: the parable of Dives and Lazarus should not lead to the assumption that riches automatically damned a man, any more than poverty saved him – the poor man may not be able readily to indulge the sin of gluttony, but he was as subject to the temptations of the remaining sins as the rich man. Dives earned hell not because of his possession of wealth, but because he would not share it with the beggar at his gate[24]. Conversely, lack of goods is not in itself a virtue[25]. Expounding the parable of the unjust steward, Wyclif describes how the secular ruler needs to deal justly with riches, and deplores 'tanta inequalitas particionis'[26]. Wyclif's fullest and most nuanced discussion of poverty comes in *De civili dominio* iii chapters 7–10. The previous two chapters examine the position of Christ and, after his death, of the apostles in the early church – this should form the true model for later christian behaviour. The early church in holding in common did not hold *civiliter* (80/20). The perfection of life revealed by this model is not one

---

[22] See, most notably, *Aubrey Gwynn*, The English Austin Friars in the Time of Wyclif (London 1940) especially 59–73; *Michael Wilks*, Predestination, Property and Power: Wyclif's Theory of Dominion and Grace, in: Studies in Church History 2 (1965) 220–36; *Gordon Leff*, Heresy in the Later Middle Ages, 2 vols. (Manchester 1967) ii.545–549; *Katherine Walsh*, A Fourteenth-Century Scholar and Primate: Richard FitzRalph in Oxford, Avignon and Armagh (Oxford 1981), especially 349–468; *James D. Dawson*, Richard FitzRalph and the Fourteenth-Century Poverty Controversy, in: Journal of Ecclesiastical History 34 (1983) 315–44.
[23] See for this *Margaret Aston* "Caim's Castles: Poverty, Politics and Disendowment, reprinted in: Faith and Fire: Popular and Unpopular Religion 1350–1600 (London and Rio Grande 1993) 95–131.
[24] Sermones 4 vols., ed. *Johann Loserth* (Wyclif Society 1887–90) i.224/1ff.
[25] De civ.dom. iii.145/28 'remanet paupertas evangelica in temporalia affluencia'.
[26] Sermones i.273/37.

of simple negation of personal possession, but of shared communication of all good things, spiritual and material[27]. The singular pronouns *meum*, *tuum* and *suum* are repugnant since they imply *proprietatem civilem* (143/19); 'paupertas ... stat in perfecta abdicacione proprietatis et per consequens in abdicacione civilis dominii' (85/13)[28]. This leads to the central concept of *paupertas evangelica* defined shortly afterwards: 'evangelica paupertas non habet nudam carenciam temporalium pro fundamento, quia illam carenciam stat viciosissimum habere temporalia quantumlibet sicientem sed fundatur in fervore caritatis quo quis gratis prescindit ab ipso possibilitatem occasionis usibilium unde Dei dileccio tardaretur' (89/13); this 'evangelica paupertas est scola Christi' (172/16). As emerges, the *pauper evangelicus* is to renounce possession *civiliter*: 'paupertas evangelica infert maius dominium quam aliquid ad quod quis secundum civilitatem potest attingere' (113/24)[29]. Since Christ refused civil possession and declined to judge *civiliter*, the most fitting poverty lies 'in caritativa abdicacione civilitatis propter Christum et eciam in voluntaria communicacione temporalium' (130/17). But this abdication depends crucially on disposition (76/8): such poverty implies true humility (120/19); to this Wyclif repeatedly returns, as 'notandum tamen quod paupertas evangelica non est nuda privacio que est temporalium carencia, sed habitus animi, quo humilis abdicat a se temporalium civilitatem ut expedicius excolat Deum suum' (151/2). At this stage, as he acknowledges, Wyclif's views are comparable to the founding ideals of the monastic and fraternal orders; in later chapters, where Wyclif is answering Woodford's objections, the departure of the contemporary religious from those ideals is more fully stressed[30].

But, as the English saying goes, fine words butter no parsnips – where does this leave those who, from adversity of birth or circumstance, cannot choose but go hungry, without clothing or lodging? Is not Wyclif's thinking limited to his preoccupation with the questions associated with clerical property? Whilst it may not be unfair to see his discussion as coloured by the claims and counterclaims of the clergy, and as framed in terms traditional in that long polemic, it would be wrong to argue that Wyclif gave no thought to the practical issues of civil society in his discussion here. The endowment of the church was intended by the laity not for the enrichment of the clergy but 'ad ministerium pauperum bona mundi' (217/17), and this is backed by gospels and epistles, and also by the canonists[31]. There may

---

[27] De civ.dom. iii.78/26; for Wyclif's views on community of property see *Anthony Kenny*, Wyclif (Oxford 1985) 46–7, 108, and note De statu innocencie, *Johann Loserth, Frederic D. Matthew* (eds.) (Wyclif Society 1922) 508/13 all things may be 'propria quoad habicionem relativam' but 'communia quoad usum'.

[28] Cf. 147/19 the Lord's prayer does not ask for 'panem meum' but for 'panem vite communem' implied by the collective 'nostrum'.

[29] Cf. De civ.dom. i.60/21, iii.73/15 where it is stated that civil possession is always tainted with sin.

[30] De civ.dom. iii.108/9; later 405/19, 419/31ff., 478/3. Woodford's De dominio civili clericorum was edited by *Eric Doyle*, in: Archivum Franciscanum Historicum 66 (1973) 49–109, and is answered in De civ. dom. iii.351–405 (caps. 18–19).

[31] The whole of chapter 14 is an anthology of canon law support for clerical poverty, culmi-

be two kinds of possession, *civiliter* and *ex nudo titulo gracie* (143/29); the second should be that to which the christian should aspire, but the need for the first in this world is freely acknowledged. Evangelical poverty is of itself a virtue, whilst civil dominion is by definition an imperfect religion which can only be justified if it leads to evangelical poverty (161/26); 'civilis possessio ... implicat veniale peccatum' (161/43). This raises, as Wyclif acknowledged, a problem for the secular ruler. God, he argues, does not order civil dominion as such in scripture, but he ordains many acts of civil dominion as meritorious; civil dominion is itself only venial sin – the deadly sin of pride and of defect of charity are often inculcated by it (167/8). The temporalities of the church would be better dispensed if they were in the hands of laymen (334/35). In *De officio regis* Wyclif observes that nothing so readily destroys a kingdom 'quo ad vitam politicam, quam immoderate aufferre ab inferioribus bona fortune' (96/25); in practice subjects are obedient *because* the king dispenses goods wisely and rules prudently – departure from this, and particularly collusion in the appropriation of goods into the dead hand of the church, encourages revolt (97/34).

Wyclif's importance as a writer on political theory in the later medieval period has long been acknowledged; the implication of analysis of that theory has, however, often been that his ideas remain remote from the realm of actuality – his views on dominion, for example, to many historians of medieval thought were speculations without possible impact on the world of England in the reign of Richard II, or anywhere else[32]. Only the schemes for disendowment, adumbrated by Wyclif and more fully developed by his followers, we are assured by such critics, had any practical application. But some precise practical implications are drawn by Wyclif in *De civili dominio* iii: if a natural heir to property that has been given to the church finds himself in poverty, it is not right that the church should remain in possession (304/17); the layman who believes a cleric to have temporalities unjustly may bring the case to a civil court (309/18), and the king should organize scrutiny of clerical possessions, which scrutiny would certainly lead to confiscation (314/2)[33]. Equally in *De officio regis* theory extends to specificities: the archbishop on admission swears allegiance to the king on behalf of the clergy (69/24), and hence admits the temporal subordination of the institutional church to the secular authority[34]; the king should not admit to England any priest unless he is prepared to swear such an oath of allegiance (108/2, cf. 154/1, 206/1); it is lawful for the king to pull down a church to build a defensive tower, or to melt chalices to pay his soldiers (185/9). Is it surprising that Wyclif's contemporaries saw his

nating (257/9–263/13) in seven conclusions concerning the implications and means of remedying this situation.
[32] See, for instance, *Leff*, (above n.22), ii.549, and *John Stacey*, Wyclif and Reform (London 1964) 63–4.
[33] De civ.dom. ii.47/8ff., 51/17 gives historical examples of confiscation of clerical property in England in the past.
[34] Cf. De civ.dom. ii.39/31 and the material from London MS BL Additional 24202 quoted below.

teaching in a much more alarming light than the modern critics: Gregory XI's bull against Wyclif in 1377 selected precisely those views on dominion from *De civili dominio* i for condemnation, and the letter that accompanied that bull to England stressed the disruptive effects that such views could have on ecclesiastical and civil society. Later opponents saw those warnings only too accurately fulfilled in the Peasants' Revolt, to which they connected Wyclif as a prime instigator. As I have tried to show, whatever the causal relation between the Oxford academic and civil uprising, Wyclif's comments on that Revolt give the lie to any modern dismissal of his interest in contemporary actuality – and those comments on that actuality were far from reassuring to either church or secular ruler.

In the light of those comments it is worth looking at the way in which Wyclif's followers continued his political concern. At some point in 1382, probably early, Nicholas Hereford had openly proclaimed that Simon Sudbury had been *juste* slain, because he had desired to correct his master, John Wyclif, whose views he (Hereford) approved – and Hereford 'semper commovendo populum ad insurrectionem'; Philip Repingdon at the Corpus Christi day sermon 'excitavit ... populum ad insurrectionem, et ad spoliandas ecclesias'[35]. There is more information about Hereford's sermon on Ascension day 1382 in Oxford which survives in a copy of a notarial account commissioned immediately by Peter Stokes, the Cistercian messenger (or more accurately spy) of archbishop Courtenay; as the wording makes clear, for the most part only a précis of Hereford's words, which had been delivered in English not in academic Latin before his congregation of the Chancellor of the university and a multitude of clerics and of lay people, is provided – given the purpose of Stokes, it is safe to assume that only the more provocative parts of the sermon were recorded[36]. The sermon, it should be remembered, was given on 15 May 1382, just eleven months after the Revolt had reached its climax in the murder of Sudbury, the destruction of the Savoy and the meeting of Richard with Wat Tyler. That this fact was in the mind of Stokes and of his notary John Fykyes is implicit in the declaredly verbatim account of Hereford's peroration, in which he lamented that the king had no officers to effect the disendowment of the clergy that he had been urging, and exhorted 'vos, o fideles Cristiani, manum apponere vt vos saltim hoc negocium ad finem debitum perducatis' (135). The corruption of all ranks of the church by their attachment to temporalities had been outlined in the preceding analysis; Hereford's description followed exactly in the steps of his master, and echoed older complaints by FitzRalph and others. Stokes could doubtless have amplified these words from his experience of the polemic,

---

[35] Fasc.Ziz. 296, 299.
[36] See the edition by *Simon Forde*, "Nicholas Hereford's Ascension Day Sermon 1382", in: Mediaeval Studies 51 (1989) 205–41. The manuscript, described 230-4, is now Oxford MS Bodley 240, where the sermon appears amongst a final miscellaneous collection of texts on pp.848b-50, but derives from Bury St.Edmunds; *Forde*, 234–6, makes a persuasive case for thinking that the text is 'a close copy of an original instrument'.

and doubtless expected his ecclesiastical masters to be capable of the same[37]. But one or two comments are recorded that are more germane to this paper. At the start of his sermon Hereford outraged Stokes by praying for the king, the queen, the queen mother, the lord duke (unspecified but obviously the Duke of Lancaster, John of Gaunt, long time protector of Wyclif and, as they hoped, of his disciples), for all the lay rulers of the kingdom, for all those 'qui sunt spirituales postpositi Dei' (32), for the Chancellor and members of the university, for the mayor and community of Oxford, but not for the pope[38]. Hereford then apparently started 'Sicut Cristus diligit plus totam comunitatem quam aliquam eius personam, sic deberet quilibet homo plus diligere et zelare totam comunitatem et eius profectum quam particulare comodum alicuius persone singularis eiusdem' (35); he claimed that he had set himself to work entirely 'propter zelum comunitatis', in which cause he was prepared to labour and if necessary to suffer (40). To this concern with the community he returns after a condemnation of the self-interest of all ranks in the church, especially of the friars; turning to his immediate congregation he reproaches the greed of the bachelors, and the even more avaricious claims of the masters 'Et cum omnes sint eiusdem professionis et vnius comunitatis, ex quo inferiores contenti sunt modica parte bonorum comunium, quare non essent contenti superiores tam modico sicut illi?' (106)[39]. Since all religious orders have more than they need for maintenance of life, 'si rex et regnum vellet eis auferre possessiones et thesauros eorum superfluous ut deberet, tunc non oporteret regem spoliare pauperem comunitatem regni per talagia sicut solet' (130). The similarity of wording between Hereford's words, as reported by Stokes, and Wyclif's comments in the *De blasphemia* is striking. Behind the notarial account, and colouring all its declaredly neutral reporting of the sermon that Ascension day, lie the events of the previous year, events that the poet John Gower described in the book that he added in first place to his completed *Vox Clamantis* as the action of 'tanta monstrorum more ferarum ... sicut arena maris'[40]. And that Stokes was not being hysterical in his reporting seems plain from Hereford's peroration, a peroration which, if it bears any resemblance to what Hereford said, urged a repeat performance of that Revolt *ad finem debitum*[41].

---

[37] See references *Penn R. Szittya*, The Antifraternal Tradition in Medieval Literature (Princeton 1986).
[38] The outrage felt comes clearly through the words: after the long sequence of prayers, with its thrice reiterated 'inquit', 'et in tota recomendacione non fecit mencionem de summo pontifice specialem' (33–4).
[39] Wyclif considered the avarice of academics, both corporately and individually, in De blasphemia 244/35ff.; compare the English texts cited below.
[40] *George C. Macaulay* (ed.), The Complete Works of John Gower, 4 vols. (Oxford 1899–1902) iv.679–80, "the great multitude of monsters like wild beasts ... a multitude like the sands of the sea".
[41] 135–8: 'Ideo oportet vos, o fideles Cristiani, manum apponere vt vos saltim hoc negocium ad finem debitum perducatis. Et tunc firmiter spero quod bene procedet, quia scio certissime quod ipse Deus omnipotens uult quod fiat.'

Hereford's sermon can be dated, and precisely dated only a year after the Revolt. With most of the Lollard texts more uncertainty about dating exists, and more likelihood that a longer passage of time had elapsed since that event. But echoes of the concerns revealed in Wyclif's *De blasphemia* and in Hereford's sermon can be repeatedly found. Modern critics fasten the more avidly on the constant criticism of the clergy. But, alongside this preoccupation, the contrasting plight of the poor is not in the texts forgotten: the clergy 'laten pore men haue nakid sidis, and dede wallis haue grete plente of wast gold'; the exactions from the commons may not in financial terms amount to large sums, but 'it is in many caasis as myche synne to rob a wedewe or a pore fadirles child of a peny or an halpeny as it were to robbe a riche man of an hundrid markis-worth godis'; bishops in taking secular power cause dissension between men 'as risyngis of the puple and comunes a3en hem and ther lordis as doolfully we sawen late'[42]. Wyclif's view of *evangelica paupertas* is recalled when an English writer claims that worldly prelates rob the church 'of the tresour of wilful povert and mekenesse'[43]. Much detail is given of the ways in which the activities of churchmen work to the detriment of the poor commons. 'The sotil amortasynge of seculer lordischipis that is don bi menene hondis in fraude of the kyngis statute' should be remedied, to the advantage of the kingdom 'in sparynge of the pore comons of taxes'; 'Now the thrid dele o the land es in her [sc.the clergy's] handes and [thei] ben waxen worldliche lordes that the comone popil es greteli anentisid therbi so ferforth that, when the kinge had nede to be holpen of his popel of taxes and other tallyages, thai ben no3t of mi3t to help the kinge'; the clergy, in following the decretal prohibition on payment of civil taxes without papal permission, give an example to the people to rebel against the king and lords[44].

The results of the continuing accretion of property to the church are spelt out in immediately apprehensible terms: a gentleman asked a bishop how secular lords and knights should live, if the clergy had all the property, to which the bishop answered that 'thai schuld be clerkis soudyoures, and lyue by her wagis'[45]. Clerical claims of the inalienability of property given to the church produce both deplorable and also ridiculous consequences: deplorable in that the process diminishes the king's *regalie* 'and than were he no kinge bot as kinge in a somer game, or elles as a kinge paintid on a wall', ridiculous in that, if followed logically, a clerk would be unable to purchase food or other necessaries of life since he could not alienate the money needed[46]. The evils of the conveyance of wealth out of the

---

[42] *Frederic D. Matthew* (ed.), The English Works of Wyclif hitherto unprinted, in: Early English Text Society 74 ([2]1902) 91/32, 417/31 and cf.127/29; the third from an unprinted tract in London BL Additional 24202, f.41. In all quotations of Middle English I have replaced thorn by th.
[43] *Thomas Arnold* (ed.), Select English Works of John Wyclif, 3 vols. (Oxford 1869–71) iii.275/13.
[44] *Matthew*, 278/34; unprinted dialogue in Durham University Library MS V.iii.6 f.10v; *Arnold*, iii.298/10.
[45] *Matthew*, 368/28.
[46] Durham dialogue f.17v; cf. *Arnold*, iii.516/2.

Views of Poverty

country to the papacy by various means is frequently deplored: 'it is opin at the i3e to kunnynge men that, thou3 oo greet hil of gold were in Ingelond, and no man outake siche Rome-renneris toke of it, 3ea, a ferthing, al the gold shulde be borun out of the rewme bi hem to straungeris withynne a certeyn tyme'[47].

The concept of the king's *regalie* is, for the writers of these texts, one of considerable potency but also a very practical matter. The *Tractatus de regibus* urges the need for the king to maintain his *regalie*, for which he needs money and men; those who claim exemption from taxation or from the processes of civil justice, as the clergy do, break the king's *regalie*, ensuring that 'kyngus bene not fulle lordes of her kyngedome'[48]. The kings and the lords are intimidated by clerks who curse them if they attempt to reclaim goods 'as 3if seculer lordis and the comyns weren no part of holy chirche'[49].

Many of these ideas are, of course, traditional; some of them are uncanny echoes of the doctrines of the accursed Marsilius of Padua – whom Gregory XI in his bull asserted had been the teacher of Wyclif[50]. Others are more distinctively derived from Wyclif, in their terminology as in their ideas. Even if Wyclif himself is rarely mentioned by name, important events in his history are sometimes specified: the friars at the Earthquake Council condemned the view that tithes are alms and can be withheld and given to poor men; the friars at the Blackfriars Council condemned as heretical the idea of disendowment; the clergy at the Earthquake Council cursed those who attempted to take anything from the church[51]. In each of these three allusions, deriving from three different texts, the Council is associated not with condemnation of Wyclif's eucharistic views, but with his views about the temporalities of the church. More specifically an unprinted text alleges that the clergy reply to charges against their ill-gotten wealth with the claim 'in this wise profesiede of vs Lincoln, Bradewardyn, Armacan, Kilmyngton, Wiclyue, and manye othere – and, in tone that ther profecie is but desiryng of veniaunce of ther owne enuye, thei hemself persheden and we ben euere the lengere the strengere'[52]. The patrimony, of Grosseteste, Bradwardine, FitzRalph and his ally Kilmyngton, would not, I think, have displeased Wyclif, and suggests that one later Lollard writer at least was aware of a heritage that derived from before 1381.

---

[47] Josiah Forshall (ed.), Thirty-Seven Conclusions of the Lollards, printed under the title of Remonstrance against Romish Corruptions (London 1851) 88, here quoted from BL Cotton Titus D.i f.49; cf. *Matthew*, 22/32, 23/15, 223/30.
[48] Tractatus de regibus, ed. *Jean-Philippe Genet*, Four English Political Tracts of the Later Middle Ages, in: Camden Society 4th series 18 (1977) 10/5; cf. *Arnold*, iii.391/8, 495/20; *Matthew*, 292/3.
[49] *Arnold*, iii.275/33.
[50] This is not the place to investigate the vexed question of that asserted influence. Wyclif never mentions Marsilius, or quotes him by name, and it seems doubtful whether the Defensor pacis was available in England before 1400; but any reader of that text followed by many of Wyclif's mature writings must be struck by the similarities.
[51] Three different texts in *Arnold*, iii.175/22, 233/3, 313/20.
[52] BL Additional 24202, f.53v.

XII

THE KING AND ERRING CLERGY: A WYCLIFFITE CONTRIBUTION

ONE of the questions that appeared in the theologians' list of questions to be asked of suspected Lollards was 'An reges et domini temporales existentes in peccato mortali eo ipso cadunt ab omni iure et titulo ac illa regna vel dominia.' This question appears between one that enquires whether anyone may preach without authority from the pope or a bishop, and another that seeks to know whether the suspect considers that the laity may freely *ad suum arbitrium* correct and judge delinquent lords. At the same position in the longer list put together by a jurist appears a somewhat different question: 'an domini temporales possunt ad arbitrium suum auferre bona temporalia ab ecclesia et a viris ecclesiasticis.'[1] Wyclif's followers would have returned a positive answer to both questions, though the enthusiasm of their reply would have been the more audible for the second.[2] Throughout the history of the movement Lollards were notable for the stridency of their objections to clerical prerogatives, and, especially in the view of their opponents, for their sympathy towards the secular rulers. Individual heretics and isolated texts applied Wyclif's views of dominion to kings and secular lords, but the theory was undoubtedly primarily used against ecclesiastics. Academic debate of Wyclif's theory of dominion was early, and the issue formed the heart of Gregory XI's condemnation in 1377.[3] But the question does not seem to have figured largely in the disputations that followed Wyclif's departure from Oxford in 1381.

One text on this issue, now surviving apparently only in three Hussite manuscripts, may be of interest. The text takes the form of a set of 'six arguments to prove that it pertains to a secular king to punish those clerics who err mortally'. The author is stated in the opening colophon to be

---

[1] For the lists see A. Hudson, 'The Examination of Lollards', *BIHR*, 46 (1973), pp. 155, 153, reprinted in *Lollards and their Books* (London, 1985), pp. 135, 133. I should like to record my gratitude to Dr Alison McHardy for her kindness in reading a draft of this paper and advising me on it; its faults should not be attributed to her.
[2] For the issues see A. Hudson, *The Premature Reformation* (Oxford, 1988), pp. 359–62 and 334–46 respectively.
[3] See Walsingham's *Historia Anglicana*, ed. H. T. Riley, *RS* (1863–4), 1, pp. 346–56; for the issue see G. Leff, *Heresy in the Later Middle Ages* (Manchester, 1967), 2, pp. 546–9 and A. Kenny, *Wyclif* (Oxford, 1985), pp. 42–55.

discipulus quidam venerabilis Doctoris Ewangelici; lest that title should escape the understanding of a reader, one scribe spells out that the author was a disciple *Magistri Johannis Wygleph*. The three manuscripts are now Prague, University Library, X.E.9 (1910), fols 206r–7v, Vienna, Österreichische Nationalbibliothek, 3928, fols 189r–90r, and 3932, fols 155v–6r. The first of these is a collection of Wyclif's works, with at the opening (fols 1r–37r) Hermes Pastor with Czech glosses; it seems to date from c.1420.[4] The other two manuscripts contain only Wyclif texts; the first item in Vienna 3932, the *Trialogus*, is dated by the scribe 1418; on palaeographical grounds Vienna 3928 is dated c.1410.[5]

The first obvious question concerns the origins of the text: granted that it is Wycliffite, does it come from Bohemia, where the surviving manuscripts are to be found, or from England? The Hussites used the term *Doctor Evangelicus* for Wyclif with perhaps greater frequency than the heretic's own countrymen; the argument would fit as well into the context of Hussite thought as into the English Wycliffite world. On the other hand, its exclusively continental preservation does not of itself preclude the possibility of English origin: the *Opus Arduum*, to name a better known and more extensive text, is of certain English source, but no manuscript has yet been found of the text in this country.[6] Fortunately, the *Sex raciones* contains within it evidence that settles the question beyond any reasonable doubt. Five of the six reasons use clauses from the coronation oath and words from the coronation service of an English king to demonstrate the author's case; the wording is quoted at length and verbatim.[7]

---

[4] See W. R. Thomson, *The Latin Writings of John Wyclyf* (Toronto, 1983), nos 53, 35, 50, 427, 414, 394, 413, 388, 431, 204, 410, 395 and GSpur.2. For a description of the manuscript see J. Truhlar, *Catalogus Codicum Manu Scriptorum Latinorum . . . Universitatis Pragensis Asservantur* (Prague, 1905–6), 2, pp. 74–5. The present text is listed by Thomson, p. 307, as GDub.16.

[5] See Thomson index; the lists of contents in both these manuscripts in *Tabulae Codicum Manu Scriptorum . . . in Bibliotheca Palatina Vindobonensi Asservatorum* (Vienna, 1869), 3, pp. 119–21 are superseded by Thomson's.

★ [6] For the *Opus Arduum* see A. Hudson, 'A Neglected Wycliffite Text', *JEH*, 29 (1978), pp. 257–79, reprinted in *Lollards and their Books*, pp. 43–65.

[7] The basic source for information on the subject is P. E. Schramm, tr. L. G. Wickham Legg, *A History of the English Coronation* (Oxford, 1937), esp. appendix, pp. 233–40, and the same author's article 'Ordines-Studien III: die Krönung in England vom 10. Jahrhundert bis zur Neuzeit', *Archiv für Urkundenforschung in Verbindung mit dem Reichsinstitut für ältere deutsche Geschichtskunde*, 15 (1938), neue folge 1.2, pp. 305–91. J. Brückmann, 'The Ordines of the Third Recension of the Medieval English Coronation Order', in T. A. Sandquist and M. R. Powicke, eds, *Essays in Medieval History presented to Bertie Wilkinson* (Toronto, 1969), pp. 99–115, has useful further material and bibliography, but the edition promised at n. 8 seems never to have appeared. A. F. Sutton and P. W. Hammond, *The Coronation of Richard III: the Extant Documents* (Gloucester and New York, 1983), esp. pp. 200–12 has valuable information, albeit relating primarily to a ceremony later than that involved here.

A Wycliffite Contribution

These provide sufficient evidence to establish an English origin for the text.

The quotations are of varying help in proving this. The longest, the fourth and fifth, are not useful: they give at length the prayers uttered by the archbishop when he hands to the king the ceremonial sword and when he consecrates the king. The first of these does indeed occur in the English *Liber Regalis*,[8] but it is also found in the ceremony for the coronation of the emperor, as, for instance, in the service used for Charles IV in 1355.[9] Similarly, the prayer used at the consecration of the king is again found in both English and imperial liturgies.[10] But the first three quotations, taken from the oath sworn by the king, are much more illuminating. They do not correspond to the imperial oath, but give the wording of the English oath.[11] It seems very unlikely, to put the case at its lowest, that a Bohemian Wycliffite should appeal to words that are distinctively English.

More difficult is the question of the date of the text. Here the citation within the *raciones* of the exact words in the coronation service should provide useful evidence. It appears, however, that though the text itself is precise enough, the details known about the oaths sworn at the relevant English coronations are less certain. The royal ceremonies possibly involved would seem to be only two: the coronations of Richard II or Henry IV, since the dating of Vienna 3928 as *c*.1410, unless this is too early, rules out that of Henry V. Both of these should have used the so-called fourth recension of the coronation ceremony. About the actual coronation of Richard II quite a lot is known. The Close Rolls preserve a *Processus factus ad Coronacionem domini Regis Anglie Ricardie secundi post conquestum Anno regni sui primo*, and descriptions of the ceremony are found in Walsingham's *Historia Anglicana* and the *Anonimalle Chronicle*.[12]

---

[8] See L. G. Wickham Legg, *English Coronation Records* (London, 1901), pp. 81–112, at p. 98.

[9] *Ordines Coronationis Imperialis*, ed. R. Elze, *MGH.F*, ns 9 (1960), no. XX.25; see also J. Loserth, 'Die böhmische Krönungsordnung bis auf Karl IV', *Archiv für österreichische Geschichte*, 54 (1876), pp. 11–36. The reason for the similarity in this, and in the next point, seems to lie in the debt of both English and imperial ceremonies to the *Ordo Romanus*; see H. G. Richardson, 'The Coronation in Medieval England', *Traditio* 16 (1960), pp. 111–202, esp. pp. 136ff. and 174–80.

[10] See *Liber Regalis*, p. 99 and P. E. Schramm, 'Die Krönung im Deutschland bis zum Beginn des Salischen Hauses', *ZSRG.K*, 24 (1935), pp. 184–332, at p. 319.

[11] For the imperial oath see *MGH* (n. 9 above), XX.2, 8; for the precise form of the English oath see below.

[12] The first is PRO Close Roll, 1 Ric. II, mem. 45, printed by Wickham Legg, *Records*, pp. 131–50; the summary in *CCR 1377–81* (1914), pp. 1–5, is not detailed enough for the present purpose; for the other two, see *Historia Anglicana*, 1, pp. 332–8 (also in *Chronicon Angliae*, ed. E. M. Thompson, RS (1874), pp. 156–62), and *The Anonimalle Chronicle 1333 to 1381*, ed.

XII

All of these accounts differ in regard to the precise wording of the oath from the form of the fourth recension service found in the *Liber Regalis*, a version apparently prepared for this occasion by Abbot Lytlington of Westminster.[13] For the coronation of Henry IV the sources are less satisfactory: a memorandum printed by Rymer from a document in the Public Record Office does not provide the oath used in the present text, and the only descriptions of the event, in the *Annales Henrici IV* and in Adam of Usk, lack the specificity of detail needed for comparison.[14] The implication, however, seems to be that Henry used the form of oath cited in the deposition procedure invoked against his predecessor.[15] Comparing the *Sex raciones* with the material for Richard II's coronation, the less distinctive quotations for the fourth and fifth *raciones* can be found with considerable precision in both the *Processus* and in Walsingham's account.[16]

The first three quotations in the *Sex raciones* from the king's own oath are more difficult to match precisely in the accounts of actual coronations. The accounts of Richard II's oath are unsatisfactory: the *Processus* and Walsingham, though they give a tripartite oath, report it in the third person rather than in direct quotation.[17] The *Anonimalle Chronicle* gives the material as a series of questions by the archbishop, followed by assent from the king, so reproducing more accurately the actual process of the ceremony.[18] Here there is reasonable agreement between Walsingham and the present text in the third section, with slightly less close similarity between the second and Walsingham's first clause; the nearest parallel to the first section in the *raciones* is with that in the *Anonimalle Chronicle*, though the correspondence is not precise. In fact, the closest parallel that I have found to the wording of the oath in the

---

V. H. Galbraith (Manchester, 1927), pp. 107–14. See the comments of L. B. Wilkinson, 'Notes on the Coronation Records of the Fourteenth Century', *EHR*, 70 (1955), pp. 581–600.

[13] Wickham Legg, *Records*, p. 147, and also *Missale ad Usum Ecclesie Westmonasteriensis*, ed. J. Wickham Legg, *HBS*, 5 (1893), 2, cols 683–708.

[14] See *Foedera*, 3, 3rd edn (1740), pp. 163–4; *Johannis de Trokelowe . . . Chronica et Annales*, ed. H. T. Riley, *RS* (1866), pp. 292–6; *Chronicon Adae de Usk*, ed. E. M. Thompson, 2nd edn (London, 1904), p. 34.

[15] *Annales Henrici IV*, p. 294, after the question concerning Henry's willingness to observe the laws, custom and liberties granted to the clergy and people by the most glorious king Edward, 'Interroganda etiam sunt et alia, quae reperies in hoc quaternione ante articulos depositos contra Regem Ricardum'; these articles are in *Annales Ricardi II*, pp. 259–77.

[16] See *Hist. Angl.*, 1, pp. 334–5, 336 (*Chron. Angl.*, pp. 158, 160). The text in the *Anonimalle Chronicle* does not include the archbishop's words in full at these points (pp. 111, 113); the account is in French with Latin words given for the liturgical material.

[17] *Processus*, ed. Wickham Legg, p. 147; *Hist. Angl.*, 1, p. 333 (*Chron. Angl.*, p. 156).

[18] *Anon. Chron.*, pp. 109–10; see Wickham Legg, ed., *Missale*, 2, pp. 684–6.

272

A Wycliffite Contribution

Sex raciones is in Bracton, where under the heading 'De sacramento quod rex facere debet in coronatione sua' appears:

> Imprimis se esse praecepturum et pro viribus opem impensurum ut ecclesiae dei et omni populo christiano vera pax omni suo tempore observetur. Secundo, ut rapacitates et omnes iniquitates omnibus gradibus interdicat. Tertio, ut in omnibus iudiciis aequitatem praecipiat et misericordiam, ut indulgeat ei suam misericordiam clemens et misericors deus, et ut per iustitiam suam firma pace gaudeant universi.[19]

Bracton does not include the two prayers cited under the fourth and fifth arguments.

In addition to the material associated with the coronation, the author draws in the last section explicitly on canon law.[20] The section is one that Wyclif had used to similar purpose. The beginning and end of the chapter are quoted twice in the *De civili dominio*.[21] Interestingly, the adverb *nonnumquam*, restricting the power of the secular ruler, is omitted when the first sentence is again quoted in the *De ecclesia*. In this instance, Wyclif comments that the chapter indicated that secular rulers are part of the Church and that therefore 'ipsorum est cohercere rebelles ecclesie, ubicunque requiritur potencia civiliter coactiva.' The ensuing list of eight cases in which a cleric is subject to secular correction is attributed to John de Deo; its material is to be found in the marginal gloss on this chapter in the copy of canon law that Wyclif for a time jointly owned.[22]

It seems likely, therefore, that the writer of *Sex raciones* obtained his knowledge of the coronation material from a variety of sources.[23] From the preceding evidence a date between 1380 and 1409 seems most likely,

---

[19] Bracton, *De Legibus et consuetudinibus Angliae*, ed. G. E. Woodbine and S. E. Thorne (Cambridge, Mass., 1968–77), 2, p. 304.

[20] *Decretum*, C.23 q.5 c.20 (col. 935).

[21] *De civili dominio*, ed. R. L. Poole and J. Loserth, *WS* (1885–1904), 1, p. 271, line 6 and 4, p. 458, line 17 (the first sentence in the latter is misquoted, apparently by accidental omission of several words). See also 2, p. 79, line 17, and p. 109, line 24.

[22] *De ecclesia*, ed. J. Loserth, *WS* (1886), pp. 13, line 27–14, line 16; see BL MS Royal 10 E.ii, fol. 219r.

[23] A text fairly widely disseminated in the fifteenth century describes 'The maner and the forme of the Coronacioun of kyngis and Quenes in Engelonde', but this, though it gives the order of the ceremonial, does not include the wording of the archbishop quoted here. The text is printed by H. Arthur, 'On a MS Collection of Ordinances of Chivalry in the Fifteenth Century', *Archaeologia*, 57 (1900), pp. 29–70, at pp. 47–55, esp. pp. 51–2; for other manuscripts of the text see G. A. Lester, *Sir John Paston's 'Grete Boke': a Descriptive Catalogue, with an Introduction, of British Library MS Lansdowne 285* (Woodbridge, 1984), pp. 20–29, 71.

since the production evidently reflects academic discussion and thus presumably originated in Oxford.[24] Interest in the manipulation of legal sources is not unique to this Wycliffite text. Closest to the form of the present example is an English tract, now surviving only incompletely in a single manuscript, which considers the legality of the oath sworn by a bishop to the pope on his consecration.[25]

The coronation oath was, of course, a traditional source of appeal in regard to the king's relation both to law and to his nobles.[26] Equally, the issue of the authority of the secular ruler over clerics within his domain was a perennial one in the relations between the papacy and the emperor, as Michael Wilks has demonstrated so fully.[27] But the Wycliffite author of the present tract seems not to have appreciated one irony in his attempt to bring together this latter issue with the coronation ceremony: that the wording he cites most fully, namely the prayers at the giving of the sword and at the enthronement, and the oath as actually administered, are spoken by the metropolitan and thus imply that the Church effectively is endowing the secular ruler with authority. As Alvarus Pelagius put it: 'rex recepit coronam et gladium ab ecclesia ... unde videtur se habere ad papam sicut manus ad caput in defendendo et ministrando ... quilibet rex ab episcopo aliquo regni sui nomine ecclesiae dantis recipit gladium, intelligendo quod in gladio recipit curam et regimen totius regni.'[28]

---

[24] For evidence that a date as late as 1409 is possible for advocacy of Wycliffite causes in Oxford see *The Premature Reformation*, pp. 82–103.
[25] Found in BL MS Additional 24202, fols 1r–13v.
[26] See Gaines Post, 'Bracton on Kingship', *Tulane Law Review*, 42 (1968), pp. 519–54, with references to earlier literature.
[27] See Michael Wilks, *The Problem of Sovereignty in the Later Middle Ages* (Cambridge, 1963), esp. pp. 217, n. 1, 236–7, 338, 425. For aspects more particularly relating to England, see P. N. Riesenberg, *Inalienability of Sovereignty in Medieval Political Thought* (New York, 1956), pp. 118–23, 126–8, and E. H. Kantorowicz, 'Inalienability: a note on canonical practice and the English Coronation Oath in the thirteenth century', *Speculum*, 29 (1954), pp. 488–502.
[29] Quoted from Alvarus's *Speculum regum* in Wilks, *The Problem*, p. 425.

A Wycliffite Contribution

Text*

Discipulus quidam venerabilis Doctoris Ewangelici facit sex raciones ad probandum quod ad regem secularem pertinet punire clericos scilicet mortaliter peccantes.

Prima earum est hec: Ad regem pertinet secularem cum plena execucione sue potestatis regalis laborare ut clerici sui seruent veram pacem. Cum ergo vera pax et peccatum mortale[1] sint contraria, cum nemo habet veram pacem nisi habuerit pacem cum Deo, sequitur quod ad regem secularem pertinet cum execucione censurarum secularium laborare ut clerici sui purgentur a peccato mortali si sint in eo. Patet consequentia cum minori et assumptum per iuramentum primum quod rex facit in sua consecracione sub hac forma: 'In Christi nomine promitto me precepturum et opere pro viribus impleturum ut ecclesia Dei et omnis populus christianus veram pacem meo arbitrio in omni tempore seruet.'

Item ad regem secularem pertinet interdicere suis clericis omne genus iniquitatum. Ergo ad eum pertinet punire clericos suos si contra suam interdiccionem aliquod genus iniquitatis seu mortalis peccati committant. Patet consequentia et antecedens per secundum iuramentum quod rex secularis facit in sua consecracione sub hac forma: 'In Christi nomine promitto ut rapacitates et omnes iniquitates omnibus gradibus interdicam.'

Item ad regem secularem pertinet precipere[2] clericis suis seruare equitatem et misericordiam in omnibus iudiciis suis. Ergo ad eum pertinet punire clericos suos si contra eius preceptum deficiant ab hac oberuancia. Cum ergo omnis clericus suus peccans mortaliter deficit contra huiusmodi preceptum[3] ab hac obseruancia eo quod omnis huiusmodi clericus dat iniquum iudicium de malo culpe scilicet quod ipsum est preeligendum bono gracie, omnis eciam huiusmodi clericus dat inmisericorde

---

* The text is based on Vienna MS 3932 (X), corrected against and collated with Vienna MS 3928 (V) and Prague University Library X.E.9 (P). Though X needs emendation, in the final section it is the only copy to give the necessary readings without correction (see notes 17–18 to the text), and hence seems to be closer than the other two copies to the original. Minor variations in word order are not recorded
[1] mortale] om. P
[2] precipere] precipue X
[3] preceptum] om. P

iudicium de seipso, scilicet quod pocius debet eligere sibi mortem quam vitam, sequitur quod ad eum pertinet punire omnem huiusmodi clericum suum. Patet conclusio et assumptum per tercium iuramentum quod rex secularis facit in sua consecracione sub hac forma: 'In Christi nomine promitto quod in omnibus iudicijs equitatem et misericordiam precipiam ut michi et vobis indulgeat misericordiam suam clemens et misericors Deus.'

Item ad regem secularem pertinet portare gladium ad destruendum falsos clericos regalie sue subiectos. Ergo a forciori ad eum pertinet destruere peccata mortalia eorum. Patet conclusio et assumptum per formam verborum quibus metropolitanus sic loquitur ad regem dum in sua consecracione tradit sibi gladium: 'Accipe,' inquit, 'gladium per manus episcoporum, licet indignas, vice tamen et auctoritate apostolorum consecratas, tibi regaliter[4] inpositum nostroque benediccionis officio in defensionem sancte[5] Dei ecclesie diuinitus ordinatum; et esto memor de quo Psalmista prophetauit dicens, "Accingere gladio tuo super femur tuum, potentissime", ut per eundem vim equitatis exerceas, molem iniquitatis potenter destruas, et sanctam Dei ecclesiam eiusque fideles propugnando protegas, nec minus sub fide falsos communi christiani nominis hostes execreris ac destruas, et uiduas[6] ac pupillos clementer adiuues ad defendas, desolata restaures, restaurata conserues, vlciscaris iniusta, confirmes bene disposita.'

Item ad regem pertinet secularem esse mediatorem inter clerum suum et plebem suam ad tuendum eos in pace mutua. Sicut ergo ad eum pertinet rectificare iniurias plebis sue ad tuendam eam in pace cum clero suo si quas faciat clero suo, sic ad eum pertinet rectificare iniurias cleri sui ad tuendum eum in pace cum plebe sua si quas faciat plebi sue. Cum ergo eo ipso quod clerus suus facit peccatum mortale facit iniuriam plebi sue, sequitur quod eo ipso quod clerus suus facit peccatum mortale saltem notorium pertinet ad eum rectificare ipsum. Patet consequencia et assumptum per formam verborum quibus metropolitanus sic loquitur ad regem dum eum consecrat: 'Sta,' inquit, 'et retine amodo locum quem huiusque paterna successione tenuisti hereditario, iudicio tibi delegatum per auctoritatem Dei omnipotentis, et presentem tradicionem nostram et

---

[4] regaliter] regulariter XPV
[5] sancte] sicut, *margin* sancte V, sic P
[6] uiduas] uiduam X

A Wycliffite Contribution

omnium episcoporum ceterumque⁷ Dei seruorum; et quanto clerum sacris altaribus propinquiorem perspicis, tanto eis pociorem in locis congruis honorem impendere memineris. Quatinus mediator Dei et hominis te mediatorem cleri et plebis in hoc regni solio confirmet.'

Item ad regem secularem pertinet habere clericos suos in racione seruorum suorum in regno suo ad debite seruiendum ei et plebi sue in catholici verbi Dei predicacione, in spirituali correccione peruersorum, et in sacramentorum Christi ministracione, in uirtuosa oracione et eciam in ducatu ad beatitudinem. Ergo ad eum pertinet punire eos pro subtraccione⁸ ipsius seruicij, si ipsum notorie faciant.⁹ Patet consequencia et assumptum per hoc quod ad regem¹⁰ secularem pertinet esse dominum suorum clericorum, et per conuersus ad eum pertinet uti eis in seruicio clericali duplici supradicto pro comodo sui regni.

Ex quibus uidetur quod licet non pertineat ad potestatem temporalem secundum racionem qua est sub spirituali potestate in ecclesia ut est regnum spirituale rectificare clericos preter licenciam spiritualis potestatis, tamen pertinet ad potestatem temporalem secundum racionem qua dicit potestatem spiritualem in ecclesia ut est regnum temporale preter licenciam spiritualis potestatis rectificare clericos. Et per conuersus ad potestatem secularem pertinet auctoritate propria iudicare de potestate spirituali et punire eam per¹¹ ablacionem temporalium secundum¹² racionem qua ipsa potestas spiritualis est subiecta potestati temporali,¹³ licet ad potestatem temporalem non pertineat auctoritate propria iudicare de potestate spirituali uel punire eam per ablacionem temporalium secundum racionem qua ipsa potestas spiritualis est relata potestati temporali in regno spirituali. Secundo uidetur quod sicut intra ecclesiam, secundum racionem qua est regnum spirituale regulatum per papam tanquam per caput, potestates seculares necessarie non essent¹⁴ nisi ut, quod non perualent sacerdotes efficere per doctrine sermonem hec potestas secularis imperet per discipline terrorem (ut dicit Canon 23 q. 5

---

⁷ ceterumque] ceterosque P
⁸ ad beatitudinem...subtraccione] *om.* P
⁹ faciant] faciat P
¹⁰ regem] regularem X
¹¹ per] et per X
¹² secundum] sed secundum X
¹³ temporali] temporali in regno temporali P
¹⁴ essent] esset P

principes,¹⁵ sic¹⁶ intra ecclesiam eandem, secundum racionem qua est regnum temporale regulatum per imperatorem tanquam per caput, potestates spirituales necessarie non essent, nisi ut seruicium clericale quod laici non possunt ministrare regno temporali, hec potestas spiritualis ex auctoritate et precepto principis secularis ministret eidem. Tercio uidetur quod non valet argumentum quo sic arguitur: clerici secundum racionem qua sunt sub potestate temporali in ecclesia ut est regnum temporale non possunt preter licenciam potestatis temporalis punire laicos, ergo clerici non possunt punire laicos.¹⁷ Sic non valet argumentum quo sic arguitur: laici, secundum racionem qua sunt sub potestate spirituali in ecclesia ut est regnum spirituale, non possunt preter licenciam potestatis spiritualis punire clericos, ergo laici non possunt punire clericos.¹⁸ Quarto patet quod, sicut omnes curati sub domino papa tenentur tanquam¹⁹ eius adiutores iuuare ipsum ad implendum suum officium papale quod habet ad castigandum per censuras²⁰ spirituales suos laicos mortaliter peccantes, sic²¹ omnes domini regi subditi tenentur tanquam eius adiutores iuuare ipsum ad implendum suum officium regale quod habet ad castigandum suos clericos mortaliter peccantes.²²

Iste sunt sex raciones quod discipulus Magistri Johannis Wygleph de hac questione utrum licet seculari clerum delinquentem castigare et dicitur quod sic.²³

---

[15] 23] 21 P; *Decretum*, C.23 q.5 c.20 (col. 936).
[16] sic] si X
[17] ergo ... laicos] *margin different hand* V, ergo non potest preter licenciam potestatis temporalis punire laycos P
[18] ergo ... clericos] *margin different hand* V, *om.* P
[19] tanquam] *om.* P
[20] per censuras] pretensuras P
[21] sic] si X
[22] sic ... peccantes] *om.* P
[23] iste ... sic] *om.* XV

XIII

Notes of an Early Fifteenth-Century Research Assistant, and the Emergence of the 267 Articles against Wyclif

FROM 1377 onwards the ideas and writings of John Wyclif were a recurrent source of trouble for the authorities at Oxford University. The tale of how the university tried to disentangle itself from the contamination of fostering a heresiarch, whilst at the same time preserving its academic independence from episcopal interference, is one that has been told several times before.[1] The purpose of this note is not to revisit the whole story but to fill in some details from a late stage in the struggle. Probably at the meeting of the Canterbury convocation of 1407 it was decided that a committee of twelve from the two universities, Oxford and Cambridge, should investigate the orthodoxy of Wyclif's theological writings, in evident pursuit of Archbishop Arundel's *Constitution* (drawn up the same year) that academic debate within the two institutions should not discuss unapproved doctrines.[2] Oxford university seems to have been slow in appointing its representatives for this task, and Arundel wrote to enquire into the delay; this prompted a reply from the university apparently written during a subsequent long vacation to excuse its dilatoriness. Arundel, probably in January 1409, responded to this by imposing more precise terms for the committee, by this time to be drawn from Oxford alone: they should scrutinize the works of Wyclif and draw up a list of errors to be submitted to him.[3] After further delays and excuses (the number of works by Wyclif, and the number of errors) the list was finally presented to Convocation on 17 March 1411 before being sent to Arundel.[4]

The task confronted by the committee was not a simple one. Though eighteen errors had previously been extracted at the order of Arundel from Wyclif's *Trialogus* in 1395–6, following which William Woodford composed his refutation of them, this time Arundel plainly had in mind

---

1. The current standard account must be J. I. Catto, 'Wyclif and Wycliffism at Oxford 1356–1430', in *The History of the University of Oxford II: Late Medieval Oxford*, ed. J. I. Catto and T. A. R. Evans (Oxford, 1992), pp. 175–261; see also J. H. Dahmus, *The Prosecution of John Wyclyf* (New Haven, 1952), and H. B. Workman, *John Wyclif* (Oxford, 1926), ii.246–93, 340–76.

2. Arundel's *Constitutions* are printed in D. Wilkins, *Concilia Magnae Britanniae et Hiberniae* (4 vols, London, 1737), iii.314–19; the sequence of events, and many of the documents relevant to them, is traced by H. E. Salter, *Snappe's Formulary and other Records*, Oxford Historical Society 80 (1924), pp. 90–137 and here especially pp. 98–100. See also Catto, pp. 244–8.

3. See Salter documents 3–6, pp. 117–120.

4. Salter document 13, pp. 128–30, and see no. 24 pp. 156–8.

something much more ambitious.⁵ The list that eventually was sent to the Archbishop contained 267 extracts from a total of fourteen of Wyclif's works; the great majority of these extracts can be precisely located in the works from which it is claimed they were drawn, though a few appear to be summaries or paraphrases.⁶ The list was printed by Wilkins from a manuscript whose authority will be discussed later; for convenience the numbers of the articles there are used throughout the present paper.

In Magdalen College lat.99 is to be found some of the preliminary listing of errors for this final presentation; the material appears on ff. 176ra–178vb and ff. 257ra–261vb. The main contents of the manuscript are copies of Richard Snettisham's abbreviation of Cowton on the *Sentences* (ff. 1ra–98va with following tabula ff. 98va–107vb), John Sharpe's abbreviation of Scotus' *Quodlibeta* (ff. 107vb–166rb with following lists of questions and their subdivisions, and alphabetically of topics ff. 166rb–170va), a brief introduction to theology (ff. 170va–173vb), an anonymous set of questions on the *Sentences* (ff. 179ra–241va), Thomas of Sutton's reply to a *quodlibet* of Scotus (ff. 241va–251rb), and an anonymous question (ff. 252ra–256vb).⁷ From the quire signatures the three main items appear to have been disordered in the manuscript as it currently stands, and the third of them was intended to come first.⁸ The material of concern here starts on ff. 176ra–178vb and continues on ff. 257ra–261vb, both sections filling the otherwise blank leaves of the final quires concluding the previous items, and the latter ending eight lines from the foot of the column. Whether this addition was written before or after the rearrangement is unclear: at the start of f. 257ra the reader is directed to the earlier part of the material *infra in isto libro*, suggesting that the addition was made before rearrangement, but at the end of f. 178vb the scribe, starting within the ruled frame, directs 'Require plures de istis conclusionibus dampnatis 4to (sic, actually 5to) folio ante finem libri pro eo quod hic non est plus spacij ad scribendum', suggesting the opposite. Since the material immediately preceding the first section of the Wyclif conclusions is a list of the Snettisham

---

5. Catto, p. 233; Wilkins, iii.229–30. For Woodford's *De causis condemnationis xviii articulorum damnatorum Iohannis Wyclif* see E. Brown, *Fasciculus rerum expetendarum* (London, 1690), i.191–265; copies of this refutation were widely distributed (see list of manuscripts in R. Sharpe, *A Handlist of the Latin Writers of Great Britain and Ireland before 1540* (Turnhout, 1997), pp. 819–20).

6. Wilkins, iii.339–49 from BL Cotton Faustina C.vii, ff. 143v–159v; see below further p. 689.

7. The first two items are listed by Sharpe nos. 1385 (pp. 510–11) and 884 (p. 315); Sutton's reply is no. 1838 (p. 683).

8. The summary listing in H. O. Coxe, *Catalogue of the Manuscripts in the Oxford Colleges* (Oxford, 1852), ii. 53–4 gives the main contents only, not including the material here of special interest. I am greatly indebted to Prof. Ralph Hanna, who is preparing a new catalogue of the manuscripts at Magdalen College, for a copy of his description and for drawing my attention to the fact that the first quire of the third main item is signed *a*, whilst that of the first is signed *h*, a sequence that would exactly fit if that final item had originally come first. On rearrangement the catchwords of f. 179 (originally the first leaf) were entered on f. 178vb.

distinctions on the four books of Cowton and of Scotus' *Quodlibeta* (ff. 174ra–175va and 175va–b respectively), no help is given to resolve the issue, since both items precede the list on either arrangement.[9] All that is clear is that the scribe of the Wyclif material fitted his contribution around texts in an already completed composite volume, and was unable to do so without the use of two blank sections.

Eight folios in double columns are closely written with extracts, most of them accompanied by precise locations, from eleven of Wyclif's writings. The worker seems to have been principally concerned with the *Opus evangelicum* and *De symonia*, the two texts which stand first in the final list of 267 articles (items 1–74 and 75–98 respectively); these cover ff. 176ra–178vb and 257ra–259va.[10] After this the listing continues to *De perfeccione statuum*, *Trialogus*, *De ordine christiano*, *Dialogus*, *De dotacione cesarea* (better known as the *Supplementum* to the *Trialogus*), the *Responsorium ad argumenta monachi de Salley* (i.e. William Rymington, known now as *Responsiones ad xliv conclusiones*), the *De libello ad argumenta Strode*, *De confessione* and *Contra versucias pseudoclerum*.[11] A little of the worker's methods emerges from the material as it stands. The long first section of the notes deriving entirely from the *Opus evangelicum* and *De symonia* is arranged under subject headings such as 'De hostia consecrata' (f. 176ra), 'De confessione priuata' (f. 176vb), 'De papa et eius statu' (f. 177ra). Before the start it has been noted that the former work is divided into four books, whose incipits are quoted; use of the second is also there noted. References in this section are to the *Opus evangelicum* where a book number precedes the chapter number, by chapter number only to the *De symonia*; *ibidem* follows any subsequent quotation from the same location if immediately after one whose full reference is cited. Approximately a hundred passages are extracted from the *Opus evangelicum*, forty from the *De symonia*; from limited checking both quotation and referencing seem to be remarkably accurate. At the end of this section (ff. 259va–b) seven passages from the *De perfeccione statuum* are given, a text mentioned briefly in the introductory note. The worker then (f. 259vb) explains to his superior that he has gone on to extract some more errors from other works. This second sequence is less systematically done: there is some attempt to provide subject headings at the start, where passages from the

---

9. Catto, p. 247 n. 235 notes that the previous brief item is in the same hand as the Wyclif material; there he signs off 'quod Rawclyff', but in default of further evidence about his identity this is not helpful.

10. An inaccurate description of this material in W. R. Thomson, *The Latin Writings of John Wyclyf* (Toronto, 1983), p. 222, n. 6 first drew my attention to it; see *The Premature Reformation: Wycliffite Texts and Lollard History* (Oxford, 1988), p. 85. Wilkins's numbering of the conclusions is used here throughout, though for his text see further below pp. 692–3.

11. Thomson nos. 426, 47, 414 408, 48, 384, 388, 44, and 420 respectively. The texts here are quoted and referenced (by page and, following a slash, line numbers) from the editions of the Wyclif Society (London, 1883–1921) save for the *Trialogus* and its *Supplementum* edited by G. Lechler (Oxford, 1869).

Trialogus and *Dialogus* are given, but this increasingly breaks down and extracts are taken in sequence from a work regardless of the subject matter. At that point the worker seems to have run out of patience, and possibly of time, and notes (f. 261vb) that many more errors could be listed but these would only repeat the sense of those already given to no useful purpose.

Comparing these notes with the final 267 conclusions, it is clear first that the worker of Magdalen 99 did not investigate three texts found in the final list: that described there as *De arte sophistica* (better known as *De logica 3*), *De civili dominio* and *De diabolo et membris* (though the title of the last seems to have been known to him, see f. 259vb).[12] Conversely Magdalen notes one passage from *De gradibus cleri*, a text not cited in the final list.[13] Secondly it emerges that the Magdalen 99 listing is *not* the final product, even for those texts included in it: in some cases the eventual article omitted the beginning or end of the extracts as here given,[14] whilst on the other hand a large number of Magdalen's extracts are not incorporated into the final listing.[15] I have located all articles derived from *Opus evangelicum* and *De symonia* in Magdalen save for one exception in each case.[16] But with the subordinate texts Magdalen's coverage is less complete. All nine of the articles from each of *De perfeccione statuum* (99–107) and *Responsiones ad Strode* (250–8) are present (ff. 259va–b and 261va respectively); but only two of the thirteen items from *De ordine christiano* in the final list are found in Magdalen (nos. 118–19 but not 108–17 and 120, f. 260rb).[17] It seems probable that another worker was (at least) primarily responsible for listing the errors in *De confessione* and *Contra versucias pseudoclerum*: though two of those from the former (259 and 263) and one from the latter (265) identify the same passages as those listed in the final column of Magdalen (f. 261vb), there are discrepancies of wording in these, in addition to the absence of nos.260–2 from the former, 264 and 266–7 from the latter. Even with texts relatively fully covered in Magdalen, such as the *Dialogus* and *Trialogus*, someone else must have repeated the reading: fifteen errors were eventually listed from the first (nos. 141–55),

---

12. Wilkins conclusions nos. 156–75, 176–219, 220–4; Thomson texts nos. 3, 28–30, 430 respectively.

13. Thomson no. 394; here f. 260ra from *Opera minora* p. 142/16–20.

14. A particularly striking example is eventual no. 71, listed as the first in Magd.99 (f. 176ra), where *Opus evangelicum* iii.159/8–160/7 is at the start summarized, then fully quoted; from this only 159/19–29 survives, with everything summarized.

15. See, for instance, f. 176va from which *Opus evangelicum* iii.174/28–175/2 is not used, or f. 177va where likewise 109/1–5, 187/27–30, 39–188/1 are quoted in succession between two extracts that became conclusions nos. 12 and 13. I would estimate that about half of the extracts in Magdalen 99 are *not* incorporated into the final list, but the proportion varies between the different works.

16. Nos. 39 and 82; the overall sense of these is certainly found in the extracts, and it seems likely they are both abbreviated paraphrases.

17. Similarly articles 226 and 236 are not in Magdalen, but the remaining twelve (225, 227–35, 237–8) from *De dotacione caesarea* are found there (f. 261ra–b); similarly articles 239–40 and 245 from *Responsiones xliv* are not found in the listing, whereas 241–4, 246–9 are present (f. 261rb–va).

of which only three are found in Magdalen 99 together with eight that were not taken over; twenty from the second were listed (nos. 121–40), of which nine are in Magdalen 99, but seven there are ignored.[18]

These facts alone make it clear that the notes in Magdalen 99 reflect a stage behind the final report of the twelve commissioners, rather than being later notes from that report. The final selection from Magdalen's listing is not without interest: though in the main topics covered repeatedly in the extracts are reduced, some unusual points are omitted. Thus in the section on the sects from the two main texts scrutinized, Magdalen quotes *Opus evangelicum* 'Dicti scribe et pharisei claudunt fidelibus istud regnum impediendo ne euangelium anglicetur', but this is not taken over into the articles; the mistaken chapter number given, 16 for 10, also suggests Magdalen is a 'fair copy' from notes or from an exemplar likewise having Arabic numerals for chapters; the final verb is an interesting substitute for the printed text's *fidelibus predicatur*, perhaps reflecting the scribe's memory of Arundel's prohibition in the seventh of the *Constitutions*.[19]

Who was responsible for the making of these extracts? To put a name to the worker seems unfortunately to be impossible, but his status can be deduced from his prefatory and concluding notes and from some observations that he interjects between the extracts. At three points he addresses the person to whom he directs his work as 'pater reuerende' (ff. 176va and 177ra), 'reuerende pater et domine' (f. 259vb); the precise status of his superior is unfortunately from this unclear – any of the twelve commissioners, or the university's chancellor, could be so addressed.[20] That the worker is not directly subordinate to Arundel, and so cannot be one of the commissioners, seems established from an allusion to the condemnation 'per reuerendissimum in Christo patrem dominum Cant' in prouinciali concilio nuper London' celebrato' (f. 260ra).[21] The date of the researcher's work can also be fixed by a reference to the deaths of Sawtry (oddly described as 'prothomartir') and Badby 'nuper London' in quadragesima'(f. 176va); Badby's burning on 5 March 1410 was evidently recent memory.[22] The reference to 'vltima temporalis commocio Lollardorum' (f. 257vb) could also reflect activity around the same time.[23] Since the report of the committee was presented

---

18. Magdalen ff. 260ra–vb; this section is the most unclear in its ordering, attempting a subject arrangement, but mixing references from these two texts and from *De ordine christiano*

19. Cf. *Opus evangelicum* ii.36/31–7; Magdalen f. 259ra; Wilkins, iii.317.

20. The list of the twelve is to be found in the manuscript of *Fasciculi zizaniorum*, Oxford Bodleian MS e Museo 86, f. 110ra, and in BL Cotton Faustina C.vii f. 138r from which it is printed by Salter, p. 130; there are no significant differences between the lists. See further below pp. 691–2.

21. See Wilkins, iii.322–3 from Arundel reg.ii.ff. 10–12v dated 1409.

22. Wilkins, iii.324–9 from Arundel reg.ii.17ff. For a detailed account of this case, and its significance within the politics of the time, see P. McNiven, *Heresy and Politics in the Reign of Henry IV: The Burning of John Badby* (Woodbridge, 1987).

23. The reference is probably to the attempted introduction in parliament of the so-called 'Lollard Disendowment Bill'; see McNiven, pp. 188–98, and the Bill printed A. Hudson, *Selections from English Wycliffite Writings* (Cambridge, 1978), no. 27.

on 17 March 1411, it seems reasonable to suggest that the work was done between Easter 1410 and the end of the year. Two other personal comments are intriguing rather than informative. One follows an extract from *Opus evangelicum* (ii.59/30–6), where the researcher interjects 'Ista conclusio in magna parte sumitur a Burnello, et sic tolerabiliter est mihi' (f. 259va); the reference is to Nigel Wireker's satire against the religious orders figured through the antics of the ass who samples each in turn.[24] This may suggest that the worker was a secular clerk, and less certainly that his superior may also have been. The second is less explicable: here, following a quotation from *De symonia* where Wyclif deplores the way in which lay patrons encourage clerical simony,[25] a question is interposed 'Cur ergo non sinitis nouum castrum?' (f. 258rb). It is tempting to see this enigmatic question as a disguised reference to Oldcastle (*castrum* but *non . . . nouum*), and more particularly to the knight's fostering of dubious chaplains through patronage – the only charge through which Oldcastle by the end of 1410 had been publicly associated with unorthodoxy.[26] Beyond these comments, little emerges from the rare observations which the researcher interpolates into his record: at one point he notes an expression of dubiety in Wyclif's wording about the eucharist, in another Wyclif's deceptive rhetoric, at another the inconsistency between two of the extracts; in a more extended comment he observes that some of Wyclif's statements could be defended scholastically 'quo ad verba', but that, preached or taught openly or secretly, they could lead the hearers to error.[27] But such observations could derive from any academic of the time.

If it is impossible to put a name to the researcher, can his superior be identified? The two copies of the list of the commissioners divide their number into three parts, four doctors of theology, four bachelors of theology and four students of theology. As has been said, the terms of address could, depending on the status of the writer, be applied to any of them. Three of the twelve were from the religious orders, John Langdon OSB, Thomas Claxton OP and William Ufford OCarm; the extractor does not seem especially interested in Wyclif's hostility to these

---

24. See Sharpe no. 1128 under the surname Witeker (p. 401) and A. G. Rigg, *A History of Anglo-Latin Literature 1066–1422* (Cambridge, 1992), pp. 102–4 and references pp. 349–50; the text was edited as *Speculum stultorum* by J. H. Mozley and R. R. Raymo (Berkeley and Los Angeles, 1960).

25. *De symonia* p. 6/32–4, article 77.

26. For the charges see the material printed in Wilkins iii.329–30; the most recent brief biography of Oldcastle is that by C. Kightly in *The History of Parliament: The House of Commons 1386–1421*, ed. J. S. Roskell et al. (Stroud, 1993), iii.866–9. Kightly associates Oldcastle with two other events of 1410 in which Lollardy is implicated, but his name is not mentioned in the surviving records of them. Less publicly Oldcastle had in September 1410 written to the Hussite gentleman Woksa of Waldstein; see my paper 'Which Wyche? The Framing of the Lollard heretic/saint', *Texts and the Repression of Medieval Heresy*, ed. C. Bruschi and P. Biller (Woodbridge, 2003), pp. 221–37 for the implications of that letter.

27. Respectively Magdalen ff. 176rb, 176va, 260rb and 259vb; the first two relate to quotations from *Opus evangelicum* ii.159/15 quoted in article 71, and ii.174/28–175/2 not used in the final list.

orders, but this may not be significant in regard to the superior. Three others were immediately from Merton: Robert Gilbert, John Luke and Thomas Rudbourne; the first two were at varying times in the first decade of the fifteenth-century room-renters at Queen's – both colleges had reason to be sensitive about Wyclif.[28] Luke and Rudbourne were in correspondence with Netter, who himself (as will be seen below) showed interest in the list.[29] Richard Flemyng, later founder of Lincoln college, was himself in difficulties with Arundel around the same time as these extracts were made, as a result of a proposition which he had defended; he stoutly rebutted the charge that the proposition showed sympathy with Wyclif, and it was evidently dropped.[30] Little seems known of Richard Cartysdale, Richard Garsdale and Robert Rowberry; the last two were northerners.[31] The possibility that the individual commissioner was Richard Snetisham might seem to be favoured by the fact that Magdalen 99 contains his abbreviation of Cowton until it is realized that this was a widely copied work, extant in several other copies of a similar date.[32] Snetisham and John Wytenham the chairman were perhaps the best established of the commissioners in Oxford, and it may be significant that Wytenham went on to act as a commissioner in the trial of Oldcastle in September 1413.[33]

Apart from Magdalen 99 only two copies seem to survive of the commissioners' final list. The better known is in a collection of letters and other documents associated with the university made in the middle of the fifteenth century, now MS Cotton Faustina C.vii ff. 143v–159v; from this Wilkins printed the material in his *Concilia*.[34] There the conclusions are numbered, and arranged under the books from which each derives; only 32 from 74 deriving from the *Opus evangelicum* are

---

28. Wyclif was briefly a probationary fellow of Merton (see Catto p. 187), and for longer room-renter at Queen's (see A. B. Emden, *A Biographical Register of the University of Oxford to A. D. 1500* (Oxford, 1957–9), iii.2103); for later interest in him at Merton, see M. Jurkowski, 'Heresy and Factionalism at Merton College in the early Fifteenth century', *Journal of Ecclesiastical History*, xlviii (1997), 658–81.
29. See Bodley 73 ff. 94v–95r.
30. See Salter, pp. 95–8.
31. For the second and third see Emden ii.744–5 and iii.1597–8; Emden appears to have considered Cartysdale as a variant spelling for Garsdale, but the two are named separately in both copies of the list. Garsdale appears in John Bale's *Scriptorum illustrium maioris Brytanniae* (Basel, 1557–9), i.560–1 under the variant Grasdale as author of five works; for a suggestion about their identity see Sharpe, no. 1332 (p. 482).
32. See Sharpe no. 1385 who notes (p. 510) that the text often travelled, as here, with Sharpe's abbreviation of Scotus's *Quodlibete* plus its *tabulae* by Peter Partridge.
33. See Emden, iii.1724–5 and 2131, and for the trial Wilkins, iii.355.
34. Folio numbers used are those in modern pencil at the foot of the leaves. The volume came from the collection of Robert Hare, a recusant of Elizabeth's reign: see A. G. Watson, 'Robert Hare's Books', in *The English Medieval Book: Studies in Memory of Jeremy Griffiths*, ed. A. S. G. Edwards, V. Gillespie and R. Hanna (London, 2000), pp. 209–32, especially p. 220 where this volume appears as no. 25. It may originally have belonged in the Royal collection, if the note of Sir Frederic Madden in the volume, saying that it was formerly in the Old Royal Library binding, is believed: see pp. 212, 231; it is, however, not included by J. P. Carley, *The Libraries of King Henry VIII* (Corpus of British Medieval Library Catalogues 7, 2000).

provided with details of book and chapter (not all of which can derive from information purveyed in Magdalen 99). Wilkins's edition does not reveal that all the indications of book source were certainly added by the same scribe after the writing of the conclusions, as were probably the book and chapter indications where given, and possibly the numbers; presumably this may suggest that all this information derived from a second copy of the text. Equally one conclusion after no. 157 and one after no. 220 are marked for excision and are not numbered.[35]

The second copy of the full 267 conclusions is found in the manuscript known as *Fasciculi zizaniorum*, Bodleian Library MS e Mus.86, ff. 110vb–119ra; this part was not printed by Shirley, and sets out in no clear order lists of condemned academic conclusions together with material from the councils of the first two decades of the fifteenth century.[36] The copy here has various discrepancies of numbering from the previous one, some at least of which are probably due to miscopying by the scribe but some of which point to an exemplar different from that available to the Faustina copyist.[37] Because of the miscopyings this list only gets as far as 262 conclusions, and the remaining four are made up by additions said to have been extracted by Thomas Netter from the *Responsiones ad argumenta Radulphi Strode*; none of these last is found in the printed listing, or in Magdalen 99.[38] In the *Fasciculi* no texts are specified to divide up the whole (though the text order is retained), though twenty-five individual references are provided; again not all of these references can derive from the notes in Magdalen 99.[39] It seems clear that these two surviving copies are independent transcriptions of the list forwarded to Archbishop Arundel in March 1411.

---

35. The first, lightly crossed through, reads 'Deus terminat seipsum maximo numero possibili materiarum punctalium ex quibus fecit mundus'; after 220 is marked for removal 'Omnis homo prescitus est dyabolus incarnatus' and an incorrect anticipation of no. 224. Wilkins has adjusted the numbering of the following four items which the scribe had wrongly divided and misnumbered.

36. See the summary of the contents in W. W. Shirley, *Fasciculi zizaniorum* (Rolls Series, 1858), pp. lxxii–lxxv; the foliation used here is that of the original scribe at the centre of each recto. For the origins of the material in this collection see J. Crompton, '*Fasciculi Zizaniorum*', *Journal of Ecclesiastical History* xii (1961), 35–45, 155–66.

37. Omitted are conclusions (on Wilkins's numbering) 23, 26, 119, 194, 226; there is in *FZ* no no. 42 (Wilkins, 44); 93–4, 164–5 are each combined into a single conclusion. The rearrangement of Wilkins nos. 1–2 points to a separate exemplar. After Wilkins no. 220 (FZ 215) a later hand, probably that of James Ussher, has added in the lower margin 'Omnis homo prescitus est diabolus incarnatus', presumably taken from Faustina. The same hand has corrected the quotations and supplemented them with sources apparently derived from Faustina.

38. In the text printed in *Opera minora* the passages are pp. 189/4–9, 189/30–35, 191/15–20, 191/30–37, all answering Strode's tenth objection, though the last is reported as answering the sixth. Wilkins's quotations derive from answers to Strode's second (250–1), third (252), sixth (253) and fifteenth (254–8).

39. This is obviously true of the four references given to extracts from *De civili dominio*, a text not available to the extractor of Magdalen 99; FZ also provides references for each of the conclusions from *Ad argumenta Strode*, to none of which Magdalen 99 adds information.

The *St Alban's Chronicle* has an abbreviated account of these affairs in Oxford under the year 1409.[40] A list of seven books scrutinized is given, together with eighteen condemned conclusions with their alleged origins. The information has, however, been somewhat garbled as well as abbreviated: attributions are incorrect, titles improperly reported and the conclusions an unordered selection.[41] Although some of the material could derive from the final report, this is not true of all (even allowing for heavy abbreviation and some misreporting); it seems likely that it derives from an independent, and probably Oxford, source.[42] Salter noted that the Junior Proctor's Book in the Oxford University Archives also contains a list of some 61 conclusions, added to a very brief account of Wyclif's condemnation on 24 counts in 1381 (*sic*, for the 1382 Blackfriars Council), notes of the addition to these of a further 21, of Wyclif's death in 1384 and of subsequent censures of him.[43] There follows a note of the condemnation in Congregation on 26 June 1410 (sic) of a list of 61 conclusions allegedly drawn from eight books listed at the end: *De sermone domini in monte* (i.e. *Opus evangelicum*), *Trialogus, Dialogus, De symonia, De gradibus ecclesie, De perfeccione statuum, De ordine christiano, De arte sophistica* (i.e. *De logica* 3), though in fact only the first four and the seventh are represented here.[44] The date of this copy is unclear: the three leaves are in a different hand from the surrounding items, and the ordering at this point is puzzling.[45] It does, however, have some interest in relation to the Magdalen material. In the first instance this series does not derive from the final listing, since, in addition to being in an entirely different order, it preserves in several cases much longer quotations from Wyclif's writings.[46] But though many of these could derive from the extracts in Magdalen, the sequence cannot descend from those earlier notes. Five of the conclusions are not replicated in Magdalen's selections, and some of its extended quotations

---

40. See *The St. Albans Chronicle 1406–1420*, ed. V. H. Galbraith (Oxford, 1937), pp. 46–50; the single manuscript is Bodley 462, here ff. 297v–299r.

41. Thus the second here, a fragment of conclusion 11 in the final list, is said to derive from *De ordine christiano* when it actually comes from the *Opus evangelicum*; conclusion 14 there is reported from a book *De imperfeccione statuum* (for *perfeccione*); though most of the conclusions relate to the eucharist, confession, the private orders or temporalities, the last relates to the conditions for sin.

42. Conclusion 7 'Nullus existens in mortali peccato est verus dominus alicuius rei' is said to derive from the *Trialogus*, but is not amongst the 267 final views, nor in the Magdalen listing from that text; it is more likely to derive from the *De civili dominio*.

43. Salter, p. 100, also Galbraith, p. 47 n. 2, corrected by Catto, p. 248 n. 236 (though what follows here suggests some further modifications). The Book is University Archives Register C, this material ff. 123r–125v; it was one of the principal sources of *Munimenta academica*, ed. H. Anstey (Rolls Series, London, 1868), but this material was not printed there.

44. See the list f. 125v at the end. The list is not in the same order as is found in the *St Albans Chronicle*, p. 47, and adds the last to it.

45. Catto, p. 248 n. 236 seems to suggest a date between 1446 and 1478 because of the items before and after; but 1446 is on a post-medieval paper leaf (f. 122) copied from another source to supply a gap.

46. Thus, for instance, its sequence of conclusions 26–37 reflects the same material as the final list 42, 34, 36, 47, 48, 138, 133, 134, 148, 135, 79, 83; similarly its number 4 (also the final list 4), the quotation from *Opus evangelicum* i 107/25–32 continues for several lines beyond the final version.

are longer than Magdalen let alone the final listing.[47] On the other hand it must have been made from a source very like Magdalen: its documented extracts all relate to the *Opus evangelicum* and replicate those in Magdalen. Given that Magdalen is, as shown above, a fair copy, and that the Proctor's Book has a decisively Oxford location, it seems probable that both were made independently from the same earlier Oxford source. It is possible that the conclusions in the Proctor's Book derive from a source other than the preliminary and final narratives that surround it: this could explain the knowledge of texts which the conclusions themselves do not quote. But even those narratives are unlikely to have come from the final material sent to Arundel, since that would have given a fuller set of texts.

The list of 267 conclusions went on from Oxford to have an afterlife as part of the dossier against Wyclif at the Council of Constance, though they seem to have been less important there than the shorter list of 45 heretical opinions.[48] The 45 conclusions included the 24 condemned at the Blackfriars Council of 1382, plus a further 21 apparently added during the struggles between Czech and German masters in Prague in 1403; the list was reported as condemned there and subsequently at Paris.[49] Although the existence of the 260 (as they seem to have become) is often mentioned in proceedings at Constance,[50] manuscripts that contain records of those proceedings do not seem usually to reiterate them in full detail.[51] A shorter list of 58, selected by Bartholdus of Wildungen, was recited there at the fifteenth session on 6 July 1415.[52] This selection was once more rearranged, back to one based on subject matter rather than text.[53] Whether by design or accident, all save one of the fourteen texts used in the original Oxford conclusions are still represented in this

---

47. Magdalen does not give the quotations from the *Trialogus*, in these conclusions 31 (=138 of final listing), 58 (=136), 60 (=139), from the *Dialogus* in 45 (=151), or from the *De ordine christiano* in 55 (=109); conclusion 24 (=52) has variants from any other listing.

48. See J. D. Mansi, *Sacrorum conciliorum nova et amplissima collectio* 27 (Venice, 1784), cols. 632–4. A brief account of the main events in relation to Wyclif is in E. C. Tatnall, 'The Condemnation of John Wyclif at the Council of Constance', *Studies in Church History*, vii (1971), 209–18; see also the points in H. A. Kelly, 'Trial Procedures against Wyclif and Wycliffites in England and at the Council of Constance', *Huntington Library Quarterly*, lxi (1999 for 1998), 1–28.

49. See M. Spinka, *John Hus: a Biography* (Princeton, 1968), pp. 62–4. Though known in England (see FZ ff. 107va–108vb), they were more familiar on the continent. For the text see N. Tanner, *Decrees of the Ecumenical Councils* (London and Washington, 1990), pp. 411–13; the article on their origin promised by Crompton, p. 159 n. 5, seems never to have appeared.

50. See H. von der Hardt, *Magnum oecumenicum Constantiense concilium* (6 vols, Frankfurt and Leipzig, 1697–1700), iv. cols. 118, 152, 191.

51. See von der Hardt's sidenote at iv. col. 156 'Hi artic. 260 in omnibus nostris manuscriptis haud reperti.'

52. Mansi cols. 748–51 and von der Hardt iv. 399–407; the list is translated, from the copy in C.-J. Hefele, trans. H. Leclercq, *Histoire des Conciles* 7 (Paris, 1916), pp. 308–13, in Tanner pp. 422–6. For the manuscripts used by von der Hardt, see C. M. D. Crowder, 'Le Concile de Constance et l'édition de von der Hardt', *Revue d'histoire écclésiastique*, lvii (1962), 409–45.

53. Thus 1–5 concern the eucharist, 6–8 other sacraments, 9–11 confession, 12–15 the priesthood, 17–24 the papacy and so on; nos. 47–55 are philosophical rather than theological points.

abbreviated form, though those sources are not cited.[54] A copy of this list is found in the manuscript of the Constance *acta* written for bishop Thomas Polton, an English representative there, now BL Cotton Nero E.v, ff. 52va–53va; after Polton's death it was purchased from his executors by Humfrey, Duke of Gloucester, and presented by him to Oxford University in February 1443/4.[55]

Even later than the Council of Constance the list of conclusions was used again by Thomas Netter in his vast *Doctrinale*: though he cited individual items throughout his work (apart from books 3–4),[56] it was in book 2 on the church that references are most common. Some interesting points emerge from a comparison of Netter's citations with the two versions of Faustina and *FZ* and the preliminary materials in Magdalen 99. Most simply, Netter's numeration differs from both of the two finished versions considered so far, but is closer to that in *FZ*: thus printed conclusion from Faustina no. 159 is 156 in *FZ* but 155 for Netter, and similarly printed nos 190 and 193 are Netter's 185 and 188 but one higher in *FZ*.[57] The discrepancies are, however, not regular (as these last examples might imply) nor reconcilable to a single explanation – some, but whether those of the *Doctrinale* or of *FZ*, must be simple transcription errors. More interestingly Netter cites one conclusion (226) which is omitted in *FZ*, though conversely two of his errors can be explained by the *FZ* version.[58] Whilst the extant *FZ* manuscript is later than Netter (being dateable to 1439 or after),[59] and therefore it would be possible to suppose that Netter had access to its antecedent, a more likely hypothesis seems to be that Netter used yet another independent copy of the conclusions. This is confirmed by certain other differences. In some cases differences between the *Doctrinale* text and the conclusions can be explained by the fact that Netter went back to the source of the latter and expanded the material: thus conclusion 19, deriving from *Opus evangelicum* iii cap.28 (as indicated in Faustina and in Magdalen 99), slightly

---

54. The exception is *Contra versutias pseudoclerum*; four conclusions, nos. 7, 13, 32 and 36 do not appear to have any counterpart in the list sent to Arundel from Oxford.

55. The list of 45 brought forward to an earlier session is ff. 19vb–20rb; the full list of 260 is not present. See C. M. D. Crowder, 'Constance Acta in English Libraries', in *Das Konzil von Konstanz*, ed. A. Frantzen and W. Muller (Freiburg, 1964), pp. 477–517 at pp. 493–4, and the exhibition catalogue *Duke Humfrey's Library and the Divinity School 1488–1988* (Oxford, 1988), no. 33 (which points out that, whilst the scribe may not have been English, the decoration of the manuscript certainly is).

56. *Doctrinale antiquitatum fidei catholicae ecclesiae*, ed. B. Blanciotti (Venice, 1757–9, reprinted Farnborough, 1967); these two books seem likely on other grounds to antedate the rest of the *Doctrinale* and probably were composed for a different purpose; the absence of references to the conclusions may suggest that they were written before the Council of Constance, even perhaps before 1411.

57. References are given first by book and chapter, followed in parentheses by volume and column number. Netter 1.13 (i.84), 2.30 (i.400), 2.35 (i.426).

58. Wilkins 226 is quoted 2.29 (i.398); Netter cites as 175 (2.81, i.682) conclusion 138 which appears in *FZ* as 135 and as 136 (2.3, i.427) conclusion 241 which in *FZ* is 236.

59. See Crompton, pp. 158–60.

abbreviates Wyclif's original text whereas Netter quotes precisely and continues with one further sentence.[60] Conclusion 10, deriving from the same text chapter 51 (as indicated in Faustina (*pace* Wilkins who prints 71) and *FZ* (but 52 in Magdalen 99)), is put in context by Netter.[61] In at least one instance Netter gives a better text of Wyclif, citing both the original reference and the conclusion: thus conclusion 144 derives from the *Dialogus* chapter 3, of which Netter gives both a longer and a more correct quotation.[62] Sometimes, however, Netter accepts the conclusion text without correction: thus he includes the interpretative sentence on the 'four sects' added to conclusion 13, even though this has no counterpart in Wyclif.[63] There seems no evidence that Netter had access to Magdalen 99, nor to a text very close to Faustina.

Thomas Gascoigne records that a bonfire of Wyclif's books was lit at Carfax in 1410 in the presence of the chancellor, Thomas Prestbury, an event he connects with the condemnation of over two hundred conclusions from the writings.[64] Salter took this to be a response to the decree in Congregation on 26 June 1410 put forward by John Wells, and consequently assumed the bonfire to have been during the summer.[65] But, if there was a connection, a later date nearer to March 1411 seems perhaps more appropriate, given the dilatoriness of the university in taking action. The texts which were available to the committee are perhaps not more interesting than those which were *not* used. Certainly, books were available in Oxford then that now survive only in
* continental, and usually Hussite, copies; notably, *De logica* 3 and *Contra versucias pseudoclerum* are extant now only in a single copy each, *De civili dominio* complete likewise only in one manuscript, all of them Hussite.[66] But, leaving aside the multiplicity of short, mostly polemical works which Wyclif wrote, it is striking that only the *De civili dominio* and the *De symonia* from the so-called *Summa theologie* were scrutinized: had the contentious *De ecclesia, De potestate pape, De apostasia, De blasphemia* been available, they would surely have been examined and a host of unacceptable sections could certainly have been

60. *Opus evangelicum* ii.104/32–40 in Netter (2.41, i.453), but only to 39 in the conclusion and in Magdalen, f. 257rb.
61. Netter 2.53 (i.520) quoting ii.188/11–16 which precedes the passage in the conclusion (188/27–30). Similarly Netter quotes *De civili dominio* i.8/31–9/1 (2.81, i.683), associating it with conclusion 176 (his 172) which derives from i.10/23–5.
62. Netter 2.46 (i.482) quotes *Dialogus* 6/23–7/10, of which the conclusion quotes only 7/7–10; Netter reads in line 7 *nimis indisposita ad convincendum alios* (as the edited text) whereas Faustina, *FZ* and Magdalen f. 260va all read *minus disposita ad conuincendum* (not *communicandum* as Wilkins prints) *aliquos*.
63. Netter 2.53 (i.536); the quotation is *Opus evangelicum* ii.188/31–5, deriving as noted in Faustina, *FZ* and Magdalen 99 from book 3 cap.51. The interpretative sentence is not found in Magdalen f. 177va.
64. *Loci e libro veritatum*, ed. J. E. Thorold Rogers (Oxford, 1881), p. 116.
65. Salter, p. 100; for Wells see Emden, iii. 2010–11.
66. See Thomson, nos. 3, 420 and 28–30.

found. The same would have been true of the *De eucharistia* or the sermons. Certainly the *Trialogus* offered a compendium of Wyclif's mature thought usefully in systematic order; this probably explains the early attention it attracted from Wyclif's enemies, though to the 267 conclusions this text was far from being the most significant contributor. Whether by 1410 Oxford's holdings of Wyclif were already diminished, or were too successfully guarded by sympathizers for use by the commission, is another story – a story that in large measure necessarily escapes our scrutiny. Publicly, however, the university did its duty,[67] and provided a list that gained notoriety far away from Oxford.

---

67. The university did its duty again in 1530 when, following an enquiry from Henry VIII, it sent a summary of its earlier conclusions and those of the Council of Constance; these are found in Oxford MS Bodley 282, ff. 109r–119r (a reference I owe to Prof. Richard Sharpe), whence they are printed by W. T. Mitchell, *Epistolae Academicae 1508–1596* (Oxford Historical Society, new series 26, 1980), nos. 202–3.

XIV

Which Wyche? The Framing of the Lollard Heretic and/or Saint

I should like to start by recalling the story behind the Wife of Bath's familiar question 'Who peyntede the leon, tel me who?', for it is the text of the present sermon.¹ The question is the lion's when shown a picture by a peasant of the killing of a lion by a man with an axe; in Marie de France's recounting of the fable the lion follows up his question by describing to the peasant how *he* would have represented a man and a lion.² The story here concerns not a peasant and a lion, but a series of ecclesiastical figures and a man called Richard Wyche, or, to use the loaded terms of conventional history, investigating authorities and a heretic.³ The story – the case, the legend – of Richard Wyche is one of the rare instances where we have two pictures, one painted by the man, the other by the lion. I propose to start by describing these two pictures, one by one, using the terminology that each uses about its own story. As will be seen, the identity of man and lion is not a fixed one.

The Official Story

It may be unfair to start this version from the end, but I will do the same with my second. The official picture of Wyche is crystallized and dominated by the account of his death: on 17 June 1440 Richard Wyche was burned as a relapsed heretic on Tower Hill in London. This fact is recorded

---

¹ *The Riverside Chaucer*, ed. L. D. Benson et al. (Oxford, 1987), 'Canterbury Tales', iii.692.
² See the edition and translation by H. Spiegel (Toronto, 1987), no. 37.
³ An account of the case is to be found in J. A. F. Thomson, *The Later Lollards 1414–1520*, 2nd edn (Oxford, 1967), pp. 15–16 and 148–50 (to which, as will emerge below, some details can be added); see also C. von Nolcken, 'Richard Wyche, a Certain Knight, and the Beginning of the End', in *Lollardy and the Gentry in the Later Middle Ages*, ed. M. Aston and C. Richmond (Stroud, 1997), pp. 127–54. Much important detail of the background to Wyche's case is to be found in M. Jurkowski, 'Heresy and Factionalism at Merton College in the Early Fifteenth Century', *JEH* 48 (1997), 658–81. Since this paper was written Rita Copeland's study of Wyche has been published in her *Pedagogy, Intellectuals, and Dissent in the Later Middle Ages: Lollardy and Ideas of Learning* (Cambridge, 2001), pp. 151–90; I have added a few points of factual disagreement to the notes here, but have not otherwise modified the text.

in various London chronicles.[4] Two weeks later, on 2 July 1440, the patent roll records the grant of Wyche's goods and chattels to the king's servant John Somerseth, Wyche having been executed 'for certain articles and untrue opinions held by him against the faith of Christ and of Holy Church'.[5] At the time of his burning Wyche was vicar of Harmondsworth, Middlesex, to which he had been presented in January 1437, the patrons being Winchester College.[6] Episcopal registers allow his previous livings to be traced: he went to Harmondsworth from Leaveland in Kent in 1434, a living in the patronage of the king; he had been admitted as vicar of West Greenwich, now known as Deptford, in 1423, and had probably held that living until he moved to Leaveland.[7] That paper trail is entirely neutral: the moves are part of the normal process of clerical appointment, and the documentation does not differentiate Wyche from any other priest. Where Wyche was before Deptford is not declared – nor need it be, there is nothing incriminating about that. Thirty years earlier a Richard Wyche appears to have resigned from the living of Hartley, also in the Rochester diocese, in June 1394; whether he is the same man is typically unresolvable.[8]

Between 1394 and 1424 Wyche, if indeed the two are the same, had, however, appeared in ecclesiastical records in a much less conventional guise. The earliest surviving document is one found in a brief collection of heresy material in BL Royal 8 F. xii, fols. 16–17.[9] There appears a formal recantation before Bishop Walter of Durham by *Ricardus Wyche, presbyter Herfordensis*, of fourteen heresies,[10] followed by a further six articles whose veracity Wyche was apparently required to affirm; he was forced to read out

---

[4] See *Six Town Chronicles of England*, ed. R. Flenley (Oxford, 1911), pp. 101 and 114; C. L. Kingsford, *Chronicles of London* (Oxford, 1905), pp. 147 and 153–4, and the material added to the same author's *English Historical Literature in the Fifteenth Century* (Oxford, 1913), p. 339. Also *CCR 1435–1441*, pp. 385–6.

[5] *CPR 1436–1441*, p. 426.

[6] See G. Hennessy, *Novum Repertorium Ecclesiasticum Parochiale Londinense* (London, 1898), p. 203, from London reg. Gilbert fols. 5r and 32v. Here, and in the following notes, references to bishops' registers are given in the form diocese, bishop's name, folio, page or opening; the registers are listed in D. M. Smith, *Guide to Bishops' Registers of England and Wales* (London, 1981).

[7] For the institution to West Greenwich see C. H. Fielding, *The Records of Rochester Diocese* (Dartford, 1910), p. 81, from Rochester reg. Langdon fol. 66r; for the move to Leaveland, *The Register of Henry Chichele*, ed. E. F. Jacob and H. C. Johnson, 4 vols., Canterbury and York Society 42 and 45–7 (Oxford, 1937–47), I, 342. The exchange of Leaveland for Harmondsworth is recorded in *CPR 1436–1441*, p. 32.

[8] Rochester reg. de Bottlesham, fol. 49v.

[9] The material directly relating to heresy cases begins with this, followed by the recantation of Purvey in 1401, the parliamentary writ for the burning of Sawtry also in 1401, and a copy of Courtenay's reissue on 13 December 1384 of the Blackfriars Council condemnation of articles from Wyclif's works. The Wyche material is reprinted in the appendix to *FZ*, pp. 501–5.

[10] The *FZ* text, p. 501, reads *Willelmus . . . Dinolmensis episcopus* but the personal name in the manuscript is clearly *Walterus*.

all of this, to sign the document, and to promise that he would not in any way propagate the heresies in future but would abide by the teachings of Holy Church. The document is formally undated, but Bishop Walter of Durham is clearly Walter Skirlawe, bishop from September 1388 till his death in March 1406; equally the final affirmation that Wyche made speaks of 'dominus Innocentius . . . papa septimus', and hence cannot have been made until October 1404 when Innocent was elected.[11] In the opening section, couched in the first person but, from its vocabulary and demeanour, almost certainly in wording provided by Wyche's accusers, Wyche acknowledges that he had failed to respond to the bishop's summons and had consequently been twice excommunicated – this is, it is reasonable to conclude, a case that has been pursued by the authorities over some time. The fourteen errors are stated in bald terms: images are not to be worshipped, each lay person is bound to know the whole gospel and to preach it, no priest should beg anything, every place is as suitable for prayer as every other, and so on; ominously the last two are 'they act wrongfully who burn men', and 'foolish are those who say that Richard Wyche has erred in any point'.[12] The six statements that Wyche was required to affirm cover matters not directly addressed in the fourteen errors: the first two provide an orthodox formulation of eucharistic doctrine, the third affirms that obedience is due to all parts of canon law, the fourth that the four orders of friars are approved by the Church and should be received and helped in their work, the fifth that no priest should preach outside his own parish save by special licence from the relevant bishop, and the sixth that anyone entering an order of mendicants, even if he were able-bodied and capable of labour, is entitled to beg. No further comment is made. We may surmise that the bishop had doubts about Wyche's opinion on all six final matters, but that is our deduction: their presence in the picture is, in view of the general economy of its delineation, doubtless significant but it would strictly be going beyond the evidence to affirm that Wyche had taught their opposite.

That recantation stands, as I have said, on its own, followed by a comparable recantation by John Purvey dateable to 1401. No word is given of Wyche's sentence, if any, after he had recited it. From other sources we learn that Skirlawe had prosecuted a number of Durham parish priests over the winter of 1402/3; the case against Wyche probably, though not declaredly, started at the same time.[13] In date the next official record derives from

---

[11] *FZ*, p. 505. Copeland (above n. 3), pp. 152–4, dates the enquiries of Bishop Skirlaw, and this document, more precisely than the evidence warrants; her statement there on the source for this document should be modified by the information given p. 184 n. 91 – only the undated reply of Wyche, discussed here pp. 228–9, appears in the manuscript of the *FZ*.

[12] *FZ*, pp. 501–3.

[13] See the material collected together by M. G. Snape, 'Some Evidence of Lollard Activity in the Diocese of Durham in the Early Fifteenth Century', *Archaeologia Aeliana* 4th s. 39 (1961), 355–61.

the instigation of Wyche himself: in the autumn of 1416 Wyche filed a suit of debt and detinue in Oxfordshire against William Warde, fellow of Merton, alleging that Warde detained from him 54s. 6d. and a book worth five marks. Four years later, 13 June 1420, Warde failed to appear and was outlawed, but in October 1421 appealed. The outcome of the case is unclear, but its process suggests Wyche was near Oxford around the time of proceedings against Oldcastle's followers.[14] From there he may have gone further south, since the next record concerning Wyche occurs in the Exchequer rolls, enigmatically granting payment to a sergeant of the sheriff of Southampton on 21 October 1417 for expenses incurred in arresting, following divers writs from the king, Wyche and another priest William Broune, and delivering them to the King's Council at Westminster 'to make disclosures to them concerning certain sums of money that belonged to Sir John Oldecastell, knight, forfeited to the king'.[15] Again no record survives of the immediate process against either man, though the potential charge now presumably involved treason as well as, or even rather than, heresy.

Two years later, however, both men appeared before the Canterbury Convocation on 20 November 1419. In the fuller record of Chichele's register some part of Wyche's earlier history is rehearsed: Wyche had been investigated by Skirlawe, and also by Richard Holme, and had been imprisoned 'for a long time . . . in northern parts'.[16] If, as seems to be implied, Holme's investigation was separate from that by Skirlawe, its date and its locality seems to have been similar.[17] The precise dates for which Wyche had remained in prison is unclear, but, it is said, Wyche had been brought south by a royal summons called *corpus cum causa* to Westminster, where he had been freed. At what point, or why, this had happened is unclear. But what is stated is that the 1417 arrest had been followed by imprisonment in the Fleet prison, whence the two had come before Chichele and Convocation. But if Chichele's clerk recorded the antecedent history in some detail, albeit maddeningly undated, he did not continue to the archbishop's own questioning: Broune was allowed to recant, but of what

---

[14] For this case, and the documents (largely unprinted) on which it is based, see Jurkowski, 'Heresy and Factionalism', pp. 679–80.

[15] *Issues of the Exchequer . . . from King Henry III to King Henry VI inclusive*, ed. F. Devon (London, 1837), pp. 352–3.

[16] *Register of Henry Chichele*, III, 57.

[17] For Holme see A. B. Emden, *A Biographical Register of the University of Cambridge to 1500* (Cambridge, 1963), pp. 311–12. Holme was commissary to Bishop Thomas Langley whilst the latter was chancellor to the king, between March 1405 and January 1407, and later to Arundel in his resumed chancellorship, January 1407 to December 1409: see R. L. Storey, *Thomas Langley and the Bishopric of Durham 1406–1437* (London, 1961), pp. 15–17, 25 and 169, and *CPR 1405–8*, p. 313. The enquiry concerning Wyche was probably under the former of these two tenures. Copeland (above n. 3), p. 184, suggests that Holme was Skirlaw's chancellor, but there is no evidence for Holme's association with Durham until the episcopacy of Langley.

is unspecified, but Wyche was returned to the Fleet prison to await a decision on appropriate action.[18]

Chichele's register gives no more. Six months later, on 15 July 1420, Wyche was released from the Fleet prison on the security of £200 from five men, three from Herefordshire or Worcestershire, two from London, to appear again at Michaelmas before the King's Council 'to answer touching what shall be laid against him.'[19] End of story. The most that it seems legitimate to deduce from this is that Chichele had not been convinced of Wyche's unorthodoxy at this point, but that questions still remained about his involvement with Oldcastle and that the charges would come before a civil court. Since Wyche was appointed to Deptford in 1423, however, it would seem that he was not found to have been seriously implicated in Oldcastle's rising.

Here then is a coherent, if incomplete, picture: from the documentation by Church and state we are allowed to see a man recurrently under suspicion, required to recant at least once in the first decade of the fifteenth century, examined by Convocation and by Council or their agents between 1417 and 1423, holding a series of livings near London, and executed on Tower Hill in 1440 after being again found guilty of heresy. The paper trail is not complete, but sufficient remains to produce a background to that final stark image of the flames on Tower Hill. But it is a schematic picture in black and white, and neither Wyche nor his opponents emerge as more than flat figures. Even the names of those opponents are few: Skirlawe, Holme, Chichele; beyond that are a shadowy host of clerical officials and underlings, minor officers responsible for arresting, supervising, producing the offender; faceless notaries and scribes who recorded in formulaic terms crucial moments of recantation or trial, but who either had not the knowledge or did not care to record anything beyond a few crucial moments. As for the central figure, we learn his name and the fact that he derived from the Hereford diocese, that he was a priest, that he had travelled, probably lived, widely in the north as well as in the vicinity of London, that equally he had resided – or at least that he had not been charged as non-resident – in several livings around London for nearly twenty years. As far as his heresy is concerned, the crime for which he was finally burned, all we are firmly told are the fourteen errors he recanted thirty-five years before that burning. No further opinions, no explanation for the views allegedly held, no reasoning for, or linkage between, the opinions. Those opinions, furthermore, were found offensive by the authorities, but no definite label was attached to them or to Wyche. Wyche had been fitted in to the stereotype of the heretic, treated in the prescribed fashion, and recorded in the traditional formulae.

---

[18] *Register of Henry Chichele*, III, 57. Dr Maureen Jurkowski kindly tells me that her searches for this writ through Public Record Office files have not uncovered it, or related, documents.

[19] *CCR 1419–1422*, p. 82.

As a transition to the next section it is worth mentioning one vignette preserved in this hostile record of chronicle and official document. At the site where the ashes from Wyche's fire were buried a shrine was set up by his followers, where they made prayers as to a saint.[20] The irony of this escapes the contemporary notice: that, to judge by several items in the recantation at the end of Skirlawe's process against him, Wyche had taught against images, pilgrimages and prayers in special places. 'Orthodox' behaviour is here decried by 'orthodox' sources; the 'heretic' would have denounced that behaviour as strongly as the 'orthodox' authorities.

The Individual's Story

Like the ecclesiastical story, this picture is radically incomplete – just as the ecclesiastical picture is riddled with holes, so half of the picture drawn by the individual does not survive. We have nothing from the second half of Wyche's career, no record from him of events after his alleged involvement with Oldcastle. But for the first decade of the fifteenth century a surprising amount of his own record survives. The first, and fullest, item is a long letter from Wyche to his friends, written whilst he was imprisoned and under interrogation by Bishop Skirlawe; when he wrote he had been excommunicated and sent to wait in prison for his degradation from clerical office.[21] No year is specified within the text, though the sequence of events from Wyche's arrest in late November through to the excommunication in the middle of the ensuing Lent is carefully set out. The purpose of the letter was apparently twofold: its final section makes requests of his friends, for prayers, for various minor objects and books (pp. 541/28–544/9), but the main part details the immensely complicated processes of the investigation, recounting conversations, specifying the interrogators and intermediaries sometimes by their office, sometimes by their name.[22] Wyche clearly apprehended that Skirlawe wanted a recantation, not just a conviction for heresy; his officials, by Wyche's account, were prepared to resort to elaborate guile to achieve this. Wyche declares he was arrested in Chester le Street (p. 531/7), and first came before Skirlawe on 7 December, accused of preaching errors, and questioned on his views about the mendicancy of the friars (p. 531/13); the bishop's

---

[20] See Caroline Barron's review of Thomson (above n. 3), in *Journal of the Society of Archivists* 3 (1967), 257–9; the place of Wyche's burning is there said to be West Smithfield, but this is contradicted by all of the chronicles listed above, n. 4.
[21] The text was printed by F. D. Matthew, 'The Trial of Richard Wyche', *EHR* 5 (1890), 530–44; references here are by page and, following a slash, added line numbers. For the final situation, see pp. 540/49–541/3.
[22] Snape, 'Lollard Activity', may be over-confident in preferring the date of the winter of 1402/3 for the events recorded; he mentions, but as less probable (p. 358), 1403/4. But the recantation reference to Innocent VII (above, p. 223) requires the end of the case to be dated after October 1404.

officials required him to swear that all Christians were bound to accept and obey all parts of canon law (p. 531/19); Wyche asked for time and counsel, was given until after dinner but then repeatedly refused to swear; he was denounced as excommunicate and consigned to prison (p. 531/22–7). A few days later he was taken before the bishop, and asked who had licensed him to preach in the diocese (p. 531/31). By this time the bishop had learned that Wyche was 'one of the sect of Lollards who do not believe the truth about the eucharist' (p. 531/40).[23] Thereafter the eucharist formed the overt central issue of enquiry, though, as Wyche apprehended, the heart of the matter was the question of ecclesiastical authority: Skirlawe was demanding that Wyche should abandon individual judgement to blind obedience. Wyche was left in prison until after Christmas (p. 532/23), but then intermittently was questioned and persuaded for at least a further two months.

There is not time here to recount the circumstantial story that Wyche sets out, a story whose time scale is precisely timetabled,[24] and whose scene is often lit by vivid visual detail and nuanced phraseology. A few points must be highlighted from this fascinating document. The first is the awareness that Wyche shows of legal procedure and its rules. Twice he attempted to stop the enquiry by questioning its legality: in one instance he disputed the validity of the charge since it named him erroneously as from the Worcester diocese (p. 541/9), in the other more extensively he claimed that, since Skirlawe and his officials had not kept to their own schedule but had failed to summon him when they had stated they would, the charges against him must lapse – only a new charge, based on new evidence, could resume the investigation – and for this he cited precedent in the southern province.[25] The second point is that, whilst the enquiry was largely conducted, as would be expected, by the bishop and his clerical officials, an unnamed knight was used as an intermediary; the purpose of the knight was to persuade Wyche to agree to swear an oath to the bishop *in corde tuo limitatum*, 'with reservation in his heart' – such an oath would, the knight averred, satisfy Skirlawe at the same time as salving Wyche's own conscience.[26] The manoeuvres on both sides about this oath dominate much of the account in the letter: Wyche ruefully admits that it was inevitable that Skirlawe would manipulate the oath, and

---

[23] Von Nolcken, 'Wyche, a Certain Knight', pp. 133–5, summarizes Wyche's Lollard views as they emerge from this text.

[24] The intervals between interrogations are clearly signalled (see pp. 533/7 and 16, 534/2, 535/2–3, 536/22 and 24, 537/13, 18 and 47, 538/14 and 18, 539/16 and 540/16). The latest date is two weeks after Ash Wednesday. For the argumentation, see von Nolcken, 'Wyche, a Certain Knight', pp. 136–9, though inevitably interpretation colours the summary.

[25] See pp. 537/14 and 540/22. It is tempting to wonder whether the precedent he has in mind was that of William Thorpe, and whether this was how Thorpe had escaped from the clutches of Bishop Braybrooke of London in early 1397 (see *Two Wycliffite Texts*, ed. A. Hudson, Early English Text Society 301 (Oxford, 1993), pp. xlix–l); for the possible connections between Wyche and Thorpe, see there pp. lviii–lix.

[26] See p. 534/30, and then persistently to p. 540/6.

would not be satisfied, contrary to what the knight had assured Wyche, with the single noncommittal promise (p. 539/31ff). The third point that deserves highlighting in this picture is the constant psychological pressure on Wyche: at an early stage Skirlawe threatened him with burning (p. 533/13), later the revocation of Purvey (in 1401) was read to him (p. 537/19), and he was threatened with the amount of evidence the officials had against him (p. 539/11), and then (rather obscurely) threatened that he must be regarded as a relapse (p. 540/11) – a condition which by current legislation meant that, even if he recanted, he could be held indefinitely in prison, and if he did not he would instantly be resigned to the lay authorities for execution.[27] Finally, as befits a personal letter, friends are named, individual messages sent, the writer's variable states of mind indicated, and his requests set out.[28] Most strikingly we are given an impression of the demeanour of the officials to Wyche. As has been said earlier, some are identified by name, some by position only – 'the archdeacon', 'the chancellor' are the most prominent. Some in both categories cannot be identified now, others can.[29] Doubtless the recipients of Wyche's letter could have named most: 'the chancellor' we can be certain they knew – certain because Wyche, very unusually in Lollard texts at one point but unnecessarily mentions *bonus Wicleff* as his teacher; 'the chancellor' at this point in the Durham diocese was Robert Wyclif, probably his nephew, the unnameable but implied *pessimus Wicleff*.[30]

Before I comment further on the picture that emerges here, it is worth turning to two other texts from the individual's side of the story – albeit neither is so long or so directly informative. The first, like the transition vignette, derives from hostile recording. In the single manuscript of the *Fasciculi zizaniorum* appears an undated reply of Richard Wyche on articles of which he has been accused, the suspect 'protesting that whatever I shall write

---

[27] See *Chichele reg.* I, cxxix–cxxxvi for early fifteenth century refinement of the rules concerning what constituted relapse.

[28] See pp. 541/28ff. Snape, 'Lollard Activity', suggested identities for some of these friends amongst the excommunicated persons of the surviving documents. For 'James' (p. 535/48), see Jurkowski, 'Heresy and Factionalism', p. 618. C. Kightly, 'The Early Lollards: A Survey of Popular Lollard Activity in England, 1382–1428' (unpublished D.Phil. thesis, University of York, 1975), p. 17 n. 3, dismissed the likelihood that *Robert Herl* (p. 542/27) is to be identified with Robert Harley who was executed in 1414 for his part in the Oldcastle rising, but in view of the connections between Wyche and Oldcastle this should perhaps be reconsidered.

[29] The archdeacon of Durham (p. 532/13 and elsewhere) till 1408 was Thomas de Weston (*Fasti Ecclesiae Anglicanae 1300–1541* VI [London, 1963], 112); Paris, a Dominican (pp. 539/19, 540/17ff), was John Paris O.P. (see A. B. Emden, *A Biographical Register of the University of Oxford to 1500*, 3 vols. [Oxford, 1957–9], III, 347 and 357; Emden, *Cambridge*, pp. 441–2; FZ, pp. 286, 498 and 343); the monk called Rome is doubtless Thomas Rome O.S.B. from Durham Cathedral Priory (Emden, *Oxford*, III, 1587–8). One who should be identifiable is the Augustinian prior of Newcastle (p. 539/19).

[30] See p. 536/14; for Robert see *CPR 1401–1405*, p. 459, where in a document of 20 October 1404 Robert de Wyclif is named as Skirlawe's chancellor.

or say which cannot be grounded in scripture I will in repentance revoke and retract, and I ask that the Church should regard as error'.[31] There follow fourteen sections – despite the identity of numbers *not* in all instances identical with those in the recantation – listing views, and, in most but not all cases, the evidence Wyche would adduce for their legitimacy.[32] Part of the first is included by Thomas Netter in his later refutation of Lollard views as deriving from 'quidam dictur Richardus Wyth respondendo pro se in libello oblato judici ad defensionem huius'.[33] The evidence cited by Wyche is primarily biblical, but in addition patristic and canon law authorities are cited, sometimes at length and most with precise referencing, together with 'venerabilis doctor Lincolniensis', that is Grosseteste.[34] Wyche emerges from this as erudite: most striking is his knowledge of the gloss on a section of the *Decretum* by 'the archdeacon', that is Guy de Baysio.[35] But, although this may help to fill out the intellectual background, little of Wyche's own reasoning emerges – or perhaps, given the source, is allowed to emerge. The veracity of the record, even if it has been abbreviated, is supported by the existence of numerous other comparable lists produced between 1380 and 1450 to justify claims that the authorities regarded with suspicion, lists which are preserved not only, as this one, in sources deriving from the ecclesiastical establishment, but also from manuscripts more favourable to innovatory ideas.[36]

The second text is the more surprising and arguably the more informative. This is a letter written by Wyche to Jan Hus, dated from London on 8 September 1410; since all the surviving seven manuscripts derive from Bohemia, there is a Czech translation in a further copy, and two copies of a reply from Hus are likewise found in Bohemia, it seems reasonable to conclude that the letter was indeed sent and reached its destination.[37] In

---

[31] *FZ*, pp. 370–82, here p. 370/2.

[32] Articles 1 and 2 are parallel to the items listed in the recantation 1 and 9, but the remainder are not the same. The articles here, like those of the recantation, are an eclectic mixture of views commonly found in Wycliffite texts (e.g. here 1 on images, 2 on mendicancy, 3 on the equal power of all good priests, 4 on the invalidity of papal excommunication) and the idiosyncratic (e.g. 8 that bastards cannot be saved, 9 that the only lawful offerings are animals).

[33] *Doctrinale* vi. 161, ed. B. Blanciotti, 3 vols. (Venice, 1757–9), III, 967, quoting most of the authorities cited in *FZ*, pp. 370–1.

[34] For patristic references see, for example, *FZ*, p. 370, from Gregory's *Registrum* x. 30 (modern xi. 13, *PL* 77, 1129), and, for canon law, *FZ*, p. 373, referring to Jerome on the epistle to Titus (*PL* 26, 562–3) found 'in canone dist. 95' (D. 95 c. 5, Friedberg, I, 332–3) from which Wyche is evidently quoting; for Grosseteste see *FZ*, pp. 381–2.

[35] *FZ*, p. 380, referring to commentary on D. 32 c. 6, 1 (Friedberg I, 117–18).

[36] For lists in Wycliffite texts cf. *An Apology for Lollard Doctrines*, ed. J. H. Todd, Camden Society old s. 20 (London, 1842).

[37] The edition in V. Novotný, *M. Jana Husi Korespondence a dokumenty* (Prague, 1920), no. 22, lists, and gives variants from, the seven manuscripts, and as 22* prints the Czech translation from the single surviving manuscript. Hus's reply is in the same edition no. 24. The heading of one copy of Wyche's letter, in Stará Boleslav MS C. 132 (now Prague, University Library, MS Cim D 79), 'Magister Richardus *Oxoniensis* ad Magistrum Johannem Hus' (my italics) is interesting. There is a modern English

many respects the content of the letter is uninstructive: it is devoted to brotherly encouragement to persistence in evangelical living and is couched in language rich in biblical resonance with parallels drawn between present suffering and the experiences of Christ and the early Church. But some interesting points emerge: Wyche has evidently heard of Hus's constancy amidst the troubles afflicting him and his friends in Bohemia, though, whether from ignorance or tact, ascribes these to 'antichrist';[38] he mentions the situation in England where 'God has so greatly strengthened the hearts of some people, that they gladly endure imprisonment, exile, and even death for the Word of God';[39] more specifically, Wyche knows the name of *Jacobellum* as a 'co-worker in the gospel' with Hus – *Jacobellum* is Jakoubek of Štríbro, one of Hus's foremost assistants.[40] Less well attested than Wyche's letter is another, dated the same day, 8 September 1410, and addressed to Woksa of Waldstein, a noble who supported Hus, deriving from Sir John Oldcastle.[41] Again the content is entirely conventional, but the interest lies in the coincident dating: even though Oldcastle's letter is addressed from his manor of Cooling in northern Kent, it is surely stretching credulity too far to think that two Englishmen should independently write on the same date to two associated figures in Bohemia on comparable lines. Though from hostile sources the outcome of the charge against Wyche of association with Oldcastle does not emerge, these letters surely guarantee its veracity – even if they do not indicate whether that association was innocent or treasonous.

Here then the individual's story is unusually full: even if the latter half of the picture, after 1410, has been torn away, the earlier half is in full technicolour, 3-D if not wrap-around, with quadraphonic sound system. But, despite all its verisimilitude and circumstantial detail, can we believe it?

---

translation of the letters by M. Spinka, *The Letters of John Hus* (Manchester, 1972), pp. 213–15 (Wyche), 45–8 (Hus's reply).

[38] Novotný, p. 76: 'Audivi, fratres, quam acriter vos turbat Antichristus, tribulaciones varias et inauditas Christi fidelibus inferendo' ('I have heard, brethren, how bitterly the Antichrist troubles you, inflicting various and unheard of tribulations on Christ's faithful'; translation is that of Spinka, p. 213).

[39] Novotný, p. 78: 'in regno nostro et alibi deus corda quorumdam adeo animaverat, quod eciam usque ad carceres, exilium et mortem gaudenter sustinent propter verbum Christi'; translation Spinka, p. 215.

[40] Novotný, p. 78: he greets the lovers of God's law 'et specialiter vestrum in ewangelio coadiutorem Jacobellum' ('and especially your co-worker in the gospel, Jakoubek'; Spinka, p. 215); for Jakoubek see H. Kaminsky, *A History of the Hussite Revolution* (Berkeley and Los Angeles, 1967), pp. 75–80, and see further pp. 98–126 for his later radicalism.

[41] Again printed in Novotný no. 21; two copies, both Bohemian, survive. Woksa was amongst those excommunicated by the archbishop of Prague 2 May 1411 (*Documenta Mag. Ioannis Hus vitam*, ed. F. Palacky [Prague, 1869], p. 430), and he appears in later documents (pp. 581, 584 and 591) favourable to Hus. Failing Woksa, the letter is directed to Zdyslaus of Zvířetic who appears also in these documents, and in the defence of Wyclif's books (below p. 234).

The Framing of the Lollard Heretic and/or Saint

There are, I would like to suggest, problems of various kinds. First of documentation. The absence of an English copy of Wyche's letter to Hus may not be surprising, but the similar absence of the longer document is odd.[42] Furthermore, why should a Bohemian audience be interested in such a detailed account of experiences in a north-country English prison, and in its requests for trivial items from unknown friends with rebarbative names, especially when that distant audience could not furnish the personal identities for the officials pictured?[43] Even if it may be granted that, along with the knight as *agent provocateur*, there was in the prison a sympathetic warder prepared to transmit the suspect's letter to his rural friends, how or why did that apparently personal document travel from northern county Durham to Bohemia?[44] To suggest that the whole document is a forgery would raise more difficulties than it solves; but simple preservation should suggest that the actual reception of the letter is revealing: that it is found so far from home must imply that its intended recipients saw it as more than locally significant, more than just a private record of a single experience. Turning attention to that wider significance, features that the historian tends to 'read over' emerge: far from being a spontaneous and artless account of personal experience, the whole is couched within a well-developed rhetorical frame. Echoes of the Pauline pastoral epistles abound, especially in the mingled exhortations and salutations to friends at the end;[45] the vocabulary of bible and hagiography combine to present the writer in the role of incipient

---

[42] John Bale's knowledge of the letter of Wyche (given by Bale as *Wichewith vel Wichewurth*) to Hus in his *Index Britanniae Scriptorum*, ed. R. L. Poole and M. Bateson, rev. C. Brett and J. P. Carley (Cambridge, 1990), p. 363, derives 'ex opusculis Ioannis Hussij' and is certainly the 1558 Nuremberg edition of texts by and documents concerning Hus (i. fol. 101r–v, with the surname *Vuychewitze*). Foxe's knowledge of the letter (see *The Acts and Monuments of John Foxe*, ed. S. R. Cattley and J. Pratt, 8 vols. [London, 1853–70], III, 506–7) almost certainly derives from the same source (surname *Wichewitze*) since it is not clear that Foxe identified its writer with the Wyche whose burning in 1440 he records elsewhere (III, 702–4).

[43] The manuscript, Prague, University Library, MS III.G.11 (Wyche fols. 89v–95v), is an interesting collection: in addition to that letter it also contains twelve sermons and twenty-three other short works by Wyclif, and the Latin version of William Taylor's 1406 sermon at St Paul's Cross London (see my paper 'William Taylor's 1406 Sermon: A Postscript', *Medium Aevum* 64 [1995], 100–6). The claim that the *Quaestio ad fratres de sacramento altaris*, usually thought to be by Wyclif, is in this manuscript ascribed to Wyche (see W. R. Thomson, *The Latin Writings of John Wyclyf* [Toronto, 1983], p. 74, recording an older view) derives from a dubious claim concerning an erasure in the medieval list of contents on fol. i (a claim repeated by von Nolcken [above, n. 3], p. 149 n. 60, and by Copeland [above, n. 3], p. 152 n. 5).

[44] A similar problem exists both with Thorpe's *Testimony*, declaredly written in prison, which survives in one medieval English copy and in two Bohemian Latin manuscripts, and with the longer *Opus Arduum* (for which see my paper in *Lollards and their Books* [London, 1985], pp. 43–65).

[45] See pp. 542/1ff, 542/27ff and 543/20ff.

saint[46] – Wyche may have preached against the worship of saints, but he had certainly absorbed the literary techniques of their biographies.[47] And his apparently private letter was carefully designed for a wider audience. That awareness of rhetoric is much more evident in the letter to Hus: this is an exercise in the consolatory epistolary style rather than a meaningful transmission of information, whether personal or sect – Hus's reply, interestingly, is the more 'informative', both in regard to the immediate situation in Bohemia and also in its use of established Wycliffite vocabulary.[48]

Reconstruction?

Look then upon this picture, and on this:
The *counterfeit presentment* of –

not two brothers, but the same person. Can one picture be made from the two? Or is the *presentment* so rhetorically coloured that the two *counterfeits* can never be combined? Of course it is possible to elicit the 'facts' from both pictures, and weld them together to provide an outline biography. In such an enterprise, however, hypotheses have to be accepted, incipient contradictions ironed out, and the danger is that the resulting picture may resemble a diagram. The interest of this case lies not just in the two, arguably unresolvable, pictures, but in the way it highlights the simplification of the cases where only *one* picture survives: usually, as with Swinderby, Robert Hook, William Drayton and probably John Purvey, it is the ecclesiastical authorities' picture which alone survives, rarely, as is almost the case with William Thorpe, the individual 'heretic's' picture.[49] But each is rhetorically framed: Thorpe's dramatic identification of antichrist with Thomas Arundel is no less contrived as propaganda than the episcopal register that brands the captive as 'hereticus, pessimus Lollardus'.[50] It is for

---

[46] See the sequence of biblical quotations and their surrounding appropriation on pp. 541/32ff and elsewhere in this concluding section, but also earlier on pp. 533/14, 536/24–537/12 and 541/20–7.

[47] In Wyche's recantation (above, pp. 222–3) hostility to saints, their images, pilgrimages to their shrines and prayers to them, is seen in errors 1–2, 7 and 11–12; in the undated *responsio* (above, pp. 228–9) in answers 1 and, implicitly, 14.

[48] See Novotný, no. 24 pp. 84–5; for the Wycliffite vocabulary, reflecting the concept of the Church as the *congregatio predestinatorum* ('the congregation of the predestined'), see the final salutation from 'Christi ecclesia de Boemia' ('The Church of Christ in Bohemia') to 'ecclesiam Christi in Anglia' ('The Church of Christ in England'); Spinka, p. 48.

[49] For some references to the documentary materials on the first two, see Hudson, *Premature Reformation*, pp. 74–7, 154 and 164; on the third, *Two Wycliffite Texts*, pp. xix–xxi, and for the fourth, *Lollards and their Books*, pp. 85–110.

[50] See Thorpe's *Testimony* in *Two Wycliffite Texts*; materials concerning the early stages of Thorpe's 'heresy' survive from hostile sources (see pp. xlvii–l). Maureen

a modern audience easier to exonerate the individual than the official, to portray sympathetically the captured and interrogated suspect than to persuade of the disinterest of a 'caesarian prelate', simpler to discern the official formulae of the episcopal or civil document than the rhetoric of hagiography. But we should be careful. Which *was* the lion, which the peasant?

The Researcher's Story

If there is an inherited rhetoric that seeks to convince in both the Official Story and the Individual's Story, there is also a conventional art of persuasion in the language of the present-day researcher. The material here must candidly be admitted as a series of hypotheses, clues that cannot in the final analysis construct a watertight case – for the present, at least. But, in the hope that more may subsequently emerge, or be seen by other investigators, it seems worth setting out the trail so far.

The final sentence of Hus's reply to Wyche's 1410 letter thanks him for the trouble he has taken over manuscripts on behalf of the Bohemians: 'quod tantis laboribus exemplaria nobis egentibus ministrastis'.[51] What were these manuscripts? It seems clear from the wording that they were more than just the letter from Wyche, or even the two from him and from Oldcastle: the reasonable implication of the words is that they were books which Hus and the Bohemians had requested, and which Wyche had supplied, or had been influential in supplying. The use of the term 'exemplaria' rather than 'manuscriptas' suggests that the books supplied were to furnish the masters from which further copies might be made. The texts which Hus and his followers are most likely to have wanted from England are those of Wyclif's writings.

Hus in this letter earlier refers, in infuriatingly allusive terms, to two of the intermediaries in the correspondence: 'Nicholas, to whom I am writing, will inform you of other things. The letter was first delivered to us on the second Sunday in Lent, because Simon was in Hungary with it.'[52] Presumably Hus could be sure that Wyche would be able to identify these two just from their Christian names. The identity of the Nicholas, who will be physically present

Jurkowski has also discovered important new information about Thorpe's arrest in 1407; for this see below, p. 236.

[51] Novotný, p. 85; Spinka, p. 48 one of the two copies reads *exempla* for *exemplaria*. Stephen Páleč also reports that Hus mentioned 'literas de Anglia et presertim unam bonam epistolam quam . . . michi scripsit Richardus Witz presbiter magistri Johannis Wicleff' (Novotný, no. 29, quoting from the extracts from Páleč's unprinted *Tractatus de ecclesia* in J. Sedlák, *M. Jan Hus* [Prague, 1915], ii.248*). Hus's letter is not among those whose authenticity has been questioned by B. Kopičková and A. Vidmanová, *Listy na Husovu obranu z let 1410–1412* (Prague, 1999).

[52] Novotný, p. 85; Spinka, p. 48; the names are identical in both copies.

when Hus's letter arrives, can be suggested with fair certainty: Mikuláš Faulfiš, to give his name in Czech form, was one of two Bohemians who visited England in 1406–7, and who, by Hus's own testimony at Constance, died travelling between Spain and England some years later.[53] His death can be shown, from documentary evidence relating to a dispute over his inheritance, to have occurred by the end of November 1411.[54] The purpose of Faulfiš's earlier journey was the collection of materials concerning Wyclif: he, and his companion Jiri Kněhnic, gathered a chip from Wyclif's tomb at Lutterworth, obtained through the assistance of Peter Payne (later to follow them back to Bohemia) a testimonial from the University of Oxford to Wyclif's repute and orthodoxy,[55] and copied at least three of Wyclif's longer theological writings. Their copy miraculously survives as Vienna, Österreichische Nationalbibliothek MS 1294: notes before and after the three texts and at the end of some chapters provide the testimony to its origins, and allow an itinerary for the two Bohemians to be constructed.[56] The 'Simon' of Hus's letter has been taken to be Simon of Tišnov, one of the masters, along with Hus himself and Jakoubek of Stříbro (the Jacobellus of Wyche's letter), who had spoken in defence of Wyclif's books in July and early August 1410 after the bonfire of the master's books ordered by the archbishop of Prague; Simon had defended *De probationibus propositionum*, better known to us as part 2 of *De logica*.[57] Suggestively, ÖNB 1294 has as a flyleaf a document naming Simon of Tišnov as the beneficiary of a newly founded chapel.[58] Equally, a connection between Simon and Faulfiš is assured by the fact that the former appears as a creditor of the latter in the legal negotiations which followed Faulfiš's death.[59]

Was Wyche then involved in some way in facilitating the production of ÖNB 1294? Directly, the answer must probably be negative: Wyche is likely to have been still in prison in the north in 1406–7. But the itinerary and

---

[53] Novotný suggests this identity with a question mark. For the 1406–7 journey see below; Hus's comment on his death is reported by Peter of Mladoňovice, printed F. Palacký, *Documenta Mag. Johannis Hus* (Prague, 1869), p. 313, trans. M. Spinka, *John Hus at the Council of Constance* (New York and London, 1965), p. 220.

[54] See *Archiv Český* 36 (1941), p. 440.

[55] The testimonial, obtained on the signature of Congregation, is printed in *Concilia Magnae Britanniae et Hiberniae A.D. 466–1717*, ed. D. Wilkins, 4 vols. (London, 1737), III, 302 from BL MS Cotton Faustina C.7, where it is dated 5 October 1406. Memory of the visit, and of the testimonial, was still vivid at Hus's trial in 1415, judging by the testimony of Peter of Mladoňovice (above n. 53) p. 313.

[56] See below for its details.

[57] For the events leading to the bonfire and the defences, see Kaminsky (above n. 40), pp. 70–4 and esp. p. 73; Simon's text is printed by J. Loserth, *Wiclif and Hus*, trans. M. J. Evans (London, 1884), pp. 309–16. Another spokesman was Zdyslaus of Zvířetic (above n. 41).

[58] See flyleaf I at the start, dated at the end 1401; mentioned in the most recent catalogue listing, *Katalog der kroatischen, polnischen und tschechischen Handschriften der Österreichischen Nationalbibliothek*, K. Schwarzenberg (Vienna, 1972), p. 12.

[59] See above, n. 54.

dates found in the manuscript warrant closer attention. Three texts appear in the manuscript, each originally in separable sets of quires;[60] their present ordering is *De veritate sacre scripture, De ecclesia* and *De dominio divino*. Copying of the first of these was, by the note added at the end of chapter 20, in train on the vigil of St James, 24 July; it was corrected, according to the note at the end, by Faulfiš and Kněhnic in Oxford on 1 February 1407.[61] The second text is said at the end of chapter 2 (fol. 134va) to have been copied at Kemerton, but its writing is only dated once, at the end of chapter 4 'in vigilia pentecostes' (fol. 141ra). The third text was copied at Braybrooke (end of book iii chapter 5), and is twice dated by liturgical occasion, Maundy Thursday and Good Friday (fols. 223va and 225va, at the end of i.10 and i.11). It seems not unreasonable to think that the shortest timetable compatible with these dates is the most likely: the Bohemians had a mission in England, but no reason to delay there. This suggests that they first copied *De veritate* in an uncertain location, possibly Oxford; they were certainly there to collect the Wyclif testimonial, and in February 1407 to correct the text. They then went to Braybrooke where they worked on *De dominio divino* in March 1407, the occasions mentioned being 24 and 25 March that year; then on to Kemerton, where they were at work on *De ecclesia* on 14 May (Whit Sunday that year fell on 15 May). Their hosts outside Oxford are not directly relevant to the present question, but can be identified as Robert Lychlade, rector at Kemerton after investigation for heresy in 1395 whilst at Oxford, and the Latimer household at Braybrooke.[62] A visit of eleven months, and a journey to three places at least, could certainly explain Hus's assumption that 'Nicholas' needed no further specification.

Indirectly, however, Wyche may be connected with the details that emerge from the notes in ÖNB 1294. In addition to the notes that date and localize the copying, a few other comments are to be found. Relevant here is a Czech couplet at the end of chapter 11 of the copy of Wyclif's *De ecclesia*:

> W Anglii wyerna dwa knyezy
> Pro slowo bozye w zalarzy wyezye   (fol. 163vb)

'In England they have imprisoned two true priests for preaching the gospel.' This note is likely to have been made at Kemerton in May or early June 1407.

---

[60] Their separation is now disguised by the indexes provided by a different hand at the end of the first two items: the second of these covers an added bifolium (now fols. 208–9) plus the first leaf of the ten-leaf quire on whose third the final text begins.

[61] Fols. 68va and 119vb; the notes relevant to the itinerary are all entered within the ruling of the columns, directly after the last word of the chapter; consequently, save at the end of the text, they cannot have been added later but must have been entered as the writing proceeded. The note concerning the correction of *De veritate* is at the foot of the column, whilst the text ends halfway down.

[62] See Hudson, *Lollards and their Books*, p. 78, and references there given.

A recent discovery by Maureeen Jurkowski suggests the news that could have provoked that couplet: on 17 April 1407 William Thorpe and his assistant John Pollyrbache were arrested in Shrewsbury, interrogated, and then in late June or early July taken under guard to imprisonment by Archbishop Arundel in Canterbury; the charges against the pair were indeed that they had preached errors.[63] Since chapter 2 had been completed by 14 May, news of the arrest could well have reached the Bohemians by the time they had copied as far as the end of chapter 11.

If this last identification is plausible, and if the earlier suggestions concerning the allusions in Hus's letter are credible, then Wyche can be linked much more closely to the group of Wycliffites influential in facilitating the transmission of books to Bohemia; indeed, if all these hypotheses are put together, a much clearer picture emerges of that transmission than has hitherto been discernible. Wyche can be seen to have been acquainted not only with two Bohemians, Nicholas and Simon, and to have known of Jakoubek of Stříbro, but also with other English Lollards. The misspelled 'Willelmi Corpp' of his prison letter can be more firmly identified with William Thorpe, long elusive not only to his contemporaries but also to modern researchers; the suggestion that Wyche's letter could have been the inspiration for Thorpe's *Testimony* gains in credibility.[64] If Faulfiš and Knĕhnic heard of Thorpe's arrest in Gloucestershire, and thought it worth recording, it reinforces the idea that the Bohemians' journeyings round England were the result of a concerted effort by a number of native Wycliffites to facilitate their endeavours. And there is no reason to suppose that ÖNB 1294 comprised the full extent of the Bohemians' new baggage on their return home: particularly in the first half of their visit there are gaps in time for more copying. One credible addition might be the exemplar for several of the texts now surviving in Prague University Library MS III.G.11: a Latin version of William Taylor's 1406 sermon at St Paul's Cross, some three dozen short works by Wyclif, and the sole copy of Wyche's prison letter.[65] William Thorpe's *Testimony* must have been a later migrant: again two Latin copies are found in Hussite territory, but the work cannot have been written at least until after 7 August 1407, or, if the colophon to the single medieval English manuscript is believed, until after the death of archbishop Arundel in February 1414.[66] Hus's thanks for the *exemplaria* become comprehensible. Dimly and tentatively, we may see two groups of associates: the Bohemians Hus, Jakoubek, Faulfiš, Tišnov, Waldstein, Zvířetic, and the English Wyche,

---

[63] M. Jurkowski, 'The Arrest of William Thorpe in Shrewsbury and the Anti-Lollard Statute of 1406', *Historical Research* 117 (2002), 273–95. I am very grateful to Dr Jurkowski for advance information on this discovery, and for her comments on an earlier draft of this paper.
[64] See my edition (above, n. 25) pp. lvii–lix.
[65] Above, n. 43 and references there.
[66] See edition pp. xxviii–xxx and lii.

Oldcastle, Thorpe, Payne, even Taylor, and the multifarious interchanges and connections between them.[67]

This story, as I warned, is full of hypotheses; the picture has been fragmented into tiny pieces, only a few of which survive – or, at least, have so far come to light. The outline that I have been suggesting would go some way to explaining Bohemian interest in Wyche. Insofar as any narrative emerges, it fills in the background to Wyche's career up to the writing of his letter to Hus in 1410. It does not help towards filling the hiatus between Wyche's release from the Fleet in 1420 and his burning for heresy in 1440: the sequence of benefice changes testifies to Wyche's presence in England during that time, but not much more. Whether he remained true to his Wycliffite beliefs throughout that time, how he propagated heresy or finally came into the authorities' power, these are only the most obvious questions that remain unanswered.

---

[67] Purvey because his 1401 recantation was mentioned to both Wyche (above, p. 228) and Thorpe (*Testimony* 499, 541–8), and both evidently knew something of his history; Taylor because Thorpe refers to the scandal of his November 1406 sermon (*Testimony* 1967–89 and notes) – a time when Faulfiš and Kněhnic were in England. The Bohemian Jerome of Prague is another tempting addition: he had been in Hungary just before Simon of Tišnov in 1411 (see F. Šmahel, 'Leben und Werk des Magisters Hieronymus von Prag', *Historica* 13 [1966], 81–111 esp. pp. 86–9).

XV

Wyclif texts in Fifteenth-century London

Debate continues about the significance of Wyclif and of Lollardy between 1384 and 1530; claims on both sides have arguably been over-stated. Investigation of the manuscripts of Wyclif's Latin works can still produce new evidence, and evidence that suggests that the situation during that century and a half was more complex, and more interesting, than has always been admitted. In 2000 an important paper by Jeremy Catto appeared, entitled 'A Radical Preacher's Handbook, c.1383'; in it Dr Catto described the contents of the manuscript now Peterhouse, Cambridge, MS 223, and argued, from an erased inscription on the second preliminary folio, that the first owner of the book was Laurence Stephen, better known as the Oxford disciple of John Wyclif under the name of Laurence Bedeman.[1] The final item in the manuscript is an incomplete copy of Wyclif's *De veritate sacre scripture* (T31),[2] and the purpose of Dr Catto's paper was to analyse the interests that lay behind the compilation as a whole, and to argue that Stephen/Bedeman was responsible for bringing these contents together, probably in Oxford before he returned to overt orthodoxy in 1383. The importance of the discovery of the ownership is that this puts Peterhouse 223 amongst the very earliest manuscripts of a text by Wyclif, copied in Oxford before Wyclif's own death. Dr Catto mentioned at the close of his paper that the manuscript had subsequently come into the hands of Dr William Lichfield, a Cambridge graduate and one time fellow of Peterhouse, who had left it to his old college at his death in 1448.[3] It is this later ownership which prompts the present enquiry.

---

[1] See *EHR* 115 (2000), 893–904; generously, at the start of the footnotes Dr Catto thanks me for reading the paper, and I reproach myself for not having realised then the importance of the later ownership of the manuscript.

[2] The text was edited by R. Buddensieg for the Wyclif Society, London, 1905–7, but not using this manuscript; the copy here ends in chapter 24 (ii.246/5); the text breaks off a line and a half before the bottom of f.281v, the seventh leaf of a probable twelve-leaf quire.

[3] The manuscript appears as a later marginal addition in the 1418 catalogue of Peterhouse books: see *The University and College Libraries of Cambridge*, ed. P.D. Clarke and R. Lovatt (*CBMLC* 10, London, 2002), p. 489 no. 173 – where, however, the Wyclif item is not mentioned by name (though the note of the incipit of the penultimate folio reveals that it was present); for the date of the addition soon after 1448 see p. 446.

William Lichfield at some point apparently owned a second copy of Wyclif's *De veritate sacre scripture*: this one is now in Oxford, Bodleian Library, MS Bodley 924.[4] Again it is incomplete, but here it is the opening of the text which is missing.[5] This copy was given by Lichfield to St Mary Overey, later Southwark cathedral, as an ownership inscription by the latter institution on the final leaf (p. 621 top margin) declares; the date of the donation is unclear. Why should Lichfield, not a man anywhere connected with Wycliffite sympathies, have owned two copies of this text? – copies which he seems to have felt important enough to warrant giving to two institutions that could be expected to preserve them, and copies with which he apparently felt no qualms about being associated? Lichfield's career began in Cambridge, of which he must have been a graduate by October 1404 when he was admitted to a fellowship at Peterhouse; he later became first Bachelor (by 1416) and Doctor of Theology.[6] After three years between 1420 and 1423 as rector of a Leicestershire village, he became rector of All Hallows the Great in London from 1423 till his death in 1448 where, as will be seen, he was active in a number of ways; he did not, however, lose touch with Cambridge, since in 1446–7 he was involved in the foundation of Godshouse, later Christ's College. The beneficiaries of Lichfield's gifts of books are therefore entirely comprehensible, and there seems every reason to accept the veracity of the donation of both manuscripts; what remains surprising is their content. The context in which Lichfield's name is probably most familiar to historians of the fifteenth century is as one of the opponents of Reginald Pecock; this confirms the other evidence pointing to Lichfield's unimpeachable orthodoxy.[7]

---

[4] A second William Lichfield who died in 1517, an Oxford graduate (see Emden, *Oxford* pp. 1145–6) whose career was also primarily in London, could have been the donor, but there is no evidence to support this. His will survives (NRA/PRO PROB.11/19 – for help in finding this I am grateful to Dr Maureen Jurkowski) but mentions no books, and, more significantly, amongst very many charitable gifts to religious causes does not include any mention of St Mary Overey. It thus seems more credible to connect Bodley 924 with the earlier man: as will become clear, duplication of owned material is provable for him beyond Wyclif.

[5] The text starts in chapter 4, i.77/9; here the defect is clearly the result of the loss of folios. As is mentioned by R.M. Ball, *Thomas Gascoigne, Libraries and Scholarship* (Cambridge Bibliographical Society Monograph 14, 2006), p. 35, there are some marginal notes in the manuscript, but it is uncertain whether they are in Lichfield's hand.

[6] See most recently R.M. Ball's biography (name spelled 'Lichefeld') in *ODNB*; also Emden, *Cambridge*, p. 368.

[7] See Wendy Scase's biography of Pecock in the *ODNB* and at more length her account in *Authors of the Middle Ages* 8 (Aldershot, 1996), especially pp. 94, 98–9, also J. Catto, 'The King's Government and the Fall of Pecock, 1457–58', in *Rulers and Ruled in Late Medieval England: Essays presented to Gerald Harriss*, ed. R. Archer and S. Walker (London, 1995), pp. 201–22. Some of the

Lichfield, however, was not the only Londoner around the middle of the fifteenth century with a considerable interest in books, some of them of surprising content. It is worth first looking at the earlier background to this situation. Much seems ultimately traceable to the interests of Richard Whittington during his lifetime and in the terms of his bequests that set up the Whittington charity.[8] These concerns primarily established what later became the Guildhall Library, but it is clear that the repercussions were felt far beyond either the immediate beneficiaries of Whittington's charity or the official Guildhall itself.[9] Influential here was John Carpenter, common clerk of the city of London from 1417 till 1438, and chief executor of Whittington's will. Carpenter owned a number of books, including a copy of Roger Dymmok's reply to the *Twelve Conclusions of the Lollards*, posted on the doors of St. Paul's Cathedral and of Westminster Hall in 1395.[10] An early master of Whittington College, from 1431 to 1444, was Reginald Pecock; he was succeeded by Thomas Eborall from 1444–64.[11] Eborall moved on to become rector of All Hallows, Honey Lane till his death in 1471, but at Whittington College in turn was followed by William Ive from 1464–1470. It may have been during Ive's term of office that Eborall and Ive together approved a copy of the Wycliffite New Testament in the later, idiomatic, version which is now in the John Rylands Library, Manchester, MS Eng.77: the inscription (f.267v) recording this was apparently written by the son of a woman who paid £4.6s.8d for the book,

---

figures here, and their careers, are mentioned for a different purpose in R.M. Ball. 'The Opponents of Bishop Pecock', *JEH* 48 (1997), 230–62 (Ball apparently did not know either Catto's paper or Scase's 1996 biography).

[8] For Whittington's career see the *ODNB* article by A.F. Sutton, and C.M. Barron, 'Richard Whittington: the man behind the myth', *Studies in London History presented to P.E. Jones*, ed. A.E.J. Hollaender and W. Kellaway (London, 1969), 197–248, J.Imray, *The charity of Richard Whittington* (London, 1968), especially pp. 1–15, 38–41; A.F. Sutton, *The Mercery of London: Trade, Goods and People, 1130–1578* (Aldershot, 2005), pp. 161–72 deals briefly with Whittington's will and the charities established.

[9] For the early development of the Guildhall Library see R. Smith, 'The Library at Guildhall in the 15th and 16th Centuries', *Guildhall Miscellany* I/1 (1952), 2–9 and I/6 (1956), 2–6, and N.R. Ker, '*Liber custumarum*, and other manuscripts formerly at the Guildhall', *Guildhall Miscellany* I/3 (1952), 37–45.

[10] For his will see T. Brewer, *Memoir of the Life and Times of John Carpenter* (London, 1856), appendix II and S.H. Cavanaugh *A Study of Books privately owned in England, 1300–1450* (unpublished Ph.D. thesis, University of Pennsylvania, 1980) i.167–70 – it is in London Guildhall, Commissary Court of London, Reg.iv (Prowet), ff.84r-85v; for an analysis of Carpenter's most remarkable engagement with books see W. Kellaway, 'John Carpenter's *Liber Albus*', *Guildhall Studies* III/2 (1978), 67–84. There is a biography by M. Davies in *ODNB*.

[11] For Eborall see Emden, *Oxford*, pp. 622–3, but there is no *ODNB* entry; Ball (1997) pp. 231, 235.

but the name of the purchaser and her son are unfortunately not specified.[12] Ive himself was the recipient of a bequest by William Wagge in 1469 of a volume, now Oxford Magdalen College 98, which contains as its final item a copy of Wyclif's *De mandatis*. A further London cleric, Thomas Graunt, can be linked with Thomas Eborall in 1452 when the two men, plus another unnamed, were commissioned to inspect the books of Andrew Teye for 'heresy, error, or treason'.[13] Graunt was an Oxford man, who by 1452 had just become a canon of St. Paul's London, and two years later became precentor there till his death in 1474. Graunt, in addition to a large number of other books, owned the copy of parts of Wyclif's *Postilla in totam Bibliam*, now St. John's College Oxford MS 171.[14]

All of these men, as is evident from the summary above, had an interest in and owned books; more details about these books will be considered below. But it is important that, in addition to their individual concern with books, they were also in contact with each other: though it would be unfair to describe them as a group, since their associations were fluctuating and casual, it seems clear that there were links between them. Most obviously, three, Pecock, Eborall and Ive, were masters of Whittington College. John Carpenter was the chief executor of Whittington's will and, especially in view of the residuary powers left in that will to the executors, was until his own death in 1442 (nearly twenty years after Whittington's) influential in the affairs of the College; though it is chronologically unlikely that he would have known Ive or even Eborall, he certainly encountered Pecock. Pecock and William Lichfield in 1441 were named in the will of Carpenter to select from amongst his books not specifically earmarked for others those that should go to the Guildhall Library;[15] at this point Lichfield had been rector of All Hallows the Great for eighteen years and Pecock had been at the College for ten years – presumably their joint nomination implies that at this point there was no overt hostility between the two men. Five years later Pecock and Lichfield were two amongst a group of Londoners, mostly clerics, who set up a fraternity aiming to establish a perpetual chantry.[16]

---

[12] For some comments on this episode see R. Hanna, *London Literature 1300–1380* (Cambridge, 2005), pp. 308–10.

[13] *CPR 1446–52*, p. 584.

[14] See his signature f.v at the end of the manuscript; it is recorded by R. Hanna, *A Descriptive Catalogue of the Western Manuscripts of St.John's College Oxford* (Oxford, 2002), pp. 236–7. A brief biography is in Emden, *Oxford* 802–3 but see V. Gillespie, *Syon Abbey* (*CBMLC* 9, 2001), p. 580 where the *Martiloge* gives the date of his death as 1471; for further details and Graunt's other books see below.

[15] See references in n. 10.

[16] Scase (1996), pp. 94–5, Ball (1997) p. 232 and n. 5.

But by about 1447, by then bishop of St. Asaph, Pecock was in trouble about his theological views, and in particular his defence of non-preaching bishops; his opponents included both Lichfield and also Thomas Eborall and these two were amongst those commended by Thomas Gascoigne for their effective preaching.[17] The association of Eborall and Ive, apart from the succession of the two at Whittington College, has already been mentioned; both men have been suggested as possible suppliers of the final section of *Gregory's Chronicle* and possibly as the main author of the work.[18] Graunt certainly knew Eborall, and his prominent position at St. Paul's makes it incredible that he did not know Ive; his direct acquaintance with Lichfield is less certain, but it seems improbable that he would not at least have heard of him.

It is worth looking in a little more detail at the books with which these five men, Carpenter, Lichfield, Eborall, Ive and Graunt can be connected; in the process a further group of names of others similarly involved with books will emerge. The earliest of them, as has been said, was Carpenter. His will indicates clearly that he owned a very considerable library of books both in Latin and French; the Dymmok text against the Wycliffites was only one amongst a collection that included, alongside a great missal and conventional devotional material, books on architecture and the arts of warfare, several that might be thought to have taxed a layman's knowledge of Latin.[19] Carpenter's concern with books and their collection is seen in the inclusion of Richard of Bury's *Philobiblon* in his own library; the specific legacies (*librum* has here been counted as singular even when the specified content might suggest plurality) number thirteen plus more generally books and quires at the discretion of the executors to two named clerks, business papers to be deposited in the Guildhall library for the use of the clerks, and (as has already been mentioned) any remaining books that, again in the view of the executors, should seem useful to be deposited in the same Guildhall library. The personal beneficiaries of this will include nine who were or had been Carpenter's clerks, five clerics – one of them Dr John Carpenter currently warden of the hospital of St. Anthony but later bishop of Worcester and probably a relation, a second John Neale, master of the hospital of St. Thomas of Acres, Cheapside, a third William Byngham then rector of St.

---

[17] Gascoigne, *Loci e libro veritatum*, ed. J.E. Thorold Rogers (Oxford, 1881), pp. 188–9 and Catto (1995), p. 205.

[18] See J.A.F. Thomson, 'The Continuation of 'Gregory's Chronicle' – a possible author?', *British Museum Quarterly* 36 no. 3 (1972), 92–7.

[19] For instances of these categories *De meditationibus et orationibus Sancti Anselmi* Prosper *De vita contemplativa*; a 'book on architecture' and another including *Dispositio et regimen bellorum duorum et acierum guerrarum*; two copies of Alanus *De planctu nature*, one of Alanus *Anticlaudianus*, or one of Innocent IV's *De miseria conditionis humane*.

John Zachary London but later a founder of Godshouse (later Christ's College) Cambridge, a fourth David Fyvian rector of St. Benet Fink,[20] and the fifth his own resident chaplain. It is also notable that Carpenter, in addition to naming those to whom the books should go after his death, records in several cases the name of the man who had previously given it to him: thus the book on architecture had come by gift from William Cleve, the Dymmok text from John Wilok, the French book had belonged to Sir Thomas Pykworth *chivaler*. The reason for naming these donors is not specifically stated, but it seems reasonable (especially in the light of evidence to be considered below) that they are mentioned in the hope that the further recipients will remember the previous owners in their prayers.

Chronologically the next of the five men is William Lichfield. Here the evidence is less ample, not least since his will appears not to survive. As has been mentioned, he left two books to Peterhouse Cambridge, the Wyclif volume from which this note started and a second book listed in the college's record as *Libellus Willelmi de Amore* but apparently not surviving; William of St Amour was, of course, a notorious opponent of the friars. But the surviving Peterhouse manuscript, that containing Wyclif's *De veritate*, itself includes material by William: however, the simple explanation that two books, separate when Lichfield left them to the college, were subsequently combined is not compatible with the evidence of the list, and it must be concluded that, in addition to his duplicate Wyclif, Lichfield also had two books containing William's contentious writings.[21] Lichfield was known as a celebrated preacher in London, and the Syon catalogue records two copies *de materiis predicabilibus* called *Mille exempla* by him, and two copies of his sermons (one possibly in English).[22] Less certain are other ascriptions to him: surviving in the present BL

---

[20] His will survives in Guildhall 9171/5, f.22v; the only book mentioned in it is a Bible, which from the wording was probably not the *Biblia abbreviata* left him in Carpenter's will. For the foundation of Godshouse cf Ball (1997) p. 232 and B. Dobson, 'Henry VI and the University of Cambridge', in *The Lancastrian Court*, ed. J. Stratford (Harlaxton Medieval Studies 13, Donington, 2003), pp. 53–67 at pp. 63–6.

[21] The editors of the list (*CBMLC 10*, UC 48, no. 172) suggest the book was his *Tractatus de periculis nouissimorum temporum*. The second folio of the William volume in the list is given as *predictas* and the penultimate as *obediencia*; neither of these agrees with the relevant folios of that item in Peterhouse 223 (ff.71–178). The equivalent information for the list no. 173 (the surviving volume) agrees with the existing state of the manuscript; this leaves the possibility that the William section was later inserted into the middle of 173, but the second and penultimate folios given are untraceable anywhere in Peterhouse 223.

[22] See *Syon Abbey* nos. 889 item v and 948 item f, and for the sermons 617 item c, 1324 item a where the 2o folio is in English – since in 617 the sermons are the third item it is impossible to know whether those there were also in the vernacular.

Royal 8 C.i is an item entered in the list of contents, f.1v, as 'Optimus tractatus de quinque sensibus secundum lichef', expanded f.143v at the end of the text to *Lichfeild* in a hand probably of the seventeenth century; this is actually an abbreviated version of part of the *Ancrene Riwle*;[23] in the current Gonville and Caius 174/95 an English poem is claimed in the colophon 'compilatus per Mag. Will. Lychefelde doctorem theologie'.[24] The second of these is very widely disseminated, though not always so ascribed, whilst Lichfield's connection with the first if any can only be that of immediate reviser. But, whilst it may be prudent to deny Lichfield any originatory connection with either of these surviving works, it is credible enough that he may have owned copies of both from whose inscriptions authorship rather than simple possession was deduced.

Unlike Carpenter and Lichfield whose lives seem to have been led almost throughout in London and its vicinity, Thomas Eborall's connection with the city is only traceable from 1444 when he became master of Whittington College; after that, however, he seems to have remained in London till his death in 1471.[25] Again no will survives, so the evidence for his ownership of books is restricted. He owned three surviving books, as *ex libris* inscriptions make plain: they are now Lambeth Palace 541 with a copy of the vernacular *Pore caitif*,[26] St. John's College Oxford 127 containing Bersuire's *Ovidius moralizatus*,[27] and a theological miscellany now BL Royal 5 C.iii whose most substantial items are the *Dicta, De cessacione legalium*, selected sermons and letters of Grosseteste, the *Compendium theologie* usually now attributed to Thomas of Strasburg and the *Incendium amoris* of Richard Rolle.[28] Bale also records Eborall in his private

---

[23] See the edition by A.C. Baugh (EETS 232, 1956), ix–x, where the ascription is recognized as possible for the adapter.

[24] See M.R. James, *A Descriptive Catalogue of the Manuscripts in the Library of Gonville and Caius College* (3 vols., Cambridge, 1907–14), i.198 at pp. 469–81 of the manuscript, and see the edition by E. Borgström, *Anglia* 34 (1911), 498–525.

[25] For his career before this see Emden *Oxford* pp. 622–3.

[26] See M.R. James, *A Descriptive Catalogue of the Manuscripts in ... Lambeth Palace* (Cambridge, 1932), no. 541 for this and other contents; also M.T. Brady, 'The Pore Caitif: an introductory study', *Traditio* 10 (1954), 529–48 at p. 532 n. 39; the copy is not one of those with Lollard additions, for which see the same author's 'Lollard interpolations and omissions in manuscripts of *The Pore Caitif*, in '*De cella in seculum*': *Religious and Secular Life and Devotion in Late Medieval England*, ed. M.G. Sargent (Cambridge, 1989), pp. 183–203.

[27] See Hanna (above n. 14); contrary to the note there, this manuscript is mentioned in Emden, *Oxford*, but in the corrections iii.xxii not in the main entry.

[28] See G.F. Warner and J.P. Gilson, *British Museum: Catalogue of ...Royal and King's Collections* (4 vols., London, 1921); the Grosseteste items are more fully listed in S.H. Thomson, *The Writings of Robert Grosseteste* (Cambridge, 1940).

notebook, now known as the *Index Britanniae scriptorum*, but not apparently in his larger *Scriptorum illustrium maioris Brytannie catalogus*, as author of visitation sermons in the diocese of London, with an incipit of 'Visita nos in salutari tuo. Psal.105' then in the possession of St. Paul's Cathedral.[29] In 1465 he was bequeathed by Nicholas Sabrisford two books containing the gospels and epistles in English.[30] Even within the limited evidence for Eborall's books, however, some patterns emerge that recall features of the collections already surveyed. In two of the surviving books Eborall recorded how he obtained them: the *Pore caitif* he was given by one John Petyrffelde, whilst the Royal miscellany he had bought from John Pye, the prominent London stationer, for 27s 6d.[31] For two of them likewise he made arrangements after his death: the St. John's Bersuire was given to master Robert Elyot for Elyot's lifetime with a prohibition on its sale and a requirement that it should be left to another who would pray for Eborall's soul; the Royal miscellany likewise was to go to Henry Mosie, once Eborall's pupil, if he should become a priest, or to John Sory and again should not be sold but given to an acquaintance 'sin autem, ab uno presbytero ad alium'.[32]

For William Ive's books there is much more evidence. His will, dated 5 October 1484 and proved 6 March 1485/6, though it gives great detail of numerous monetary bequests, infuriatingly does not name any books; but it leaves a book (singular) to each of five specified clerics, books (plural) to both New College and Magdalen Colleges Oxford and a book (singular) to the college of the Virgin Mary in Winchester.[33] By the time of his death Ive had been chancellor of Salisbury for some fifteen years, but had been warden of the chapel of Holy Trinity in St. Mary's Winchester, and had retained connections with William Waynflete, bishop there till 1486; his gifts to New College, described as the college of Winchester in Oxford, and to Winchester itself are thus not surprising.[34] Apart from the volume already mentioned, now Magdalen lat.98,

---

[29] See the edition of Bale's *Index* p. 437; as the editors point out, Tanner describes this as only *olim* in such possession; for the fate of St. Paul's Cathedral medieval collection see the headnote to the entry for the present library in Ker, *MMBL* i. 240.

[30] Emden, *Oxford*, 623 under Eborall, quoting the will of Sabrisford (now NRA/PRO PROB 11/5, ff.55v–56r).

[31] See C.P. Christianson, *A Directory of London Stationers and Book Artisans 1300–1500* (New York, 1990), pp. 145–8.

[32] See inscriptions, in Lambeth 541 f.172r, in St.John's f.i^v, in Royal the inscription is now lost but was recorded at the end of the manuscript before its rebinding by the 18th-century librarian David Casley (see cat. i.107).

[33] NRA/PRO PROB 11/7, ff.173v–174.

[34] See Emden, *Oxford*, 1008–9 and the *ODNB* entry by Simon Walker.

none of Ive's gifts to that college survives, though Magdalen records indicate that he also left copies of Jerome's epistles and of Alexander Nequam.[35] New College seems to have paid for the carriage of Ive's books from Winchester to Oxford in 1488–9, suggesting that the quantity was considerable.[36] Surviving is the book now New College 32, a handsome copy of Lombard's commentary on the Psalter.[37] Ive, like Lichfield, was also an author: Bale lists a series of six works, four without incipit, which he knew from a volume in the possession of William Hanley.[38] The first of these, the '*De mendicitate Christi*' (title not given in the manuscript, but the incipit *Preteriens aliquando et aspiciens* agrees) survives incompletely in a manuscript now Bodleian Lat.th.e.25 (incipit f.2), and it is probable that some at least of Bale's other titles represent parts of this.[39] The work was a contribution to the controversy aroused by the preaching of the London Carmelites Thomas Halden, John Milverton and Harry Parker in the 1460s, who claimed that Christ and his apostles had owned nothing and begged their subsistence;[40] Ive disputed this claim. The rubrics to the surviving fragments of Ive's work provide a fairly exact timetable of those contributions: the first

---

[35] Noted by Emden; Magdalen College Libri computi i. f.175 for 1488–9 where the cost of their binding is noted; I am grateful to the Archivist at the College for allowing me access to this and other records.

[36] Again noted by Emden; New College Bursars' Accounts no. 7448, where eight pence is recorded as the payment but no further details given; again I am grateful to the Archivist for access to the records.

[37] A note of the gift appears on the front flyleaf; on the final text leaf a hand later than that of the text noted the price as *xxx s.*, and there is also a heavily erased inscription; since the manuscript is of the early thirteenth century it is clear that it came to Ive secondhand. There is no mention of Ive, or of this book, in R.W. Hunt, 'The Medieval Library', *New College Oxford 1379–1979*, ed. J. Buxton and P. Williams (Oxford, 1979), pp. 317–45.

[38] Bale *Index* p. 129 (Hanley has not been identified by Brett and Carley, see p. xxv) and *Catalogus* i.610.

[39] Bale's other titles: *Lecturas Oxonii lectas, inc.Super Babylonis flumina aliquan* (see the extant copy f.17v the third tract), *In minores prophetas (lib.12), De Christi dominio, Sermones ad clerum, Determinationes quoque*. The Bodleian typescript catalogue entry states that a quire is missing after f.9 and another after f.26; whilst at the second point the Ive text breaks off incomplete (and the remaining folios were originally a separate manuscript of another author's text), it is not to me clear that anything is missing after f.9 despite an oddity in the catchwords. In 1609 a copy of Ive's work, perhaps to be identified with this sole extant copy, was in the Lumley Library (S. Jayne and F.R. Johnson, *The Library of John, Lord Lumley: the Catalogue of 1609* (London, 1956), p 297); the Bodleian typescript entry only traces the firm history of the extant copy back to 1844.

[40] See F.R.H. du Boulay, 'The Quarrel between the Carmelite Friars and the Secular Clergy of London, 1464–1468', *JEH* 6 (1955), 156–74; du Boulay did not know Ive's text here discussed. The controversy is reported in Gregory's *Chronicle of London*, see *The Historical Collections of a Citizen of London in the Fifteenth Century*, ed. J. Gairdner (Camden Society, 2nd ser.17, 1876), pp. 203, 228–32. For some comments cf Ball (1997) p. 251.

(f.6) was delivered in the schools of St. Paul's in London on 14 December (*in crastino sancte lucie virginis*) 1464 and the second on the sixteenth of the same month; a third (f.17v) was given and disputed in Oxford on 9 February 1465; the last rubric states that Ive subsequently preached, 'read' and disputed the question of Christ's *dominium et regalium* both in Oxford and at the schools in St. Paul's London on 10 May 1465 (f.24, this last could well have given Bale his title *De Christi dominio*). This text has two points of interest for the purpose here: first in the Oxford determination (f.20v) Ive openly points out that the view of the Carmelites that Christ did not have *regiam potestatem et temporale dominium* is not far from that of John Wyclif 'cuius sentencia erat sacerdotes succedere Christo secundum naturam hominis et principes seculares secundum naturam deitatis', named as 'Wyclyffe quem eciam ... pro heretico condempnant'.[41] The second point is that at the end of the second surviving tract a colophon in the main hand (f.17v) reads 'Q. (ie *quod*) M.I. Hychecok, tunc socius collegii Whytyngton. Scripsit hychecok manu sua' (the last four words in red). It should presumably be deduced from the *tunc* that this colophon has been taken over from the exemplar, and does not, despite its prominence, relate to the scribe of the surviving manuscript.[42] Hitchcok appears as a beneficiary in Ive's will, at which time he was vicar of Odiham and Brixworth, as one of those left a book at the discretion of Ive's executors.

Hitchcock was himself an Oxford graduate of the 1450s, and acted in various minor administrative positions for the University; he became fellow of Whittington College in 1462, vicar of Odiham in 1472 and of Brixworth in 1484; he died in 1495.[43] In Oxford he acted as keeper of three of the loan chests, positions which, since the pledges were usually books, suggest his knowledge of texts; whilst still in Oxford he bought a copy of Grosseteste's commentary on the *Posterior Analytics* from another Oxford graduate, and when he was fellow of Whittington College he bought in 1462 from John Smyth then priest of St. James beside Whittington College a Latin Bible which he subsequently left to another.[44] Hitchcok like Ive thus links the worlds of academic Oxford,

---

[41] F.15r; the scribe entered *Cave* in the margin beside the passage on f.20v. Ive refers to the same view earlier ff.9v–10r, but without explicitly naming its advocate. For this view see Wyclif, for example *De blasfemia*, ed. M.H. Dziewicki (WS, 1893), 110/4; but it should be noted that he, as he remarked, drew the view from a text ascribed to Augustine in the medieval period, PL 35.2284.

[42] And the manuscript does not appear in Andrew Watson's *Dated and Dateable Manuscripts c.435–1600 in Oxford Libraries* (2 vols., Oxford, 1984).

[43] See Emden, *Oxford*, 929.

[44] The first is now National Library of Wales, MS Gwysany 16, for which see H.D. Emanuel, 'The Gwysany Manuscripts', *National Library of Wales Journal* 7 (1952), 326–43 at p. 337; the second

of Whittington College in London and the more distant but still educationally informed worlds of Winchester and Salisbury dioceses. It will be recalled that Ive was bequeathed the book which contains Wyclif's *De mandatis* by William Wagge: Wagge himself has affiliations with two of those worlds, of Oxford and of both Winchester and Salisbury dioceses.[45]

Thomas Graunt's involvement with books matches or even exceeds that of William Ive. Mention has already been made of his Wyclif volume, now St.John's College Oxford MS 171. But he can be connected with a large number more: the most obviously interesting of these in the present context is a copy of anti-Wyclif(fite material that survives as British Library MS Harley 31, containing Woodford's *Questiones LXXII de sacramento altaris* and his tract against Wyclif's *Trialogus*, Winterton's *Absolucio* again answering Wyclif's views on the eucharist and tracts probably originating as rebuttals of Walter Brut's views documented during his trial of 1393; Graunt entered his name several times in the book.[46] He was also the owner of the assemblage of Latin poems, now the first part of Oxford MS Bodley 496 (ff.1–254), a collection including a number of satirical, and anticlerical, works.[47] Record survives of two gifts to the University Library, and of one to Canterbury College, both in Oxford; two further surviving books contain signs of his ownership.[48] But a much larger gift was assigned to St.Paul's, some time between 1458 and Graunt's death in 1471: at least four of these still survive amongst the 1624 gift of Thomas Reid to the library of the

---

is Bodleian MS Auct.D.5.19, where the purchase is recorded f.i^v and the legacy (the erased name is probably Henry Cooper) on f.742v. He was also executor of the will of Walter Hopton, who himself (see Emden, *Oxford,* 961) owned All Souls 88.

[45] See Emden, *Oxford,* 1954 which records his graduation as BA and MA in the mid 1440s, his licence to preach in the Salisbury diocese in 1445, and his connection with St. Mary's Winchester from 1465 to his death in 1469.

[46] See Graunt's name ff.94v, 143v, 181r, 215v, 223r, 242r; for the Brut material see A. Blamires and C.W. Marx, 'Woman not to preach: A Disputation in British Library MS Harley 31', *Journal of Medieval Latin* 3 (1993), 2–63.

[47] See A.G. Rigg, *A History of Anglo-Latin Literature 1066–1422* (Cambridge, 1992), summary p. 312.

[48] The contents of those given to the University Library are not specified; they are recorded *Epistolae academicae Oxon.(Registrum F)*, ed. H. Anstey (OHS 36, 1898), ii.382, 397 dated 1467 and 1471; a note of 1472 recording carriage cost for books given by Graunt (see *Mediaeval Archives of the University of Oxford* ii, ed. H.E. Salter (OHS 73, 1921) 308) may record a third and more substantial gift. The gift to Canterbury College survives as BL MS Additional 22572, containing Felton's sermons, and is described by W.A. Pantin, *Canterbury College Oxford* i (OHS ns 6 (1947), 111–12, and see also ii (OHS ns 7, 1947), 192, iii (OHS ns 8, 1950), 111 and iv (OHS ns 30, 1985), 101. The other books are Oriel College Oxford MS 55, a scientific manuscript, and Southampton King Edward VI Grammar School, a thirteenth-century Bible (for which see N.R. Ker, *MMBL* iv, 333).

university of Aberdeen, and a further three were amongst 52 precious books recorded in the Treasury at St. Paul's in 1486.[49] These were all standard texts: a glossed Psalter, Peter Comestor, Gregory, Augustine, Rufinus and the *Legenda aurea*;[50] even those not kept in the Treasury were handsome volumes.[51] Our knowledge of Graunt's gifts to St. Paul's derives from the surviving books and from a later fifteenth-century listing of particularly prized volumes; how large the total benefaction was cannot be guessed.

More evidence, though fewer surviving books, is available for Graunt's munificence to Syon Abbey: Graunt was recognized as a major benefactor in the house's *Martiloge*.[52] A total of 26 books are marked as his gifts in the early sixteenth-century *Registrum* of the brothers' library; their contents covered a considerable range of patristic (Augustine, pseudo-Chrysostom etc.) and mainstream medieval theology and pastoral materials (Hugh of St. Victor, Bernard, Grosseteste, Holcot, Waleys, Peraldus, unattributed sermons).[53] One of the gifts, however, was almost certainly another copy of part of Wyclif's *Postilla in totam Bibliam*, overlapping with, but more extensive than the surviving Graunt volume, St. John's Oxford 171. The contents were *Postillator quidem* on Job, Ecclesiastes, Psalms, *Cantica canticorum*, Lamentations, Proverbs, Wisdom and Ecclesiasticus, in that order. The *secundo folio* was *diluculo*, making it plain that this book was not the St. John's manuscript.[54] The ordering of the biblical books is eccentric, with Ecclesiastes after Job and Lamentations after *Cantica*;

---

[49] Graunt's will is Guildhall 9171/6, f.167v. I am grateful to James Willoughby of the *CBMLC* for information about the surviving records of Graunt's gifts, and especially for the evidence concerning the Treasury books; the gifts are mentioned also in N. Ramsay, 'The Library and Archives to 1897', in *St.Paul's: the Cathedral Church of London 604–2004*, ed. D.Keene, A. Burns and A. Saint (New Haven and London, 2004), 413–25 at p. 417 (though the catalogue volume there given with a 2004 date of publication is not yet out). For the books see M.R. James, *A Catalogue of the Medieval Manuscripts in the University Library Aberdeen* (Cambridge, 1932) p. 124; the manuscripts with signs of Graunt's ownership in them are 10, 219, 240 and 244. It is possible that Aberdeen University Library MS 11 was also one of Graunt's donations: on f.i^b there is a very effective erasure, which James suggests may have been an inscription of gift by Graunt.

[50] The Treasury books were the first two, plus a third 'tractans de vocabulis verborum et nominum'; the Aberdeen four are, in the order given here, 10, 219, 244 and 240.

[51] Aberdeen MSS 219 and 244 are elegant specimens of the late twelfth or early thirteenth century; MS 11, if Graunt's gift, follows this pattern since it is another twelfth-century book, this time of Jerome's letters.

[52] See Gillespie *CBMLC* 9, 580.

[53] The books are indexed under Graunt's name in the list of donors.

[54] Unhelpfully, the word is Job 1:5, and so will occur in any commentary on Job; in St. John's its first occurrence is f.2r eight lines from the bottom. Allowing for a larger folio size in the Syon copy, the lengths of the overlapping commentaries are proportionate (assuming that the Syon details have run together the Psalter and *Cantica* folios).

but it is identical with the sequence in which Wyclif commented on this section of the Old Testament.⁵⁵ If this suggestion is plausible, then the Syon copy contained more of the commentary than now survives either in England or Bohemia.⁵⁶ Finally, it is worth mentioning that Graunt is recognized as the compiler of a surviving index to Roger of Waltham's *Compendium morale*,⁵⁷ and it may be that some of the indexes recorded in other surviving gifts were also his.⁵⁸

A number of implications seem worth highlighting from this assemblage of details. First, in an important article Wendy Scase has drawn attention to the links between Pecock, Carpenter and the so-called 'common profit' group of manuscripts. This is a group of five books of almost exclusively English content, all of which include at the start inscriptions explaining that the book in question had been made 'of þe goodes' of a specified person, who wished the book to go after his or her death to another person who should pray for the soul of the donor but also ensure that the book was again passed on with a similar commitment 'as longe as þe booke endureth'.⁵⁹ The names which appear in these inscriptions are identifiable with London merchants or their families; the contents of the books are devotional or didactic works mostly directed at lay people; the books themselves are small volumes with little decoration and certainly valuable for their subject matter rather than their appearance. It seems that the scheme involved investment by those of substance, of the merchant class rather than the aristocracy, in the production of the books for the benefit of themselves and others, and the 'repayment' of this investment by the prayers of those who subsequently held and used the books. Scase pointed to the similarity of this scheme to the proposals of Pecock to facilitate lay readership of books. She also noted a comparable scheme that was set up in

---

⁵⁵ Listed under G.14, p. 135. See T320–324. Beryl Smalley, 'Wyclif's *Postilla* on the Old Testament and his *Principium*', in *Oxford Studies presented to Daniel Callus* (OHS ns 16 (1964), pp. 253–96 at p. 253, clearly thought that the order required comment: she does not say that it is unparalleled, but the nearest analogy she provides, that of Peter Aureol, recognized that Wyclif had switched the Job-Ecclesiastes 'disputative et dialectica' sequence to before the 'ymnica et... poetica' group. See also her 'John Wyclif's *Postilla super Totam Bibliam*', BLR 4 (1953), 186–205 at pp. 190–92.

⁵⁶ Proverbs to Ecclesiasticus is not extant (T325–7).

⁵⁷ See Sharpe, no. 1755 listing four copies.

⁵⁸ For instance, the index to Gregory in Aberdeen UL 10, to Augustine in 219, and to the *Legenda aurea* in 240; in all cases Graunt's name was attached to the index, suggesting that he was, at least, its scribe. Graunt's career and books would repay further investigation.

⁵⁹ W. Scase, 'Reginald Pecock, John Carpenter and John Colop's 'Common-profit' Books: Aspects of Book Ownership and Circulation in Fifteenth-Century London', *Medium Aevum* 61 (1992), 261–74.

York in 1402, though there the initiator was a clerk and the library of books was intended for use by other clergy.[60] A scheme very close to that in York seems to be envisaged by the inscription of donation that appears in one of the books owned by William Ive: in the lower margin of f.2 in MS Magdalen College 98 appears a Latin note recording that William Wagge, once rector of St. Mary's Winchester, had given the book to Ive in 1469 on condition that Ive should perform his funeral rites and requiem mass for the souls of Wagge and all the faithful departed; Ive was also to ensure after Wagge's death that the book was passed on at his own death with the same condition, 'et sic deinceps de viro in virum quamdiu liber durauerit'.[61] The similarity in wording between this Latin inscription and the vernacular notes in the English books is striking. In this case Ive's Latin is the later, but Carpenter's will, in which the request for prayers and the bequests of books both appear though separated, suggests this may be misleading.

The second striking point which emerges is that Wyclif's works are treated in exactly the same way as others – there is absolutely no sign that Arundel's *Constitutions* removed his writings from the ordinary processes of circulation and bequest. The period covered by the three clerics, Lichfield, Ive and Graunt, who owned and passed on works by Wyclif extend in London from 1423 (Lichfield's first London position) to 1471 (the year of Graunt's death), though the dates of their possession and gifts may be shorter – Lichfield was the first to die in 1448, though may have given the book to St Mary Overey before that, Graunt likewise (since no books are mentioned in his will) probably passed on his before his death.[62] Two of the three certainly left Wyclif books to established libraries, Lichfield to both Peterhouse Cambridge and St. Mary Overey Southwark, Ive to Magdalen College Oxford. Graunt's disposition of his certain Wyclif volume is unclear: ownership inscriptions from the sixteenth and very early seventeenth centuries may suggest that he did not give it to

---

[60] Scase p. 263; see J.A. Hoeppner Moran, 'A "common profit" library in fifteenth-century England and other books for chaplains', *Manuscripta* 28 (1984), 17–25; see also N. Orme, 'A Bristol Library for the Clergy', *Bristol and Gloucestershire Archaeological Society Transactions* 96 (1978), 33–52.

[61] I am very grateful to Prof. Ralph Hanna for providing me with a copy of his description of the manuscript (intended for a new complete catalogue of Magdalen manuscripts) which includes a transcription of this marginal note. Another similar formulation appears in the will of Hugh Damlett, rector of St. Peter's Cornhill from 1447 to 1476 (Guildhall MS 9171/6 f.189r), where a copy of his own sermons is bequeathed to Edward Story, bishop of Carlisle, on condition that at Story's death he leave it to another poor priest desirous of preaching 'et sic quamdiu durare poterit'.

[62] The addition of Wagge to these three does not extend the period, since he died in 1469; Hitchcok (see above pp. 10–11) did not die until 1495 but his connections with London seem to have ended in 1472.

St. Paul's.⁶³ But if the suggestion above about the identity of the *Postillator quidem* is correct, then he also gave a Wyclif book to a house noted for its originary connections with orthodoxy. Did they know what the contents of their four surviving books were? That cannot be regarded as certain in the case of Lichfield's Peterhouse manuscript.⁶⁴ In the copy he left to St. Mary Overey the final colophon (p. 621) reads 'Explicit de veritate sacre scripture', followed by an erasure whose length and incompleteness is compatible with the words 'doctoris euangelici', using Wyclif's Latin byname.⁶⁵ Ive's *De mandatis* was likewise attributed in a scribal colophon (f.117r), again at some point erased;⁶⁶ Graunt's surviving section of the *Postilla* is anonymous, and the Syon copy evidently did not ascribe the commentary. But neither Ive nor Graunt was ignorant of Wyclif's ideas: Ive's own writing makes that explicit (see above p. 10), whilst Graunt's ownership and frequent signatures in the manuscript now Harley 31 shows his interest in anti-Wycliffite polemic. What is absolutely clear is that these three, together with Eborall, Wagge and Hitchcok, were unimpeachably orthodox: the inscriptions in their books and the terms of their wills make clear their enthusiastic fostering of prayers for the dead, all held recognized clerical positions of some eminence, Lichfield and Eborall were noted preachers against Pecock, Eborall is linked with Ive in the validation of an English Bible, Eborall with Graunt in the investigation of the books of a man suspected of heresy or even treason.

Certainly most of the books mentioned here, and all by Wyclif, are in Latin: the men owning them were all clerics, so this is not surprising. But it should be remembered that, though most recent discussions have concentrated on the clause that affected the vernacular, Arundel's *Constitutions* were directed at the clergy and the academic community: not only under what conditions they could preach, but also the books that they were prohibited from discussing, reading or disseminating.⁶⁷ The expectation, which did not need to be spelled

---

⁶³ See the inscriptions noted by Hanna (2002) p. 237.

⁶⁴ The text was not recognized by M.R. James, *A Descriptive Catalogue of the Manuscripts in the Library of Peterhouse* (Cambridge, 1899), 276–7.

⁶⁵ A later reader of the text (p. 553) notes his deduction from views on predestination in the text that the author was Wyclif.

⁶⁶ Ralph Hanna suggests from the quire signatures that the *De mandatis*, now the second item, was originally the first, and that the rearrangement was intended to obscure 'the heretical text'; the date of any such adjustment, and whether it was before or after Ive's gift to Magdalen, is unclear.

⁶⁷ See Wilkins iii.314–19; for a recent influential paper that concentrates on the implications of the *Constitutions* for vernacular writing see N. Watson, 'Censorship and Cultural Change in Late Medieval England: Vernacular Theology, the Oxford Translation Debate and Arundel's *Constitutions*', *Speculum* 70 (1995), 822–64.

out in explicit words, was that these books would be in Latin. It is, however, here perhaps worth adding a fifth figure, involving a vernacular text, to those already examined. John Wakeryng, master of St. Bartholomew's Smithfield from 1422 to 1466,[68] owned a copy of the compilation made from the Wycliffite *Glossed Gospels* that is now in York Minster Library MS XVI.D.2.[69] Wakeryng seems not to have been a graduate;[70] St. Bartholomew's was less than a quarter of a mile from Whittington College, albeit just outside the City's walls. His long tenure at the hospital overlapped with the London careers of Carpenter, Lichfield, Eborall, Ive and Graunt. Interestingly, like many of the books already mentioned, Wakeryng had inherited his volume from another priest, John Kynt or Kynthust.[71] As master of St. Bartholomew's, Wakeryng had legal dealings with John Shirley, the most familiar of mid fifteenth-century scribes and bookmen, and also with John Pye of the Stationers' Company from whom Eborall had obtained one of his books.[72] Wakeryng probably died not long after he ceased to be master of St. Bartholomew's, and his will seems not to survive. What he did with his book is unclear, but in 1531 it was left by archbishop William Warham, a notable book collector, to Dr Oliver Godfrey;[73] it seems not unreasonable to think that transmission between Wakeryng and Warham had been through the same clerical channels as are recorded before the first and after the second. Again, though nothing has been traced of Kynt or Kynthust, the orthodoxy of Wakeryng, Warham and Godfrey cannot be questioned; Warham was responsible for an investigation into Lollardy in Kent in 1511–12.[74] However reluctant most Lollards seem to have been to enter their

---

[68] See *Cartulary of St. Bartholomew's Hospital*, ed. N.J.M. Kerling (London, 1973), p. 175; Thomas Graunt appears alongside Wakeryng as a witness to a deed in 1455 (no. 1116).

[69] The manuscript is described in *MMBL* iv. 695–6.

[70] He was probably a younger kinsman of the John Wakeryng (d.1425) who eventually became bishop of Norwich in 1415: see the *ODNB* entry for the bishop by R.G. Davies.

[71] See the inscriptions f.i^{verso} and f.225r, in the first of which the name is badly scuffed and appears as Kynt.

[72] See Christianson (above n. 31) pp. 159–60 and 147; for Shirley, in addition to the references there, more recently M. Connolly, *John Shirley: Book Production and the Noble Household in Fifteenth-Century England* (Aldershot, 1998).

[73] The inscription is f.ii^{verso}; Emden, *Oxford*, 1988–92 (Emden's identification of the text is incorrect, and derives from a post-medieval note there) and 778 respectively; Godfrey himself died in 1550.

[74] See the edition by N. Tanner, *Kent Heresy Proceedings 1511–12* (Kent Records 26, Maidstone, 1997). Warham's will is printed in *Wills from Doctors' Commons*, ed. J.G. Nichols and J. Bruce (Camden Society 83, 1863), pp. 21–7; it does not mention Godfrey, nor any individual recipients of books other than Warham's own nephew, but it does specify substantial categories of books to be given to New College and All Souls in Oxford and to Winchester College (details of identifications of the first two groups are in Emden).

names in their vernacular books of heresy, not all English works associated with them and not all owners apparently felt this. The *Glossed Gospels* are certainly not at the radical end of the spectrum of Lollard texts, and all the quotations that make up their sole content are reassuringly attributed to established figures such as Augustine, Gregory, Jerome;[75] but perusal of the so-called 'topics' in the York manuscript might have given an episcopal investigator reason to question an owner otherwise suspected of unorthodoxy.[76]

This survey of the written materials associated with these six men, Carpenter, Eborall, Ive, Lichfield, Graunt and Wakeryng suggests that categories that speak of 'orthodox' / 'heretical' in regard to books or individuals in the fifteenth century are simplistic. Certainly, study of episcopal records of the investigation of 'heresy' or of the polemical tracts of Woodford, Radcliffe, Netter or others might indicate that such a clear-cut distinction can be made. But this is to read the highly charged dossiers for the prosecution in isolation and at a distance. On the ground and at the time, the situation was not only less clear but also less adversarial. None of those mentioned in my cursory investigation, and the limits of that investigation could have been greatly extended without leaving London, was ever investigated for 'heresy' – on the contrary, all of them occupied positions where 'orthodoxy' would seem to have been axiomatic, and were involved in transactions, often testamentary, that lay at the heart of conventional piety. Those connected with books that have been labelled 'Wyclif(fite' disposed of their possessions in the traditional form, with no indication that they perceived anything exceptional about them, to named individuals or to institutional libraries – there is no sign that they saw any risk in naming those from whom they had obtained them or to whom they were leaving them. The same situation can be found with a number of other copies of Wyclif's works, more isolated in geographical incidence, given or left to institutional libraries in the fifteenth century.[77] Was London a particular case? a place where more tolerance or broad-mindedness might be shown? There seems no reason to think so; on the contrary, the evidence recently so clearly demonstrated by Maureen Jurkowski for London's importance in the supply of written materials to Lollard adherents might suggest that sensitivity

---

[75] It is worth noting that another copy of the *Glossed Gospels*, now British Library MS Additional 41175, was owned by John Crowlond, an Oxford graduate (see Emden, *Oxford* 520) and rector of South Ockendon in Essex, and was given by him to Geoffrey Downes, a Cambridge graduate (Emden, *Cambridge* 170, 193) who left it to a relation with the provision that after his death it should go to the chapel of Pott Shrigley (now Cheshire) – see Ker, *MLGB*, p. 324.

[76] For details about the 'topics' see *PR* 254–8.

[77] See no. XVI here.

to unorthodox texts would have been particularly acute there.[78] Piety in the fifteenth century was a seamless spectrum from the most extreme Lollard radicalism to Netter-ish extreme conservatism, even paranoia; perhaps more importantly, save at the two extremes there was an interest in written materials covering the widest range of opinions, necessarily in the vernacular for most (but by no means all) laymen but also in Latin for the more learned (clergy, but also men like John Carpenter). Pecock's problems may seem to contradict this: his investigation for heresy, an investigation that turned on his written books as well as on his rash spoken words, surely indicates the limits of acceptable opinion? The affair is, however, a particularly obscure one from which, unless new evidence should come to light, it may be difficult to draw any conclusion: many of Pecock's own writings have not survived, even if they were ever written, any detailed records of the trials equally have disappeared, the chroniclers tell a somewhat evasive and muddled tale.[79] It would be rash to draw any general conclusions from this isolated and in many ways extraordinary case. The group of London clerics and their books outlined here demonstrates that general conclusions can be equally hazardous in the history of Wyclif's books and even ideas in the period between the Blackfriars Council of 1382 and the Reformation Parliament of 1529–36.

---

[78] See her paper 'Lollard Book Producers in London in 1414', in *TCWB* 201–26.

[79] Many issues seem to have been involved, some that were less than absolutely clear cut: ecclesiastical practice (whether bishops should preach), the acceptability of arguing with the Lollards in English, along perhaps with a long simmering local feud (involving various London men, including Eborall and Lichfield, whose history of association with Pecock is belied by their public opposition to him in 1447).

XVI

The Survival of Wyclif's Works in England and Bohemia

1. The English manuscripts

Today less than a half of Wyclif's writings survive in manuscripts in England: when did this situation first arise? The sequence of legislation, civil and ecclesiastical, that required the resignation or confiscation of books, pamphlets or rolls containing the works of Wyclif and his followers, from as early as 1382 onwards, might suggest that little would survive in this country to provide witness to their radical ideas.[1] But Wyclif worked in Oxford until his enforced exile to Lutterworth, and wrote in Latin: both he and his opponents were accustomed to the processes of normal academic argument, which allowed for the ferocious discussion of all issues without the constraints of immediate censorship, and which did not immediately assume that all the views of a master who was advancing radical opinions on one issue would necessarily be equally problematic.[2] University education at this date was, after all, predicated on the disputation, a method which expected the student to assume the role of either protagonist or defendant on views about which he might personally hold the opposite (or have no opinion).[3] As I have argued in earlier chapters (see nos. V and VI), even in his exile it is clear Wyclif maintained close links with Oxford; this section will confirm that works written in Lutterworth speedily became available in the university. The account here has concentrated on those English copies that are traceable in England: a few English copies went abroad, mostly,

---

[1] See H.G. Richardson, 'Heresy and the Lay Power under Richard II', *EHR* 51 (1936), 1–28, *PR* 60–119 and Catto *HUC*, 175–261.

[2] Counter-examples to this claim could, of course, be found, such as that of Eckhart (see *ODCC*), but the case of FitzRalph whose views on the friars were certainly unwelcome in many quarters, shows that even in the second half of the fourteenth century the validity of the rest of a master's teaching (as here with the *Summa de questionibus Armenorum* and even *De pauperie Salvatoris*) was not automatically impugned.

[3] For the early stages see O. Weijers, *La 'disputatio' à la Faculté des arts de Paris (1200–+1350 environ): Esquisse d'une typologie* (Turnhout, 1995).

where their history can be traced, probably within fifty years of Wyclif's death.⁴ Many of them contain logical or philosophical texts, and were transmitted along with other similar texts of English origin.⁵

The story of the medieval transmission of Wyclif's writings in England after his death in 1384 can conveniently be divided into three parts: the first extends up to the condemnation of the 267 conclusions in Oxford in 1411 and the bonfire of his books at Carfax in Oxford a few months before that;⁶ the second takes the account beyond those events up to the early sixteenth century and the third, more selectively, into the post-Reformation period. The concluding date is somewhat flexible: I shall look at evidence from after 1560 that indicates the continued existence of medieval manuscripts containing Wyclif; I shall not be concerned with the post-Reformation views about Wyclif, whether from the side that might be thought to have been sympathetic or from the successors to the earlier suppression. As will become clear, the division between the two earlier sections is not as dramatic as might be expected. The 1411 condemnation might be thought to have completed the process of Arundel's Constitutions, and to have shown Oxford's acquiescence (whatever individual reservations might remain) in the suppression of Wyclif's ideas. Two political events which followed that condemnation in the ensuing five years seemingly confirmed the dynamic of repression: the Oldcastle rising of January 1414, which conveniently fulfilled the opposition prophecy that Wycliffism entailed treason,⁷ and the formal condemnation of a set of over forty of Wyclif's views at the eighth session of the Council of Constance in May 1415, dramatically confirmed two months later by the burning of Jan Hus whom the councillors saw as the close disciple of Wyclif.⁸ But the details of evidence for the transmission of Wyclif's actual texts do not bear out the apparent inevitability of this story.

---

⁴ Details about many of these are given in J. Catto, 'Some English Manuscripts of Wyclif's Latin Works', *SCH, Subs* 5 (1987), pp. 353–9. One of the most striking cases, though not included by Catto, is the Salamanca copy of Wyclif's *De proposicionibus insolubilibus* (T5), whose arrival in the library can be dated between 1437 and 1440 (see G. Beaujouan, 'Manuscrits scientifiques médiévaux de l'Université de Salamanque, *Bibliothèque de l'École des Hautes Études Hispaniques* 32 (1962), pp. 148–51.

⁵ See the entries under T2–3, 5–6, 20–21; the context is set in *English Logic in Italy in the 14ᵗʰ and 15ᵗʰ Centuries*, ed. A. Maieru (Naples, 1982).

⁶ See no. XIII for the details.

⁷ For this view see M. Aston, 'Lollardy and Sedition, 1381–1431', reprinted with additional notes in her *Lollards and Reformers: Images and Literacy in Late Medieval Religion* (London, 1984), 1–47.

⁸ The material is conveniently printed and translated in *Conciliorum oecumenicorum decreta*, ed. N.P. Tanner (London, 1990), i.411–16, 421–31 where 58 views of Wyclif chosen from amongst the 267 conclusions condemned in Oxford are listed immediately before the condemnation of

The evidence here is of varying kinds. Most simply it consists in books and their ownership: copies of texts whose making is dateable (ideally by evidence other than purely paleographic where precision is hard to come by), or whose ownership is known. Here it is also important to distinguish between copies which were, at least originally, ascribed and those which appear anonymously and where, at least in some instances, it may be legitimate to doubt whether the origins of the text were apprehended. In several books the author's name has been visibly erased or deleted, sometimes irretrievably, though the gap may be sufficient testimony to the compromising nature of what has been removed; until a scientific test has been devised to date erasure and deletion, this leaves an obscurity of the time of removal. Superficially less informative is the evidence of library catalogues, of records of donations to institutions: the latter may provide a precise date of the gift, the former is likely only to establish (sometimes imprecisely) the period at which the book was available. But this type of witness is in some ways more interesting: the very fact that the book was thought worth giving to an institution, that the institution accepted it, entered its ownership mark in the book and the book in its library catalogue suggests that the material was thought to be of more than transient interest and that some care would be taken to retain it. Arundel and his successors would hardly have endorsed such a valuation. Even if the London Carmelites before 1430 might have justified their holdings of Wyclif by the use made of such material by Thomas Netter for the polemic in his *Doctrinale*,[9] such an excuse can hardly have been available to all of the institutional owners. Thirdly, there is the evidence of quotation from Wyclif in the works of his opponents: quotation, rather than mention of titles, seems crucial here since the latter may not imply any meaningful familiarity with the work in question. As will emerge, this category is most in evidence, and most persuasive, at the early period: after the listing of conclusions that took the form of quotation from works for the purposes of condemnation (as in the 1411 listing), it may be important to exclude any individual quotations that could derive from such sources.

a) Before the 1410 bonfire

Perhaps the earliest surviving copy of Wyclif's work is a short extract from the *De potestate pape* entered into the notebook of the Benedictine Adam de Stocton, almost certainly around 1380: revealingly, the extract was first noted as 'Hec

---

Hus; for the latter's asserted agreement with them and his discipleship of Wyclif see especially p. 427.

[9] See below pp. 16–19.

uenerabilis doctor Magister Johannes Wyclyf in quadam sua determinacione anno domini 1379' but the second and third words were altered by Stocton to 'execrabilis seductor'.[10] The change is a useful barometer of Wyclif's reputation, but its implications are not carried through quite predictably. Individual copies of Wyclif's writings that are dateable to the last quarter of the fourteenth century are of very varied type and with varied acknowledgement of authorship and of ownership. The handsome but textually mediocre collection that is now Cambridge Trinity College B.16.2 (above no. VIII) contains ascribed texts along with unascribed but with the clear implication that all were by the same author; some of those ascriptions were erased. No indication is provided of the intended or actual owner of this expensive book. The much less visually impressive Cambridge Gonville and Caius MS 337/565 likewise has some erased ascriptions, and its ownership around 1403 by three Oxford masters was declared by their, now partially erased, inscription.[11] If the John Rodby who wrote his ownership claim on the first folio of a copy of Wyclif's *De mandatis*, now Cambridge Trinity College B.15.28, is to be identified with the fellow of Pembroke Hall Cambridge and later rector of Cosgrove (Northants.), this likewise is an early example of ownership.[12] The copy of *De veritate sacre scripture* found in Peterhouse Cambridge MS 223 is anonymous, but has been shown by Jeremy Catto to have been owned by Laurence Bedeman (*alias* Stephen), an Oxford man who was linked to Wyclif by his participation in the preaching expedition to Odiham, diocese of Winchester, in 1382 whose other participants were Nicholas Hereford, John Aston and Robert Alington.[13] Given Bedeman's renunciation of heretical views by November 1382, it seems clear

---

[10] The manuscript is now TCD 115, Wyclif item pp. 176–9, see the details about the manuscript most recently in M.L. Colker, *Trinity College Library Dublin: Descriptive Catalogue of the Medieval and Renaissance Latin Manuscripts* (2 vols., Aldershot, 1991), i. 238–44; the Wyclif material is pp.176–9; for the subsequent transmission see below p. 14. Colker (p. 243) says the hand of pp. 176–89 is not Stocton's, though he agrees the note is; I am not convinced that there is a change of hand, and p. 175, the first leaf of the quire in which the Wyclif extract occurs, continues in the hand of the previous material which, following the colophon, Colker accepts as Stocton's.

[11] See my paper 'The Debate on Bible Translation, Oxford 1401', reprinted in *LB* 67–84 at p. 79.

[12] See top f.1; for Rodby see Emden *Cambridge* p. 494; Rudby was fellow 1376, held various livings before the latest at Cosgrove to which he was admitted in 1398. The copy of *De mandatis* starts at cap.15, as is acknowledged by the scribe's note; a few marginal notes of caution appear (eg ff.58r and v, 68r and 78v).

[13] See J. Catto, 'A Radical Preacher's Handbook, c.1383', *EHR* 115 (2000), 893–904, who gives details both about the book and about Bedeman's history; further details about this manuscript are above no. XV 1, 6–7.

that the manuscript was put together within Wyclif's lifetime.¹⁴ If this copy was made for a sympathiser, the copy of *De incarnacione verbi* made for, and possibly by, Nicholas Fawkes OSB in 1389 for his house at Glastonbury, now Oxford Oriel College 15, has no such explanation. Fawkes cannot have been ignorant of the origins of the work, since the name is transcribed at the work's end (a colophon subsequently erased though a note with the name on f.233vb was not), but the relatively brief text appears alongside other, mostly weightier, discussions of academic questions; Wyclif remains here an unremarked part of normal debate.¹⁵

Oriel 15 belongs both to the category of manuscripts whose individual owners, or their writers, are known and also the institution that acquired a Wyclif text. The interest of the Durham Benedictine house, and of its dependency Durham College in Oxford, in Wyclif has been described above (no. IX). Briefly, by c. 1400 Durham priory owned copies of 'Confessio Joh. Wicliff de sacramento altaris' (T39, now Cambridge Jesus College 59), of the *Sermones quadraginta* (T257–95. now Lambeth Palace 23), of three chapters of book III of the *De civili dominio* (T30, now Durham Registrum Papireum (N)), and of Wyclif's *Complaint* (T403, now London BL Cotton Vitelius E.xii).¹⁶ Durham College Oxford had further been given by Robert Rypon a copy of a *Summa Wyclyffe*, probably containing the whole or parts of *De logica*. Another institution that acquired Wyclif material in this period was The Queen's College Oxford: in 1401 or 1402 they accepted a copy of *De mandatis Wicliff* as security for a loan: admittedly the text is not one of Wyclif's more outspoken or radical writings, but the authorship of the book was acknowledged in the transaction and the copy had some financial value, indeed twice the value of a small book of the *Sentences* pledged by the same person at the same time.¹⁷

Turning to the third category, knowledge that is evidenced by quotation, usually in texts written by Wyclif's opponents, there are obvious instances in

---

¹⁴ The whole seems to be in the same, rather variable, hand; though the four sections of the manuscript are separable as booklets, medieval quire signatures run throughout in a single sequence, indicating that the whole was together from an early date.

¹⁵ See L. Minio-Paluello, 'Two Erasures in MS Oriel College 15', *BLR* 4 (1953), 205–7; the other contents are FitzRalph, Holcot, Swyneshed, Nicholas Aston, and an anonymous *De communicatione idiomatum* (ff.222v–224v); the Wyclif text is ff.225ra–243ra and running heads read 'W. de incarnacione verbi'. How long Glastonbury retained the book is uncertain: most of the Glastonbury library catalogues are too early to include this, and neither Leland nor Bale in their listings include it.

¹⁶ For the last see the additional note to no. IX; it was recognized by James Carley, to whom I am indebted for the information.

¹⁷ See N.R. Ker, 'Wyclif Manuscripts in Oxford in the Fifteenth Century', *BLR* 4 (1953), 292–3; the *De mandatis* was valued at 13s 4d, the smaller book at 6s 8d.

controversies begun during his own lifetime. These, however, hardly testify to the issue of the long-term transmission of Wyclif's works, and so will only selectively be reviewed here. Both sides of the arguments at Oxford in the early 1370s with the Carmelite John Kenningham survive incompletely, but, although the opponent's side appears only incorporated into the Carmelite collection, the *Fasciculi zizaniorum* of 1439 or later, there seems no reason in this case at least to doubt that the material goes back nearly seventy years; Kenningham quotes his adversary's views.[18] From the other end of Wyclif's controversial career come the unprinted sets of accusations made by the Cistercian William Rymyngton, the first of which provoked Wyclif's *Responsiones ad xliv conclusiones* whilst the second probably dates from just after Wyclif's death; again Rymyngton cites Wyclif's answers.[19]

More interesting is the case of William Woodford, an adversary with whom Wyclif exchanged views and notes at Oxford but who continued to write against the heretic after his death. Here, as might be expected, it is possible to trace a change of practice over time and according to occasion: in Woodford's responses to Wyclif's current teaching in Oxford, as for example 'magister meus ... ultima hebdomada in quadam lectione', though it may be possible to map those answers on to Wyclif's written text, no precise reference is provided within the answer itself and minor variations predictably occur.[20] By the writing of *Questiones lxxii de sacramento altaris* Wyclif's views had already been condemned at the Blackfriars Council though the master himself was still alive: here there is close reference to the *De eucharistia minor confessio* (T39), usually dated 10 May 1381, but otherwise only unspecific references to Wyclif's earlier teaching or to ideas expressed 'in aliis questionibus quos posuit in materia ista', or 'in eodem tractatu et ex multis dictis suis'; whether Woodford had seen either *De apostasia* or *De eucharistia*, at least in the forms in which they have

---

[18] For a reasonable reconstruction of the stages of the debate see Thomson under T378–80. Wyclif's side of the debate likewise only survives in part, in the academic collection now Cambridge Corpus Christi College 103, a manuscript whose origins and early history seem impossible to trace. Wyclif's work appears in two parts of the manuscript, T4 pp. 47a–87b and T378 and 380 at pp. 419a–428b; both works are ascribed to Wyclif by a note, medieval but probably not in the hand of the scribes, at their openings.

[19] Rymyngton's texts survive in MS Bodley 158, ff.199r–217r and 188r–197r respectively; Wyclif's text is T384 printed *Opera minora* pp. 201–57, surviving only in four Bohemian copies.

[20] See, for instance, E. Doyle's edition of 'William Woodford's *De dominio civili clericorum* against John Wyclif', *Archivum Franciscanum Historicum* 66 (1973), 49–109 at pp. 76–90; Woodford's discussion is itself taken up in *De civili dominio* iii. 351–405. See Woodford's comment, quoted by A.G. Little, *The Grey Friars in Oxford* (OHS 20, 1892), p. 81.

come down to us, is entirely unclear.²¹ In his *Quattuor determinationes*, which date from 1389–90 and were given in Oxford when Woodford was Regent Master in the Franciscan School, apart from references to Wyclif's *De religione* by chapter, and a single reference to *De apostasia*, Woodford seems to avoid direct quotation from Wyclif.²² Woodford's most widely attested work, his *De causis condemnationis articulorum 18 damnatorum Joannis Wyclif*, undertaken by the commission of archbishop Arundel in 1397, derives from the *Trialogus* (T47) to which Woodford had close access; he quotes a number of passages from its fourth book.²³ Also referred to is the Supplement to the *Trialogus*, the *De religione* again, and several quotations are given with precise references from *De civili dominio*.²⁴ Compared with the evidence that Netter provides, evidence that will be considered later, Woodford reveals little about the transmission of Wyclif's works: the *Trialogus* was a conveniently systematic account of the heretic's final positions on many issues, and thus offered an ideal focus for orthodox refutation – it is hardly surprising that it was used in many counter-offensives, nor conversely that it should have been eliminated from English transmission; otherwise Woodford used largely texts with which he had debated in the Oxford schools.²⁵ What the sequence of Woodford's writings do reveal is the gradual realisation that documentation of the adversary's opinions was valuable: precision of reference becomes increasingly evident in refutations and condemnations between the 1390s and 1430. When the Oxford committee of twelve between January 1409 and March 1411 set about scrutinizing Wyclif's writings and listing their errors, they seem to have had a fair range of material to draw on, as has been indicated previously.²⁶ All of the texts must have been in front of the investigators or their assistants, and there is no reason to think the work was done anywhere other than in Oxford. The tally of works includes

---

²¹ For the date see E. Doyle, 'William Woodford, OFM (c.1330–c.1400): his life and works together with a study and edition of his *Responsiones contra Wiclevum et Lollardos*', *Franciscan Studies* 43 (1983), 17–187 at p. 40; the text is unprinted, and I have used MS Bodley 703, here ff.128va, 130rb for citations of Wyclif's text, ff.129ra, 161vb–162ra, 162vb–163ra for Wyclif's earlier views, f.128va for the vague references.

²² See Doyle (1983), p. 42 for the date; for the *De religione* see above no. IV 197–8; I have used the unpublished edition of Woodford's work by M.D. Dobson (1932) where the reference to *De apostasia* is p. 147/22.

²³ Doyle (1983), pp. 50–53; the errors had been submitted by representatives of Oxford university (see Wilkins iii.227–30). For these quotations see E. Brown, *Fasciculus rerum expetendarum* (2 vols., London, 1690), i.194, 199, 204 etc.

²⁴ Brown (1690), i.217 to the Supplement (though the reference is not exact), 218 to *De religione*, 238, 240, 241 etc to *De civili dominio* i.

²⁵ The only exception to this appears to be Wyclif's *De religione*.

²⁶ See above no. XIII.

some written after Wyclif's withdrawal to Lutterworth: *Trialogus* (T47) and *Opus evangelicum* (T374–7), the latter unfinished at his death, are the most notable examples. Equally several of these texts scanned no longer exist complete in England: *Trialogus* and its supplement (T48), *De arte sophistica* (T3) and *De civili dominio* (T28–30) are the obvious cases.

b) 1410–Bale

The bonfire at Carfax in Oxford in 1410, following the listing of these 267 erroneous conclusions from fourteen of Wyclif's works was presumably fuelled, at least in part, by the books from which those conclusions were taken; it was doubtless designed to remove the pernicious sources of the continuing attraction of Wyclif's ideas in the University. But if the aim was to eradicate Wyclif, his opinions, writings and followers from English ecclesiastical history, all these continuing acts of suppression were only partially successful. After 1411 it is perhaps surprising to find evidence for those writings in Oxford library holdings: Queen's no longer possessed the copy of *De mandatis* (above p. 5) when John Bale visited in the 1530s or early 1540s, but this could be explicable by its redemption on repayment of the loan. Bale, however, did record at Queen's what, if it were a single volume, must have been a considerable holding: it contained *De veritate sacre scripture, De blasphemia, De statu innocencie* and, before the last mentioned, an obscure *De anime immobilitate*, perhaps part of the lost commentary on Aristotle for which there is other evidence.[27] This volume reveals a situation that will be met repeatedly here: the volume could hardly be overlooked, yet Queen's no longer possesses it even though it was apparently still in place after the worst of the directed suppression. A similar case, with a college that preserved its medieval library much better than Queen's, is that of the Balliol manuscript mentioned by Bale containing several of Wyclif's philosophical works: apart from unspecified *Questiones*, the volume also contained *De insolubilibus, De universalibus, De tempore, De materia et forma, De composicione hominis, and De ydeis*.[28] Bale's *Index* is likewise the source of information that in the 1540s Pembroke College Cambridge owned a third substantial volume containing both philosophical and theological works, *De*

---

[27] Bale *Index* p. 269; the identifiable items are T31, 37 and 27. It is perhaps worth noting that the Provost of Queen's from 1426 to 1432 was Roland Byres, cited before archbishop Arundel for speaking against his *Constitutions* (Emden *Oxford*, 334 for reference). For the Aristotle commentary see I. Mueller, 'A "Lost" Summa of John Wyclif', *SCH, Subs* 5 (1987), 179–83.

[28] See Bale *Index* p. 269; the items are T5, 11, 12, 20, 21 and 18; for the history of Balliol's library see R.A.B. Mynors, *Catalogue of the Manuscripts of Balliol College Oxford* (Oxford, 1963), Introduction and pp. 384–7.

trinitate, De veritate sacre scripture, Confessio de sacramento altaris, De fide catholica and *De statu innocencie* and two other unidentified works.²⁹ In this instance Bale provides incipits for the texts in this now lost manuscript.

A fourth university volume noted by Bale is probably not lost, but it seems that at some point it has been considerably modified and reduced in scope. Bale notes that the University Library in Cambridge owned a copy of Wyclif's *De dominio ciuili* with the incipit 'Detectis vtrumque parumper erroribus'; it has been suggested that the volume in question is that now with the shelfmark Ll.5.13.³⁰ At the front of this book is a flyleaf with a list of contents in a medieval hand (not that of the text which now follows), stating that a 'tractatus de dominio ciuili' comes first, followed by 'tractatus de mandatis cum tabula...', and 'Lincolniensis de lingua'; what actually follows is only Wyclif's *De mandatis*. A post-medieval hand which made additions to the list of contents also headed the beginning of this text 'Lincolniensis De Dominio Ciuili' (f.2r), and added on f.36r 'Tractatus de mandatis' at the beginning of chapter 15; both of these seem best explained as efforts to make the surviving contents match the prefaced list. The third item, Grosseteste's *De lingua,* is certainly lost, though it may have been that which induced the writer of the added headings to ascribe 'De dominio ciuili' also to the earlier master.³¹ Bale's incipit is not that of *De lingua* nor that of Wyclif's *De dominio civili*; nor is it that of the opening of *De mandatis* as that text currently stands in the manuscript; equally it could not have been obtained from the list of contents. But it is the incipit of chapter 15 of this last text, and this chapter begins a new quire.³² So it is possible that, when Bale saw it, the second part of the text (which in two surviving manuscripts

---

²⁹ Bale *Index* pp. 265–6; the identified items are T17, 31, 39, 40 and 27; the two unidentified are a fourth entitled 'De cessatione legalium' with an incipit 'Redeundo autem ad propositum de', which, as the editors of the *Index* note, corresponds to Grosseteste's work of that title but the incipit is that of the penultimate chapter of *De veritate*, which cross-references in Wyclif recognize as a separate entity (see above no. IV 199), and 'Ad quendam discipulum' with the incipit 'Pauper discipulus Iesu Christi' – this second could well be a lost letter of Wyclif's.

³⁰ Bale *Index* p. 266; see *CBMLC* 10 (2002), p. 78 at no. 22.

³¹ And perhaps a second, probably seventeenth-century hand, to add at the end of the *De mandatis* (f.108va) after the medieval 'Explicit tractatus mandatorum fructuosissimus', the words 'Robertus Grostheade Episcopus Lincolniensis' at the head of the leaf.

³² See Loserth's text p. 152/1; the original scribe left a five-line gap at the end of chapter 14, though this has been filled with a near contemporary note extending into the lower margin (transcribed by Loserth pp. 151–2). Chapters 1–14 are contained in present quires 1–3 (ff.2–35), the last of which is a ten of which the final leaf is cut away; chapters 15–30 are in quires 4–10 (ff.36–108v, the last quire being of four leaves of which all but the first are blank), followed by quires 11–12 containing an index to the entire text.

stands alone without the opening chapters)³³ came before the first, and that it was subsequently reordered, though the chapter numbers at the head of each recto seem to be in the original scribe's hand. Whether the manuscript ever contained *De civili dominio* thus remains (infuriatingly) unclear.³⁴

By the first half of the fifteenth century Bedeman's copy of *De veritate sacre scripture* had been passed to the preacher Dr William Lichfield, who in turn left it to his old college, Peterhouse in Cambridge.³⁵ More contentious material was in the possession of Henry Abyngdon, *custos* of Merton College Oxford in 1436/7: that year he lent to John Hanham, also of the college, a number of books stated to be 'libri proprii, non de domo'.³⁶ Two of these were certainly works by Wyclif, as can be confirmed by the *secundo folio* which is given: his *De civili dominio* (T28) and his *De trinitate* (T17); the final book listed as *Super Euangelia*, given the *secundo folio* 'peruertens totam' may well be a set of Wyclif's sermons.³⁷ It seems, however, that at his death in 1437 Abyngdon did not see fit to leave these three amongst the books he gave to Merton.³⁸ Two years later Thomas Markaunt bequeathed to Corpus Christi College Cambridge three volumes that included Wyclif texts:³⁹ the first was a collection of six philosophical works, the second the second book of the *De logica* (T2) and the third a miscellany including *Opiniones Wyklef cum aliis*; the first certainly included *De universalibus, De tempore, De materia et forma* and possibly *De ydeis, De benedicta incarnacione* and a part of the lost *De anima* commentary.⁴⁰ This was a legacy as large as Abyngdon's holdings, but overtly less dangerous in

---

³³ Namely Cambridge Trinity College B.15.28 (above p. 4), and Cambridge UL Ii.3.29 (below p. 13).

³⁴ The source in *CBMLC* 10 p. 78 item 22 is the inventory drawn up for the Marian commissioners in 1557; the editors imply (p. 73) that the Wyclif item might have been deliberately suppressed from the entry.

³⁵ See above no. XV 1–2.

³⁶ See F.M.Powicke, *The Medieval Books of Merton College* (Oxford, 1931), p. 76.

³⁷ Powicke confirmed the first only; the second is in Breck's edition p. 4/16 (reading *assentire cum hoc* for Powicke's *assentiri cum hos*); the third is most likely to be the set printed by Loserth as *Sermones* i, but the *secundo folio* seems not findable near the start of that set, despite its typically Wyclif ring; the same is true of the item 'Tractatus phisicus de materia et forma' which sounds like T20.

³⁸ Powicke pp. 194–5.

³⁹ For more details of the terms of Markaunt's bequest see C.R. Cheney, 'A Register of Manuscripts borrowed from a College Library, 1440–1517: Corpus Christi College, Cambridge MS 232', *Transactions of the Cambridge Bibliographical Society* 9 (1987), 103–29.

⁴⁰ See most recently Clarke and Lovatt, (2002), pp. 200 and 205, nos. 43, 44 and 67; the editors do not identify the works under no. 43, apparently misled by the first item in the manuscript attributed to Robert Allington into thinking all the works were of the same authorship – items 2–4 are respectively T11, 12 and 20, the next may be part of the *De anima* commentary, whilst

its contents. When John Leland visited the library c.1535 he noted only one Wyclif volume 'Tres tractatus siue libelli Ioannis Wyclif de rebus sophisticis et dialecticis': this is likely to have been the second that Markaunt had left to the college, and suggests that its contents were more extensive than the earlier bequest indicated.[41] At his death in 1458 master John Allwarde left to Exeter College Oxford a book (now MS 6) containing two extracts ascribed to 'doctor euangelicus' from the *Sermones quadraginta*; since the whole is written by a single late fourteenth-century hand, it seems likely that Allwarde obtained the book when he was in Oxford, as a fellow of Exeter in 1408 and later as the college's rector in 1416/17 and 1418/19.[42]

Perhaps a more surprising gift, both because of its content and because of its destination, appears amongst the books in the 1459 inventory of Canterbury College Oxford: 'Item sermones I. Wycliffe R. Lynton' 2° fo. *methaphisicis*': from the *dicta probatoria* it is possible to be sure that this was Wyclif's set of Sunday gospel sermons, put together after his retirement to Lutterworth.[43] Lynton was warden of the College between 1443 and 1448, and it is hard to think that he was unaware of Wyclif's earlier, unhappy affiliation with the College and his eventual eviction.[44] Surprising from a different perspective is the case of Oriel College: between 14 February and 10 March 1454 the College paid out two sums of money for the purchase of copies first of *De civili dominio* and *De blasphemia* (costing 7s 6d) and second of a book 'cum multis continentis Wycliff' (costing 3s 6d). The second is infuriatingly vague, but the first must have been a very substantial volume, and one containing some of Wyclif's more inflammatory statements especially about the relation between civil and ecclesiastical powers. The first book, purchased from Andrew Mankswell, a fellow of the college, was to be bound and provided with library chains.[45] What

---

items 6–7 are T18 and 22; the final item may be, as Clarke suggests, the work listed by Thomson as GSpur.1 *De necessitate futurorum*, though this is otherwise known only in Bohemian copies.

[41] See Clarke and Lovatt *CBMLC* 10 p. 240, item 10.

[42] See J.H.A. van Banning, 'Two uncontroversial fragments of Wyclif in an Oxford manuscript', *JTS* ns 36 (1985), 338–49 and A.G. Watson, *A Descriptive Catalogue of the Medieval Manuscripts of Exeter College Oxford* (Oxford, 2000), pp. 10–11.

[43] See *Sermones* i.4/6; the list is printed in W.A.Pantin, *Canterbury College Oxford* i (OHS ns 6, 1947), p. 12 no. 23.

[44] See Catto *HUO* ii.187–8 for references.

[45] The purchase was noted by N.R. Ker, 'Wyclif Manuscripts in Oxford in the Fifteenth Century', *BLR* 4 (1951–2), 292–3; Ker suggests that the *De dominio ciuili* could have been the copy owned previously by Abyngdon, but there is no mention of the second item in the earlier loan note. The list edited and discussed by W.J. Courtenay, 'The Fourteenth-century booklist of the Oriel College Library', *Viator* 19 (1988), 283–90 is too early to include these volumes. For Mankswell see Emden *Oxford*, 1215.

prompted the purchase, a much more deliberate act than the reception of a gift, or how long the books continued in Oriel's possession are questions that remain unanswered – it would be interesting to know the reactions of Thomas Gascoigne, at the time already a benefactor of Oriel, to the purchases.[46] Later still a copy of *De scismate* 'Magistri Johannis W.' (T410) was included in a volume left to Merton College by John Maynsforth at his death some time between 1461 and 1488 (now Oxford MS Bodley 52); since the book was probably written by Maynsforth himself, it may date back to his time as a fellow of the college in 1426.[47] William Ive, a man associated with Winchester and London who died in 1485/6, left books to various individuals and institutions, amongst them Magdalen College Oxford: his copy of Wyclif's *De mandatis* is now MS lat.98 there with his ownership inscription.[48]

Oxford and Cambridge colleges were not the only institutions which continued to hold Wyclif's books well into the fifteenth century. Whilst archbishop Arundel might not have been altogether surprised to learn that Oxford colleges did not observe his prohibition on the continued, or new, ownership of these proscribed works, he might have found it a little more remarkable that various monastic and fraternal libraries are recorded as having owned them. The gift early in the fifteenth century by Peter Fader, vicar choral, to Salisbury cathedral of a volume containing mostly anti-Wycliffite materials, a volume now split into two parts, might have been less bothering, despite the fact that it contains three short but radical works by the heresiarch himself.[49] In a similarly hostile environment are the two copies of Wyclif's *Confessio* (T39) made by John Malberthorp, fellow of Lincoln College Oxford, for his own use; the other contents of the collections, and Malberthorp's comments throughout the volumes show a sharply anti-Wyclif bias.[50] Bodley 716 containing Wyclif's

---

[46] See Emden *Oxford*, 746, R.M. Ball, 'The Opponents of Bishop Pecock', *JEH* 48 (1997), 230–62 at pp. 245–8 for Gascoigne and Oriel's books, and the same author's *Thomas Gascoigne, Libraries and Scholarship* (Cambridge Bibliographical Society Monograph 14, 2006), esp. pp. 13–14, 19–20.

[47] The item is at ff.100v–102v; for Maynsforth see Emden *Oxford*, 1250 and Powicke pp. 207–9 (the inscription is present at f.59).

[48] See above no. XV 4, 8–9.

[49] The two parts are now Bodleian Arch Seld.B.26, ff.35–94 and Digby 173; the Wyclif items are in the former, T400 ff.83va–85va, T401 ff.85va–87vb and T383 ff.88ra–90ra, the second and third clearly ascribed. See N.R. Ker, ed.A.G. Watson, *Books, Collectors and Libraries: Studies in the Medieval Heritage* (London, 1985), p. 180.

[50] Emden *Oxford*, 1198–9; the two manuscripts are now Eton College 47 (Wyclif material ff.119r–121v) and BL Harley 635 (Wyclif material ff.202v–205v) – this second manuscript not known to Thomson; the contents of the first and the overlap with the second are fully analysed in Ker's *MMBL* 2.686–8.

New Testament *Postilla* (T345–71) was purchased by John Cranewys OSB of Bury St Edmunds, where he was sacrist and archdeacon between 1426 and 1435; the text was ascribed more than once by its original scribe, though at some point the name was erased.[51] The abbey's library catalogues are too early to include this book, but it appears to have been annotated by several users there.[52] By about 1454 the manuscript containing the *De universalibus* (T11) and the *De tempore* (T12), now Lincoln Cathedral 159, was recorded in the catalogue of books chained in the newly-constructed library; the second text is ascribed at its conclusion.[53] An incomplete and unascribed copy of the *De mandatis* (T26) was given to Norwich cathedral priory by John Molet, prior there from 1454 to his death in 1471.[54] A donation inscription in a now incomplete copy of *De veritate sacre scripture* (T31) records that it was given to St Mary Overey's in Southwark, 'ex dono magistri Lichefelde', the William Lichfield whose other copy of the same text went to Peterhouse Cambridge.[55]

Startling are the holdings of the Leicester abbey of Augustinian canons, the house to which Philip Repingdon had been attached during his Wyclif discipleship in Oxford and of which he was later abbot. The library was an impressive one, and the catalogue, probably drawn up shortly before 1463 but surviving in a copy made between 1477 and 1494, contains nearly 1700 books. The recent editors of the catalogue recognize three as containing Wyclif texts: one the *Trialogus* (T47), another following immediately after this and described

---

[51] For Cranewys see Emden *Oxford*, 510. See the purchase inscription f.iii^v; this was the manuscript that led Beryl Smalley to her discoveries about the *Postilla* (see her papers, 'John Wyclif's *Postilla super totam Bibliam*, *BLR* 4 (1953), 186–205 and 'Wyclif's *Postilla* on the Old Testament and his *Principium*', *Oxford Studies presented to Daniel Callus* (OHS ns 16, 1964), 253–96). The Bury library catalogues are too early to show this purchase (see Sharpe et al., *CBMLC* 4, 1996, B12–14). The Bodleian *Summary Catalogue* ii.no. 2630 states that the mark 'A.8.1' derives from Pembroke College Cambridge, but it does not appear in any of the listings from that college (Clarke and Lovatt, *CBMLC* 10, 2002, UC 42–47), nor in Ker *MLGB* p. 31.

[52] As noted by A. Gransden, 'Some Manuscripts in Cambridge from Bury St Edmunds Abbey: Exhibition Catalogue', revised and reprinted in *Bury St Edmunds: Medieval Art, Architecture, Archaeology and Economy*, ed. A. Gransden (The British Archaeological Association Conference Transactions 20, 1998), 228–85 at p. 243.

[53] See R.M. Thomson, *Catalogue of the Manuscripts of Lincoln Cathedral Chapter Library* (Cambridge, 1989), pp. 127–9.

[54] The manuscript is now Cambridge University Library Ii.3.29, and the text is here ff.1ra–49vb and consists of chapter 15 to the end. For Molet see J. Greatrex, *Biographical Register of the English Cathedral Priories of the Province of Canterbury c.1066–1540* (Oxford, 1997), pp. 541–2.

[55] See MS Bodley 924, inscription p.621; the text begins in chapter 4 (i.77/9); the author's name originally occurred in the colophon and is still visible despite erasure; see above no. XV 2.

as *Logica eiusdem* and a third entered as *Sermones Wyclyf*.[56] A fourth can be added to this: as the second item in a manuscript of Grosseteste's *Dicta*, appearing under the heading of *Lincoln'* is 'W. de mandatis' – the initial can surely be expanded to Wyclif.[57] None of these books survive. But one that belonged to Exeter Cathedral in 1506 does: this is the ascribed copy of the *De mandatis* (T26) in what is now MS Bodley 333, and had, as the inscription on f.iii[v] states, been given to the library by Henry Webber, dean of Exeter from 1459–77. It was presented to the Bodleian by the current dean and chapter in 1602.[58]

Records for the holdings of the friars in England are almost everywhere deplorably lacking: Leland's notes are often the only source of information. Stocton's notebook, already mentioned, passed at some point after his death to the Cambridge Austin friars.[59] It is from Leland's jottings that we learn that the London Austin friars had a copy of 'Wiclif de legibus et de veneno', probably to be identified with *De mandatis* (T26), and that the London Dominicans owned 'Wicliuus de paupertate Christi contra ecclesiasticos', whilst the London Franciscans had 'Opinio Uuicliui de uniuersalibus'.[60] It has been suggested that MS Bodley 703 may derive from the Oxford Franciscan house: it contains mainly Woodford's writings against Wyclif, but also has copies of the heretic's *De eucharistia minor confessio* (the only one that carries a date) and of the second determination against Binham.[61] Leland also says that the London Carmelites were provided with a copy of Wyclif's *Opus evangelicum* (T374–5) and also of his *De apostasia* (T36), whose margins had been annotated with the information that Wyclif had derived his eucharistic heresy from the man 'quem Wicliuus Ambrosium aut Ambrosii discipulum nominat'.[62] It is very tempting to think that this book had been used by Thomas Netter in the course of his composition of the *Doctrinale* in the 1420s, that he may have been instrumental

---

[56] Ed. T. Webber and A.G. Watson, *The Libraries of the Augustinian Canons* (*CBMLC* 6, 1998), p. 231 nos. 611 and 612, the second amplified at p. 310 as no. 1107 and at p. 378 at no. 1661, and the third p. 269 no. 858; *dicta probatoria* are attached to all three.

[57] See p. 228 no. 590; the 2° fo is here, of course, no help since it applies to the *Dicta*.

[58] See *Summary Catalogue* no. 2245; Ker *MLGB* p. 84; Emden *Oxford*, 2005.

[59] See Ker, *MLGB* p. 24 and Colker's catalogue (above n. 10) pp. 243–4.

[60] *The Friars' Libraries*, ed. K.W. Humphries (*CBMLC* 1, 1990), respectively p. 8 no. 9, p. 202 no. 22 = T402, and p. 220 no. 24 = T11.

[61] T39 and 383; the suggestion, deriving from marginalia, is in Ker, *MLGB* p. 142 with a query.

[62] *CBMLC* 1, p. 182 no. 26.

in the acquisition (or at least the retention) of the volume, and that he may have been the annotator.[63]

Whether Netter used these two copies of Wyclif's very contentious writings or not, it is obvious why the London Carmelite house might have had a use for the books that would have satisfied the requirements of Arundel's Constitutions: Netter's order was, after all, one that had taken a lead in polemical anti-Wyclif writing.[64] It is slightly less easy to explain the considerable holdings of the brothers' library at Syon Abbey:[65] whilst Henry V's founding ideals for the house certainly included the affirmation of orthodoxy, no explicit anti-Wyclif treatise seems attributable to any of its community. The immediate explanation would seem to be that the books were, like the majority of Syon's holdings, brought to the Abbey by individual brethren when they joined the house; they did not, in other words, reflect any communal interest or purpose. Thus John Bracebridge in the 1420s gave a volume including two of Wyclif's commentaries on Aristotle: the extant 'super 8 libros phisicorum Aristotelis', and the lost 'super tres libros methereorum.[66] More contentious material was contained within four other miscellaneous volumes, though all are relatively short items and it is reasonable to suppose that they may well have been preserved for their other, non-Wyclif contents. One, a volume that contained some English as well as Latin works, was again given by John Bracebridge; it contained, ascribed, Wyclif's letter to Urban VI and his *De iuramento Arnaldi*.[67] Another brother, John Weston gave a volume again of short items, one of which was 'Scriptum I.Wyclif in materia schismatis'; this was presumably the *De dissensione paparum*.[68] A third volume, given by Stephen Sawndre (d. 1513), listed an item later erased <*Wyclyf*> *de peregrinacione*: the identity of this is uncertain, and it may have been

---

[63] Both works are heavily cited in the *Doctrinale*. The identity of the authority whom Wyclif cited as 'Auctor de officiis', or as Fulgentius or rarely Ambrose, was one that excited Netter considerably: see his discussion *Doctrinale* V.25, 47 (ii.171, 293).

[64] Others were Peter Stokes, John Kenningham, Richard Lavenham and Richard Maidstone, for all of whom see R. Copsey, 'The Carmelites in England 1242–1540: surviving writings', *Carmel in Britain* 3 (2004), 341–417.

[65] The comments that follow are heavily indebted to Vincent Gillespie's work both as editor of *CBMLC* 9 (2001), and as author of 'The Mole in the Vineyard: Wyclif at Syon in the Fifteenth Century', in *TCWB* 131–62.

[66] The book is SS2.45 on p. 450 originally numbered C.15; the first item is T6, surviving only in Venice Biblioteca Marciana lat.VI.173; for a copy of the second in the Carolinum in Prague see above no. I 12.

[67] *Syon* SS1.882, N.28; the items are T404 and 397.

[68] See *Syon* SS.1.978, originally O.36; T410.

by one of Wyclif's followers rather than by the master himself.[69] Two other volumes at Syon are only known from the index to Betson's catalogue, and had apparently been purged from the library itself by the time that the main catalogue was made; their donors are unknown. One contained <*Wyclyf*> *in Epistola ad ducem Lancastriensem*, a letter now unfortunately no longer extant, the other <*Wyclyf*> *de sacramento altaris cum aliis de quibus cauendum est* which, given its apparent length, could have been either *De apostasia* or *De eucharistia*.[70] Another Oxford man, Thomas Graunt, a considerable bibliophile who owned parts of Wyclif's *Postilla in totam Bibliam*, now Oxford St. John's College 171, gave a second volume that seems likely to have been other parts of the same work to Syon Abbey; he died in 1471.[71] In addition to these volumes, the house owned no less than three copies of the *Floretum*.[72] Although, as has been said, there was a purging of many of these manuscripts in the sixteenth century, it is unclear whether this was on doctrinal grounds: many other books were deaccessioned at this time to make way for the enormous influx of printed volumes which were added to the Syon library.[73]

The third source of information described at the start of this chapter is quotations by polemical writers. By far the most important in this category after the 1410 bonfire is, of course, Thomas Netter in his *Doctrinale antiquitatum fidei*:[74] not only is this the most extensive attempt to refute Wyclif that was written, but also it carries through that polemic by means of repeated quotations from the heretic's own writings, most of them annotated with precise identifications. Netter's most frequent quarries were all late works from Wyclif's Lutterworth period, the *Trialogus* (T47) and its supplement (T48 usually called by Netter *De dotacione ecclesie*), the *Opus evangelicum* (T374–7) and the sermons on the Sunday

---

[69] *Syon* SS1.227, D.49. Wyclif himself wrote no independent treatise on the subject, and only touches on it in other works with such brevity that it seems unlikely that any section concerning the topic would have been excerpted as an independent tract.

[70] The first is *Syon* SS2.121 (K.34); that Wyclif and Gaunt were in touch at various stages of the former's life is clear: see *ODNB*. The second is SS.2.208 (S.6); the suggestion I made to Prof. Gillespie about the identity of the text, and there cited, should be disregarded since it does not take account of the foliation given; T36 or 38 are more likely.

[71] *Syon* SS1.135 (G.14); see above no. XV 4, 12–13.

[72] *Syon* SS1.695, 1.717, 1.723–4 which last two-volumed set seems, because of overlap, to be separate from the incomplete second volume; but the inclusion of 1.1137 in the index p. 785 attached to the *Floretum* seems unlikely in view of the designated contents and their brevity (see p. 358).

[73] See Gillespie's comments, *Syon* pp. li–lvi.

[74] The account of Netter's activity here is a shortened version of a paper due for belated publication in *Carmel in Britain*.

epistles.⁷⁵ Of Wyclif's logical and philosophical works Netter only quotes the *De universalibus* and *De ydeis*, and refers to the *De tempore*.⁷⁵ But, whilst this reveals that he did not share the conviction of some modern commentators that Wyclif's eucharistic errors were the inevitable consequence of his philosophical position, Netter is more concerned with strictly theological and ecclesiological issues; it could be rash to suppose that no other texts were available to him. More significant are the gaps in Netter's quotation from the more evidently contentious books of the *Summa theologie* : he certainly knew *De potestate pape* (though this may not have reached him until late in his work on book 5),⁷⁷ *De apostasia* and *De blasfemia*,⁷⁸ had access (perhaps only when working on book 6) to *De statu innocencie* and (perhaps only when working on book 5) to *De veritate sacre scripture*.⁷⁹ Outside the *Summa* he equally must have had a copy of *De composicionis homini*, *De benedicta incarnacione* and *De eucharistia*.⁸⁰ But of the *Summa* it seems clear that Netter did not know *De ecclesia* or *De officio regis*, and probably not *De symonia*.⁸¹ All of these could have furnished him with further

---

⁷⁵   For instances from each volume see *Trialogus* 1.4 (i.49), 1.6 (i.56), 1.10 (i.71) etc., 5.doct.8 (ii.22), 5.12 (ii.90), 5.17 (ii.122) etc., 6.doct.5 (iii.20), 6.11 (iii.100), 6.86 (iii.558) etc.; *Opus evangelicum* 2.5 (i.262), 2.6 (i.267), 2.8 (i.274) etc., 5.doct.12 (ii.36), 5.1 (ii.44), 5.2 (ii.49) etc., 6.7 (ii.81), 6.25 (iii.174), 6.26 (iii.180) etc.; Sunday epistles 1 doct.5 (i.18), 2.16 (i.324), 2.19 (i.334) etc., 5.doct.4 (ii.13), 5.3 (ii.54), 5.14 (ii.99) etc., 6 (iii.44), 6.7 (iii.78), 6.8 (iii.88) etc.

⁷⁶   Respectively 1.17 (i.99), 1.13 (i.105), 5.68 (ii.413); 1.1 (i.34, 35), 1.2 (i.39, 41), 1.3 (i.45), 1.4 (i.47, 51), 1.5 (i.53), 1.6 (i.56), 1.18 (i.104), 5.49 (ii.302); 1.6 (i.56). I have not been able to identify the two quotations 5.78 (ii.472–3) said to derive from Wyclif's *Summa*, chapters *de quidditate* and *de numero praedicamentorum*.

⁷⁷   The quotations from a *De pape* in 3.quaestio authoris (i.701), 4.39 (i.955), 4.45 (i.977) derive from the English text of that name (see Matthew pp. 458–32); there is a reference but no quotation in book 5 cap.36 (ii.235), and lengthy quotations begin only at cap.116 (ii.680), continuing through that book 5.117 (ii.688), 5.120 (ii.708), 5.121 (ii.713) etc. and into the next 6.28 (iii.198), 6.29 (iii.210), 6.46 (iii.305) etc. The subject matter of Wyclif's text would seem to have been relevant to book 2.

⁷⁸   For references to these see respectively 5.24, 28, 29 etc (ii.163, 187, 194); 5.25, 59, 83 etc (ii.164, 360, 501).

⁷⁹   See respectively 6.144, 163 (iii.870, 1000); 5.82 (ii.493). Obviously any deduction from absence of citation must be tentative, but both texts, and especially the second, would seem to be relevant to Netter's discussion elsewhere in the *Doctrinale*.

⁸⁰   Citations of the first appears in book 1 (eg 31, 32, 34 (i.169, 174, 186); 39, 40, 41 (i.208, 210, 213), and of the second book 5.78, 86 (ii.471, 516). The third is frequently called on in book 5, eg caps.17, 23, 25 (ii.122, 153, 164).

⁸¹   I have been unable to identify Netter's two quotations from a text he describes once as 'in tractatu suo barbarico *De Simonia* (5.13, ii.96) and once simply by title (5.24, ii.158); in the latter he claims to be quoting chapter 20 but Wyclif's Latin work of that name has only eight. Neither quotation comes from the 1411 list (Wilkins nos. 75–98) of which Netter quotes no. 97 (5.122, ii.715).

quotations to demonstrate Wyclif's execrable heresy.[82] More intriguing is the situation regarding *De civili dominio*: it is mentioned only in book 2, where four passages are given in quick succession: two of these are said to derive from the 1411 Oxford list, though only one is a precisely accurate quotation.[83] All have correct references to the text by chapter only, though in the same cluster is an erroneous citation of *De dominio divino*, actually once more *De civili dominio*.[84] It seems likely that Netter did not directly know either of these texts, but that a list of heterodox conclusions from them had come to him – a list whose correspondence with the 1411 list was only partial in verbal detail, though its similarities were clear. The earlier availability of such a list from *De civili dominio* to the Benedictine Adam Easton was mentioned above as a contribution to Gregory XI's 1377 condemnation of Wyclif.[85]

From amongst the large number of Wyclif's shorter works it is hardly surprising that Netter seems only to have known a selection, though he comments on their great number (5.24, ii.164). The *Dialogus* and *De officio pastorali* provided convenient short statements of some of Wyclif's central errors; others, such as *De confessione* or *De oratione*, are cited in limited sections according to their topic.[86] Interestingly Netter's citations do not entirely replicate those works used in the 1411 Oxford list: that list, for example, used *Logica* 3 (under the title *De arte sophistica*) and the 44 conclusions against Rymington,[87] neither cited by Netter (apart from his unlocated repetitions of the list), whilst conversely Netter seems to have had a range of short works on which the Oxford masters were silent.[88] One limitation on Netter's knowledge of Wyclif is, after the absence of *De civili dominio*, most striking: he evidently only had access to one of the sets of the sermons, those on the Sunday epistles.[89] As

---

[82] The absence of *De ecclesia* is the most surprising (even though it does not survive complete now in an English copy), because of its evident relevance to Netter's second book on the same topic.

[83] Three references to *De civili dominio* are 2.81–3 (i.682, 682–3, 683, 690), the first said to be conclusion 194 (Wilkins 199), the third to be conclusion 172 but actually a paraphrase (Wilkins 176).

[84] The reference under the wrong title is at 2.82 (i.687) to 2 (*De civ.dom.* i.11/6–13).

[85] See above no. V 65–8.

[86] Apart from the works already mentioned, the texts used by Netter are (using Thomson's numbers for brevity) T44, 46, 50, 53, 372, 386, 394, 407, 408, 412, 414, 415, 423, 424, 426–31.

[87] Conclusions 156–75 from T3 and 239–49 from T384.

[88] For instance T414 *De ordine christiano* (5.123, ii.722), T429 *De quattuor sectis novellis* (2.57, i.542), T372 exposition of Matthew 23 (2.67, i.597).

[89] This set is various described as *secunda pars sermonum* 2.16 (i.324), 2.20 (i.346) etc, as *tertia pars* 5.135 (ii.787), 5.142 (ii.817)etc, or as epistle sermons 2.48 (i.493), 2.66 (i.592)etc. Since the lower numbering disappears after 5.76 (ii.458), it would seem as though either Netter used a

mentioned, these he cited repeatedly throughout the *Doctrinale*. But he never mentions the sermons on the Sanctorale or the late *Sermones viginti*, both of which would have provided ample ammunition on a number of issues.[90] He was aware of Wyclif's set on the Sunday gospels and its probable heterodoxy, but cites it only once and then on the declared authority of a quotation from it in the Lollard compilation, the *Floretum*.[91] Here, if nowhere else, it seems certain that a Wyclif work was not available to Netter.

Netter's case is evidently a special one. Where he obtained his materials depends on the length of time over which he was working on his vast project. It seems probable that the dates of the three letters of dedication to pope Martin V between 1422 and 1430 mark only the termination of each section; their initiation was in all probability many years earlier.[92] This opens the likelihood that some of Netter's sources came to his notice in Oxford, even possibly before the 1410 bonfire; Netter's own whereabouts in the period from then onwards may not be entirely relevant.

As has been indicated, many of the copies of Wyclif's works which found their way into institutional libraries in the fifteenth and early sixteenth centuries did so by the gift of individuals. In the majority of cases the works were certainly attributed (and this is in many instances the reason for our ability to identify them) – they were not given in ignorance of their origin. This raises a number of interesting questions: by what right, and for what reason, did the individuals hold works whose ownership was proscribed? why did those individuals consider an ecclesiastical or academic institution, whose orthodoxy was presumably by the time of gift not in question, to be a suitable repository for the books? Why did the institutions accept the books, or rather, having accepted them, why did they register them within the permanent record of a library catalogue? Perhaps the lingering interest in Wyclif's ideas explains the holdings of Oxford or even Cambridge colleges, and of their fellows; the concern to refute the more radical may account for possession by, for instance, the London Carmelites. The money spent by Oriel College Oxford in the 1450s is hard to account for unless one of these (more probably the first?) was in question. It is more difficult to answer the questions concerning individual owners.

---

different manuscript later in his work, or that different information came to him about the set. By internal indications the higher number is correct.

[90] The sermons are numbered in Thomson individually, and the sets here are respectively 115–75 and 237–56; the second set is made clear from the manuscript preservation and the Hussite catalogue of Wyclif's works.

[91] 5.145 (ii.834), correctly located in the *Floretum* entry for *confessio*.

[92] See *PR* pp. 51–2.

c) From Bale onwards

This question of individual ownership arises again in the first source of evidence provided by John Bale. Reference has already been made to his material in his so-called *Index* on Wyclif works owned by Balliol and Queen's Colleges Oxford, by Pembroke College and the University Library in Cambridge. But Bale also lists a number of works in the possession of individual owners, most of them by title and by incipit – since both are always cited by Bale in Latin, the incipit allows in many instances greater certainty about the identity of the work than the title which may be common to both a Latin tract by Wyclif himself and an English work.[93] By the time of Bale's cataloguing it is clear that ownership could derive from reforming sympathies: this could be clearly the case with Richard Grafton who owned a substantial volume of Wyclif's logical and philosophical works, the *Logice continuacio, De logica tractatus tercius* (broken down into five separate sections, each marked as a *liber*), *De universalibus, De ydeis, De materia et forma, De composicione hominis* (again split into two separate books).[94] Robert Stoughton owned a less substantial volume which overlapped with this: an impressive list of apparently separate works is in fact the *Logice continuacio* (in two parts) and the *De logica tractatus tercius* only, the latter divided again into ten separate works.[95] Humfrey Perkins' book was smaller, being a copy of *De officio pastorali* (the incipit corresponds with the Latin and not with the English tract of the same name).[96] Some obscurity surrounds the holdings of John Leland, Bale's friend and mentor: Bale gives first a list of three titles, without incipits, 'Ex museo Ioannis Lelandi': one of these is probably identifiable with the Latin *De cruciata*, but the other two, though with credible Wyclif subjects, cannot be firmly identified.[97] These two then recur at the head of a longer list of works, all with incipits, 'Ex bibliotheca Ioan.Lelandi'; despite the additional information they remain uncertain. But the remainder is either a very large

---

[93] Bale's first listing consists of eight works 'Ex diuersis Bibliothecis'; these involve both languages, though this is not always declared.

[94] T2, 3, 11, 18, 20 and 21 respectively; no complete copy of the first two or of T20 survives now in England. For Grafton see *ODNB* and briefly Bale *Index* pp. xxiii–xxiv.

[95] See *Index* pp. 273–4; T2 and 3 and p. xxxiii. The fourth and penultimate sections are not readily identifiable from titles or divisions in the printed text (which used only a single Bohemian manuscript), but their subjects are compatible with this explanation.

[96] T53 and see p.xxx; for the English see Matthew pp. 408–57 from Manchester Rylands Eng.86, the only surviving copy.

[97] See *Index* p. 271; the first is probably T411, the second 'De ablatis restituendis' and the third 'De excommunicandis' could be respectively T405 and T407 or 413, but, as the incipits subsequently given in the longer list (and repeated in *Catalogus* nos. 144 and 146) suggest, were more probably extracts from longer works.

single volume, or more probably, two substantial books. First is a copy of the *Trialogus* and of its supplement *De dotacione ecclesie*: the presence of the latter makes it improbable that the first was the print of [1525], since that did not contain the supplement; neither of these works now survives in England. There is then a sequence of eleven shorter, polemical tracts which together make up a significant collection.[98] Even if, however, the reason behind the immediate mid-sixteenth century ownership noted by Bale is evident enough in the sympathy of these men with the discussions of the earlier radical, the question remains of the whereabouts (and reasons for those whereabouts) of these manuscripts through the preceding century or more. Whether they had been in institutional or private ownership, this group recorded by Bale gives evidence that a much wider variety of Wyclif's works was still extant in England than was clear in the institutional holdings, whether from the testimony of library catalogues and shelfmarks or from Bale himself.

Bale, however, provides a good deal more information on Wyclif than is declared in the unpublished *Index*: in both his *Summarium* (1548) and his *Catalogus* (1557–9) Bale gives a biography of Wyclif, followed by a list of his writings.[99] As in the *Index*, some works are given by both title and incipit, some only by title; equally as in the *Index* English and Latin works, the former disguised in Latin dress, are mingled indiscriminately with consequent difficulty of identification in cases where no incipit is provided. The listing in the *Catalogus* resumes and expands considerably upon the earlier *Summarium* listing: the order is altered (though for no perceptible reason), further items are added along with a number more incipits, only one item in the earlier work is untraceable in the later, namely a text entitled *De purgatorio sectae Christi* without incipit.[100] The discussion here will consequently focus on the later work. The listing in the *Catalogus* consists of an impressive 238 titles (numbers are not given in the edition). Despite the number, however, certain features of the list have made it easy to criticize: some titles, as in the *Index*, derive from taking chapters in what is now known as a single book as separate works (thus the separate items made

---

[98] T408, 416, 395, 404, 393, 423, 430, 409, 405, 394 (with variant incipit) plus, before the last, chapter 31 only of T408; of these items no English copy of any save 408, 404, 430, 405 and 394 survives; the editors of the *Index*, p. 272 n. 8, state that only one manuscript of T408 contains chapter 31 of the text, but ÖNB 3932, unknown to Pollard, the editor of the Wyclif Society edition, is another witness to it (see above no. I 10). For a fuller discussion of Leland's Wyclif holdings see the Appendix to James Carley's paper in *TCWB* pp. 184–7.

[99] The first is *STC* 1295 where the material relevant here is ff.154v–157v, the second, *Scriptorum illustrium maioris Brytannie ... Catalogus* (2 vols., Basel, 1557–9), i.450–56.

[100] See f.156v; it is tempting to identify this with T428, of which otherwise Bale shows no knowledge. The possible source of this entry will be considered below pp. 25–6

out of the chapters of *De logica tractatus tercius* in Grafton's and Stoughton's volumes are listed again individually, though the two sets are amalgamated); some works are certainly not by Wyclif (for instance Thomas of Wimbledon's sermon on *Redde rationem uillicationis tuae* appears p. 453); English and Latin works are jumbled together without distinction (within the first sixteen items seven are shown by their incipits to be certainly, and in one further case probably, English texts).[101] These evident defects have led to a tendency on the part of scholars to decry Bale's value as serious evidence for knowledge of Wyclif's writings. But, whilst Bale was no systematic modern bibliographer, and whilst modern impatience with one who knew and had seen many books that we no longer have but who described them imperfectly is understandable, it is perverse to reject what Bale does reveal. Certainly, leaving aside the features mentioned, there are unresolvable problems: many items that have only a title are unidentifiable (for instance, the probably Latin *De formis idealibus* or the declaredly English *Metaphysicam uulgarem* or *Glossas uulgares*); some even with an incipit are uncertain (is *Commentarios in Psalterium* with an incipit *Magnam abundantiam consolationis di.* the wrongly-included Psalter commentary of Richard Rolle, or one of the revisions of that commentary that derive from Wycliffite circles?);[102] some titles seem inappropriate or even downright erroneous (*De uelocitate motus localis* is said to begin with words that are identical to the incipit of *De potestate pape*).[103] But, whilst it would be highly foolish to suggest that all of Bale's 238 items can be identified, it seems equally indefensible to dismiss the entire list as worthless.

Most important to my present concern here is not the tally of works itself, but the evidence that Bale's listing provides about the survival of *copies* of Wyclif's works in England. Here I want to argue that, unless there is a positive reason for doubt, it is justifiable to suppose that the citation of an incipit is evidence that Bale had seen a copy of the work in question; citation of a title alone is more dubious, since these could have been gained from secondary sources such as Netter. An obvious objection to my main claim would be that

---

[101] Bale lists six sets of sermons, five with incipits, as items 9–14; item 13 must be the English Sunday gospel set because of its distinctive opening at 1 Trinity, and items 11–12 and 14 probably are likewise vernacular sets since they are cited in the same form (but reverse order) in *Index* p. 266 in a volume owned by Henry Reynold; no. 6 in the *Catalogus* may derive from the same volume (the order of items in *Index* agrees with that of Magdalene College Cambridge Pepys 2616 whose early origins are unknown); item 4 is Matthew pp. 264–74; the dubious case is no. 6 which could be either the English or the Latin commentary on Matthew 24 (*EWS* ii.328–65 or T373), though the incipit agrees better with the former.

[102] For which see *PR* 259–64, an account which will be updated in my forthcoming edition; the text also appears in the *Index* p. 265.

[103] T34, though admittedly they are the uninformative 'Iam ultimo restat uidere quid'.

the information could have come to Bale at secondhand, from some anterior listing. The question is in this instance the identity of such a prior list, one which included incipits? Neither the author Bale knew as Boston of Bury, nor Trithemius in the *Liber de scriptoribus ecclesiasticis* (Basel, 1494) which he cited, include Wyclif, even though the information given about the authors covered may have provided Bale with his format.[104] The only prior list relating to Wyclif is, to the best of my knowledge, the catalogue of the works found in four Bohemian manuscripts which has been described above (no. III); that does include incipits. But the chances that Bale had seen a copy of this seem very slim: the most persuasive reason for thinking that he had *not* is surely that he would have included much more information, both in regard to titles and in regard to incipits, if he had. It is notable that all the information on these two matters included by Bale in his *Index*, there grouped according to codexes that he had seen, is reproduced in the *Catalogus* – in other words, Bale worked economically and made the best use of his information.[105] As has been said, the fifteenth-century catalogue was a Bohemian production, and there is no evidence that it was ever available in England or known to Bale.

If the reasoning seems persuasive, what certain *new* information does Bale's *Catalogus* offer? – new, that is, that supplements the other information so far discussed about the survival of Wyclif's Latin works in England First, Bale includes here the items which are to be found in the single surviving manuscript of the *Fasciculi zizaniorum* which by 1557 Bale himself owned:[106] these are T39 *De eucharistia minor confessio*, T41 *De eucharistia conclusiones duodecim*, T398 *Responsio ad quesita regis et concilii*, T400 *Libellus ad parliamentum regis*, and T404 *Epistola missa pape Urbano*. Then there is a group of texts which now survive in English copies which Bale may, or may not, have seen: T40 *De fide sacramenti* (only known

---

[104] For Bale's ownership of the text now known to be by Henry of Kirkestede see item 61 in the list of books Bale lost in his flight from Ireland in 1553 (H. McCusker, 'Books and Manuscripts formerly in the Possession of John Bale', *The Library* 4th ser.16 (1935), 144–65); see Rouse and Rouse in *CBMLC* 11 (2004), lxxxix; the second is mentioned, for example, in *Index* p. 478. See most usefully R. Sharpe 'The English Bibliographical Tradition from Kirkestede to Tanner', in *Britannia Latina*, ed. C.J.F Burnett and C.N.J. Mann (Warburg Studies, London, 2005), 86–128.

[105] This extends to the subdivisions of works which Bale took to be separate items; see above for those in Grafton's and Stoughton's copies of *De logica tractatus tercius* which are reproduced as different items in the *Catalogus*. Thomson gives the listing details for each item that he has identified in the *Catalogus*; my own here differs in a few instances, usually on the side of greater doubt. Thomson was not concerned with Bale's knowledge of manuscripts as opposed to texts.

[106] Now Oxford Bodleian MS e Mus.86; Bale's annotations and additions are found throughout the manuscript; it is no. 47 in the 1553 list of his books, and some of the items from it are further enumerated at nos. 299–307.

in Trinity College B.14.50), T378–80 *Determinaciones contra Kynyngham* (only known in Corpus Christi College Cambridge 103), T383 *Determinationes contra Binham* (known in two medieval copies in England),[107] T399 *Protestacio* (found in Walsingham's *St Albans Chronicle*, from a manuscript of which Bale probably derived this), T414 *De ordine christiano* (found in Manchester Eng.86). There are two items which, because of the biblical nature of their incipits, could be either Latin or English works on Matthew 23–24, T372–3; if they are the former, again they are found in Manchester Eng.86.[108] Then there are two texts, T403 *Peticio ad regem et parliamentum* and T431 *De fundacione sectarum* that are found in a manuscript now in Florence but of English origin; the first appears in a single copy in England.[109] The identity of one of Bale's texts is uncertain: his *Ad 14 argumenta Strodae* lacks an incipit, and it is unclear to which of Wyclif's four responses to Strode, none of which has exactly fourteen points, this refers: three of them, T385–7, are not found now in any English copy, and the fourth, T388, only survives here in two part leaves used as pastedowns in a fifteenth-century binding.[110] Beyond these there are four items in Bale's *Catalogus* for which no English copy now survives, and whose survival so long in England is not elsewhere attested: these are T50 *De septem donis Sancti Spiritus*, T381 the *Determinacio ad argumenta magistri Outredi*,[111] T407 *De clavibus ecclesie* and T435 *De solucione Sathane*. Further work on Bale, his notes and his contacts, may well produce further identifications; but even on this showing it seems that Bale had a considerable number of Wyclif texts at some point in his hands.

As well as his cataloguing activities, Bale was a collector of books, chiefly manuscripts. The value he set upon his collection becomes evident in his attempts to regain the books after they had been lost to him in his flight from Ireland in 1553: a listing of these is provided in his own *Catalogus* ii.159–67.[112] Bale retrieved few if any of his books, and few of the remainder have been

---

[107] These are now Bodley 703 and Bodley Arch Seld.B.26; the copy in Lambeth Palace 537 was made in 1609, too late for Bale.

[108] T414 is ff.21v–24v, T372 ff.69r–82v and T373 ff.55r–64v; the English texts are printed *EWS* ii.366–78 and 328–65 respectively.

[109] This is that now in Florence Bibl.Laurentiana Plut.XIX.33, in which T383 is also found; the other English copy of T403 is now BL Cotton Vitellius E.xii.

[110] Now Trinity College Cambridge O.4.43; see the paper by F.Mantello in *Speculum* 54 (1979), 100–103.

[111] This is found only in Paris BN lat.3184; but since this is a French copy which belonged to Carmelite houses in Clermont and then Paris (see *Bibliothèque national: Catalogue général des manuscrits latins* iv (nos. 3014–3277, Paris, 1958), p. 323), before entering the royal library, it is very unlikely to have been seen by Bale. For an earlier Carmelite owner, Lawrence Burrell (d. 1504) of the Narbonne province, see Sharpe (2005[1] – see below n. 135), p. 88 n. 13.

[112] Reproduced and numbered by McCusker (1935) 149–62.

subsequently located.¹¹³ One of his major treasures, appearing as no. 47 in his list, was the collection known as *Fasciculus zizaniorum*, now Oxford Bodleian e Museo 86; this has numerous annotations and additions in Bale's own hand. From it Bale derived knowledge of much material relevant to the events of 1381 to 1415.¹¹⁴ Bale's copies of the *De mandatis* and of the *Trialogus* have not been identified; the second could have been the printed text, though it is listed with the addition 'Et xxiiij tractatus'.¹¹⁵ One manuscript from which Bale's *Catalogus* listing seems certainly to derive, and which was in his possession is now Trinity College Dublin 244; Bale sent this to Lord Francis Russell, afterwards earl of Bedford, in 1552, as is declared in the description of the manuscript Bale entered at the back of the notebook containing his *Index*.¹¹⁶ This, however, contains no Latin texts. More tentatively, it seems at first consideration attractive that Bale knew the anthology of Latin and English texts now Manchester John Rylands Library Eng.86: this contains ten of Wyclif's Latin writings, including an idiosyncratic version of the *Dialogus*. Eight of these are listed in the *Catalogus*,¹¹⁷ most of them with incipits; a ninth is the sole item that appears in the *Summarium* but not the *Catalogus*;¹¹⁸ most strikingly this manuscript starts T394 *De gradibus cleri* with chapter 3, the incipit provided by Bale. The one Latin item in the manuscript that seems hard to trace in Bale is T415 *De nova prevaricacione mendatorum*, here ff.90r–96v.¹¹⁹ Bale's list of the items in one of Leland's manuscripts in his *Index* includes one with the incipit of chapter 31 of the *Dialogus* (T408); this chapter is found only in Manchester Rylands Eng.86 and in ÖNB 3932 but there seems no reason why Bale should

---

¹¹³ See most recently W. O'Sullivan, 'The Irish 'remnaunt' of John Bale's manuscripts', in *New Science out of Old Books: Studies in Manuscripts and Early Printed Books in Honour of A.I. Doyle*, ed. R. Beadle and A.J. Piper (Aldershot, 1995), pp. 374–87.

¹¹⁴ The edition by W.W.Shirley (Rolls Series, 1858) only covers part of the manuscript.

¹¹⁵ Items 176 and 177; it is tempting to wonder whether the latter is the same manuscript that is mentioned in the *Index* (p. 271) as belonging to Leland, though the number of short tracts is here larger.

¹¹⁶ Oddly, the relevant page has never been printed; it is MS Selden Supra 64, f.267r–v. The list concludes with five items 'Ex paruo libro ad eundem misso' which are found, along with other material, in Trinity College Dublin 245; it is tempting to identify the two (and 245 is smaller in size than 244), but the five items are in the manuscript in a different order from that in the list.

¹¹⁷ I do not, for reasons given above no. I 1n., include T391 which is a brief quotation on f.117r without heading from two of Wyclif's *Sermones quadraginte*; the other text in the manuscript is T415 which may be Bale's *De purgatorio piorum* but its incipit does not agree.

¹¹⁸ See above, p. 21; it is T425 *Purgatorium secte Christi*.

¹¹⁹ Thomson's queried identification with *Catalogus* 124 is not convincing since neither title nor incipit agree.

pick it out for separate mention.[120] The case must at present remain attractive but unproven.

Bale provided in his *Summarium* (ff.154v–155r, 157v–158r) a brief biography of Wyclif, somewhat enlarged in the *Catalogus* (i.450–1, 455–6); both owe much to Leland. This sketch was in turn enlarged by Bale's friend John Foxe in the various editions of his *Actes and Monuments*. Foxe himself in the 1570 edition states that he has found copies of Wyclif's *De sensu et veritate scripturae, De ecclesia* and *De eucharistia confessio* and intends to publish them, a project which he never accomplished; the first and last of these texts (T31 and 39) Foxe could have encountered in a number of places, the second (T32) is more intriguing.[121] Alongside these three biographers, all of whom can be shown to have consulted widely in the manuscript sources about Wyclif, his followers, his opponents and his times, there are numerous other accounts and references in the two centuries that followed the coming of Lutheranism to England. Interesting though these are in the history of sectarian writing, most of them offer lean pickings for anyone concerned to trace the transmission of Wyclif's own writings: some may contain a reference or two, but few add to the body of solid evidence. Three of these later writers may exemplify the situation. Thomas James (d. 1629), Sir Thomas Bodley's first librarian, published in 1600 his *Ecloga Oxonio-Cantabrigiensis*, which lists under Wyclif's name seven items: four of these, two declared to be in English, are cited on the evidence of manuscripts in St. Benet's, that is Corpus Christi, College Cambridge,[122] the other three from two manuscripts in a private library.[123] Thomas James went

---

[120] *Index* p. 272; the second was not known to the editors. Chapters 29–32 of the *Dialogus* (see above no. I 9–11) were omitted by the scribe on first writing, and have been added with a directive after another item; had Bale not understood the directive, it would be expected that he would have regarded chapter 29 as the start of a new item.

[121] See the 1570 edition (online version), book 5 p. 547; the only English copies of T32, and those solely chapter 7, are those now in TCD 242 and in Florence Laurentian Plut.XIX.33, neither of whose ownerships can be traced back to 1570.

[122] STC 14453; ii.58–9. These are now MSS 103 containing the two Latin works, T4 and T378, and 296 and 336 containing English material. M.R. James's table of correspondence between the current numbering and that of Thomas James (*A Descriptive Catalogue of the Manuscripts in the Library of Corpus Christi College Cambridge* [Cambridge, 1912], i.xliv–xlviii) does not identify current 296 as the earlier 355 (but rather as 362).

[123] One of these was Lumley 296, now BL Royal 7 B.iii, containing T22 *De verbi incarnacione* and T39 *De eucharistia minor confessio*. The second, described as 'Controuersia inter Io.Wiclef et Monachos', seems to refer to one of the determinations against Binham (T383) of which James himself subsequently made a copy, now Lambeth 537 dated on its title page 1609; the source of this is unstated but was probably what is now MS Bodley 703, as is confirmed by notes in MS Lambeth 580, pp. 65–8. For the Lumley library see S. Jayne and F.R. Johnson, *The Library of John, Lord Lumley: the Catalogue of 1609* (London, 1956).

on to publish *An Apologie for Iohn Wickliffe* in 1608.¹²⁴ In this he quotes from a number of Wyclif's works, Latin and English, most of which are marginally annotated to explain their sources and to locate these in native libraries. There is a large degree of overlap between this and the notebook of his nephew, Richard James, that is usually dated about 1620–36 – so large, indeed, as to lead one to wonder whether Richard was actually transcribing here the notes his uncle had compiled before publication.¹²⁵ Both refer to T31 *De veritate sacre scripture* (probably from the copy now Bodley 924 given to the Library in 1601), T26 *De mandatis* (from Bodley 333, given 1602), from the T39 *De eucharistia minor confessio* (probably from Bodley 703, given in 1604), and with the same unusual title 'Determinatio .. de dominio contra unum monachum' T383 the second determination against Binham (probably also from Bodley 703).¹²⁶ There is a similar overlap in the vernacular sources quoted.¹²⁷ To the sources in Thomas's *Apologie* the notebook of his nephew adds some further works: T410 *De scismate* is quoted from MS Bodley 52, T400 *Libellus ad parliamentum regis* and T401 *De condemnacione xix conclusionum*, both probably from what later came to be Bodleian Arch.Seld.B.26,¹²⁸ T408 *Dialogus* said to be in the Royal Library but now lost,¹²⁹ T430 *De dyabolo et membris eius* from an unstated source,¹³⁰ and extracts from T409 *Speculum secularium dominorum* for which no source is given

---

¹²⁴ STC 14445, printed at Oxford.

¹²⁵ Richard was born in 1591, so it seems unlikely that he could have collected the extracts from Bodleian Library books before the 1608 publication of Thomas's *Apologie*. The relevant notebook is now Bodleian MS James 3; I have used the headnote to the James collection in *SC* ii.750–51 for the dating and the entry for this copy, p. 752. My observations on MS James 3 have been assisted by notes on it made some years ago by Dr Stephen Halasey.

¹²⁶ The *Apologie* reference is given before those from the notebook: T26 p. 7/pp. 89–107; T31 p. 9/pp. 107–78; T39 p. 28/pp. 261–2; T383 p. 18/pp. 262–8; references to the first two in the *Apologie* are common. Acquisition dates derive from the *Summary Catalogue*.

¹²⁷ These used Bodleian MSS 647 (acquired 1605), 938 (given 1605), 3 (given 1605).

¹²⁸ T410 pp. 228–9 (the manuscript given 1605), T400 pp. 304–14 and T401 pp. 314–25; MS Arch.SeldenB.26 is a composite manuscript: the relevant section here is ff.35–94 which seems to have belonged to Thomas Allen, then to Ussher before passing to John Selden whose library came to the Bodleian in 1659 (see A.G. Watson, 'Thomas Allen of Oxford and his manuscripts', in *Medieval Scribes, Manuscripts and Libraries: Essays presented to N.R. Ker*, ed. M.B. Parkes and A.G. Watson (London, 1978), pp. 279–313 especially pp. 298–9, 312.

¹²⁹ The extracts from the *Dialogus* occur pp. 346–52; the manuscript no longer exists in the Royal collection, nor does it appear in Carley's lists of the King's Libraries (*CBMLC* 7, 2000); the only copy of the text now in England is that in Manchester Eng.86.

¹³⁰ The only English copy still extant is that in BL Cotton Vespasian D.xxii, ff.21r–29r, of whose origins nothing appears to be known (see C.G.C. Tite, *The Early Records of Sir Robert Cotton's Library* (London, 2003), p. 184).

and no English manuscript now survives.[131] This last may be compared with a manuscript copy made late in the seventeenth century, and now preserved as Lambeth Palace 1058: the text is an incomplete copy of T49 *De fide catholica*.[132] Of this text no other English copy survives. These last two examples serve as a salutary reminder of the incompleteness of our knowledge.

Bibliographers after Bale, when they include Wyclif, build on his information.[133] The second edition of William Cave's *Scriptorum ecclesiasticorum historia literaria* (London, 1688) includes Wyclif only in its appendix contributed by Henry Wharton (pp. 40–43) and published the following year; this makes good use of James's *Ecloga* in addition to Bale. Casimir Oudin's *Commentarius de scriptoribus ecclesie antiquis...* (3 vols., Leipzig, 1722) in turn rehearses much of the same material.[134] Thomas Tanner, however, is a more productive source of new information. His *Bibliotheca Britannico-Hibernica* was published in 1748; as its title page made clear, it drew on earlier English surveys, but, in addition to repeating much of Bale's listing in the same sequence, some refinements on earlier knowledge of the works and details of new manuscripts are mentioned in the dense footnotes.[135] Like Bale, Tanner includes English works usually with Latin titles, but since he provides English incipits the material is clearer – these English works are not considered here but the numerous manuscripts mentioned show Tanner's extensive knowledge. Tanner recognized that *De arte sophistica* in the 1411 list (which he knew from Twyne's transcription) was to be identified with the third book of what he called *Summulas logicales*;[136] he noticed that Wyclif mentioned the *De symonia* at the end of *De veritate sacre scripture*, though knew the text itself only from the extracts in that same 1411 list.[137] For part of his listing (p. 770 col.b – p. 771 col.b) he is following Bale's list

---

[131] See MS James 3, pp. 354–7.

[132] The manuscript is a notebook, and the Wyclif item is pp. 1–23 covering the text in *Op.min.* pp. 92–108/26. H.J. Todd, *A Catalogue of the Archiepiscopal Manuscripts ...* (London, 1812), p. 251 says the hand is that of Archbishop Tenison (archbishop 1695–1715); other items are dated 1691 and 1692. Loserth used all seven known medieval manuscripts, all Bohemian, but his variants suggest (as would be expected) that none of them was the exemplar for this transcript.

[133] The Catholic John Pits, *Relationum historicarum de rebus Anglicis* (Paris, 1619) includes no heretics, and hence omits Wyclif.

[134] See iii.cols.1038–1048; Oudin does, however, mention the contents of the manuscript now Florence Biblioteca Medicea Laurentiana Plut.XIX.33 (iii.1042).

[135] Entry pp. 767–72. For Tanner see now R. Sharpe, 'The English Bibliographical Tradition from Kirkestede to Tanner', in *Britannia Latina*, ed. C.S.F. Burnett and C.N.J. Mann (Warburg Studies, London 2005), 86–128, and 'Thomas Tanner (1674–1735), the 1697 Catalogue, and *Bibliotheca Britannica*', *The Library* 7th ser. 6 (2005), 381–421.

[136] Tanner p. 768 note i; Twyne's copy is now MS Twyne 2, ff.213v–222.

[137] Tanner p. 769 note n; for this reference see *De ver.* iii.310/2.

in the *Catalogus*, and is evidently trying to match Bale's information against manuscripts he himself knew.[138] He twice mentions Lincoln Cathedral 159 as containing *De universalibus* (T11) and *De tempore* (T12). He knew Corpus Christi College Cambridge 103 (of T4 and T378–80), Lambeth 23 (of T257–84), Bodley 52 (of T410) and the later BL Royal 7 B.iii (once Lumley 297 of T22 and 39); he was also aware of Trinity College Cambridge B.16.2, and mentions it three times. His knowledge of some of these may have come through his own and others' contributions to Bernard's *Catalogue*,[139] and he also used Wharton's appendix to Cave.[140] Tanner also mentions *De sermone Domini in monte* (that is *Opus evangelicum*) and *De ente universali et attributis divinis*, and rather misleadingly (since its language implies that they are in the vernacular) *Homilies upon the epistles and gospels*, all in the Trinity manuscript.[141] *De perfeccione statuum* (T426) is cited on the basis of Twyne's copy of the 1411 list.[142] Perhaps most striking is Tanner's knowledge of the Syon holdings of Wyclif: cited as 'olim in bibl.mon.Syon' are *Super tres lib.meteoror, Super viii lib.Physic., De peregrinatione, Epistola ad ducem Lancastriae* and *De materia schismatis*.[143] Tanner had clearly studied the manuscript of the Syon catalogue, now Corpus Christi College Cambridge 141 (perhaps alerted by James's *Ecloga* where it is no. 224 in the library).[144]

2. The survival of the Bohemian manuscripts

The vast majority of the surviving Bohemian copies of Wyclif's works are now to be found in libraries in Prague and Vienna. The first of these is hardly surprising, though their transmission through the upheavals of the sixteenth and seventeenth centuries was hazardous and obscure. The second is, however, startling: neither Vienna itself nor its surrounding neighbourhood were seriously affected by the Hussite movement (though Jerome of Prague visited the city in 1410 and had fled from trial there), nor were there any

---

[138] Tanner p. 770 note n* and p. 771 note n*.

[139] E. Bernard, *Catalogi librorum manuscriptorum Angliae et Hiberniae* (Oxford 1697). In the note p. 771 col.a Tanner seems to suggest that T404, the letter to pope Urban VI, is to be found in Lambeth Palace 104, but this seems to be a mistake: ff.211r–221v contains material relating to Wyclif's tenure of the headship of Canterbury College c.1368–70, including a bull of pope Urban V, but not Wyclif's later letter (see Pantin, OHS ns 8, 1950, 184–206 esp. 198–201). For Tanner's part in Bernard see Sharpe (2005²), pp. 385–7.

[140] See above p. 28 and Sharpe (2005²), p. 404.

[141] Tanner p. 769 note n* and p. 771 note n*.

[142] P. 771 col.a; see MS Twyne 2, f.217v.

[143] P. 771 col.b; for these see above no. XV 12–13 and here pp. 15–16.

[144] *Ecloga* i.85; Tanner does not indicate any secondary source.

conciliar councils assembled there that could account for an interest in matters Wycliffite.[145] Yet in the present Österreichische Nationalbibliothek in Vienna some 46 manuscripts containing works now accepted as by Wyclif are to be found; to my knowledge, there are no works by Wyclif himself in other Austrian collections.[146] Furthermore, almost all of them can be shown to have been present in the Imperial Library (whose collections form the basis for today's library) by 1576. The story of how they came to be there is one of the stranger sequences in the history of the transmission of Wyclif's works. Since it covers a large number of important copies, I will deal with this group first.

Firm evidence for the existence of these manuscripts in the Imperial Library comes from the catalogue of the collection made in 1576 by the first official Librarian, the Dutch bibliographer Hugo Blotius.[147] Blotius used the shelfmarkings then in use, consisting of a capital letter plus a number, and gave a brief summary of the contents of each volume together with an indication of the material of which the manuscript was made. Since the same shelfmarks were written into each manuscript in pencil, usually on a flyleaf but sometimes on the first folio, it is possible in most cases to link Blotius's items with the volumes under their present-day numbers; this is considerably helped by the fact that few of the books have been rebound since the sixteenth century. Of the 46 manuscripts containing works by Wyclif now in the Library, all but seven were identified by the editor of Blotius's catalogue.[148] Two more can be added with fair certainty.[149] Only one manuscript of the remaining five, now ÖNB 3927, consists entirely of works by Wyclif; all of the others are miscellanies, in which (excepting 5204) Wyclif items occur late in the volume,

---

[145] See references above no. I 13 n.52 but here especially L. Klicman, *Processus iudiciarius contra Jeronimum de Praga habitus Viennae a.1410–1412* (Prague, 1898) and the same author's paper in *Mittheilungen des Instituts für Österreichische Geschichtsforschung* 21 (1900), 445–57, and more recently P.P. Bernard, 'Jerome of Prague, Austria and the Hussites', *Church History* 27 (1958), 3–22.

[146] A copy of the *Floretum* is, however, found in the Klosterneuburg library: see my paper 'A Lollard Compilation in England and Bohemia'. reprinted *LB* 31–42 at p. 35.

[147] The listing is edited from ÖNB nova 4451 by H. Menhardt, 'Das älteste Handschriftenverzeichnis der Wiener Hofbibliothek von Hugo Blotius 1576', *Österreichische Akademie der Wissenschaften Phil.-hist.Klasse Denkschriften* 76 (1957).

[148] Menhardt does not provide identifications for current ÖNB 1338, 1725, 3927, 4343, 4701, 5204, 5239. The arrangement of the categories by alphabetical initial and number does not appear to help identification, though all Wyclif volumes are in categories M, N, O or P.

[149] Blotius usually gives the first item as the main content. Current ÖNB 1725 is clearly O4355 described as 'Registrum super tres tractatus de divino dominio in 8° in membrana scriptus', for which see above no. VII 333–6; less certainly ÖNB 1338 is O4378 'Speculum saecularium dominorum, iunctis aliis variis opusculis de mendaciis fratrum etc., Liber in membrana in 4° scriptus', where the first item (T409) mentioned occurs on ff.20vb–26va, the second (T419) on f.30rb, but the first items, ff.1ra–20va are not provided with a title by the scribe.

and which may be hidden under one of Blotius's less distinctive descriptions. 3927 is one of the very few relevant volumes that *was* rebound in the nineteenth century, and all old shelfmarks have been lost along with the old flyleaves. From other evidence to be considered below, it is certain that it was in the Imperial Library by the time that Blotius worked there, though it is not clear why it is apparently missing from his listing.[150] A second manuscript, a miscellany, now 5204, appears, for reasons to be explained below, also to have been certainly in the collection by 1576. Blotius confirms that by his day the two copies of the *Opus arduum*, the one of the *Floretum* and the manuscript containing Thorpe's investigation were also in the Library.[151]

It seems safe to deduce that by 1576 all the Wyclif holdings were already in Vienna. Their origins, however, were undoubtedly in Bohemia, and their arrival in the Imperial collection seems certain to be dependent upon the activities and unexpected death of one man, Kaspar von Niedbruck. Von Niedbruck was born about 1525, and early in his life came, under the influence of Calvin and Melancthon, to be a convinced reformer. By 1550 he had, however, entered the service of the archduke, later emperor, Maximilian, on whose behalf he undertook numerous diplomatic journeys; though he has sometimes been described as Maximilian's librarian, it seems unlikely he ever fulfilled such a formal role or had time to do so.[152] Von Niedbruck's interest in the antecedents to the reformers of his own day was much fostered, though not instigated by, Flacius Illyricus with whom he maintained a frequent correspondence, of which letters from 1552–7 survive.[153] Flacius was already heavily engaged in the work which was published under the title of the *Magdeburger Centurien*,[154]

---

[150] The contents of Blotius's N4167 'De simonia plurimorum doctorum varia in 4° scriptus in charta, iunctis aliis quaternionibus in membra' might be appropriate, since Wyclif *De symonia* (T35) is the first substantial item, ff.53–74; but the size is wrong (it is of a similar size to those Blotius describes elsewhere as folio), and there is no sign now of the final quires of parchment.

[151] Of the first text current ÖNB 4526 is Blotius M3920 and 4925 is M3933; of the second 4492 is O4346, and of the third current 3936 is O4224. For the first and second see *LB* 43–65 and 13–42, for the third EETS 301 (1993), xxviii–xxix.

[152] A brief account is in F. Unterkircher's contribution to *Geschichte der Österreichischen Nationalbibliothek*, ed. J. Stummvoll (Vienna, 1968), pp. 67–71; a fuller review of the archduke's confessional sympathies is in P.S. Fichtner, *Emperor Maximilian II* (New Haven and London, 2001), especially pp. 32–49 and notes.

[153] The surviving letters between the two were edited by K. Viktor Bibl, 'Der Briefwechsel zwischen Flacius und Nidbruck', *Jahrbuch der Gesellschaft für die Geschichte des Protestantismus in Österreich* 17 (1896), 1–24, 18 (1897) 201–38, 19 (1898), 96–110, 20 (1899), 83–116.

[154] There are two recent book-length studies of Flacius Illyricus: Martina Hartmann, *Humanismus und Kirchenkritik: Matthias Flacius Illyricus als Erforscher des Mittelalters* (Beiträge zur Geschichte und Quellenkunde des Mittelalters 19, Stuttgart, 2001) and O.K. Olson, *Matthias Flacius and the Survival of Luther's Reform* (Wiesbaden, 2002). Unfortunately, though both deal

but also in the assembling of a large library of 'reforming texts' at Regensburg. Doubtless initiated first through diplomatic channels, but much fostered by his evangelical colleagues, von Niedbruck was in touch with many sources in the old Hussite areas of Bohemia. Urged on by Flacius, he sought to obtain from his friends and acquaintances copies of the works of Hus and his followers and of Wyclif whom he saw as Hus's mentor. Flacius evidently urged secrecy, concealed his own name under a variety of pseudonyms, and was often noted by von Niedbruck as Φ, that is 'Philos', 'Friend'.

Von Niedbruck's efforts in Bohemia were multifarious and persistent. One of his correspondents after 1553 was Mathaeus Kollín, Czech in origin and teacher of Greek in Prague in the sixteenth century;[155] Kollín provided von Niedbruck with information about owners of materials that might be of interest, and was persuaded by him to act as an intermediary in obtaining books 'on loan' from their current owners.[156] At first the purpose of the 'loan' seems to have been to allow for the copying of the materials, and for the translation of works from Czech into German, work which, partly because of the suspicion of the owners, should be done in Prague; even for this von Niedbruck encountered considerable opposition. In the summer of 1556 von Niedbruck came to Prague himself, and eventually persuaded the Carolinum to allow him to take back to Vienna on loan a collection of forty-nine books. The assurances of their safe return were, however, defeated by the unexpected and untimely death of von Niedbruck on 26 September 1557. Because he died intestate, all von Niedbruck's property was forfeit to the emperor; this covered everything in his possession, and hence the books were never returned.

The list of the books from the Carolinum loaned to von Niedbruck survives, and has been subject to a good deal of scrutiny.[157] By no means all

---

with Flacius's gathering of texts and his association with von Niedbruck, it is clear that neither has investigated the Bohemian sources for his work. I have also been able to consult online R. Diener's Harvard dissertation *The Magdeburg Centuries: A Bibliothecal and Historical Analysis* (1979); this, though it gives much detail of the relations between von Niedbruck and Flacius, has little to say about the acquisition of manuscripts from Bohemia.

[155] The surviving correspondence was edited by F. Menčík, *Dopisy M.Matouše Kollína z Chotěřiny a jeho přátel ke Kašparovi z Nydbrucka* (Prague, 1914); this provides almost all the evidence here.

[156] See F. Menčik, 'Casper Nydbrucks Verhältniss zu den Calixtinern in Böhmen', *Jahrbuch der Gesellschaft für die Geschichte des Protestantismus in Oesterreich* 18 (1897), 48–55.

[157] See F.M. Bartoš, 'Vzácný Dokument z dějin knihovny Karlovy University', *Jihočeský sborník historický* 17 (1948), 31–4, K. Schwarzenberg, 'Bücher der Österreichischen Nationalbibliothek aus dem Prager Karolinum', *Biblos* 19 (1970), 97–103 with correction 20 (1971), 103. There are also some less systematic assertions in K. Schwarzenberg, *Katalog der kroatischen, polnischen und tschechischen Handschriften der Österreichischen Nationalbibliothek* (Vienna, 1972) under individual listings.

of the volumes listed are of reformist interest, let alone of works by Wyclif; nor is it always easy, in default of markings that would identify items in the list with surviving volumes, to be sure which of the present holdings of the library derive from the Carolinum. Wyclif's name appears twice in the list and a distinctive title (*De dominio divino*) adds a third book: these three volumes have been identified as ÖNB 4529, 4514 and 3935.[158] Contents listed anonymously, or amongst miscellanies, have led to the identification of a further eleven manuscripts that have Wyclif items within them.[159] The Carolinum collection, however, only accounts for fourteen out of the 46 Vienna holding of Wyclif manuscripts. But von Niedbruck seems certainly responsible for the assembly of many more. His candour to the Bohemians from whom, or through whose offices, he obtained these or other books about the use to which they would be put, or their eventual destination seems questionable. Flacius, as has been said, had urged him on to obtain the books, and it seems plain that some were intended to be forwarded to him. The Φ symbol that indicated Flacius's name was entered into some volumes, and it seems reasonable to think that these were intended to be sent to him: such a symbol appears on ÖNB 1294 and 4516; neither of these are clearly identifiable in the Carolinum list.[160] Those two did not reach Flacius, though, as I will outline later, some Bohemian manuscripts did. It is clear from his correspondence that von Niedbruck was from time to time in Regensburg with Flacius.[161]

Von Niedbruck was particularly anxious to persuade his correspondent Mathaeus Kollín to help in acquiring books from Lymburg, now the small town of Nymburk, some thirty miles north east of Prague; news about the town library there had reached him from another correspondent Humbert Languet.[162] He succeeded in obtaining a list of the contents of the library, and

---

[158] See Schwarzenberg (1970), 102, following for the first and third Bartoš; in the list they are items 32–3, 46.

[159] Items 1=3930, 2=1622, 4=4505, 5=4536, 6=4527, 7=4515, 8=3933 (correcting Schwarzenberg's mistranscription of Bartoš's number), 9=3928, 18=4504, 35=4307, 45=4483 according to Schwarzenberg, usually following Bartoš.

[160] F. Unterkircher, *Die datierten Handschriften der Österreichischen Nationalbibliothek von 1401 bis 1450* (Vienna, 1971), i.100 states that the second had come from the Carolinum to von Niedbruck, but he does not provide a matching number from the list. On the front board of 1622 is stuck a small piece of paper on which the symbol Φ can be conjectured, but its form is not altogether convincing.

[161] See letters, Menčik p. 97.

[162] See letters on both sides dated between November 1553 and December 1555, Menčik pp. 20, 25, 30, 38, 50–58, 71, 74; most important here is the list of Nymburk books pp. 50–52 text. Menčik also prints (pp. 50–51 n. 2) a list of Nymburk books found in ÖNB 7980 f.23a^v (for the manuscript see above no. III 4), but its relation to the list in Niedbruck's letter is not clear.

sought eagerly to get access to it; the townsfolk were apparently very unwilling, though the dean of the town proved willing to send his own rich collection.[163] Amongst the Wyclif manuscripts now in Vienna a number can be connected with the place by a small inscription 'Lymburg' found in the margin: these are now ÖNB 1337, 1339, 1387, 1647 and 4522.[164] The first two of these are part of the set of seven manuscripts, now 1337–43, using parchment (rather than the normal paper of Bohemian manuscripts of this date), and having an identical format, similar layout and hands, which together contain a substantial proportion of Wyclif's works; since only two very short works appear twice within this set, it seems a reasonable assumption that the set was the larger part of what was intended as a complete collection of those works.[165] An eighth manuscript of the same format is now Wolfenbüttel Helmstedt Guelf 565, once belonging to Flacius; though formal proof is not available, it was doubtless supplied by von Niedbruck. If two of the eight volumes derive from Nymburk, it seems justifiable to think that all reached von Niedbruck from that source. Whether this set, or the singletons 1387, 1647 and 4522, belonged to the town library or to the dean seems impossible to ascertain; whichever was the case, it was an astonishingly rich collection.

This adds a further nine to the Carolinum fourteen volumes, making a total of exactly half of the 46 current Vienna Wyclif manuscripts. Connections of the remaining half with von Niedbruck are more difficult to trace. In view of the links between von Niedbruck and Flacius Illyricus, this is a convenient point to deal with his holdings of Wyclif manuscripts, a holding that was smaller than had been intended because of Niedbruck's unexpected death. Much of the surviving contents of Flacius's library came into the collections of the Wolfenbüttel Library, and there four manuscripts containing Wyclif texts are now to be found.[166] Of these one, Guelf 565, as I have suggested, came to

---

[163] See Menčík pp. 17, 30, 32, 35–6, 38, 48, 53–4, 58, F.M. Bartoš, 'Nad Husitským sborníkem z Nymburka', *Jihočeský sborník historický* 83 (1960), 123–7; I. Hlaváček, 'Dva přispěvky k dějinám našich knihoven předhusitské doby', *Časopis Národního Muzea řada historická* 150 (1981), 25–36 only deals with material earlier than that relevant here.

[164] In 1337 see f.ii^{va}, in 1339 front pastedown bottom left, in 1387 on the front parchment flyleaf top recto left, in 1647 foot of f.Iv (with offset on f.IIr), in 4522 on leather pasted down inside front cover bottom. 4522 and its connection with Nymburk is set out by F. Bartoš (1960), 123–7; Schwarzenberg (n.157) adds 4518 and 4302, though the evidence in these latter cases is not clear to me from the manuscripts themselves.

[165] K. Stejskal comments on the similar decoration of ÖNB 1337, 1339 and 1341 in 'Nové poznatky o iluminovaných rukopisech Husitské doby', *Český časopis historický* 93 (1995), 419–25 at p. 422, but does not locate the workshop.

[166] All are noted as having belonged to Flacius in O. von Heinemann, *Die Handschriften der herzoglichen Bibliothek zu Wolfenbüttel i: Die Helmstedter Handschriften* i–iii (Wolfenbüttel, 1884–8) under

Flacius through the offices of von Niedbruck from Nymburk in Bohemia.[167] 1126, on the flyleaf of which Flacius wrote 'De officio pastorali liber incerti authoris', has some Czech words in a colophon (f.46) and on the parchment covering, but its transmission is unclear. 669, a miscellany with two short Wyclif texts (T204 and 404), was, according to a note on the front flyleaf, bought in Prague in 1433 by Heinrich Toke, Domherr at Magdeburg and legate to the Council of Basel in 1431; how it came to Flacius, who identified the contents as 'Hussi et Wiclefi quedam scripta' (f.1r), is unknown, but it seems unlikely that it had left Germany after Toke's purchase.[168] Finally 306: this contains on a flyleaf a Polish eulogy of Wyclif 'edita ab Andrea de Dobschino, olim magistro artium studii Cracowiensis'.[169] This was Andrzej Gałka, active in Krakow between 1420 and 1449, who died probably soon after leaving the city under investigation for heresy. Given Gałka's enthusiasm for Wyclif, it is likely that the whole manuscript belonged to him.[170] Again Flacius probably acquired it from a German or Polish source. If von Niedbruck was involved in the transmission of any of these, then Flacius must have obtained them by 1557; it seems possible, however, that some material went direct from Prague to Flacius.[171] A few years later, in 1561, Flacius apparently sent to England, again in pursuit of manuscripts of Wyclif, a list of the books he already possessed: the titles are not all transparent, but items can credibly be matched against the contents of the present 306, 565 and 1126;[172] in the remaining 669 there are only two brief Wyclif texts, neither in a prominent position, though both with Wyclif's name attached. This same list, however, reveals that Flacius must have

---

the relevant numbers.

[167] Hartmann (2001), pp. 110 and 237 suggests the manuscript perhaps came from Kloster Reichenbach in the Oberpfalz, but gives no reasons; the suggestion seems to derive from K.Schottenloher 'Handschriftenschätze zu Regensburg in Dienste des Zenturiatoren (1554–1562), *Zentralblatt für Bibliothekswesen* 34 (1917), 65–82 at pp. 79–80 where again no evidence is given.

[168] See Hartmann (2001), pp. 106 and 238; also W. Milde, 'Metamorphosen: Die Wandlung des Codex durch den Leser oder der dritte Aspekt der Handschriftenkunde – Ein Überblick', *Gutenberg-Jahrbuch* 70 (1995), 27–36 at p. 30.

[169] The eulogy was printed from another source by M. Schlauch, 'A Polish Vernacular Eulogy of Wycliff', *Journal of Ecclesiastical History* 8 (1957), 53–73 at pp. 71–2.

[170] See P. Kras, 'Hussitism and the Polish Nobility', in *Lollards and the Gentry in the Later Middle Ages*, ed. M. Aston and C. Richmond (Stroud, 1997), pp. 183–98 esp. p. 186, and his 'Wyclif's Tradition in Fifteenth Century Poland: the Heresy of Andrzej Gałka of Dobczyn', in *The Bohemian Reformation and Religious Practice* 5, ed. Z.V. David and D.R. Holeton (Prague, 2004) pp. 191–210.

[171] See Menčik p. 15, a letter dated to October 1553.

[172] See N.L. Jones, 'Matthew Parker, John Bale, and the Magdeburg Centuriators', *Sixteenth Century Journal* 12 (1981), 35–49 at p. 45 n. 35. As Jones explains, the list existed in a manuscript once in the collection belonging to Baroness Lucas of Wrest Park, whose present whereabouts is unknown.

owned more than currently survives at Wolfenbüttel: leaving aside titles whose identity is less than certain, the penultimate item 'Ejusdem de universalibus et ideis' must refer to the two philosophical works of those names (T11 and 18), neither of which now survives in Wolfenbüttel. No manuscripts of Wyclif's Latin works seem to have reached Flacius from England, but it seems likely that the very handsome copy of the Wycliffite Bible now Wolfenbüttel Guelf A.2.Aug. 2, came to Flacius from the collection of John, Lord Lumley (1534?–1609).[173]

With all the Vienna Wyclif manuscripts present in the Imperial collection by 1576, and with the strong probability that all were brought to Vienna at the instigation of Kaspar von Niedbruck, the group is obviously a closed collection and an artificial one. It is, however, strikingly important in its contents, including as it does amongst other treasures the single surviving example of a Wyclif manuscript written in England and itself taken back to Bohemia (ÖNB 1294), the major part of a complete Wyclif *opera* series (ÖNB 1337–43), and a vast volume heavily annotated perhaps by Peter Payne (ÖNB 1387).[174] Whether by good fortune or by skilful selection, von Niedbruck assembled a remarkable group: almost all of the lengthy works are represented in it,[175] together with a very large number of the short polemical texts; without the collection (ÖNB 1340–41) *De civili dominio* would only survive in an abbreviated and somewhat garbled form. But, however dubious the means by which von Niedbruck gained control over the manuscripts and however unfortunate their permanent removal from Bohemia may have been, it is arguable that more of them survived in Vienna than might have done in their original home: the depredations of books, and particularly of reformist books, in Bohemia during the Thirty Years War and especially after the Battle of the White Mountain were enormous. One of the most celebrated removals during that War was, of course, that of Hus's own copy of five of Wyclif's philosophical works (now Stockholm Kunglig. Biblioteket Lat.A.164)[176] – one which shows that disruption came from both Protestant and Catholic sides, and also that von Niedbruck had not succeeded

---

[173] See S.R. Jayne and F.R. Johnson, *The Lumley Library: the Catalogue of 1609* (London, 1956), p. 11 and note, and Y. Terasawa, 'A Manuscript of the Wycliffite Bible (Early Version)', in *History and Structure of English*, ed. Y. Terasawa et al. (Tokyo, 1981), 33–50.

[174] The suggested responsibility for the annotation is from S.H. Thomson, 'A note on Peter Payne and Wyclif', *Medievalia et Humanistica* 16 (1964), 60–63.

[175] A few parts of the *Summa de ente*, particularly of its second half (T13–16, 19), *De materia et forma* (T20), *De potestate pape* (T34), and the Old Testament part of the *Postilla* are the exceptions.

[176] See M. Hedlund, *Katalog der datierten Handschriften ... in Schweden* i (Uppsala, 1980), p. 15 and J. Daňhelka, 'Das Zeugnis des Stockholmer Autographs von Hus', *Die Welt der Slaven* 27 (1982), 225–33.

in locating all the significant manuscripts. From close to the present-day border of the Czech Republic should be noted also the Wyclif(fite material now in Bautzen and Herrnhut.[177]

Turning now to the collections in Bohemia itself, the first notable feature is their appearance in a number of libraries: three libraries in Prague itself, two in Olomouc, one in Brno, and in each case it is clear that the materials derive from a number of sources. In Prague itself, the significant and longstanding groups are those in the National (formerly University) Library and in the Metropolitan Chapter Library; the two Wyclif manuscripts in the National Museum Library are of recent acquisition.[178] Of these more can be said about the National Library collection. Given its association with the University, and its home in the Clementinum building, it might be thought that it should have inherited what remained of the Carolinum library after the loan to von Niedbruck. This, however, is too optimistic an expectation. From 1408 Prague synodal statutes had banned the ownership of Wyclif's books, though these prohibitions may not have had much immediate effect.[179] The current library, however, like the university in which it is housed, was the creation of the Jesuit order, charged with the reconversion of the Czech lands in the aftermath of the defeat at the White Mountain; as Truhlář, the cataloguer of the manuscript collection, observed, the wonder is that so many copies of the works of Wyclif and Hus appear within it.[180] Of the holdings of the medieval university and its colleges some lists survive;[181] the earliest dates from the end of the fourteenth century and is not informative. But the others, dating from the second half of the fifteenth century, one for Queen Hedvika's College (or the Lithuanian College), and another in two divisions for the College of the Bohemian Nation, are more

---

[177] That in the former has been described recently by T. Krzenck, 'Die Bautzener Hussitica der ehemaligen Gersdorfschen Bibliothek', *Studie o Rukopisech* 31 (1996), 153–78 The Herrnhut manuscript, AB II.R.1.16a is a notebook that deserves further scrutiny; it contains five Wyclif sermons (T200–2, 203, 208), and other extracts. I am grateful to the librarians at both places for the opportunity to examine their material.

[178] They are, notwithstanding important: I E 6, obtained in 1847 with T413, and XIII F 9, bought in 1869, containing the Epistle section of the *Postilla* (T349–70).

[179] J. Kadlec, 'Synods of Prague and their Statutes', *Apolinaris* 54 (1991), 227–93 at pp. 232–4.

[180] J. Truhlář, *Catalogus codicum manu scriptorum qui in C.R.Bibliotheca Publica atque Universitatis Pragensis asservantur* (Prague, 1905), .ix.

[181] They were reproduced in facsimile by J. Bečka and E. Urbánková, *Katalogy knihoven kolejí Karlovy University* (Prague, 1948), a publication made to mark the 400th anniversary of the founding of the Charles University; I remain deeply indebted to the kindness of Prof. I. Hlaváček, who in 1992 generously gave me a copy of this.

interesting.[182] All of these contain works either ascribed to Wyclif, by surname or by Latin by-name, or with titles identifiable with his.[183] The catalogues for both libraries provide a classification by capital letter and number, and the marks of an apparently identical system are still visible in many of the surviving manuscripts. However, when an attempt to match these is made, it becomes clear that some serious reclassification, either in the marking of the books or in the catalogues, must have occurred:[184] of the surviving Wyclif manuscripts only one can be certainly identified with an item in the catalogue of the Bohemian College, namely V.G.19 which contains the pressmark E.43 and can be recognized in the long description.[185] A second, IV.H.17, which before excision contained a copy of Thorpe's investigation, appears as P.22.[186] More hesitantly, the current V.A.3, bearing the mark D20 contains the same contents, Wyclif's *De mandatis*, as the catalogue of the Lithuanian College D21.[187] More serious doubts affect other possible matches.[188] This is a poor tally of the 49 manuscripts containing Wyclif's own writings that are to be found in the

---

[182] See the brief introduction to the facsimile, and the paper by J. Truhlář, 'Dva staré katalogy knih kolejí Pražskych', *Vestnik České Akademie* 13 (1904), 98–105.

[183] In the first of these lists an incipit is also given, for instance D21 'Super x precepta doctor ewangelicus premissa sentencia' and similarly D22; the lists of the Bohemian College give author and title only, for instance K2[6] 'vniuersalia Wykleff Tractatus de ydeis', and similarly F7, M1, M2, M13, M50, and in the second part P18, whilst listings such as P11 give seven recognizable titles but no clear authorship, to which P12 and P22 may tentatively be added.

[184] See F. Šmahel, 'Knihovní katalogy Koleje Národa Českého a Koleje Rečkovy', *Acta Universitatis Carolinae* 2 (1961), 59–85, now updated (but not in regard to Wyclif manuscripts changed) as 'Bibliothekskataloge des Kollegs der Böhmischen Nation und des Reček-Kollegs' in *Die Prager Universität im Mittelalter* (Leiden, 2007), pp. 405–39; earlier analyses include J. Loserth, 'Der älteste Katalog der Prager Universitäts-Bibliothek', *Mitteilungen des Instituts für österreichische Geschichtsforschung* 11 (1890), 301–18.

[185] See Šmahel (2007), p. 439, catalogue p. 118; the Wyclif item in the manuscript is T385, ff.86r–87v, and is listed as 'Questio Magistri Richardi Strode' without authorship (as in the volume).

[186] The material was on ff.122–144, as noted by Truhlář in his description of the manuscript; in the medieval catalogue (p.162) the item appears as 'Tractatulus Wilhelmi Anglici Torp de responsionibus ad doctores'.

[187] See p. 14, not identified by Šmahel.

[188] Thus in the listing of the Bohemian college it is tempting to identify M1 (p. 71) with current PUK V.H.16, but this contains the old shelfmark B,3 and the order of contents is not clear, or from the second listing (p. 160) to see a similarity of the ordering and contents of P11 with ÖNB 4527, though that now contains no appropriate mark.

University Library.[189] One identifiable Carolinum manuscript, M13, is certainly now in Vienna.[190]

Of one late fifteenth-century collector's manuscripts a very large number survives into the present University Library. Václav Koranda the younger, administrator of the Bethlehem Chapel in Prague from 1471 to 1497, assembled an impressive personal library, identifiable largely because of the distinctive monogram which he entered in each of the books. Of 27 volumes owned by him and now in the Prague University Library three include Wyclif items (now V.F.9, V.G.10 and VIII.F.13), though only in the first as the predominant component.[191] In addition several of Koranda's manuscripts reached Vienna, including those now ÖNB 1294, 3930 and 4516, the first two of which are extremely important volumes.

Little can be said of the background of the nineteen Wyclif volumes currently in the Prague Metropolitan Chapter Library. Four of them contain library shelfmarks of a kind similar to those used by the two colleges of the Carolinum, but the same problem of identification exists;[192] one (now M.54) belonged to Alexander Třeboňsky at the end of the fifteenth century;[193] a third (now C.118) has associations with Nymburk about 1437.[194] Again, given the views of the ecclesiastical authorities in charge of the library, the surprise is perhaps that so many manuscripts are to be found there; it is hardly unexpected that they are probably of diverse backgrounds. Outside Prague copies of Wyclif's works are to be found in Olomouc and in Brno, both in Moravia and

---

[189] A later list of Wyclif material 'ex registris vniuersitatis et collegii Caroli 4ti' appears in ÖNB 7980 f.8 (for the manuscript see above no. III 4): only titles are given, insufficient for the identification of individual copies

[190] See p. 71. ÖNB 5204 corresponds to the first two items (the second is the only Bohemian copy of Robert Allington's *Suppositiones* – see Sharpe (1997) 523), and has the signature M13 on the outer case.

[191] See E. Urbánková, 'Zbytky knihovny M.Václava Korandy ml. v Universitní Knihovně v Praze', *Ročenka UK v Praze 1956* (Prague, 1958), 135–61, supplemented by P. Spunar, 'Několik doplňků k rekonstrukci knihovny Václava Korandy ml.' *Listy filologické* 91 (1968), 147–50.

[192] PMK B.53 is marked N.10, C.73 is marked N.9, D.50 has two signatures, N.27 and N.31, N.19 is marked N.8.

[193] See I. Hlaváček, 'Alexius Třeboňský a katalog jeho knihovny z Konze 15 stol.', *Sborník historický* 6 (1958), 223–52 at pp. 241, 249; the catalogue was probably made shortly before Třeboňsky's death c. 1496.

[194] See A. Podlaha, *Soupis Rukopisů Knihovny Metropolitní Kapitoly Pražské* (Prague, 1922), i.315; PMK D.105 containing the *Rosarium* belonged to M. Prokop of Kladruby in the first half of the fifteenth century (see J. Kadlec, 'Die Bibliothek des M.Prokop aus Kladrub', *Mediaevalia Bohemica* 1–2 (1969), 315–20 at p. 316).

beyond the main Hussite areas.¹⁹⁵ But, as research is gradually revealing, interest in reformist ideas was not limited to those main areas, and this is confirmed by the survival of individual manuscripts in Krakow and Wroclaw in present-day Poland, as well as those in Germany.¹⁹⁶

Comment was made above about the quality of the Vienna holdings of Wyclif material. Von Niedbruck, the assembler of those manuscripts, did not, however, manage to remove all the important texts from Bohemia. Even if the Prague holdings include a higher proportion of apparently informal, perhaps student, collections in which Wyclif texts, often short, exist alongside a multiplicity of other brief items (examples would be PUK III.G.16, V.F.17, V.G.10, or PMK A.84 or D.50), there are some handsome and well produced copies also. Examples of this latter type are PUK VIII.C.3 containing the *De veritate sacre scripture* with a portrait, presumably of Wyclif, in the opening initial;¹⁹⁷ or PMK C.73 with copies of the *De blasfemia, De apostasia* and *De potestate pape* plus two shorter texts. Less attractive to the eye, but important because of their content are PUK III.G.11 with, alongside a large number of Wyclif's own writings, the Latin version of William Taylor's 1406 sermon and the 1403/4 letter of the English Wycliffite Richard Wyche, or X.E.11, the collection of indexes to seventeen of Wyclif's works, or PMK O.29 containing many extracts or short works by Wyclif together with the Latin text of Thorpe's investigation.¹⁹⁸ Looked at by another measure: there are three texts (T43, 51 and 392) that would be unknown were they not preserved in manuscripts now in Prague, five if they did not survive in copies now in Vienna (T13, 46, 48, 407, 425); but, with the exception of T48 *De dotacione ecclesie*, all are brief, and the balance between the two places not greatly discrepant. What is more important is that the collections must be seen as a single whole of Bohemian origin, and that without their combined testimony we would be largely ignorant of Wyclif's most important works.

---

¹⁹⁵ For these see Thomson's manuscript index; a modern catalogue of the Brno volumes is by V. Dokoupil, *Soupis rukopisných fondů Universitní knihovny v Brně* 2 (Prague, 1958).

¹⁹⁶ P. Kras has studied interest in present-day Polish lands in 'Hussitism and the Polish Nobility', in *Lollardy and the Gentry in the Later Middle Ages*, ed. M. Aston and C.Richmond (Stroud, 1997), pp. 183–98, and more widely in *Husyci w piętnastowiecznej Polsce* (Lublin, 1998). The Wyclif copies in Brno derive from the Dietrichstein library at Mikulov in south Moravia.

¹⁹⁷ Reproduced several times, for instance on the cover of the Bodleian Library's 1984–5 exhibition catalogue *Wyclif and his Followers*; for another probable portrait in PMK C.38, f.17rb see the frontispiece here.

¹⁹⁸ For these see Thomson's index pp. 314–15; for the first my note 'William Taylor's 1406 Sermon: a Postscript', *Medium Aevum* 64 (1995), 100–106 and F.D. Matthew, 'The Trial of Richard Wyche', *EHR* 5 (1890), 530–44 and here no. XIV; for the last my edition *Two Wycliffite Texts*, EETS 301 (1993), pp. xxix–xxx.

The extent of the dissemination of Wyclif's texts in Hussite Bohemia is an issue that cannot here be considered further. The hazards through which the surviving copies have passed suggests that, as in England, much is likely to have been lost. Any attempt to assess how much would need to consider the evidence of quotation from Wyclif in Bohemian sources. A quick search through volumes of Hus's works published since the beginning of the twentieth century reveals a wide range of quotation there from most of the major works and many shorter ones.[199] Disciples of Hus such as Jacobellus of Stříbro,[200] and opponents such as Stephen Páleč likewise quote from the texts.[201] Some of these quotations may have derived from the handbooks, the *Floretum* and *Rosarium*, but by no means all – many of the texts used were not excerpted for those collections. Much investigation remains to be done, both in the period when the Hussite movement was being established, and also in the later period up to the time of the Thirty Years War.[202]

3. Conclusions

In view of the incompleteness of the enquiry, especially in the Bohemian area, few general conclusions can be drawn. It seems fair to say, however, that both in England and in Bohemia attempts to eliminate knowledge of Wyclif's texts by the orthodox ecclesiastical authorities were of very limited effect: in both areas access to his writings seems to have been widely possible throughout the fifteenth century. Yet in neither area did any text find its way into print. The only printed editions of a work by Wyclif until the middle of the nineteenth century were two prints of the *Trialogus* (T47, without its Supplement T48)

---

[199] See above no. I 14 n. The extent of Hus's debt to Wyclif is, of course, an extremely contentious question on which widely divergent views have been advanced; the interpretation of the range and frequency of Hus's quotations is not relevant to the subject here. A useful list of passages from Wyclif in Hus's *De ecclesia* is in A. Patschovsky, 'Ekklesiologie bei Johannes Hus' in *Lebenslehren und Weltenwürfe im Übergang vom Mittelalter zur Neuzeit*, ed. H. Boockmann, B. Moeller and K. Stackmann (Göttingen, 1989), pp. 370–99 at pp. 375–6.

[200] See, for instance, P. de Vooght, *Jacobellus of Stříbro* (Bibliothèque de la Revue d'histoire ecclésiastique 54, Louvain, 1972), especially pp. 108–14, 319–29.

[201] See the material in his *Tractetus de ecclesia*, parts of which are printed in J. Sedlak, *M. Jan Hus* (Prague, 1915), ii.*202–304.

[202] Some relevant material is in V. Mudroch, 'John Wyclif's *Postilla* in Fifteenth-Century Bohemia', *Canadian Journal of Theology* 10 (1964), 118–23, the same author's *The Wyclyf Tradition* (Athens, Ohio, 1979), and Z.V. David, *Finding the Middle Way: the Utraquists' Liberal Challenge to Rome and Luther* (Washington, 2003).

put out in Germany, the first in 1525 and the second in 1753.²⁰³ Rather than advancing the circulation of these texts, print may actually have hindered it — for it seems that the pressure on library space, at least in England in the early sixteenth century, caused the removal of older, handwritten books. The fate of Wyclif's works was no different from that of many medieval writers whose texts had never been suspected of heresy: they were removed to make room for newer, more accessible printed volumes. In England the shift from Latin to English as the medium of academic, even theological, discourse, hastened the process. Paradoxically, just when religious opinion was moving nearer towards the ideas put out by Wyclif, when he was coming to be seen as 'the morning star of the Reformation', his writings became much less easy to find. The dissolution of the religious houses, a dissolution for which Wyclif himself had argued, released a flood of books whose value, academic, financial or historical, was only too slowly apprehended. Ironically Archbishop Arundel's anathema on all writings by Wyclif turned back on the institutions which, against that anathema, had preserved them. In Bohemia the effects of the Reformation were more complicated and less rapid in their resolution, not least because developments there were tied to events in the emerging political patterns in the Austrian and German areas. One minor episode in those events, the attempts of von Niedbruck and Flacius Illyricus to influence the archduke Maximilian and the unexpectedly sudden death of the former, had a disproportionate effect on the survival and distribution of Wyclif manuscripts: ensuring that some highly important ones escaped destruction, but taking them outside their historic territory.

In both England and Bohemia, political and ecclesiastical events far beyond the purview of their author and his immediate disciples or opponents took a major role in shaping our view of Wyclif and his writings. But equally the role of sheer chance should not be underestimated. Before it is concluded that the absence from England of any complete copy of the *Trialogus* (T47), the *De eucharistia* (T38) and six books of the *Summa theologie* (T28–30, 32, 33 and 34) shows the success of archbishop Arundel and other orthodox opponents, it should be recalled that the survey above has detailed the existence of three, perhaps four, copies of *De civili dominio* (T28–30) in the fifteenth century. Though that work had been at the root of the first condemnation of Wyclif by pope Gregory XI in 1377, it apparently remained in circulation as late as the

---

[203] The first printed probably at Mainz or Worms, the second under the care of L.P. Wirth of Frankfurt and Leipzig. The Wycliffite *Opus arduum*, a commentary on the Apocalypse written in prison by an English disciple between Christmas 1389 and Easter 1390, was also put into print in abbreviated form, probably at Wittenberg, in 1528 with a preface thought to be by Luther (who seems to have been unaware of the English origin of the text); see my paper *LB* 43–65.

1450s when Oriel College purchased a copy to be bound and chained in the library. All of those copies are now lost, and chance seems to have had a large hand in such a situation. Looking at the surviving manuscripts from another perspective, it is striking what a large proportion of the English copies can be traced at some stage before they reached their present home: few can be located throughout their history, but about two thirds are identifiable at some stage in their transmission. But again is this significant? One major exception is arguably in its coverage, if not in the quality of its texts, the most important English manuscript, now Trinity College Cambridge B.16.2: it, like the present Trinity College Dublin 242 and 243, contains only Wyclif items, but nothing is known of the origins or medieval provenance of any of them.

Wyclif's own history must be regarded as exceptional; even more exceptional is the history of his ideas and their impact during and after their originator's lifetime. The studies here have not for the most part been concerned with those ideas, but rather with their transmission. Here the amount of evidence available is extraordinarily large, allowing us to trace the modifications made from early drafts to revised and 'published' texts, to see the efforts through analyses and indexes to make their long and complicated arguments accessible to the scholar and the preacher, and in the Hussite catalogue to authenticate their status. New editions of the texts, new electronic methods of scrutinizing them, even the discovery of further copies (including the identification in secondary sources of lost manuscripts) will certainly further enlarge our understanding of Wyclif's legacy; but even in its current state the picture is one of remarkable and fascinating detail.

APPENDIX I: ADDITIONAL NOTES

Since the publication of papers here reproduced, a number of works have appeared which would have been mentioned in my work, had they existed when the material was written. The following list is not exhaustive, but includes those which are relevant to several of the papers here.

K. Ghosh, *The Wycliffite Heresy: Authority and the Interpretation of Texts* (Cambridge, 2002).
S. Lahey, *Philosophy and Politics in the Thought of John Wyclif* (Cambridge, 2003).
I.C. Levy, *John Wyclif: Scriptural Logic, Real Presence, and the Parameters of Orthodoxy* (Marquette, 2003).
ed. I.C. Levy, *A Companion to John Wyclif, late medieval theologian* (Leiden, 2006).
O. Marin, *L'archevêque, le maître et le dévot: Genèses du mouvement réformateur pragois, Années 1360-1419* (Paris, 2005).
F. Šmahel, *Die Prager Universität im Mittelalter: Gesammelte Aufsätze* (Leiden, 2007): an extensive collection of papers in German and English, many of which were originally published in Czech.
M. Wilks, *Wyclif, Political Ideas and Practice,* with introduction by A. Hudson (Oxford, 2000): twelve papers, including one previously unpublished.
Oxford Dictionary of National Biography (Oxford, 2004): a considerable number of entries concern relevant people, most notably that on John Wyclif (by Anthony Kenny and myself).

New editions of the following chronicles used in several of the papers here are:
Knighton's Chronicle, 1337–1396, ed. G.H. Martin (Oxford, 1995).
The Chronicle of Adam Usk, 1377–1421, ed. C. Given-Wilson (Oxford, 1997).
The St Albans Chronicle: Volume I 1376–1394, eds J. Taylor, W.R. Childs and L. Watkiss (Oxford, 2003).
No adjustment has been made in references that were written before these appeared, but they are obviously used in the new material here.

Cross references in the footnotes to forthcoming papers are not usually annotated here unless the reference is not transparent or the relevant papers are not included in the present volume.

II. From Oxford to Prague: the writings of John Wyclif and his English followers in Bohemia (1997)

Further details about possible means of transmission appear here no. XIV.
p. 644: for more details about Biceps see W. Zega, *Filozofia Boga w 'Questiones Sententiarum' Mikolaja Bicepsa* (Warsaw and Bydgoszcz, 2002).
p. 645 n. 12: see M. Harvey, 'Adam Easton and the Condemnation of John Wyclif, 1377', *EHR* 113 (1998), 321–34.
p. 647 n. 21: F. Šmahel contributed a new biography of Payne to *ODNB* (2004).
p. 654: on the *Opus arduum* see further C.V. Bostick, *The Antichrist and the Lollards: Apocalypticism in Late Medieval and Reformation England* (Leiden, 1998).
p. 655: for more on the poem *Heu quanta desolacio* see my paper 'Peter Pateshull: One-Time Friar and Poet?', in *Interstices: Studies in Middle English and Anglo-Latin Texts in Honour of A.G. Rigg*, eds R.F. Green and L.R. Mooney (Toronto, 2004), pp. 167–83.

III. The Hussite catalogue of Wyclif's works

This is a completely revised, and much expanded, version of a paper first published (without the edition of the Catalogue) as 'The Hussite Catalogues of Wyclif's Works' in *Husitství – Reformace – Renesance: Sborník k 60. narozeninám Františka Šmahela* i, eds J. Pánek, M. Polívka, N. Rejchrtová (Prague, 1994), pp. 401–17. The use of the plural 'Catalogues' there, and elsewhere in my references, was an error of judgment: all four copies of the material represent the same text, and the singular should have been used.

IV. Cross-referencing in Wyclif's Latin works (1999)

p. 196 n. 7: see here no. VII.
p. 197: see here no. VI.
pp. 206–8: for further consideration of the position of *De officio regis* within the *Summa theologie* see here nos. V and X.

V. The development of Wyclif's *Summa theologie* (2003)

p. 65: in addition to no. XI here, see also my paper 'Piers Plowman and the Peasants' Revolt: a Problem Revisited', *Yearbook of Langland Studies* 8 (1994), 85–106.

p. 66: for Biceps, see further in the study referenced above no. II p. 644.

VI. Wyclif's Latin sermons: questions of form, date and audience (2001)

p. 238: for further material on the *Postilla in totam Bibliam* see P. Gradon, 'Wyclif's *Postilla* and his Sermons', in *TCWB* pp. 67–77.

The Appendix to this paper, concerning the *Sermones quadraginta* (not discussed in paper VI), derives from my article 'Aspects of the "Publication" of Wyclif's Latin Sermons', in *Late-Medieval Religious Texts and their Transmission: Essays in Honour of A.I. Doyle*, ed. A.J. Minnis (Cambridge, 1994), pp. 121–9.

VII. *Accessus ad auctorem*: the case of John Wyclif (1999)

p. 324 n. 3: see above no. III for an expanded revision of the paper mentioned.

p. 340: for a comparable effort of organization see *Henry of Kirkestede 'Catalogus de libris autenticis et apocrifis'*, eds R.H. and M.A. Rouse (*CBMLC* 11, 2004).

IX. Wyclif and the north: the evidence from Durham (1999)

To the copies of Wyclif's works from Durham mentioned here should be added the copy of his so-called *Complaint* (T403) in the Durham section of BL Cotton Vitellius E.xii, ff. 79r–81r, discovered by James Carley (see his paper in *TCWB* p. 185 n. 88); I am much indebted to him for his information and discussion.

p. 87: for more details of Wyclif's birth and family connections see *ODNB* Wyclif.

p. 97: a biography of Uthred (under Boldon, Uthred) by Jeremy Catto appears in *ODNB*.

X. *Peculiaris regis clericus*: Wyclif and the issue of authority (1999)

p. 63 n. 2: a fuller biography of Sir John Oldcastle is available in *The House of Commons 1386–1421*, vol. iii, eds J.S. Roskell, L. Clark and C. Rawcliffe

(Stroud, 1993), 866–9 by Charles Kightly, and by J.A.F. Thomson in *ODNB*.

p. 68 n. 16: the Lichfield material has now been printed as *Lollards of Coventry, 1486–1522*, eds S. McSheffrey and N. Tanner (Camden Fifth Series vol. 23, 2003).

XI. *Poor preachers, poor men*: views of poverty in Wyclif and his followers (1998)

Fourteenth-century views of poverty are further examined by H. Barr, *Socioliterary Practice in Late Medieval England* (Oxford, 2001), pp. 128–57, and by D. Aers, *Sanctifying Signs: Making Christian Tradition in Late Medieval England* (Notre Dame, 2004), pp. 99–178.

p. 45 n. 19: for Harvey's paper see above no. II p. 645.

XII. The king and erring clergy: a Wycliffite contribution (1991)

p. 270 n. 6: see further Bostick, above no. II p. 654.

XIII. Notes of an early fifteenth-century research assistant, and the emergence of the 267 articles against Wyclif (2003)

p. 696 and n. 66: the inclusion of *De logica* 3 here is erroneous and should be deleted: no complete copy survives in England, but there are two copies in the hands of English scribes, one now in Italy, the other in Spain (see T3), and there are two Hussite copies. Several of the other texts used by the committee, T44, 48, 384, 426 are only extant now in Hussite copies.

XIV. Which Wyche? The framing of the Lollard heretic and/or saint (2003)

p. 231 n. 43: further scrutiny of the text and of the list of contents in PUK III.G.11 convinces me there is no justification for any association in the manuscript of Wyche with the *Questio ad fratres de sacramento altaris*.

APPENDIX II: SUPPLEMENT TO MANUSCRIPT LISTINGS

Supplement to the manuscript listings in Williel R. Thomson, *The Latin Writings of John Wyclyf: An Annotated Catalog* (Toronto, Pontifical Institute of Mediaeval Studies, Subsidia Mediaevalia 14, 1983).

The following list of additions and corrections to Thomson's catalogue deals only with the details of medieval manuscripts and modern editions; it does not cover Thomson's commentary on the texts, his dating of the manuscripts, his indications of inclusion of a text in the Hussite catalogue of Wyclif's writings (for which see above no. III) or in Bale's lists. Some lost manuscripts, not mentioned for the most part by Thomson, can be traced in the previous chapters here. Corrections to the foliation of Cambridge Trinity College B.16.2 can be found in no. VIII, and are not repeated here. In the list 'correct' usually concerns the manuscript folio references, occasionally the library shelfmark, provided by Thomson. The first work listed was not known to Thomson, but, given the broad categories of his *Catalog*, belongs before his first item.

?1a *Sumula sumularum*: a brief introduction to elementary logic ascribed, with some misspelling, to Wyclif in[1]
Cambridge Mass., Harvard Houghton Lat.338, ff.1r–8v
Oxford, Bodleian Library Lat. misc. e.79, ff.43ra–45vb
Seville, Biblioteca Capitular y Colombina Cod.5–1–12, ff.52r–54v

2. *Logice continuacio*
add: fragments of a manuscript used in binding, now Oxford, Bodleian Library Lat. misc.b.27, ff.1–2.[2]
extract: Oxford, New College 289, ff.37–8, consisting of pp. 75/3–83/14.

3. *De logica tractatus tercius*
add: fragments of a manuscript used in binding, now Oxford, Bodleian Library Lat.misc.b.27, ff.3–10.

---

[1] See note at end.
[2] See my note in *BLR* 19 (2006), 244–50.

5. *De proposicionibus insolubilibus*
edited as *Summa insolubilium* by P.V. Spade and G.A. Wilson (Binghamton, Medieval and Renaissance Texts and Studies 41, 1986), who add
Prague, Metropolitan Chapter M.145 (1506), ff.59v–86v
Worcester, Cathedral Library Q.54, ff.108r–109r (fragment)
They do not mention Thomson's Vienna, ÖNB 5239, ff.146r–147v (fragment).

6a. Commentary on Aristotle's *Meteora* (lost)
Thomson p. 13 n. 1 rejected this work, a copy of which is listed in the catalogue of the Bridgettine library at Syon (for which see now Gillespie *CBMLC* 9, p. 450). But the existence of a second copy of 'Wigleff super Metheorum' in the catalogue of the library of Hedvika's College at the University of Prague (see no. I 12 above), suggests, since the two references must be independent, that the work should be accepted.

11. *De universalibus*
Now edited by I.J. Mueller, trans. A. Kenny and introduction by P.V. Spade, *John Wyclif's Tractatus de universalibus* (2 vols., Oxford, 1985).

12. *De tempore*
correct: Prague UK IV.H.9 (773), ff.95ra–113vb
X.E.11 (1912), ff.173ra–175rb (index)
The disordering in the Pavia manuscript here and in other items is the result of errors in the binding. The correct quiring appears to be: $1-3^{12}$, 4^{12} but inner 5 bifolia are now in quire 9, 5^{12} but second and third bifolia should be reversed (to 49, 51, 50, 52), 6^{12} but inner 5 bifolia are now in quire 4, 7^{12}, 8^{12} but central two bifolia should be reversed (to 90, 89, 92, 91), 9^{12} but inner 5 bifolia are now in quire 6, 10^{12}, 11^{12} lacks 11–12 cut away and probably blank. Adjusting for these displacements, the order of items is T11, 20, 12, 18, 21, 22.[3]

13. *De ente predicamentali*
Note: chapters 17–18 (157/6–178/34) are identical with chapters 9–10 of T16 *De volucione dei* (202/32–221/22). For the absence of this text from Cambridge, Trinity College B.16.2 see above no. VIII 63–4.

---

[3] According to the catalogue (L. de Marchi and G. Bertolani, *Inventario dei Manoscritti della R.Biblioteca Universitaria di Pavia* (Milan, 1894), p. 170, the binding is nineteenth century, but it is unclear whether the incorrect ordering goes back beyond that. My work on this manuscript has been from microfilm only.

16. *De volucione dei*
Note: for identity of chapters 9–10 here and chapter 17–18 in *De ente predicamentalis* see above 3.
Prague UK IX.E.6 (1762) lacks the whole of chapters 9–10 and part of chapter 13 (pp. 231/28–233/13), but it does include chapter 12 that is now missing from Cambridge, Trinity College B.16.2 (and hence from the printed edition).

18. *De ydeis*
correct: Prague UK VIII.F.1 (1555), ff.73va–87ra
              XXIII.F.58 (Lobkovice 153), ff.167r–187r
   Vienna ÖNB 4523, ff.133r–156r

19. *De potencia productive dei ad extra*
For further evidence that chapters 12–14 may have had an existence independent of this tract see above no. VIII 58–9.

20. *De materia et forma*
add: Pavia, BU 311, ff.35v–37vb, 98ra–107rb, 48ra (for the disordering see T12 above)
correct: Prague UK VIII.F.1 (1555), ff.39rb–53rb
              XXIII.F.58 (Lobkovice 153), ff.141r–166v

26. *De mandatis divinis*
add: Brno University Library Mk 38, ff.29v–166v
correct: Paris, BN f.l.15869, ff.109r–112v (to 56/5 only)
         Prague, MK A.71/1 (116), ff.109r–112v; (not A.70); text ends p. 56/5

28–30. *De civili dominio*
Listing is confusing, since it suggests wider preservation than is in fact the case.
Complete is the text in the companion volumes:
Vienna ÖNB 1340, ff.1ra–260vb: book iii only
             1341, ff.1ra–251vb: books i and ii only
Substantial parts are in:
Paris, BN f.l.15869, ff.70r–103r, 112r–120v, 120v–125r: book i (but missing 27/6–38/23 and 106/33–119/22), book ii caps.1–12 (but missing 110/21–129/1), book iii. caps.24, 27 (512/21–538/18, 626/19–647/31 disordered); the whole variably compressed.
Extracts: Durham, Dean and Chapter Registrum Papireum N, ff.109r–124v,
       book iii, caps.24, 26–7 (see above no. IX 91–3)

Florence, BLaur Plut.XIX.33 sin. ff.174r–182v, book iii.cap.27
Prague, MK D.123 (693), f.162 (notes only)
   MK O.29 (1613), ff.234v–236r (notes only)
   UK V.H.27 (1004), ff.59r–65r, book ii. cap.15
      X.E.6 (1907), f.61v, book iii. from cap.27 (extract only)
For the indexes in PUK IV.G.27, X.E.11 and ÖNB 1725 see above no. VII 333–44.

31. *De veritate sacre scripture*
add: extracts in Prague, MK D.123 (693), f.160r–181v (extracts from caps. 1–11)
Note that the details concerning the Bautzen manuscript, which Thomson could not confirm, are correct: the extract, neither attributed nor titled in any way, is a copy, verbally modified at the start, of i.350/11–353/12.

34. *De potestate pape*
correct: Prague MK C.118 (550), ff.82v–96v (copy of index)

36. *De apostasia*
For the overlap between this and T39 see below under the latter and above no. I 2–3.

37. *De blasfemia*
Note that 270/25–271/29 is quoted by Walsingham from a *cedula*, see *The St Albans Chronicle i.1376–1394*, eds J. Taylor, W.R. Childs and L. Watkiss (Oxford, 2003), 584–6; the manuscripts involved are:
   Cambridge, Corpus Christi College 195, pp. 320–21
   London, BL Royal 13 E.ix, f.291ra
   BL Harley 3634, f.186rb–va
   London, College of Arms, Arundel 7, p. 356
   (London, BL Cotton Otho C.ii – this section was burned in the Cotton fire)[4]

39. *De eucharistia minor confessio*
add: London, British Library Harley 635, ff.202v–205v
extracts in Brno UK Mk 109, f.179v: though this is an extract only from the extension (see below), its heading 'doctor ewangelicus in Confessione fidei Sepe confessus sum subdit inter cetera' makes clear that the extractor knew

---

[4] For another work of Wyclif in some copies of the same chronicle see below T399.

its relation to the complete text, the beginning of which appears, with a few omissions, f.183r–v (ending at *FZ* text p. 117/11).
Note that only one copy, Oxford, Bodley 703 (the majority of whose other contents are by Wyclif's opponent, William Woodford), is dated; consequently, the reliability of this precise dating must be regarded as questionable (see above no. I 2–3). All the copies in English libraries are of the shorter text; all the continental copies are of the longer text. The supplementary material in the latter was printed by E. Stein, 'An unpublished fragment of Wyclif's *Confessio*', *Speculum* 8 (1933), 503–10.
The shorter text consists entirely of passages also found in T36 *De apostasia*: pp. 213/2–16, 219/32–221/13, 222/40–229/37, 230/21–231/9; this is recognized by the heading in Prague UK XI.E.3, f.54v (the first copy in that manuscript) 'Exponitur ista pro confessio doctoris de sacramento Eukaristie libro de apostasia capitulo 16 circa g'. The extension in the longer version found in continental manuscripts derives largely from material found also in T209, a sermon for Corpus Christi day (*Sermones* iii.278/7–286/30).

44. *De eucharistia et penitencia*
correct: Bautzen, Stadt und Kreisbibliothek 8°7, ff.14r–20v.

45. *De vaticinacione sive de prophecia*
correct: Prague MK C.73 (504), ff.259vb–262vb
Prague UK III.F.11 (514), ff.223va–226rb
Vienna ÖNB 1337, ff.20vb–24rb

47. *Trialogus*
correct: Prague UK X.E.11 (1912) (not XI.E.3), ff.113rb–146ra, index.

48. *De dotacione ecclesie*
Note that this is described by medieval writers either under this title or, notably by Netter, as *De ecclesia et membris*; it rarely appears as *Supplementum trialogii*.
correct: Vienna, ÖNB 1338, f.82ra–99ra.

50. *De septem donis spiritus sancti*
correct: Prague UK X.E.9 (1910), ff.132r–137v

51. *[Differencia inter peccatum mortale et veniale]*
Note that this is an extract from T30 *De civili dominic* book iii, cap.24, and also that each of the three surviving manuscripts ends at a different place. The

Hussite catalogue, however, lists it (above no. III as no. 73) as a separate work with the explicit of the longest of the surviving copies.
correct: Prague MK A.71/1 (not A.70) (116), ff.275v–276v, ends *De civ.dom.*
iii.517/2.
MK C.38 (462), ff.182va–183rb, ends iii.515/40
UK V.E.17 (911), ff.180r–183v, ends iii.518/32

52. *De peccata in spiritum sanctum*
add: Basel Öffentliche Bibliothek, Universität Basel, A.x.66, f.305r.[5]

53 *De officio pastorali*
add: Brno UK Mk 38 (II.94), ff.11v–29v
Prague MK D.120 (690), ff.110r–159v
correct: Prague UK XIII.F.21 (2359) (not XII.F.21), ff.35r–61v
The source of Lechler's text was Vienna ÖNB 1337, and not the Prague copy mentioned.

54–299 *Sermones*
These are listed here by number only. Thomson's designation (which largely follows Loserth) is usually liturgically reasonable; it should, however, be noted that Loserth's base text, Cambridge Trinity College B.16.2, very rarely contains any indication of occasion. For the date of these sermons and various other details about their ordering and composition see above no. VI.
Set 1, Sunday gospels: note that extracts, sometimes abbreviated, of 92 (252/32–253/32, 254/15–255/10), 93 (259/9–32), 100 (304/18–305/8) appear in the augmented version of Jan Hus's *Leccionarium bipartitum* found in Prague UK III.B.19 (428), ff.118v, 122r–v and 164v respectively, and the first passage also in a second manuscript of the same Hus work, Prague UK III.B.3 (412), f.88r. This section of the *Leccionarium* has not been edited and more extracts may be recognized when it is printed, and it should then emerge whether these sections are present also in the other copies of Hus's work. For more on the two Prague manuscripts see below nos. 176–234.

102
correct: Vienna ÖNB 4529, ff.128r–131r

---

[5] Noted F.M. Bartoš, 'Husitika a bohemika nekolike knihoven německých a švýcarských', *Věstnik královské české společnosti nauk* 5 (1931), 55–7. I am grateful to the manuscript librarian for sending me photocopies of the Wycliffite texts in the volume. The hand is Bohemian.

124
correct: Vienna ÖNB 3928, ff.18ra–19va (there is no irregularity in the manuscript)

125
correct: Vienna ÖNB 3928, ff.19va–21rb

141
For a fuller analysis of the existence of *De sex iugis* prior to the compilation of the sermons see above, no. VI 231–3.

151
correct: Vienna ÖNB 3928, ff.73ra–75rb

152
correct: Vienna ÖNB 3928, ff.75rb–77va

153
correct: Vienna ÖNB 3928, f.77va

162
correct: Vienna ÖNB 3931, ff.105ra–107vb

176–234
In Prague UK III.B.19 (428), ff.2–250v appears a copy of the summer section of Jan Hus's *Leccionarium bipartitum*. At the start of most sermons is added a copy of Wyclif's epistle sermon for the same occasion, used as a protheme; most of these copies are verbally identical, as indicated below, though the polemical section may be curtailed. The editor of the winter section of Hus's work, Professor Anežka Vidmanová-Schmidtová, kindly tells me that this arrangement is peculiar to the single manuscript, though, to judge by the printed *Pars Hiemalis* (Prague, 1988), there may be some further brief quotations in others. The material is listed here by sermon number, followed by folio references in this manuscript; the coverage in Loserth's edition is given in brackets by page/line number.

185: ff.249r–250v (69/31–75/21); 200: ff.2v–4v (complete); 201 ff.8r–10v (complete); 202: ff.17v–20r (complete); 203: ff.23r–28v (complete); 204: ff.32v–34r (224/26–230/20); 205: ff.38v–42v (complete); 206: ff.48v–49v (248/26–251/30); 207: ff.57r–59r (257/22–261/15); 208: ff.66r–68r (267/8–273/13); 209: ff.76v–79v (complete); 210: ff.81v–85v (complete);

APPENDIX II

211: ff.91r–93v (297/11–303/15); 212: ff.97r–98v (306/2–310/3); 213: ff.102v–104r (315/4–318/25); 214: ff.107v–110r (complete); 215: ff.115r–118r (complete); 216: ff.120v–121v (341/2–344/22); 217: ff.124v–125v (352/11–355/31); 218: ff.128v–130r (365/16–369/36); 219: ff.134v–137r (complete); 220: ff.140v–144r (complete); 221: ff.147v–150r (complete); 222: ff.154v–156r (402/3–407/15); 223: ff.160r–163r (complete); 224: ff.168v–171v (complete); 225: ff.175v–178r (429/35–434/15); 226: ff.181r–184v (complete); 227: ff.188v–190r (447/14–451/20); 228: ff.194r–197r (complete); 229: ff.200r–203r (complete); 230: ff.208r–211r (473/19–481/32); 231: ff.215v–216v (483/2–487/14); 232: ff.221v–225v (complete); 233: ff.230r–231r (502/2–503/35); 234: ff.233v–237r (511/2–518/2); also 235: ff.245r–246v (1/3–6/24); 236: ff.247v–249r (11/30–16/33)

201
correct: Herrnhut, ff.41r–42v (199/25–202/3, 204/15–205/40)

202
correct: Herrnhut ff.48r–51v (complete)
        Olomouc ff.202v–204r
        Vienna 1387 ff.110va–111va
For the status of *De incarcerandis fidelibus* see above no. VI 232–3.

203
correct: Herrnhut ff.55r–56v (213/5–215/17)

204
add: Naples, Biblioteca Nazionale, VII D.9, ff.156v–162r (text of *De religione privata II*)[6]
For the status of *De religione privata II*, see above, no. VI 232–3.

205, 206
remove: the extracts from these listed by Thomson in Oxford, Bodleian Library e Mus.86, ff.53v–54r (on the medieval numbering by the scribe) derive from the list of conclusions compiled in 1411 in response to archbishop Arundel's requirements of Oxford University; since quotations from other works found in that list (for which see above no. XIII) are not included in the *Catalog* it seems illogical to include these two sets.

---

[6] See above no. VI 232 n. 40 for this manuscript.

APPENDIX II

208
correct: Herrnhut, ff.145r–147r (267/ 8–271/23)

209
For the overlap between this and the continental version of T39 see above no. I 2–3.

217
correct: Wo 565, ff.233va–238rb

218
correct: Wo 565, ff.238va–241vb

232
add: PUK III.B.3 (412), ff. 197r–199r (491/28–496/7)[7]

235–236
Note: for the original position of these two sermons see above, no. VI 247.

235
add: PUK III.B.19 (428), ff.245r–246v (1/2–6/24)[8]
correct: TCD 242, pp. 404a–408a

236
add: PUK III.B.19 (428), ff.247v–249r (11/29–16/33)

237–256
Note: these sermons form the group recognized in the Hussite catalogue as *Sermones viginti*, written by Wyclif 'in fine vite sue'. See above nos. III and VI 239–43.

252
add: Vienna ÖNB 3927, ff. 120va–122ra

---

[7] This is another copy of the summer section of Hus's *Lecciorarium bipartitum*: it certainly does not contain most of the Wyclif material found in PUK III.B.19, but does include this substantial part of T232. Prof.V.dmanová's stemma in her paper 'K textové tradici letní části Husova *Leccionaria bipartita*', *Listy filologické* 109 (1986), 147–55 at p. 153 shows these two manuscripts as related, and considerably distant from all other copies.

[8] For the manuscript see above under 176–234.

257–296

Note: these sermons form the group *Sermones quadraginta*, dating from a relatively early date in Wyclif's career; for the editorial rearrangement they have undergone see above no. VI Appendix. Siegfried Wenzel identified a further manuscript of the set in Cambridge, Pembroke College 199, ff.142ra–221vb, see his 'A New Version of Wyclif's *Sermones quadraginta*', *JTS* ns 49 (1998), 155–61; the following list gives Thomson's numbers followed by folio references in this copy:
257: ff.142ra–144rb; 258: ff.144va–146rb; 259: ff.146rb–149ra; 260: ff.149ra–151vb; 261: ff.151vb–153va; 262: ff.153va–155rb; 263: ff.155rb–158ra; 264: ff.158ra–159vb; 265: ff.159vb–162ra (ends incomplete p. 271/3); 267: f.163vb (begins incomplete p. 290/13); 268: ff.163vb–165rb; 269: ff.165rb–167va; 270: ff.167va–168va; 271: ff.168vb–170ra; 272: ff.170ra–172ra; 273: ff.172ra–173vb; 274: ff.174ra–176va; 275: ff.176va–177vb; 276: ff.178ra–181ra; 277: ff.181ra–182rb; 278: ff.182rb–183vb; 279: ff.183vb–185rb; 280: ff.185rb–187vb; 281: ff.187vb–190ra; 282: ff.190ra–191rb; 283: ff.191va–192va; 284: ff.192va–193vb; 285: ff.193vb–195ra; 286: ff.195ra–196rb; 287: ff.196rb–200rb; 288: ff.200rb–201ra; 289: ff.201rb–203vb; 290: ff.203vb–206va; 291: ff.206va–208vb; 292: ff.208vb–211vb; 293: ff.211vb–213rb (p.464/2–466/21 are displaced to after p. 469/2); 294: ff.213rb–216va; 295: ff.216va–218va; 296: ff.218va–221vb.

260 and 261
add: extracts in Manchester, John Rylands Library Eng.86, f.117r (200/27–201/5 and 233/10–26).[9]

269 and 275:
add extracts in Oxford, Exeter College 6, ff.267r (299/24–300/13) and 266r (341/29–342/36) respectively.[10]

297:
add: Prague UK III.B.19 (428), ff.237v–239r (492/32–497/31)

299
Note: this is a sermon for a Graduation, and is described in the Hussite catalogue item 33 'Recommendacio assumencium gradus' (see above no. III).

---

[9] Classified as a separate text by Thomson as 391, and printed 'An unknown letter by John Wyclyf...', *Medieval Studies* 43 (1981), 531–6.

[10] See J.H.A. van Banning, 'Two uncontroversial fragments of Wyclif in an Oxford manuscript', *JTS* ns 36 (1985), 338–49.

APPENDIX II

300 *De demonio meridiano*
A medieval list of contents at the front of PUK V.F.9 (931) indicates the volume once contained this text (after existing f.75v), but it is no longer present.

301–371 [*Postilla super totam Bibliam*]
correct: Prague, National Museum XIII.F.9 (not XXX.F.9).

322
correct: OSJ, ff.109v–312v

323
sequence should be corrected: OSJ, f.313r,
OSJ, ff.313r–324r
OSJ, ff.324v–327v
OSJ, ff.327v–363r

324
sequence should be corrected: OSJ, ff.363v–364r
OSJ, ff.364r–374v

331
second set correction: OMC 117, ff.132ra–184rb

348
sequence should be corrected: OBod, f.51ra–va
OBod, ff.51va–69va

349
correct: PNM, ff.2r–25r

350
correct: OBod, ff.83vb–94va
PNM, ff.25r–50v

351
correct: OBod, f.94va–101va
PNM, ff.50v–67r

352–370
The sequence of folio references to PNM needs substantial correction. The following list gives Thomson's numbers followed by the folios in this manuscript:
352: f.67r–v; ff.67v–76r; 353: f.76r–v; ff.76v–84r; 354: f.84r; ff.84r–89r; 355: ff.89r–93v; 356: ff.93v–99r; 357: ff.99r–101v; 358: ff.102r–109r; 359: ff.109v–113v; 360: ff.113v–116r; 361: 116v–117r; 362: f.117r–v; ff.117v–132r; 363: ff.132r–133v; ff.133v–157r; 364: f.157r; ff.157r–162v; 365: f.162v–168r; 366: ff.168v–172v; 367: ff.172v–173r; ff.173r–178r; 368: ff.178r–179r; 369: f.179r–v; 370: ff.179v–180v.

372 *Exposicio textus Matthei xxiii*
correct: Vienna ÖNB 3930, ff.128rb–141rb

374 *Opus evangelicum*
add: extract in Prague, MK C.38 (462), ff.175ra–182rb (i.caps.52–58).

385 *Responsio ad decem questiones*
correct: Vienna, ÖNB 3929, ff.274va–276ra
Note: the colophon at the end of all three surviving manuscripts (all Bohemian) indicates that the text was found 'inter cartas magistri Roberti Stonam, qui mortuus est in Pisis in concilio 1409'; for Stonham see Emden, *Oxford* iii.1789–90.

390 *De octo questionibus pulchris*
delete: Prague, MK D.123 (693)
correct: Vienna, ÖNB 1387, ff.106rb–107ra

391: delete this item which consists of two extracts from the *Sermones quadraginta* with a linking sentence between; see above under 260 and 261.

393 *De amore*
add: Basel Öffentliche Bibliothek, Universität Basel, A.x.66, f.304r–v

395 *Epistola missa archiepiscopo Cantuariensi*
add: Basel Öffentliche Bibliothek, Universität Basel, A.x.66, ff.376v–377r

398 [*Responsio*] *ad quesita regis et concilii*
correct: Prague, UK III.B.5 (414), ff.3rb–5rb

399 *Protestacio*
This text appears in the longer version of *The St Albans Chronicle* i 1376–1394, eds J. Taylor, W.R. Childs and L. Watkiss (Oxford, 2003), pp. 198–210; the manuscripts in question are: London, BL Royal 13 E.ix, ff.250va–251vb
    London, BL Harley 3634, ff.153va–154vb
    London, BL Cotton Otho C.ii, ff.120v–122r
    London, College of Arms Arundel 7, pp. 222–6
    Cambridge, Corpus Christi College 195, pp. 228–32

401 *De condemnacione xix conclusionum*
add: Vienna, ÖNB 3930, ff.125ra–127vb

402 *De paupertate Christi*
add: Padua, Antoniana MS 226, f.260r–v, ending incomplete in mid folio at 22/27 (the middle of conclusion 5)[11]
    Prague, MK D.105 (674), ff.201r–219v (lacks 68/3–70/29 because of loss of leaf)
correct: Prague, MK B.17/1 (310), ff.184v–201r

403 [*Peticio ad regem et parliamentum*]
add: London, BL Cotton Vitellius E.xii, ff.79r–81r (using the modern pencil numbering of the remounted leaves)[12]

406 *De officio regis conclusio*
add: Basel Öffentliche Bibliothek, Universität Basel, A.X.66, f.305r

408 *Dyalogus*
correct: Munich, BSB clm 15771, ff.35r–50r
    Vienna, ÖNB 3932, f.72vb–89vb

409 *Speculum secularium dominorum*
correct: Vienna, ÖNB 4522, ff.133r–139r

410 *De scismate*
delete Thomson's note 1: there are no chapters in the text, nor are any specified in the Hussite catalogue (item 68). Note that Prague UK X.E.9, ÖNB 1337 and

---

[11] Noted by F. Stegmüller, *Repertorium Biblicum medii aevi* 9 (Madrid, 1977), no.5083 in his listing of Wyclif's relevant works. I am grateful to the librarian for photographs.

[12] Identified by Prof. James Carley.

4527 have the colophon 'Explicit epistola missa ad episcopum Nortwicensem propter cruciatam' (ie to bishop Despenser about the 1383 crusade).

416 *Epistola missa ad simplices sacerdotes*
correct: Basel Öffentliche Bibliothek, Universität Basel, A.X.66, ff.304v–305r

417 *Quattuor imprecaciones*
add: Prague, MK C.118 (550), f.16r

419 *De mendaciis fratrum*
add: Wisbech Town Museum 8, f.34r[13]
delete: Prague UK X.C.23 (1876)

422 *De novis ordinibus*
correct: Munich, BSB clm 15771, ff.29r–31v

427 *De triplici vinculo amoris*
correct: Munich, BSB clm 15771, ff.19r–26v
A medieval list of contents in PUK V.F.9 (931) indicates that the volume once contained this text (after T300 itself list after existing f.75v), but it is no longer present.

429 *De quattuor sectis novellis*
add: Brno, University Library Mk 38, ff.1r–11r

433 *Descripcio fratris*
add: Vienna, ÖNB 4527, f.19v[14]
    Wisbech, Town Museum 8, f.34r

434 *De religionibus vanis monachorum*
add: Vienna, ÖNB 4308, ff.124r–125r
Note: there is an Occitan version of this text in Cambridge, University Library Dd.15.29, ff.177r–179v.[15]

---

[13] The manuscript contains also T433 below, incorporated into a copy of the English Wycliffite sermons (see *EWS* i.92–4).

[14] Written at the foot of the leaf, but in the main hand of the text.

[15] For this manuscript see A. Brenon, 'The Waldensian Books' in *Heresy and Literacy, 1000–1530*, eds P. Biller and A. Hudson (Cambridge, 1994), pp.137–59.

GDub.2 [*Tractatus*] *de probacionibus proposicionum*
Note: this should be deleted: Simon of Tišnov's *protestacio* gives the incipit of the text he was defending, from which it is clear that the text was Thomson's 2 *Logice continuacio*.[16]

GDub.8 *Epistola pulcra m.jo.anglici*
Add: London, BL Cotton Faustina C.vii, ff.138v–139v, printed by H.E. Salter, *Snappe's Formulary and other Records* (Oxford Historical Society 80, 1924), pp. 130–32.

GDub.10–11 *Epistola ad ducem Lancastriensem* and *De peregrinacione*
See now Gillespie *CBMLC* 9, pp. 467 (number K.34) and 78–9 respectively.

GDub.16
See edition above no. XII.

GDub.18
add: Vienna ÖNB 5204, f.66r–v

GSpur.2 *De ymaginibus*
correct: Brno Mk 102 (II.123), ff.169v–181v.
The text was edited J. Nechutová under the title 'Nicolai de Dresda "De imaginibus"', *Sborník prací filosofické fakulty brněnské university*, series E.15 (1970), 211–40.

GSpur.5 *Commentarius in Apocalypsim* (*Opus arduum*)
add: Brno, University Library Mk 28 (II.206), ff.126r–216r
For discussion of the authorship see *LB* pp. 56–62, and for the text generally C.V. Bostick, *The Antichrist and the Lollards: Apocalypticism in Late Medieval and Reformation England* (Leiden, 1998), esp. pp. 76–113.

GSpur 12, 13, 14: Thomson p. 310 states that these are ascribed to Wyclif in the Hussite catalogue: this is not the case.

GSpur.14
add: Vienna, ÖNB 3929, f.250ra–261rb where it is headed 'Posicio discipuli M.Johannis'.

---

[16] See J. Loserth, trans. M.J. Evans, *Wiclif and Hus* (London, 1884), p. 312.

Note: Brno Mk 109 (II.28) contains a collection of extracts, made in the second half of the fifteenth century, including some very brief quotations from Wyclif: some of these, but not all, are mentioned in the catalogue entry;[17] they are not detailed here. ÖNB 4308, ff.113v–121r, has extracts, some of them ascribed, from Wyclif's sermons, polemical works short and long and even from *De universalibus* (T11); again they are not detailed here. There are many other similar collections of Bohemian origin, often involving many scribes and sometimes involving diverse booklets bound together: short unattributed texts of Wyclif and extracts from his works may still be found when these are fully analysed.

Appended note on item 1a
All three of these manuscripts contain material that they describe as *Sumula sumularum*; in the Harvard copy this is ascribed at the start to *Iohannis Wiclif*, in the Seville copy at the end of the section to *Iohannis Eclif*,[18] in the Oxford copy again at the end of the section to *Iohannis ecaf* (or possibly *eclif*). All three manuscripts are Italian in origin. The entire contents of the Seville and Oxford manuscripts are identical; the material involves the complex *Logica Oxoniensis*,[19] and the equally complex *Sophismata asinina* ascribed to William Heytesbury.[20] The Harvard quire ends incomplete. Its relationship to the other two manuscripts is not clear, but it certainly contains other matter beyond their material, including some passages that overlap with *De logica* i.[21]

---

[17] V. Dokoupil, *Soupis Rukopisů Mikulovské Dietrichsteinské Knihovny* (Prague, 1958) pp. 202–9.

[18] The manuscript is described J.F.S. Guillén, *Catálogo de Manuscritos de la Biblioteca Colombina de Sevilla* (Seville, 2002), pp. 41–2.

[19] See L.M.de Rijk, '*Logica Oxoniensis*: An Attempt to reconstruct a Fifteenth Century Oxford Manual of Logic', *Medioevo* 3 (1977), 121–64; de Rijk mentions the Oxford manuscript, but not either of the other two.

[20] See the edition and study by F. Pironet (Paris, 1994).

[21] As described in the seminar paper 'A New Work by John Wyclif?', in *The Marks in the Fields*, eds R.G. Dennis and E. Falsey (Cambridge Mass., 1992), pp. 30–37; I am grateful to Dr William Stoneman for drawing my attention to this paper.

INDEX OF WYCLIF'S WRITINGS DISCUSSED

Note: titles given are normally those used by Thomson, sometimes in slightly abbreviated form, but adjusted to the usage of the present book; Thomson's numbering is given in brackets following the title. References to Appendix II (excluding corrections that only involve folio numbering) are in the form 'App. followed by the item number of the work there'; references to the Hussite catalogue edited in III are given after the others (if any) in the form 'Cat. followed by the number under which the work is there entered'. Incidental references are not here cited; for details of manuscripts see Appendix II and the index of manuscripts.

Ad argumenta Wilelmi Vyrinham determinaciones (T382–3): XVI 12, 14, 24, 27; Cat. 78, 48
Ad xiv argumenta Strode (cf T385–7): XVI 24

Contra versucias pseudoclerum (*De versuciis antichristi* T420): XIII 688, 697; Cat. 69

De actibus anime (T4): III 8; V 70; XVI 26n, 29
De amore (T393): VII 338; XVI 21n; Cat. 65
De apostasia (T36): I 2–3; II 646; III 31; IV 197, VI 233–4; VII 331, 333, 338; XVI 6–7, 14, 16, 17, 40; Cat. 114
De benedicta incarnacione (De verbi incarnacione) (T22): I 8–9; IV 196, 198, 200, 212; VII 325–6, 331, 338; XVI 5, 10, 17, 26n, 29; Cat. 60
De blasfemia (T37): III 2–3; IV 197; V 65; VI 238; VII 331, 333–4, 340; X 76; XI 44–7; XVI 8, 11–12, 17, 40; App. 37; Cat. 115
De Christo et suo adversario Antichristo (T412): XVI 18n; Cat. 76
De citacionibus frivolis (T413): XVI 20n, 37n; Cat. 81
De civili dominio (T28–30): I 13; II 644, 648; III 30; IV 193, 197–203, 213–14; V 58, 60–61, 65–8; VI 236; VII 325, 331, 334, 337–8; IX 91–3; X 70; XI 45, 47–9; XII 273; XIII 689; XVI 5, 7–11, 18, 36n; App. 28–30, 51; Cat. 106–8
De clavibus ecclesie (T407): XVI 18n, 20n, 24, 40
De composicione hominis (T2): XVI 8, 17, 20; Cat. 86
De concordacione fratrum (T432): VII 338; Cat. 17
De condemnacione xix conclusionum (T401): V 69; XVI 12, 27; Cat. 21
De confessione (T44): XIII 688; XVI 18; Cat. 27
De contrarietate duorum dominorum (T423): XVI 18n, 21n; Cat. 80
De cruciata (T411): XVI 20; Cat. 13
De demonio meridiano (T300): App. 300; Cat. 22, 39
De diabolo et membris eius (T430): XIII 689 XVI 18n, 21n, 27; Cat. 38
De dominio divino (T23–5): I 4, 6–7; II 641; III 3, 11, 33; IV 199, 210–11; V 59, 62–3; VII 331, 334, 338; X 70; XIV 235; XVI 18, 33; Cat. 101–3
De dotacione ecclesie (Supplementum Trialogi) (T48): II 648; III 31–2; VII 338; XIII 688; XVI 7, 16, 21, 40; Cat. 92
De duobus generibus hereticorum (T418): III 26; Cat. 32
De ecclesia (T32): I 2, 7; II 641, 648, 651–2; IV 193, 198–206, 213; V 61–2, 69; VII 325, 327, 329, 333–4, 338; XII 273; XIV 235; XVI 17, 26, 41n; Cat. 110
De ente in communi (T7): IV 212; VIII 56; XVI 29
De ente primo in communi (T8): VIII 56
De ente predicamentali (T13): VIII 63–4; App. 13

De eucharistia (T38): II 646, 648; IV 193, 198; V 59; VII 325, 329, 331, 333–4, 338–9; XVI 6, 16, 17, 42; Cat. 84

De eucharistia conclusiones (T41): XVI 23

De eucharistia et penitencia (T44): Cat. 27

De eucharistia minor confessio (T39): I 2–3; V 68; VI 233; IX 89–90; XI 43; XVI 6, 9, 12, 14, 23, 26–7, 29; App. 39; Cat. 79

De fide catholica (T49): IV 195; XVI 9, 28; Cat. 82

De fide sacramenti (T40): III 8; XVI 23

De fratribus ad scolares (T392): XVI 40

De fundacione sectarum (T431): VII 338, 340; XVI 18n, 24; Cat. 56

De gradibus cleri (T394): III 26; VII 338; XIII 689; XVI 18n, 21n, 25; Cat. ?29, 67, 91

De incarcerandis fidelibus (see T202): III 26; VI 232–3; VII 339; Cat. 23

De intelleccione dei (T14): IV 196, 210, 212; VIII 57

De iuramento Arnaldi (T397): I 2; V 69; XVI 15; Cat. 44

De libello ad argumenta Strode (T388): XIII 688; Cat. 62

De logica I–II (T1–2): I 7–8; III 32; IX 94; XIV 234; XVI 5, 10, 14, 20; App. 1–2; Cat. 98

De logica tractatus tercius (*De arte sophistica*) (T3): I 8; III 32; IV 200, 214; XIII 689; XVI 8, 18, 20, 22, 23n, 28; App. 3; Cat. 98

De mandatis (T26): III 5, 11n; IV 210; VI 233; VII 325–9, 331–2, 334, 337–8; XV 4–5, 8, 11; XVI 4, 5, 8, 9, 12–14, 25, 27, 38n; App. 26; Cat. 104

De materia et forma (T20): II 647; VII 328, 333–5; XVI 8, 10, 20, 36n; App. 20; Cat. 16

De mendaciis fratrum (T419): App. 419; Cat. 59

De nova prevaricancia mandatorum (T415): VII 338; XVI 18n, 25; Cat. 8

De novis ordinibus (T422): VII 338; Cat. 77

De octo questionibus pulcris (T390): III 24, 29; Cat. 2, 4

De officio pastorali (T53): IV 207; VII 338; XVI 18, 20, 35; Cat. 7

De officio regis (T33): II 648; III 2; IV 199, 206–8; V 60–61; VII 325, 330–31, 333–4, 338, 340; X 71–7; XI 45, 49; XVI 17; Cat. 111

De oratione (T46): XVI 18, 40; Cat. 28

De oratione dominica (T424): XVI 18n; Cat. 10

De ordine christiano (T414): VII 338; XIII 688; XVI 18n, 24; Cat. 1

De paupertate Christi (conclusiones XXXIII) (T402): I 4; III 26; VII 338; XVI 14n; Cat. 26

De peccato in spiritum sanctum (T52): App. 52; Cat. 57

De perfeccione statuum (T426): VII 338; XIII 688; XVI 18n, 29; Cat. 11

De potencia productiva dei ad extra (T19): IV 198; VIII 58–9, 61–2; App. 19

De potestate pape (T34): II 648; IV 195, 205; V 63; VII 325, 327, 332–4, 338; XVI 3–4, 17, 22n. 36n, 40; Cat. 112

De proposicionibus insolubilibus (T5): XVI 2n, 8; App. 5

De quattuor sectis novellis (T429): IV 195; XVI 18n; App. 429; Cat. 75

De religione: IV 197–8; V 61; XVI 7

De religione privata II (see T204): VII 232–3

De religionibus vanis monachorum (T434): App. 434

De salutacione angelica (T425): XVI 40; Cat. 66

De sciencia dei (T15): VIII 57–8, 61–2, 66–7

De scismate (T410): XVI 12, 15, 27, 29; App. 410; Cat. 68

De septem donis Spiritus Sancti (T50): XVI 18, 24; Cat. 18

De servitute civili (T405): XVI 20n, 21n; Cat. 12

De sex iugis (see T141–2, 145–7): VI 231–3; VII 339; Cat. 88

De solucione Sathane (T435): III 24; XVI 24; Cat. 2

De statu innocencie (T27): II 650; III 7, 9, 11; IV 198, 210; V 58; XVI 8–9, 17; Cat. 93, 105

De symonia (T35): II 648; IV 199, 213; V 63; VII 325, 329, 331, 333–5, 337–8; XIII 688–9; XVI 17, 28, 31n; Cat. 113

De tempore (T12): II 647, 650; III 28; IV 196, 212; VII 325–8, 331, 333, 338–9; VIII 57, 62–3; XVI 8, 10, 13, 17, 28; App. 12; Cat. 47

De trinitate (T17): II 648, 650; IV 212; VII 328; VIII 58, 63–6; XVI 9, 10; Cat. 83

De triplici vinculo amoris (T427): II 645; VII 338; XVI 18n; App. 427; Cat. 87

INDEX OF WYCLIF'S WRITINGS DISCUSSED

De universalibus (T11): II 647–8, 650;
    IV 195, 212; VII 325–6, 328;
    VIII 57, 62–3, 66; XVI 8, 10, 13,
    14n, 17, 20, 28, 36, 38n; App. 11;
    Cat. 46
De veritate sacre scripture (T31): II 543–4,
    652; III 9; IV 193, 197–206; V 63–5,
    69; VII 325–7, 329, 332–4, 336–8;
    XIV 235; XV 1–2, 6; XVI 4, 8–10,
    13, 17, 26–7, 28, 40; App. 31
    Cat. 109
De versuciis antichristi (T420): Cat. 69
De volucione dei (T16): VIII 58; App. 16
De ydeis (T18): II 647, 650; IV 195, 212;
    VII 328, 333; VIII 58; XVI 8, 10,
    17, 20, 36, 38n; Cat. 85
Descripcio fratris (T433): App. 433
*Determinacio ad argumenta magistri
    Outredi* (T381): IX 97–101; XVI 24;
    Cat. 36
*Determinaciones contra Kylyngham Car-
    melitam* (T378–80): I 1–2; II 649;
    XVI 6, 24, 26n, 29
Dialogus (T408): I 9–12; II 646; III 9, 24;
    IV 215; VII 328, 330, 338;
    XIII 688–9; XVI 18, 21, 25, 27;
    Cat. 5
*Differencia inter peccatum mortale et veni-
    ale* (T51): XVI 40; App. 51 Cat. 73

Epistola missa ad simplices saceractes
    (T416): III 5; XVI 21n; Cat. 90
Epistola missa archiepiscopo Cantuariensi
    (T395): VII 338; XVI 21n; Cat. 89
Epistola missa episcopo Lincolniensi
    (T396): Cat. 43
Epistola missa pape Urbano (T404):
    VII 338; XVI 21n, 23; Cat. 40
Errare in materia fidei (T43): XVI 40
Exhortatio cuiusdam doctoris (T389):
    Cat. 50
Exposicio Matthei 23 (T372): XVI 18n, 24;
    Cat. 19
Exposicio Matthei 24 (T373): XVI 24;
    Cat. 70

Libellus ad parliamentum regis (T400):
    I 3–4; V 69; XVI 12, 23, 27; Cat. 61
Litera parva ad quendam socium (T387):
    Cat. 3

Opus evangelicum (T374–7): I 4–5;
    II 648; III 7, 26, 29; IV 194;
    VII 329, 331–2, 339; VIII 61, 68;
    XIII 688–90, 694–5; XVI 8, 14, 29;

Cat. 24, 31, 52–5

Peticio ad regem et parliamentum (T403):
    III 8; XVI 5, 24
Postilla in totam Bibliam (T301–371): I 12;
    III 7, 10; VI 238; VII 330, 339;
    XV 4, 12; XVI 13, 16, 36n, 37n;
    App. 301–371; Cat. 99
Protestacio (T399): I 3–4; III 8; XVI 24;
    App. 399
*Purgans errores circa universalia in
    communi* (T10): IV 212; VIII 56
Purgans errores circa veritates in communi
    (T9): IV 196; VIII 56
Purgatorium secte Christi (T428):
    XVI 18n, 21n, 25n; Cat. 74

Quattuor imprecaciones (T417): III 5;
    App. 417; Cat. 71
Questiones ... super viii libros physicorum
    (T6): II 649; XVI 15, 29

Recommendacio assumencium gradus
    (T299): III 26–7; App. 299; Cat. 33
Responsio ad decem questiones (T385):
    I 13; III 8n; XVI 38n
Responsio ad quesita regis et concilii
    (T398): I 2; V 69; IX 96; XVI 23;
    Cat. 34
*Responsiones ad argumenta cuiusdam
    emuli veritatis* (T388): Cat. 62
*Responsiones ad argumenta Radulphi
    Strode* (T386): XIII 693; XVI 18n,
    24; Cat. 54
Responsiones ad xliv conclusiones (T384):
    VII 338; XIII 688; XVI 6, 18;
    Cat. 63

Sermones (T54–299): VI *passim*; VIII 67;
    XVI 10, 14
Sermones quadraginta (T257–96): III 10,
    27; IV 193, 215; VI 239, VI app.;
    VII 331–2; VIII 60–61; IX 90–91;
    XVI 5, 11, 25n, 29; App. 257–96;
    Cat. 41
Sermones super epistolas (T176–234):
    VI 235–8; VII 331; VIII 60, 67–8;
    XVI 16–18; App. 176–234;
    Cat. 42, 96
Sermones super evangelia de sanctis
    (T115–175): III 32; VI 234–5;
    VIII 59–60; XVI 19; Cat. 94–5
Sermones super evangelia dominicalia
    (T54–114): VI 233–4; VII 331;
    VIII 59, XVI 11–12; App. 54–114,

Cat. 25
Sermones viginti (T237–56): III 10, 30;
    VI 239–43; VIII 59–61; XVI 19;
    Cat. 72
Speculum secularium dominorum (T409):
    VII 338; XVI 21n, 27, 30n; Cat. 14
Summa de ente (T7–19): IV 212;
    VIII 56–65; XVI 36n
Summa philosophie (T7–19): III 8
Summa theologie (T26–37): III 5, 7, 11;
    V *passim*; XVI 17, 42
Sumula sumularum (T *absent*): III 7n;
    App. 1a

Trialogus (T47): II 646; III 24; IV 194;
    V 70; VII 328, 330–31, 333, 338;
    XIII 686, 688–9; XVI 7–8, 13, 16,
    21, 25, 41–2; Cat. 6

Lost works

Aristotle *De anima*, commentary on:
    XVI 8, 10
Aristotle *Meteora*, commentary on: I 12;

XVI 15, 29; App. 6a

De peregrinatione (GDub.11): XVI 15, 29;
    App. GDub.11

Epistola ad ducem Lancastriensem
    (GDub.10): XVI 16, 29

Dubious or spurious works

Cantica canticorum, commentary on
    (GSpur. 3): III 3n

De necessitate futurorum (GSpur. 1): III 10;
    XVI 11n; Cat. 45
Discipulus quidam venerabilis doctoris
    (GDub. 16): III 10, 27; XII *passim*;
    App. GDub.16; Cat. 37

[Extra information for GDub.2, 8, 18
    and for GSpur. 2, 5, 12, 13, 14 are
    found in App. II under the relevant
    number.]

INDEX OF MANUSCRIPTS

Note: References to Appendix II (excluding corrections that only involve folio numbering) are in the form 'App. followed by the item number of the work there'.

a) Manuscripts containing material by Wyclif

Assisi, Biblioteca Communale
  662: I 7n, 8n

Basel, Universitäts- und offentliche Bibliothek
  A.X.66: App. 52, 393, 395, 406
Bautzen, Stadt- und Kreisbibliothek
  Q° 24: XVI 37n
  8° 7: II 651; XVI 37n
Brno, Universitní Knihovna
  Mk 38: VII 328n, 329, 343; App. 26, 53, 429
  Mk 62: I 10n
  Mk 109: I 3n; V 69n; VI 233n; App. 39 and see endnote there

Cambridge
  Corpus Christi College, 103: XVI 6n, 24, 26n, 29
  Gonville and Caius College, 337/565: I 6n, 7n, 8n, 9n; II 650; IV 211n; V 63n; VII 326–42; VIII 70; XVI 4
  Jesus College, 59: I 3n; V 69n; IX 89; XVI 5
  Pembroke College, 199: VI 224n; App. 257–96
  Peterhouse, 223: II 652n; IV 202–3; XV 1; XVI 4, 10
  Queens' College, 15: II 652n; IV 202–3
  Trinity College, B.4.50: III 8n; XVI 24
    B.15.28: III 29; VII 327n; XVI 4, 10n
    B.16.2: I 5n; III 29, 30; IV 196, 198, 209; VI 224–48; VII 325n, 342; VIII 53–80; XVI 4, 29, 43; App. 54–299
    O.4.43: VIII 70, 74; XVI 24n
  University Library
    Dd.15.29: App. 434
    Ii.3.29: VII 327n; XVI 10n, 13
    Ll.5.13: VII 331–44; XVI 9–10
Cambridge USA, Harvard Houghton Library
  Lat.338: III 7n; App. 1a

Dublin, Trinity College
  115: IV 213 XVI 3–4
  241: I 5n; II 650
  242: III 29; V 62n; VII 327–44; VIII 68; XVI 26n, 43
  243: II 652r; IV 202–3, 211n; V 59n; VII 342; XVI 43
Durham, Chapter Muniments
  Registrum Papireum (Reg.N): IV 214; IX 91–3; XVI 5; App. 30

El Escorial
  e.II.6: I 7n, 8n; VII 325n, 342
Erfurt, SB Ampl.
  Q° 253: III 32
Eton College
  47: I 3n; V 59n; XVI 12n

Florence
  Biblioteca Medicea Laurenziana
    Plut.XIX.33: I 10n; III 8n, 9n; V 62n; IX 92–3; XVI 24n, 26n, 28n
  Biblioteca Nazionale Centrale
    Conv.Sopp. E.3.379: I 10n

Herrnhut, Archiv der Brüder-Unität
  AB.II.R.1.16a: VI 225–48; XVI 37

Krakow, Biblioteka Jagiellonska
  848: VII 342
  1855: VII 342

Lincoln, Cathedral Chapter Library

159: VII 328, 342; VIII 57, 65, 70; XVI 13, 29
London
 British Library
  Additional 5902: I 4n
  Cotton Vespasian D.xxiii: XVI 27n
  Cotton Vitellius E.xii: III 8n; IX supplementary note; XVI 5, 24n; App. 403
  Harley 635: I 3n; XVI 12n; App. 39
  Royal 7 B.iii: I 3n, 8n, V 69n; VII 342; XVI 26n, 29
  Royal 7 E.x: II 652n; IV 202–3
 Lambeth Palace Library
  23: VII 331–44; IX 90–91; XVI 5, 29
  537: XVI 27n
  1058: XVI 28

Manchester, John Rylands Library
 Eng.86: I 10–11; III 9n; IV 215n; XVI 20n, 24–6, 27n; App. 260, 261
Munich, Bayerische Staatsbibliothek
 clm 15771: I 10n

Naples, Biblioteca Nazionale
 VII.D.9: VI 232n; App. 204

Olomouc
 Kapitolní Knihovna
  C.O.115: II 652n; IV 202–3
  C.O.118: III 26; VI 232n
 Státní vědecká Knihovna
  I.V.34: I 10n
Oxford
 Bodleian Library
  Arch.Seld. B.26: I 4n; XVI 12n, 24n, 27
  Bodley 52: XVI 12, 27, 29
  Bodley 333: XVI 14, 27
  Bodley 703: I 3n; V 61n, 68n; VI 233n; IX 89n; XVI 7n, 14, 24n, 27
  Bodley 716: VIII 74; XVI 12–13
  Bodley 924: II 652n; IV 202–3; XV 2; XVI 13, 27
  e Mus. 86: V 69n; XIII 690, 693, 696–7; XIV 228–9; XVI 23–5; App. 205–6
  James 3: I 9n; XVI 27–8
  Lat.misc.b.27: I 7n; App. 2–3
  Lat.misc.e.79: III 7n; App. 1a
 Exeter College
  6: XVI 11; App. 269, 275
 Magdalen College
  lat. 98: XV 4, 8, 14; XVI 12
 New College
  289: I 8n; App. 2
 Oriel College
  15: I 8n; IV 213; VII 342; VIII 74; XVI 5
 St John's College 171: XV 4, 11, 12; XVI 16

Padua, Biblioteca Antoniana
 226: I 4n; App. 402
Paris, Bibliothèque nationale
 f.l.3184: I 4n; III 9n, 26, 28; IX 97n; XVI 24n
 f.l.15869: I 13; II 644n; IV 214; V 68n; VII 327; IX 100n; App. 26, 28–30
Pavia, Biblioteca Universitaria
 311: I 8n; VII 327n, 336n; App. 12, 20
Prague
 Knihovna Metropolitní Kapituli
  A 71/1: VII 329, 343; IX 92n; App. 26, 51
  A.84: II 652n; IV 202–3; XVI 40
  B.17/1: I 10n; III 26
  B.53: II 652n; IV 202–3; VII 342; XVI 39n
  C.38: I 5n, 10n; II 652n; III 11; IV 202–3; V 58n; VII 326n, 333n, 336n, 337, 342–4; IX 92n; XVI 40n; App. 51, 374
  C.73: III 33; VII 327n, 342, 344; XVI 39n, 40
  C.116: VI 231n
  C.118: II 652n; VII 333–44; XVI 39; App 417
  D.35: I 8n; VII 342
  D.50: III 25; XVI 39n, 40
  D.105: I 4n; XVI 39n; App. 402
  D.120: App. 53
  D.123: III 26; VI 231n, 232n; VII 332, 344; App. 28–30, 31, 390
  F.20: VII 343
  L.36: VII 342
  M.54: VII 342; XVI 39
  M.145: App. 5
  N.19: I 7n; XVI 39n
  N.48: VI 231n
  O.29: XVI 40
 Národný Museum I.E.6: XVI 37n
  III.B.11: I 11n
  XIII.F.9: XVI 37n; App. 301–371
 Národný (formerly Universitní) Knihovna
  III.B.3: App. 54–299

INDEX OF MANUSCRIPTS

III.B.5 II 652; IV 202–3; VII 342
III.B.19: VI 225–6, 229n, 232n;
   VIII 73; App. 54–114, 175–234,
   297
III.F.11: III 33; VII 327n, 342
III.F.20: VII 330, 343
III.G.10: II 647; VII 342
III.G.11: II 654, 655n; III 11, 26;
   VI 225–48; VII 343; IX 102n;
   XIV 226–37; XVI 40
III.G.16: I 13n; XVI 40
IV.A.18: I 5n; II 648; III 29; VII 332,
   343; VIII 68
IV.D.22: VII 342
IV.G.27: IV 204n; VII 333–44
IV.H.9: VII 342
V.A.3: VII 336, 344; XVI 38
V.E.14: I 8n
V.E.17: IX 92n; App. 51
V.F.9: III 10n, 25, 28; VII 343;
   XVI 39; App. 427
V.F.17: III 26; XVI 40
V.G.10: XVI 39
V.G.19: I 13n; XVI 38
V.H.16: VII 342
V.H.27: VI app. 126n
V.H.33: I 7n
VIII.C.3: II 652n; IV 202–3;
   XVI 40
VIII.F.1: VII 336n, 342, 344
VIII.F.13: I 10n; XVI 39
VIII.G.6: VII 342
VIII.G.23: VII 342
VIII.G.32: II 648; VII 336, 342, 344
IX.E.3: I 7n
IX.E.6: IV 198; VIII 57–9, 62, 66;
   App. 16
X.C.23: I 10n; VII 343; App. 419
X.D.11: II 651; IV 201, 207n;
   V 60n; VII 325, 327n, 342
X.E.9: III 27; VI 232n, 241n;
   VII 335, 342–4; X 78n,
   XII 270–78
X.E.11: II 652n; VII 331, 333–44;
   XVI 40; App. 47
X.E.24: II 655n
X.G.1: III 11; V 58n; VII 343–4
X.H.17: VII 343
XI.E.3: I 3n, 4n; II 642n; V 61n,
   69n; VI 233n; VII 342
XIII.F.21: II 655n; VII 343
XXIII.F.58: VII 342

Salamanca, Biblioteca Universitaria
   2358: XVI 2n

Seville, Biblioteca Colombina
   5–1–12: III 7r.; App. 1a
Stockholm, Kunglig Biblioteket
   Lat.A.164: II 548; VII 328n, 342–3;
   XVI 36

Vatican
   Borgh.lat.29: I 4n, 10n; III 9n, 24
   Vat.lat.4313: VII 342
Venice, Biblioteca Nazionale Marciana
   Lat.VI.172: I 651; VII 327n, 342
Vienna, Österreichische Nationalbibliothek
   1294: I 6n; II 643, 651–2; IV 201–3;
   V 63n; VII 325, 329, 342–4;
   XIV 234–6; XVI 33, 36, 39
   1337: I 10n; III 11, 25–7, 29; VI 231n,
   232n, 241n, 243n; VII 344;
   XVI 34, 36
   1338: I 10n; III 31; XVI 30n, 34, 36
   1339: I 6n; III 11; V 58n, 59n, 63n;
   VII 326n, 336n, 342, 344; XVI 34,
   36
   1340: III 33; IV 208; V 59n, 68;
   VII 336n, 342, 344; XVI 34, 36
   1341: III 33; IV 208, V 59n, 68;
   VII 336n, 337, 342, 344; VIII 74;
   IX 100n; XVI 34, 36
   1342: V 59n; VII 330, 336n, 343;
   XVI 34, 36
   1343: V 59n; VII 336n, 342, 344;
   XVI 34, 36
   1387: I 3n, 4n, 8–10nn, III 26, 31;
   V 69n; VI 232n; VII 336n, 342, 344;
   XVI 33, 34, 36
   1622: I 10n VII 342; XVI 33n
   1647: I 5n; II 648; III 29; VIII 68;
   XVI 34
   1725: II 652n; VII 333–44; XVI 30n
   3927: VI 225n, 239n; VII 329, 342–3;
   XVI 30; App. 252
   3928: III 27, 30; VI 225–48; VIII 60;
   X 79n; XII 270–78; XVI 33n
   3929: I 4n, 6n, 13n; II 651, 656n; III 25,
   27, 29, 31; IV 201; V 63n; VI 243n;
   VII 325, 342; App. G5pur 14
   3930: I 10r; III 25; VI 232n; VII 330,
   343; XVI 33n, 39; App. 401
   3931: VI 225–48; VIII 60
   3932: I 10–11; III 27; VI 231n, 239n;
   VII 330, 342–3; X 79n; XII 270–78;
   XVI 25
   3933: II 649; III *passim*; IV 207n;
   V 57n; VII 336n, 342–4; XVI 33n
   3934: VI 225–48; VIII 59–60
   3935: I 6n II 649; III *passim*; V 63n;

VII 328n, 336n, 343–4; XVI 33
3937: II 648; VII 342
4302: I 10n; XVI 34n
4307: I 8n; II 10n; III 8n; VII 325n, 342;
  VIII 56, 63, 65; XVI 33n
4308: App. 434 and see endnote there
4316: VII 342–3; VIII 72
4343: I 3n; III 26; V 69n; VI 231n;
  XVI 30n
4483: XVI 33n
4504: I 8n; VII 342; XVI 33n
4505: I 10n; III 29, 31; VII 336, 344;
  XVI 33n
4514: II 649; III *passim*; IV 207n;
  VII 336, 342, 344; XVI 33
4515: I 10n; VII 342; XVI 33n
4516: XVI 33, 39
4518: XVI 34n
4522: IV 204n; VI 231n; VII 338–9,
  344; XVI 34
4523: I 7n; III 32; VII 342
4527: III 25; VI 232n, 241n; VII 343;
  XVI 33n; App. 433
4529: VI 225–48; VIII 59–60; XVI 33
4536: I 10n; III 25; VII 335, 342–4;
  XVI 33n
4701: I 10n; XVI 30n
4937: III 3n, 10n, 28
5204: XVI 30–31, 39; App. GDub 18
5239: XVI 30n
7980 II 649; III *passim*; XVI 33n, 39n

Wisbech Town Museum
  8: App. 419, 433
Wolfenbüttel, Herzog August Bibliothek
  Guelf 306: III 33; VI 225–48; VIII 73;
    XVI 35
  565: II 656n; V 59n; VI 225–48;
    VII 344; VIII 59, 67; XVI 34–5
  669: VI 232n; XVI 35
  1126: VII 342; XVI 35
Worcester, Chapter Library
  Q.54: App. 5
Wroclaw, Biblioteka Uniwersytecka
  IV.F.7: VII.342

b) Other manuscripts mentioned

Aberdeen, University Library
  10, 11, 219, 240, 244: XV 11–12

Brno, Universitní Knihovna
  Mk 28: II 653; App. GSpur 5
  Mk 102: App. GSpur 2

Cambridge
  Corpus Christi College
    141: XVI 29
    195: App. 37, 399
    232: XVI 10n
    296: XVI 26n
    336: XVI 26n
  Gonville and Caius College
    174/95: XV 7
  Magdalene College
    Pepys 2616: XVI 22

Dublin, Trinity College
  244: XVI 25
  245: XVI 25n
Durham
  Cathedral Library
    A.IV.33: IX 98
    C.IV.25: IX 95–6
    Priory Registrum Magnum (III): IX 94
  University Library
    V.iii.6: XI 52n

Herrnhut, Archiv der Brüder-Unität
  I.61: II 655

London
  British Library
    Additional 24202: X 79; XI 52;
      XII 274n
    Additional 22572: XV 11n
    Cotton Cleopatra B.iii: II 656n
    Cotton Faustina C.vii: II 642n, 655n;
      XIII 690–98; XIV 234n;
      App. GDub 8
    Cotton Nero E.v: XIII 696
    Cotton Otho C.ii: App. 38, 399
    Harley 31: XV 11, 15
    Harley 3634: App. 38, 399
    Harley 4894: IX 94
    Royal 5 C.iii: XV 7
    Royal 8 C.i: XV 7
    Royal 8 F.xii: XIII 222–3
    Royal 10 E.ii: VI 237n
    Royal 13 E.ix: App. 38, 399
  College of Arms
    Arundel 7: App. 38, 399
  Lambeth Palace Library
    104: XVI 29n
    541: XV 7
    580: XVI 26n

Manchester, John Rylands Library
  Eng.77: XV 3

INDEX OF MANUSCRIPTS

Oxford
  Bodleian Library
    Bodley 3: XVI 27n
    Bodley 158: XI 44n; XVI 6n
    Bodley 240: XI 50n
    Bodley 462: XIII 694n
    Bodley 496: XV 11
    Bodley 647: XVI 27n
    Bodley 938: XVI 27n
    Digby 98: II 656n
    Douce 273: X 77
    Lat. th.e.25: XV 9–10
    Selden supra 64: XVI 25n
    Twyne 2: XVI 29n
  Magdalen College
    Lat.99: XIII *passim*
  New College
    32: XV 9
  Oriel College
    55: XV 11n
  St John's College
    137: XV 7
  University Archives, Junior Proctors'
    Book: XIII 694–5

Prague
  Knihovna Metropolitní Kapituli
    C.19: II 644
    C.105: II 646
    D.12: II 656n
    D.16: II 653

Národný (*formerly* Universitní)
  Knihovna
    III B.3: App. 232
    IV.G.19: II 653
    IV.H.17: XVI 38
    V.B.2: II 653
    V.D.12: III 3n
    IX.D.7 III 3n
    Cim D.79 (*ol.m* Stará Boleslav C.132):
      XIV 229n

Southampton, King Edward VI Grammar
  School: XV 11n

Vatican
  Pal.lat. 994: II 656n
Vienna, Österreichische Nationalbibliothek
  1430: II 646n
  3936: XVI 31n
  4492: XVI 31n
  4526: XVI 31n
  4925: XVI 31n
  nova 4451: XVI 30n

Wolfenbüttel, Herzog August Bibliothek
  Guelf A.2.Aug.2: XVI 36

York, Minster Library
  XVI.D.2: XV 16–17
  XVI.I.1: IX 95

GENERAL INDEX

Note: references to Appendix II are by item number

Aberdeen, King's College: XV 12
Abyngdon, Henry: XVI 10
Alington, Robert: XVI 4, 10, 39
Allwarde, John: XVI 11
Alnwick, William, bishop of Norwich: X 66
Ancrene Riwle: XV 7
Annales Henrici IV: XII 272
Anne of Bohemia: II 645
Anonimalle Chronicle: XII 271
Aristotle: V 70
    De anima: IV 200
    Meteora: I 12; V 70; XVI 15
Arundel, Thomas, archbishop of
    Canterbury: II 654; IX 94; X 64, 67,
    80; XIII 686–7, 693; XIV 232, 236;
    XVI 8, 50
    Constitutions: VII 323; X 64; XIII 686,
    690; XV 14, 15; XVI 2, 15
Ashbourne, Thomas IX 99
Aston, John: XVI 4
Augustine: V 69; X 78
    Retractiones: III 6
Avignon: VI 236; IX 100; X 70
Aycliffe (Acley), John de: IX 96

Badby, John: XIII 690
Bale, John: I 15; III 1; IV 199; XV 8–9 ;
    XVI 8–29, 35–6
Ball, John: XI 41–2
Bankin, John: IX 99
Barnard Castle: IX 87–8
Basel, Council of:VII 324; IX 94–5;
    XVI 35
Baysio, Guy de: XIV 229
Beauchamp, Sir William: II 643
Bedeman (*alias* Stephen), Laurence:
    XV 1; XVI 4
Bernard, Edward: XVI 29
Bersuire, *Ovidius moralizatus*: XV 7
Berton, William: XI 43
Betson, Thomas: XVI 16
Biceps, Nicholas: I 13; II 644; V 66–7

Binham, William: III 9, 28; IX 100; XVI 14
Blackfriars Council: III 8; V 66–7;
    VI 236–7, 240; XI 53; XIII 694;
    XV 18; XVI 6
Blotius, Hugo: XVI 30–31
Boldon, Uthred of: III 9, 27; IX 96–101
Boniface VIII, pope: X 71
'Boston of Bury': XVI 23
Bracebridge, John: XVI 15
Bradwardine, Thomas:XI 53
Braybrooke (Northants.): I 6; II 642; X 66;
    XIV 235
Brinton, Thomas, bishop of Rochester: XI 41
Brixworth: XV 10
Bromyard, *Opus trivium*: IX 90
Broune, William: XIV 224
Bryt, Henry: VIII 70
Burton, Robert: IX 95
Bury, Richard of: XV 5
Bury St Edmunds: XVI 13
Byngham, William: XV 5

Caistor: IX 87
Cambridge university: XIII 686; XV 1
    Austin friars: XVI 14
    Christ's College: XV 2, 6
    Corpus Christi College: XVI 10–11, 26
    Pembroke College: XVI 4, 8–9
    Peterhouse: XV 1, 6, 14; XVI 10
    University Library: XVI 9–10
Carpenter, John: XV 3–5
Carpenter, John, later bishop of Worcester:
    XV 5
Cartysdale, Richard: XIII 692
Cave, William: XVI 28
Charles IV: XII 271
Chaucer, Geoffrey: I 15
Chester le Street: XIV 226
Cheyne family: X 65
Chichele, Henry, archbishop of Canterbury:
    X 65, 67, 80; XIV 224
Claxton, Thomas: XIII 691

GENERAL INDEX 11

Clement VII, pope: X 71, 79
Cleve, William: XV 6
Constance, Council of: I 15; II 643, 646; III 1; XIII 695–8; XIV 234; XVI 2
Constantine, Donation of: X 75
Cooling (Kent): XIV 230
Cosgrove (Northants.): XVI 4
Courtenay, William, archbishop of Canterbury: III 8; VI 237; X 80; XI 50
Cranewys, John: XVI 13

De heretico comburendo 1401: X 64
Deptford: XIV 222
Despenser crusade: VI 240–42
Despenser, Henry, bishop of Norwich: X 71; App. 410
Drayton, Thomas: X 65–6; XIV 222
Durham: VII 332; IX 89–103; XIV 223; XVI 5
Dymmok, Roger: XV 3, 5

Easton, Adam: II 645; V 65–8; VI 236; IX 99; X 30; XI 45; XVI 18
Eborall, Thomas: XV 3–17
Edward III: X 70
Egglestone abbey: IX 88
Elyot, Robert: XV 8
Emyldon, Robert: IX 95
Essex: XI 42

Fader, Peter: XVI 12
Fasciculi zizaniorum: XI 42; XIII 693–7; XIV 228; XVI 23, 25
Faulfiš, Mikuláš: I 7; II 642; VII 329; XIV 233–7
Fawkes, Nicholas: IV 214; XVI 5
Fillingham (Lincs.): IX 88
Finchale (Durham): IX 94, 97
FitzRalph, Richard (Armacan.): II 645–6; V 62; X 70; XI 47
Flacius Illyricus: XVI 31–6, 42
Flemyng, Richard, bishop of Lincoln: X 66; XIII 692
Floretum/Rosarium: II 653–4; VI 227; VII 332, 341; XVI 16, 31, 41
Folkhyrd, Quentin: II 655
Foxe, John: I 15; XVI 26
Fyvian, David: XV 6

Gaľka, Andrzej: XVI 35
Garnier, Arnald: I 2; IX 87
Garsdale, Richard: XIII 692
Gascoigne, Thomas: IX 94; XIII 697; XV 5; XVI 12

Gaunt, John of, duke of Lancaster: I 12; X 70; XI 42, 51
Gilbert, Robert: XIII 692
Glastonbury abbey: IV 214; XVI 5
Glossed Gospels: VII 341; XV 16–17
Gloucester, parliament of: I 2; IV 200; V 61
Godfrey, Oliver: XV 16–17
Gosele, John: VII 70
Gower, John: I 15; XI 51
Grafton, Richard: XVI 20
Graunt, Thomas: XV 4–17; XVI 16
Gregory XI, pope: I 3; II 645; IV 207, 213; V 60, 65–7; VI 236; IX 99; X 64, 70; XI 43, 50, 53; XII 269; XVI 42
Gregory's Chronicle: XV 5
Grosseteste, Robert, bishop of Lincoln: IV 199; V 69; VI 228; XI 53; XIV 229; XV 7, 10; XVI 9, 14

Halden, Thomas: XV 9
Hanham, John: XVI 10
Hanley, William: XV 9
Harmondsworth (Middx.): XIV 222
Hartley (Kent): XIV 222
Haulay, Robert: IV 200; V 61; X 72
Heidelberg: I 13
Henry IV: II 643, X 67, 79; XII 271
Henry V: X 65, 80; XII 271; XVI 15
Hereford, Nicholas II: 656; X 80; XI 50–52; XVI 4
Hereford, diocese of: XIV 222, 225
Heu quanta desolacio: II 655
Higden, Ranulph: VII 332; IX 90
Hitchcok, John: XV 10–11, 15
Hnatnice, Matthias de (Matthias Engliš): II 653
Hoke, Robert: X 66; XIV 232
Holme, Richard: XIV 224
Humfrey, duke of Gloucester: XIII 696
Hus, Jan: I 13–16; II 643–4, 648, 654; III 1, 4; VI 225; VII 328; X 66; XIV 229–37; XVI 2, 41; App. 54–299

Innocent VII, pope: XIV 223
Ireland, Thomas of, *Manipulus florum*: III 6–7
Ive, William: XV *passim*; XVI 12

Jacobellus *see* Štríbro, Jakoubek of
James, Richard: XVI 27–8
James, Thomas: XVI 26–8
Jandun, John of: X 70
Jenštejn, Jan of: II 647
Jerome: XV 10

De viris illustribus III 6
Jerome of Prague: I 13, 15–16; II 643, 646, 653

Kemerton (Glos.): II 642; XIV 235
Kilmington, Richard de: XI 53
Kilwardby, Robert: VII 325
Kirklees: IX 88
Kirkstede, Henry of: XVI 23
Kňehnice, Jiři: II 642, 644, VII 329; XIV 234
Knighton, Henry: XI 42
Koranda, Václav: XVI 39

Langchestre, Robert of: IX 96
Langdon, John: XIII 691
Langland, William: I 15
Lanquet, Humbert: XVI 33
Latimer, Sir Thomas: II 643; X 66
family of XIV 235
Leaveland (Kent): XIV 222
Leicester abbey: XVI 13–14
Leland, John: XVI 11, 14, 20–21
Liber regalis: XI 272
Lichfield, William: XV *passim*, XVI 10, 13
Logica Oxoniensis: I 7–8; App. 1a
Lombard, Peter: XV 9
London: II 656; VI 224, 235; VI app 124; IX 100; XIII 690; XV 17–18
　All Hallows the Great: XV 2
　All Hallows Honey Lane: XV 3
　Austin friars: XVI 14
　Carmelite friars: XVI 14
　Dominican friars: XVI 14
　Fleet prison: XIV 224–5
　Franciscan friars: XVI 14
　Guildhall: XV 3–4
　St Anthony's hospital: XV 5
　St Bartholomew Smithfield: XV 16
　St Benet Fink: XV 6
　St James beside Whittington College: XV 10
　St Paul's: XV 3, 4, 8, 10–12
　St Paul's Cross: XIV 236
　St John Zachary: XV 6
　St Thomas of Acres Cheapside: XV 5
　Savoy palace: XI 42
　Tower: XI 42
　Tower Hill: XIV 221, 225
　Whittington College: XV 3, 7, 10
Luke, John: XIII 692
Lumley, John Lord: XVI 36
Lutterworth: II 642; V 69; VI 224, 227, 235, 237, 241; IX 88; XIV 234
Lychlade, Robert: II 643; XIV 235

Lymburg (Nymburk): XVI 33–5, 39
Lynton, Robert: XVI 11
Lytlington, Nicholas, abbot of Westminster: II 272

Magdeburg: XVI 35
Malberthorp, John: I 3n; XVI 12
Mankswell, Andrew: XVI 11
Mardisley, John: IX 99
Marie de France: XIV 221
Markaunt, Thomas: XVI 10
Marsilius of Padua: X 70; XI 53
Martin V, pope: XVI 19
Maximilian II, archduke and later emperor: XVI 31, 42
Maynsforth, John: XVI 12
Milverton, John: XV 9
Mladoňovice, Peter of: II 647
Molet, John: XVI 13
Mosie, Henry: XV 8
Mychel, John: VIII 70

Neale, John: XV 5
Nequam, Alexander: VII 332; IX 90; XV 9
Netter, Thomas of Walden, *Doctrinale* I 4, 11; II 651; III 26; V 59, 69; XIII 692–3; 696–7; XIV 229; XV 17; XVI 14–19
Neville, Thomas: VIII 55
Niedbruck, Kaspar von: III 3–4; XVI 31–5, 42
Norwich: IX 100, XVI 13
Nymburk/Lymburg: XVI 33–6, 39

Odiham: XV 12, XVI 4
Oldcastle, Sir John: II 655; X 63, 65; XIII 691; XIV 224–5, 230–7; XVI 2
Opus arduum: II 653–4; XII 270; XVI 31
Oudin, Casimir: XVI 28
Overey, St Mary: XV 2, 14; XVI 13
Oxford: I 6–7; II 642, 645–6; IV 194; VI 235–8; VII 325; IX 87, 95, 100; X 65; XI 45, 50; XII 274; XIII *passim*; XIV 224, 235; XV 9–10; XVI 6–8;
　1411 condemnation at: IV 208; XIII *passim*; XVI 2, 18
　Balliol College: IX 88; XVI 8
　Canterbury College: VIII 55, 69; XVI 11
　Carfax: XIII 697
　Durham College: IX 94, 100, 102; XVI 5
　Exeter College: VIII 70; XVI 11
　Greyfriars: VII 340

Lincoln College: XVI 12
Magdalen College: XV 8, 14
Merton College II 643; IX 88; XVI 10, 12
New College: XV 8–9
Oriel College: XVI 11, 43
Queen's College: VIII 70; XVI 5, 8
St Edmund Hall: X 66
St Mary's church: IX 101

Páleč, Stephen: XVI 41
Paris: I 13; II 644, 647
Paris, William of, *De fide et legibus*: IX 89
Parker, Harry: XV 9
Partridge, Peter: I 12
Payne, Peter: I 14; II 642, 647, 654;
    VII 333–8; X 63–5; XIV 234–6;
    XVI 36
Peasants' Revolt 1381: VI 238; X 80;
    XI 42–53
Pecock, Reginald: XV 2, 13,18
Pelagius, Alvarus: XII 274
Perkins, Humfrey: XVI 20
Petyrffelde, John: XV 8
Piccolomini, Aeneas Sylvius, pope Pius II:
    II 642
Pickingham, Osbert of: II 646
Pisa, Council of: I 13; III 8
Pollyrbache, John: XIV 236
Polton, Thomas: XIII 696
Pore caitif: XV 8
Prague: II 643, 647, 657; VII 325; X 63, 69;
    XIII 695
    Bohemian College: III 4; XVI 38
    Carolinum: I 12, III 3–4, 14; V 70;
        VII 323; XVI 32–8
    Clementinum: XVI 37
    Queen Hedvika's (or Lithuanian)
        College: XVI 37
Prestbury, Thomas: XIII 697
Příbram, Jan: VII 335
Purvey, John: XIV 223, 228, 232
Pye, John: XV 8, 16
Pykworth, Sir Thomas: XV 6

Radcliffe, Nicholas: XV 17
Ramsey: VI 236
Ranconis, Adalbertus: II 646
Regensburg: XVI 32–3
Reid, Thomas: XV 11
Repingdon, Philip: X 66; XI 50; XVI 13
Richard II: II 645; X 73, 79; XI 45;
    XII 271–2
Rodby, John: XVI 4
Rokycana, John: III 33

Rolle, Richard: XV 7; XVI 22
Rome: II 644
Rome, Thomas: IX 102
Rowberry, Robert: XIII 692
Rudbourne, Thomas: XIII 692
Russell, Lord Francis: XVI 25
Rymington, William: XVI 6
Rypon, Robert: IX 94; XVI 5

Sabrisford, Nicholas: XV 8
St Albans abbey: I 15; IX 95; XI 42
St Albans Chronicle: XIII 694; XVI 24
St Amour, William of: XV 6
Salisbury cathedral: XVI 12
Sarum rite: VI 227–30
Sawndre, Stephen: XVI 15
Sawtry, William: XIII 690
Shakyl, John: IV 200; V 61; X 71
Sharpe, John: XIII 687
Shrewsbury: XIV 236
Skirlaw, Walter, bishop of Durham: II 654;
    IX 87, 102; X 66; XIV 222–9
Slawkowicz, Paul of: III 2
Smyth, John: XV 9
Snettisham, Richard: XIII 687, 692
Somerseth, John: XIV 232
Sory, John: XV 8
Southampton: XIV 224
Stocton, Adam de: XVI 3–4, 14
Stokes, John: II 646
Stokes, Peter: II 656; VI 236; XI 50–51
Stonham, Robert: I 13; II 650n; III 8
Stoughton, Robert: XVI 20
Strasburg, Thomas of XV 7
Stříbro, Jakoubek of (Jacobellus): II 654;
    XIV 230, 234
Sudbury, Simon of, archbishop of
    Canterbury: X 76; XI 42, 46, 50
Sutton, Thomas of: XIII 687
Swalwell, Thomas: IX 95
Swinderby, William: XIV 232

Tabula septem custodiarum: VII 340
Tanner, Thomas: XVI 28–9
Taylor, William: II 654; X 66 XIV 236;
    XVI 40
Teye, Andrew: XV 4
Thirty Years War: XVI 36, 41
Thornbury, Philip: IX 87
Thorpe, William: II 654; X 66; XIV 232,
    236; XVI 31, 38, 40
Tišnov, Simon of: XIV 233–4
Toke, Heinrich XVI 35
Třeboňsky, Alexander: XVI 39
Trithemius: XVI 23

Twelve Conclusions of the Lollards: XV 3
Twyne, Brian: XVI 29
Tyler, Wat: XI 80

Ufford, William: XIII 691
Urban VI, pope: IV 206; V 67; VI 240–42; X 71, 79
Usk, Adam of: XII 272
Usk, John of, abbot of Chertsey: X 73

Valdštejn, Voksa of: II 655; XIV 230
Vienna: I 13; II 643; XVI 29–36
Voragine, Jacobus de (Januensis): VII 332; IX 90

Wagge, William: XV 4, 14
Wakeryng, John, bishop of Norwich: X 66
Walsingham, Thomas I 3; III 8; VI 224; VI app 124; XI 41–3; XII 271–2; App. 37, 399
Waltham, Roger of: XV 13
Warde, William: XIV 224
Warham, William, archbishop of Canterbury: XV 16–17
Waynflete, William, bishop of Winchester: XV 8
Webber, Henry: XVI 14
Wells, John, OSB (d.1388): VI 236
Wells, John (d.1417): XIII 697
Westbury on Trym: IX 88
West Greenwich: XIV 222

Westminster: XIV 224
 Westminster Hall: XV 3
 Westminster Abbey: I 2; IV 200, 206
Weston, John: XVI 15
Wharton, Henry: XVI 28
White Mountain, battle of: XVI 36
Whittington, Richard: XV 3
Wildungen, Bartholdus of: XIII 695
Wilok, John: XV 6
Wimbledon, Thomas of: XVI 22
Winchester, college of BVM: XIV 222; XV 8, 14
Winterton, Thomas: XV 11
Wireker, Nigel: XIII 691
Woodford, William: I 2; IV 197, 213; V 61, 68; XI 48; XIII 686; XV 11, 17; XVI 6–7; App. 39
Worcester diocese: XIV 227
Wyche, Richard: II 654; IX 102; X 66; XIV *passim*; XVI 40
Wyclif, Robert: IX 87, 103; XIV 228
Wyclif, Simon: IX 87
Wyclif, William: IX 87
Wycliffe (village, NYorks): IX 87
Wycliffite Bible: I 1, 14; XV 3
Wytenham, John: XIII 692

York: IX 88; XV 14

Znojmo, Stanislaus of: II 647
Zvířetic, Zdyslaus of: XIV 230, 236

For Product Safety Concerns and Information please contact our EU
representative GPSR@taylorandfrancis.com
Taylor & Francis Verlag GmbH, Kaufingerstraße 24, 80331 München, Germany

www.ingramcontent.com/pod-product-compliance
Lightning Source LLC
Chambersburg PA
CBHW071239300426
44116CB00008B/1100